For Aaron
affectionately
Claire

1937 - 1947 - (1977 reprint)

COMPOSERS
in America

Da Capo Press Music Reprint Series

MUSIC EDITOR
BEA FRIEDLAND
Ph.D., City University of New York

This title was recommended for Da Capo reprint by
Dr. Léonie Rosenstiel

COMPOSERS
in America

BIOGRAPHICAL SKETCHES

OF CONTEMPORARY COMPOSERS

WITH

A RECORD OF THEIR WORKS

BY

CLAIRE R. REIS

With a New Introduction by
WILLIAM SCHUMAN

(Revised and Enlarged Edition)

DA CAPO PRESS • NEW YORK • 1977

Library of Congress Cataloging in Publication Data

Reis, Claire Raphael.
  Composers in America.

(Da Capo Press music reprint series)
Reprint of the ed. published by Macmillan, New York.
1. Composers—United States—Biography. 2. Music,
American—Bio-bibliography. I. Title.
ML390.R38 1977   780'.92'2 [B]   77-4158
ISBN 0-306-70893-0

This Da Capo Press edition of *Composers in America* is,
apart from the new Introduction by William Schuman,
an unabridged republication of the revised and enlarged
edition published in New York in 1947. It is reprinted
by arrangement with Macmillan Publishing Co., Inc.

Published by Da Capo Press, Inc.
A Subsidiary of Plenum Publishing Corporation
227 West 17th Street, New York, N. Y. 10011

INTRODUCTION

There are two reasons to justify the re-issuing of Claire Reis's *Composers in America:* first, the specifics of the book itself and, second, a reminder to more recent generations of the special contribution its author continues to make to the music of our time.

To read *Composers in America* three decades after its initial publication is to envy those who will now have that extraordinary pleasure and enlightenment for the first time. This book was and remains an original. To my knowledge, no other survey exists wherein the composers of a particular period were themselves the suppliers of all the pertinent data and have all been brought together in one huge family portrait.

It is a fascinating exercise to study the list of diverse composers and to see where each was at the same given moment. The book covers compositions created from 1916 to 1946. Some of the composers were already advanced in years, others were merely beginning, still others were in their middle years. And these wide variations in age are recorded on a special clock which, though stopped at a fixed point, indicates the morning, afternoon, or evening for each composer.

The achievements, for example, of a precocious 24-year-old, gave absolutely no inkling that he would subsequently become a composer identified with experimental techniques rather than continue as a traditionalist. And what of a certain 72-year-old? It is hard to realize that with all of his accomplishments then long behind him, he was still unknown to the general public. Now, with hindsight, it seems unbelievable that his recognition was so long delayed. And, in the instance of one of today's most celebrated of American composers, there was certainly no hint at all, even in his 38th year, that he would so soon astonish the music world through the vast complexity and originality of his stunning concepts.

But, to move on, the excitement of the book is so much more than in its brief biographies and meticulous cataloguing. Its fascination, as I have noted, is in capturing the total creative life in music at a certain point in American history and making a still photograph of it. Depending on each composer's age, we have a picture that we can dust off and look at again, as we do a graduation picture, a baby picture, or that of a golden wedding anniversary, all reminding us of what we were.

If we compare today with 30 years ago, we find that growth in the number of known composers in the United States could be tenfold, yet history tells us that the select few, those who rise to the top, will not increase numerically. Certainly, a newly-written volume would include many new names and I am resisting the temptation of mentioning any. But, it is highly unlikely that there will be a comparable compendium for 1946 to 1976, which brings me now to the second point of the importance of this reprint.

For composers, Claire Reis is the ideal patron. In her home, leading creative figures in music of all schools and nationalities have been welcome these many, many years. She has provided a meeting place, a center with a special warmth and camaraderie. It would be, however, the most extreme injustice to give the impression that she has served composers only through the social amenities. Claire Reis knows that composers are the true seminal force for all of music. If the thought is commonplace, dedicated service in its implementation is rare.

The focus of Mrs. Reis's professional life is a never-ending crusade for the creative artist. Concern for the living composer is fundamental to the survival of the art of music. The contributions of a Claire Reis, for this reason, continue to be unique.

WILLIAM SCHUMAN

January, 1977

COMPOSERS IN AMERICA

THE MACMILLAN COMPANY
NEW YORK · BOSTON · CHICAGO · DALLAS
ATLANTA · SAN FRANCISCO

MACMILLAN AND CO., Limited
LONDON · BOMBAY · CALCUTTA · MADRAS
MELBOURNE

THE MACMILLAN COMPANY
OF CANADA, Limited
TORONTO

COMPOSERS
in America

BIOGRAPHICAL SKETCHES

OF CONTEMPORARY COMPOSERS

WITH

A RECORD OF THEIR WORKS

BY

CLAIRE R. REIS

Revised and Enlarged Edition

THE MACMILLAN COMPANY

NEW YORK · 1947

I hold that man is in the right who is most closely in league with the future.

—HENRIK IBSEN

ACKNOWLEDGMENTS

I am profoundly indebted to Aaron Copland for his wise counsel and encouragement in preparing this volume. Appreciation is also due to Lawrence Morton, who contributed valuable information about the composers of film music. I wish also to express my gratitude to Walter Kramer, William Schuman, Carlton Sprague Smith, Edward Waters, and Hugo Winter for their friendly advice. I am grateful to May Gober Grey for her painstaking interest in preparing the manuscript for publication, to Rita Minter and H. Adler, as well as to the American Music Center and the New York Music Library for their assistance in the research for this book.

FOREWORD

The twentieth century is yielding generation after generation of prolific composers in America as orchestras, choral societies, ensembles, and bands burst into being in communities all over the country. Performance rights for the premieres of new symphonies are sought by renowned conductors, and unpublished works are eagerly tried out by the students and the faculties in leading educational centers. Although contemporary music may still be subject to critical appraisal within the confines of the concert hall, yet the vocabulary of music has gradually crept into the idiom of everyday speech and the man on the street is familiar with composers who would have been unknown to him a generation ago. The present trend is illustrated by an amusing caption in a recent newspaper account of a murder trial, reading: "Witness sobs in Stravinsky-like rhythms." But despite many bright portents which mark the advance of contemporary music, its acceptance in America has been as cautiously conceded as the acknowledgment of any new art form.

American composers themselves have had a high stake in bringing about the recognition of good music during the last few decades and these men have exerted a stimulating influence upon the public through their activities in various professions existing within the field of music. Many have become composer-teachers, others composer-critics, -conductors, -publishers, -authors. In addition to the immeasurable benefit derived by contemporary music, the dual profession has been economically important to the individual composer.

Educational institutions are a focal point today for a progressive music movement, and the creative musician has had a large share in this activity. Among the American composers on faculties of music across the country I cite at random: Theodore Chanler at the Peabody Conservatory of Music; Aaron Copland at the Berkshire Music Center; Norman Dello Joio at Sarah Lawrence College; Albert Elkus at the University of California; Howard Hanson at the Eastman School of Music; Roy Harris at Colorado College; Philip James at New York University; Werner Josten at Smith College; Robert McBride at Bennington College; Walter Piston at Harvard University; Quincy Porter at Yale University; William Schuman at the Juilliard School of Music; Roger Sessions at the University of California; Randall Thompson at Princeton University. It is natural that when talented students encounter the inspiring mind of the creative artist they feel encouraged to follow a career of music.

The roster of composer-critics includes Marion Bauer, Arthur Berger, Felix Borowski, Paul Bowles, Herbert Elwell, Arthur Shepherd, Deems Taylor, Virgil Thomson. The composer-conductors include Nicolai Berezowski, Leonard Bernstein, Lehman Engel, Rudolph Ganz, Morton Gould,

Eugene Goossens, Werner Janssen, Leopold Stokowski. Composer-publishers number Henry Cowell, Harrison Kerr, A. Walter Kramer. Composer-authors include George Antheil, Marc Blitzstein, Colin McPhee, Richard Goldman, Joseph Schillinger, Elie Siegmeister.

Commissions, scholarships, prizes, and publication awards also have done a great deal to promote the composer in America during the past three decades. The list is imposing; mention should be particularly made of the American Academy of Arts and Letters; the American Academy in Rome, Prix de Rome Award; Bearns Prize; Bispham Memorial Medal; Boston Symphony Award; Music Critics' Circle awards; Elizabeth Sprague Coolidge prizes and commissions; Coolidge Foundation prizes and commissions (Library of Congress); Composers Press competitions; Alice M. Ditson awards (Columbia University); George Gershwin Memorial fellowships; Guggenheim Foundation fellowships; Juilliard commissions, publications, and fellowships; Koussevitzky Music Foundation commissions; F. K. Kulas American Composers Fund (Cleveland Musical Art Association); League of Composers American commissions *; Metropolitan Opera Company American Award; National American Composers and Conductors awards; National Federation of Music Club awards and contests; National Institute of Arts and Letters awards; Pan American Union contests; Paderewski Prize; Pulitzer Prize; Rachmaninoff Memorial Fund; Society for the Publication of American Music competitions; Town Hall Composition awards. Awards and commissions by radio networks and local stations include the ABC awards; BMI awards; CBS commissions; NBC contests; RCA prizes; RCA Victor awards; WHAM commissions. But despite a large group of awards and commissions the composer's livelihood if solely dependent upon royalties is still one of the most perilously earned in all the fields of art.

The past thirty years has seen a rapid growth of contemporary music. *Composers in America,* which I compiled nine years ago, listed significant living composers, American-born or American citizens, with biographical material and a record of their works. But in revising and expanding this volume it has seemed more important to present a survey of music written in America by serious composers during the past thirty years, regardless of the fact whether the composer was still alive, or whether this was the land of his birth or of his citizenship at the time of publication. I have included, therefore, works written by musicians no longer living which, however, belong to this period as well as a few compositions written shortly before 1915 (the date at which this record begins), because the music seemed prophetic of the period to follow. Together with the brief biographies of more than three hundred and thirty composers will be found a record of fellowships, awards, and commissions, works which were broadcast and recorded and mention of some of their major performances. I have tried to list with each work the year in which it was completed, the name of the publisher, and the length of time required for performance.

I have found it necessary to select the composers from a wider group

---

* The League of Composers awarded its seventieth commission in 1946.

in order to do justice to a certain section of contemporary music. Those musicians are represented who have had at least one major performance, and who have written major classical compositions in the larger form—orchestral, choral, stage, or film works—and chamber music including sonatas and suites. Transcriptions of works paraphrased from folk melodies have been generally omitted as well as short songs and short solo instrumental pieces. A supplementary list of composers at the end of the book credits men and women of merit whose work may not fit into any of the above categories, young composers of promise, and, finally, several musicians I could not reach for detailed information.

The volume records, among the works of foreign composers, only those which were written in America; however, in the brief biographies of these men, an attempt has been made to indicate some of their early important achievements. In a few cases it has been difficult to determine whether works of composers who have traveled extensively in Europe as well as America, and who have often composed on tour, were actually written in America. Rachmaninoff is an outstanding example, and in his case only those works are listed which he wrote after he made America his permanent home.

After much consideration it seemed best to omit from these pages composers whose major works have been written as operettas or musical comedies. For it would be impossible to include their record without also giving consideration to the many songs by which they have become equally well known; to do so would have taken me too far afield into the department of popular music. A reference book is indeed greatly needed which will devote itself exclusively to the works of Irving Berlin, Reginald de Koven, Duke Ellington, Rudolph Friml, Walter Hendl, Victor Herbert,* Jerome Kern, Cole Porter, Richard Rodgers, Sigmund Romberg, Harold Rome, Vincent Youmans, and others. But although this important section of our music literature is not included here, the influence of these composers is recognized as a great part of our American heritage.

We can look to the films as a new medium for the advancement of serious music. A story has gone the rounds concerning a composer who provided music for a film and was subsequently taken to task by the director because the public became so interested in the music that its attention was diverted from the picture. This was perhaps true five or ten years ago; but Hollywood today has a greater regard for good music. In fact, Kurt Weill writes amusingly about a lady who closes her eyes as soon as she has taken her seat in the movie theater so that she can listen to the music undisturbed by the picture which is shown with it.† The League of Composers carried out an interesting experiment at the Museum of Modern Art in 1941, when it circulated a questionnaire among the members of a large

---

* Victor Herbert is one of the composers who might rightfully have a place in this volume because of the symphonies he wrote; but his name will forever be chiefly associated with operettas and songs.

† "Music in the Movies," by Kurt Weill, *Harper's Bazaar*, Sept., 1946.

audience at a program of music composed for the films, requesting them to cite the names of any composers who had written scores for the films. Only sixty-four among the sophisticated audience could name one or two film composers. But if this experiment were repeated today, undoubtedly the answers would be more rewarding.

The documentary films, probably more than others, have used music scores as an integral part of their narratives. But the movie industry as a whole is increasingly conscious of the active role that music can play in the films. The inclusion in this book of film material will perhaps be valuable in focusing the attention of the critics and the public upon the importance of contemporary scores for motion pictures.

Few of the established composers of serious music write regularly for films. The majority of scores produced each year—some four-hundred-odd—are written by composers who find that their time is restricted to this work alone. Occasionally such musicians later adapt their film music to symphonic suites or concert pieces; however, although their education and their early careers were in the field of classical music, a large proportion of the composers now living in Hollywood are essentially film writers. In this book, therefore, only the film scores of these composers are listed, and their earlier works, written for other mediums, are not included. Works of these film composers, however, are included in the body of the text because such music belongs more and more in the mainstream of American composition; therefore, it should receive the same attention and criticism that is given to music for concert or opera.

The radio and the recording industries are two other outstanding mediums, developed during this century, by means of which the American composer ought to be able to discover further outlets for his talents as well as a source of increased income. The potential audience which radio commands, via a thousand or more stations throughout the country, reaches into the millions; and this medium could become particularly important to contemporary music. Occasionally certain networks have granted commissions to composers for original radio scores, and now and again radio stations do carry sustaining programs of contemporary music. The annual WNYC American Music Festival, for example, is indicative of a growing interest on the part of the broadcasting stations in presenting the American works of living composers. But the number of contemporary works on radio programs still represents far too small a percentage of the music now on the air. An increasing number of catalogues of contemporary recorded music and the existence of many new recording companies are hopeful omens for the future of modern music; for recordings make it possible to hear repetitions of new works which might be performed infrequently in the concert hall.

Simultaneously with a quickening in the musical activity of native-born Americans, and of American citizens of foreign birth, a certain body of important music has been composed by European musicians who have come to this country more recently. Fascism has sent many of the great European composers to our shores during the past decade; in consequence, American students who formerly would have gone to Paris, Rome, or Berlin for their musical education are studying with European masters in many different parts of the United States.

These European artists came to us first as visitors; but many have taken permanent root in our country. While a certain number have inspired music activities in small communities others have found visiting or permanent positions in the music departments of colleges and universities. Paul Hindemith, for example, found a teaching position in Yale University, Ernst Krenek in Vassar College, Darius Milhaud in Mills College, Arnold Schoenberg in the University of California, Igor Stravinsky lectured at Harvard University. These men have added to our music culture and in turn they have been influenced by the American life. It seems important, therefore, for an accurate picture of music in America since 1915, to include a record of the works written by foreign-born composers who are now living here.

Our music has been the richer for the presence of these men. Yet we need have no fears that American music will always bear the mark of the European tradition. To what extent has the American composer been able to blend an inherited music culture with the music education he has acquired into an integrated and individualized style?—that is the test he has faced! Serge Koussevitzky once remarked: "Some have criticized me for playing American music, saying America has not produced a Beethoven or a Brahms. I replied: 'Why should it? We have the spirit of Beethoven and Brahms always with us. But America is producing something new, youthful and vital in music. We should honor the American composer.' "

CLAIRE R. REIS

NEW YORK CITY
July, 1946

ABBREVIATIONS

ABC	American Broadcasting Company
ACA	American Composers Alliance
ASCAP	American Society of Composers, Authors and Publishers
BBC	British Broadcasting Company
BMI	Broadcast Music, Incorporated
CBS	Columbia Broadcasting System
COLUMBIA	Columbia Phonograph Company, New York City
DECCA	Decca Record Corporation, New York City and London
H.M.V.	"His Master's Voice" (The Gramophone Company), London
I.S.C.M.	International Society for Contemporary Music
MBS	Mutual Broadcasting System
M.G.M.	Metro-Goldwyn-Mayer
NAACC	National Association of American Composers and Conductors
NBC	National Broadcasting Company
N.M.Q.R. (or N.M.R.)	New Music Quarterly Recordings, Bennington, Vermont
O.W.I.	Office of War Information
PARLOPHONE	The Parlophone Company, London
R.C.A.	Radio Corporation of America
R.K.O.	Radio-Keith-Orpheum Corporation
S.M.I.	Société Musicale Indépendante
S.P.A.M.	Society for the Publication of American Music
VICTOR	RCA Victor Company, Camden, New Jersey

BIOGRAPHIES AND RECORDS OF COMPOSERS IN AMERICA

JOSEPH ACHRON

Born in 1886 at Losdzeye, Lithuania, and died in 1943. At five years of age he began to study theory and violin. After his first public appearance in Warsaw, at the age of eight, he continued his studies and entered the St. Petersburg Conservatory. He was a pupil of Auer and Liadov and later studied orchestration with Steinberg; he taught himself counterpoint.

In 1913 he became head of the violin and chamber-music department in the Kharkov Conservatory in Russia. From 1916 to 1918 he was in the Russian army, and following these years he concertized extensively and became head of the violin master class and chamber-music department of the Leningrad Artists' Union. In 1925 he came to the United States and made his home in New York for nine years. He then moved to Hollywood, California.

Many of his orchestral works have been played by leading orchestras in America and in Europe, and many of his works for chamber music and for stage have been performed and broadcast. A program of his compositions was broadcast over WOR. The Second Sonata was chosen in Berlin by the I.S.C.M., and the "Golem Suite" for the Venice I.S.C.M. Festival. There have been records made by the Victor, Brunswick, and Gramophone companies of the violin pieces. He has translated Rimsky-Korsakov's *Practical Manual of Harmony* into English. The League of Composers commissioned him to write a string quartet, and his Third Violin Concerto was commissioned by Jascha Heifetz.

COMPOSITIONS

ORCHESTRAL WORKS	DURATION	PUBLISHER	DATE
FIRST CONCERTO, OPUS 60	26 minutes	Universal Edition,	1925
violin, orchestra		Vienna	
		orch. score ms.	
		for hire	
KONZERTANTEN KAPELLE, OPUS 64	3 "	Manuscript	1928
voice, orchestra			
DANCE OUVERTURE	15 "	Manuscript	1933
SECOND CONCERTO, OPUS 68	25 "	Manuscript	1933
violin, orchestra			
THIRD CONCERTO, OPUS 72	22 "	Manuscript	1933
violin, orchestra			

CHAMBER ORCHESTRA

GOLEM SUITE	10 minutes	Manuscript	1932

CHORAL WORKS

SALOMÉ'S DANCE, OPUS 61	10 minutes	Manuscript	1925
mixed voices, percussion, piano			
EVENING SERVICE OF THE SABBATH,			
OPUS 67	21½ "	Bloch Publishing Co.	1932
mixed voices, baritone, organ			

CHAMBER MUSIC

ELEGY, OPUS 62	77 minutes	Manuscript	1927
string quartet			
FOUR IMPROVISATIONS, OPUS 63	14 "	Manuscript	1927
string quartet			
SINFONIETTA, OPUS 71	13½ "	Manuscript	1935
string quartet			

JOSEPH ACHRON (*Continued*)

STAGE WORKS	PUBLISHER	DATE
INCIDENTAL MUSIC TO "THE 10TH COMMANDMENT" (recomposed after Goldfaden) *orchestra, solo voices, chorus*	Manuscript	1926
INCIDENTAL MUSIC TO "KIDDUSH HASHEM" *orchestra, solo voices, chorus*	Manuscript	1928
INCIDENTAL MUSIC TO "STEMPENYU" *orchestra, solo voices, solo violin, chorus*	Manuscript	1929
INCIDENTAL MUSIC TO "MONISH" *solo voice, orchestra or piano*	Manuscript	1929
INCIDENTAL MUSIC TO "THE WITCH OF CASTILE" *orchestra, solo voices, chorus*	Manuscript	1930
INCIDENTAL MUSIC TO "GOLEM" *cello, trumpet, horn, piano*	Manuscript	1931

FILM MUSIC	STUDIO	
SPRING NIGHT (A NIGHT WITH PAN) *Ballet for the Screen*	Paramount	1935

PAUL HASTINGS ALLEN

Born in Boston, Massachusetts, in 1883. He studied in Italy for twenty years. His Symphony in D major was awarded first prize in the Paderewski Competition of 1910. Since his return to the United States he has been active in musical circles at Harvard.

Among his works which have been performed are "Il Filtro," an opera, and "Milda," which was produced in the leading opera houses in Italy.

COMPOSITIONS

ORCHESTRAL WORKS	DURATION	PUBLISHER	DATE
SERENADE	25 minutes	Row & Co. *American agents*	1928
EX HOCTE	60 "	Row & Co. *American agents*	1930
SYMPHONY IN D, No. 2	45 "	Row & Co. *American agents*	1937

CHAMBER ORCHESTRA			
SUITE—five pieces	30 minutes	Manuscript	1928
DANS LA NUIT	5 "	Manuscript	1928
THREE PIECES	18 "	Manuscript	1928

CHORAL WORKS			
THREE WOMEN'S CHORUSES *harp, horn, piano*	12 minutes	Manuscript	1929
SEVEN MADRIGALS	30 "	Row & Co. *American agents*	1930
LEFT BUT THE POWER	6 "	Row & Co. *American agents*	1932

PAUL HASTINGS ALLEN (*Continued*)

CHAMBER MUSIC	DURATION	PUBLISHER	DATE
CLARINET QUARTET	22 minutes	Manuscript	1929
TRIO	15 "	Manuscript	1929
oboe, clarinet, bassoon			
CELLO SONATA IN D	15 "	Manuscript	1932

STAGE WORKS			
MILDA	1⅛ hours	Sonzogno, Italy	1915
LAST OF THE MOHICANS	2¾ "	G. Ricordi & Co.	1916

MARTHA ALTER

Born in New Bloomfield, Pennsylvania, in 1904. She received her early musical training from her mother. She graduated from Vassar College and received her Master of Musicology degree from Columbia University and her Master of Music degree from the Eastman School of Music. She studied composition with Bingham, Goldmark, Gow and Rogers and piano with Chittenden and Hutcheson. She was awarded the Kendrick-Ryland Fellowship, the Associate Alumnae Fellowship (the first person to have held this for two years), the Salmon Fund for Research Award and the 75th Anniversary Publication Award from Vassar. She also held a Teaching Fellowship at the Eastman School of Music.

She has taught at Vassar and at present is Assistant Professor of Music in Connecticut College. She was a visiting lecturer and has frequently appeared as pianist in her own works.

Her compositions have had numerous performances in colleges throughout the country and have been played by leading orchestras. The orchestral ballet, "Anthony Comstock" ("A Puritan's Progress"), was presented at the Festival of American Music in Rochester. "Rhythmic Dance for Orchestra" was broadcast over an NBC network, the "Bric-a-Brac Suite" was heard over a CBS network and some of her compositions have been played over a New London radio station.

COMPOSITIONS

ORCHESTRA	DURATION	PUBLISHER	DATE
BILL GEORGE—march and song	6 minutes	Vassar College	1932
baritone, orchestra		Publication	
SINFONIETTA FOR ORCHESTRA	8 "	Photostat	1932
SUITE from the ballet	20 "	The Edwin A.	1934
"ANTHONY COMSTOCK" or		Fleisher Music	
"A PURITAN'S PROGRESS"		Collection	

CHAMBER ORCHESTRA			
BILL GEORGE—March and Song	6 minutes	Manuscript	1932
baritone, 21 instruments			

MARTHA ALTER (*Continued*)

CHORAL WORKS	DURATION	PUBLISHER	DATE
PEACE	5 minutes	Photostat	1940
(text: Bacchylides)			
women's voices, piano			
TWO PLATO SETTINGS: COUNTRY			
GODS AND COUNTRY MUSIC	5¼ "	Galaxy Music	1942
women's voices, flute, piano		Corporation	

CHAMBER MUSIC

TRIO		Manuscript	1925
violin, cello, piano			
PIANO SONATA	10 minutes	Manuscript	1927
TRIO		Manuscript	1927
clarinet, cello, piano			
SUITE OF THREE DANCES	6 "	Manuscript	1928
violin, jazz percussion, piano			
SEXTET	4 "	Blue Print	1933
flute, oboe, clarinet,		Process	
trumpet, horn, bassoon			
SUITE OF SONGS AND DANCES	16 "	Blue Print	1936
two pianos		Process	
WEDDING MUSIC	8 "	Blue Print	1937
oboe, cello, piano		Process	
SIMON LEGREE—a Negro sermon	6 "	Blue Print	1938
(text: Vachel Lindsay)		Process	
baritone, two pianos			
HARPSICHORD SONATA	10½ "	Blue Print	1941
		Process	
BLACKOUT—a dramatic chamber work	12 "	Blue Print	1941
baritone, two trumpets,		Process	
jazz percussion, piano			

STAGE WORKS

GROCERIES AND NOTIONS—	entire	Vassar Experimental	1931
operetta in 3 acts	evening	Theater Publication	
(music by Martha Alter			
and Gertrude Brown)			
girls' or mixed voices, piano			
ANTHONY COMSTOCK OR	45 minutes	Manuscript	1934
A PURITAN'S PROGRESS			
ballet for 4 solo dancers,			
dance group, full orchestra			
MUSIC FOR CHRISTMAS PAGEANT	7 "	Manuscript	1942
Hammond organ, microphone			
voice, dance group			
MUSIC OF THE STRATOSPHERE—	12 "	Manuscript	1945
THROUGH SPACE, THROUGH TIME,			
AND BEYOND			
dance group, orchestra or piano			
A DIMENSIONAL FANTASY	6 "	Manuscript	1946
dance group, piano, percussion			

DANIELE AMFITHEATROF

Born in St. Petersburg, Russia, in 1901. He began his piano studies at the age of six. He received his diploma for composition from the Royal Conservatory in Italy, where he studied under Respighi. In Rome he also studied organ at the Pontifical Academy of Sacred Music of the Vatican. From 1924 to 1929 he was engaged as pianist, organist and chorus assistant at the Augusteo in Rome, and while there he worked under Molinari as orchestra conductor.

He was artistic director of the Genoa and Trieste Radio and also conductor and manager for the Italian Broadcasting Company in Turin. He conducted on the Continent. He came to America in 1937 and was engaged as Associate Conductor of the Minneapolis Symphony Orchestra. He has appeared as a guest conductor of the Boston Symphony Orchestra. Since 1939 he has been scoring pictures in Hollywood for the major motion-picture studios.

As a composer of concert music he is well known in the United States and abroad, where many of his compositions for orchestra have been performed. "De Profundis Clamavi" and the "Prelude to a Requiem Mass" were presented by the NBC Symphony and the Los Angeles Symphony. The "American Panorama" was recorded in Paris by Pathé and also by Columbia Records. It won the Grand Prix du Disque in 1937. "De Profundis Clamavi" was broadcast over an NBC coast-to-coast network.

COMPOSITIONS WRITTEN IN AMERICA

ORCHESTRAL WORKS	DURATION	PUBLISHER	DATE
CONCERTO FOR PIANO AND ORCHESTRA	29 minutes	Manuscript	1937–46
DE PROFUNDIS CLAMAVI	18 "	Manuscript	1944

FILM MUSIC	STUDIO	DATE
CRY HAVOC	M.G.M.	1943
LOST ANGEL	M.G.M.	1943
LASSIE COME HOME	M.G.M.	1943
I'LL BE SEEING YOU	Selznick-International	1944
DAYS OF GLORY	R.K.O.	1944
MISS SUSIE SLAGLE'S	Paramount	1945
GUEST WIFE	United Artists	1945
THE VIRGINIAN	Paramount	1945
SUSPENSE	Monogram	1946
SONG OF THE SOUTH	Walt Disney	1946

GEORGE ANTHEIL

Born in Trenton, New Jersey, in 1900. He is of Polish parentage. He began his studies in music at the Philadelphia Conservatory with Smith and Von Sternberg and later he became a pupil of Bloch. In 1932 and 1933 he won a Guggenheim Fellowship. For five years he concertized as pianist in Central Europe, England and France.

In 1922 his first symphony, "Zingareska," was performed by the Berlin Philharmonic Orchestra, and his use of jazz in a symphonic work produced protests by some of the composers in the audience. He then went to live in Paris. After a short visit to America to present the première of his "Ballet Mecanique," which introduced several mechanical pianos and electrical appliances, he returned to Vienna and Berlin. The work was chosen by the International Festival at Baden-Baden. In 1928 he became Assistant Music Director of the Berlin Stadtheater. His interest in opera and film music led him to Hollywood, where he has written the music for a series of films. He has contributed articles to magazines on many musical subjects, also on astronomy and glands, two subjects which he studies as hobbies.

Many of his orchestral works and much of his chamber music have been performed abroad and in the United States. "Archipelago" and the Fourth Symphony were broadcast with the NBC Orchestra and also broadcast in Europe. The "Airplane Sonata" has been recorded by N.M.Q.R. At present he is working on a commission from the Dallas Symphony for a Violin Concerto and is completing a Piano Concerto.

COMPOSITIONS

ORCHESTRAL WORKS

	DURATION	PUBLISHER	DATE
ZINGARESKA	20 minutes	Manuscript	1921
BALLET MECANIQUE	30 "	Photostat	1925
SYMPHONY IN F	45 "	Photostat	1926
PIANO CONCERTO	25 "	Manuscript	1926
CAPRICCIO	10 "	Universal Edition	1930
ARCHIPELAGO	10 "	Manuscript	1933
AMERICAN SYMPHONY	25 "	Manuscript	1937
SYMPHONY No. 4	29 "	Boosey & Hawkes	1942
DECATUR IN ALGIERS	5 "	Boosey & Hawkes	1943
HEROES OF TODAY	7 "	Boosey & Hawkes	1945
OVER THE PLAINS	8½ "	Boosey & Hawkes	1946
FIFTH SYMPHONY—TRAGIC	40 "	Boosey & Hawkes	1946
VIOLIN CONCERTO	27 "	Boosey & Hawkes	1946
violin, orchestra			

CHAMBER ORCHESTRA

JAZZ SYMPHONY	18 minutes	Manuscript	1925
22 instruments			
SUITE FOR ORCHESTRA	8 "	Photostat	1926
20 instruments			
CRUCIFIXION	7 "	Manuscript	1927
string orchestra			
COURSE	10 "	Manuscript	1935
5 instruments			

CHORAL WORKS

ELECTION FROM "TRANSATLANTIC"	15 minutes	Universal Edition	1929

GEORGE ANTHEIL (*Continued*)

CHAMBER MUSIC	DURATION	PUBLISHER	DATE
FIRST VIOLIN AND PIANO SONATA	15 minutes		1923
SECOND VIOLIN AND PIANO SONATA	8 "	Manuscript	1923
THIRD VIOLIN AND PIANO SONATA	8 "	Manuscript	1924
FIRST STRING QUARTET	15 "	Manuscript	1924
SECOND STRING QUARTET	25 "	Manuscript	1928
CONCERTO FOR FLUTE, BASSOON, PIANO	15 "	Manuscript	1930
CHAMBER CONCERTO FOR EIGHT INSTRUMENTS	15 "	Manuscript	1932
FEMME 100 TÊTES	16 "	Manuscript	1933
piano			
STRING QUARTET No. 3	20 "	Boosey & Hawkes	1946
SONATINA FOR VIOLIN			
violin, piano			

STAGE WORKS

OEDIPUS—incidental music		Oesterheld Verlag	1928
FIGHTING THE WAVES—ballet	30 minutes	Manuscript	1929
TRANSATLANTIC—opera	3 hours	Universal Edition	1929
FLIGHT—chamber opera	40 minutes	Manuscript	1930
ballet for marionettes			
HELEN RETIRES—opera	2½ hours	Universal Edition	1932
Book by John Erskine			
DREAMS—ballet	32 minutes	Manuscript	1935
25-piece orchestra			

FILM MUSIC

	STUDIO		
ONCE IN A BLUE MOON	Paramount		1935
THE SCOUNDREL	Paramount		1935
THE PLAINSMAN	Paramount		1936
MAKE WAY FOR TOMORROW	Paramount		1937
SPECTER OF THE ROSE	Republic Pictures		
(concert version)			

LOUIS APPLEBAUM

Born in Toronto, Canada, in 1918. He started his piano studies at the age of nine. He attended schools in Toronto, and in 1940 he came to New York to study with Harris and Wagenaar. His early compositions won two prizes in the competition sponsored by the Canadian Performing Society.

In 1936 he started to teach at the University of Toronto. In 1939 he began to write for the National Film Board of Canada, which was created by the Canadian government to serve as the official film outlet for government agencies and also for the Canadian armed forces. In 1942 he joined the staff as composer-conductor. He helped to produce the first Canadian film about a symphony orchestra as part of a music-and-film-education program. He has participated in experimental work in film and music and has also been Music Director for the Toronto Symphony Orchestra film.

LOUIS APPLEBAUM (*Continued*)

He has written film scores for some Hollywood productions. He is planning to come to New York to do research in sound production for motion pictures and also to lecture and write on music for films.

Many of his smaller works were broadcast over the Canadian Broadcasting Company networks and presented at the Toronto Conservatory. The Second String Quartet was performed by the League of Composers.

COMPOSITIONS

ORCHESTRAL WORKS	DURATION	PUBLISHER	DATE
RONDO FOR ORCHESTRA	8 minutes	Manuscript	1938
PIECE FOR ORCHESTRA	6 "	Manuscript	1938

CHAMBER MUSIC			
STRING QUARTET NO. 1	16 minutes	Manuscript	1939
STRING QUARTET NO. 2	21 "	Manuscript	1941
FOUR THUMBS AND SIXTEEN FINGERS *piano, 4 hands*	12 "	Manuscript	1942

FILM MUSIC	STUDIO	PUBLISHER	DATE
ACTION STATIONS	National Film Board of Canada		1942
THIRTEEN PLATOON	National Film Board of Canada		1943
TRANS-CANADA EXPRESS	National Film Board of Canada		1943
FORTRESS JAPAN	National Film Board of Canada		1944
TOMORROW THE WORLD	United Artists and Lester Cowan	Sam Fox Publishing Co.	1944
SUFFER LITTLE CHILDREN	National Film Board of Canada		1945
ORDEAL BY ICE	National Film Board of Canada		1945
FOOD, SECRET OF THE PEACE	National Film Board of Canada		1945
THE STORY OF G.I. JOE	Lester Cowan Producer	Sam Fox Publishing Co.	1945
NEW FACES COME BACK	National Film Board of Canada		1946

RICHARD ARNELL

Born in London, England, in 1917. From 1935 to 1938 he studied with John Ireland at the Royal College of Music in London.

He won the Ernest Farrar Prize in 1938 and came to the United States in 1939. Since 1941 he has been teaching composition privately. From 1943 to 1945 he was music consultant to the New York office of BBC.

His overture "The New Age" and his Violin Concerto have been performed by the National Orchestral Association, New York City. Several other works have been performed in New York and St. Louis and were broadcast over the NBC and CBS networks and also over WQXR, New York.

RICHARD ARNELL (*Continued*)

COMPOSITIONS

ORCHESTRAL WORKS

	DURATION	PUBLISHER	DATE
OVERTURE—THE NEW AGE	8 minutes	Manuscript *for hire*	1939
OVERTURE—"1940"	13 "	Manuscript	1940
CONCERTO FOR VIOLIN AND ORCHESTRA IN ONE MOVEMENT	20 "	Mills Music, Inc.	1940
SINFONIA, QUASI VARIAZIONI	18 "	Manuscript	1941
FANTASIA FOR ORCHESTRA	17 "	Manuscript	1941–42
SYMPHONY NO. 2	22 "	Manuscript	1943
SYMPHONY NO. 3	47 "	Manuscript	1945

CHAMBER ORCHESTRA

DIVERTIMENTO NO. 1 *piano, 12 instruments*	18 minutes	Manuscript	1939
CLASSICAL VARIATIONS *strings*	12 "	Associated Music Publishers	1939
DIVERTIMENTO NO. 2 *11 instruments*	20 "	Manuscript	1940
SONATA FOR CHAMBER ORCHESTRA *11 instruments*	6 "	Manuscript	1942
SYMPHONY NO. 1 *11 instruments*	26 "	Manuscript	1943
CEREMONIAL AND FLOURISH *brass ensemble, 10 instruments*	5 "	Manuscript	1946

CHORAL WORKS

THREE CHILDREN'S SONGS *mixed chorus, a cappella*	10 minutes	Manuscript	1939
SECULAR CANTATA (Algernon Swinburne) *mixed chorus, orchestra*	20 "	Manuscript	1941
CANTATA—THE WAR GOD (Stephen Spender) *soprano solo, mixed chorus, orchestra*	27 "	Manuscript	1944

CHAMBER MUSIC

STRING QUARTET NO. 1	12 minutes	Manuscript	1939
STRING QUARTET NO. 2	15 "	Manuscript	1941
VIOLIN SONATA *violin, piano*	15 "	Manuscript	1941
PIANO QUARTET *piano, strings*	27 "	Manuscript	1942
ORGAN SONATAS No. 1, No. 2	12–15 "	Manuscript	1942
SONATAS FOR UNACCOMPANIED STRING INSTRUMENTS	8 " each	Manuscript	1942–44
PIANO SONATA	26 "	Manuscript	1943
STRING QUARTET NO. 3	17 "	Manuscript	1945
OBOE QUINTET *oboe, strings*	20 "	Manuscript	1945

FILM MUSIC

THE LAND (concert version—suite)		Dept. of Agriculture	1941
FARM FRONT		Dept. of Agriculture	1942

ERNST BACON

Born in 1898 in Chicago, Illinois. He was educated at the Lewis Institute and Northwestern University and received his degree of Master of Arts from the University of Chicago. He began his musical studies first with his mother. He then studied in Chicago and continued later in Vienna studying piano, composition and conducting. Among his teachers were Bree, Bloch and Goossens.

He concertized as pianist in Germany and in the United States. He became Assistant Conductor of the Rochester Opera Company and teacher of piano at the Eastman School of Music. He has conducted at various festivals in the West, has lectured at the San Francisco Conservatory of Music, and has been a director of the Federal Music Project. In 1932 he won the Pulitzer Prize for Music and has also held a Guggenheim Fellowship. From 1934 to 1935 he was Music Editor of *Argonaut*. At present, he is head of the Department of Music at Syracuse University.

His symphonic compositions have had major performances by major orchestras in various cities throughout the country. "A Tree on the Plains" was commissioned by the League of Composers and has had numerous performances. In 1946 "From These States" was presented at the Columbia University Contemporary Music Festival by the NBC Symphony and was broadcast from coast to coast. He has written many songs and works for two pianos which have been published and which have also been played by many chamber groups and soloists.

COMPOSITIONS

ORCHESTRAL WORKS	DURATION	PUBLISHER	DATE
SYMPHONY No. 1 *piano, orchestra*	35 minutes	Associated Music Publishers *for hire*	1932
SYMPHONY No. 2	26 "	Associated Music Publishers *for hire*	1937
"FORD'S THEATRE"—suite	23 "	Associated Music Publishers *for hire*	1943
"FROM THESE STATES"—suite	20 "	Associated Music Publishers *for hire*	1943

CHORAL WORKS			
"ECCLESIASTES"—cantata *soprano, baritone solo,* *mixed chorus, orchestra*	35 minutes	Manuscript	1936
"FROM EMILY'S DIARY"—cantata *soprano, alto solo, women's* *chorus, orchestra*	25 "	G. Schirmer, Inc. *piano score* *parts available*	1944

STAGE WORKS			
"TAKE YOUR CHOICE"—musical comedy	1 hour	Manuscript	1936
"A TREE ON THE PLAINS"—music-play *soprano, alto, tenor, baritone,* *bass and lesser parts*	1 "	Associated Music Publishers *for hire*	1942

SAMUEL BARBER

Born in West Chester, Pennsylvania, in 1910. He began to study music at the age of six and to compose when he was seven years old. He entered the Curtis Institute of Music when he was thirteen and studied piano and singing with Vengerova and De Gogorza; he was chiefly interested, however, in his work in composition, which he studied under Scalero for six years. He was awarded the Prix de Rome in 1935 and the Pulitzer Prize for Music in 1935 and 1936. He received a Guggenheim Fellowship in 1945.

His First Symphony had its première in Rome in 1936 and was played at the Salzburg Music Festival in 1937. It was given its American première in Cleveland in 1937 and has been recorded by Columbia.

His orchestral works have had major performances by the leading symphony orchestras in the United States and Europe. "Music for a Scene from Shelley" was played in London, Rome and Finland and throughout this country. The "Adagio for Strings" has been a frequently performed American composition in England, and it has been presented on the European continent and in this country many times; it has also been recorded by Victor. Victor has likewise recorded "Essay for Orchestra" and "Dover Beach." There have been frequent performances of his chamber works in America and Europe, and his choral works have been sung by the Robert Shaw Collegiate Chorale, the Curtis Institute Madrigal Chorus and by choruses in England. The Concert Hall Society has recently recorded the "Capricorn Concerto."

COMPOSITIONS

ORCHESTRAL WORKS	DURATION	PUBLISHER	DATE
OVERTURE TO "THE SCHOOL FGR SCANDAL," OPUS 5	8 minutes	G. Schirmer, Inc. *miniature score; parts for hire*	1932
MUSIC FOR A SCENE FROM SHELLEY, OPUS 7	8 "	G. Schirmer, Inc. *miniature score; parts for hire*	1933
SYMPHONY NO. 1, OPUS 9	18½ "	G. Schirmer, Inc. *miniature score; parts for hire*	1936
ADAGIO FOR STRINGS, OPUS 11	7 "	G. Schirmer, Inc.	1936
I HEAR AN ARMY, OPUS 10 *voice, orchestra*	2½ "	G. Schirmer, Inc. *score and parts for hire*	1936
SURE ON THIS SHINING NIGHT, OPUS 13 *voice, orchestra*	2 "	G. Schirmer, Inc. *score and parts for hire*	1937
ESSAY FOR ORCHESTRA, OPUS 12	7½ "	G. Schirmer, Inc. *miniature score; parts for hire*	1937
VIOLIN CONCERTO, OPUS 14	22 "	G. Schirmer, Inc. *violin and piano score published; orchestra score and parts for hire*	1939
NOCTURNE, OPUS 13 *voice, orchestra*	3½ "	G. Schirmer, Inc. *score and parts for hire*	1940

SAMUEL BARBER (*Continued*)

ORCHESTRAL WORKS (*Continued*)	DURATION	PUBLISHER	DATE
SECOND ESSAY, OPUS 17	9½ minutes	G. Schirmer, Inc. miniature score; parts for hire	1942
MONKS AND RAISINS, OPUS 18 voice, orchestra	2 "	G. Schirmer, Inc. score and parts for hire	1943
CAPRICORN CONCERTO FOR FLUTE, OBOE, TRUMPET AND STRINGS, OPUS 21	14 "	G. Schirmer, Inc.	1944
SYMPHONY No. 2, OPUS 19	26 "	G. Schirmer, Inc. score and parts for hire	1944
CELLO CONCERTO, OPUS 22	24 "	G. Schirmer, Inc. score and parts for hire	1945

BAND MUSIC

COMMANDO MARCH		G. Schirmer, Inc.	1943

CHORAL WORKS

THE VIRGIN MARTYRS, OPUS 8, No. 1 4 part women's chorus a cappella		G. Schirmer, Inc.	1935
LET DOWN THE BARS, O DEATH, OPUS 8, No. 2 4 part mixed chorus a cappella		G. Schirmer, Inc.	1936
A STOPWATCH AND AN ORDNANCE MAP, OPUS 15 men's voices, 3 kettledrums (4 horns, 3 trombones, tuba ad lib.)		G. Schirmer, Inc. vocal score; brass parts for hire	1940
REINCARNATIONS, OPUS 16 4 part mixed chorus a cappella		G. Schirmer, Inc.	1936–40

CHAMBER MUSIC

SERENADE FOR STRING QUARTET OR STRING ORCHESTRA, OPUS 1		G. Schirmer, Inc.	1929
DOVER BEACH, OPUS 3 medium voice, string quartet		G. Schirmer, Inc.	1931
SONATA FOR VIOLONCELLO AND PIANO, OPUS 6		G. Schirmer, Inc.	1932
STRING QUARTET, OPUS 11		G. Schirmer, Inc.	1936
EXCURSIONS, OPUS 20—four piano pieces		G. Schirmer, Inc.	1944

SAMUEL L. M. BARLOW

Born in New York City, N. Y., in 1892. He is the son of Judge Barlow and a descendant of Joel Barlow the poet, who was Ambassador to Napoleon I. While still at school he began to write and publish music, and his first commission came at the age of nineteen when he was asked to write the incidental music for Guimera's tragedy "Maria Rosa." He studied at Harvard University and continued his musical training with Goetschius and Robinson in New York. In 1923 he went to Rome to study with Respighi.

Before and after the First World War he took an active interest in New York City music and taught in the settlements and lectured for the Board of Education. He was the first Chairman of the New York Community

SAMUEL L. M. BARLOW (*Continued*)

Chorus. He is Chairman of the Music Division of the Independent Citizens Committee for Arts, Sciences and Professions; he is a Governor of the American Composers Alliance; Secretary of the Iranian Institute; Chairman of the American Committee for the Arts; Director of the China Aid Council; Vice-President of the American Committee for Spanish Freedom. He has lectured at the University of Puerto Rico and in other countries. He is a contributor to the League of Composers' quarterly magazine, *Modern Music,* and the author of *Report on South America, Art and Politics* and other works.

He appeared as soloist with his Concerto for Piano and Orchestra with the Rochester Symphony and later in Europe. His opera "Mon Ami Pierrot" was the first opera written by an American to be given in Paris. The Overture to this work has been played repeatedly by the symphonic orchestras in North and South America and in Europe. "Three Songs with Orchestra," "Alba," "Babar" and "Amphitryon" have been presented in Europe, Brazil and the United States. Many of the works for chamber music have been played in Europe and America. "Cherry Tree" was recorded with Elsie Houston and the Columbia Recording Company is preparing a record of "Jim Crow Car" with Paul Robeson.

COMPOSITIONS

ORCHESTRAL WORKS	DURATION	PUBLISHER	DATE
ALBA—POÈME SYMPHONIQUE	10 minutes	Manuscript	1927
BALLO SARDO	26 "	Manuscript	1928
CONCERTO	30 "	Manuscript	1931
piano, orchestra			
SPANISH QUARTER		Manuscript	
OVERTURE—MON AMI PIERROT	12 "	Choudens	1934
BABAR—POÈME SYMPHONIQUE	18 "	Manuscript	1936
		for hire	
LEDA	8 "	Manuscript	1939
SOUSA AD PARNASSUM	4 "	Manuscript	1939

CHAMBER ORCHESTRA			
THREE SONGS FROM CHINESE	5 minutes	Manuscript	1924
6 instruments, piano, tenor			
VOCALISE	5 "	Manuscript	1926
30–50 instruments			
ALBA—first form	10 "	Manuscript	1927
35 instruments, soprano			
AMPHITRYON 38	14 "	Manuscript	1937
small orchestra		G. Schirmer, Inc.	

CHAMBER MUSIC			
BALLAD	7 minutes	Manuscript	1933
quartet			
SCHERZO	10 "	Manuscript	1933
quartet			
SPANISH QUARTER—suite		Manuscript	
for piano solo			
JARDIN DE LE NOTRE—suite		Joubert	
for piano solo			
CONVERSATION WITH CHEKHOV	10 "	Manuscript	1940
trio for piano, violin, cello			

SAMUEL L. M. BARLOW (*Continued*)

STAGE WORKS	DURATION	PUBLISHER	DATE
MON AMI PIERROT—opera	80 minutes	Choudens	1934
full orchestra			
AMANDA—opera	80 "	Manuscript	1936
full orchestra			
AMPHITRYON 38	50 "	Manuscript	1937
12 piece orchestra		G. Schirmer, Inc.	

WAYNE BARLOW

Born in Elyria, Ohio, in 1912. He studied at the Eastman School of Music with Hanson, Rogers and Royce. He was also a pupil of Schoenberg. Since 1937 he has been a member of the faculty of the Eastman School of Music, where he teaches theory and composition. He was commissioned by station WHAM, Rochester, to write a nocturne for small orchestra. He is especially interested in the study of acoustics.

His major compositions have been performed by leading orchestras in various cities of the United States. CBS and NBC have broadcast "Winter's Past" and Nocturne; Victor has recorded "Winter's Past." He is now completing a serenade for orchestra and a concerto grosso for brass and orchestra.

COMPOSITIONS

ORCHESTRAL WORKS	DURATION	PUBLISHER	DATE
THREE MOODS FOR DANCING	15 minutes	Manuscript	1940

CHAMBER ORCHESTRA			
RHAPSODY, "THE WINTER'S PAST"	5 minutes	Carl Fischer, Inc.	1938
oboe, strings			
LYRICAL PIECE	5 "	Carl Fischer, Inc.	1945
clarinet, strings			
NOCTURNE	6 "	Manuscript	1946
18 instruments			

CHORAL WORKS			
SONGS FROM THE SILENCE OF AMOR	12 minutes	Manuscript	1937
soprano solo, small orchestra			
MADRIGAL FOR A BRIGHT MORNING	2½ "	J. Fischer & Bro.	1942
mixed chorus, a cappella			
THE 23RD PSALM	5 "	J. Fischer & Bro.	1943
mixed chorus, organ or orchestra			

STAGE WORKS			
THE BLACK MADONNA—ballet	25 minutes	Manuscript	1941
large orchestra			

JOHN R. BARROWS, JR.

Born in Glendale, California, in 1913. He first studied the horn at the East-
man School in Rochester, and studied composition, cello, and horn at the
Yale School of Music. He was a pupil of Baumgartner, Donovan, and Smith.
He won a scholarship in composition at Yale and honorable mention in the
NBC Chamber Music Contest of 1936. He played first horn with the San
Diego Symphony and with the New Haven Symphony, also soloist in small
ensemble.

He was in the armed services for four years and was the Assistant Leader
of the Official AAF Band of Washington, D. C. The Three Marches for
Military Band was written during this period and was played in many
concerts and broadcasts here and in England. Nocturne was played by
the San Diego Symphony. The Quintet for woodwinds was given at the
festival of American Music at Yaddo and at Saratoga Springs and was
broadcast over WJZ. The Divertimento was broadcast over WICC Mutual network. "Would Be Gentleman" with incidental music was presented
at the New Haven Federal Theatre.

COMPOSITIONS

CHAMBER ORCHESTRA

	DURATION	PUBLISHER	DATE
VARIATIONS	12 minutes	Manuscript	1935
French horn, 5 strings			
NOCTURNE	6 "	Manuscript	1935
English horn			
CONCERTINO	15 "	Manuscript	1937
piano			
SUITE FOR STRING ORCHESTRA		Manuscript	1937

CHAMBER MUSIC

QUINTET	23 minutes	Manuscript	1936
woodwinds			
STRING QUARTET No. 1	18 "	Manuscript	1936
DIVERTIMENTO	15 "	Manuscript	1937
string trio			
SONATA	15 "	Manuscript	1937
French horn, piano			
SONATA	14 "	Manuscript	1937
cello, piano			
SONATINA	13 "	Manuscript	1937
piano			
STRING QUARTET No. 2		Manuscript	1937
VIOLA SONATA		Manuscript	1937
TRIO		Manuscript	1937
flute, horn, bassoon			
FLUTE SONATA		Manuscript	1937
SONATA FOR BASSOON		Manuscript	1937

BAND MUSIC

CONCERT MARCH No. 1	4 minutes	Manuscript	1943
MARCH OF THE GREMLINS	3 "	Manuscript	1944
CONCERT MARCH No. 2	4 "	Manuscript	1945

STAGE WORKS

INCIDENTAL MUSIC TO "WOULD BE GENTLEMAN"	2 hours	Manuscript	1935
theatre orchestra			

HANS BARTH

Born in Leipzig, Germany, in 1896. He came to America at the age of six. He received a scholarship at the Leipzig Conservatory under Professor Rechendorf. At the age of twelve he gave recitals in New York City. He subsequently studied with various New York and European teachers and made his début in 1917.

He has made a special study of tonal and octave divisions and is the inventor of a portable, sectional, quarter-tone piano, for which instrument he has written extensively. He has concertized in America as well as in Europe, playing the harpsichord, piano and quarter-tone piano. He has appeared with many of the major orchestras and has introduced some of his works for the quarter-tone piano on their programs. The Philadelphia, Cincinnati and Havana orchestras have played the Concerto for Quarter-Tone Strings and Quarter-Tone Piano, and the Sonata, Op. 14, has had many performances all over the United States. Courses and lectures on music have been given by him in various cities. His book, *Technic,* is used all over the United States and Canada, as well as in Europe. He has been Director of the Yonkers Institute of Musical Art and has taught piano at the David Mannes Music School. He is at present Director of the National School for Musical Culture in New York City. He is now completing a Symphony No. 2 and a Sonata No. 3 for piano.

COMPOSITIONS

ORCHESTRAL WORKS

	DURATION	PUBLISHER	DATE
CONCERTO FOR PIANO, OPUS 11 ½ tone	25 minutes	Manuscript	1928
CONCERTO FOR STRINGS, OPUS 15 ¼ tone strings, ¼ tone piano	10 "	Manuscript	1930
QUINTET FOR STRINGS AND PIANO ¼ tone	9 "	Manuscript	1930
DRAMA SYMPHONY, OPUS 25 ½ tone	30 "	Manuscript	1940
TEN ETUDES FOR PIANO AND ORCHESTRA, OPUS 26 ½ tone	35 "	Manuscript	1943

CHAMBER MUSIC

	DURATION	PUBLISHER	DATE
SONATA FOR PIANO No. 1, OPUS 7	14 minutes	Manuscript	1929
SONATA FOR PIANO No 2, OPUS 14	12 "	Associated Music Publishers	1932

STAGE WORKS

	DURATION	PUBLISHER	DATE
MIRAGIA—operetta	2½ hours	Manuscript	1928
SAVE ME THE WALTZ—incidental music to play	2 "	Crawford Music Corp.	1939

BELA BARTOK

Born in Nagyszentmiklos, Hungary, in 1881, and died in New York in 1945. His father was director of a School of Agriculture and his mother was a school teacher. At the age of eight he began to compose and he made his first public appearance as composer-pianist two years later. He studied at the Royal Academy of Music in Budapest for four years, where he studied composition and piano.

In co-operation with Zoltan Kodály he began a collection of Hungarian folk music. The first joint publication which appeared in 1906 was called "Hungarian Folksongs for Voice and Piano." Following this work Bartok's own "Twenty Songs" and "Szekely Ballads" appeared. More than six thousand folk songs of Slavic origin and two hundred Arab melodies were gathered during his researches, and his volume "Hungarian Folk Music" is a standard work in this field. In 1907 he was made Professor of Piano at the Royal Academy of Music in Budapest. He came to America in 1927 and in 1928, where he was soloist with major orchestras, playing his Rhapsody and Piano Concerto, No. 1; he also appeared as pianist in programs of his own chamber music. In 1939 he returned to the United States and played at the Congressional Library in Washington and at a program in his honor presented by the League of Composers in New York.

In 1941 he became a resident of New York, where he remained until his death. During this period he was commissioned by Menuhin to write a sonata for violin, and by the Koussevitzky Music Foundation to write the Concerto for Orchestra, which was first performed by the Boston Symphony Orchestra. Columbia University commissioned him to transcribe the Milman Parry Collection of Jugoslav folk-music recordings. "Village Scenes," for chamber orchestra and vocal quartet, was written for the League of Composers and first performed by Koussevitzky at Town Hall.

His works for stage have been performed at the Budapest Opera House. "The Wooden Prince," first presented in 1917, was followed by "Bluebeard's Castle." "The Wonderful Mandarin," a pantomime with full orchestra, was written for a text by the Hungarian author Melchior Lengyel. Many of Bartok's orchestral works have been performed by major orchestras in Europe and in America and his chamber music has been presented by the leading ensemble groups in all parts of the world.

COMPOSITIONS WRITTEN IN AMERICA

ORCHESTRAL WORKS	DURATION	PUBLISHER	DATE
CONCERTO	37 minutes	Boosey & Hawkes	1943
CONCERTO FOR PIANO, No. 3	21 "	Boosey & Hawkes	1945
CONCERTO FOR VIOLA (unfinished)		Manuscript	1945

CHAMBER MUSIC			
SONATA FOR VIOLIN	15 minutes	Boosey & Hawkes	1943

STANLEY BATE

Born in Devonshire, England, in 1912. In 1932 he won the All England Open Scholarship for study at the Royal College of Music under Vaughan Williams. The Octavia Travelling Scholarship, won in 1936, enabled him to go to Paris, where he worked with Nadia Boulanger, and to Berlin, where he studied with Paul Hindemith at the Hochschule. He was awarded a Guggenheim Fellowship in 1942.

During his student years in London, he won the Ernest Farrar Prize, the Cobbett Prize for String Quartet and the Arthur Sullivan Memorial Prize for the outstanding scholar of his year. On his return to England in 1938, he was commissioned to write a Concertino for Piano and Orchestra for the Eastbourne Festival of Music. He was music director and composer of incidental music for various theatrical groups. During the years of the war he was in London organizing "morale" music and "blackout" concerts. In 1941 he toured Australia under the auspices of the British Council for Cultural Relations, lecturing on British and contemporary music and appearing in concerts of his own and other modern works. He came to the United States in April, 1941. His American début took place in 1942, when he appeared as soloist in the first performance of his Piano Concerto. In 1943, he wrote the incidental music for Kingsley's play "The Patriots." In 1945, he went on a tour of Brazil and gave a series of programs; he also broadcast in Latin America.

His Sinfonietta No. 1 was performed at the I.S.C.M. Festival in Berkeley in 1942. Other works have been frequently performed and broadcast in England, the United States and Latin America.

COMPOSITIONS WRITTEN IN AMERICA

ORCHESTRAL WORKS	DURATION	PUBLISHER	DATE
CONCERTO No. 2, OPUS 28 *piano, orchestra*	30 minutes	Manuscript	1941
SINFONIETTA No. 2, OPUS 39	15 "	Manuscript	1943
SYMPHONY No. 3, OPUS 29	28 "	Manuscript	1943
CONCERTO No. 1, OPUS 42 *violin, orchestra*	35 "	Manuscript	1943
INCANTATIONS, OPUS 43 (poems: Eugene Jolas) *tenor or soprano solo*	15 "	Manuscript	1945
CONCERTO No. 1, OPUS 46 *viola, orchestra*	40 "	Manuscript	1945–46

CHAMBER MUSIC			
SONATINAS *piano*	7 minutes each	Associated Music Publishers	1941–45
FIVE PIECES FOR STRING QUARTET, OPUS 23	8 "	Schott	1943
STRING QUARTET No. 2, OPUS 41	15 "	Schott	1943
OVERTURE TO A RUSSIAN WAR RELIEF, OPUS 37 *2 pianos*	7 "	Manuscript	1943
THREE PIECES FOR TWO PIANOS, OPUS 38	24 "	Associated Music Publishers	1944
PIANO SONATA No 1, OPUS 45	20 "	Schott	1945
PIANO SUITE, OPUS 44	15 "	Schott	1945
SONATA No. 1, OPUS 47 *violin, piano*	15 "	Manuscript	1945

STANLEY BATE (*Continued*)

STAGE WORKS	DURATION	PUBLISHER	DATE
VARIATIONS ON A THEME—ballet	35 minutes		1945
full orchestra			
FOLK SONG BALLET	25 "		1945–46
THE PATRIOTS—incidental music			
(Kingsley)			

FILM MUSIC	STUDIO		
THE FIFTH YEAR	British Library	Associated Music	1945
full orchestra	of Information	Publishers	

MARION EUGENIE BAUER

Born in Walla Walla, Washington, in 1887. She is of French parentage. Her mother was a professor of languages in the Northwest, and her father a musician. Her first teacher of music was her sister, the well-known music critic, Emilie Frances Bauer. She studied also with Heffley, Huss, Rothwell, Pugno, Gédalge, Boulanger, and Campbell-Tipton.

She is Associate Professor in the Music Department of New York University, a faculty member of the Juilliard School of Music, and is the New York editor of *Musical Leader*. She has been a visiting professor at Carnegie Institute of Technology, Mills College and Cincinnati Conservatory of Music and teacher in the Juilliard summer school. Since 1932 she has been an annual lecturer at Chautauqua. Author of *Twentieth Century Music* and *Musical Questions and Quizzes,* and contributor to many magazines on music, she is also co-author with Ethel R. Peyser of *How Music Grew* and *Music Through the Ages*. She is a member of the Board of Directors of the League of Composers and the American Music Center and of the Board of Governors of the American Composers Alliance; Vice-President of the Society for the Publication of American Music and of the Chautauqua Society of Greater New York; Chairman of the Young Composers Contests of the National Federation of Music Clubs.

Her orchestral works have been presented by the Worcester Festival Orchestra and the Chautauqua Symphony Orchestra in New York and in Syracuse. The choral works have been performed in New York, in Cleveland and Detroit and at the Worcester Festival. Her chamber music has been frequently performed, and many of these works have been broadcast over network and local stations, including NBC, CBS, WNYC and WQXR. The Symphonic Suite for String Orchestra won honorable mention in the Sigma Alpha Iota Contest for compositions by women. The Concertino for Oboe, Clarinet and String Quartet was commissioned by the League of Composers and broadcast over CBS in 1940.

COMPOSITIONS

ORCHESTRAL WORKS	DURATION	PUBLISHER	DATE
INDIAN PIPES	4 minutes	Manuscript	1929
(orchestrated by Martin			
Bernstein)			

MARION EUGENIE BAUER (*Continued*)

ORCHESTRAL WORKS (*Continued*)	DURATION	PUBLISHER	DATE
ORIENTALE	2 minutes	Manuscript	1932
accompaniment to song			
SUN SPLENDOR	6 "	Manuscript	1936
SYMPHONIC SUITE FOR STRING			
ORCHESTRA, OPUS 34	15 "	Manuscript	1940
CONCERTO FOR PIANO AND			
ORCHESTRA, OPUS 36	14 "	G. Schirmer, Inc.	1943

CHAMBER ORCHESTRA

A LAMENT ON AFRICAN THEMES	6 minutes	Manuscript	1928
(slow movement from string quartet)			
string orchestra			
FAUN SONG	3 "	Manuscript	1934
contralto, chamber orchestra			
PAN—choreographic sketch	12 "	Manuscript	1937
7 instruments, piano			
CONCERTINO FOR OBOE, CLARINET AND			
STRING QUARTET, OPUS 32b	8 "	Arrow Press	1939/1943
string orchestra optional			

CHORAL WORKS

THE LAY OF THE FOUR WINDS	7 minutes	A. P. Schmidt Co.	
men's voices, piano accompaniment			
THREE NOELS	6 "	A. P. Schmidt Co.	1929
women's voices, a cappella			
HERE AT HIGH MORNING	3 "	H. W. Gray Co.	1931
men's voices, a cappella			
FAIR DAFFODILS	4 "	A. P. Schmidt Co.	
trio for women's voices			
THE THINKER, OPUS 35		Galaxy Music Corp.	1938
mixed chorus			
A GARDEN IS A LOVESOME THING,			
OPUS 28		G. Schirmer, Inc.	1938
CHINA, OPUS 38		J. Fischer & Bro.	1943–44
mixed chorus, orchestra			

CHAMBER MUSIC

VIOLIN SONATA NO. 1, OPUS 14	20 minutes	Manuscript	1922
FANTASIA QUASI UNA SONATA	20 "	G. Schirmer, Inc.	1928
violin, piano			
STRING QUARTET	17 "	Manuscript	1928
SUN SPLENDOR	6 "	Manuscript	1930
two pianos			
DANCE SONATA	18 "	Manuscript	1932
SUITE FOR OBOE AND CLARINET		Manuscript	1932
SONATA FOR VIOLA AND PIANO, OPUS 22	18 "	Manuscript	1935
SUITE FOR SOPRANO AND STRING			
QUARTET	15 "	Manuscript	1935
SONATINA FOR OBOE AND PIANO,			
OPUS 32a	8 "	Manuscript	1940
CONCERTINO FOR OBOE, CLARINET			
AND STRING QUARTET, OPUS 32b	8 "	Arrow Press	1939/1943
TRIO SONATA, OPUS 40		Manuscript	1944
flute, cello, piano			

STAGE WORKS AND FILM MUSIC

PROMETHEUS BOUND—incidental music	entire	Manuscript	1930
two pianos and flutes	evening		
PAN—choreographic sketch for film	12 minutes	Manuscript	1937
flute, oboe, clarinet, string quartet,			
piano			

MRS. H. H. A. BEACH
(née Amy Marcy Cheney)

Born in Henniker, New Hampshire, in 1867 and died in 1944. She came from a family dating back to the earliest colonial settlers. There was musical talent in her mother's family for several generations; her father came from a family of scholars and was greatly interested in mathematics. At the age of four she began studying the piano with her mother, and at a very early age she began to compose. She later studied piano and harmony with Perabo, Baermann and Hill. She taught herself fugue, counterpoint and instrumentation. At the age of sixteen she toured in the United States as a pianist and appeared with the Boston and Chicago Symphony orchestras. She toured in Europe, where she played her own Concerto with many of the orchestras. She divided her energies between composing and playing in concerts.

In 1893 she was commissioned to write a composition to dedicate the Woman's Building at the Chicago World's Fair. The "Song of Welcome" was written in 1898 for the Omaha Exposition and the "Panama Hymn" in 1915 for the San Francisco Panama-Pacific Exposition. Her choral works and chamber music have been performed extensively in America and in Europe. Several works have been recorded by Victor.

COMPOSITIONS

ORCHESTRAL WORKS	DURATION	PUBLISHER	DATE
CONCERTO IN C# MINOR *piano, orchestra*		A. P. Schmidt Co.	

CHORAL WORKS			
THOU KNOWEST, LORD	12 minutes	G. Schirmer, Inc.	1915
LET THIS MIND BE IN YOU!	10 "	John Church Co.	1923
BENEDICTUS ES DOMINE	6 "	A. P. Schmidt Co.	1924
LORD OF THE WORLDS ABOVE	9 "	Oliver Ditson Co.	1925
BENEDICITE OMNIA OPERA	7 "	A. P. Schmidt Co.	1927
CANTICLE OF THE SUN	20 "	A. P. Schmidt Co.	1928
CHRIST IN THE UNIVERSE	20 "	H. W. Gray Co.	1931
HEARKEN UNTO ME	11 "	A. P. Schmidt Co.	1934
CANDY LION		G. Schirmer, Inc.	
4 part women's chorus			
DOLLADINE		G. Schirmer, Inc.	
4 part women's chorus			
DUSK IN JUNE		G. Schirmer, Inc.	
4 part chorus			
PANAMA HYMN		G. Schirmer, Inc.	
soprano, alto, tenor, bass, *orchestra, organ*			
PRAYER OF A TIRED CHILD		G. Schirmer, Inc.	
sopranos, altos			
A THANKSGIVING FABLE		G. Schirmer, Inc.	

CHAMBER MUSIC			
VARIATIONS	20 minutes	G. Schirmer, Inc.	1916
flute, string quartet			
SUITE FOR TWO PIANOS	25 "	John Church Co.	1922
STRING QUARTET	20 "	Manuscript	1929
VARIATIONS ON BALKAN THEMES	20 "	A. P. Schmidt Co.	1935
two pianos			
TRIO	15 "		1939

JOHN BEACH

Born in Gloversville, New York, in 1877. He studied at the New England Conservatory of Music in Boston. Among his piano teachers were Johns and Bauer; his teachers of composition were Chadwick and Loeffler and later Gédalge in Paris and Malipiero in Italy. He taught piano and theory at the University of Minnesota, in New Orleans and in Boston. At present he is living in La Crescenta, California.

His principal orchestral works, "Asolani" and "Orleans Alley," have had major performances with the Minneapolis Orchestra and the Philadelphia and New Orleans orchestras. "Phantom Satyr" has been performed as a symphonic work and also given in its stage version with the Rochester Orchestra and the Eastman School Ballet. Most of the music for chamber orchestra or small ensemble has had performances in America or in Europe.

COMPOSITIONS

ORCHESTRAL WORKS

	DURATION	PUBLISHER	DATE
ASOLANI	20 minutes	Manuscript	1920
PHANTOM SATYR	12 "	Manuscript	1924
ORLEANS ALLEY	12 "	Manuscript	1925

CHAMBER ORCHESTRA

	DURATION	PUBLISHER	DATE
ANGELO'S LETTER *tenor or baritone, 17 instruments*	20 minutes	Manuscript	1926
ENTER BUFFOON *11 instruments*	8 "	Manuscript	1929

CHAMBER MUSIC

	DURATION	PUBLISHER	DATE
NAÏVE LANDSCAPES *piano, flute, oboe, clarinet*	10 minutes	Manuscript	1917
POEM FOR STRING QUARTET	12 "	J. & W. Chester	1920
CONCERT FOR SIX INSTRUMENTS *violin, viola, cello, flute,* *oboe, clarinet*	15 "	Manuscript	1929

STAGE WORKS

	DURATION	PUBLISHER	DATE
PIPPA'S HOLIDAY—dramatic prelude *soprano and orchestra*	30 minutes	Manuscript	1916
PHANTOM SATYR—ballet *large or small orchestra*	12 "	Manuscript	1924
MARDI GRAS—ballet *small orchestra*	30 "	Manuscript	1925

JOHN J. BECKER

Born in Henderson, Kentucky, in 1886. He studied with Middleshulte, Kruger, Gulli, Von Fielitz, Keller and Busch and received his Bachelor of Arts and Doctor of Music degrees from the Wisconsin Conservatory. He has been a contributor to many magazines, including *Musical Quarterly, Northwest Music Herald* and the *Musical Observer,* and was Associate Editor of New Music Publications. He is now on the Executive Board of New Music Publications and New Music Recordings and also on the Advisory Committee of the American Composers Fellowship group. He was Director of Music at Notre Dame University and Conductor of its Glee Club, Professor of Fine Arts at the College of St. Scholastica, and conductor of many orchestral and choral groups. He has lectured in many colleges on musical subjects, and at the present time he is Director of Music and composer in residence at Barat College of the Sacred Heart in Illinois.

His Symphony No. 3 was performed by the New York Philharmonic Symphony, and his Symphony No. 2 was played at the Frankfurt Music Festival in Germany. Many of his works have been presented frequently in the United States. His First and Third Symphonies were broadcast. The "Credo" for a cappella men's chorus has been recorded by N.M.Q.R. He is preparing at present a Symphony No. 7, a musical stage work for television, and "Man and Shadow" based on the poem by Kreymborg.

COMPOSITIONS

ORCHESTRAL WORKS	DURATION	PUBLISHER	DATE
SYMPHONY NO. 2		Manuscript for hire	1920
SYMPHONY NO. 3—SYMPHONIA BREVIS	18 minutes	New Music for hire piano copy for sale	1929
CONCERTO ARABESQUE piano solo, orchestra	12 "	New Music parts for hire	1930
CONCERTO PASTORALE—A FOREST RHAPSODIE 2 flutes, orchestra	8 "	Manuscript for hire	1933
CONCERTO horn solo, orchestra	15 "	New Music parts for hire	1933
SOUNDPIECES NOS. 1 AND 2 strings		Manuscript for hire	1937
CONCERTO viola solo, orchestra	18 "	Manuscript for hire	1937
SYMPHONY No. 4—dramatic episodes	25 "	Manuscript for hire	1938
CONCERTO No. 2 (Satirico) piano, orchestra	15 "	Manuscript for hire	1938
FIRST ORCHESTRAL SUITE— RAIN DOWN DEATH	12 "	Manuscript for hire	1939
SECOND ORCHESTRAL SUITE— WHEN THE WILLOW NODS	15 "	Manuscript for hire	1940
DANCES FROM ANTIGONE	15 "	Manuscript for hire	1940

JOHN J. BECKER (*Continued*)

ORCHESTRAL WORKS (*Continued*)	DURATION	PUBLISHER	DATE
SYMPHONY No. 6—symphony of democracy *speaker, high-school chorus, orchestra*	25 minutes	Manuscript *for hire*	1942
VICTORY MARCH	5 "	Manuscript *for hire*	1942
SYMPHONY No. 5—homage to Mozart	15 "	Manuscript *for hire*	1943
THE SWAN GOOSE—legend	10 "	Manuscript *for hire*	1944

CHAMBER ORCHESTRA

CONCERTO ARABESQUE *piano solo, 12 instruments*	12 minutes	New Music *parts for hire*	1930
CONCERTO *horn, 18 instruments*	15 "	New Music *parts for hire*	1933
SOUNDPIECES *strings (small group)*		Manuscript *for hire*	1937
FIRST ORCHESTRAL SUITE— RAIN DOWN DEATH *10 instruments*	12 "	Manuscript *for hire*	1939
SECOND ORCHESTRAL SUITE— WHEN THE WILLOW NODS *10 instruments*	15 "	Manuscript *for hire*	1940
SYMPHONY No. 5—homage to Mozart *10 instruments*	15 "	Manuscript	1943

CHORAL WORKS

ROUGE BOUQUET *male chorus a cappella, trumpet, solo piano*	13 minutes	Manuscript *for hire*	1917
OUT OF THE CRADLE ENDLESSLY ROCKING *narrator, soprano, tenor, mixed chorus, orchestra*	20 "	Manuscript *for hire*	1929
MISSA SYMPHONICA *male chorus a cappella*	40 "	New Music *for hire*	1933
LINCOLN'S GETTYSBURG ADDRESS *speaker, mixed chorus, orchestra*	12 "	Manuscript *for hire*	1941
MASS IN HONOR OF THE SACRED HEART *men's or women's voices a cappella*	20 "	Manuscript *for hire*	1944
MOMENTS FROM THE PASSION *soli, men's or women's voices a cappella*	50 "	Gamble Hinge Co.	1945

CHAMBER MUSIC

FOUR SONGS FOR SOPRANO AND STRING QUARTET	6 minutes	Manuscript	1919
A HEINE SONG CYCLE—8 songs *high voice*	15 "	Manuscript	1924
PSALMS OF LOVE—CYCLE—4 songs	15 "	Manuscript	1935
SOUNDPIECE No. 3—sonata for violin and piano	10 "	Manuscript	1936
SOUNDPIECES Nos. 1-2-4 *string quartets and quintets*		Manuscript	1937
SOUNDPIECE No. 5—sonata for piano	12 "	New Music	1938

JOHN J. BECKER (*Continued*)

CHAMBER MUSIC (*Continued*)	DURATION	PUBLISHER	DATE
SOUNDPIECE No. 6—sonata for flute and clarinet	15 minutes	Manuscript for hire	1940

STAGE WORKS

	DURATION	PUBLISHER	DATE
DANCE FIGURE *singer, dance group, large orchestra*	15 minutes	Manuscript for hire	1933
OBONGO—DANCE PRIMITIVE *dance group and 29 percussion instruments*	15–20 "	Manuscript for hire	1933
A MARRIAGE WITH SPACE—a new stage form *for solo and mass recitation, solo and dance group, large orchestra*	45–50 "	Manuscript for hire	1933
LIFE OF MAN—prologue and 4 acts (Andreiev)—a new music dramatic form		Manuscript	1937
DANCE *dance group, piano, 5 percussion instruments*	10 "	Manuscript for hire	1939
RAIN DOWN DEATH—1 act *small orchestra, 30 players*	20 "	Manuscript for hire	1939
WHEN THE WILLOW NODS—1 act play *small orchestra, 30 players*	40 "	Manuscript for hire	1939
PRIVILEGE AND PRIVATION—1 act play *small orchestra, 30 players*	35 "	Manuscript for hire	1940
ANTIGONE (Sophocles)	80 "	Manuscript	1940
"DEIRDRE OF THE SORROWS"— (Synge) lyric drama in 1 act, 3 scenes *large opera orchestra*	1½ hours	Manuscript	1945

JEANNE BEHREND

Born in Philadelphia, Pennsylvania, in 1911. She graduated from the Curtis Institute of Music in 1934. She studied piano with Hoffmann, Saperton and Landowska and composition with Scalero, Chasins and Toch.

She taught in the Curtis Institute and at Western College in Ohio. She is very active as a concert artist, appearing as soloist and with leading orchestras. Her interest in Latin-American music has resulted in a series of lecture-recitals given at the Pan American Association in Philadelphia and the Pan American Union in Washington. She is the first woman to be sent by the United States State Department on a South American concert tour as a good-will ambassador; she visited Brazil, Uruguay, Argentina, Chile and Peru. She was awarded the Bearns Prize (Columbia University) in 1936 for the orchestral suite, "From Dawn Until Dusk," and for the Teasdale Songs.

Her compositions have been performed in many parts of the country. "From Dawn Until Dusk" was broadcast by the NBC Orchestra over an NBC network.

JEANNE BEHREND (*Continued*)

COMPOSITIONS

ORCHESTRAL WORKS	DURATION	PUBLISHER	DATE
FROM DAWN UNTIL DUSK—suite	15 minutes	Elkan-Vogel *for hire*	1939

CHORAL WORKS			
EASTER HYMN *solo soprano, chorus, small orchestra; or organ, 2 harps*	8 minutes	Manuscript	1940–41
FANTASY ON SONG OF UNITED NATIONS (Shostakovitch) *solo soprano, soprano chorus, 2 pianos*	7 "	Manuscript	1942

CHAMBER MUSIC			
FROM DAWN UNTIL DUSK—suite *piano*	13 minutes	Elkan-Vogel	1934
SONATA *piano*	45 "	Manuscript	1935
THREE DIALOGUES *viola d'amore, piano*	7 "	Manuscript	1940
STRING QUARTET	10 "	Manuscript	1940
SONATINA *piano*	10 "	Manuscript	1942
LAMENTATION *viola, piano*	7 "	Manuscript	1944
SIX SONGS—song cycle (Teasdale)	12 "	Manuscript	1932–43

ROBERT RUSSELL BENNETT

Born in Kansas City, Missouri, in 1894. He began his study of musical instruments at the age of nine with his parents, continuing with Busch in his native city. In 1926 he went to Paris to work with Nadia Boulanger. He received a Guggenheim Fellowship in 1927 and 1928, and continued his studies in Paris, Berlin and London.

At the age of sixteen he started to earn his living as a pianist, copyist, arranger and orchestrator for musical comedies, and since 1930 he has been working for various film studios in Hollywood. For twenty years he has devoted part of his time to the composition of symphonic, choral and chamber music. In 1940 he began his activity as a radio conductor with a weekly program, "Russell Bennett's Notebook," over Mutual network, and early in 1944 he acted as Guest Conductor for six broadcasts of the WOR Sinfonietta, including one program of his own works. He also conducted the Ford program. His "Abraham Lincoln Symphony" and "Sights and Sounds" won awards in the RCA Victor Symphonic Contest of 1930. In 1942 he received the Award of Merit of the National Association for American Composers and Conductors.

ROBERT RUSSELL BENNETT (*Continued*)

In 1936 the League of Composers commissioned him to write an orchestral work called "Hollywood," which was played by the NBC Orchestra on their tenth-anniversary program. "Eight Etudes for Symphony Orchestra" was commissioned by CBS in 1938. The opera "Maria Malibran" was presented in 1935 by the Juilliard School. His works have had frequent concert and radio performances throughout the United States and also in Berlin. "Hexapoda" was recorded by Columbia.

COMPOSITIONS

ORCHESTRAL WORKS

	DURATION	PUBLISHER	DATE
CHARLESTON RHAPSODY	12 minutes	Manuscript	1926
PAYSAGE FOR ORCHESTRA	15 "	Manuscript	1928
SIGHTS AND SOUNDS	28 "	Harms, Inc.	1929
ABRAHAM LINCOLN SYMPHONY	30 "	Harms, Inc.	1929
MARCH FOR TWO PIANOS AND ORCHESTRA	14 "	Manuscript	1930
ADAGIO EROICO	8 "	Manuscript	1933
CONCERTO GROSSO *small dance band as soli*	13 "	Manuscript	1933
HOLLYWOOD—Scherzo	15 "	Manuscript	1936
EIGHT ETUDES FOR SYMPHONY ORCHESTRA	18 "	Manuscript	1938
SYMPHONY IN D FOR THE DODGERS	20 "	Manuscript	1941
NOCTURNE AND APPASSIONATA *piano, orchestra*	13 "	Manuscript	1941
CONCERTO FOR VIOLIN AND ORCHESTRA	21 "	Manuscript	1941
THE FOUR FREEDOMS SYMPHONY	18 "	Robbins Music Corp.	1943
OVERTURE TO AN IMAGINARY DRAMA	7 "	Manuscript	1946
SYMPHONY	38 "	Manuscript	1946
A SYMPHONIC STORY OF JEROME KERN	16 "	T. B. Harms Co.	1946
A SYMPHONIC PICTURE OF CAROUSEL	16 "	Williamson	1946
A DRY WEATHER LEGEND *flute, orchestra*	7 "	Manuscript	1946

CHAMBER ORCHESTRA

TOY SYMPHONY *5 woodwinds*	18 minutes	Manuscript	1928
EARLY AMERICAN BALLADE—on melodies of Stephen Foster *30 or fewer instruments*	6 "	Manuscript	1932
VARIATIONS ON A THEME BY JEROME KERN *20 instruments*	10 "	Manuscript	1934
CLASSIC SERENADE FOR STRING ORCHESTRA	12 "	Manuscript	1941

BAND MUSIC

SIX TONE POEMS FOR BAND (for the Lagoon of Nations, New York World's Fair)	15 minutes	Manuscript	1939

CHORAL WORKS

LORELEI VARIATIONS *women's voices with piano*		Manuscript	1929
NIETZSCHE VARIATIONS *women's voices with piano*		Manuscript	1929

ROBERT RUSSELL BENNETT (*Continued*)

CHAMBER MUSIC	DURATION	PUBLISHER	DATE
THREE SONGS		Manuscript	1927
string quartet and soprano			
SONATA FOR VIOLIN AND PIANO	25 minutes	Manuscript	1927
SONATA FOR ORGAN	20 "	Edwin F. Kalmus	1929
SONATINA		Manuscript	
harp, flute, cello			
WATER MUSIC—on "A Sailor's Hornpipe"		Manuscript	
2 violins, viola, cello			
DANCE SCHERZO	4 "	Manuscript	1937
5 woodwinds			

STAGE WORKS			
ENDIMION—5-act operette-ballet	1¾ hours	Manuscript	1927
AN HOUR OF DELUSION—1-act opera	30 minutes	Manuscript	1928
MARIA MALIBRAN—3-act opera			1935
THE ENCHANTED KISS—1-act opera	1¼ hours	Manuscript	1944

EVELYN BERCKMAN

Born in Philadelphia, Pennsylvania, 1900. She studied by herself to develop her musical talents, but ill health retarded her career for seven years.

Besides composing, she has done editorial work and written articles for the *North American Review, Musical Courier* and other magazines, as well as program notes for the Philharmonic Symphony Chamber Orchestra.

Her works have been presented by symphony orchestras in America, and in London her compositions were given by the British Association of Women Composers. "Dr. Johnson's Tour" was presented with the League of Composers, the New School for Social Research and the Bennington Artist Series. There have been broadcasts of her works over WOR, WEAF and WEVD, and also from Brussels. Recently she has composed for radio and theater.

COMPOSITIONS

ORCHESTRAL WORKS	DURATION	PUBLISHER	DATE
DIE NEBELSTADT	7 minutes	M. Sénart	1924
soprano solo, orchestra			
STURM	7 "	M. Sénart	1924
soprano solo, orchestra			
SWANS	5 "	Manuscript	1925
ABOARD THE MORNING STAR	17 "	Manuscript	1932
TOURS, XVITH CENTURY	8 "	Manuscript	1936
SORBONNE		Manuscript	1937

CHAMBER ORCHESTRA

PUNCH AND JUDY DANCES		Manuscript	1937

EVELYN BERCKMAN (*Continued*)

CHAMBER MUSIC	DURATION	PUBLISHER	DATE
SPRINGTIME IN THE ORCHARD	5 minutes	Manuscript	1929
soprano, string quartet			
THE QUIET POOL	3 "	Manuscript	1929
soprano, string quartet			
THE FAR LAND	4 "	Manuscript	1930
soprano solo, 7 instruments			
THE SOLDIER'S TRADE	5 "	Manuscript	1930
soprano solo, 7 instruments			
ARCHANGELS—suite for 3 harps	20 "	Manuscript	1932
INCANTATION; PERCUSSION; THE WEB;			
CIRCUS DAY	14 "	Manuscript	1934
harp, flute, cello			
DR. JOHNSON'S TOUR OF THE HEBRIDES	8 "	Manuscript	1936
soprano, flute			

STAGE WORKS			
FROM THE ODYSSEY—ballet	12 minutes	Manuscript	1931
soprano solo, women's chorus, 7			
instruments, corps de ballet			
COUNTY FAIR—ballet	22 "	Manuscript	1937
corps de ballet, 3 solo dancers,			
full orchestra			

NICOLAI T. BEREZOWSKY

Born in St. Petersburg, Russia, in 1900. He graduated with honors at the age of sixteen from the Imperial Capella in St. Petersburg. His musical activities in Russia as concert master of the Saratov National Opera House and first violinist of the Moscow Bolshoi Theatre led to the position of Music Director of the School of Modern Art in 1921. He came to New York in 1922 and began his studies again at the Juilliard Graduate School of Music with Paul Kochanski and Rubin Goldmark. He won two scholarships in composition and violin and graduated from the Juilliard School in 1928.

For five years he was first violinist with the New York Philharmonic Symphony Orchestra. He was first violinist of the League of Composers String Quartet and a member of the Coolidge String Quartet of the Library of Congress. In 1931 he began to work with the Columbia Broadcasting System and since 1940 he has become a Columbia Broadcasting artist. He has been Guest Conductor of the Boston, Philadelphia, Cincinnati and National symphony orchestras as well as CBS and WJZ Symphonies.

His Symphonies No. 1 and No. 3 have been performed by the major orchestras throughout this country. Symphony No. 4 was presented by the Boston Symphony with the composer conducting. His Concertos for Viola, Violin and Harp have had performances in New York, Boston, Chicago, Philadelphia and Mexico City. There have been major performances of his orchestral and chamber music also in many countries of Europe and in Canada, and almost all of these works have had radio performances. His chamber music was presented at the Coolidge Festival,

NICOLAI T. BEREZOWSKY (*Continued*)

at the Paris Exposition of 1937 and by various chamber-music ensembles at the League of Composers concerts. The Quintet for Wood-Winds has been recorded by N.M.Q.R., and the String Quartet has been recorded by the Victor Company. The League of Composers commissioned a work for radio in 1934. He received a commission from the Elizabeth Sprague Coolidge Foundation (Library of Congress). In 1936 he was one of the winners in the National Broadcasting Company's competition, and he also received their orchestral award. In 1944 he won the Academy of Arts and Letters grant in recognition of the distinguished position he held in contemporary music. He is now completing an oratorio for soloist, chorus and orchestra, called "Gilgamesh."

COMPOSITIONS

ORCHESTRAL WORKS

	DURATION	PUBLISHER	DATE
SYMPHONY No. 1	35 minutes	Edition Russe	1925
HEBREW SUITE	25 "	Edition Russe	1928
SYMPHONY No. 2	30 "	Edition Russe	1929
VIOLIN CONCERTO	25 "	Edition Russe	1930
FANTASIE	14 "	Associated Music	1931
with 2 pianos		Publishers	
SINFONIETTA	12 "	C. C. Birchard & Co.	1931
CONCERTO LIRICO FOR THE CELLO	20 "	Edition Russe	1934
SYMPHONY No. 3	28 "	Edition Russe	1936
STRING QUARTET WITH ORCHESTRA	22 "	Associated Music	1937
		Publishers	
VIOLA CONCERTO	24 "	for sale	1941
CLARINET CONCERTO	22 "	for sale	1941
SOLDIER ON THE TOWN	3 "	Manuscript	1942
		for hire	
SYMPHONY No. 4	35 "	Manuscript	1943
		for hire	
HARP CONCERTO	20 "	for sale	1944
CHRISTMAS OVERTURE	9 "	Manuscript	1944
		for hire	

CHAMBER ORCHESTRA

INTRODUCTION AND ALLEGRO	9 minutes	Weiner	1927
11 instruments			
SUITE	12 "	for sale	1938
7 brass instruments			

CHORAL WORKS

CANTATA	35 minutes	Manuscript	1927
soprano, tenor, bass mixed			
chorus, orchestra			
HYMN	3 "	for sale	1944
mixed chorus			
BOWDOIN HYMN	3 "	for sale	1944
mixed chorus			

CHAMBER MUSIC

PIANO SONATA	25 minutes	Manuscript	1926
SEXTET No. 1	25 "	Edition Russe	1928
WOODWIND QUINTET No. 1	30 "	Edition Russe	1928
FANTASIA FOR TWO PIANOS	12 "	Associated Music	1930
		Publishers	

NICOLAI T. BEREZOWSKY (*Continued*)

CHAMBER MUSIC (*Continued*)	DURATION	PUBLISHER	DATE
QUARTET NO. 1	15 minutes	Edition Russe	1930
DUO FOR VIOLA AND CLARINET	10 "	Sprague-Coleman	1931
STRING QUARTET, OPUS 16	20 "	Edition Russe	1931
STRING QUARTET	18 "	Manuscript	1934
WOODWIND QUINTET NO. 2	20 "	Mills	1937
STRING SEXTET	25 "	Associated Music Publishers	1940
BRASS SUITE		Mills	

ARTHUR VICTOR BERGER

Born in New York City in 1912. He went to New York University and received his Master of Arts degree from Harvard University. He was a pupil of Nadia Boulanger, Walter Piston, Darius Milhaud, and Vincent Jones. He was given a fellowship from the Longy School of Music, the Paine Travelling Fellowship from Harvard, and the Council of Learned Societies Fellowship.

He taught at Mills College, North Texas State College, and at Brooklyn College. He was a member of the music staff of the *Boston Transcript* and Editor of *Musical Mercury* and *Listen*. At the present time, he is a member of the *New York Herald Tribune* staff. His articles have appeared in *Modern Music, Musical Quarterly*, the *New Republic*, and *Harper's Bazaar*. He is on the Board of Governors of the American Composers Alliance.

The Quartet for Woodwinds was performed by the League of Composers and by the San Francisco Woodwind Quintet. His Serenade was played by the Eastman-Rochester Symphony and the Little Symphony, which also presented the "Three Pieces for Strings."

COMPOSITIONS

CHAMBER ORCHESTRA	DURATION	PUBLISHER	DATE
SERENADE—in one movement *17 instruments minimum*	10 minutes	Manuscript	1944
THREE PIECES FOR STRINGS	8½ "	Manuscript	1944
CHORAL WORKS			
92ND PSALM	3½ minutes	Manuscript	1946
CHAMBER MUSIC			
WORDS FOR MUSIC PERHAPS— 3 songs from the Yeats Cycle *high voice, piano*	7½ minutes	Manuscript	1940
QUARTET IN C MAJOR FOR WOODWINDS *flute, oboe, clarinet, bassoon*	12 "	Manuscript	1941
THREE PIECES FOR STRING QUARTET	8 "	Manuscript	1944
STAGE WORKS			
ENTERTAINMENT PIECE—ballet *3 dancers modern style, piano solo*	12 minutes	Manuscript	1940

WILLIAM BERGSMA

Born in Oakland, California in 1921. He studied at Stanford University and also attended the Eastman School of Music, where he studied composition with Hanson and orchestration with Rogers. He won the Bearns Prize and the Society for the Publication of American Music Award. He also received a grant from the National Institute of Arts and Letters and the Guggenheim Fellowship for creative work.

He recently became a member of the Composition Department of the Juilliard School of Music.

His works were performed by the Boston "Pops" Orchestra, the Eastman-Rochester Philharmonic, Gordon Quartet, the New York Philharmonic Orchestra, and the San Francisco Orchestra. Network and local stations, including CBS, MBC, NBC, WNYC, and WQXR, have broadcast his compositions. The Second Quartet was played on the Columbia Festival in 1945 over WNYC, and his "Six Songs" was presented on the WNYC American Festival the same year. "Siesta and Happy Dance" from "Gold and the Señor Commandante" was recorded by RCA Victor. He has received commissions from the Collegiate Chorale, the Koussevitzky Music Foundation and Town Hall. At present he is preparing an orchestral work.

COMPOSITIONS

ORCHESTRAL WORKS	DURATION	PUBLISHER	DATE
PAUL BUNYAN SUITE	12 minutes	Carl Fischer, Inc.	1938
from the ballet			
school orchestra			
SIESTA AND HAPPY DANCE	4 "	Hargail Music Press	1941
from the ballet			
MUSIC ON A QUIET THEME	8 "	Arrow Press	1943
SUITE FROM A CHILDREN'S FILM	8 "	G. Schirmer, Inc.	1945

CHAMBER ORCHESTRA			
SYMPHONY FOR CHAMBER ORCHESTRA	15 minutes	Hargail Music Press	1942
23 instruments		*for hire*	

CHORAL WORKS			
TIME FOR SLEEP (Benét)	4 minutes	Manuscript	1945
4 part chorus, piano			
ON THE BEACH AT NIGHT (Whitman)	5 "	Manuscript	1946
4 part chorus, a cappella			

CHAMBER MUSIC			
SUITE FOR BRASS QUARTET	6 minutes	Carl Fischer, Inc.	1940
FIRST QUARTET	18 "	S.P.A.M.	1942
string quartet			
SECOND QUARTET	25 "	Hargail Music Press	1944
string quartet			
SIX SONGS (E. E. Cummings)	15 "	Carl Fischer, Inc.	1945
high voice, piano			

STAGE WORKS			
PAUL BUNYAN—ballet	33 minutes	Manuscript	1937
puppets, solo dancers,			
orchestra			
GOLD AND THE SEÑOR COMMANDANTE—	17 "	Manuscript	1941
ballet		Fleisher Collection	
orchestra, 1 set			

FILM MUSIC
TITIAN—THE BOY PAINTER

PUBLISHER
Manuscript
Palo Alto Children's
Theatre

DATE
1945

LEONARD BERNSTEIN

Born in Lawrence, Massachusetts, in 1918. He was educated at Boston Latin School and graduated from Harvard University in 1939, where he studied composition under Walter Piston and Edward Burlingame Hill. He studied piano with Helen Coates and Heinrich Gebhard. The following two years were spent at the Curtis Institute of Music in Philadelphia, where he studied conducting under Fritz Reiner, orchestration with Randall Thompson, and continued his piano studies with Isabella Vengerova. After two summers at Tanglewood, where he studied conducting with Serge Koussevitzky, Bernstein became Koussevitzky's assistant for the summer of 1942.

At the age of twenty-five Bernstein was engaged by Arthur Rodzinski as Assistant Conductor of the Philharmonic Symphony Orchestra for the season 1943–44 and made his début at Carnegie Hall in November, 1943. He returned to this orchestra as Guest Conductor for a series of concerts in 1945. In the past two seasons he has conducted major symphony orchestras all over the country and at present is Music Director and Conductor of the New York City Center Orchestra. For the first festival of the I.S.C.M. at Prague following the Second World War, Leonard Bernstein was invited to conduct the American programs. He has also appeared in a series of programs with the London Philharmonic Orchestra. He conducted the first performances in this country of the opera "Peter Grimes," by Benjamin Britten, at Tanglewood in 1946.

His first orchestral work, "Jeremiah," a symphony for orchestra and mezzo-soprano, had its première with the Pittsburgh Symphony and has been played by the Boston Symphony, the New York Philharmonic Orchestra, and other orchestras throughout the country. It has been broadcast by NBC. This work won the award of the Music Critics Circle in 1943–44. It has been recorded by RCA Victor and the St. Louis Symphony. The ballet, "Fancy Free," in collaboration with the choreographer, Jerome Robbins, was commissioned by the Ballet Theatre and had its première at the Metropolitan Opera House in 1944; it has since had repeated performances all over the country. A Suite for concert performance has been played frequently by the orchestras. The score is recorded by Decca. Following several works which Bernstein wrote for chamber music, including a Clarinet Sonata which is recorded by Hargail, he wrote the score for the musical "On the Town," which was produced in New York in 1944 and

LEONARD BERNSTEIN (*Continued*)

ran on Broadway for two years before touring throughout the country. The ballet "Facsimile" was also commissioned by the Ballet Theatre Company and had its première in 1946.

COMPOSITIONS

ORCHESTRAL WORKS	DURATION	PUBLISHER	DATE
SYMPHONY, "JEREMIAH"	27 minutes	Harms, Inc.	1942
mezzo soprano, orchestra.		for hire	
SUITE FROM BALLET "FANCY FREE"	15 "	Harms, Inc.	1944
		for hire	
CHORAL WORKS			
HASHKIVENU	6 minutes	Harms, Inc.	1945
tenor solo, mixed chorus,			
organ			
CHAMBER MUSIC			
CLARINET SONATA	10 minutes	M. Witmark & Sons	1942
clarinet, piano			
I HATE MUSIC—song cycle	6 "	M. Witmark & Sons	1943
soprano			
SEVEN ANNIVERSARIES FOR PIANO	10 "	M. Witmark & Sons	1943
STAGE WORKS			
ON THE TOWN			1944
complete Broadway production			
FANCY FREE—ballet			1944
full orchestra			
FACSIMILE—ballet		Manuscript	1946

ABRAHAM WOLFE BINDER

Born in New York City in 1895. He received his musical education at Columbia University and studied with Mason and Riebner. In 1917 he received the Mosenthal Fellowship in composition.

His interest in Jewish music led him during his initial visit to Palestine in 1925 to gather and publish the first collection of songs of the New Palestine and the Chalutsim (Pioneers). A second volume of Palestinian songs was published in 1933. He has been instrumental in introducing the popular Palestinian music into this country. He has been Director of Music of the Y.M.H.A., New York City, and founder and Director of the Y.M.H.A. Choral Society since 1918, instructor in Jewish liturgical music at the Jewish Institute of Religion in New York since 1922 and Professor since 1937. He has been choirmaster of the Free Synagogue since 1923. In 1929 he was appointed musical editor of the third edition of the *Union Hymnal* by the Central Conference of American Rabbis. He is the author of many articles on various phases of Jewish music, and he has lectured

ABRAHAM WOLFE BINDER (*Continued*)

throughout the country before community centers, colleges, universities and Hillel Foundations. He gave a concert of his compositions in Town Hall in 1929 and in 1931 was Guest Conductor of the Manhattan Symphony Orchestra and of the Palestine Symphonic Ensemble.

His orchestral work "He Chalutsim" was given its première in 1933 by the Palestine Symphony Orchestra in Tel-Aviv and Jerusalem, and it was also performed by the Manhattan Symphony Orchestra in New York. "Holy Land Impressions" has been presented by the Detroit Symphony Orchestra. The Oboe Trio was broadcast by the Palestine Broadcasting Company from Jerusalem, and many of his works have been broadcast in this country. He has made two Victor albums of recordings with his Free Synagogue Choir, "Music of the Synagogue" and "Songs of Palestine."

COMPOSITIONS

ORCHESTRAL WORKS	DURATION	PUBLISHER	DATE
HOLY LAND IMPRESSIONS—			
SYMPHONIC SUITE No. 1	20 minutes	Manuscript	1927
HE CHALUTSIM (THE PIONEERS)—			
overture	12 "	Manuscript	1929
SYMPHONIC SUITE No. 2	20 "	Manuscript	1929
SYMPHONIC SUITE No. 3	20 "	Manuscript	1934
FANTASY—overture	12 "	Mills Music Co.	1938
LAMENT	7 "	Mills Music Co.	1944

CHAMBER ORCHESTRA			
CONCERTANTE FOR STRING ORCHESTRA	15 minutes	Mills Music Co.	1938
CONCERTINO FOR STRING ORCHESTRA	14 "	Mills Music Co.	1945

CHORAL WORKS			
HIBBATH SHABBATH—Sabbath service	1 hour	Bloch Publishing Co.	1927
12 PALESTINIAN FOLK SONGS			
FOR MIXED CHORUS		Bloch Publishing Co.	1930
RINNATH SHABBATH—Sabbath service	55 minutes	Bloch Publishing Co.	1932
KABBALATH SHABBATH—Sabbath service	90 "	Bloch Publishing Co.	1940
AMOS ON TIMES SQUARE—cantata	30 "	Bloch Publishing Co.	1941
6 AMERICAN FOLK SONGS FOR			
MIXED CHORUS		Elkan-Vogel Co.	
4 VOLUMES OF PALESTINIAN			
FOLK SONGS		Bloch, Metro, Marks	1945

CHAMBER MUSIC			
STRING QUARTET	15 minutes	Manuscript	1935
TRIO FOR OBOE, CELLO AND PIANO	20 "	Manuscript	1936
SONATINA FOR PIANO No. 1	15 "	Manuscript	1936
SONATINA FOR PIANO No. 2	20 "	Manuscript	1941
TRIO FOR VIOLIN, CELLO AND PIANO	15 "	Manuscript	1943
VARIATIONS ON A YEMENITE THEME	10 "	Leeds Music Co.	1944

STAGE WORKS			
THE ROAD TO PEACE—			
operetta for children	1 hour	Manuscript	1936
ESTHER, QUEEN OF PERSIA—			
dramatic narrative		Manuscript	

SETH BINGHAM

Born in Bloomfield, New Jersey, in 1882. He studied theory with Parker, composition with D'Indy and organ with Widor, Guilmant and Jepson. In 1904 he graduated from Yale University with the degree of Bachelor of Arts and in 1908 received the degree of Bachelor of Music. He won the Yale Prize for organ playing, the Heald and Steinert prizes for composition and a fellowship from the American Guild of Organists, of which he is now Vice-President. He has held the post of organist in several Presbyterian churches. From 1908 to 1919 he was instructor of organ at Yale University. Today he is Associate Professor of Music at Columbia College and is head of the Theory Department.

Some of his works for large orchestra and chamber orchestra have been heard in Chicago, Cleveland, Boston, New York and New Haven. "Wilderness Stone" was performed several times in New York and broadcast by NBC in a nationwide hook-up over WEAF and also over WJZ. "The Breton Cadence" has been broadcast over NBC. He has written a great many organ works which have been published and which have also been performed by prominent soloists.

COMPOSITIONS

ORCHESTRAL WORKS

	DURATION	PUBLISHER	DATE
PASSACAGLIA	13 minutes	Manuscript	1918
MEMORIES OF FRANCE—suite	22 "	Manuscript	1920
PIONEER AMERICA—suite	18 "	Manuscript	1925
THE BRETON CADENCE—suite	20 "	Manuscript	1928
CONCERTO	16 "	Manuscript	1946
organ, orchestra			

CHAMBER ORCHESTRA

SUITE FOR WIND	26 minutes	Manuscript	1915
9 instruments			
TAME ANIMAL TUNES	25 "	Manuscript	1918
18 instruments			

CHORAL WORKS

LET GOD ARISE—motet		A. P. Schmidt Co.	1916
men's chorus			
THE STRIFE IS O'ER—motet		J. Fischer & Bro.	1916
mixed chorus			
COME THOU ALMIGHTY KING—motet		Carl Fischer, Inc.	1916
mixed chorus			
SEVEN ENGLISH LOVE LYRICS	20 minutes	H. W. Gray Co., Inc.	1921
women's voices, a cappella			
WILDERNESS STONE	1¼ hours	H. W. Gray Co., Inc.	1933
narrator, soli, chorus, orchestra			
POEMS OF PASSION—choral cycle	24 minutes	Manuscript	1935
mixed chorus, a cappella			
CANTICLE OF THE SUN	40 "	Manuscript	1942
mixed chorus, orchestra			

CHAMBER MUSIC

STRING QUARTET IN B FLAT	23 minutes	Manuscript	1916
FIRST SUITE FOR ORGAN	20 "	G. Schirmer, Inc.	1923
HARMONIES OF FLORENCE—suite			
for organ	18 "	G. Schirmer, Inc.	1928

SETH BINGHAM (*Continued*)

CHAMBER MUSIC (*Continued*)	DURATION	PUBLISHER	DATE
PIONEER AMERICA—suite for organ		H. W. Gray Co., Inc.	
PASTORAL PSALMS—suite for organ	16 minutes	Carl Fischer, Inc.	1937
BAROQUES—suite	14 "	Galaxy Music Corp.	1943

STAGE WORKS

LA CHARELZENN—opera	2½ hours	Manuscript	1917

MARC BLITZSTEIN

Born in Philadelphia, Pennsylvania, in 1905. He began to study music at the age of five and appeared as solo pianist with the Philadelphia Orchestra when he was fifteen. He has composed music from his earliest years. Scalero in New York, Boulanger in Paris and Schoenberg in Berlin were his composition teachers and piano study was pursued under Silotti.

In addition to his activities as a composer, he has lectured frequently at many colleges and universities. He has written a great many critical articles for *Modern Music, Musical Quarterly, Boston Transcript, Querschnitt* and *Revue-Musicale.* He taught at the New School for Social Research and at the Downtown Music School, which he helped to organize. He is a member of the American Music League, the League of American Writers and a member of the Board of Directors of the League of Composers. In 1942 he enlisted in the U. S. Army and was overseas until 1945. He was Director of Music at the American broadcasting station in Europe in 1944–45, and directed the U. S. Army Negro Chorus in a work dedicated to the U. S. Army Negro troops, called "Airborne Symphony," which was first performed at Albert Hall, London, and twice with the New York City Center Orchestra and the Shaw Chorale, conducted by Leonard Bernstein, with Welles and Corwin as narrators. He did the musical research for "True Glory" while serving with the armed forces.

A one-act opera was commissioned by the League of Composers, and in 1937 CBS ordered a radio song play called "I've Got the Tune." In collaboration with Virgil Thomson he arranged the music for the film "Spanish Earth." His opera to his own text, "The Cradle Will Rock," has been given frequent performances in New York City; "Triple Sec," written for the New York "Garrick Gaieties," has been given by the Philadelphia Society for Contemporary Music. Many of his pieces for chamber music have been presented at the Copland-Sessions Concerts, The League of Composers and the Yaddo Festival. He wrote the incidental music for the Mercury Theatre's production of "Julius Caesar" and for Buchner's "Danton." In 1941 "No for an Answer" was performed at the Mecca Temple. "Freedom Morning" has been presented by the London Symphony, the RAF Symphony, the Philadelphia Orchestra and the New York Philharmonic Symphony Society and has been broadcast. Excerpts from the

MARC BLITZSTEIN (*Continued*)

films "True Glory" and "Native Land" have been shown and broadcast in Europe.

There are recordings of "The Cradle Will Rock" in the Musicraft Album and "No for an Answer" in the Keynote Album. "Purest Kind of a Guy" with Paul Robeson is recorded by the Columbia Phonograph Company. He received an award from the American Academy of Arts and Letters in 1946. He is now completing a score for a play.

COMPOSITIONS

ORCHESTRAL WORKS	DURATION	PUBLISHER	DATE
ROMANTIC PIECE FOR ORCHESTRA	16 minutes	Manuscript	1930
PIANO CONCERTO	24 "	Manuscript for hire	1931
VARIATIONS FOR ORCHESTRA	17 "	Manuscript	1934
FREEDOM MORNING	12 "	G. Schirmer, Inc.	1943

CHAMBER ORCHESTRA			
GODS mezzo-soprano, string orchestra, cello soloist	8 minutes	Manuscript for hire	1926

CHORAL WORKS			
THE CONDEMNED—choral opera 4 choruses (men's and women's voices) with orchestra	40 minutes	Manuscript for hire	1933
CHILDREN'S CANTATA	25 "	Manuscript for hire	1935
AIRBORNE SYMPHONY speaker, solo tenor, solo baritone, male chorus, orchestra	1 hour	Manuscript	1943–44

CHAMBER MUSIC			
PIANO SONATA	6 minutes	Manuscript	1927
"Is 5" SONGS—Cummings texts soprano	18 "	Manuscript	1929
STRING QUARTET	19 "	Manuscript	1930
SERENADE FOR STRING QUARTET	18 "	Manuscript	1932

STAGE WORKS			
TRIPLE SEC—opera-farce chamber orchestra	15 minutes	B. Schott's Söhne	1928
PARABOLA AND CIRCULA—one-act opera solo baritone and dancers	60 "	Manuscript for hire	1929
CAIN—ballet	30 "	Manuscript for hire	1930
THE HARPIES—one-act opera 8 singers, chamber orchestra	16 "	Manuscript	1931
SEND FOR THE MILITIA—speaking number voice and piano	10 "	Manuscript	1935
THE CRADLE WILL ROCK—opera voices, orchestra	2 hours	Random House	1936
I'VE GOT THE TUNE—radio song play voices, orchestra, effects	30 minutes	Manuscript	1937
NO FOR AN ANSWER		Manuscript	1937–40
SCORE FOR AN UNTITLED OPERETTA	1½ hours	Manuscript	1945
ANDROCLES AND THE LION—incidental music	25 minutes		1946

MARC BLITZSTEIN (*Continued*)

FILM MUSIC	STUDIO	PUBLISHER	DATE
SURF AND SEAWEED *chamber orchestra*		Manuscript *for hire*	1931
CHESAPEAKE BAY RETRIEVER	Pedigreed Pictures, Inc.		1936
SPANISH EARTH (collated by Blitzstein and Thomson)	Contemporary His- torians, Inc.		1937
VALLEY TOWN concert version—suite	Willard Van Dyke	Manuscript *for hire*	1940
NATIVE LAND concert version—suite	Frontier Films	Manuscript *for hire*	1941
NIGHT SHIFT	O.E.M. (Gov't)		1942

ERNEST BLOCH

Born in Geneva, Switzerland, in 1880. At the age of eleven he began to compose. He also studied the violin as a child, and one of his teachers was the renowned Ysaye. His composition teachers included Dalcroze, Rasse and Knorr.

He became Professor of Composition and lectured on aesthetics at the Geneva Conservatory. He conducted concerts in Switzerland, and in 1916 he came to America as conductor for the dancer, Maud Allen. In New York he joined the faculty of the David Mannes Music School. In 1920 he became the Director of the Cleveland Institute of Music, and in 1925 he moved to California to direct the San Francisco Conservatory. A patron of arts who had befriended him arranged a fund with an income for him to live on for ten years, and from 1930 to 1940 this fund enabled him to devote himself to creative work without teaching.

In 1910 his opera "Macbeth" was first produced in Paris and years later it was given again in Naples. In 1919 his Suite for Viola and Piano won the Coolidge Berkshire Prize at the Berkshire Festival. In 1927–28 the orchestral work "America" won the prize offered by the magazine, *Musical America,* and in 1930 he was one of the winners in the Victor Company's symphonic contest. He was made an honorary member of the Royal Academy of St. Cecilia in Rome, and he has been elected a member of the American Academy of Arts and Letters, which awarded him the Gold Medal in 1942. The "Jewish Sacred Service," which he was commissioned to write, has been presented in America and in Europe. Entire programs of his symphonic and chamber music have been given on the Continent and in the United States and broadcast. His works are on the programs today of all the leading orchestras and chamber-music ensembles all over the world. RCA Victor Company, Columbia and the Parlophone companies have recorded many of his works.

ERNEST BLOCH (*Continued*)

COMPOSITIONS

ORCHESTRAL WORKS

	DURATION	PUBLISHER	DATE
TROIS POÈMES JUIFS	25 minutes	G. Schirmer, Inc.	
TWO PSALMS AND A PRELUDE *soprano or tenor, orchestra*	15 "	G. Schirmer, Inc.	
PSALM 22 *baritone or alto, orchestra*	5 "	G. Schirmer, Inc.	
SCHELOMO—Hebrew rhapsody *cello, orchestra*	20 "	G. Schirmer, Inc.	1915
ISRAEL SYMPHONY *2 sopranos, 2 altos, bass, orchestra*	30 "	G. Schirmer, Inc.	1916
SUITE FOR VIOLA AND ORCHESTRA	25 "	G. Schirmer, Inc.	1919
IN THE NIGHT—nocturne	6 "	G. Schirmer, Inc.	1923
POEMS OF THE SEA	12 "	G. Schirmer, Inc.	1923
AMERICA—an epic rhapsody	45 "	C. C. Birchard & Co.	1925
HELVETIA—a symphonic fresco	25 "	C. C. Birchard & Co.	1929
VOICE IN THE WILDERNESS—symphonic poem *cello, orchestra*	25 "	G. Schirmer, Inc. *for sale and hire*	1936
EVOCATIONS—symphonic suite	17 "	G. Schirmer, Inc. *2 piano transcription and full score; parts available*	1937
VIOLIN CONCERTO	35 "	Boosey & Hawkes	1937
SUITE SYMPHONIQUE (Ouverture-Passacaglia-Finale)	20 "	Boosey & Hawkes	1944

CHAMBER ORCHESTRA

CONCERTO GROSSO *string orchestra, piano obbligato*	25 minutes	C. C. Birchard & Co.	1925
FOUR ÉPISODES *piano, strings, wind instruments*	15 "	C. C. Birchard & Co.	1926

CHORAL WORKS

ADONAI ELOHIM—from Israel *2 sopranos, 2 altos, bass, orchestra or piano*		G. Schirmer, Inc.	
SACRED SERVICE *baritone, mixed chorus, orchestra or organ*	55 minutes	C. C. Birchard & Co. Carisch	1932

CHAMBER MUSIC

STRING QUARTET IN B MINOR	50 minutes	G. Schirmer, Inc.	1916
SCHELOMO—HEBREW RHAPSODY *cello, piano*	20 "	G. Schirmer, Inc.	1916
SUITE IN FOUR MOVEMENTS *viola, piano*	25 "	G. Schirmer, Inc.	1919
VIOLIN SONATA *violin, piano*	25 "	G. Schirmer, Inc.	1920
BAAL SHEM *violin, piano*	15 "	Carl Fischer, Inc.	1923
POÈME MYSTIQUE *violin, piano*	20 "	F. E. C. Leuckart	1924
QUINTET *piano, string quartet*	30 "	G. Schirmer, Inc.	1924

ERNEST BLOCH (*Continued*)

CHAMBER MUSIC (*Continued*)	DURATION	PUBLISHER	DATE
THREE NOCTURNES	15 minutes	Carl Fischer, Inc.	1924
piano, violin, cello			
MÉDITATION HÉBRAÏQUE	10 "	Carl Fischer, Inc.	1924
cello, piano			
FROM JEWISH LIFE		Carl Fischer, Inc.	1924
cello, piano			
THREE LANDSCAPES	15 "	Carl Fischer, Inc.	1924
string quartet			
IN THE MOUNTAINS	10 "	Carl Fischer, Inc.	1924
piano trio or string quartet			
PRELUDE—RECUEILLEMENT	5 "	Carl Fischer, Inc.	1924
string quartet			
MELODY		Carl Fischer, Inc.	1929
violin, piano			
PIANO SONATA	22 "	Carisch	1936
SECOND STRING QUARTET	33 "	Boosey & Hawkes	1945

EUGENE MacDONALD BONNER

Born in Washington, North Carolina, in 1889. He received his early musical training at the Peabody Conservatory of Music in Baltimore. He studied composition with Bois and Brockway, piano with Bachner and Hutcheson and organ under Philips. From 1911 to 1917 he lived in Europe, where he studied composition and instrumentation with Scott, Lehmann and Bedford. Returning to the United States in 1917, he joined the heavy artillery. At the close of World War I he remained in Paris, and from 1921 until 1927 he studied instrumentation and conducting under Wolff, Musical Director of the Opéra Comique.

On his return to New York City in 1927 he was critic and Music Editor of the *Outlook Magazine,* holding that post for two years. He has been associate critic on the *Brooklyn Eagle* and also critic on the *Daily Mirror, Cue Magazine* and the *New York Herald Tribune.* He has been Managing Editor of the *Musical Record* and has written articles for various magazines and newspapers. He was awarded the Munich Fellowship in 1937.

Of his works, "Whispers of Heavenly Death" and "Celui Qui Epousa une Femme Muette" have been performed by the Baltimore Symphony Orchestra; "Flutes" in London, Brussels and Geneva; "Piano Quintet" in Brussels and London; and "Venetian Glass Nephew" and "Young Alexander" in New York City. His "Suite Sicilienne" was broadcast over Station WOR, Concertino for Piano and String Orchestra was heard over WQXR and by the Wallenstein Symphonic Strings, and "Taormina" was presented over WNYC.

COMPOSITIONS

ORCHESTRAL WORKS	DURATION	PUBLISHER	DATE
WHISPERS OF HEAVENLY DEATH	25 minutes	Manuscript	1922
Three Whitman poems for voice and orchestra		*score and parts for hire*	

EUGENE MacDONALD BONNER (*Continued*)

ORCHESTRAL WORKS (*Continued*)	DURATION	PUBLISHER	DATE
WHITE NIGHTS—a prelude	15 minutes	Manuscript score and parts for hire	1925
TAORMINA—a little suite	14 "	Manuscript for hire	1939

CHAMBER ORCHESTRA

INCIDENTAL MUSIC FOR "THE YOUNG ALEXANDER" wood, brass, harp, percussion	21 minutes	Manuscript	1929
CONCERTINO FOR PIANO AND STRING ORCHESTRA	13 "	Manuscript for hire	1945

CHAMBER MUSIC

FLUTES voice, 4 instruments	15 minutes	J. & W. Chester, Ltd.	1923
PIANO QUINTET	20 "	Maurice Sénart	1925
SUITE SICILIENNE violin, piano	20 "	Maurice Sénart	1926

STAGE WORKS

BARBARA FRIETCHIE—opera full orchestra	3 hours	Manuscript	1921
CELUI QUI EPOUSA UNE FEMME MUETTE—opera full orchestra	1½ "	Manuscript	1923
THE VENETIAN GLASS NEPHEW—opera chamber orchestra	2 "	Manuscript	1927
THE GODS OF THE MOUNTAIN—opera full orchestra	1½ "	Manuscript	1936
FRANKIE AND JOHNNIE—opéra comique medium size orchestra	2½ "	Manuscript	1945

FRANZ BORNSCHEIN

Born in Baltimore, Maryland, in 1879. He is a graduate of the Peabody Conservatory of Music. He is a composer, violinist, and conductor, and is now at Peabody teaching composition, harmony, conducting, and violin pedagogy. He is a member of the Advisory Board of the National Academy of Music, a contributor to various musical magazines, an editor for several music publishers, and has received several awards in national and international music competitions. He has made frequent appearances as guest conductor.

The operetta, "The Willow Plate," was first produced by the Baltimore Civic Opera Company in 1932. The Baltimore Symphony has performed his orchestral compositions, including "Leif Ericson," "The Mission Road," "The Earth Sings." The National Symphony of Washington, D. C., has performed his "Southern Nights," "Ode to the Brave" and "Moon Over Taos." The Chicago Symphony, New York Symphony and Los

FRANZ BORNSCHEIN (*Continued*)

Angeles Symphony Orchestra have premiered his scores. The National Federated Music Clubs biennial program in 1940 featured his setting of Poe's "Conqueror Worm" for chorus and symphony orchestra.

COMPOSITIONS

ORCHESTRAL WORKS

	DURATION	PUBLISHER	DATE
CAPE COD IMPRESSIONS—suite	15 minutes	Manuscript	1935
LEIF ERICSON—symphonic poem	15 "	Carl Fischer, Inc.	1936
SOUTHERN NIGHTS—symphonic poem	12 "	Carl Fischer, Inc.	1936
THE MISSION ROAD—symphonic poem	14 "	Manuscript	1937
MOON OVER TAOS	5 "	Manuscript for hire	1943
solo flute, strings, harp, timpani and Indian drum			
THE EARTH SINGS	15 "	Manuscript for hire	1944
ODE TO THE BRAVE	15 "	Manuscript for hire	1945
LAMENT	15 "	Manuscript for hire	1945
PHANTASY	18 "	Manuscript for hire	1945

CHORAL WORKS

VISION OF SIR LAUNFAL	45 minutes	J. Fischer & Bro.	1928
tenor, baritone, mixed chorus			
THE MINUTE MAN	40 "	Oliver Ditson Co.	1930
mixed chorus, orchestra			
TUSCAN CYPRESS	35 "	J. Fischer & Bro.	1931
mixed chorus, orchestra			
ARETHUSA	14 "	J. Fischer & Bro.	
women's voices			
ENCHANTED ISLE	15 "	J. Fischer & Bro.	1933
women's voices			
DAY	12 "	Manuscript	1935
women's voices with piano			
CONQUEROR WORM	16 "	Manuscript	1936
women's voices with piano			
JOY	30 "	Manuscript	1944
mixed chorus, orchestra			

CHAMBER MUSIC

PIANO QUINTET	30 minutes	Manuscript	1942

STAGE WORKS

THE WILLOW PLATE—operetta	60 minutes	C. C. Birchard & Co.	1932

FELIX BOROWSKI

Born in Burton, Westmorland, England, in 1872. He studied in London and later graduated from the Conservatory of Music in Cologne, Germany. In 1897 he came to America to be Director of the Department of Composition and History of Music at the Chicago Musical College. From 1916 to 1925 he was President of this college. From 1926 to 1932 he was Superintendent of the Civic Music Association in Chicago, and for many years he edited the Chicago Symphony Orchestra program books. He was Music

FELIX BOROWSKI (*Continued*)

Editor of the *Chicago Evening Post* and the *Chicago Herald* and music critic in Chicago for the *Christian Science Monitor*. He lectured at Northwestern University at Evanston, Illinois, and was Professor of Musicology.

The Concerto for Piano and Orchestra has been played by the Chicago and Minneapolis Symphony orchestras. "Two Pieces for String Orchestra," the Allegro de Concert, Elégie Symphonique, "Youth," "Peintures," "Le Printemps Passionné" and other works have been played by the Chicago Symphony Orchestra. Other performances were given by the symphony orchestras in Cleveland, Cincinnati, New York, Philadelphia, St. Louis, Detroit, Hollywood and at the Ann Arbor Festival. A great many presentations have been given of his chamber works. He is at present Music Editor of the *Chicago Sun*.

The ballet pantomime "Boudour" was produced by the Chicago Opera Company and in New York and Boston; it also toured in South America. The ballet "A Century of the Dance" was commissioned by the Ford Motor Company for the Chicago Exposition. Many of his works written before 1915 are not listed here.

COMPOSITIONS

ORCHESTRAL WORKS	DURATION	PUBLISHER	DATE
ALLEGRO DE CONCERT FOR ORGAN AND ORCHESTRA	10 minutes	Manuscript	1915
ELEGIE SYMPHONIQUE	8 "	Manuscript	1917
PEINTURES	25 "	Manuscript	1917
LE PRINTEMPS PASSIONNÉ—poème	10 "	Manuscript	1920
YOUTH—fantasie-overture	12 "	Manuscript	1922
ECCE HOMO—tone poem	12 "	Manuscript	1923
SEMIRAMIS—tone poem	12 "	Manuscript	1924
SYMPHONY NO. 1, D MINOR	27 "	Manuscript for hire	1932
SYMPHONY NO. 2, E MINOR	26 "	Manuscript for hire	1933
SYMPHONY NO. 3, G MAJOR		Manuscript	1937
REQUIEM FOR A CHILD		Manuscript	1944

CHAMBER ORCHESTRA			
OVERTURE TO A PANTOMIME	5 minutes	Manuscript	1925
RHAPSODY FOR ORGAN AND CHAMBER ORCHESTRA	10 "	Manuscript	1926

CHAMBER MUSIC			
QUARTET, G MAJOR	12 minutes	Manuscript	1928
STRING QUARTET NO. 3, D MINOR		Manuscript	1944

STAGE WORKS			
BOUDOUR—ballet-pantomime, 1 act	45 minutes	Manuscript	1918
PIERROT IN ARCADY—ballet-pantomime		Manuscript	1920
A CENTURY OF THE DANCE—ballet in 5 episodes *chamber orchestra*	1 hour	Manuscript	1934
FERNANDO DEL NONSENTSICO—satirical opera in 3 acts *chamber orchestra*	1 "	Manuscript	1935
THE LITTLE MATCH GIRL (Hans Christian Andersen) *narrator, orchestra*		Manuscript	1943

PAUL BOWLES

Born in New York City in 1911. He is a pupil of Aaron Copland and Virgil Thomson. He has traveled in Spain, North Africa, the Sahara, the Antilles and South and Central America to study the folk music of those countries. In 1941 he received the Guggenheim Fellowship. He joined the staff of the *New York Herald Tribune* as Music Critic in 1942.

Since 1936 he has provided incidental scores for fourteen Broadway productions, many of which had major presentations by the Theatre Guild, the Group Theatre, Orson Welles, Herman Shumlin and Eddie Dowling. He has had many performances of his chamber music in New York and in other cities in the United States, as well as in London and in Rome. His works have been broadcast over WABC, WQXR, WOR, WEVD, WJZ, WNYC and KGY. New Musical Quarterly Recordings have been made of Huapango I and II, "Cafe Sin Nombre" and the Sonata for Flute and Piano; "Sayula" and "El Bejuco" have been recorded in the Art of This Century Albums. The Sonata for Two Pianos is now being recorded by the Concert Hall Society. Recent songs and piano solos have had a great many performances and many are published but are not listed here.

COMPOSITIONS

ORCHESTRAL WORKS

	DURATION	PUBLISHER	DATE
SUITE FOR SMALL ORCHESTRA	10 minutes	Manuscript	1933
SUITE FROM "PASTORELA"	12 "	Manuscript	1941
DANZA MEXICANA	2 "	Manuscript	1941
PROLOGUE, SONG AND DANCE FROM "SENTIMENTAL COLLOQUY"	12 "	Manuscript	1944

CHAMBER ORCHESTRA

	DURATION	PUBLISHER	DATE
MEDIODIA *flute, clarinet, trumpet, piano, strings*	5 minutes	Manuscript	1937
ROMANTIC SUITE *6 wind and string instruments, percussion, piano*	8 "	Manuscript	1939

CHORAL WORKS

	DURATION	PUBLISHER	DATE
PAR LE DETROIT—cantata	12 minutes	Manuscript	1933
TORNADO BLUES	5 "	G. Schirmer, Inc.	1939

CHAMBER MUSIC

	DURATION	PUBLISHER	DATE
SONATA FOR OBOE AND CLARINET	9 minutes	Manuscript	1931
SONATA FOR FLUTE AND PIANO	15 "	Manuscript	1932
SCENES D'ANABASE *tenor, oboe, piano*		Parts 1, 2, 4—Manuscript Part 3—New Music Part 5—Cos Cob Press	1932
PIANO SONATINA NO. 1	8 "	Elkan-Vogel	1932
PAR LE DETROIT—cantata *soprano, male quartet, reader, harmonium*	12 "	Manuscript	1933

PAUL BOWLES (*Continued*)

CHAMBER MUSIC (*Continued*)	DURATION	PUBLISHER	DATE
NOCTURNE FOR TWO PIANOS	4 minutes	Manuscript	1935
PIANO SONATINA No. 2	5 "	Boletin Latino-Americano	1935
MUSIC FOR A FARCE	8 "	Manuscript	1938
clarinet, trumpet, piano, percussion			
SUITE FOR TWO PIANOS	9 "	Manuscript	1939
CANCIONES ESPAÑOLAS—four songs	5 "	Manuscript	1943
THREE PASTORAL SONGS	6 "	Manuscript	1945
tenor, piano, string ensemble			
SONATINA FOR TWO PIANOS	10 "	Manuscript	1945

STAGE WORKS

YANKEE CLIPPER—ballet	40 minutes	Manuscript	1936
full orchestra			
DENMARK VESEY (Charles Henri Ford)—			
opera in 3 acts		Manuscript	1937
PASTORELA—ballet		Manuscript	1941
2 male voices, full orchestra			
THE WIND REMAINS (Garcia Lorca)—			
opera, one act		Manuscript	1943
SENTIMENTAL COLLOQUY		Manuscript	1944
full orchestra			
FACSIMILE—ballet (Jerome Robbins—			
Ballet Theatre)		Manuscript	1946

INCIDENTAL MUSIC FOR PLAYS

HORSE EATS HAT	1936
(Orson Welles, producer)	
DOCTOR FAUSTUS	1936
(Orson Welles, producer)	
MY HEART'S IN THE HIGHLANDS	1939
(Saroyan-Theatre Guild)	
LOVE'S OLD SWEET SONG	1940
(Saroyan-Theatre Guild)	
TWELFTH NIGHT	1940
(Theatre Guild)	
LIBERTY JONES	1941
(Theatre Guild)	
WATCH ON THE RHINE	1941
(Shumlin)	
JACOBOWSKY AND THE COLONEL	1944
(Theatre Guild)	
THE GLASS MENAGERIE	1945

FILM MUSIC

AMERICA'S DISINHERITED	Southern Tenant Farmers' Union	1937
ROOTS IN THE EARTH	U.S. Dept. of Agriculture	1940
CONGO	Belgian Government	1944

GENA BRANSCOMBE

Born in Picton, Canada, in 1881. She is of pioneer ancestors who settled on Manhattan Island (New Amsterdam) in 1640. Among her teachers of music were Ganz and Borowski; during her stay in Berlin she was a pupil of Humperdinck. On her return to New York she studied conducting at New York University and continued her musical studies at the Institute of Musical Art.

She has received several awards for compositions. In 1928 the National League of American Pen Women awarded her a prize for a choral drama set to her own text, "Pilgrims of Destiny." She has been President of the Society of American Women Composers and Vice-President of the National Association for American Composers and Conductors. She has appeared as Conductor of the MacDowell Chorus of New Jersey and guest conductor with many other choral and orchestral organizations. In 1941 she conducted the National Chorus of the Federation of Women's Clubs in celebration of fifty years of women's achievements. She was National Chairman of the Music and Folk Song Committee of the Federation of Women's Clubs. She has conducted the Branscombe Choral Society since its founding.

"Pilgrims of Destiny" has been frequently presented by large choral groups, by the Boston Festival Orchestra and other organizations in New York, Plymouth, Salem, etc., and has been broadcast by the NBC Orchestra. "Youth of the World" was performed by the chorus of the University of the Philippines and the orchestra of Manila, by Queen Alexandra's House Choir in London and by the Festival Chorus and Chicago Women's Symphony Orchestra, as well as broadcast. Her other choral and orchestral works have had frequent performances all over the United States. The chamber music has also been heard frequently in many cities throughout the United States. She has had repeated broadcasts over WOR, WEAF, WABC, WJZ and by the Canadian Broadcasting Commission. "Coventry's Choir" was performed in New York in 1944. She is writing a work for the stage.

COMPOSITIONS

ORCHESTRAL WORKS	DURATION	PUBLISHER	DATE
QUEBEC—symphonic suite *short trumpet solo,* *French horn solo*	20 minutes	Manuscript	1928
PROCESSION	14 "	Manuscript	1935
ELÉGIE	4 "	Manuscript	1937
PAVANE	5 "	Manuscript	1946
GAILLIARD	6 "	Manuscript	1946
RIGAUDON	4 "	Manuscript	1946

CHAMBER ORCHESTRA

QUEBEC SUITE *11 instruments*	20 minutes	Manuscript	1928
MAPLES *oboe solo, English horn solo,* *22 instruments*	3½ "	Manuscript	1935
BALADINE *22 instruments*	3 "	Manuscript	1935

GENA BRANSCOMBE *(Continued)*

CHAMBER ORCHESTRA *(Continued)*	DURATION	PUBLISHER	DATE
BLOW SOFTLY MAPLE LEAVES *low voice, woodwinds, brass*	4 minutes	H. W. Gray Co., Inc.	1946

CHORAL WORKS

THE PHANTOM CARAVAN *men's voices, orchestra*	14 minutes	John Church Co.	1926
THE DANCER OF FJAARD *soprano, alto solos, women's* *voices*	10 "	Arthur P. Schmidt Co.	1926
A WIND FROM THE SEA *women's voices, chamber orchestra*	5 "	Arthur P. Schmidt Co.	1926
PILGRIMS OF DESTINY *solo voices, mixed chorus,* *orchestra*	1½ hours	Oliver Ditson Co. Theodore Presser	1929
YOUTH OF THE WORLD *women's voices, large orchestra*	11 minutes	M. Witmark & Sons	1932
SUN, AND THE WARM BROWN EARTH *women's voices, orchestra*	2½ "	C. C. Birchard & Co.	1934
COVENTRY'S CHOIR *soprano solo, women's voices,* *piano, organ, percussion*	5½ "	G. Schirmer, Inc.	1944

CHAMBER MUSIC

SONATA FOR VIOLIN AND PIANO	12 minutes	Manuscript	1920
CARNIVAL FANTASY *violin, piano, 6 instruments*	4½ "	Arthur P. Schmidt Co.	1932
A LUTE OF JADE—cycle *soprano, woodwinds*	9 "	Arthur P. Schmidt Co.	1937
ACROSS THE BLUE AEGEAN SEA *soprano, harp, flute, 2 clarinets,* *French horn*	3 "	Galaxy Music Corp.	1939

STAGE WORKS

FINALE FROM ACT II OF "THE BELLS OF CIRCUMSTANCE"—unfinished opera *soprano and tenor solos, chorus,* *chamber orchestra*		Manuscript	1928

HENRY DREYFUSS BRANT

Born in Montreal, Canada, in 1913, he studied at the Juilliard School with Goldmark in composition and Friskin in piano. He won the Loeb, the Coolidge, and the Seligman prizes. He later studied under George Antheil.

He is a member of the Board of Governors of the American Composers Alliance. He is an instructor at Columbia University in scoring and arranging for radio, films and stage. He is active as a composer and arranger of music for dramatic radio shows on major networks of CBS, NBC and ABC. He has orchestrated for the American Ballet and for Paramount Pictures, also Benny Goodman and Kostelanetz. Brant has become a collector of unusual wind instruments and has had frequent public appearances as soloist for the Chinese oboe, double flageolet, tin whistles, etc.

His orchestral works have been performed by the New York Philharmonic

HENRY DREYFUSS BRANT (*Continued*)

Symphony Society, the Detroit Symphony, the All American Youth Orchestra with Stokowski conducting, the WOR Sinfonietta and the Columbia Broadcasting Symphony. He has had stage performances with the Ballet Theatre and Ballet Caravan in New York City and on tour. His chamber works have been performed by the League of Composers, the New School for Social Research and the Pan American Association. Local stations and many of the major networks have frequently broadcast his chamber music. A commissioned work was first presented at the Festival of American Music at Yaddo, Saratoga Springs.

He is at present writing a Sermon, Ballad, Skit and Celebration for orchestra.

COMPOSITIONS

ORCHESTRAL WORKS

	DURATION	PUBLISHER	DATE
SYMPHONY IN B	30 minutes	Manuscript	1931
FOUR CHORAL PRELUDES	16 "	Manuscript	1932
INTRADA AND RICERCATA	25 "	Manuscript	1933
PRELUDE AND FUGUE	12 "	Manuscript	1934
GALLOPJIC COLLOQUY—scherzo ballad	23 "	Manuscript	1934
SYMPHONY IN C MINOR, OPUS 25	30 "	Manuscript	1937
GOOD WEATHER OVERTURE	5 "	Manuscript	1940
FANTASY AND CAPRICE	14 "	Manuscript	1941
violin, orchestra			
CONCERTO FOR SAXOPHONE AND			
ORCHESTRA	20 "	Manuscript	1942
alto saxophone			
DEDICATION IN MEMORY OF A			
GREAT MAN	10 "	Manuscript	1945

CHAMBER ORCHESTRA

	DURATION	PUBLISHER	DATE
VARIATIONS	15 minutes	New Music	1930
CONCERTO	20 "	Manuscript	1932
solo flute, 10 instruments			
FIVE AND TEN CENTS STORE MUSIC	12 "	Manuscript	1932
solo piano, 20 instruments			
LYRIC PIECE	6 "	Manuscript	1933
THE MARX BROTHERS—3 faithful			
portraits	12 "	Manuscript	1938
piccolo			
PRELUDE AND FUGUE	12 "	Manuscript	1938
octet—string quartet, woodwind			
quartet			

CHORAL WORKS

	DURATION	PUBLISHER	DATE
IN ZURU	5 minutes	Manuscript	1936
solo male falsetto, a cappella mixed			
chorus			

CHAMBER MUSIC

	DURATION	PUBLISHER	DATE
SONATA	22 minutes	Manuscript	1931
2 pianos			
SUITE	20 "	Manuscript	1932
flute, string quartet			
HANDORGAN MUSIC—choral-variations, nocturne	20 "	Manuscript	1933
2 pianos			
LYRIC CYCLE	14 "	Manuscript	1937
soprano, 3 violas, piano			

HENRY DREYFUSS BRANT (*Continued*)

STAGE WORKS	DURATION	PUBLISHER	DATE
DIS CHORD—musical burlesque, 2 acts	2 hours	Manuscript	1932
2 leads, large orchestra, chorus			
MISS O'GRADY—theatre-opera,			
1 act, 3 scenes	90 minutes	Manuscript	1936
chorus, 3 leads, orchestra, 1 set			
ENTENTE CORDIALE—satire with			
music, 1 act	40 "	Manuscript	1936
chorus, 3 leads, orchestra, 1 set			
ALISAUNDE—platform opera,			
earth-rite satire		Manuscript	
THE GREAT AMERICAN GOOF—ballet	40 "	Manuscript	1940
complete dance group,			
symphony orchestra			
CITY PORTRAIT—ballet	35 "	Manuscript	1940
dance group, symphony			
orchestra			

FILM MUSIC			
THE PALE HORSEMAN	2 reels	Manuscript	1945
		U.S. Office of War	
		Information	
CAPITOL STORY	2 "	Manuscript	1945
		U.S. Office of War	
		Information	

CARL ERNEST BRICKEN

Born in Shelbyville, Kentucky, in 1898. He studied composition with Scalero and piano under Leopold and Bert at the David Mannes Music School. He also studied piano with Cortot in Paris and Weisse in Vienna. In 1922 he received a Bachelor of Arts degree from Yale University. He won the Pulitzer Prize for 1929 and the Guggenheim Fellowship for 1930–31.

From 1920 to 1922 he was Conductor of the Yale Symphony Orchestra. From 1925 to 1928 he taught piano at the Mannes School of Music and during 1929–30 theory at the Institute of Musical Art, New York. He served as Guest Conductor of the Chicago Symphony in the summer of 1934. From 1931 to 1944 he was Professor and Chairman of the Department of Music of the University of Chicago and Conductor of the University of Chicago Symphony Orchestra. In 1944 he became Resident Conductor of the Seattle Symphony Orchestra and has been guest conductor on various occasions with university orchestras. He has had many articles published on musical criticism.

There have been recent performances of his Sonata for Violin and Piano, other chamber music and the Symphony No. 2.

CARL ERNEST BRICKEN (*Continued*)

COMPOSITIONS

ORCHESTRAL WORKS	DURATION	PUBLISHER	DATE
SUITE FOR ORCHESTRA	15 minutes	Manuscript	1931
PRELUDE FOR ORCHESTRA		Manuscript	1932
SYMPHONY IN D MINOR, No. 1		Manuscript	1935
SYMPHONY IN F MAJOR, No. 2		Manuscript	1936

CHAMBER MUSIC			
STRING QUARTET IN C MINOR	25 minutes	Manuscript	1925
SONATA FOR CELLO AND PIANO		Manuscript	1926
VARIATIONS ON AN OLD ENGLISH THEME 2 *pianos*		Manuscript	1926
PIANO QUINTET IN D MINOR	25 "	Manuscript	1930
SONATA FOR VIOLIN AND PIANO, F♯ MINOR		Manuscript	1944

RADIE BRITAIN

Born in Amarillo, Texas, in 1903. She began her music studies at the age of seven at Clarendon College, Texas, and graduated seven years later with high honors. At the American Conservatory in Chicago she studied piano under Heniot Levy and organ under Von Dusen. In 1920 she received the Bachelor of Music degree.

After teaching at Clarendon College for four years, she went to France and Germany. In Paris she studied organ with Dupré and in Germany, composition with Noelte. She made her début in Munich as a composer. She has been a member of the National League of American Pen Women. Many of her compositions have won prizes: "Heroic Poem" for orchestra— International Prize at Hollywood Bowl, 1930; "Epic Poem" for string quartet—first prize, national contest of American Pen Women; "Nirvana" —first prize, Texas Federation of Music Clubs; "Theme and Variations on the Old Gray Mare"—prize in Texas, 1934; and "Baby I Can't Sleep," a song—first prize, Federation of Music Clubs. She won the first national prize sponsored by the Boston Women's Symphony for "We Believe" and the first prize for the Suite for Strings from Sigma Alpha Iota. She was awarded the Juilliard Publication Prize for "Light" in 1945 and a prize sponsored by Delta Omicron. She is a life member of the Texas Federation of Music Clubs.

Many of her compositions have been played throughout the United States and have been broadcast over MBS, NBC and many local stations.

COMPOSITIONS

ORCHESTRAL WORKS	DURATION	PUBLISHER	DATE
HEROIC POEM	13 minutes	Manuscript	1929
SYMPHONIC INTERMEZZO	6 "	Manuscript	1929
OVERTURE TO PYGMALION	6 "	Manuscript	1930
RHAPSODIE PHANTASIE	14 "	Manuscript	1931
piano, orchestra			
LIGHT	12 "	Manuscript	1935
SOUTHERN SYMPHONY	25 "	Manuscript	1937
ONTONAGON SKETCHES	19 "	Manuscript	1939
SATURNALE	14 "	Manuscript	1939
PHANTASY FOR OBOE AND ORCHESTRA	8 "	Manuscript	1941
FRANCISCAN SKETCHES	11 "	Manuscript	1941
WE BELIEVE	9 "	Manuscript	1942
CACTUS RHAPSODY	12 "	Manuscript	1945

CHAMBER ORCHESTRA			
NOCTURNE	7 minutes	Manuscript	1934
9 instruments			
INFANT SUITE	11 "	Manuscript	1935
10 instruments			
PASTORALE	7 "	Manuscript	1939
SUITE FOR STRINGS	18 "	Manuscript	1940
PRISON	3 "	Manuscript	1940

CHORAL WORKS			
DRUMS OF AFRICA	5 minutes	M. Witmark & Sons	1934
mixed chorus or 2 tenors, 2 basses			
PRAYER	3 "	G. Ricordi & Co.	1934
mixed chorus			
DICKY DONKEY	2 "	Carl Fischer, Inc.	1939
mixed chorus or 2 sopranos, 2 altos			
NOONTIDE	3 "	Arthur P. Schmidt	1940
2 sopranos, 2 altos			
FAIRY OF SPRING	3 "	Arthur P. Schmidt	1940
2 sopranos, alto			
LASSO OF TIME	3 "	Neil Kjos	1940
2 tenors, 2 basses			
IMMORTALITY	4 "	Arthur P. Schmidt	1940
mixed chorus			
ISE COMIN LORD TO YOU	4 "	Clayton Summy	1941
mixed chorus			

CHAMBER MUSIC			
STRING QUARTET	17 minutes	Manuscript	1929
EPIC POEM	12 "	Manuscript	1934
string quartet			
PIANO PRELUDE IN G FLAT	3 "	Neil Kjos	1940
WESTERN SUITE		Lyon & Healy	1940
piano			

STAGE WORKS			
SHEPHERD IN THE DISTANCE—ballet		Manuscript	1930
large orchestra, drop curtain			
UBIQUITY—music drama	45 minutes	Manuscript	1937
medium orchestra, solo,			
chorus, boys' chorus			
HAPPYLAND—children's operetta	1½ hours	Manuscript	1945
solos and chorus			

HAROLD BROWN

Born in New York City in 1909. He studied violin with Bostelmann and Dittler and received his Bachelor of Arts degree from Columbia College, where he studied with Bingham. He was awarded the Mosenthal Fellowship for composition and continued his studies with Boulanger in Paris. He also studied with Copland, Barzin, and at the Pius X School of Music. At present, he is violist with the Baltimore Symphony Orchestra.

His works have been performed by the Eastman-Rochester Philharmonic Orchestra and have been presented by the Sinfonietta over MBS and by NBC. In preparation are a Symphony No. 2, a Divertimento No. 2, a Concerto for Viola and Orchestra, and a Sonata for Violin and Piano.

COMPOSITIONS

ORCHESTRAL WORKS	DURATION	PUBLISHER	DATE
SYMPHONY No. 1	18 minutes	Manuscript	1938–45
ORCHESTRA SUITE No. 1	30 "	Manuscript	1940
DIVERTIMENTO FOR SMALL ORCHESTRA	8½ "	Manuscript	1945
CHAMBER ORCHESTRA			
SUITE FOR STRING ORCHESTRA	18 minutes	Manuscript	1937
CHORAL WORKS			
CHORAL SETTING No. 1	7 minutes	Arrow Music Press	1939
(G. M. Hopkins)			
women's voices a cappella			
CHAMBER MUSIC			
TWO EXPERIMENTS	6 minutes	Manuscript	1931
flute, clarinet, bassoon			
STRING QUINTET	16 "	Manuscript	1934
STRING QUARTET	10 "	Manuscript	1944

MARK BRUNSWICK

Born in New York City in 1902. He studied with Goldmark and Bloch. He was later a pupil of Boulanger and Sessions. For the past twenty years he has been teaching theory, composition and other related subjects. He has taught at the Studios of Music Education, at the Greenwich House Music School and at the Music Institute, Kenyon College, and is now on the faculty of Brooklyn College. From 1938 to 1943 he was Chairman of the National Committee for Refugee Musicians. He is President of the United States Section of the I.S.C.M. and is a member of the American Musicological Society. He has written articles for *Modern Music* and the *Musical Quarterly* and also program notes for New Friends of Music.

His works have been performed in New York City, Black Mountain, North Carolina, St. Paul, Kenyon, Ohio, and in Vienna and Barcelona.

MARK BRUNSWICK (*Continued*)

COMPOSITIONS

ORCHESTRAL WORKS	DURATION	PUBLISHER	DATE
LYSISTRATA—suite	25 minutes	Manuscript	1936
SYMPHONY FOR CHORUS AND ORCHESTRA		Manuscript	1937
SYMPHONY IN B FLAT	25 "	Manuscript	1945
full or chamber orchestra of 12 instruments			

CHORAL WORKS			
FRAGMENT OF SAPPHO—motet	8 minutes	Universal Edition	1932
4 mixed voices, a cappella			

CHAMBER MUSIC			
TWO MOVEMENTS FOR STRING QUARTET	25 minutes	Universal Edition	1926
FANTASIA FOR VIOLA SOLO	23 "	Manuscript	1932

STAGE WORKS			
BALLET SUITE—text from Aristophanes' "Lysistrata"	25 minutes	Manuscript	1936
orchestra, chorus of women's voices, mezzo-soprano solo			

CHARLES FAULKNER BRYAN

Born in McMinnville, Tennessee, in 1911. He received his Bachelor of Music degree from the Nashville Conservatory in 1934 and his Bachelor of Science and Master of Arts degrees from Peabody College for Teachers, where he was awarded a teacher's fellowship. His teachers were Martin and Sorantin. In 1945–46, he attended Yale University.

From 1935–39, he was Director of Music at the Tennessee Polytechnic Institute. While there, he wrote and produced the operetta "Rebel Academy" and began "White Spiritual Symphony" based on folk music of the Tennessee hill country. He was also staff composer and arranger for a Nashville radio station. In 1940, he was Director of the Federal Music Project for Tennessee, and in 1942 was made Director for the Southeastern Region. In 1943, he was Civilian Defense Consultant for the Fourth Service Command, and in 1944–45 he was State Director of Civilian Defense for Tennessee. He was awarded a Guggenheim Fellowship in 1945. He is very interested in American folk-song and has collected many southern folk tunes. He is co-author of *American Folk-Songs for High School*, published by C. C. Birchard and Company.

His folk-song choral compositions have been performed in principal cities of the United States and also in England. Four of the choral compositions were heard at the Music Educators National Conference. The "White Spiritual Symphony" was performed by the Cincinnati Symphony Orchestra. He has had broadcasts of these works over local stations and by short-wave overseas.

CHARLES FAULKNER BRYAN (*Continued*)

COMPOSITIONS

ORCHESTRAL WORKS	DURATION	PUBLISHER	DATE
KINGDOM OF SORROW OVERTURE	8 minutes	Manuscript	1935
WHITE SPIRITUAL SYMPHONY	19 "	Manuscript	1946

CHAMBER ORCHESTRA			
REBEL ACADEMY OVERTURE	7 minutes	Manuscript	1939
HOEDOWN	5 "	Manuscript	1939
piano			
FOLK DANCE	4 "	Manuscript	1941

CHORAL WORKS			
KING OF PEACE CANTATA	1½ hours	Manuscript	1941
CHARLOTTOWN	2 "	J. Fischer and Brothers	1943
I HAVE A MOTHER IN HEAVEN	2 "	J. Fischer and Brothers	1943
PROMISED LAND	1 "	J. Fischer and Brothers	1943

CHAMBER MUSIC			
POEMS (Suite)	14 minutes	Manuscript	1942
harp, two violins			

STAGE WORKS			
KINGDOM OF SORROW	50 minutes	Manuscript	1934
REBEL ACADEMY—operetta in two acts	2 hours	Manuscript	1939

CECIL BURLEIGH

Born in Wyoming, New York, in 1885. At the age of nine the family moved to Omaha, Nebraska, and he began studying the violin. When he was fifteen he preferred improvising at the piano to studying the violin. As a young student he often wrote incidental music for the literature he had to read in school. From 1903 to 1905 he spent in Berlin, studying theory and composition with Hugo Leichtentritt. He moved to Sioux City in 1911 to teach at Morningside College, then in 1914 to Missoula, Montana, where he taught at the State University. In 1919 he resumed study in New York in orchestration with Walter Rothwell. Since 1921 he has taught violin and composition, advanced composition, and modern harmony at the University of Wisconsin.

Three Concertos for Violin and Orchestra and "Mountain Pictures" have had performances by the symphonic orchestras in Chicago, Minneapolis, St. Louis, Detroit, Cleveland, Los Angeles, Boston and Portland, as well as in many European cities and Capetown, South Africa. His chamber music has had performances in the United States and in Mexico.

CECIL BURLEIGH (*Continued*)

COMPOSITIONS

ORCHESTRAL WORKS	DURATION	PUBLISHER	DATE
First Concerto for Violin	18 minutes	Clayton F. Summy	1915
Second Concerto for Violin	15 "	Carl Fischer, Inc.	1919
Third Concerto for Violin	20 "	Carl Fischer, Inc.	1928
Evangeline—tone poem	12 "	Carl Fischer, Inc.	1929
Mountain Pictures	15 "	Carl Fischer, Inc.	1930
Leaders of Men	20 "	Manuscript	
Trilogy of Symphonies:			
Creation	16 "	Manuscript	
Prophecy	20 "	Manuscript	
Revelation	15 "	Manuscript	

CHAMBER ORCHESTRA			
The Village Dance (from the Musea)	12 minutes	G. Schirmer, Inc.	1921
		Manuscript	

CHAMBER MUSIC			
Sonata (from the Life of St. Paul)	18 minutes	G. Schirmer, Inc.	1921
Hymn to the Ancients	16 "	Manuscript	
string quartet, piano			
Quartet No. 1—Illusion	18 "	Manuscript	
string quartet			
Quartet No. 2—Transition	18 "	Manuscript	
string quartet			
American Processional	17 "	Manuscript	1945
violin and piano			
Mountain Scenes	12 "	Manuscript	1945
violin and piano			

DAVID BUTTOLPH

Born in New York City in 1902. He studied at the Institute of Musical Art. He was a pupil of Helena Augustin, Percy Goetschius and A. Madley Richardson. He studied in Vienna with Clemens Krauss and Hugo Rohr.

He coached opera singers for a year at the National Theatre in Munich. He has also been a conductor and arranger for NBC. Since 1933, he has been a composer for films at 20th Century-Fox, Paramount, Republic and Universal. His works for films are listed here.

COMPOSITIONS

FILM MUSIC	STUDIO	DATE
Western Union	Fox	1941
Immortal Sergeant	Fox	1942
This Gun for Hire	Paramount	1942
Bahama Passage	Paramount	1942
Buffalo Bill	Fox	1943
Corvette K-225	Universal	1943
Hitler Gang	Paramount	1944
House on 92nd Street	Fox	1945
Somewhere in the Night	Fox	1946
Shock	Fox	1946

CHARLES WAKEFIELD CADMAN

Born in Johnstown, Pennsylvania, in 1881 and died in 1946. He studied with Von Kunits and Paur in Pittsburgh, where he first became prominent as organist and as Music Editor of the *Pittsburgh Dispatch*. His earliest effort was in the field of comic operas and operettas. His interest in Indian music, extending from 1909 to 1925, began with a visit to an Omaha Reservation, where he made phonograph records of Indian tribal music. He lectured on Indian music and customs and later wrote two Indian operas, "Shanewis" and the "Sunset Trail." "Shanewis" was the first American opera to be presented for two consecutive years at the Metropolitan Opera House in New York. He also wrote the first opera for radio for NBC. His song "From the Land of the Sky Blue Water," based on an Indian melody, is probably one of the most popular American songs; this composition is greatly responsible for Cadman's reputation as an arranger of Indian melodies. He received his Doctor of Music degree from the University of Southern California.

His orchestral works have had numerous performances by major orchestras throughout the country and in England. His operas "Shanewis" and "A Witch of Salem" have been repeated often in Chicago and New York. Besides the songs based on American Indian material, there are several other songs and excerpts from "Shanewis" recorded by Victor and Columbia and, in England, by H.M.V.

COMPOSITIONS

ORCHESTRAL WORKS	DURATION	PUBLISHER	DATE
THUNDERBIRD SUITE	14 minutes	Boosey & Co.	
DARK DANCERS OF THE MARDI GRAS	10 "	Edition Musicus	1933
piano, orchestra			
AMERICAN SUITE	10 "	Composers Press	1937
SYMPHONY NO. 1 IN E MINOR	35 "	Manuscript	1939
(Pennsylvania)			
AURORA BOREALIS	17 "	Manuscript	1942
piano, orchestra			
HUCKLEBERRY FINN—overture	15 "	Manuscript	1945

CHAMBER ORCHESTRA			
TO A VANISHING RACE	3 minutes	John Church Co.	1925
strings			
AMERICAN SUITE	10 "	Composers Press	1937
strings			

CHORAL WORKS			
THE SUNSET TRAIL	25 minutes	White Smith Music Co.	1925
mixed chorus			
THE FATHER OF WATERS	30 "	Oliver Ditson Co.	1928
mixed chorus			

CHAMBER MUSIC			
PIANO SONATA IN A	22 minutes	White Smith Music Co.	1915
VIOLIN SONATA IN G	18 "	J. Fischer & Bro.	1930
QUINTET IN G MINOR	25 "	Manuscript	1935
piano, strings			
A MAD EMPRESS REMEMBERS	15 "	Mills Music Co.	1944
cello, piano			

CHARLES WAKEFIELD CADMAN (*Continued*)

STAGE WORKS	DURATION	PUBLISHER	DATE
A GARDEN OF MYSTERY—opera in one act	1 hour	J. Fischer & Bro.	1915
SHANEWIS—opera in two acts	1½ hours	White Smith Music Co.	1917
THE WILLOW TREE—opera for radio	25 minutes	Manuscript	1925
A WITCH OF SALEM—opera in two acts	2 hours	Oliver Ditson Co.	1926

JOHN CAGE

Born in Los Angeles, California, in 1912. He studied with Weiss, Schoenberg and Cowell. He has been on the faculties of the Cornish School in Seattle, Mills College, California, and the School of Design in Chicago. He has organized various groups of players and has presented fourteen concerts of music for percussion orchestra and for the "prepared" piano since 1939. During the war, he was engaged in library research for a company under government contract and is still doing this work. He is at present investigating further possibilities for the "prepared" piano and writing chamber music.

Fizdale and Gold performed the first of his "Three Dances" for "prepared" piano in Town Hall. Three of his works for percussion orchestra, "Construction in Metal," "Second Construction," and "Third Construction," are scored for such instruments as sleigh bells, oxen bells, Turkish and Chinese cymbals, wind glass, tin cans and teponaxtli. His compositions have been played in many cities, including New York and San Francisco, and in colleges throughout the country. "The City Wears a Slouch Hat" for "sound" orchestra was commissioned by CBS in 1942.

COMPOSITIONS

ORCHESTRAL WORKS	DURATION	PUBLISHER	DATE
PERCUSSION ORCHESTRA			
CONSTRUCTION IN METAL *for seven players*	9 minutes	Manuscript	1939
SECOND CONSTRUCTION *for four players*	6 "	Manuscript	1940
THIRD CONSTRUCTION *for four players*	15 "	Manuscript	1941
MARCH *for five players*	7 "	Manuscript	1942
AMORES *for three players*	9 "	New Music Society	1943
ELECTRICAL ORCHESTRA WITH PERCUSSION			
IMAGINARY LANDSCAPE No. 1 *for four players*	9 minutes	Manuscript	1939
IMAGINARY LANDSCAPE No. 2 *for four players*	3 "	Manuscript	1940
IMAGINARY LANDSCAPE No. 3 *for six players*	3 "	Manuscript	1942

JOHN CAGE *(Continued)*

ORCHESTRAL WORKS *(Continued)* DURATION   PUBLISHER   DATE

PREPARED PIANO

	DURATION	PUBLISHER	DATE
THE PERILOUS NIGHT—suite	15 minutes	Manuscript	1944
A BOOK OF MUSIC FOR 2 PIANOS	28 "	Manuscript	1944
THREE DANCES	19 "	Manuscript	1945
two pianos			

WORK FOR RADIO

THE CITY WEARS A SLOUCH HAT			1942
percussion orchestra			

JOHN ALDEN CARPENTER

Born in 1876 at Park Ridge, Illinois. While a student at Harvard University he studied music under Professor Paine. In 1897, after graduating from the university, he entered the firm of George B. Carpenter & Company, Chicago merchants in mill, railway, and vessel supplies. His interest in music soon led him to renew his studies and he went to Rome in 1906 to work with Sir Edward Elgar. In 1908 on his return to Chicago he became the pupil of Ziehn. In 1922 he took his degree of Master of Arts at Harvard University. The French Legion of Honor was conferred upon him in 1924, and in 1933 the University of Wisconsin made him a Doctor of Music.

Although he held the position of Vice-President of Carpenter & Company from 1912 to 1936, he continued to compose during those years. His first orchestral performance in 1915 was at Orchestra Hall in Chicago when "The Adventures in a Perambulator" met with great success, and it has since been performed by the major orchestras in America and in Europe. The Concertino for Piano and Orchestra and the concert version of "Skyscrapers" have also had frequent performances by the major orchestras in America and in Paris. There have been presentations of "Sea Drift" and the Violin Concerto by the symphony orchestras in Chicago, New York, Cleveland, etc.

Following the success of his ballet "Krazy Kat," Diaghileff asked him to write a ballet which would embody the bustle and racket of American life, expressed in the terms of the prevalent American musical vernacular. "Skyscrapers" was the result of this suggestion and, with Robert Edmond Jones, the ballet was produced at the Metropolitan Opera House in New York in 1926; later it had many performances in Germany. The "Birthday of the Infanta" had been produced as a ballet by the Chicago Opera Company in 1919. His chamber music has been played frequently; the Piano Quintet was commissioned for the Library of Congress Festival in 1935 by the Elizabeth Sprague Coolidge Foundation. The choral work "Song of Faith" was performed at the Washington Bicentennial in 1932. Many of these works have been broadcast frequently and there are Victor records of "Adventures in a Perambulator," "Skyscrapers" and "Gitanjali." His most recent work is a symphonic suite, "The Seven Ages," which was first performed by the New York Philharmonic Symphony Orchestra in 1945.

JOHN ALDEN CARPENTER *(Continued)*

COMPOSITIONS

ORCHESTRAL WORKS	DURATION	PUBLISHER	DATE
ADVENTURES IN A PERAMBULATOR—suite	24 minutes	G. Schirmer, Inc.	1915
CONCERTINO	26 "	G. Schirmer, Inc.	1917
piano, orchestra			
BIRTHDAY OF THE INFANTA—ballet suite	28 "	G. Schirmer, Inc.	1919
KRAZY KAT—ballet			
(concert version)	10 "	G. Schirmer, Inc.	1922
SKYSCRAPERS—ballet			
(concert version)	15 "	G. Schirmer, Inc.	1926
SEA DRIFT	14 "	G. Schirmer, Inc.	1933
CONCERTO	23 "	G. Schirmer, Inc.	1937
violin, orchestra			
SYMPHONY I	18 "	G. Schirmer, Inc.	1940
SYMPHONY II	21 "	G. Schirmer, Inc.	1941
DANSE SUITE	12 "	G. Schirmer, Inc.	1942
THE ANXIOUS BUGLER	5 "	G. Schirmer, Inc.	1943
THE SEVEN AGES—symphonic suite	19 "	G. Schirmer, Inc.	1945

CHAMBER ORCHESTRA			
WATER COLORS—Chinese song suite			
for mezzo soprano	10 minutes	G. Schirmer, Inc.	1918
GITANJALI—song suite for			
mezzo soprano	22 "	G. Schirmer, Inc.	1932

CHORAL WORKS			
SONG OF FAITH	11 minutes	G. Schirmer, Inc.	1931
mixed chorus, orchestra			
SONG OF FREEDOM	5 "	G. Schirmer, Inc.	1941
unison chorus, orchestra			
(also band arrangement)			

CHAMBER MUSIC			
STRING QUARTET	20 minutes	G. Schirmer, Inc.	1928
PIANO QUINTET	20 "	G. Schirmer, Inc.	1934
piano, string quartet			

STAGE WORKS			
BIRTHDAY OF THE INFANTA—ballet	28 minutes	G. Schirmer, Inc.	1919
KRAZY KAT—ballet	10 "	G. Schirmer, Inc.	1922
SKYSCRAPERS—ballet	30 "	G. Schirmer, Inc.	1926

ELLIOTT COOK CARTER, JR.

Born in New York City, N. Y., in 1908. He studied music under Piston, Holst, Hill and Davison, and received his Master of Arts degree from Harvard University in 1930. From 1932 to 1935 he studied with Boulanger in Paris.

In 1936 he became Music Director of the Ballet Caravan and remained with them for two years, during which time he also contributed many articles to magazines and was music critic on the staff of the League of Composers' quarterly magazine, *Modern Music*. He has contributed articles to the *Saturday Review of Literature* and to the *New York Herald Tribune*.

ELLIOTT COOK CARTER, JR. (*Continued*)

In 1940 he became Director of the Music Department of St. Johns College, Annapolis. In addition to teaching music, he directed the Glee Club, taught mathematics, Greek, physics and philosophy. In 1942 he obtained leave of absence in order to join the Office of War Information as music consultant.

His ballet "Pocahontas" was first performed by the Ballet Caravan in New York City under the auspices of the League of Composers and the American Lyric Theatre. His Symphony No. 1 was played by the Rochester Symphony at the Festival of American Music. The Harvard Glee Club presented "The Defense of Corinth" and "Tarantella" in New York and on tour. "The Harmony of Morning" was presented at the centennial program of Temple Emanu-El. He has had frequent broadcasts of his chamber music and choral music over network and local stations including NBC, WABC and WNYC. The incidental music for the Mercury Theatre production of "The Merchant of Venice" was recorded by the Columbia Recording Company, and "The Defense of Corinth" was brought out by the Advertisers Recording Service. He received the Juilliard Award for the Suite from "Pocahontas" in 1940, first prize for "Holiday Overture" given by the Independent Music Publishers in 1944 and awards given by the American Composers Alliance with B.M.I. for a work for radio orchestra, "Prelude, Fanfare and Polka," and a Suite for Quartet of Alto-Saxophones in 1945. In 1938 he received the prize given by WPA in conjunction with Columbia Records and CBS. He is at present completing a piano sonata and a second symphony.

COMPOSITIONS

ORCHESTRAL WORKS

	DURATION	PUBLISHER	DATE
SUITE FROM "POCAHONTAS"	20 minutes	Edwin F. Kalmus	1939
SYMPHONY NO. 1	27 "	Manuscript	1942
medium sized orchestra			
HOLIDAY OVERTURE	10 "	Arrow Music Press	1944

CHAMBER ORCHESTRA

WARBLE FOR LILAC TIME	8 minutes	Manuscript	1943
soprano, small orchestra			
PRELUDE, FANFARE AND POLKA	8 "	B.M.I.	1944

CHORAL WORKS

TARANTELLA	6 minutes	Manuscript	1936
men's voices, orchestra			
TO MUSIC	7 "	Manuscript	1938
mixed chorus a cappella			
HEART NOT SO HEAVY AS MINE	5 "	Arrow Music Press	1939
mixed chorus a cappella			
THE DEFENSE OF CORINTH	16 "	Manuscript	1941
men's voices, piano 4 hands			
THE HARMONY OF MORNING	7 "	Manuscript	1945
women's voices, small orchestra			
MUSICIANS WRESTLE EVERYWHERE	3 "	Manuscript	1945
mixed chorus a cappella			

ELLIOTT COOK CARTER, JR. *(Continued)*

CHAMBER MUSIC	DURATION	PUBLISHER	DATE
FLUTE SONATA	14 minutes	Manuscript	1934
flute, piano			
FIRST STRING QUARTET	25 "	Manuscript	1935
SECOND STRING QUARTET	16 "	Manuscript	1937
PASTORAL FOR ENGLISH HORN			
(or viola, or clarinet) AND PIANO	8 "	New Music	1940
SUITE FOR QUARTET OF ALTO-			
SAXOPHONES	6 "	B.M.I.	1942
PIANO SONATA	18 "	Manuscript	1945

STAGE WORKS			
INCIDENTAL MUSIC AND CHORUSES			
FOR SOPHOCLES' "PHILOCTETES"	30 minutes	Manuscript	1933
men's chorus, oboe, percussion			
INCIDENTAL MUSIC AND CHORUSES			
FOR PLAUTUS' "MOSTELLARIA"	20 "	Manuscript	1936
bass solo, men's chorus, 10			
piece chamber orchestra			
POCAHONTAS—ballet in one act	40 "	Manuscript	1939
symphony orchestra			
MINOTAUR—ballet	23 "	Manuscript	1946

ERNEST CARTER

Born in Orange, New Jersey, in 1886. He received his Bachelor of Arts degree from Princeton University and his Master of Arts and LL.B. degrees from Columbia University. He studied theory and composition with Freudenberg in Berlin, piano with Mason, and organ with Egide in Berlin and with Bartlett in New York City. He is the editor of various college song books, including the *Princeton Song Book.*

Of his stage works, a one-act opera, "The White Bird," was performed in Chicago, Germany, Riverside, California, and New York City; "The Blonde Donna," an opéra comique in three acts, was heard in New York City, Brooklyn, and California; "Namba; or The Third Statue," a one-act dance pantomime, was given in Columbus, Ohio, Stamford, Conn., and New York City.

COMPOSITIONS

CHAMBER MUSIC	DURATION	PUBLISHER	DATE
STRING QUARTET IN G MAJOR		Manuscript	

STAGE WORKS			
THE WHITE BIRD—one-act opera	1½ hours	Manuscript	1917
26–30 instruments		orch. parts and	
		stage set for hire	
NAMBA; OR THE THIRD STATUE—			
one-act dance pantomime	35 minutes	Manuscript	1924
26–30 instruments		orch. parts and	
		stage set for hire	

MARIO CASTELNUOVO-TEDESCO

Born in Florence, Italy, in 1895. His opera "La Mandragola," first performed in Venice in 1926, won the Italian Prize for Opera. His other operas, all written in Europe, are "Bacco in Toscana," "Savonarola," "The Giants of the Mountain" and "Aucassin et Nicolette." He is the composer of seven overtures to plays by Shakespeare, symphonic music, concertos for various instruments, chamber music, piano music and over two hundred songs. He came to the United States in 1939 and lives in Beverly Hills, California. One of his activities now is writing music for films.

Several of his European compositions had their first performance in this country, e.g. the Violin Concerto "The Prophets" was given in 1934 and the Cello Concerto in 1935 by the New York Philharmonic under Arturo Toscanini. His Second Piano Concerto was performed by the same orchestra under John Barbirolli, with the composer as soloist. His orchestral works written in America have had performances by the New York Philharmonic, the Boston Symphony Orchestra and the Los Angeles Philharmonic Orchestra. "Deux Etudes d'Ondes" and "La Vieille Vienne" have been recorded by French Polydor with the composer as the pianist, "Chant Hebraïque" has been recorded by Parlophone and "Vivo e Energico," by H.M.V.

COMPOSITIONS WRITTEN IN AMERICA

ORCHESTRAL WORKS	PUBLISHER	DATE
CYPRESSES	Manuscript	
OVERTURE TO "KING JOHN"	Manuscript	
INDIAN SONGS AND DANCES	Manuscript	
AN AMERICAN RHAPSODY	Manuscript	
FIGARO	Manuscript	
violin, orchestra		
OVERTURE TO A FAIRY TALE	Manuscript	1945
SERENADE	Manuscript	
guitar, orchestra		
FIVE HUMORESQUES ON FOSTER'S THEMES	Manuscript	

CHAMBER MUSIC		
DIVERTIMENTO FOR TWO FLUTES	Manuscript	
SONATA FOR VIOLIN AND VIOLA	Manuscript	
SONATA FOR CLARINET AND PIANO	Manuscript	

CHORAL WORKS		
SACRED SERVICE FOR THE SYNAGOGUE	Manuscript	

FILM MUSIC		
AND THEN THERE WERE NONE	Popular Pictures, Inc.	

NORMAN CAZDEN

Born in New York City, N. Y., in 1914. He studied piano with Ravitch and with Newstead at the Institute of Musical Art. He received the student's and teacher's diplomas. At the Juilliard Graduate School, where he edited *Dynamics,* the student magazine, he was a pupil of Hutcheson and Wagenaar. He received his Bachelor of Science degree in social science from the New York City College and his Master of Arts degree in music from Harvard University, where he studied composition with Piston and Copland. He received fellowships at the Juilliard School in 1927 and 1939, at Harvard University 1943–45, the Westminster Choir Award in 1936, the George Arthur Knight Prize in 1945 and the John Knowles Paine Travelling Fellowship, 1945–46.

He has written considerable material for educational use; he was formerly on the musical staff of the New Dance Group, and he has helped to formulate the musical programs for workers' clubs in New York City. He has concertized extensively throughout the eastern part of the United States. At present he teaches piano and theory at the Juilliard School.

His compositions have been performed in New York City, Newark, Princeton, New Haven and other cities and broadcast over WJZ. He is now working on a symphony.

COMPOSITIONS

ORCHESTRAL WORKS	DURATION	PUBLISHER	DATE
PREAMBLE, OPUS 18	7¾ minutes	Associated Music Publishers Manuscript *for hire*	1938
ON THE DEATH OF A SPANISH CHILD, OPUS 20	5 "	Weaner-Levant	1939
THREE DANCES, OPUS 28	9 "	Associated Music Publishers Manuscript *for hire*	1940

CHAMBER ORCHESTRA			
CONCERTO FOR TEN INSTRUMENTS, OPUS 10 *piano, viola, solo*	15 minutes	Associated Music Publishers Manuscript *for hire*	1937
SIX DEFINITIONS, OPUS 25 *21 instruments*	9½ "	Associated Music Publishers	1939

CHAMBER MUSIC			
SONATINA, OPUS 7 *piano*	7 minutes	New Music	1935
STRING QUARTET, OPUS 9	13½ "	Associated Music Publishers Manuscript *for hire*	1936
SONATA, OPUS 12 *piano*	16½ "	American Music Center *for hire*	1938
THREE CHAMBER SONATAS, OPUS 17 *clarinet, viola*	10 " each	American Music Center *for hire*	1938
QUARTET, OPUS 23 *violin, clarinet, viola, cello*	13½ "	American Music Center *for hire*	1939

NORMAN CAZDEN (*Continued*)

CHAMBER MUSIC (*Continued*)	DURATION	PUBLISHER	DATE
AMERICAN SUITE, OPUS 31 *cello, piano*	12 minutes	American Music Center *for hire*	1940
QUINTET, OPUS 32 *2 violins, viola, 2 cellos*	11 "	American Music Center *for hire*	1941
SONATA, OPUS 33 *horn, piano*	8½ "	American Music Center *for hire*	1941
SONATA, OPUS 36 *flute, piano*	13½ "	American Music Center *for hire*	1941
SUITE, OPUS 43 *violin, piano*	14½ "	American Music Center *for hire*	1943

STAGE WORKS

	DURATION	PUBLISHER	DATE
FIVE AMERICAN DANCES, OPUS 14 *piano, modern dance*	9 minutes	American Music Center *for hire*	1938
ETCETERA, OPUS 35 *piano, recitation, dance*	5 "	Manuscript	1941
THE LONELY ONES, OPUS 44 *piano, cartoons, dance*	7 "	Manuscript	1944

THEODORE CELLA

Born in Philadelphia, Pennsylvania, in 1897. He studied in Philadelphia, Boston and New York City. Martini and Maquarre were his teachers in piano and harmony. After studying composition in Europe, he returned to the United States to continue his studies with Loeffler. As a member of the Boston Symphony Orchestra, he played under Muck, Rabaud and Monteux.

His composition "Through the Pyrenees" was presented for the first time with the New York Philharmonic. Under the composer's leadership "The Lido" received performances with the Boston Symphony, the Philharmonic Symphony Society of New York and the Philadelphia orchestras; "On a Transatlantic Liner" was given by the Philharmonic Symphony Society of New York, Boston Symphony, and Philadelphia orchestras; "Carnival" was heard with the Boston Symphony and New York Philharmonic; the latter orchestra also gave his "Alpine Impressions." "On a Transatlantic Liner" was broadcast over a coast-to-coast hook-up; Divertimento was broadcast from WOR.

COMPOSITIONS

ORCHESTRAL WORKS	DURATION	PUBLISHER	DATE
ON A TRANSATLANTIC LINER	8 minutes	Manuscript	1931
CARNIVAL	9 "	Manuscript	1931
THROUGH THE PYRENEES	10 "	Manuscript	1932
THE LIDO—symphonic sketch	10 "	Manuscript	1934
ALPINE IMPRESSIONS	12 "	Manuscript	1937
CARNEGIE HALL—suite	25 "	Manuscript	1945

CHAMBER ORCHESTRA

	DURATION	PUBLISHER	DATE
ROMANCE *for strings*	8 minutes	Manuscript	1925
NOTTURNO *string quartet*	9 "	Manuscript	1928
DIVERTIMENTO	7 "	Manuscript	1933

JULIUS CHAJES

Born in Lwow, Poland, in 1910. He began his piano studies with his mother and then continued to study with many teachers, including Moriz Rosenthal. He attended the Vienna Conservatory of Music and the Vienna University and won the Honor Prize in 1933 at the first International Competition for Pianists in Vienna. In 1937 he won a "Judischer Kultur-band" competition for a choral work. He was head of the Piano Department at the Music College in Tel-Aviv, Palestine. He did extensive research work on ancient Hebrew music in Jerusalem.

He came to the United States in 1938 and made his American début as pianist in Town Hall and over the Columbia network. In 1939–40 he was a Professor of Composition at the New York College of Music. At present he is Director of Music at the Detroit Jewish Community Center. He is the co-founder and Artistic Director of the Detroit Friends of Opera, Inc., and he is a teacher of composition at the Detroit Institute of Musical Art. In 1945 he founded the Society for the Advancement of Jewish Music and is at present its chairman. He is also music chairman of the Detroit Round-table of Catholics, Jews, and Protestants, and board member of the Detroit Musicians League.

His compositions have had numerous performances in Europe and in Palestine. His works have also been presented in Kansas City, Washington, D. C., New York and Detroit. The "Song for Americans" was broadcast over WOR from coast to coast and in Canada. At present he is preparing liturgical music for a Friday evening service and an orchestration of "Palestinian Melodies."

COMPOSITIONS WRITTEN IN AMERICA

ORCHESTRAL WORKS	DURATION	PUBLISHER	DATE
PALESTINIAN SUITE	16 minutes	Manuscript for hire	1940

CHORAL WORKS			
ZION RISE AND SHINE mixed chorus, orchestra	12 minutes	Trans-Continental Music Corp.	1939
HARKEN TO MY PRAY'R mixed chorus a cappella		Bloch Publishing Co.	1940
SABBATH EVENING SERVICE chorus, organ			1946

CHAMBER MUSIC			
PALESTINIAN SUITE clarinet, string quartet, piano	16 minutes	Manuscript	1938

THEODORE WARD CHANLER

Born in Newport, Rhode Island, in 1902. He began to study piano at the age of six and ten years later started to compose. He was a pupil of Ebell in piano and composition and of Arthur Shepherd in harmony. In 1919 he attended the Institute of Musical Art in New York, studying piano with Buhlig and counterpoint with Goetschius. Several years later he worked with Bloch in Cleveland and in 1923 went abroad to spend a year and a half at Oxford University. After three years of study in Paris with Boulanger, he returned to the United States.

In 1934 he went to Boston, becoming for a short time Music Editor of the *Boston Herald*. In 1940 he received the Guggenheim Fellowship and the League of Composers-Town Hall Award for which he composed "Four Rhymes from Peacock Pie." He has been a member of the League of Composers' Board of Directors since 1943 and a regular contributor to the League of Composers' quarterly magazine, *Modern Music*. In 1945 he accepted a position on the faculty of Peabody Conservatory in Baltimore.

His Sonata for Violin and Piano was performed in Paris by the Société Musicale Indépendante and at the Copland-Sessions Series in New York City. "Four Rhythms from Peacock Pie" was first sung by Dorothy Maynor at Town Hall in 1941. The "Second Joyful Mystery" was first performed by Bartlett and Robertson at Town Hall in 1943. At present he is working on two movements for two pianos to be played with the "Second Joyful Mystery." He is also writing a book on modern music, which will be published by Macmillan.

COMPOSITIONS

CHORAL WORKS	DURATION	PUBLISHER	DATE
MASS FOR TWO WOMEN'S VOICES	20 minutes	Manuscript	1930
organ accompaniment			
ANN GREGORY (W. B. Yeats)	5 "	Manuscript	1942
mixed chorus a cappella			
CHAMBER MUSIC			
SONATA FOR VIOLIN AND PIANO	15 minutes	Manuscript	1927
FIVE SHORT COLLOQUIES—suite for piano	6 "	Manuscript	1936
EIGHT EPITAPHS—song cycle	13½ "	Arrow Press	1937
medium voice, piano			
SECOND SERIES OF EPITAPHS		Manuscript	1937
SECOND JOYFUL MYSTERY—fugue	7 "	Associated Music	1943
2 pianos		Publishers	
THE CHILDREN—suite	18 "	G. Schirmer, Inc.	1945
voice and piano			
STAGE WORKS			
PAS DE TROIS—ballet	8 minutes	Manuscript	1942
piano			

ABRAM CHASINS

Born in New York City, N. Y., in 1903. He has toured in Europe and America giving piano recitals and appearing as soloist with leading orchestras, often playing his own compositions. From 1932 to 1938 his major activities were in radio, and as radio artist he was the first to initiate a Master Class of the Air in a weekly network series of talking-playing broadcasts over CBS and NBC. From 1926 to 1935 he was a member of the piano faculty of the Curtis Institute of Philadelphia, and in 1940 he was a member of the Berkshire Music Center at Tanglewood. He has lectured at leading universities and musical institutions. He is the author of many articles and has made extensive research which has been incorporated in scientific and music books. He is now music consultant to the *New York Times* radio station WQXR. He received four government citations during World War II for voluntary war work in music and radio.

His Concerto in F Minor has been heard with symphonic organizations in Philadelphia, New York, Vienna, Munich and Havana. "The Parade" has been performed in New York, Boston, Philadelphia, Los Angeles, Paris and Oslo, Norway. "Three Chinese Pieces" was given by the New York Philharmonic, Curtis Symphony (Philadelphia) and the Roxy Symphony. The Second Piano Concerto was performed by the Philadelphia Orchestra, with the composer as soloist, also by the New York Philharmonic. His piano and two-piano works are among the standard works in teaching and concert repertory and are frequently broadcast. Many of his works have been recorded by Victor and Gramophone.

COMPOSITIONS

ORCHESTRAL WORKS	DURATION	PUBLISHER	DATE
First Piano Concerto in F Minor	20 minutes	J. Fischer & Bro.	1929
Three Chinese Pieces	10 "	J. Fischer & Bro.	1929
A Shanghai Tragedy			
Flirtation in a Chinese Garden			
Rush Hour in Hong-Kong			
(also arranged for piano)			
Parade	7 "	J. Fischer & Bro.	1930
Second Piano Concerto in			
F# Minor	20 "	J. Fischer & Bro.	1932

CHAMBER MUSIC			
Blue Danube Waltzes	8 minutes	J. Fischer & Bro.	1925
2 *pianos*			
Twenty-Four Preludes for Piano	35 "	Oliver Ditson Co.	1928
Three Violin Preludes	7 "	Oliver Ditson Co.	1935
violin, piano			
Carmen Fantasy	9 "	J. Fischer & Bro.	1937
2 *pianos*			
Melody	3½ "	Carl Fischer	1938
2 *pianos, also 1 piano*			

LOUIS CHESLOCK

Born in London, England, in 1899. He came to the United States in 1901. He entered the Peabody Conservatory of Music; in 1917 he received a certificate in violin, in 1919 a certificate in harmony and an artist diploma in 1921. He studied violin under Van Hulsteyn and Gittelson and composition with Strube.

In 1916 he became a violinist in the Baltimore Symphony Orchestra and was guest-composer-conductor in 1928 and in 1944. Between 1932 and 1937, he was assistant concert master. Since 1917 he has been a violin instructor and since 1922 an instructor in harmony. He was a member of the American Musicological Society. In 1921 he was awarded the Peabody Alumni Prize in composition; in 1923 he received honorable mention in the Chicago Theatre Symphonic Contest, and he was among the prize winners in the *Chicago Daily News* Contest for compositions for piano, violin, violoncello and orchestra. In 1938 he received honorable mention in the New York Women's Symphony Orchestra Contest for his Overture to the opera "The Jewel Merchants." He won the National Composers' Clinic Contest for the choral work "The Congo" and also honorable mention in their contest in 1944.

His works have been performed in Baltimore, Washington, D. C., Akron, Chicago and many other cities. There have been broadcasts of some of his works by local radio stations.

COMPOSITIONS

ORCHESTRAL WORKS	DURATION	PUBLISHER	DATE
VIOLIN CONCERTO	20 minutes	Manuscript	1921
'NEATH WASHINGTON MONUMENT— tone poem		Manuscript	1922
CATHEDRAL AT SUNDOWN—tone poem		Manuscript	1922
AT THE RAILWAY STATION—tone poem		Manuscript	1922
TWO DANCES: POLISH DANCE; SPANISH DANCE	6 "	Manuscript	1923
SYMPHONIC PRELUDE	15 "	Manuscript	1927
SYMPHONY—four movements	20 "	Manuscript	1932
VALSE VODKA	15 "	Manuscript	1935
LEGEND OF SLEEPY HOLLOW	15 "	Manuscript	1936
FRENCH HORN CONCERTO	18 "	Manuscript	1936
small orchestra			
BIBLICAL DANCE		Manuscript	1937
SUITE FROM "DAVID"— Prelude, Pastorale, Dance	17 "	Manuscript	1938
tenor voice in Pastorale			

CHAMBER ORCHESTRA

	DURATION	PUBLISHER	DATE
TWO MINIATURES: SLUMBER SONG; SERENADE	6 minutes	Manuscript	1930
5 instruments			
SHIRE AMI—rhapsody	7 "	Manuscript	1932
5 instruments			
THEME AND VARIATIONS	10 "	Manuscript	1934
8 instruments			
TWO LITTLE DANCES IN D MINOR	5 "	Manuscript	1940
11 instruments			

LOUIS CHESLOCK (*Continued*)

CHORAL WORKS	DURATION	PUBLISHER	DATE
BLOW, BLOW, THOU WINTER WIND	5 minutes	Manuscript	1927
men's voices, piano			
150TH PSALM	6 "	Manuscript	1931
mixed chorus, orchestra			
23RD PSALM	4 "	Manuscript	1933
a cappella			
THE CONGO	20 "	Manuscript	1942
baritone solo, mixed chorus,			
orchestra or piano			

CHAMBER MUSIC			
VIOLIN SONATA	20 minutes	Manuscript	1920
piano			
STRING QUARTET	20 "	Manuscript	1930
SONG CYCLES	10 "	Manuscript	1937
soprano or tenor			
SONATINA FOR VIOLONCELLO AND PIANO	18 "	Manuscript	1939
CONCERTINO FOR VIOLIN AND PIANO	7 "	Manuscript	1943

STAGE WORKS			
THE JEWEL MERCHANTS—opera in 1 act	1¼ hours	Manuscript	1930
3 voices, small orchestra			
DAVID		Manuscript	1937
CINDERELLA—ballet; 3 scenes	35 minutes	Manuscript	1941
3 woodwinds, 3 brass instruments,			
timpani, percussion, harp,			
strings; 2 stage sets			

ISRAEL CITKOWITZ

Born in Skiernewice, Russia, in 1909. He came to this country as an infant. He has studied with Copland and Sessions and, for several years in Paris, with Boulanger. He has been a member of the faculty of the Dalcroze School of Music, where he taught composition.

Modern Music and *Musical Mercury* have published several critical articles by him; *Poetry* has printed some of his verses. His main interests are choral and chamber music. The modern poets, Hart Crane, Stephen Spender, and others, have inspired him to set music to their verses.

His String Quartet was performed at the first Yaddo Festival, Saratoga Springs; Andante for String Quartet, by the League of Composers and the Société Musicale Indépendante (S.M.I.), Paris; Sonatine, by the S.M.I. and the Vienna Section of the I.S.C.M. In New York City the Dessoff Choirs gave "The Lamb," and the New Singers gave "Songs of Protest." "Song Cycle to Words of Joyce" was heard with the League of Composers at the second Yaddo Festival and at the London Section of the I.S.C.M.

ISRAEL CITKOWITZ (*Continued*)

COMPOSITIONS
(list incomplete)

CHORAL WORKS	DURATION	PUBLISHER	DATE
THE LAMB	4 minutes	Manuscript	1936
a cappella		*for hire*	
SONGS OF PROTEST	8 "	Manuscript	1936
a cappella		*for hire*	

CHAMBER MUSIC			
PASSACAGLIA	8 minutes	Manuscript	1927
piano			
SONATINE	7 "	Manuscript	1929
piano			
SONG CYCLE TO WORDS OF JOYCE	13 "	Cos Cob Press	1930
voice, piano			
STRING QUARTET	13 "	Manuscript	1932
ANDANTE TRANQUILLO	6 "	Manuscript	1932
string quartet			
SONG CYCLE (Blake)	10 "	Manuscript	1934
voice, string quartet			
SONG CYCLE TO WORDS OF FROST	12 "	Manuscript	1936
voice, piano			

AVERY CLAFLIN

Born in Keene, New Hampshire, in 1898. He started taking piano lessons at the age of seven and made some early attempts at composition between the ages of ten and fifteen. He graduated from Harvard in 1920. Although he is now the Vice-President of the French-American Banking Corporation, he continues his interest in music.

A scene from his opera "Hester Prynne" based on *The Scarlet Letter* (for which the composer's wife wrote the libretto) was performed by The Friends and Enemies of Modern Music at Hartford during the winter of 1935. The First Symphony was performed in January, 1944, by the Sioux City Symphony and in South Carolina and Iowa.

Claflin is working on a one-act opera based on "La Grande Breteche" by Balzac.

COMPOSITIONS

ORCHESTRAL WORKS	DURATION	PUBLISHER	DATE
MOBY DICK SUITE	30 minutes	Manuscript	1929
SYMPHONY IN D MINOR	50 "	Manuscript	1936
SYMPHONY II (DIRGE FOR 1941)	32 "	Manuscript	1944
BALLET MUSIC FROM HEWLETT	18 "	Manuscript	1944
ALLEGRO	5 "	Manuscript	1944

CHORAL WORKS			
TWO SHORT CHORUSES FOR FEMALE VOICES (Max Jacob and E. E. Cummings)	15 minutes		1926
a cappella or 2 piano accompaniment			

AVERY CLAFLIN (*Continued*)

CHAMBER MUSIC	DURATION	PUBLISHER	DATE
TRIO FOR PIANO, VIOLIN AND VIOLONCELLO	20 minutes		1921
STRING QUARTET	40 "	Manuscript	1937

STAGE WORKS			
THE FALL OF USHER—opera in 1 act *full orchestra*	40 minutes	Manuscript	1921
HESTER PRYNNE—opera in 3 acts	2½ hours	Manuscript	1934

ARTHUR COHN

Born in Philadelphia, Pennsylvania, in 1910. He studied violin, pedagogy and theory at Combs Conservatory in Philadelphia. He was a pupil of Jacobinoff and Happich. In 1933 he was awarded a fellowship in composition at the Juilliard School, where he worked with Goldmark.

He organized the Dorian Quartet and in 1933 the Stringart Quartet, which specialized in contemporary music and toured for five seasons. He was concert master of the Philadelphia Civic orchestra and co-founder of the Chamber Orchestra and Composers' Laboratory of Philadelphia. At present he is Administrative Director of the Symphony Club in Philadelphia and conducts both the large orchestra and chamber orchestra and teaches. He is head of the Music Department of the Philadelphia School for Social Science and Art and also lectures. From 1933 to 1943 he was administrator of the Free Library of Philadelphia project for copying contemporary composers' music, and in 1940 he was appointed Director of the Fleisher Collection of the Free Library. He contributes articles to *Modern Music* and has served as guest critic for the *Rochester Times Union*. He has appeared as guest conductor with various musical ensembles.

He was awarded first prize in the national contest of the American Society of Ancient Instruments in 1938, and in 1941 he was awarded a prize by the National Symphony Orchestra for an orchestral work. Major performances of his works have been given in Washington, Philadelphia, New York and on tour. CBS has broadcast "Four Preludes for String Quartet" over a national hook-up and NBC has broadcast String Quartet No. 4, as well as "Four Preludes for String Orchestra," over a national hook-up; WQXR has also broadcast some of his chamber music. String Quartet No. 4 was recorded by Yaddo. At present he is collaborating on several books on music and is preparing a treatise on the orchestra and orchestration. He is also at work on a Suite for Piano and a symphony.

COMPOSITIONS

ORCHESTRAL WORKS	DURATION	PUBLISHER	DATE
SUITE FOR ORCHESTRA, OPUS 3	25 minutes	Manuscript	1931
FIVE NATURE STUDIES (Second Suite for Orchestra), OPUS 12	35 "	Manuscript	1932

ARTHUR COHN (*Continued*)

ORCHESTRAL WORKS (*Continued*)	DURATION	PUBLISHER	DATE
RETROSPECTIONS, OPUS 11 *string orchestra*	20 minutes	Manuscript	1933
FOUR PRELUDES, OPUS 27 *string orchestra*	17 "	Elkan-Vogel *for hire*	1937
SUITE FOR VIOLA AND ORCHESTRA, OPUS 28	30 "	Elkan-Vogel *for hire*	1937
FOUR SYMPHONIC DOCUMENTS, OPUS 30	25 "	Elkan-Vogel *for hire*	1939
QUINTUPLE CONCERTO, OPUS 31 *treble viol, viola d'amore, viola da* *gamba, bass viol, harpsichord and* *full orchestra*	45 "	Elkan-Vogel *for hire*	1940
HISTRIONICS, OPUS 32 *large string orchestra*	20 "	Elkan-Vogel *for hire*	1940
CONCERTO FOR FLUTE AND ORCHESTRA, OPUS 37	50 "	Elkan-Vogel *for hire*	1941
VARIATIONS *solo clarinet or alto saxophone,* *string orchestra*	7½ "	Elkan-Vogel	1945

CHORAL WORKS

MASS SONG, OPUS 25 *mixed chorus, a cappella*	5 minutes	Manuscript	1935
DULCE ET DECORUM EST, OPUS 8, No. 2 *mixed chorus, a cappella*	5 "	Manuscript	1938

CHAMBER MUSIC

STRING QUARTET No. 1—FOUR PRELUDES, OPUS 1	17 minutes	Manuscript	1928
STRING QUARTET No. 2—SIX MINIA- TURES, OPUS 4	9 "	Manuscript	1930
SUITE, OPUS 2 *viola, piano*	30 "	Manuscript	1930
SONATA, OPUS 6 *violin, piano*	35 "	Manuscript	1932
STRING QUARTET No. 3—CONCEPTIONS IN BRONZE, OPUS 7	20 "	Manuscript	1932
THE POT BELLIED GODS, OPUS 8, No. 1 *baritone, string quartet*	22 "	Manuscript	1933
MUSIC FOR BRASS INSTRUMENTS, OPUS 9 *4 trumpets, 3 trombones*	5 "	Manuscript	1933
SUITE IN E MINOR, OPUS 10 *violin, piano*	14½ "	Manuscript	1933
TRANSCRIPTIONS, OPUS 5 *string quartet*	15 "	Manuscript	1934
THE TWELVE, OPUS 15 *string quartet, declaimer*	16 "	Manuscript	1934
PARAPHRASE ON A FOLK TUNE, OPUS 17, No. 1 *string quartet*	3 "	Manuscript	1935
STRING QUARTET No. 4—HISTRIONICS, OPUS 24	25 "	Manuscript	1935
THREE IMPRESSIONS, OPUS 26, No. 1 *string quartet*	2 "	Manuscript	1935
MACHINE MUSIC, OPUS 20, No. 2 *2 pianos*	5 "	Manuscript	1937
MUSIC FOR ANCIENT INSTRUMENTS, OPUS 29 *treble viol, viola d'amore, viola da* *gamba, bass viol, harpsichord*	22 "	Manuscript	1938
MUSIC FOR BASSOON AND PIANO. OPUS 39	6 "	Elkan-Vogel	1944

ARTHUR COHN (*Continued*)

STAGE WORKS	DURATION	PUBLISHER	DATE
PRODUCING UNITS, OPUS 20, No. 1	6 minutes	Manuscript	1934
dance ensemble, piano			
TRIAL—a satire, OPUS 21	5 "	Manuscript	1934
dance ensemble, piano			
MUSIC TO "TOO LATE TO DIE," OPUS			
16—play in 3 acts	40 "	Manuscript	1935
16 instruments, 26 players			

FILM MUSIC			
BET IT'S A BOY, OPUS 38	16 minutes	Manuscript	1941
for lantern slides with piano quintet (also arranged for concert)			

ROSSETTER GLEASON COLE

Born on a farm near Clyde, Michigan, in 1866. In 1874 he moved to Ann Arbor, Michigan, where he was educated in the public schools and graduated from the University of Michigan. He won a three-year free scholarship in the Royal Master-school for Composition under Max Bruch in Berlin. In 1930 he was made an alumnus member of the University of Michigan chapter of Phi Beta Kappa.

He served three terms as President of the Music Teachers' National Association and four terms as Dean of the Illinois Chapter of American Guild of Organists. He has been Professor of Music in Ripon College (Wisconsin), Grinnell College (Iowa) and the University of Wisconsin. From 1908 to 1939 he was head of the Music Department of Columbia University Summer Sessions in New York City. Since 1909 he has resided in Chicago, where he is head of the Theory Department and Dean of the Cosmopolitan School of Music. In 1934 his opera "The Maypole Lovers" was awarded the David Bispham Memorial Medal.

His orchestral works have all been performed in the United States, and many of them have had several performances by the Chicago Symphony Orchestra. "The Rock of Liberty" for chorus was performed in Springfield, Chicago and Madison by various choral organizations.

COMPOSITIONS

ORCHESTRAL WORKS	DURATION	PUBLISHER	DATE
OVERTURE "PIONEER," OPUS 35	13 minutes	Manuscript	1918
SUITE No. 1 FROM "THE MAYPOLE			
LOVERS"	15 "	Manuscript	1934
HEROIC PIECE, OPUS 39	9 "	Manuscript	1938
orchestra, organ; rescored for orchestra alone			
SUITE No. 2 FROM "THE MAYPOLE			
LOVERS"	18 "	Manuscript	1942
RHAPSODY, OPUS 30	9 "	Manuscript	1943

ROSSETTER GLEASON COLE (*Continued*)

CHORAL WORKS	DURATION	PUBLISHER	DATE
THE ROCK OF LIBERTY, OPUS 36 soli, women's voices, orchestra	90 minutes	A. P. Schmidt Co.	1920
CHAMBER MUSIC			
SONATA IN D MAJOR, OPUS 8 piano, violin	30 minutes	A. P. Schmidt Co.	1917
STAGE WORKS			
THE MAYPOLE LOVERS—3 act romantic opera symphony orchestra	2 hrs., 10 min.	Manuscript	1931

ULRIC COLE

Born in New York City in 1905. She began studying piano at the age of five. Her early piano compositions, written when she was eight years old, were published later in England as a book of children's pieces. She studied with Goetschius, Goldmark, Grunn and Lhevinne and received fellowship awards from the Juilliard Graduate School.

She has appeared as guest artist with the Cincinnati Symphony and with Frank Black's String Symphony in performances of her Divertimento for String Orchestra and Piano and also with the Gordon Quartet playing her Quintet for Piano and Strings. Her compositions have been presented in concert by the National, Rochester and Toronto symphony orchestras, the Wallenstein String Symphony and others; they have also had major broadcasts over the Mutual and NBC networks and WNYC and WQXR. In 1946 the Concerto No. 2 for Piano and Orchestra was premiered by the Cincinnati Symphony under the direction of Goossens.

COMPOSITIONS

ORCHESTRAL WORKS	DURATION	PUBLISHER	DATE
CONCERTO FOR PIANO AND ORCHESTRA	25 minutes	Manuscript	1930
TWO SKETCHES FOR STRING ORCHESTRA	10 "	Manuscript for hire	1937
DIVERTIMENTO FOR STRING ORCHESTRA AND PIANO	16 "	J. Fischer & Bro. for sale or hire	1938
CONCERTO FOR PIANO AND ORCHESTRA, No. 2	30 "	Manuscript	1942
CHAMBER MUSIC			
SONATA FOR VIOLIN AND PIANO	20 minutes	S.P.A.M.	1927
SONATA FOR VIOLIN AND PIANO, No. 2	17 "	Manuscript	1929
SUITE FOR TRIO piano, violin, cello	18 "	Manuscript	1931
QUARTET 2 violins, viola, cello	17 "	Manuscript	1932
FANTASY SONATA FOR PIANO	9 "	Manuscript	1933
SUITE FOR STRING QUARTET	18 "	Manuscript	1936
QUINTET FOR PIANO AND STRINGS	16 "	S.P.A.M.	1936
ROUND DANCE FOR STRINGS	7 "	Manuscript	1940

EDWARD TONER CONE

Born in Greensboro, North Carolina, in 1917. He graduated from Princeton University in 1939 and received his Masters degree in fine arts from Columbia University in 1941. He studied composition with Roger Sessions and piano with Karl Ulrich Schnabel. Until he entered the U. S. Army in 1942, he was part-time instructor of music at Princeton University.

His Violin and Piano Sonata was performed by the League of Composers and later by I.S.C.M. The League of Composers also performed his Clarinet Quintet. The Musical Art Quartet played his String Quartet in Baltimore.

COMPOSITIONS

ORCHESTRAL WORKS	DURATION	PUBLISHER	DATE
ORCHESTRAL WORK	12 minutes	Manuscript	1942
CHORAL WORKS			
THE LOTUS-EATERS *men's voices, orchestra*	20 minutes	Manuscript	1939
EXCURSIONS *a cappella chorus*		Manuscript	1946
LET US NOW PRAISE FAMOUS MEN— a commemorative anthem *tenor solo, male chorus, organ*	15 "	Manuscript	1946
CHAMBER MUSIC			
STRING QUARTET	15 minutes	Manuscript	1939
SONATA *violin, piano*	20 "	Manuscript	1940
CLARINET QUINTET *string quartet, clarinet*	15 "	Manuscript	1941
DIVERTIMENTO *woodwinds*		Manuscript	1946
PRELUDE AND VARIATIONS *piano four hands*		Manuscript	1946

FREDERICK SHEPHERD CONVERSE

Born in Newton, Massachusetts, in 1871, and died in Massachusetts in 1940. He attended Harvard University, where he studied music with Paine and graduated with highest honors. Later he worked with Chadwick, Rheinberger and Baermann. After a brief attempt to make a career in business he decided to study music again and went to Munich to the Royal Academy of Music. He returned to the New England Conservatory in Boston, teaching harmony, and in 1900 joined the faculty at Harvard University, where he taught composition and became Assistant Professor in the Music Department. Later he returned to the New England Conservatory as Dean of Music.

The David Bispham Medal was awarded him for his opera "The Pipe of Desire," an early work which was produced in Boston and in 1910 at

FREDERICK SHEPHERD CONVERSE (*Continued*)

the Metropolitan Opera House in New York. The Boston Opera Company also produced another work called "The Sacrifice." His orchestral music has been performed by major orchestras in many cities of the United States, also in Paris, Vienna, Berlin and London. Several of his works for chamber music have been broadcast over NBC. He became a member of the American Academy of Arts and Letters in 1937.

COMPOSITIONS

ORCHESTRAL WORKS

	DURATION	PUBLISHER	DATE
AVE ATQUE VALE—tone poem	13 minutes	Manuscript	1916
SYMPHONY C MINOR, No. 1	40 "	Manuscript	1920
SYMPHONY E MAJOR, No. 2	35 "	Manuscript	1921
ELEGIAC POEM	18 "	Manuscript	1926
FLIVVER TEN MILLION—fantasie	13 "	C. C. Birchard & Co.	1927
CALIFORNIA—Festival Scenes	15 "	C. C. Birchard & Co.	1928
AMERICAN SKETCHES—symphonic suite	30 "	Edwin F. Kalmus	1933
SYMPHONY F MAJOR, No. 3			

CHORAL WORKS

THE PEACE PIPE—cantata	45 minutes	C. C. Birchard & Co.	
mixed chorus, baritone solo, orchestra			
THE ANSWER OF THE STARS—cantata	12 "	C. C. Birchard & Co.	1920
PSALM—I WILL PRAISE THEE, O LORD		C. C. Birchard & Co.	1929
mixed chorus, organ, piano, brass			
THE FLIGHT OF THE EAGLE—cantata	30 "	C. C. Birchard & Co.	1930

CHAMBER MUSIC

TRIO FOR VIOLIN, CELLO AND PIANO	35 minutes	Manuscript	1931
STRING QUARTET E MINOR, No. 3		Manuscript	
SONATA FOR VIOLIN AND PIANO		Manuscript	
QUARTET, OPUS 17			
CONCERTO FOR VIOLIN, OPUS 12			
violin, piano			

STAGE WORKS

THE IMMIGRANTS—opera	Manuscript	
SINBAD THE SAILOR—opera	Manuscript	1917
PURITAN PASSIONA—incidental		
music to Mackaye's "Jeanne d'Arc"	Oliver Ditson Co.	

FILM MUSIC
SCARECROW SKETCHES

AARON COPLAND

Born in Brooklyn, New York, in 1900. He was first educated at the public schools in Brooklyn and graduated from high school in 1918. His sister first taught him the piano and he continued his musical studies with Wolfsohn, Wittgenstein and Adler. In 1918 he began to study theory with Goldmark, who taught him for four years. In 1921 he enrolled as a first student of composition at the Fontainebleau School of Music and subse-

AARON COPLAND (Continued)

quently studied in Paris with Nadia Boulanger. During this period he also studied piano for a short time with Viñes. In 1925 he received the Guggenheim Fellowship and it was renewed the following year.

His interest in American contemporary music has led him to take an active part in various associations. In coöperation with Roger Sessions he organized the Copland-Sessions Concerts, which presented American music during the years of 1928 to 1931. He was Director of the American Festival of Contemporary Music at Yaddo, during the first two years of its existence. He is an active member of the League of Composers' Board of Directors and a Director of the MacDowell Association, the Koussevitzky Music Foundation and the American Music Center; for eight years he was President of the American Composers Alliance. In 1935 and in 1944 he was lecturer on music at Harvard University, and from 1927 to 1937 he lectured at the New School for Social Research. He has taught composition at the Berkshire Music Center and in 1945 was appointed Assistant Director of that school. He has frequently contributed articles on music to many magazines including *American Mercury, Modern Music* and the *New Republic*. He is the author of two books: *What to Listen for in Music* (1938) and *Our New Music* (1941).

His orchestral works have been played frequently by orchestras throughout the United States as well as in South America, Mexico, England and France. His chamber works have had many performances in America and in Europe, as well as at many music festivals. "The Second Hurricane," an opera for high-school performance, produced in New York City, has been frequently performed in other parts of the country. In 1945 the ballet, "Appalachian Spring," commissioned by the Elizabeth Sprague Coolidge Foundation (Library of Congress), won the Pulitzer Prize for music and was chosen by the New York Critics Circle as the outstanding work in the dramatic category for that year. He has also received commissions from the League of Composers for a work for chamber orchestra, "Music for the Theatre," first performed by the Boston Symphony, and a commission for an orchestral work, "Statements," first presented by the Minneapolis Symphony. CBS commissioned a work for radio which received a coast-to-coast broadcast. Other major works have been broadcast over NBC, CBS and BBC. The Columbia Phonograph Company has recorded the Piano Variations, "Vitebsk," Nocturne, "Ukulele Serenade" for violin and piano and "Two Pieces for String Quartet." RCA Victor has recorded "Music for the Theatre," "El Salón México" and "Appalachian Spring." N.M.Q.R. has recorded the "Vocalise for Voice and Piano." The RCA Victor Company Award was given to him in 1930 for his "Dance Symphony." The Concert Hall Society has recorded the Piano Sonata and Three Pieces from "Our Town."

COMPOSITIONS

ORCHESTRAL WORKS	DURATION	PUBLISHER	DATE
CORTÈGE MACABRE (from Grohg)	8 minutes	Manuscript	1923
SYMPHONY FOR ORGAN AND ORCHESTRA	25 "	Manuscript	1924

AARON COPLAND *(Continued)*

ORCHESTRAL WORKS *(Continued)*

	DURATION	PUBLISHER	DATE
FIRST SYMPHONY	25 minutes	Cos Cob Press	1925
DANCE SYMPHONY	20 "	Cos Cob Press	1925
CONCERTO FOR PIANO AND ORCHESTRA	18 "	Cos Cob Press	1926
SYMPHONIC ODE	20 "	Manuscript	1929
SHORT SYMPHONY	15 "	Manuscript	1933
STATEMENTS	17 "	Boosey & Hawkes	1935
EL SALÓN MÉXICO	12 "	Boosey & Hawkes	1936
MUSIC FOR RADIO	12 "	Boosey & Hawkes	1937
OUTDOOR OVERTURE	9 "	Boosey & Hawkes	1938
BILLY THE KID—suite from the ballet	20 "	Boosey & Hawkes	1938
QUIET CITY	11 "	Boosey & Hawkes	1940
solo trumpet, English horn, *string orchestra*			
OUR TOWN—music from the film score	11 "	Boosey & Hawkes	1940
LINCOLN PORTRAIT	14 "	Boosey & Hawkes	1942
speaker, orchestra			
FANFARE FOR THE COMMON MAN	3 "	Boosey & Hawkes	1942
brass and percussion only			
FOUR DANCE EPISODES FROM "RODEO"	16 "	Boosey & Hawkes	1942
BUCKAROO HOLIDAY			
CORRAL NOCTURNE			
SATURDAY NIGHT WALTZ			
HOE-DOWN			
DANZON CUBANO	6 "	Boosey & Hawkes	1942
LETTER FROM HOME	7 "	Boosey & Hawkes	1944
APPALACHIAN SPRING—ballet suite	21 "	Boosey & Hawkes	1944
THIRD SYMPHONY	40 "	Boosey & Hawkes	1946

CHAMBER ORCHESTRA

	DURATION	PUBLISHER	DATE
MUSIC FOR THE THEATRE	20 minutes	Cos Cob Press	1925
five parts			
TWO PIECES FOR STRING ORCHESTRA	10 "	Arrow Music Press	1928
PRELUDE FROM FIRST SYMPHONY	6 "	Manuscript	1934
PRAIRIE NIGHT AND CELEBRATION			
DANCE (from Billy the Kid)	6 "	Boosey & Hawkes	1938
JOHN HENRY—railroad ballad	4 "	Manuscript	1940
MUSIC FOR MOVIES	15 "	Boosey & Hawkes	1942
HOE-DOWN (from Rodeo)	3 "	Boosey & Hawkes	1942
for string orchestra			

CHORAL WORKS

	DURATION	PUBLISHER	DATE
THE HOUSE ON THE HILL	5 minutes	E. C. Schirmer Music Co.	1925
(E. A. Robinson)			
women's voices a cappella			
AN IMMORALITY (Ezra Pound)	5 "	E. C. Schirmer Music Co.	1925
women's voices, piano			
WHAT DO WE PLANT?	4 "	Boosey & Hawkes	1936
2 part with piano, for junior high- *school chorus*			
THAT'S THE IDEA OF FREEDOM	4 "	C. C. Birchard & Co.	1937
(from The Second Hurricane)			
mixed chorus, piano or orchestra			
LARK (Genevieve Taggart)	5 "	E. C. Schirmer Music Co.	1938
baritone solo, mixed chorus a cappella			
LAS AGACHADAS (Shake-Down Song)	4 "	Boosey & Hawkes	1942
mixed chorus a cappella			
THE YOUNGER GENERATION (from			
The North Star)	2 "	Boosey & Hawkes	1943
3 or 4 part chorus, piano			
SONG OF THE GUERRILLAS (from			
The North Star)	3 "	Boosey & Hawkes	1943
baritone solo, men's voices, *piano or orchestra*			

AARON COPLAND *(Continued)*

CHAMBER MUSIC

	DURATION	PUBLISHER	DATE
As It Fell upon a Day	8 minutes	New Music	1923
soprano, flute, clarinet			
Two Pieces	10 "	Manuscript	1928
string quartet			
Vitebsk—study on a Jewish melody	11 "	Cos Cob Press	1929
violin, cello, piano			
Piano Variations	10 "	Cos Cob Press	1930
Elegies	6 "	Manuscript	1932
violin, viola			
Sextet (after the Short Symphony)	15 "	Manuscript	1937
string quartet, clarinet, piano			
Piano Sonata	23 "	Boosey & Hawkes	1941
Danzon Cubano for Two Pianos	6 "	Boosey & Hawkes	1942
Violin Sonata	17 "	Boosey & Hawkes	1943

STAGE WORKS

Miracle at Verdun—incidental music for the play by Hans Chlumberg	15 minutes	Manuscript	1931
Grohg—ballet in one act	30 "	Manuscript	1932
1 male dancer, 3 female dancers, corps de ballet, symphony orchestra			
Hear Ye, Hear Ye!—ballet in one act	35 "	Manuscript	1934
chamber orchestra, solo dancers, ballet			
The Second Hurricane—a play-opera for high-school performance	1½ hours	C. C. Birchard & Co.	1937
7 solo parts, choruses of high-school children and adults, chamber orchestra			
Billy the Kid—ballet	35 "	Manuscript	1938
woodwinds by twos, orchestra			
Quiet City—incidental music for Irwin Shaw's play	15 "	Manuscript	1939
The Five Kings—incidental music for Orson Welles' adaptation from Shakespeare	20 "	Manuscript	1939
Rodeo—ballet	25 "	Manuscript	1942
woodwinds by twos, orchestra			
Appalachian Spring—chamber ballet	35 "	Manuscript	1944

FILM MUSIC

	STUDIO	PUBLISHER	DATE
The City—documentary film concert version—"New England Countryside," "Sunday Traffic"—in suite	Civic Films Inc.	Boosey & Hawkes *for hire*	1939
Of Mice and Men concert version— excerpts: "Barley Wagons," "Threshing Machines"	Hal Roach, Inc.	Boosey & Hawkes *for hire*	1939
Our Town concert version—suite	Sol Lesser	Boosey & Hawkes	1940
The North Star concert version—Song of the Guerrillas *male chorus, orchestra*	Samuel Goldwyn	Boosey & Hawkes *for hire*	1943
The Cummington Story— documentary film	Office of War Information	Manuscript	1945

HENRY DIXON COWELL

Born in Menlo Park, California, in 1897. He is the grandson of an Episcopal Dean of Kildare, Ireland. His father moved to America and became a California newspaper editor for athletics, and his mother was a writer of books and magazine articles. He began to study the violin at the age of five, and in his eighth year he decided to become a composer and gave his instrument away with the intention of acquiring more perfect hearing by developing his mind. He introduced the term "tone cluster," which has forced its way into the musical vocabulary. At the University of California he received his first real training in music with Seeger. After serving in the army during World War I he returned to study with Woodman at the Institute of Applied Music. In 1923 he concertized in Europe as a pianist, and in 1931 and 1932 he received a Guggenheim Fellowship which took him to the University of Berlin to specialize in the study of comparative musicology.

He is a crusader for new musical resources, which is the title of one of his books published in 1930. His symposium, *American Composers on American Music,* was published by the Stanford University Press. His book entitled *The Nature of Melody* is a text on melody writing. He is the founder of the *New Music Quarterly,* New Music Orchestra Series, and New Music Quarterly Recordings and is a member of many contemporary music societies. He organized several series of lectures on music in the New School for Social Research and lectures there at present. He has been instructor in music at Stanford University, Mills College and the University of California. With Professor Leon Theremin's collaboration he developed the "rhythmicon," an instrument designed to produce all kinds of rhythms and cross-rhythms, which was first presented in a demonstration in New York in 1932.

Concerto for piano and orchestra, "Synchrony," Symphonietta, "Reel," "Old American Country Set," "Tales of Our Countryside," "Fanfare," "Liberty Horn Pipe" and many other orchestral works have been performed frequently in the United States, Havana, South America and in France. His chamber music has been heard all over Europe and America, also at the Festivals of American Music at Yaddo, the Federation of Music Clubs Convention and the League of Composers. He was commissioned by the League of Composers and by the Cincinnati Symphony. Many of his works have been broadcast by CBS and NBC and local stations. "The Building of Banba" was presented as a ballet at the Halcyon California Festival. Columbia has recorded the "Tales of Our Countryside" and Movement for String Quartet. "Six Casual Developments," Suite for Woodwinds and "Ostinati with Chorales" have been recorded by N.M.R. Several works were recorded by O.W.I. for use by the army.

COMPOSITIONS

ORCHESTRAL WORKS	DURATION	PUBLISHER	DATE
SYMPHONY	45 minutes	Manuscript	1918
COMMUNICATION	8 "	Manuscript	1920

HENRY DIXON COWELL (*Continued*)

ORCHESTRAL WORKS (*Continued*)

	DURATION	PUBLISHER	DATE
VESTIGES	10 minutes	Manuscript	1924
SOME MUSIC	12 "	Manuscript	1927
CONCERTO	18 "	M. Sénart	1929
piano, orchestra			
SYNCHRONY	15 "	Edition Adler	1930
TWO APPOSITIONS	10 "	Manuscript	1931
RHYTHMICANA	20 "	Manuscript	1931
for rhythmicon, orchestra			
ORCHESTRAL SUITE	12 "	Manuscript	1932
IRISH SUITE IN THREE MOVEMENTS	12 "	Manuscript	1933
FOUR CONTINUATIONS	16 "	Manuscript	1934
full string orchestra			
OLD AMERICAN COUNTRY SET	15 "	Associated Music Publishers	1937
SYMPHONY No. 2 (Anthropos)	23 "	Edition Adler	1938
SYMPHONIC SET, OPUS 17	12 "	Arrow Music Press	1939
ANCIENT DESERT DRONE	7 "	Associated Music Publishers	1940
PASTORAL AND FIDDLER'S DELIGHT	8 "	G. Schirmer, Inc.	1940
TALES OF OUR COUNTRYSIDE	12 "	Associated Music Publishers	1940
SCHOONTHREE	5 "	Mercury Music Corp.	1940
PURDUE OVERTURE	8 "	Manuscript	1940
SYMPHONY No. 3 (Gaelic)	23 "	Associated Music Publishers	1942
CELTIC SET	10 "	G. Schirmer, Inc.	1943
SUITE	18 "	Manuscript	1943
piano, string orchestra			
HYMN AND FUGUING TUNE, No. 2	7 "	Associated Music Publishers	1944
string orchestra			
UNITED MUSIC	8 "	Associated Music Publishers	1944
HYMN AND FUGUING TUNE, No. 3	8 "	Associated Music Publishers	1945
full orchestra			
HYMN AND FUGUING TUNE, No. 5	8 "	Manuscript	1945
string orchestra			
BIG SING	10 "	Manuscript	1945
SYMPHONY No. 4			1946
TO AMERICA—festival overture		Broadcast Music Inc.	1946
mixed chorus, two simultaneous orchestras			

CHAMBER ORCHESTRA

SYMPHONIETTA	15 minutes	Edition Adler	1928
14 instruments			
CONCERTO—Irish suite	15 "	Manuscript	1929
12 strings, piano			
POLYPHONICA	6 "	Manuscript	1930
12 instruments			
EXULTATION	5 "	Edition Adler	1930
10 strings			
HEROIC DANCE	5 "	Manuscript	1931
9 instruments			
COMPETITIVE SPORT	5 "	Manuscript	1931
9 instruments			
STEEL AND STONE	5 "	Manuscript	1931
9 instruments			
SUITE IN THREE MOVEMENTS	9 "	Manuscript	1935
12 instruments			
SIX CASUAL DEVELOPMENTS	12 "	Manuscript	1935
5 instruments			

HENRY DIXON COWELL (*Continued*)

BAND MUSIC

	DURATION	PUBLISHER	DATE
SUITE IN FIVE MOVEMENTS *full band*	15 minutes	Manuscript	1936
REEL IRISH *full band*	5 "	Manuscript	1936
CELTIC SET	10 "	G. Schirmer, Inc.	1939
VOX HUMANA	10 "	Manuscript	1939
SHIPSHAPE OVERTURE	8 "	G. Schirmer, Inc.	1940
FESTIVE OCCASION	8 "	Manuscript	1943
CONCERTO PICCOLO *piano and band*	15 "	Manuscript	1943
HYMN AND FUGUING TUNE, No. 1	5 "	Leeds Music Corp.	1944
ANIMAL MAGIC	8 "	Leeds Music Corp.	1944

CHORAL WORKS

THE THISTLE FLOWER *women's voices, a cappella*	5 minutes	Manuscript	1928
THE COMING OF LIGHT *soprano, alto, tenor, bass,* *a cappella*	6 "	Harold Flammer	1939
FIRE AND ICE *2 tenors, baritone, bass,* *orchestra or band*	5 "	Boston Music Co.	1942
AMERICAN MUSE *soprano, alto, piano*	7 "	Music Press	1943

CHAMBER MUSIC

ENSEMBLE *2 violins, viola, 2 cellos*	15 minutes	Associated Music Publishers	1925
SEVEN PARAGRAPHS—trios *violin, viola, cello*	10 "	Manuscript	1926
QUARTET	20 "	Manuscript	1927
SUITE *violin, piano*		Associated Music Publishers	
SIX CASUAL DEVELOPMENTS *clarinet, piano*	12 "	Manuscript	1934
MOVEMENT *string quartet*	8 "	New Music	1934
MOSAIC QUARTET *string quartet*	10 "	New Music	1935
SEVEN ASSOCIATED MOVEMENTS *violin, piano*	15 "	Manuscript	1935
UNITED QUARTET *string quartet*	15 "	Manuscript	1936
THREE OSTINATI WITH CHORALES *oboe, piano*	12 "	Manuscript	1937
VOCALISE *soprano, flute, piano*		Manuscript	1937
AMERIND SUITE *piano*	15 "	Axelrod	1938
TOCCANTA *soprano, flute, cello, piano*		Manuscript	1939
CELTIC SET *2 pianos*	10 "	G. Schirmer, Inc.	1940
TWO BITS *flute, piano*		Gundy-Bettoney	1941
HOW OLD IS SONG *violin, piano, strings*		Manuscript	1942–44
ACTION IN BRASS *5 brass instruments*		Edition Musicus	1943
SONATA *violin and piano*	16 "	Associated Music Publishers	1945

HENRY DIXON COWELL (*Continued*)

STAGE WORKS	DURATION	PUBLISHER	DATE
THE BUILDING OF BANBA—ballet	1 hour	Manuscript	1922
soprano, alto, tenor, two basses,			
chorus, 14 piece orchestra			
ATLANTIS—ballet	30 minutes	Manuscript	1926
3 voices, theatre orchestra			

FILM MUSIC

MR. FLAGMAKER		Mary E. Bute, Producer	1942

RUTH CRAWFORD (SEEGER)

Born in East Liverpool, Ohio, in 1901. She began to teach piano at the School of Musical Art in Jacksonville, Florida, in 1918. Moving to Chicago in 1921, she studied for a year with Palmer and then entered the American Conservatory and studied harmony, counterpoint, composition, and orchestration with Weidig and piano with Levy and Djane Herz. She taught at the American Conservatory from 1925 to 1929 and also at the Elmhurst College of Music. She received first prize in a national composition contest conducted by Sigma Alpha Iota sorority in 1927, and a Juilliard Scholarship for study with Weidig during 1927–29. In 1930 she received a Guggenheim Fellowship, and spent 1930 and 1931 in Berlin and Paris.

The past eleven years have been spent in Washington, D. C., where her husband, Charles Seeger, is Chief of the Music Division of the Pan American Union. She was Music Editor of *Our Singing Country,* by John A. and Alan Lomax. This work included transcription from phonograph discs of several hundred songs recorded in the field. She has also made many piano settings of traditional American songs, and has used these songs extensively with children of all ages.

Her music has been performed in New York, Chicago, San Francisco, as well as in European cities. In 1933 her "Three Songs for Contralto, Oboe, Piano and Percussion, with orchestral Ostinato" was chosen as one of two works to represent America at the International Festival of the I.S.C.M. in Amsterdam. The Andante from her String Quartet has been recorded by N.M.Q.R.

COMPOSITIONS

CHAMBER ORCHESTRA	DURATION	PUBLISHER	DATE
TWO MOVEMENTS FOR CHAMBER			
ORCHESTRA	6 minutes	Photostat	1926
9 instruments			
THREE SONGS	8 "	New Music	1932
contralto, 17 instruments			
RISSOLTY ROSSOLTY	3 "	Manuscript *for hire*	1941
10 wind instruments, timpani, strings			

RUTH CRAWFORD (SEEGER) (*Continued*)

CHORAL WORKS	DURATION	PUBLISHER	DATE
TWO CHANTS FOR WOMEN'S CHORUS *a cappella*	5 minutes	Manuscript	1930

CHAMBER MUSIC			
NINE PRELUDES FOR PIANO		New Music	1926
SONATA FOR VIOLIN AND PIANO	12 minutes		1927
SUITE FOR FOUR STRINGS AND PIANO	15 "	Photostat	1927
THREE MOVEMENTS FOR WINDS AND PIANO	8 "		1928
FOUR DIAPHONIC SUITES *2 celli, 2 clarinets, oboe and flute*	6 "	Manuscript	1930
STRING QUARTET	12 "	New Music	1931

PAUL CRESTON

Born in New York City, N. Y., in 1906. He comes of Italian parentage. He began to study the piano at the age of eight. Later he became a pupil of Randegger and of Dethier. He studied organ with Yon and taught himself harmony, theory and composition.

Besides composing he is active as a teacher of piano and composition and an organist; he has done research in accoustics, musico-therapy and aesthetics. He has been associated with the American Broadcasting Company in the "Hour of Faith" program and has written the background music for the "Hall of Fame" and the "Storyland Theatre" programs.

In 1938 and 1939 he received Guggenheim Fellowships. The National Association of American Composers and Conductors gave him a citation of merit in 1941 and again in 1943. In 1945 he received a grant from the Alice Ditson Fund (Columbia University). The American Academy of Arts and Letters awarded him a grant in 1943, and in the same year he received the New York Music Critics Award for his Symphony No. 1. He was commissioned by Kostelanetz, Petrides, ABC and CBS.

His compositions have been performed at the Yaddo and the Princeton festival of American music, also at the New School for Social Research and at Bennington College. His orchestral works have been performed in New York, Cincinnati, Philadelphia, Pittsburgh, Boston, Washington and other cities in this country, as well as in Canada, Russia and Mexico. His chamber music has had frequent performances and several of his works have been played in South America, Honolulu, Guam and through the Pacific Islands, and also in England. NBC, CBS, MBC and ABC have broadcast some of his orchestral works, and a world-wide network over NBC broadcast one of his recent orchestral compositions. His Scherzo from Symphony No. 1 has been recorded by Columbia and the Suite for Saxophone and Piano, by N.M.Q.R.

PAUL CRESTON (*Continued*)

COMPOSITIONS

ORCHESTRAL WORKS

	DURATION	PUBLISHER	DATE
THRENODY, OP. 16	12 minutes	Manuscript *for hire*	1938
TWO CHORIC DANCES, OP. 17B	12 "	Manuscript *for hire*	1938
SYMPHONY No. 1, OP. 20	20 "	Manuscript *for hire*	1940
CONCERTINO, OP. 21 *marimba, orchestra*	15 "	Manuscript *for hire*	1940
PRELUDE AND DANCE, OP. 25	7 "	Manuscript *for hire*	1941
CONCERTO, OP. 26 *E flat alto saxophone, orchestra*	16 "	Manuscript *for hire*	1941
A RUMOR, OP. 27	5 "	Manuscript *for hire*	1941
PASTORALE AND TARANTELLA, OP. 28	10 "	Manuscript *for hire*	1941
DANCE VARIATIONS, OP. 30 *soprano, orchestra*	5 "	Manuscript *for hire*	1942
FANTASY, OP. 32 *piano, orchestra*	8 "	Manuscript *for hire*	1942
CHANT OF 1942, OP. 33	10 "	Manuscript *for hire*	1943
FRONTIERS, OP. 34	10 "	Manuscript *for hire*	1943
SYMPHONY No. 2, OP. 35	25 "	Manuscript *for hire*	1944
DAWN MOOD, OP. 36	6 "	Manuscript *for hire*	1944
POEM, OP. 39 *harp, orchestra*	15 "	Manuscript *for hire*	1945

BAND MUSIC

LEGEND, OP. 31 FOR BAND	7 minutes	Leeds Music Corp.	1942

CHAMBER ORCHESTRA

OUT OF THE CRADLE ENDLESSLY ROCKING *15 instruments*	12 minutes	Manuscript	1934
PARTITA *flute, violin, strings*	15 "	Sprague-Coleman	1937
TWO CHORIC DANCES, OP. 17a *5 woodwinds, piano, percussion, strings*	12 "	Manuscript *for hire*	1938

CHORAL WORKS

THREE CHORALES FROM TAGORE *a cappella*	10 minutes	G. Schirmer, Inc.	1936
MISSA PRO DEFUNCTIS *tenor, baritone, organ*	15 "	Manuscript	1938
DIRGE *soprano, alto, tenor, baritone, piano*	4 "	Manuscript	1940

CHAMBER MUSIC

THREE POEMS FROM WALT WHITMAN *cello, piano*	9 minutes	Manuscript	1934
SUITE, OP. 6 *alto saxophone, piano*	10 "	New Music	1935
STRING QUARTET, OP. 8	18 "	Manuscript	1936

PAUL CRESTON (*Continued*)

CHAMBER MUSIC (*Continued*)	DURATION	PUBLISHER	DATE
SONATA, OP. 9 *piano*	15 minutes	Manuscript	1936
SUITE, OP. 13 *viola, piano*	12 "	Pro-Art	1937
SUITE, OP. 18 *violin, piano*	11 "	Manuscript	1939
SONATA, OP. 19 *alto saxophone, piano*	13 "	Axelrod	1939

STAGE WORKS			
IRON FLOWERS—incidental music *music for piano only*	20 minutes	Manuscript	1933
A TALE ABOUT THE LAND—ballet *piano*	15 "	Manuscript	1940

FILM MUSIC			
BROUGHT TO ACTION—music for U. S. Navy film		Manuscript	1945

BAINBRIDGE CRIST

Born in Lawrenceburg, Indiana, in 1883. At the age of five his mother taught him the piano, and later he studied the flute under Theodore Hahn. When the family moved to Washington, D. C., he entered George Washington University, where he obtained his degree of Bachelor of Laws. He practiced law in Boston for six years, but during his spare time he continued to compose and to play the flute in the Boston Orchestral Club. The desire to devote his entire time to music finally led him to abandon his career as a lawyer, and he left for Europe to study singing, theory and orchestration under Juon and Landi.

On his return to America in 1915 he taught singing. He later returned to Europe to prepare some of his pupils for the opera. From his earliest years he has been interested in literary and mythological subjects in relation to music.

His orchestral works have been frequently performed in Europe and in America by many of the major symphonic orchestras, and there have been broadcasts of "Vienna–1913" over ABC and other networks, "Chinese Procession" over NBC, and also of "Caprice," "La Nuit Revécue," "Evening," "Romance" and other works. "C'est Mon Ami" has been recorded by the Columbia Company.

COMPOSITIONS

ORCHESTRAL WORKS	DURATION	PUBLISHER	DATE
A BAG OF WHISTLES		Oliver Ditson Co. *voice and piano* *for hire*	1915
THE PARTING—poem *voice, orchestra*	17 minutes	Carl Fischer, Inc.	1916

BAINBRIDGE CRIST (*Continued*)

ORCHESTRAL WORKS (*Continued*)	DURATION		PUBLISHER	DATE
O COME HITHER			Carl Fischer, Inc.	1918
coloratura soprano, orchestra				
DROLLERIES FROM AN ORIENTAL				
DOLL'S HOUSE—suite of 6 songs			Carl Fischer, Inc.	1920
ABISHARIKA	10 minutes		Carl Fischer, Inc.	1921
violin, orchestra			*for hire*	
COLOURED STARS—suite of 4 songs			Carl Fischer, Inc.	1921
INTERMEZZO			Carl Fischer, Inc.	1921
CHINESE, ARABIAN AND NAUTCH DANCES			Carl Fischer, Inc.	1922
DREAMS			Carl Fischer, Inc.	1924
YEARNING			Carl Fischer, Inc.	1924
NOCTURNE			Carl Fischer, Inc.	1924
AN OLD PORTRAIT			Carl Fischer, Inc.	1924
REMEMBER			Carl Fischer, Inc.	1930
voice, orchestra				
NOONTIME			G. Schirmer, Inc.	1931
voice, orchestra				
EVENING			G. Schirmer, Inc.	1931
voice, orchestra				
BY A SILENT SHORE			G. Schirmer, Inc.	1932
voice, orchestra				
KNOCK ON THE DOOR			G. Schirmer, Inc.	1932
voice, orchestra				
VIENNA–1913	6	"	M. Witmark & Sons	1933
CHINESE PROCESSION			M. Witmark & Sons	1933
JAPANESE NOCTURNE			M. Witmark & Sons	1933
LA NUIT REVÉCUE	9	"	Manuscript	1933
			for hire	
FRIVOLITÉ			Manuscript	1934
			for hire	
ROMANCE			Manuscript	1935
			for hire	
HYMN TO NEFERTITI	15	"	Manuscript	1936
			for hire	
FÊTE ESPAGNOLE	6	"	Manuscript	1937
			for hire	
FESTIVAL OVERTURE	8	"	Manuscript	1939
			for hire	
HINDU RHAPSODY	8	"	Manuscript	1939
			for hire	
PLACE PIGALLE	4	"	Carl Fischer, Inc.	1940
(piano version)				
AMERICAN EPIC–1620—a tone	13	"	Manuscript	1941
poem			*score and parts*	
			available	
AMERICA—MY BLESSED LAND	3	"	Manuscript	1942
voice, or chorus, and orchestra			*score and parts*	
			available	
HOWDY FOLKS (memorial poem to				
Will Rogers)	8	"	Manuscript	1943
voice, orchestra			*published for*	
			voice and piano	

STAGE WORKS

LE PIED DE LA MOMIE	30 minutes		Manuscript	1915
choreographic drama, 2 scenes			*for hire*	
PREGIWA'S MARRIAGE—A Javanese ballet	30	"	Manuscript	1920
one scene			*for hire*	
THE SORCERESS	30	"	Manuscript	1926
			for hire	

CHARLES CUSHING

Born in Oakland, California, in 1905. He studied violin, piano, clarinet and viola. He received his Bachelor of Arts and Master of Arts degrees from the University of California. In 1929 he was awarded the Prix de Paris Fellowship for advanced study in France. In Paris, he attended the École Normale de Musique and also studied composition with Boulanger and violin with Nauwinck.

He is Associate Professor of Music at the University of California, and Director of the University of California Concert Band, for which he has written several works. He has contributed articles to *Modern Music* and other musical publications.

His compositions have been performed in various cities of the San Francisco Bay region. "Carmen Saeculare," a commissioned choral work, was premiered in the Greek Theater in Berkeley, California, under the composer's direction. He has had broadcasts over San Francisco radio stations.

COMPOSITIONS

CHORAL WORKS

	DURATION	PUBLISHER	DATE
CARMEN SAECULARE (Horace)—ode *mixed chorus and orchestra*	25 minutes	Manuscript *vocal score for hire*	1935
PSALM XCVII *mixed chorus, band*	12 "	Manuscript *vocal score for hire*	1939
WINE FROM CHINA (translations from the Chinese)—six songs *men's chorus with piano, four hands*	15 "	Manuscript *vocal score for hire*	1945

CHAMBER MUSIC

STRING QUARTET NO. 1 IN F MINOR	22 minutes	Manuscript	1929
FIRST SONATA IN F MAJOR *violin, piano*	15 "	Manuscript	1929
SUITE FOR PIANO: MARCH-TANGO-VALSE	13 "	Manuscript	1930
SONG SUITE: CINQUAINES	10 "	Manuscript	1930
SECOND SONATA FOR VIOLIN AND PIANO	18 "	Manuscript	1932
STRING QUARTET NO. 2 IN A	20 "	Manuscript	1936
THREE ECLOGUES *two clarinets, bassoon*	10 "	Manuscript	1938
SONG SET: GAY APOSTASY	6 "	Manuscript	1945
LYRIC SET *soprano, flute, viola*	10 "	Manuscript	1946

STAGE WORKS

THE THESMOPHORIAZUSAE (Aristophanes) *15 numbers for orchestra with women's voices*		Manuscript	1933

INGOLF DAHL

Born in Hamburg, Germany, in 1912 of Swedish parents. He studied piano and composition in Sweden and in Switzerland.

He was conductor in the Municipal Opera House in Zurich, and gave piano recitals in Switzerland. He came to America in 1935 and became an arranger and orchestrator for commercial radio programs. He also arranged music for films and appeared as pianist and conductor of contemporary music at the Hollywood Theater Alliance, "Evenings on the Roof," and the Music Guild of Los Angeles. He worked with Stravinsky and was commissioned by him for arrangements of "Dances Concertantes" and "Scenes de Ballet." At the present time, he is director of the orchestra and lecturer at the University of Southern California.

His compositions have had many performances in Zurich and in Los Angeles, especially on the programs "Evenings on the Roof." He is now completing an "Elegy" for string orchestra and a "Fanfare Overture for Orchestra."

COMPOSITIONS

CHAMBER MUSIC	DURATION	PUBLISHER	DATE
RONDO FOR PIANO FOUR HANDS	9 minutes	Manuscript	1938
SUITE FOR PIANO	20 "	Manuscript	1941
ALLEGRO AND ARIOSO	10 "	Manuscript	1942
flute, oboe, clarinet, horn, bassoon			
MUSIC FOR 5 BRASS INSTRUMENTS	14 "	Manuscript	1944
2 trumpets, horn, 2 trombones			
VARIATIONS ON A SWEDISH FOLKTUNE	9 "	New Music, Inc.	1945
flute solo			
CONCERTINO IN ONE MOVEMENT	10 "	Manuscript	1946
clarinet, violin, cello			
THE DEEP BLUE DEVIL'S BREAKDOWN	5 "	Manuscript	1946
2 pianos, 8 hands			
DUO FOR CELLO AND PIANO	20 "	Manuscript	1946

WALTER DAMROSCH

Born in Breslau, Germany, in 1862. He came to America when he was nine years old. His father's active musical life paved the way for his early career, and when Leopold Damrosch died, the son became Conductor of the Oratorio Society and of the New York Symphony. In 1894 he organized a new opera company which for five years gave German operas. He was the first to introduce Wagner's operas in many cities of the United States. For several years he conducted the Philharmonic Orchestra, but when the New York Symphony Society was reorganized in 1891 he returned as its Conductor and held this position for many years. He inaugurated concerts for young people in America, with explanatory remarks about the music. During World War I he was requested by General Pershing to reorganize

WALTER DAMROSCH (*Continued*)

the American Army Bands and improve their musical status. The School for Bandmasters and Band Musicians was therefore established at Chaumont and the War Department appointed some of the foremost French musicians as professors. The Fontainebleau Summer School of Music for American students grew out of this movement.

Since 1927 much of his time has been given to radio broadcasting. He was the first musician to conduct an orchestra with a nationwide hook-up from the Pacific Coast to the East. He organized the NBC Music Appreciation Hour for school children all over the United States and Canada, and he has conducted many of the evening orchestral programs.

The incidental music to the Greek dramas "Iphigenia in Aulis," "Medea" and "Electra" was first given in the open-air theater of the University of California. The opera "Scarlet Letter" was first introduced in Boston, and "Cyrano" was produced in New York. In 1937 "The Man without a Country" was given its première at the Metropolitan Opera House. "Abraham Lincoln's Song" was played at the Music Educators' National Conference. "Danny Deever" is played today in every country and has been recorded by Victor. "The Opera Cloak," a one-act opera, was performed by the New Opera Company in 1942. He is a member of the National Institute of Arts and Letters and President of the American Academy of Arts and Letters.

COMPOSITIONS

CHORAL WORKS

	PUBLISHER	DATE
MANILA TE DEUM *chorus and orchestra*	John Church Co.	
ABRAHAM LINCOLN SONG *baritone solo, chorus and orchestra*	M. Witmark & Sons	1935
THE VIRGIN MARY TO THE CHILD JESUS *2 motets for 6 voices*	John Church Co. *vocal score*	
THE CANTERBURY PILGRIMS *cantata*	John Church Co. *vocal score*	
DUNKIRK—BALLAD FOR BARITONE SOLO *chorus and orchestra*	G. Schirmer, Inc.	1943

CHAMBER MUSIC

SONATA, OPUS 6 *violin, piano*	John Church Co.	
THE LOOKING GLASS *voice, piano*	Manuscript	
DANNY DEEVER *(also male voices)*	John Church Co.	

STAGE WORKS

CYRANO DE BERGERAC—opera	G. Schirmer, Inc.	
DOVE OF PEACE—opera	G. Schirmer, Inc.	
SCARLET LETTER—opera	Breitkopf & Härtel	
INCIDENTAL MUSIC TO "MEDEA," "ELECTRA," AND "IPHIGENIA"	Manuscript	
THE MAN WITHOUT A COUNTRY—opera	G. Schirmer, Inc.	1936
THE OPERA CLOAK—opera	Manuscript	1942
ELEPHANTS IN CONGRESS—comic opera	Manuscript	1944

MABEL WHEELER DANIELS

Born in Swampscott, Massachusetts, in 1879. She graduated magna cum laude from Radcliffe College, where she was Director and soloist of the Glee Club. After composing three operettas for women's voices, she began to study composition and orchestration with Chadwick. Later, while a pupil of Thuille in Munich, she took the regular course at the Conservatory and was awarded a prize in singing. Upon her return to the United States, her book, *An American Girl in Munich,* was published. She has received several prizes for composition, including a National Federation of Music Clubs Award. For some years she was Director of Music at Simmons College, Boston, and at present she is a Trustee of Radcliffe College.

Her compositions have been performed in many cities throughout the country and have been broadcast over NBC and WOR, as well as on WQXR and other local stations.

COMPOSITIONS

ORCHESTRAL WORKS	DURATION	PUBLISHER	DATE
PIRATES' ISLAND	6 minutes	J. Fischer & Bro. *for hire*	1932
DEEP FOREST—prelude *version for full orchestra*	6½ "	J. Fischer & Bro. *for hire*	1934
IN MEMORIAM	5½–6 "	Manuscript	1945

CHAMBER ORCHESTRA			
DEEP FOREST—prelude for little symphony orchestra *13 instruments*	6½ minutes	J. Fischer & Bro.	1931

CHORAL WORKS			
THE HOLY STAR *mixed chorus, orchestra*	6 minutes	A. P. Schmidt Co.	1928
A HOLIDAY FANTASY *mixed chorus, orchestra*	7½ "	A. P. Schmidt Co.	1928
EXULTATE DEO *mixed chorus, orchestra*	7 "	A. P. Schmidt Co. *orch. parts, for hire*	1929
THE CHRIST CHILD *mixed chorus a cappella*	4 "	A. P. Schmidt Co.	1931
THE SONG OF JAEL *cantata for soprano solo, mixed chorus, full orchestra*	20 "	J. Fischer & Bro.	1937
DUM DIANAE VITREA *women's voices*	5¼ "	J. Fischer & Bro.	1942
FLOWER WAGON *women's voices*	4 "	J. Fischer & Bro.	1944

CHAMBER MUSIC			
SONGS OF ELFLAND *soprano soli, women's voices, flute, harp, strings, percussion*	13 minutes	A. P. Schmidt Co.	1924
PASTORAL ODE *flute and strings*	7 "	J. Fischer & Bro.	1940
THREE OBSERVATIONS FOR THREE WOODWINDS	7 "	Manuscript	1943
FOUR OBSERVATIONS FOR FOUR STRINGS		Manuscript	1945

WILLIAM LEVI DAWSON

Born in Anniston, Alabama, in 1899. He graduated from the Tuskegee Institute in 1921 and then studied composition and orchestration at Washington College, Topeka, Kansas. He later studied theory and counterpoint at the Homer Institute of Fine Arts in Kansas City under Busch, and received the degree of Bachelor of Music in 1925. He went to Chicago and in 1927 he received the Master's degree in composition from the American Conservatory of Music where he studied with Weidig and Otterstrom.

He has held several positions as Director of Music in Topeka and in Kansas City and for three years was a member of the Chicago Civic Orchestra as first trombonist. He has been Director of the School of Music at Tuskegee Institute and also Director of the Tuskegee Choir. In 1930 and 1931 he won the Rodman Wanamaker contest for composition.

His "Negro Folk Symphony, No. 1" has had performances with the Philadelphia Orchestra in Philadelphia and New York, and with the Birmingham Civic Symphony and it has been broadcast by the Columbia Broadcasting System.

COMPOSITIONS

ORCHESTRAL WORKS	DURATION	PUBLISHER	DATE
NEGRO FOLK SYMPHONY, No. 1	35 minutes	Manuscript for hire	
SCHERZO	15 "	Manuscript	1930

CHORAL WORKS			
OUT IN THE FIELDS		Manuscript	1928
BREAK, BREAK, BREAK with orchestra		Manuscript	1929
AIN'-A THAT GOOD NEWS a cappella		Manuscript	1937

CHAMBER MUSIC			
TRIO IN A violin, cello, piano		Manuscript	1925
SONATA IN A violin, piano		Manuscript	1928

ROBERT MILLS DELANEY

Born in Baltimore, Maryland, in 1903. He began to study violin at the age of five. When his family moved to Wenonah, New Jersey, he was sent to the Military Academy and continued his lessons with Schradieck and Geiger. After two years of traveling around the world, he settled in Italy and returned to his musical studies. In 1921 he came back to America and entered the College of Music at the University of Southern California. From 1922 to 1927 he was in France studying at the École Normale de Musique and privately with Boulanger, Capet and Honegger. In 1929–30 he was awarded a Guggenheim Fellowship for two years, and in 1933 he won the Pulitzer

ROBERT MILLS DELANEY (*Continued*)

Prize for his setting of Stephen Vincent Benét's "John Brown's Body." He has also been awarded six Boston Music Fund Scholarships.

He has taught theory at the School of Music in Concord, Massachusetts, and directed the music at the Santa Barbara School in California. During the war, he worked with the Simonds Saw and Steel Company and at the Naval Air Station in California. Later, he worked abroad with the American Field Service. At present he is teaching theory and composition at Northwestern University in Evanston, Illinois.

"Work 22" was presented in Boston and was broadcast over CBS. "Western Star" had its first performance in California, and "Going to Town" was first presented in Rochester. "John Brown's Song" has been repeatedly performed in Rochester and Boston and has been broadcast over MBS networks and over WHAM in Rochester. His chamber music has been widely presented in America and in Europe.

COMPOSITIONS

ORCHESTRAL WORKS	DURATION	PUBLISHER	DATE
THE CONSTANT COUPLE—suite	20 minutes	Manuscript *for hire*	1926
DON QUIXOTE SYMPHONY	38 "	Manuscript *2 pianos only*	1927
PASTORAL MOVEMENT—tone poem	11 "	Manuscript	1930
SYMPHONIC PIECE NO. I	21 "	Manuscript *for hire*	1935
SYMPHONIC PIECE NO. II	19 "	Manuscript	1937
WORK 22—overture	5½ "	Manuscript	1939
GOING TO TOWN—suite	24 "	Manuscript	1941
SYMPHONY NO. I	25 "	Manuscript	1942

CHAMBER ORCHESTRA			
ADAGIO *violin solo, string orchestra*	9 minutes	Manuscript *for hire*	1935

CHORAL WORKS			
TWO CHORUSES FOR WOMEN'S VOICES *a cappella*	8 minutes	E. C. Schirmer Music Co.	1930
TWO CHORUSES FOR MIXED VOICES *a cappella*	10 "	E. C. Schirmer Music Co.	1930
BLAKE CYCLE *chorus, orchestra*	20 "	Manuscript	1930
JOHN BROWN'S SONG—choral symphony	26 "	E. C. Schirmer Music Co.	1931
NIGHT (text—William Blake) *string orchestra, piano*	20 "	E. C. Schirmer Music Co. *for hire*	1934
THREE ARRANGEMENTS FOR WOMEN'S VOICES *piano 4 hands*	7 "	E. C. Schirmer Music Co.	1934
CHORALIA—SIX ARRANGEMENTS FOR WOMEN'S VOICES *piano 2 and 4 hands*	16 "	E. C. Schirmer Music Co.	1936
CHORALIA NO. II *piano 2 hands*	1½ hours	Manuscript	1937
MY SOUL THERE IS A COUNTRY *chorus, orchestra*		Manuscript	1937
WESTERN STAR *5-part chorus, orchestra*	65 minutes	Manuscript	1944

ROBERT MILLS DELANEY (*Continued*)

CHAMBER MUSIC	DURATION	PUBLISHER	DATE
SECOND STRING QUARTET	15 minutes	Manuscript	1930
THIRD STRING QUARTET	28 "	Manuscript	1930
VIOLIN SONATA	22 "	Manuscript	

NORMAN DELLO JOIO

Born in New York City in 1913, he is a descendant of a long line of Italian musicians. His father, a composer and organist, was his first teacher. He studied the organ with Pietro Yon at the age of fifteen, and later continued his musical education at the Institute of Musical Art, where he studied organ and piano with Gaston Dethier. His academic training was at Hallows School and at New York City College.

He started his professional career at the age of twelve by assisting his father as organist; later he held many positions as organist and choirmaster in many New York churches. At the age of twenty he had his own jazz band, which performed extensively in the East. From 1941 to 1943 he was Musical Director of the ballet company, Dance Players. At present he is teaching composition at Sarah Lawrence College in Bronxville. The Piano Trio was awarded the Elizabeth Sprague Coolidge Composition Award, and in 1939 he received a fellowship at the Juilliard Graduate School and studied with Wagenaar. In 1940 and 1941 he received a fellowship to study at the Berkshire Music Center with Hindemith, and the following two winters he continued with him at the Yale School of Music. He has been awarded two successive Guggenheim Fellowships (1944–5, 1945–6) and was awarded a grant by the American Academy of Arts and Letters in 1946. He also won the Town Hall Award for the "Magnificat" for orchestra.

Two ballets were commissioned by Eugene Loring's Dance Players, entitled "Prairie" and "The Duke of Sacramento." A third ballet, "On Stage," was commissioned by Ballet Associates and has been performed for two seasons at the Metropolitan Opera House; it has also toured extensively throughout the United States and Canada. Robert Shaw and the Collegiate Chorale have commissioned the Symphony for Voices and Orchestra set to "Western Star" by Stephen Vincent Benét, which was premiered at Carnegie Hall in 1945. Other commissioned works include "The Mystic Trumpeter," also commissioned by Robert Shaw and the Collegiate Chorale; "To a Lonely Sentry," for orchestra, commissioned by the League of Composers; "A Jubilant Song," for chorus and piano, commissioned by Schirmer for the Columbia University Music Festival; a Harp Concerto commissioned by Edna Philips for the Philadelphia Symphony Orchestra; a Trio for Flute, Cello, and Piano commissioned for the LeRoy, Foster, Scholz Trio; a Duo Concertante for two pianos, commissioned for

NORMAN DELLO JOIO (*Continued*)

Gearhart and Morley; a Piano Sonata commissioned by Sidney Foster; and
a Duo Concertato, for cello and piano, commissioned by Janos Scholz.
His works have been played frequently by major symphony orchestras and
ensemble groups and many of them have been broadcast over major radio
networks.

COMPOSITIONS

ORCHESTRAL WORKS

	DURATION	PUBLISHER	DATE
SINFONIETTA	20 minutes	G. Schirmer, Inc. for hire	1941
DUKE OF SACRAMENTO—suite	35 "	Manuscript	1942
MAGNIFICAT	16 "	G. Schirmer, Inc.	1943
TO A LONE SENTRY	8 "	G. Schirmer, Inc. for hire	1943
AMERICAN LANDSCAPE	21 "	G. Schirmer, Inc.	1944
RICERCARI *piano, orchestra*	20 "	G. Schirmer, Inc.	1946

CHAMBER ORCHESTRA

CONCERTINO FOR PIANO	20 minutes	Manuscript	1939
CONCERTINO FOR FLUTE	14 "	Manuscript	1940
CONCERTINO FOR HARMONICA	12 "	Manuscript	1942
CONCERTO FOR HARP	15 "	Manuscript	1942

CHORAL WORKS

VIGIL STRANGE *a cappella*	7 minutes	Weaner-Levant	1942
MYSTIC TRUMPETER *with French horn*	11 "	G. Schirmer, Inc.	1943
WESTERN STAR *orchestra, narrator, soloists*	42 "	Manuscript	1944
A JUBILANT SONG *chorus, piano*		G. Schirmer, Inc.	

CHAMBER MUSIC

SONATA NO. 1 *piano*	10 minutes	Hargail Music Press	1942
SONATA NO. 2 *piano*	13 "	G. Schirmer, Inc.	1943
SUITE FOR PIANO		G. Schirmer, Inc.	
SUITE FROM "ON STAGE" *piano*		G. Schirmer, Inc.	
DUO CONCERTANTE *2 pianos*	15 "	Manuscript	1943
SEXTET FOR 3 RECORDERS AND STRINGS (or 3 woodwinds)	9 "	Hargail Music Press	1943

STAGE WORKS

PRAIRIE—ballet *full orchestra*	25 minutes	G. Schirmer, Inc. for hire	1942
DUKE OF SACRAMENTO—ballet *2 pianos or full orchestra*	40 "	Manuscript	1942
ON STAGE!—ballet *full orchestra*	30 "	G. Schirmer, Inc.	1945

WILLIAM D. DENNY

Born in Seattle, Washington, in 1910. He studied at the University of California with Elkus, Stricklen and Thompson and then in Paris with Dukas. He is a Fellow of the American Academy in Rome.

He was on the faculty of the music departments of Harvard University and Vassar College. At present, he is an Assistant Professor of Music at the University of California.

The Concerto for Orchestra was performed by the San Francisco Symphony Orchestra. Broadcasts of his works include the Sinfonietta for String Orchestra by the NBC Symphony over WJZ and the Suite for Chamber Orchestra by the Sinfonietta over WOR.

COMPOSITIONS

ORCHESTRAL WORKS	DURATION	PUBLISHER	DATE
Concertino for Orchestra	12 minutes	Manuscript	1937
Sinfonietta for String Orchestra	18 "	Manuscript	1940
Overture for Strings	8 "	Manuscript	1946

CHAMBER ORCHESTRA			
Suite for Chamber Orchestra *11 instruments*	10 minutes	Manuscript	1940

CHORAL WORKS			
Quem Vidistis, Pastores? *mixed chorus, a cappella*	5 minutes	Manuscript	1946

CHAMBER MUSIC			
Sonata for Viola and Piano	17 minutes	Manuscript	1944

PAUL DESSAU

Born in Hamburg, Germany, in 1894. He studied music in Berlin. He won the Schott Prize in 1925 and the Herzka Prize in 1934. He came to the United States in 1939 and, after spending several years in New York City, settled in Hollywood.

His works have been performed in Berlin, Prague and at the Music Festival in Donaueschingen. "Les Voix de Paul Verlaine" was given in New York in 1942 under the auspices of the I.S.C.M.

COMPOSITIONS WRITTEN IN AMERICA

FILM MUSIC	STUDIO	DATE
Combat Fatigue	Training Picture for the Navy	1946
The Wife of Monte Christo	P.R.C.	1946

R. NATHANIEL DETT

Born in 1882 in Drummondville, Canada, and died in 1943. He first studied at the Lockport Conservatory of Music and later took his degree of Bachelor of Music at Oberlin College. At the Eastman School he received a Master's degree and then went to Paris to study with Boulanger. In 1920 he won the Harvard Bowdoin Prize for his essay "The Emancipation of Negro Music," and in 1927 he received the first award of the Harmon Foundation for creative music. He was made an honorary member of the Coleridge-Taylor Society in England and a life member of Pi Kappa Lambda at Oberlin College. He received the award of the Palm and Ribbon from the Royal Belgian Band by order of the Queen of Belgium. He was in charge of the music at Hampton Institute in Virginia and conducted the Hampton choral group in concerts.

His special interest was in the development of Negro music. He published five books of Negro spirituals; the Negro anthem which he wrote was used on a tour with a choir throughout Europe and in the United States (sponsored by the Elizabeth Sprague Coolidge Foundation). He wrote verse and a number of his poems have been published. He wrote the oratorio "The Ordering of Moses," based on Biblical text and Negro folklore, which was presented at the Cincinnati Music Festival.

Among his other works "Listen to the Lambs" has had many performances in America and in Europe. "The Chariot Jubilee" has been heard in Boston, Syracuse, Cleveland and Oberlin. There have been broadcasts of his music over NBC and WHAM. "Juba Dance" and "Follow Me" are recorded by Victor. He was commissioned by the CBS to write a work for radio.

COMPOSITIONS

ORCHESTRAL WORKS	DURATION	PUBLISHER
ENCHANTMENT SUITE—with harp	18 minutes	Manuscript
LISTEN TO THE LAMBS—fantasia for violin	8 "	Manuscript
JUBA DANCE FROM "IN THE BOTTOMS"	4 "	Clayton F. Summy
TROPIC WINTER—orchestral suite		Manuscript
SYMPHONY IN E MINOR		Manuscript

CHAMBER MUSIC		
MAGNOLIA *piano suite*	15 minutes	Clayton F. Summy
IN THE BOTTOMS *piano suite*	15 "	Clayton F. Summy
ENCHANTMENT *piano suite*	12 "	John Church Co.
CINNAMON GROVE *piano suite*	12 "	John Church Co.
TROPIC WINTER *piano suite*	15 "	Clayton F. Summy
SYMPHONIC SUITE IN E MINOR *piano suite*	23 "	Manuscript

There are so many Negro spirituals and choral works that it is impossible to list them here.

ADOLPH DEUTSCH

Born in London, England, in 1897. He was educated at the Royal Academy of Music in London. He was a pupil of Clara Schumann. On his arrival in America, he continued his studies in composition, conducting and orchestration.

He has been an arranger for theatrical and radio orchestras and conductor of the orchestras in many Broadway productions. He has written many articles on film music, has participated in musicians' congresses and is active in musical organizations. At present he is a composer and conductor of motion-picture scores for Warner Brothers and is Vice-President of the Screen Composers' Association.

The Philadelphia Orchestra and the New York Philharmonic Symphony performed his "Scottish Suite," which was commissioned by Paul Whiteman. The "March of the United Nations," based on themes from the film score of "Action in the North Atlantic," was played by Stokowski. "Overture Romantic," "Northwest Suite" and "Free France March" are adapted from the film scores for concert performance. His works for films and concert arrangements are listed here.

COMPOSITIONS

FILM MUSIC	STUDIO	PUBLISHER	DATE
THE GREAT GARRICK (concert version—OVERTURE ROMANTIC)	Warner Bros.	Manuscript	1937
THEY DRIVE BY NIGHT	Warner Bros.		1940
HIGH SIERRA	Warner Bros.		1940
THE MALTESE FALCON	Warner Bros.		1941
NORTHERN PURSUIT (concert version—NORTHWEST SUITE)	Warner Bros.	Manuscript	1942
ACTION IN THE NORTH ATLANTIC (concert version—MARCH OF THE UNITED NATIONS)	Warner Bros.	Manuscript	1943
UNCERTAIN GLORY (concert version—FREE FRANCE MARCH)	Warner Bros.	Manuscript	1943
THE MASK OF DIMITRIOS	Warner Bros.		1944
NOBODY LIVES FOREVER	Warner Bros.		1944
THREE STRANGERS	Warner Bros.		1945

DAVID LEO DIAMOND

Born in Rochester, New York, in 1915. He began to study music at the age of eight. In 1928 he enrolled as a pupil at the Cleveland Institute, studying violin and harmony with De Ribaupierre. From 1932 to 1934 he worked with Rogers at the Eastman School of Music. He was a pupil of Sessions and Boepple at the New Music School. During the summer of 1937 he studied composition with Boulanger at Fontainebleau.

DAVID LEO DIAMOND (*Continued*)

His Sinfonietta for Orchestra was awarded the Elfrida Whiteman Fellowship in 1935. He received the Juilliard Publication Award in 1937 for his "Psalm for Orchestra." In 1937 he was commissioned by the League of Composers in the American Commission Series to write his Quintet for Flute, String Trio and Piano. In 1938 and 1941 he was awarded the Guggenheim Fellowship, and in 1941 he also won the Award from the American Society for the Publication of American Music. In 1942, he received the American Academy in Rome Award, and in 1943 he won the Paderewski Prize for the Piano Quartet. He also received a grant from the National Academy of Arts and Letters and in 1945 a commission from the Koussevitzky Music Foundation.

His works have been performed by the Boston Symphony, Minneapolis Symphony, New York Philharmonic, St. Louis Symphony, San Francisco Symphony, Rochester Philharmonic and other orchestras, also by the Orchestra of Radio-Zurich.

COMPOSITIONS

ORCHESTRAL WORKS	DURATION	PUBLISHER	DATE
PSALM	7 minutes	Edwin F. Kalmus	1936
CONCERTO FOR VIOLIN AND ORCHESTRA	20 "	Manuscript Fleisher Collection	1936
SUITE FROM BALLET: TOM	15 "	Manuscript Fleisher Collection	1937
VARIATIONS FOR SMALL ORCHESTRA	15 "	Manuscript Fleisher Collection	1937
ELEGY IN MEMORY OF RAVEL *brass, harps and percussion or strings and percussion*	8 "	Manuscript Fleisher Collection	1937
OVERTURE	7 "	Manuscript	1937
ARIA AND HYMN	14 "	Manuscript Fleisher Collection	1937
HEROIC PIECE FOR SMALL ORCHESTRA	11 "	Manuscript	1938
CONCERTO FOR CELLO AND ORCHESTRA	20 "	Manuscript	1938
MUSIC FOR DOUBLE STRING ORCHESTRA, BRASS AND TIMPANI	25 "	Manuscript Fleisher Collection	1938
CONCERT PIECE	11 "	Manuscript Fleisher Collection	1939
FIRST SYMPHONY	20 "	Boosey & Hawkes *for hire*	1940
SECOND SYMPHONY	35 "	Associated Music Publishers *for hire*	1943
ROUNDS FOR STRING ORCHESTRA	12 "	Elkan-Vogel	1944
THIRD SYMPHONY	25 "	Manuscript	1945
FOURTH SYMPHONY	16 "	Manuscript	1945

CHAMBER ORCHESTRA			
HOMMAGE À SATIE	6 minutes	Manuscript Fleisher Collection	1934
CONCERTO	15 "	Manuscript Fleisher Collection	1940

DAVID LEO DIAMOND (Continued)

CHORAL WORKS

	DURATION	PUBLISHER	DATE
THIS IS THE GARDEN (E. E. Cummings) a cappella	5 minutes	Carl Fischer	1935
THREE MADRIGALS (James Joyce) a cappella	6 "	Edwin F. Kalmus	1937
TWO CHORUSES (E. E. Cummings) 3 part women's voices, a cappella	8 "	Manuscript	1940
YOUNG JOSEPH (Thomas Mann) 3 part women's chorus, string orchestra	6 "	Manuscript	1944

CHAMBER MUSIC

SONATINA FOR PIANO		Manuscript	1935
PARTITA FOR OBOE, BASSOON AND PIANO	10 minutes	Manuscript	1935
FOUR LADIES—song cycle	7 "	Manuscript	1935
CONCERTO FOR STRING QUARTET	20 "	Manuscript	1936
TRIO FOR STRINGS	20 "	Manuscript	1937
QUINTET FOR FLUTE, STRING TRIO AND PIANO	15 "	G. Schirmer, Inc.	1937
QUARTET FOR PIANO AND STRING TRIO	23 "	Manuscript	1938
SONATA FOR CELLO AND PIANO	20 "	New Music	1938
FIRST STRING QUARTET	15 "	Manuscript	1940
CONCERTO FOR TWO SOLO PIANOS	15 "	Manuscript	1941
SECOND STRING QUARTET	20 "	Manuscript	1943
SONATA FOR VIOLIN AND PIANO	20 "	Manuscript	1945
THIRD STRING QUARTET	19 "	Manuscript	1946

STAGE WORKS

TOM—a ballet in four episodes (scenario by E. E. Cummings) mixed chorus, large orchestra	2 hours	Manuscript	1936
THE DREAM OF AUDUBON (scenario by Glenway Westcott)	40 minutes	Manuscript	1941
THE TEMPEST—score for Margaret Webster's production	30 "	Manuscript	1944

FILM MUSIC

A PLACE TO LIVE (documentary film for the Phila- delphia Housing Association)		Manuscript	1940

RICHARD FRANK DONOVAN

Born in New Haven, Connecticut, in 1891. He studied at the Yale University School of Music, the Institute of Musical Art, New York, and for a short time in Paris under Widor. He taught at Smith College and the Institute of Musical Art and is now a member of the faculty of Yale University School of Music. He is one of the conductors of the New Haven Symphony Orchestra, Conductor of the Bach Cantata Club of New Haven, and organist and director of the choir at Christ Church, New Haven. He has been a member of the committee for the Yaddo Festivals of Contemporary American Music. His "Design for Radio" won the Publication Award in the 1945 contest sponsored by Broadcast Music, Inc.

"Ricercare for Oboe and Strings" was performed by the Saidenberg Little

RICHARD FRANK DONOVAN (*Continued*)

Symphony in New York and the Cornell University Orchestra at the Festival of Contemporary American Arts. The Serenade for Oboe, Violin, Viola and Violoncello was performed in New York, and the "Fantasy on American Folk Ballads" was given in New Haven by the Yale Glee Club and the New Haven Symphony Orchestra. "Smoke and Steel" was broadcast over WEAF. The Serenade for Oboe, Violin, Viola and Violoncello, the Suite for Piano and the Songs for Soprano and String Quartet were recorded by N.M.R. His Trio was recorded by Yaddo Recordings. Some of his works were recorded by O.W.I. for broadcast abroad. He is now at work on a symphony. He has written many works for chorus, organ and voice which are not listed here.

COMPOSITIONS

ORCHESTRAL WORKS	DURATION	PUBLISHER	DATE
WOOD-NOTES *flute, harp, string orchestra*	12 minutes	Manuscript Fleisher Music Collection	1925
SMOKE AND STEEL—symphonic poem	15 "	Manuscript	1932
OVERTURE FOR ORCHESTRA	10 "	Manuscript *for hire*	1946

CHAMBER ORCHESTRA

SYMPHONY FOR CHAMBER ORCHESTRA	25 minutes	Manuscript	1937
RICERCARE FOR OBOE AND STRINGS *large or small string section*	6¼ "	Boosey & Hawkes, Inc.	1938
SUITE FOR OBOE AND STRINGS *large or small string section*	16½ "	Manuscript *for hire*	1943
DESIGN FOR RADIO *radio unit of 26 players* *woodwinds, piano, strings, percussion*	9½ "	Manuscript	1944

CHORAL WORKS

CHANSON OF THE BELLS OF OSENEY *women's voices, piano*	6 minutes	Galaxy Music Corp.	1930
TO ALL YOU LADIES NOW AT LAND *tenor or soprano solo, men's* *voices, orchestra or piano*	7 "	Galaxy Music Corp.	1932
FOUR UNACCOMPANIED CHORUSES *women's voices*	15 "	Edwin F. Kalmus	1937
FANTASY ON AMERICAN FOLK BALLADS *men's voices, orchestra or* *piano 4 hands*	12 "	J. Fischer & Bro.	1940
GOOD ALE *men's voices, piano*	6 "	Carl Fischer, Inc.	1945
HOW SHOULD I LOVE? *women's voices, piano*	6 "	Manuscript	1946

CHAMBER MUSIC

SEXTET FOR WIND INSTRUMENTS AND PIANO *flute, oboe, clarinet, bassoon,* *horn, piano*	18 minutes	Manuscript	1932
SUITE FOR PIANO	7 "	New Music	1933
FOUR SONGS FOR SOPRANO AND STRING QUARTET	11 "	Manuscript	1933
TRIO *violin, cello, piano*	8 "	Arrow Music Press, Inc.	1937
SERENADE FOR OBOE, VIOLIN, VIOLA AND VIOLONCELLO	4¾ "	New Music	1941

ARCADY DUBENSKY

Born in Viatka, Russia, in 1890. He became a member of the Viatka cathedral choir when he was eight years old. At thirteen he played violin in the theater orchestra and continued to sing in the cathedral choir. In 1904 he went to Moscow and, receiving a scholarship in the Moscow Conservatory of Music, studied with Grjimali and Iljinsky. Two years after graduating from the conservatory he became first violinist of the Moscow Imperial Opera Orchestra and began studying conducting with the ballet director, Arends. In 1919 he left Russia and since 1921 has lived in New York, where he has been a member of the Philharmonic Symphony Orchestra.

His compositions have been given by the leading symphonic organizations in various cities in the United States and abroad; they include "Fugue for Eighteen Violins," Caprice for Piccolo-Flute, "Russian Bells," "Valse-Fantasy," "Tom Sawyer Overture," "The Raven," "Romance with Double-Bass," Suite for Nine Flutes and Andante and Scherzo. Many smaller works are played often in concerts and broadcasts. "The Raven," "Gossips" and the "Fugue for Eighteen Violins" have been recorded by Victor. He has also had broadcasts over WEAF, WOR and WNYC.

COMPOSITIONS

ORCHESTRAL WORKS

	DURATION	PUBLISHER	DATE
SYMPHONY IN G MINOR		Manuscript	1916
SUITE		G. Schirmer, Inc.	1927
INTERMEZZO AND COMPLIMENT		G. Schirmer, Inc.	1927
THREE COMPOSITIONS FOR ORCHESTRA		G. Schirmer, Inc.	1928
ANDANTE AND SCHERZO FOR FLUTE AND ORCHESTRA		Manuscript	1928
RUSSIAN BELLS—symphonic poem	10 minutes	Manuscript	1928
VALSE		Manuscript	1930
CAPRICE FOR PICCOLO-FLUTE WITH ORCHESTRA		G. Ricordi & Co.	1930
GOSSIPS	3 "	Carl Fischer, Inc.	1930
THE RAVEN—melo-declamation		G. Ricordi & Co.	1931
PRELUDE AND FUGUE		Manuscript	1932
RAJAH—Arabian dance	2 "	Associated Music Publishers	1932
REMINISCENCES—andante		Associated Music Publishers	1932
OLD RUSSIAN SOLDIERS' SONG	2 "	Associated Music Publishers	1932
LEGEND		Manuscript	1932
ITALIAN OVERTURE—for children's concerts		Manuscript	1936
SERENADE		Manuscript	1936
POLITICAL SUITE		Manuscript	1936
TOM SAWYER—overture	7 "	G. Ricordi & Co.	1936
FANFARE—introduction to "The Star Spangled Banner"	1 "	G. Ricordi & Co.	1939
STEPHEN FOSTER, THEME, VARIATIONS, FINALE	15 "	Manuscript for hire	1941
PRELUDE AND FUGUE IN B FLAT MINOR	8 "	Manuscript for hire	1942
ORIENTALE, SONG AND DANCE	8 "	Manuscript for hire	1945

CHAMBER ORCHESTRA

	DURATION	PUBLISHER	DATE
VALSE—fantasy for C-bass and piano		Manuscript	1916
SUITE ABC—for children's concerts		Manuscript	1932
FUGUE FOR EIGHTEEN VIOLINS		G. Ricordi & Co.	1932
VARIATIONS FOR EIGHT CLARINETS		Manuscript	1932
PRELUDE AND FUGUE FOR FOUR C-BASSES		Manuscript	1934
SUITE FOR FOUR TRUMPETS		Manuscript	1934
SUITE FOR NINE FLUTES		Manuscript	1935
1 piccolo, 1 alto flute, 7 gr. flutes			
ANDANTE IN F	4 minutes	Associated Music	1935
string orchestra or quartet		Publishers	
SUITE FOR STRING ORCHESTRA	14 "	G. Ricordi & Co.	1936
PRELUDE FOR STRING ORCHESTRA	3½ "	Manuscript	1936
RONDO AND GIGUE FOR STRING ORCHESTRA		Manuscript	1937
ANDANTE RUSSE	4 "	G. Ricordi & Co.	1939
string orchestra			
RUSSIAN SONG AND DANCE	3 "	G. Ricordi & Co.	1939

CHORAL WORKS

JOYOUS LIGHT—prayer	3 minutes	Manuscript	1938
a cappella			

CHAMBER MUSIC

PASSACAGLIA FOR VIOLIN AND CELLO		Manuscript	1931
STRING QUARTET IN C		Manuscript	1932
THEME AND VARIATIONS FOR FOUR HORNS		Manuscript	1932
STRING SEXTET IN C		Manuscript	1933
PRELUDE AND FUGUE FOR FOUR			
BASSOONS	4 minutes	G. Ricordi & Co.	1933

STAGE WORKS

ROMANCE WITH DOUBLE-BASS—opera			
miniature		Manuscript	1916
3 acts with prologue and epilogue			
DOWN TOWN—opera in 3 acts		Manuscript	1930
THE RAVEN—melo-declamation		G. Ricordi & Co.	1931
ON HIGHWAY—opera in one act	60 minutes	Manuscript	1936
TWO YANKEES IN ITALY—one act opera	50 "	Manuscript	1944
		for hire	

FILM MUSIC

FOUR COMPOSITIONS FOR ORCHESTRA		G. Schirmer, Inc.	1928
MOWGLI—music for Booth			
Tarkington's play			1940

JOHN WOODS DUKE

Born in Cumberland, Maryland, in 1899. He attended Peabody Conservatory from 1915 to 1918, where he studied composition with Strube. From 1919 to 1923 he lived in New York City. He became a pupil of Cannon in piano, and he studied counterpoint with Brockway. He spent the years 1929 and 1930 in Europe working with Schnabel and Boulanger. He was Chairman of the Yaddo Music Committee for the summer of 1936.

In 1923 he joined the faculty of Smith College, where he holds the rank of Professor of Music. He was Program Chairman of the National Association of American Composers and Conductors in 1944–45. He has appeared as pianist in various cities and has been engaged in editorial work for the

Ampico Laboratories. He has composed a great many songs, frequently using texts of American poets. His record of small works is not listed here.

The "Carnival Overture" has been presented in Boston, Indianapolis and New York. The Concerto for Piano and Strings and many of his chamber works have had frequent performances in various cities and at the Yaddo Festival of American Music. The NBC Quartet has played the String Quartet No. 2, WQXR has broadcast the Concerto for Piano and Strings, and the "Carnival Overture" was heard on the American Festival of Music over WNYC. Many of his songs and chamber compositions have had numerous broadcasts. At present he is preparing a Second String Quartet and a group of songs to the texts of Elinor Wylie.

COMPOSITIONS

ORCHESTRAL WORKS	DURATION	PUBLISHER	DATE
OVERTURE IN D MINOR *string orchestra*	10 minutes	Manuscript	1928
CONCERTO FOR PIANO AND STRINGS	20 "	Manuscript	1938
CARNIVAL OVERTURE	8 "	Manuscript *for hire*	1941

CHORAL WORKS			
POLE STAR FOR THIS YEAR (text by MacLeish) *mixed chorus a cappella*	5 minutes	Manuscript *for hire*	1939

CHAMBER MUSIC			
SUITE FOR VIOLONCELLO ALONE	12 minutes	Manuscript	1934
THREE SONGS IN PRAISE OF DEATH *voice, string quartet*	10 "	Manuscript	1935
FANTASIE IN A MINOR *violin, piano*	8 "	Manuscript	1937
TRIO FOR VIOLIN, VIOLA AND CELLO		Manuscript	1937
STRING QUARTET NO. I, E MINOR	15 "	Manuscript *for hire*	1941
TRIO IN D MAJOR *violin, cello, piano*	17 "	Manuscript *for hire*	1943

VLADIMIR DUKELSKY
(Vernon Duke)

Born in Psckoff, Russia, in 1903. His ancestry is Georgian and Spanish. He has had a dual career as composer of classical and of popular music. At the age of eight he had already written a ballet in fourteen acts and from his thirteenth year on he wrote prolifically. He studied composition in Russia with Glière and piano with Dombrovsky and entered the Kiev Conservatory of Music at the age of thirteen.

VLADIMIR DUKELSKY (*Continued*)

In 1920 during the civil war he moved to Turkey, where he lived for two years. He next went to Paris and London. While in Paris in 1924 Diaghilev heard his Piano Concerto and thereupon commissioned the ballet "Zephyr and Flora," which was presented in the Russian Ballet's repertoire all over Europe. In 1929 he moved to America. He tried to write jazz during the years in Constantinople, but it was only after his arrival in America that he succeeded in selling his tunes and in publishing a two-piano arrangement of George Gershwin's "Rhapsody in Blue." Since 1926, when his operetta "Yvonne" was produced in London, he has written both popular and classical music, using the name of Vernon Duke for his musical comedies and all compositions in lighter vein.

"The End of St. Petersburg" had its première with the Schola Cantorum and the Philharmonic Symphony Orchestra. The major symphonic works, which have had repeated performances, include the Symphony No. 1, played in Boston, New York, and Paris, and the Symphony No. 2 performed in Boston, Chicago, Paris, Warsaw, London and New York. His ballets have been produced in New York and in Paris, and there have been frequent performances of many of his chamber works. The light music has often been broadcast. His Concerto for Violin has had performances in Boston and New York, The Cello Concerto was performed in Boston, New York and Montreal and broadcast over WABC. "Entr'acte" was broadcast over CBS.

COMPOSITIONS

ORCHESTRAL WORKS

	DURATION	PUBLISHER	DATE
CONCERTO, C MAJOR *piano*	20 minutes	Heugel	1924
SYMPHONY NO 1, F MAJOR	16 "	Manuscript	1928
SYMPHONY NO. 2, D FLAT MAJOR	17 "	Manuscript	1929
DÉDICACES *soprano solo, piano solo, orchestra*	20 "	Manuscript	1935
CONCERTO FOR VIOLIN AND ORCHESTRA	28 "	Carl Fischer, Inc.	1942
CONCERTO FOR CELLO AND ORCHESTRA	25 "	Carl Fischer, Inc.	1943
ODE TO THE MILKY WAY	6 "	Manuscript	1945

CHAMBER ORCHESTRA

DUSHENKA *duet for women's voices and chamber orchestra*	6 minutes	Edition de Musique	1927
BALLADE FOR PIANO AND CHAMBER ORCHESTRA	11 "	Manuscript	1931
PUBLIC GARDENS OVERTURE *(revised for chamber orchestra)*	6 "	Manuscript	1945

CHORAL WORKS

EPITAPH *soprano solo, mixed chorus, orchestra*	10 minutes	Manuscript	1932
THE END OF ST. PETERSBURG—oratorio *3 soloists, chorus, orchestra*	40 "	Manuscript	1937

VLADIMIR DUKELSKY *(Continued)*

CHORAL WORKS *(Continued)*	DURATION	PUBLISHER	DATE
VICTORIAN STREET BALLADS (5) *women's voices, piano*	10 minutes	Carl Fischer, Inc.	1943
MOULIN-ROUGE (poem by A. Symons) *soprano solo, mixed chorus, piano*	5 "	Carl Fischer, Inc.	1944
A SONG ABOUT MYSELF (John Keats) *mixed chorus, piano*	6 "	Manuscript	1945

CHAMBER MUSIC			
SONATA, E FLAT MAJOR *piano solo*	14 minutes	Edition Russe	1927
TRIO (Variations) *flute, bassoon, piano*	11 "	Edition Russe	1930
HOMAGE TO BOSTON *suite for piano*	12 "	Sprague Coleman	1937
SURREALIST SUITE FOR PIANO	10 "	Sprague Coleman	1939
THREE PIECES FOR WOODWINDS AND PIANO	10 "	Carl Fischer	1940
SONG CYCLES		Carl Fischer and Sprague Coleman	

STAGE WORKS			
ZEPHYR AND FLORA—ballet *large orchestra*	35 minutes	Edition Russe	1925
DEMOISELLE PAYSANNE—opera in 2 acts (text by Pushkin)	1 hour	Manuscript	1928
PUBLIC GARDENS—ballet *large orchestra*	35 minutes	Manuscript	1935
ENTR'ACTE—ballet *medium size orchestra*	30 "	Manuscript	1938–45

HENRY EICHHEIM

Born in Chicago, Illinois, in 1870, and died in 1942. He received his early musical education at the Chicago College of Music. His first position was as violinist with the Thomas Orchestra. In 1890 he joined the Boston Symphony and for twenty-two years he remained with them as one of the first violinists. For four years he conducted the Symphony Orchestra at Winchester, Massachusetts. He conducted his own works in America and in Europe. On his tours through the Orient he became interested in the music of the East, collecting a great deal of musical material and a number of unusual instruments. He introduced in his compositions the native street cries of Korea and Siam which led him to use the native bells and gongs. "Oriental Sketches" was written for the Elizabeth Coolidge Festival. "Java" represents one of the first serious attempts to reconstruct the music of the East and bring it to the attention of the western concert audience. He was a Fellow of the Asiatic Society of Japan.

His orchestral works have been performed by the major symphonic orchestras of the United States, and the ballets have been given repeated

HENRY EICHHEIM (*Continued*)

performances on the stage or in symphonic version in America and in Europe. "Oriental Impressions" received the Award from the Society for Publication of American Music. "Japanese Nocturne" has been recorded by Victor.

COMPOSITIONS

ORCHESTRAL WORKS	DURATION	PUBLISHER	DATE
ORIENTAL IMPRESSIONS		Manuscript	1922
14 Oriental instruments		*for hire*	
CHINESE LEGEND—ballet	5 minutes	Manuscript	1924
Oriental instruments			
BURMA—orchestra suite	15 "	Manuscript	1927
special bells, disks			
JAVA—1st movement of triptych	12 "	Manuscript	1929
special Javanese instruments			

CHAMBER ORCHESTRA			
ORIENTAL IMPRESSIONS		S.P.A.M.	1921
Oriental instruments		G. Schirmer, Inc.	
MALAY MOSAIC	20 minutes	Manuscript	1924
12 instruments			

STAGE WORKS			
CHINESE LEGEND—ballet	25 minutes	Manuscript	1924
A BURMESE PWE—ballet	20 "	Manuscript	1926
THE MOON, MY SHADOW AND I—	10 "	Manuscript	1926
a Chinese ballet			
soprano, women's chorus			

HANS EISLER

Born in Leipzig, Germany, in 1898. He was educated at the Academy of Music in Vienna and also studied in Berlin. He was a pupil of Arnold Schoenberg. In 1924 he won a prize for composition.

From 1925 to 1933 he taught in Berlin. In 1934 he came to New York, where he was Professor of Music at the New School for Social Research. From 1939 to 1942 he served as Director of Research for a project on films and music established by the Rockefeller Foundation. At present he is teaching at the University of Southern California, where he has classes in composition and advanced counterpoint. He wrote a great many works for orchestra, also chamber music, choral works and songs, as well as works for stage and films before coming to this country. "Goliath," an opera in three acts, had many presentations in Europe, as did many of his earlier films and other works, notably the cantatas "Tempo der Zeit" and "Die Massnahme" and the songs from the film "Kuhle Wampe."

He is at present writing music for a Charlie Chaplin film. His recent book on music for films in collaboration with T. W. Adorno was published by the Oxford University Press.

HANS EISLER (*Continued*)

COMPOSITIONS WRITTEN IN AMERICA

ORCHESTRAL WORKS	DURATION	PUBLISHER	DATE
SYMPHONY	1 hour	Manuscript	1936
5 PIECES FOR ORCHESTRA	18 minutes	Manuscript	1938

CHAMBER ORCHESTRA			
CHAMBER SYMPHONY *15 instruments*	16 minutes	Manuscript	1938
SUITE *9 instruments*	20 "	Manuscript	1939

CHAMBER MUSIC			
STRING QUARTET	16 minutes	Manuscript	1937

STAGE WORKS

NIGHT MUSIC (Clifford Odets)	Manuscript
MEDICINE (Bernard Shaw)	Manuscript
GALILEO (Bert Brecht)	Manuscript
FURCHT UND ELEND DES DRITTEN REICHES (Bert Brecht)	Manuscript
MOTHER COURAGE (Bert Brecht)	Manuscript

FILM MUSIC	STUDIO		DATE
THE FOUR HUNDRED MILLIONS	Independent		1938
FORGOTTEN VILLAGE	Independent		1940
RAIN (concert version—FOURTEEN WAYS TO DESCRIBE RAIN)	Joris Ivens		1940
WHITE FLOODS	Frontier Film		1941
HANGMEN ALSO DIE	United Artists		1943
NONE BUT THE LONELY HEART	R.K.O.		1944
SPANISH MAIN	R.K.O.		1945
DEADLINE AT DAWN	R.K.O.		1945
SCANDAL IN PARIS (concert version—suite)	United Artists		1945

ALBERT ISRAEL ELKUS

Born in Sacramento, California, in 1884. He studied at the University of California and received his degrees of Bachelor of Arts in 1906 and Master of Arts in 1907. Among his music teachers were Lhevinne, Bauer, Prohaska, Weil and Fuchs. In 1929 he went to Mills College to lecture on music, and after a few years he became instructor of piano at the college. From 1922 to 1935 he taught piano, theory, and composition at the San Francisco Conservatory of Music and musical theory at the Dominican College and at San Rafael, California. From 1931 to 1935 he lectured at the University of California and then became Professor of Music.

In 1937 he became Chairman of the Department of Music of the University, where he is at present. He is actively connected with various educational institutions, among them the National Association of Music Execu-

ALBERT ISRAEL ELKUS *(Continued)*

tives of State Universities, the Music Educators National Conference and Music Teachers National Association. He is a member of the American Musicological Society, the I.S.C.M., the League of Composers, the San Francisco Composers Forum and various civic committees. He received the Juilliard Publication Award in 1936. He is co-editor of *The Letters and Papers of Oscar Weil.*

Most of his orchestral works have been played by the symphonic organizations of San Francisco, Los Angeles and Detroit, and the "Concertino on Lezione III of Ariosto" has also been heard in England, France and Sweden.

COMPOSITIONS

ORCHESTRAL WORKS	DURATION	PUBLISHER	DATE
IMPRESSIONS FROM A GREEK TRAGEDY	17 minutes	Edwin F. Kalmus	1921
ON A MERRY FOLK TUNE *(arranged for 2 pianos, 4 hands)*	4 "	J. Fischer & Bro.	1924
CHAMBER ORCHESTRA			
CONCERTINO ON LEZIONE III OF ARIOSTO *cello, string orchestra with timpani; also cello, piano*	12 minutes	Universal Edition	1917
CHORAL WORKS			
I AM THE REAPER (Henley) *men's voices, piano accompaniment*		H. W. Gray Co.	1921
CHAMBER MUSIC			
SERENADE FOR STRING QUARTET		Manuscript	1921

HERBERT ELWELL

Born in Minneapolis, Minnesota, in 1898. He was a student of the University of Minnesota and then came to New York in 1919 to study composition with Ernest Bloch. In 1922 he went abroad and studied with Nadia Boulanger for several years. He received the Fellowship from the American Academy in Rome in 1926 and lived in Paris, Rome and London for seven years.

In 1932 he succeeded James H. Rogers as Music Critic for the *Cleveland Plain Dealer,* and from 1930 to 1936 he was program-note annotator for the Cleveland Symphony. From 1928 to 1945 he was head of the Advanced Theory and Composition Department at the Cleveland Institute of Music and for the last ten years of that period was Assistant Director of the Institute. He is now teaching composition at the Oberlin Conservatory of Music. In 1942 he received the Juilliard Publication Award, and in 1945 he won the award of the Paderewski Fund for the Encouragement of American Composers for a work called "Lincoln."

HERBERT ELWELL (*Continued*)

His Suite from "The Happy Hypocrite" was performed in Paris, Rome and various cities in the United States. The ballet for this work was also presented in New York at the Dance Repertory Theatre. Introduction and Allegro has been played by the New York Philharmonic Symphony, the Cleveland Orchestra and the St. Louis Orchestra. His chamber music has been performed in Cleveland, New York and on tour. "Three Songs" for orchestra and voice has been broadcast internationally. He has written a great many songs and short instrumental pieces which it is impossible to list in this record.

COMPOSITIONS

ORCHESTRAL WORKS

	DURATION	PUBLISHER	DATE
SUITE FROM "THE HAPPY HYPOCRITE"	18 minutes	C. C. Birchard & Co.	1925
INTRODUCTION AND ALLEGRO	12 "	Juilliard Publication	1941

CHORAL WORKS

I WAS WITH HIM—cantata	15 minutes	Manuscript	1942
tenor solo, men's voices, piano			
FIVE SONGS	11 "	Manuscript	1944
baritone solo, men's voices a cappella			
LINCOLN	30 "	Manuscript	1945
baritone solo, mixed chorus, orchestra			

CHAMBER MUSIC

QUINTET FOR STRINGS AND PIANO	30 minutes	Manuscript	1923
PIANO SONATA	15 "	Oxford University Press	1926
DIVERTIMENTO FOR STRING QUARTET	7 "	Manuscript	1929
STRING QUARTET IN E MINOR	20 "	Manuscript	1938
SONATA FOR VIOLIN AND PIANO	18 "	Manuscript	1939
BLUE SYMPHONY	22 "	Manuscript	1943
medium voice and string quartet			

STAGE WORKS

THE HAPPY HYPOCRITE—ballet		Manuscript	1925

LEHMAN ENGEL

Born in Jackson, Mississippi, in 1910. He studied at the Cincinnati Conservatory and Cincinnati College of Music and also under a fellowship with Rubin Goldmark at the Juilliard Graduate School. Later he worked with Roger Sessions.

He has composed and conducted music for the theater and radio. For four years he conducted concerts and broadcasts of the Madrigal Singers, which he founded, and made many recordings with them for Columbia. During World War II he conducted war concerts for many renowned artists and then was put in charge of music for Navy films, in which position he composed and recorded scores for many films of all kinds. He edited

LEHMAN ENGEL (*Continued*)

Renaissance to Baroque (three centuries of choral music) and has contributed articles to leading newspapers and music journals. He is President of the Arrow Music Press, Inc. His Sonata for Cello and Piano received the S.P.A.M. Award in 1946.

His choral works have had performances in New York, Princeton, Moscow, Vienna and in other cities. His ballets have toured throughout the United States. There are innumerable stage productions for which he has written the incidental music. The music he wrote for radio has been presented over many networks in the United States and in Canada. His music has been recorded by Victor, Columbia, Decca, Brunswick and Gamut in both albums of music and of drama for theater.

COMPOSITIONS

ORCHESTRAL WORKS	DURATION	PUBLISHER	DATE
JUNGLE DANCE	5 minutes	Manuscript	1930
INTRODUCTION AND ALLEGRETTO	5 "	Manuscript	1932
SCIENTIFIC CREATION	5 "	Manuscript	1935
TRADITIONS	10 "	Manuscript	1935
SINFONIETTA NO. 1	14 "	Manuscript	1938
SYMPHONY NO. 2	19 "	Manuscript	1945
THE CREATION	30 "	Manuscript	1945
male narrator			
CONCERTO FOR VIOLA AND ORCHESTRA	20 "	Manuscript	1945
OVERTURE—for the end of the war	6 "	Manuscript	1945

CHAMBER ORCHESTRA

EXCERPTS FROM "JOB"	10 minutes	Manuscript	1932
with tenor solo			
CEREMONIALS	15 "	Manuscript	1932
with baritone solo			

CHORAL WORKS

RAIN	5 minutes	J. & W. Chester, Ltd.	1932
mixed chorus			
CHANSONS INNOCENTES	5 "	Arrow Press	1932
women's voices, piano			
REST	3 "	Manuscript	1936
mixed chorus			
SONGS OF INNOCENCE	20 "	Arrow Press	1940
mixed chorus			
SONGS OF MYSELF	20 "	Manuscript	1940
mixed chorus			

CHAMBER MUSIC

STRING QUARTET NO. 1	15 minutes	Manuscript	1934
SONATA FOR PIANO	12 "	Arrow Press	1936
THE GATES OF PARADISE	6 "		1940
variations for piano			
SONATA FOR CELLO AND PIANO	20 "	Manuscript	1945

STAGE WORKS

ATAVISMS			1932
EKSTASIS			1932
CEREMONIALS			1932
SARABANDE			1933
IMPERIAL GESTURE			1934
PHOBIAS—ballet			
MEDEA—short opera	30 minutes	Manuscript	1934

LEHMAN ENGEL (*Continued*)

INCIDENTAL MUSIC FOR THEATER   DATE

WITHIN THE GATES	1934
THE BIRDS	1935
MURDER IN THE CATHEDRAL	1935
HORSE PLAY	1936
THE EMPEROR'S NEW CLOTHES	1936
A HERO IS BORN	1936
HAMLET	1937
SHOEMAKER'S HOLIDAY	1937
TRIAL OF A JUDGE	1937
EVERYWHERE I ROAM	1938
MME. CAPET	1938
ROBIN LANDING	1938
HEAVENLY EXPRESS	1938
FAMILY PORTRAIT	1939
THE TIME OF YOUR LIFE	1939
A MIDSUMMER NIGHT'S DREAM	1939
THUNDER ROCK	1939
A KISS FOR CINDERELLA	1939
MACBETH	1940
THE TROJAN WOMEN	1940

FILM MUSIC   STUDIO   DATE

N. P. PATIENTS	U. S. Navy	1944
FURY IN THE PACIFIC	U. S. Navy	1945
FLEET THAT CAME TO STAY	U. S. Navy	1945
WELL DONE	U. S. Navy	1945
IRRITABILITY	U. S. Navy	1945

CARL EPPERT

Born in Carbon, Indiana, in 1882. He studied harmony and piano at the American Conservatory in Chicago with Harris and Wells. From 1907 to 1914, while in Berlin, he was a pupil of Kaun, Nikisch and Kunwald. He received the National Broadcasting Company Orchestra Award in 1932 for the composition "Traffic." The first prize in the Chicago Symphony Orchestra's Golden Jubilee Contest for American composers was awarded him in 1941 for the Suite No. 1 of the "Ballet of the Vitamins." He also received a special award from the Juilliard Foundation for the reproduction of score and parts of his Symphony No. 4, "Timber."

From 1903 to 1907 he was organizer and Conductor of the Terre Haute Symphony Orchestra. In 1913 he was guest conductor in Germany, and for several years he taught theory in Berlin as assistant to Hugo Kaun. He was Dean at the Milwaukee Institute of Music. He has been Dean of all theoretical branches of the Wisconsin College of Music. He founded and conducted the Milwaukee Civic and Symphony orchestras from 1923 to 1927.

Performances of his orchestral works have been with many of the major orchestras of the country. His two symphonic works for band, "The Road to Mecca" and "Symphonic Tonette," have been played and broadcast by the U. S. Navy, Army, and Marine bands. His male chorus, "The Fog Bell," has had many performances in Boston, Milwaukee, Minneapolis and elsewhere. He has had many broadcasts over CBS and NBC networks.

CARL EPPERT (*Continued*)

COMPOSITIONS

ORCHESTRAL WORKS	DURATION	PUBLISHER	DATE
ARABIAN SUITE, OPUS 16	25 minutes	Manuscript score and parts for hire	1915
THE PIONEER, OPUS 40—tone poem	16 "	Manuscript score and parts for hire	1925
THE WANDERER'S NIGHT SONG, OPUS 31—tone poem	10 "	Manuscript score and parts for hire	1933
THE ARGONAUTS OF FORTY-NINE, OPUS 35—symphonic fantasy	15 "	Manuscript score and parts for hire	1934
A SYMPHONY OF THE CITY (No. 1)— grand symphonic cycle in 4 parts	53 "	Manuscript score and parts for hire	1934
SYMPHONY NO. 3 IN C MINOR, OPUS 67	35 "	Manuscript score and parts for hire	1936
ESCAPADE, OPUS 68	11 "	Manuscript for hire	1937
VITAMINS SUITE NO. 1, OPUS 69	15 "	Manuscript for hire	1937
SYMPHONY NO. 4 IN F, "TIMBER," OPUS 70	30 "	Manuscript for hire	1938
BALLET OF THE VITAMINS, SUITE No. 2, OPUS 69b	15 "	Manuscript for hire	1939
ESCORT TO GLORY, OPUS 75 (symphonic romance)	14 "	Manuscript for hire	1941
SYMPHONY NO. 7, OPUS 77 "THE IMAGE OF AMERICA"	1 hour	Manuscript for hire	1945

CHAMBER ORCHESTRA

SERENADE FOR STRING ORCHESTRA, OPUS 23	10 minutes	Manuscript score and parts for hire	1917
CONCERT WALTZ SUITE, OPUS 47	15 "	Manuscript for hire	1930
A LITTLE SYMPHONY, OPUS 65	18 "	Manuscript score and parts for hire	1935
A CAMEO SYMPHONY, SYMPHONY No 5, OPUS 71	19 "	Manuscript for hire	1939
SYMPHONY NO. 6 IN G MINOR, OPUS 72 double string orchestra and solo strings	24 "	Manuscript for hire	1939
CONCERTO GROSSO flute, oboe, clarinet, bassoon, string orchestra	23 "	Manuscript for hire	1940

ALVIN DERALD ETLER

Born in Battle Creek, Iowa, in 1913. He studied at Western Reserve University with Arthur Shepherd and Melville Smith. He also studied with Paul Hindemith.

He has played in many chamber-music groups and has taught privately. He was a member of the Indianapolis Symphony. Since 1942, he has been on the faculty of the Yale University School of Music. In 1940 and 1941 he was awarded two Guggenheim Fellowships.

His works have been performed by the symphonic orchestras and at the Yaddo and Columbia University festivals and broadcast.

In 1939 the League of Composers commissioned the "Music for Brass," which was heard over the CBS networks. The Sonata for Oboe, Clarinet and Viola was premiered by the I.S.C.M. in 1945. He recently completed a Quartet for Strings and is now working on a Concerto for Wind and Strings, a Quintet for Wind and Strings and a Sonata for Viola and Piano.

COMPOSITIONS

ORCHESTRAL WORKS

	DURATION	PUBLISHER	DATE
SYMPHONIETTA I	14 minutes	Manuscript for hire	1940
SYMPHONIETTA II	20 "	Manuscript for hire	1941

CHAMBER ORCHESTRA

MUSIC FOR CHAMBER ORCHESTRA	13½ minutes	Manuscript for hire	1938

CHORAL WORKS

FIVE SONGS FOR FIVE PEOPLE mixed chorus	15 minutes	Manuscript	1935

CHAMBER MUSIC

TRIO FOR STRINGS violin, viola, cello	18 minutes	Manuscript	1934
SIX FROM OHIO—suite oboe, violin, viola, cello	18 "	Manuscript	1936
FIVE SPEEDS FORWARD—suite flute, oboe, viola, bassoon	12 "	Manuscript	1939
MUSIC FOR BRASS 2 trumpets, 2 horns, 2 trombones, 1 tuba	9 "	Manuscript	1939
SONATA oboe, clarinet, viola	14 "	Manuscript	1944
QUARTET FOR STRINGS	21 "	Manuscript	1945

ARTHUR FARWELL

Born in St. Paul, Minnesota, in 1872. He began his musical career after graduating from the Massachusetts Institute of Technology. He began to study harmony by himself and, upon graduating from college, took up the study of composition with Norris. Four years later he went to Germany to study with Humperdinck and Pfitzner and with Guilmant in Paris. In 1899 he returned to America and lectured at Cornell University on the history of music. For some years he studied the songs of the Indians and the folk material of the Californians of Spanish descent, and some of his works are based on Indian themes. He founded the Wa-Wan Press in Massachusetts for the purpose of publishing works by progressive American composers. He was connected with the origin and development of the community-chorus movement.

From 1909 to 1913 he was chief critic on the staff of *Musical America,* and from 1910 to 1913 he was Supervisor of Municipal Music in the parks and recreation piers in New York City. During the following three years he was Director of the Music School Settlement in New York and in 1918 he became acting head of the Music Department at the University of California, where he continued to organize choruses and to compose music for community music dramas. From 1921 to 1925 he held the Composer's Fellowship of the Pasadena Music and Art Association. In 1927 he became head of theory in the Music Division of Michigan State College, holding this post until 1939. He won the state-national competition of the National Federation of Music Clubs for "Symbolistic Study No. 6—Mountain Vision," which was awarded a broadcast over CBS. He has had many performances of his orchestral works by major orchestras, and his choruses and chamber music have also had frequent performances. "Dawn" and "A Ruined Garden" were broadcast over NBC, and "Navajo War Dance" was presented over NBC and CBS.

COMPOSITIONS

ORCHESTRAL WORKS

	DURATION	PUBLISHER	DATE
SYMBOLISTIC STUDY NO. 3	18 minutes	Manuscript	1922
(after Walt Whitman)			
MARCH! MARCH!—symphonic hymn	8 "	Manuscript	1922
orchestra alone or with choral songs			
SYMPHONIC SONG ON "OLD BLACK JOE"	8 "	Manuscript	1924
orchestra, audience			
THE GODS OF THE MOUNTAIN—suite	18 "	Manuscript	1927
SYMBOLISTIC STUDY No 6, "MOUNTAIN VISION"	14 "	Manuscript	1931
(piano concerto in one movement) string orchestra and second piano			
MOUNTAIN SONG—a symphonic work in five movements with incidental songs by mixed chorus	1 hour	Manuscript	1931
PRELUDE TO A SPIRITUAL DRAMA	10 minutes	Manuscript	1932
RUDOLPH GOTT SYMPHONY	45 "	Manuscript	1934

CHAMBER ORCHESTRA

	DURATION	PUBLISHER	DATE
NAVAJO WAR DANCE	3 minutes	Manuscript	1923
18 instruments			
DAWN—Omaha Indian themes	5 "	Manuscript	1923
18 instruments, piano ad lib.			

ARTHUR FARWELL (*Continued*)

CHORAL WORKS	DURATION	PUBLISHER	DATE
GLORIA	4 minutes	Manuscript	1920
mixed chorus			
FOUR CHORUSES ON INDIAN THEMES	10 "	G. Schirmer, Inc.	1937
8 parts, a cappella			

CHAMBER MUSIC			
THE HAKO—string quartet	11 minutes	Manuscript	1922
THE GODS OF THE MOUNTAIN—suite	18 "	Manuscript	1927
violin, cello, piano			
SONATA FOR VIOLIN AND PIANO	30 "	Manuscript	1927
SONATA IN G MINOR	13 "	Manuscript	1934
solo violin			
THE HOUND OF HEAVEN	15 "	Manuscript	1935
tenor solo, piano			
QUINTET IN E MINOR	32 "	Manuscript	1937
2 violins, viola, violoncello, piano			

STAGE WORKS			
CALIBAN—Shakespeare Tercentenary Masque	3 hours	Published	1916
THE EVERGREEN TREE—Christmas Community Masque	2 "	Published	1917
LA PRIMAVERA, Santa Barbara Community Music Drama	2½ "	Manuscript	1920
THE PILGRIMAGE PLAY (Story of the Christ), Hollywood	3 "	Manuscript	1921
GRAIL SONG—a dramatic ceremony	50 minutes	Manuscript	1925
chamber orchestra, 35 dancers, chorus			

ARTHUR FICKENSCHER

Born in Aurora, Illinois, in 1871. He is a graduate of the Royal Conservatory of Munich, Germany. As a pianist he has toured with many famous singers. He was affiliated with several schools of music, and later he established his own voice studios in San Francisco, Berlin and New York. In 1920 he became head of the Department of Music at the University of Virginia and retired in 1941.

He is the inventor of "The Polytone," an instrument with sixty tones to the octave devised for research in pure intonation, and has made extensive researches in this field. At present he is a resident of California and is devoting his time to composition.

His works have been performed in New York, Grand Rapids, Berkeley, Richmond and in many other cities in the United States, Germany and Australia. His songs have been broadcast.

COMPOSITIONS

ORCHESTRAL WORKS	DURATION	PUBLISHER	DATE
VISIONS	15 minutes	Manuscript	1915
soprano, full orchestra			
WILLOWWAVE AND WELLAWAY	36 "	Blue Print Process	1925
full orchestra			

ARTHUR FICKENSCHER (*Continued*)

ORCHESTRAL WORKS (*Continued*)	DURATION	PUBLISHER	DATE
DAY OF JUDGMENT *full orchestra*	15 minutes	Blue Print Process *score and parts* *for hire*	1927
OUT OF THE GAY NINETIES *full orchestra*	9 "	Blue Print Process *score and parts* *for hire*	1934
VARIATIONS ON A THEME IN MEDIEVAL STYLE *string orchestra*	11 "	Manuscript	1937
CLASSICAL VARIATION FANTASY *full orchestra*	18 "	Blue Print Process	1944
AUCALETE *full orchestra*	20 "	Blue Print Process	1945

CHAMBER ORCHESTRA

DIES IRAE *10 instruments*	11 minutes	Blue Print Process *score and parts* *for hire*	1927

CHORAL WORKS

AUCASSIN AND NICOLETTE *soprano, alto, tenor, baritone,* *mixed chorus, full orchestra*	28 minutes	Manuscript	1915
FRENCH FOLK SONGS *mixed chorus, a cappella*		G. Schirmer, Inc.	
FRENCH FOLK SONGS *male chorus*		C. C. Birchard & Co.	
I KNOW A MAIDEN FAIR TO SEE *women's voices*		G. Schirmer, Inc.	
LENTEN ANTHEM		C. C. Birchard & Co.	
COMMUNION SERVICE		G. Schirmer, Inc.	
THE LAND EAST OF THE SUN *soprano, alto, tenor, baritone,* *mixed chorus, full orchestra*	90 "	Blue Print Process	1945

CHAMBER MUSIC

EVOLUTIONARY QUINTET *piano, string quartet*	45 minutes	Blue Print Process	1933
OUT OF THE SEVENTH REALM *piano, string quartet*	20 "	Associated Music Publishers	1940
SMILE NAE SAE SWEET *strings, flute and voice*	4 "	Blue Print Process	

STAGE WORKS

THE CHAMBER BLUE—mimo-drama *soprano, alto, tenor, women's* *chorus, full orchestra, dancers*	40 minutes	Blue Print Process	1935

AMEDEO de FILIPPI

Born in Ariano, Italy, in 1900. He came to the United States in 1905. He studied with Lichstein, Avitabile and Haschek. He was awarded a four-year fellowship in composition at the Juilliard Graduate School, where he studied with Goldmark.

AMEDEO de FILIPPI (*Continued*)

He has been soloist and conductor for various theatrical companies and under different pseudonyms has composed and arranged music for many publishers, theaters and film companies. Since 1930 he has written music for radio presentations heard over CBS. He also teaches composition. His works have been performed in many cities of the United States and have been broadcast. The Victor Recording Company and Columbia Recordings have recorded some of his works.

COMPOSITIONS

ORCHESTRAL WORKS

	DURATION	PUBLISHER	DATE
SUITE	18 minutes	Manuscript	1920
FIVE ARABIAN SONGS *voice, orchestra*	14 "	Manuscript	1925
CONCERTO	15 "	Manuscript	1928
SYMPHONY	35 "	Manuscript	1930
TWELFTH NIGHT OVERTURE	9 "	Manuscript *for hire*	1937
RAFTSMAN'S DANCE	6 "	Manuscript *for hire*	1939
MEDIEVAL COURT DANCES	18 "	Manuscript *for hire*	1939
CONCERTO	14 "	Concord Music Publishers	1940

CHAMBER ORCHESTRA

	DURATION	PUBLISHER	DATE
TWO SONNETS FOR CONTRALTO *10 instruments*	8 minutes	Manuscript	1920
SERENADE FOR STRINGS *5 instruments*	10 "	Manuscript	1930
PROVENÇAL AIRS *strings*	18 "	Manuscript *for hire*	1938
MUSIC FOR RECREATION *strings*	15 "	E. Assher	1938
DIVERSIONS FOR STRINGS	14 "	Manuscript *for hire*	1939

CHORAL WORKS

	DURATION	PUBLISHER	DATE
CHILDREN OF ADAM *mixed chorus, orchestra*	20 minutes	Manuscript	1926
THREE POEMS (Thoreau) *mixed voices, a cappella*	6 "	Manuscript	1938
THREE POEMS (W. Whitman) *men's voices, brass instruments*	7 "	Manuscript	1939

CHAMBER MUSIC

	DURATION	PUBLISHER	DATE
PIANO SONATA	18 minutes	Manuscript	1922
SIX SONATINAS FOR PIANO	36 "	Manuscript	1926
STRING QUARTET	18 "	Manuscript	1926
PRELUDE, PASSACAGLIA AND TOCCATA FOR PIANO	12 "	Manuscript	1927
PIANO QUINTET	22 "	Manuscript	1928
SONATA FOR VIOLA AND PIANO	14 "	Manuscript	1929
DANCE SUITE FOR VIOLIN AND PIANO	10 "	Manuscript	1929

AMEDEO de FILIPPI (*Continued*)

STAGE WORKS	DURATION	PUBLISHER	DATE
R. E. LEE (Drinkwater)—incidental music, small orchestra		Manuscript	1925
THE GREEN COCKATOO—one-act opera	50 minutes	Manuscript	1927
MALVOLIO—opera in 2 acts		Manuscript	1937
LES SYLPHIDES—ballet			

FILM MUSIC	STUDIO		
BLOCKADE	Pathé Films		1930
LEATHERNECK	Pathé Films		1930
JAZZ AGE	Pathé Films		1930
TRIAL MARRIAGE	Columbia Pictures		1930
HOUSEKEEPER'S DAUGHTER	Columbia Pictures		1938
EVERYTHING ON ICE	Republic		1938

VIVIAN FINE

Born in Chicago, Illinois, in 1913. She studied composition with Sessions and piano with Whiteside. She is active as a pianist, teacher and composer.

Her works have been performed by the I.S.C.M., the League of Composers, the Music Guild of Philadelphia and the Grupo Renovacion (Buenos Aires). The Music Guild of Philadelphia, in 1943, gave her an award for the Suite for Oboe. The Violin Suite was played in 1946 by the Forum Group of the I.S.C.M. WABF (FM) and WNYC have broadcast her works several times. At present she is writing a work for two pianos.

COMPOSITIONS

ORCHESTRAL WORKS	DURATION	PUBLISHER	DATE
DANCE SUITE	15 minutes	Manuscript	1939
CONCERTO FOR PIANO AND ORCHESTRA	18 "	Manuscript	1944

CHORAL WORKS			
THE PASSIONATE SHEPHERD TO HIS LOVE *women's voices, a cappella*	10 minutes	Manuscript	1938

CHAMBER MUSIC			
PRELUDE FOR STRING QUARTET		Manuscript	1937
SUITE FOR OBOE AND PIANO	10 minutes	Manuscript	1939
PIANO SUITE IN E FLAT	9 "	Manuscript	1939
SUITE FOR VIOLIN	10 "	Manuscript	1940

STAGE WORKS			
RACE OF LIFE—ballet *piano solo, or chamber orchestra*	20 minutes	Manuscript	1938
"OPUS 51"—ballet *piano and percussion*	30 "	Manuscript	1940
WE TOO ARE EXILES—ballet *piano and percussion*	30 "	Manuscript	1940
MUSIC FOR PLAY "DOLLARS AND CENTS" *piano and voices*		Manuscript	1941

ROSS LEE FINNEY

Born in Wells, Minnesota, in 1906. He received a Bachelor of Arts degree from Carleton College. He was a pupil of Ferguson at the University of Minnesota, and studied with Boulanger, Berg and Sessions, and with Hill at Harvard University. He received the Guggenheim Fellowship, and the Pulitzer scholarship, also the Connecticut Valley Prize (Hartford Festival). At present he is Professor of Music at Smith College. He is Editor-in-Chief of the Smith College Music Archives, and co-editor of the Valley Music Press. During the Second World War he served with the O.S.S. in France.

His compositions include orchestral, choral, chamber and stage works, which have been given at the Yaddo Festival, by the League of Composers, the Composers Forum, Rochester Philharmonic, Boston "Pops" and Minneapolis Symphony Orchestra. Broadcasts have been made by the NBC Music Guild, NBC Symphony Orchestra, Mutual Network and Band Wagon. Piano works have been performed by soloists on tour.

COMPOSITIONS

ORCHESTRAL WORKS

	DURATION	PUBLISHER	DATE
CONCERTO	25 minutes	Manuscript	1934
piano, orchestra			
OVERTURE FOR A DRAMA	15 "	Manuscript	1937
PRELUDE	8 "	Manuscript	1937
BLEHERIS	14 "	Manuscript	1938
tenor, orchestra			
COMMUNIQUE (Symphony)	23 "	Manuscript	1943
VARIATIONS, FUGUEING AND RONDO	12 "	Manuscript	1943
CONCERTO	30 "	Manuscript	1944
violin, orchestra			

CHAMBER ORCHESTRA

SYMPHONY FOR STRING ORCHESTRA	25 minutes	Manuscript	1937
BARBER SHOP BALLAD	4 "	Manuscript	1939
radio orchestra			
SLOW PIECE	5 "	Valley Music Press	1940
string orchestra			
CONCERTINO	10 "	Manuscript	1941
piano, string orchestra			

CHORAL WORKS

JOHN BROWN	10 minutes	Manuscript	1929
men's chorus, orchestra			
POLE STAR FOR THIS YEAR	13 "	Manuscript	1939
tenor solo, chorus			
OH, BURY ME NOT ON THE LONE PRAIRIE	3 "	Volkwein	1940
2 sopranos, 2 altos			
or 2 tenors, 2 basses			
WHEN THE CURTAINS OF NIGHT	2 "	Volkwein	1940
2 sopranos, 2 altos			
or 2 tenors, 2 basses			
TRAIL TO MEXICO	4 "	Volkwein	1941
2 tenors, 2 basses			
PILGRIM PSALMS	40 "	Manuscript	1945
mixed chorus, orchestra			

CHAMBER MUSIC	DURATION		PUBLISHER	DATE
TRIO	20 minutes		Manuscript	1931
piano, violin, cello				
PIANO SONATA NO. 1	12	"	Manuscript	1932
PIANO SONATA IN D MINOR	17	"	New Music	1933
SONATA FOR VIOLIN AND PIANO	20	"	Manuscript	1934
STRING QUARTET IN F MINOR	25	"	Arrow Music Press	1935
EIGHT POEMS BY ARCHIBALD MACLEISH	30	"	Manuscript	1937
soprano or tenor, piano				
STRING QUARTET IN D MINOR	25	"	Manuscript	1937
SONATA FOR VIOLA AND PIANO	20	"	Manuscript	1937
TRIO IN D MINOR	18	"	Manuscript	1938
piano, violin, cello				
PASTORAL	20	"	Manuscript	1939
flute (violin), piano				
STRING QUARTET IN G MINOR	18	"	Manuscript	1940
SONATA FOR CELLO AND PIANO	18	"	Manuscript	1941
PIANO SONATA NO. 3 IN E	20	"	Valley Music Press	1942

DANTE FIORILLO

Born in New York City in 1905. He began to compose at an early age and is self-taught in composition.

He is particularly interested in education, has taught in several schools, and is Music Editor for the Educational Music Publishers of New York City. He received an award from the Society of Professional Musicians in 1938 and a Pulitzer Award in 1939. He has also had two Guggenheim Awards

His works have been performed throughout the country by many organizations. His Concerto for Oboe, Horn, Piano, Timpani, Sousaphone and String Orchestra was played in Town Hall. The "Gregorian String Quartet" was broadcast over WEAF and affiliated NBC stations. WABC and CBS broadcast his "Music for Strings." WOR and WQXR have also presented many of his compositions. The American Youth Orchestra has performed his Prelude and Passacaglia in Carnegie Hall. At present, he is working on a series of organ music, music for chorus, and a book to be called *A New Technique in Composition.*

COMPOSITIONS

ORCHESTRAL WORKS	DURATION		PUBLISHER	DATE
PRELUDE AND PASSACAGLIA	15 minutes		Manuscript *for hire*	1927
9 SYMPHONIES	30	" each	Manuscript *for hire*	1928–45
CONCERTO FOR PIANO	30	"	Manuscript *for hire*	1940
MUSIC FOR ORCHESTRA AND CHORUS	35	"	Manuscript	1941
MUSIC FOR CELLI, BASSI, TIMPANI AND CHORUS	35	"	Manuscript *for hire*	1943
CONCERTO FOR ORCHESTRA AND CHORUS	35	"	Manuscript *for hire*	1944

DANTE FIORILLO (*Continued*)

CHAMBER ORCHESTRA	DURATION		PUBLISHER	DATE
MUSIC FOR STRINGS	25 minutes		Manuscript for hire	1926
CONCERTINO FOR PIANO AND STRINGS	15	"	Manuscript	1927
PRELUDE AND FUGUE FOR ORCHESTRA	12	"	Manuscript	1928
MUSIC FOR CHAMBER ORCHESTRA	23	"	Manuscript for hire	1932
CONCERTO FOR STRINGS AND SOLO INSTRUMENTS	25	"	Manuscript for hire	1935
solo oboe, horn, piano, timpani, sousaphone				
CONCERTO FOR HARPSICHORD WITH CHAMBER ORCHESTRA	14	"	Manuscript for hire	1938
MUSIC FOR STRING ORCHESTRA AND CHORUS	30	"	Manuscript	1940
MUSIC FOR STRING ORCHESTRA AND 2 CLARINETS	25	"	Manuscript	1945

CHORAL WORKS				
MASS FOR ALTO VOICE, VIOLIN AND CELLO	28 minutes		Manuscript	1940

CHAMBER MUSIC				
SONATA FOR VIOLA AND PIANO	15 minutes		Manuscript	1925
GREGORIAN STRING QUARTET	30	"	Manuscript	1927
SONATA FOR CELLO AND PIANO	18	"	Manuscript	1928
STRING QUARTET A MINOR	28	"	Manuscript	1932
PRELUDE AND FUGUE FOR STRING QUARTET	14	"	Manuscript	1937
PIANO SONATINA	15	"	Manuscript	1945

STAGE WORKS				
"ONE WORLD"—incidental music *full orchestra*			Manuscript	1945
"PINOCCHIO"—incidental music *full orchestra*			Manuscript	1945

JERZY FITELBERG

Born in Warsaw, Poland, in 1903. He studied at the Academy of Music in Berlin. He lived in Paris until 1940, when he came to America.

He has had major performances in the capitals of Europe, and since he has been in the United States, his works have been performed in New York, Boston, Washington and Rochester. He received the Elizabeth Sprague Coolidge Prize in 1936 for his Fourth String Quartet which was written before he came to America. He also received a prize from the Polish Government for his Second String Quartet. Recently, he was given a grant from the American Academy of Art and Letters. His compositions have been broadcast in Warsaw and Luxembourg. He has written film music for "Poland Fights On" and "Prewar Poland" for the Polish Government. The Nocturne for Orchestra had its première in 1946 by the New York Philharmonic Orchestra.

JERZY FITELBERG (*Continued*)

COMPOSITIONS WRITTEN IN AMERICA

ORCHESTRAL WORKS

	DURATION	PUBLISHER	DATE
EPITAPH	9 minutes	Associated Music	1943
violin		Publishers	
NOCTURNE	15 "	Associated Music	1944
		Publishers	
POLISH PICTURES—suite for orchestra	17 "	Manuscript	
SYMPHONY FOR STRINGS	30 "	Manuscript	
SINFONIETTA FOR ORCHESTRA	20 "	Manuscript	

CHAMBER ORCHESTRA

CONCERTO FOR STRINGS	16 minutes	Universal Edition	1928
24 instruments			
FIRST VIOLIN CONCERTO	15 "	Editions Pro Musica	1928
36 instruments			
THE GOLDEN HORN—for strings	20 "	Associated Music	1942
36 instruments		Publishers	

CHORAL WORKS

THREE POLISH FOLKSONGS	6 minutes	G. Schirmer, Inc.	1942
women's voices			

CHAMBER MUSIC

SONATINE FOR 2 VIOLINS	14 minutes	J. & W. Chester	1935
SONATA FOR 2 VIOLINS AND			
2 PIANOS	20 "	J. & W. Chester	1938
FIFTH STRING QUARTET	24 "	Manuscript	1945

FILM MUSIC

POLAND FIGHTS ON		1945
Polish Government		
PREWAR POLAND		1945
Producer Julien Bryan		

GEORGE FOOTE

Born in Cannes, France, in 1886. He graduated from Harvard University, where he received honors in music. He studied with Koch and Klatte in Berlin and with Hill in the United States. He was also a piano pupil of Noyes and Wilson.

He was assistant in the Music Department at Harvard University from 1921 to 1923, and was President of the South End Music School in Boston until 1943.

"Variations on a Pious Theme" and "In Praise of Winter" were performed by the Boston Symphony Orchestra and the Providence and Rochester symphonies. His other compositions, including Trio for Flute, Harp and Violin and "We Go Forward," have been played in Boston, Duluth and New York. At present, he is preparing some waltzes for orchestra.

GEORGE FOOTE (*Continued*)

COMPOSITIONS

ORCHESTRAL WORKS	DURATION	PUBLISHER	DATE
VARIATIONS ON A PIOUS THEME	9 minutes	Manuscript	1931
LITTLE SYMPHONY	19 "	Manuscript	1929

CHORAL WORKS			
98TH PSALM *chorus, organ*	10 minutes	Manuscript	1934

CHAMBER MUSIC			
TRIO FOR PIANO, VIOLIN AND CELLO	20 minutes	Manuscript	1923
TRIO FOR FLUTE, HARP AND VIOLIN	19 "	Manuscript	1933

STAGE WORKS			
WE GO FORWARD—religious pantomime	45 minutes	Manuscript	1943

RUDOLF FORST

Born in New York City in 1900. He began his musical education at the age of eight. He received all his instruction in New York City, working at the violin and theory under various teachers but teaching himself composition. At Columbia University he did postgraduate work with Daniel Gregory Mason.

For three years he was a violin instructor at New York College of Music and Music Director of radio station WLWL, New York City. In 1936 he received one of the awards of the National Broadcasting Company Music Guild for a string quartet. He is a member of the music department of Radio City Music Hall and is an editor for Edition Musicus in New York.

Several of his works have been performed in the West, as well as in New York, by major orchestras. He has had numerous broadcasts over WOR and WQXR. At present he is completing a Concerto for Piano and Orchestra.

COMPOSITIONS

ORCHESTRAL WORKS	DURATION	PUBLISHER	DATE
FRAGMENT POÉTIQUE	10 minutes	Manuscript	1930
SYMPHONIA BREVIS	17 "	Manuscript	1933
OZARK RHAPSODY	15 "	Manuscript	1937
SYMPHONY		Manuscript	1937
MORNING IN OLD MEXICO	5 "	Manuscript	1938
CONCERTO FOR CELLO AND ORCHESTRA	25 "	Manuscript	1941
SYMPHONY FOR ORCHESTRA	17 "	Manuscript	1943

RUDOLF FORST (*Continued*)

CHAMBER ORCHESTRA	DURATION	PUBLISHER	DATE
MUSIC FOR TEN INSTRUMENTS	14 minutes	Manuscript	1935
SYMPHONIETTA FOR STRING ORCHESTRA	14 "	Affiliated Music Corp.	1936
SONATA DA CAMERA	16 "	Manuscript	1937
DIVERTIMENTO FOR SMALL ORCHESTRA	22 "	Manuscript	1937
ADAGIO FOR STRING ORCHESTRA	5 "	Edition Musicus	1945
THRENODY FOR STRING ORCHESTRA	5 "	Edition Musicus	1945

CHORAL WORKS			
THE LIGHT IN THE TEMPLE—cantata *solo voices, chorus, orchestra*		Manuscript	1946

CHAMBER MUSIC			
QUARTET FOR STRINGS	19 minutes	Edition Musicus	1936
TWO PIECES FOR STRING QUARTET AND GUITAR	10 "	Manuscript	1937
TRIO FOR FLUTE, VIOLA AND HARP	15 "	Manuscript	1940

LUKAS FOSS

Born in Berlin, Germany, in 1922. He studied at the Paris Conservatory and graduated from the Curtis Institute of Music in Philadelphia. He was a pupil of Hindemith, Herford, Koussevitzky and Reiner.

He won the Pulitzer Scholarship in 1942 for the "Suite to the Tempest of Shakespeare" and received a citation from the New York Critics' Circle in 1944 for "The Prairie," a cantata. In 1945 he was awarded a Guggenheim Fellowship and is the youngest composer ever to have been given this award. He studied and also conducted at the Berkshire Music Center and became official pianist of the Boston Symphony, which position he holds today. He has also been guest conductor and lecturer.

His compositions have had major performances by the Boston Symphony, CBS Symphony Orchestra, the Collegiate Chorale, the New York Philharmonic Orchestra, the Pittsburgh Symphony and the Westminster Choir. "The Prairie," a cantata for chorus, solo voices and orchestra, and the Piano Concerto were broadcast on "Invitation to Music" over WABC. In 1945 his ballet, "The Gift of the Magi," was given its New York première at the Metropolitan Opera House. "Dedication" for violin and piano was recorded by Hargail. At present, he is working on commissions for the Cleveland Orchestra, the League of Composers and the Koussevitzky Music Foundation.

COMPOSITIONS

ORCHESTRAL WORKS	DURATION	PUBLISHER	DATE
THE PRAIRIE—symphonic piece	14 minutes	Manuscript Schirmer Rental Library	1943
PIANO CONCERTO	23 "	Manuscript Schirmer Rental Library	1943

LUKAS FOSS (*Continued*)

ORCHESTRAL WORKS (*Continued*)	DURATION	PUBLISHER	DATE
ODE TO THOSE WHO WILL NOT RETURN	12 minutes	Manuscript Schirmer Rental Library	1944
SYMPHONY IN G	33 "	Manuscript Schirmer Rental Library	1944
BALLET SUITE	14 "	Manuscript Schirmer Rental Library	1945
SONG OF ANGUISH *baritone solo, orchestra*	19 "	Manuscript	1945
THE SONG OF SONGS *soprano solo, orchestra*	20 "		1946

CHAMBER ORCHESTRA

SUITE TO THE TEMPEST OF SHAKESPEARE		Manuscript	1941

CHORAL WORKS

THE PRAIRIE *soprano, alto, tenor, bass soli, chorus, orchestra*	54 minutes	G. Schirmer, Inc.	1942
TELL THIS BLOOD *mixed chorus, a cappella*	4 "	Manuscript	1945

CHAMBER MUSIC

SET OF THREE PIECES FOR TWO PIANOS	26 minutes	G. Schirmer, Inc.	1940

STAGE WORKS

GIFT OF THE MAGI—ballet *6 dancers, large or small orchestra*	20 minutes	Manuscript	1945

JOHAN FRANCO

Born in Zaandam, Holland, in 1908. Upon graduation from the First College of The Hague, he went to Amsterdam to study composition with Willem Pijper.

In Europe he wrote a symphony, shorter orchestral works and chamber music. He also set to music poems by English and Netherland poets, including Shakespeare, Bacon, Tennyson and Browning. He came to the United States in 1934. In 1938 he contributed the section on contemporary Dutch composers to Oscar Thompson's *Cyclopedia of Music and Musicians*. During his service in the army he composed a "Hymn for the Air Corps" and set to music Tennyson's prophecy of air power in "Locksley Hall."

His First Symphony was first performed by the Rotterdam Philharmonic Orchestra in 1934. The "Concerto Lirico" was given in Brussels in 1939 and in New York in 1944. "Baconiana" and the Suite for String Orchestra were heard in New York in 1946.

JOHAN FRANCO (*Continued*)

COMPOSITIONS WRITTEN IN AMERICA

ORCHESTRAL WORKS	DURATION	PUBLISHER	DATE
PERIPETIE—symphonic poem	12 minutes	Manuscript	1935
INTRADA	5 "	Manuscript	1938
flute, orchestra			
SYMPHONY No. 1	20 "	Associated Music Publishers *for hire*	1939
SYMPHONY No. 2—concertante *piano*	15 "	Associated Music Publishers *for hire*	1940
BACONIANA—symphonic poem	8 "	Associated Music Publishers *for hire*	1941

CHAMBER ORCHESTRA

	DURATION	PUBLISHER	DATE
CONCERTO LIRICO *violin, chamber orchestra*	15 minutes	Associated Music Publishers *for hire*	1937
SERENADE CONCERTANTE *piano, chamber orchestra*	12 "	Manuscript	1938
LOCKSLEY HALL *mezzo soprano, chamber orchestra*	4 "	Manuscript	1943
SUITE FOR STRING ORCHESTRA	20 "	Manuscript	1945
THREE RADIO PIECES *solo violin, string orchestra*	10 "	Manuscript	1945

CHORAL WORKS

	DURATION	PUBLISHER	DATE
126TH PSALM *mixed chorus, a cappella or organ*	4 minutes	Manuscript	1943
HYMN FOR THE AIR CORPS *women's chorus, organ*	4 "	Manuscript	1943

CHAMBER MUSIC

	DURATION	PUBLISHER	DATE
TWO SONATAS, PARTITA, THEME AND VARIATIONS *piano*		Manuscript	1934–45
THREE INVENTIONS *violin, violoncello*	4 minutes	Manuscript	1937
INTRADA *violin, violoncello, organ*	8 "	Manuscript	1938
THREE INVENTIONS *3 trombones*	6 "	Manuscript	1940
TWO PIECES FOR STRING QUARTET	8 "	Manuscript	1941
SONATA *violin solo*	8 "	Manuscript	1944
SUITE FOR STRINGS	15 "	Manuscript	1945
SUITE FOR VIOLIN AND PIANO	10 "	Manuscript	1946

ISADORE FREED

Born in Brest-Litovsk, Russia, in 1900. He came to the United States as a child and made his home in Philadelphia. He attended the University of Pennsylvania, where he received his degree of Bachelor of Music. A gold medal from the Philadelphia Conservatory of Music was later awarded to him. He studied composition under Bloch in New York City and with D'Indy in Paris. His piano instructors were Weiss in Berlin, Boyle in Philadelphia and Margulies in New York City. He was also a student of organ at the Schola Cantorum in Paris.

He has been on the faculty of the Curtis Institute in Philadelphia and also heads the Music Department of Temple University's Tyler School of Fine Arts. Since 1944 he has directed the Composition Department of the Julius Hartt Musical Foundation in Hartford. He is active as a choral conductor and is Co-Editor of "Masters of Our Day" series of contemporary educational piano music. He was founder and Director of the Composers Laboratory of Philadelphia. He received the S.P.A.M. Publication Prize for the "Triptych" for violin, viola, cello and piano, and he won the twentieth annual Euridice Choral Award for a chorus, "Postscripts."

His orchestral works have been presented in San Francisco, Washington, Philadelphia, New York and Paris by the major symphony orchestras and broadcast by NBC. His chamber and choral music has been played frequently in many cities in the United States and in Europe. At present he is working on a two-act opera, "The Princess and the Vagabond."

COMPOSITIONS

ORCHESTRAL WORKS

	DURATION	PUBLISHER	DATE
PYGMALION—symphonic rhapsody	15 minutes	Manuscript	1926
VIBRATIONS—symphonic suite	15 "	Manuscript	1929
JEUX DE TIMBRES—symphonic suite	18 "	Editions Eschig	1931
TRIPTYQUE—suite for string orchestra	12 "	La Sirène Musicale	1932
PASTORALES—suite of miniatures	12 "	Manuscript for hire	1936
MUSIC FOR STRINGS	16 "	Manuscript for hire	1937
VIOLA RHAPSODY	9 "	Carl Fischer, Inc.	1939
VIOLIN CONCERTO	20 "	Manuscript for hire	1939
FIRST SYMPHONY	26 "	Manuscript for hire	1942
APPALACHIAN SKETCHES	15 "	Manuscript for hire	1942
A FESTIVAL OVERTURE	12 "	Manuscript for hire	1944

CHAMBER ORCHESTRA

BALLAD *piano, 5 strings, 5 winds*	12 minutes	Manuscript	1925

CHORAL WORKS

DAREST THOU NOW, O SOUL *women's voices, piano*	5 minutes	H. W. Gray Co., Inc.	1926
SACRED SERVICE FOR THE SABBATH *mixed chorus, organ*	30 "	Bloch Publishing Co.	1937

ISADORE FREED (*Continued*)

CHORAL WORKS (*Continued*)	DURATION	PUBLISHER	DATE
PSALM 118	8½ minutes	Transcontinental	1941
2 *versions: mixed and women's chorus, orchestra*			
POSTSCRIPTS—choral suite	10 "	Carl Fischer, Inc.	1942
women's chorus, piano			
ISLAND SECRET	6 "	Carl Fischer, Inc.	1944
women's chorus, piano			

CHAMBER MUSIC			
SUITE FOR VIOLA AND PIANO	15 minutes	Manuscript	1923
FIRST STRING QUARTET (Folk Moods)	10 "	Manuscript	1925
RHAPSODY FOR CLARINET, STRING QUARTET AND PIANO	10 "	Manuscript	1925
SONATA FOR VIOLIN AND PIANO	16 "	Manuscript	1926
SECOND STRING QUARTET	16 "	Manuscript	1930
SONATA FOR PIANO	14 "	Editions Eschig	1933
THIRD STRING QUARTET	18 "	Manuscript for hire	1936
TRIO FOR FLUTE, HARP AND VIOLA	15 "	Manuscript for hire	1940
SUITE FOR HARP	12 "	Manuscript	1942
TRIPTYCH FOR VIOLIN, VIOLA, CELLO AND PIANO	18 "	G. Schirmer, Inc.	1943
SHEPHERD'S HOLIDAY	7 "	Manuscript	1944
voice, viola, piano			

STAGE WORKS			
VIBRATIONS—ballet	20 minutes	Manuscript	1928
2 *pianos, chamber orchestra*			
HOMO SUM—opera in 1 act	30 "	Manuscript	1930
4 *voices, chamber orchestra*			

ANIS FULEIHAN

Born on the Island of Cyprus in the Near East in 1900. He came to the United States in 1915 and studied piano with Jonas and theory with Milligan and Loth. He began his concert career as pianist-composer in 1919. In 1925, he returned to the Near East to make a study of Mediterranean folk music and musical idioms. He came back to America in 1928 and since then has made his home in New York, teaching, lecturing and composing.

He joined the staff of music publishers at Schirmer's in 1932. He has appeared as soloist with major orchestras in the United States and Canada, has given many lectures and has conducted radio programs. He received a Guggenheim Fellowship in composition in 1939.

His orchestral works have been performed throughout the United States and in London by the major symphony orchestras. His piano compositions have been played in this country from coast to coast. An entire program of his music was presented on "Invitation to Music" over WABC, and a similar one was offered over WQXR. BBC, WEAF, WJZ and WOR have

ÀNIS FULEIHAN (*Continued*)

also broadcast his works. His ballets were written for and produced by the Neighborhood Playhouse and were performed on tour by Bohm and the Denishawn Dancers.

COMPOSITIONS

ORCHESTRAL WORKS	DURATION	PUBLISHER	DATE
MEDITERRANEAN	14 minutes	G. Schirmer, Inc. *parts for hire*	1930
PREFACE TO A CHILD'S STORY BOOK	9 "	G. Schirmer, Inc. *for hire*	1931
SYMPHONY	22 "	G. Schirmer, Inc. *for hire*	1936
CONCERTO No. 1 *piano, string or full orchestra*	21 "	G. Schirmer, Inc.	1937
CONCERTO No. 2 *piano, orchestra*	22 "	G. Schirmer, Inc.	1937
FANTASY FOR VIOLA AND ORCHESTRA	10 "	G. Schirmer, Inc. *for hire*	1938
FIESTA—overture	8 "	G. Schirmer, Inc. *for hire*	1940
SYMPHONIE CONCERTANTE FOR STRING QUARTET AND ORCHESTRA	27 "	Manuscript *for hire*	1940
CONCERTO FOR TWO PIANOS AND ORCHESTRA	22 "	G. Schirmer, Inc. *for hire*	1940
INVOCATION	7 "	G. Schirmer, Inc. *for hire*	1941
EPITHALAMIUM—variations for piano and string orchestra	14 "	G. Schirmer, Inc.	1941
SIX ETUDES FOR ORCHESTRA	25 "	G. Schirmer, Inc.	1942
THREE CYPRUS SERENADES	12 "	G. Schirmer, Inc. *for hire*	1943
COMEDY OVERTURE	8 "	G. Schirmer, Inc. *for hire*	1944
CONCERTO FOR VIOLIN, PIANO AND ORCHESTRA	21 "	Manuscript *for hire*	1944
CONCERTO FOR THEREMIN AND ORCHESTRA	12 "	Manuscript *for hire*	1944

CHAMBER ORCHESTRA			
DIVERTIMENTO FOR OBOE, TRUMPET, HORN, BASSOON AND STRINGS	10 minutes	Manuscript *for hire*	1943

CHAMBER MUSIC			
UNSOPHISTICATED PRELUDES FOR STRING QUARTET	11 minutes	Manuscript	1921
MUSIC FOR PUPPETS *flute, oboe, clarinet, bassoon*	13 "	Manuscript	1931
QUARTET FOR STRINGS	20 "	Manuscript	1940
PASTORAL SONATA *flute, piano*	10 "	Manuscript	1940
SONATA No. 1 *piano*	18 "	G. Schirmer, Inc.	1940

ANIS FULEIHAN (*Continued*)

CHAMBER MUSIC (*Continued*)	DURATION	PUBLISHER	DATE
SUITE FOR CELLO AND PIANO	10 minutes	Manuscript	1942
CYPRIANA—suite of five pieces for piano	16 "	G. Schirmer, Inc.	1943
SONATA NO. 2 *piano*	14 "	Manuscript	1944
TOCCATA FOR TWO PIANOS	17 "	Manuscript	1944
SONORITIES FOR PIANO—5 movements	12 "	Manuscript	1945
FIFTEEN SHORT PIECES FOR PIANO—suite	12 "	Carl Fischer, Inc.	1945
SONATINE NO. 1 *piano*	5 "	Delkas	1945
SONATINE NO. 2 *piano*	6 "	Delkas	1945

DONALD SANBORN FULLER

Born in Washington, D. C., in 1919. He was a student at Yale University and studied composition with Richard Donovan and David Stanley Smith. He received a Juilliard Graduate School Fellowship and studied with Bernard Wagenaar. He worked with Aaron Copland at the first session of the Berkshire Music Center and also with Darius Milhaud at Mills College.

He has taught theory at the Chautauqua School of Music. He became an Associate Editor of *Modern Music,* for which he wrote many reviews.

His Sonatina for Oboe, Clarinet and Piano was performed by the League of Composers and by the I.S.C.M. at their 1941 Festival in California. It was also played over WQXR. His Songs to the texts of Robert Frost have been broadcast over WNYC. The League of Composers has performed his Trio for Clarinet, Cello and Piano. At the present time, he is working on a Sonata for Two Pianos and a Suite for Orchestra.

COMPOSITIONS

ORCHESTRAL WORKS	DURATION	PUBLISHER	DATE
ANDANTE FOR ORCHESTRA	8 minutes	Manuscript	1941
SYMPHONIC MOVEMENT	13 "	Manuscript	1942

CHAMBER MUSIC			
SONATINA FOR PIANO	7 minutes	Manuscript	1939
TRIO FOR CLARINET, CELLO AND PIANO	15 "	Manuscript	1939
SONATINA FOR OBOE, CLARINET AND PIANO	8 "	Manuscript	1940
PIANO SONATA	16 "	Manuscript	1946

FLORENCE GRANDLAND GALAJIKIAN

Born in Maywood, Illinois, in 1900. She began studying piano at the age of five. She graduated from the Northwestern University School of Music and Chicago Musical College. Her teachers were Noelte, Borowski, Saar, Hemington, Oldberg, Raab and Goldmark. In 1932 she was given the National Broadcasting Company Orchestral Award for her Symphonic Intermezzo; in 1936 Respighi offered her a scholarship in Rome, but he died that year.

She has made extensive tours as a concert pianist and has appeared as soloist with the Chicago Symphony Orchestra. At present she teaches piano and composition privately. In 1940 the Illinois Federation of Music Clubs gave her an award for the String Quartet. "For Freedom," a work for band and solo voices, was used by the O.W.I. on many of the allied-controlled broadcasting stations for propaganda purposes. Many of her works have been given in Chicago, New York, Portland and other cities and have been broadcast over NBC.

COMPOSITIONS

ORCHESTRAL WORKS	DURATION	PUBLISHER	DATE
SYMPHONIC INTERMEZZO	12 minutes	Carl Fischer, Inc. Manuscript *for hire*	1931
TRAGIC OVERTURE	12 "	Carl Fischer, Inc. Manuscript *for hire*	1934

CHORAL WORKS			
REVEILLE *men's voices, piano*	5 minutes	Manuscript	1930
LORD, HEAR MY VOICE *mixed chorus, organ*	5 "	Manuscript	1931
SONG OF JOY *women's voices, piano*	4 "	Carl Fischer, Inc.	1932

CHAMBER MUSIC			
ANDANTE AND SCHERZO *string quartet*	15 minutes	Manuscript	1935

STAGE WORKS			
TRANSITIONS—ballet *choreographic drama, corps de ballet, solo dancer, chamber orchestra*	45 minutes	Manuscript	1937

PAOLO GALLICO

Born in Trieste, Italy, in 1868. He studied at the Vienna Conservatory, where he received a gold medal and the silver Gesellschaft Medal. He studied piano with Eppstein and composition with Fuchs and Bruckner.

After making several tours in Europe, he came to the United States in 1892 and appeared as pianist with the principal orchestras. He is a teacher

PAOLO GALLICO (*Continued*)

of piano, composition and orchestration. His work "The Apocalypse," a dramatic oratorio, received the first prize of the National Federation of Music Clubs in 1921.

"Euphorion," "The Apocalypse" and "Septet" have been widely played. The New York Oratorio Society, the Los Angeles Symphony Orchestra, the New York Symphony Society, the Detroit Symphony and the Society of the Friends of Music have presented his works.

COMPOSITIONS

ORCHESTRAL WORKS	DURATION	PUBLISHER	DATE
EUPHORION—symphonic episode	15 minutes	Manuscript	1922
RHAPSODIE MONDIALE	13 "	Manuscript	1927
RHAPSODIE MONTEREYAN	14 "	Manuscript	1929
SYMPHONY—one movement	16 "	Manuscript	1939

CHORAL WORKS			
THE APOCALYPSE—dramatic oratorio 6 solo voices, mixed chorus, full orchestra	1½ hours	G. Schirmer, Inc. for sale and hire	1920

CHAMBER MUSIC			
SEPTET piano, string quartet, horn, contralto	35 minutes	Manuscript	1924
PIANO QUINTET piano, string quartet	3 "	Manuscript	1936
STRING QUARTET	30 "	Manuscript	1942

STAGE WORKS			
HARLEQUIN—lyric opera in three acts		Manuscript	1926

RUDOLPH GANZ

Born in Zurich, Switzerland, in 1877. He studied in Strasbourg and later with Busoni in Berlin. He came to America at the turn of the century, after receiving an offer to become head of the Piano Department of the Chicago Musical College.

He has had a long career as Conductor of the St. Louis Symphony Orchestra and has been guest conductor and pianist of major orchestras in this country, England and France. In 1933, he became President of the Chicago Musical College. He is Conductor of the Young People's and Children's Concerts of the New York Philharmonic Symphony, of the San Francisco Symphony Orchestra and of the Chicago Symphony. He is President of the Edward MacDowell Association and Chairman of the Independent Citizens Committee of the Arts, Sciences, and Professions, Midwest Division.

The "Animal Pictures," a symphonic suite, has been performed in New York, Detroit, San Francisco, Chicago and other cities. Concerto in E Flat and "Four Symphonic Demonstration Pieces" have also been played by

RUDOLPH GANZ (*Continued*)

major orchestras throughout the country and he has also conducted them in many cities.

COMPOSITIONS WRITTEN IN AMERICA

ORCHESTRAL WORKS	DURATION	PUBLISHER	DATE
SYMPHONY IN E, OPUS 1	30 minutes	Manuscript	
CONZERTSTUECK IN B MINOR, OPUS 2 *piano*	15 "	A. P. Schmidt	
ANIMAL PICTURES—suite of 20 pictures	23 "	Carl Fischer, Inc.	1932
CONCERTO IN E FLAT, OPUS 32 *piano*	23 "	Carl Fischer, Inc.	1941
FOUR SYMPHONIC DEMONSTRATION PIECES, OPUS 33	12 "	Mills Music Co.	1944

CHORAL WORKS			
THE CADETS OF GASCOGNE *men's voices a cappella*	4 minutes	H. W. Gray Co.	
A MEMORY *women's voices a cappella*	2 "	G. Schirmer, Inc.	

SAMUEL GARDNER

Born in Elizabethgrad, Russia, in 1891. He came to the United States as a young child and lived in Providence. He began to study the violin at the age of six, completing his training with Winternitz in Boston and with Kneisel in New York City. He graduated from the Institute of Musical Art in 1913, where he studied composition with Goetschius. In 1918 he won the Pulitzer Prize in composition and the Loeb Prize for his Symphonic Poem.

He was a member of the Kneisel Quartet in 1914 and of the Chicago Symphony Orchestra from 1915 to 1916. In 1917 he became a member of the Elshuco Trio, and since 1918 he has toured as a concert violinist. He has been engaged as guest conductor by various symphony orchestras.

His Piano Quintet in F Minor was first performed at the Coolidge Festival in Pittsfield, Massachusetts, and "Broadway" was given by the Boston Symphony Orchestra. He played his own Violin Concerto with the New York Philharmonic Orchestra.

COMPOSITIONS

ORCHESTRAL WORKS	DURATION	PUBLISHER	DATE
BROADWAY	16 minutes	Manuscript	1924
SYMPHONIC POEM			
VIOLIN CONCERTO			

CHAMBER MUSIC			
PIANO QUINTET IN F MINOR *piano and strings*	25 minutes	Oliver Ditson Co.	1918
PRELUDE AND FUGUE			
VARIATIONS FOR STRING QUARTET			
STRING QUARTET, NO. 2	20 "	Manuscript	1944

EDWIN GERSCHEFSKI

Born in Meriden, Connecticut, in 1909. He attended Yale University and received a degree of Bachelor of Music at the Yale School of Music. He has a diploma for piano and teaching from the Tobias Matthay Pianoforte School in London, England. His teachers in composition have been Smith, Donovan, Corder and Baumgartner; his instructors in piano, Simonds, Samuels, Matthay and Schnabel. At Yale he received the Kellogg Prize and the Charles Ditson Fellowship for study abroad, and at the Matthay School he was awarded the Jeffrey Reynolds Scholarship and a silver medal for piano.

He has given recitals for the Association of American Colleges. He won the New York World's Fair Award for his band music. At present he is Dean of the Converse College School of Music.

Outstanding among his compositions is "Streamline" (a symphonic work for band), presented in Chicago and Interlachen and also by the United States Navy Band at Annapolis. "Test Tubes" and the Symphony have been played by several orchestras and broadcast over NBC and other national hook-ups. "Guadalcanal Fantasy" (dedicated to the Marine Corps) and the Suite for Full Orchestra have been performed over radio networks.

COMPOSITIONS

	DURATION	PUBLISHER	DATE
ORCHESTRAL WORKS			
CLASSIC SYMPHONY	17 minutes	Belwin	1931
OVERTURE IN THE STYLE OF THE 18TH CENTURY	4½ "	Manuscript	1931
CONCERTINO FOR PIANO AND ORCHESTRA	6 "	Manuscript	1932
SUITE FOR FULL ORCHESTRA	16 "	Manuscript	1936
MARCH FOR ORCHESTRA	4 "	Manuscript	1945
CHAMBER ORCHESTRA			
TODAY—overture	4½ minutes	Manuscript	1938
8 wind instruments and strings			
INTRODUCTION, FUGATO AND FINALE	9 "	Manuscript	1942
SYMPHONIC BAND WORKS			
STREAMLINE	3 minutes	M. Witmark & Sons	1936
DISCHARGE IN E	5 "	Manuscript	1937
SYMPHONY FOR BAND		Manuscript	1937
GUADALCANAL FANTASY	5 "	Manuscript	1943
CHAMBER MUSIC			
PRELUDES FOR PIANO	18 minutes	Manuscript	1932
PIANO SONATINE	10 "	Manuscript	1933
QUARTET FOR TWO VIOLINS AND TWO VIOLAS	9 "	Manuscript	1933
SONATINE FOR VIOLIN AND PIANO	14 "	Manuscript	1934
PIANO QUINTET	18 "	Manuscript	1935
VARIATIONS FOR STRING QUARTET	15 "	Manuscript	1937
MOVEMENT IN THREE SPEEDS	8 "	Manuscript	1938
trumpets, trombones, horns, tuba			
LITTLE SYMPHONY FOR VIOLINS AND VIOLAS	9 "	Manuscript	1941
FILM MUSIC			
AMERICAN TARANTELLA (arranged for piano solo)		Expanding Cinema, Inc.	1939

GEORGE GERSHWIN

Born in Brooklyn, New York, in 1898 and died in 1937. He began to study music when he was thirteen. His first teacher was Hambitzer. Later he studied harmony with Goldmark and composition with Schillinger. He taught himself orchestration. At the age of sixteen he found a job as "song plugger" with J. H. Remick & Company, but left this shortly to go on a tour as accompanist for a singer. The first composition he published was a song, written at the age of eighteen. Popular recognition came three years later when he wrote "Swanee." After this success he wrote many popular songs and musical comedies which were produced with great success.

His introduction to the field of serious music was in 1924. The Whiteman program, called "An Experiment in Modern Music," introduced Gershwin as the composer for this occasion of "A Rhapsody in Blue." This was the work which first won him consideration among composers of serious music. Others followed which belong with the "Rhapsody in Blue." At the same time he continued to write musical comedies that were produced on Broadway. In 1935 he completed the score of his opera "Porgy and Bess," which was produced by the Theatre Guild. After a long run in New York it toured the United States and Europe and has had several revivals in the United States. He was awarded the David Bispham Medal for this work and was elected an honorary member of the St. Cecilia Academy of Music in Rome. Later he developed an interest in art and many of his oil paintings have been exhibited.

The "Rhapsody in Blue," the Concerto in F, "An American in Paris" and the Second Rhapsody have been played by the major orchestras in many cities of America and Europe and are constantly being broadcast. The "Rhapsody in Blue," "An American in Paris" and excerpts from "Porgy and Bess" are recorded by Victor. Concerto in F is recorded by Columbia.

COMPOSITIONS

ORCHESTRAL WORKS

	DURATION	PUBLISHER	DATE
RHAPSODY IN BLUE *piano solo*	12 minutes	Harms, Inc.	1923
CONCERTO IN F—*piano solo*	30 "	Harms, Inc.	1925
AN AMERICAN IN PARIS	15 "	The New World Music Publishers	1928
SECOND RHAPSODY—*piano solo*	14 "	The New World Music Publishers	1932
CUBAN OVERTURE	9 "	The New World Music Publishers	1932

STAGE WORKS

PORGY AND BESS—opera	3 hours		1935

FILM MUSIC

	STUDIO	DATE
SHALL WE DANCE?	RKO Radio Pictures, Inc.	1937
DAMSEL IN DISTRESS	RKO Radio Pictures, Inc.	1937
GOLDWYN FOLLIES (work incomplete at time of death)	United Artists	1937

VITTORIO GIANNINI

Born in Philadelphia, Pennsylvania, in 1903. He began his first studies in violin with his mother. Later he studied with Tua and Letz. He was awarded a scholarship at the Conservatory in Milan and also at the Juilliard Graduate School. He was a pupil of Trucco and of Goldmark.

He has received the American Grand Prize of Rome and the awards of the Juilliard Publication and the Society for the Publication of American Music. He is a Fellow of the American Academy in Rome. He was a member of the faculty of Queens College, New York City, and the Hartt School of Music, Hartford, Connecticut, and at present is on the faculty of the Juilliard School of Music and the Manhattan School of Music.

Many of his works have been performed all over the United States and in Europe. Broadcasts have been given by CBS and NBC. His symphony "In Memoriam" was performed at the ·inauguration of the New York State Theodore Roosevelt Memorial. The opera "Lucrezia" was first produced in Munich, Germany. In 1938 he was commissioned by CBS to write a radio opera.

COMPOSITIONS

ORCHESTRAL WORKS

	DURATION	PUBLISHER	DATE
PRELUDE AND FUGUE FOR STRING ORCHESTRA	7 minutes	Manuscript for hire	1926
SUITE IN FOUR MOVEMENTS	15 "	Manuscript for hire	1931
APRIL NOCTURNE—from cantata "Springtime"	6 "	Manuscript for hire	1933
SYMPHONY IN MEMORIAM	30 "	Manuscript for hire	1935
CONCERTO FOR PIANO AND ORCHESTRA	25 "	Manuscript for hire	1935
CONCERTO FOR ORGAN AND ORCHESTRA		Manuscript	1937
BALLET—from opera "Casanova"	20 "	Manuscript for hire	1938
PRELUDE CHORALE AND FUGUE FOR ORCHESTRA	25 "	Manuscript for hire	1939
CONCERTO FOR TWO PIANOS AND ORCHESTRA	20 "	Manuscript for hire	1940
CONCERTO FOR VIOLIN AND ORCHESTRA	20 "	Elkan-Vogel piano and violin reduction for sale	1944
CONCERTO FOR TRUMPET AND ORCHESTRA	18 "	National Assn. Music Schools	1945

CHAMBER ORCHESTRA

	DURATION	PUBLISHER	DATE
LIFE'S SPAN—FOR VOICE AND STRING ORCHESTRA	6 minutes	G. Ricordi & Co.	1935
TRIPTYCH FOR VOICE AND STRING ORCHESTRA	12 "	Manuscript for hire	1937

VITTORIO GIANNINI *(Continued)*

CHORAL WORKS

	DURATION	PUBLISHER	DATE
STABAT MATER	2 hours	Manuscript	1919
soli, double chorus, orchestra			
SPRINGTIME	50 minutes	Manuscript	1933
soprano, tenor, chorus, orchestra		*for hire*	
REQUIEM	2¼ hours	Universal Edition,	1936
soli, chorus, orchestra		Vienna	
LAMENT FOR ADONA	10 minutes	G. Ricordi & Co.	1940
women's voices			
MISSA "ADESTE FIDELIS"	30 "	Manuscript	1943
men's voices, organ			

CHAMBER MUSIC

SONATA FOR VIOLIN AND PIANOFORTE	25 minutes	Manuscript	1926
MADRIGAL FOR VOCAL AND STRING			
QUARTET	12 "	G. Ricordi & Co.	1929
QUARTET FOR STRINGS	30 "	Juilliard Publication	1930
QUINTET FOR STRINGS AND PIANOFORTE	30 "	S.P.A.M.	1930
SONATA FOR PIANOFORTE	15 "	G. Ricordi & Co.	1934
TRIO FOR VIOLIN, VIOLONCELLO,			
PIANOFORTE	20 "	G. Ricordi & Co.	1934
QUINTET FOR FLUTE, OBOE, CLARINET,			
BASSOON AND HORN	15 "	Manuscript	1934
SONATA FOR VIOLIN AND PIANO—			
one movement	12 "	Manuscript	1940
SONATA FOR VIOLIN AND PIANO	18 "	Manuscript	1945

STAGE WORKS

LUCREZIA—opera in a prologue and 3 acts	3 hours	Drei Masken Verlag	1932
THE SCARLET LETTER—opera in 4 acts	2½ hours	Simrock & Co.	1935
FLORA—opera in 3 acts	2¼ "	Manuscript	1937
BEAUTY AND THE BEAST—radio opera	27 minutes	Manuscript	1938
		for hire	
BLENNERHASSET—radio opera	27 "	Manuscript	1939
		for hire	

FILM MUSIC

HIGH OVER THE BORDERS		N. Y. Zoological Society with U. S. and Canadian Govts.

MIRIAM GIDEON

Born in Greeley, Colorado, in 1906. She studied at Boston University. Her teachers in composition were Saminsky and Sessions. She is on the music faculty of Brooklyn College.

Her works have been performed by the I.S.C.M., the League of Composers and the London Symphony Orchestra. The Madrigals, a choral work, and the Lyric Piece for String Quartet were played at the 1946 American Music Festival over WNYC. Her Sonata for Flute and Piano was broadcast by the I.S.C.M. over WABF. The Canzona was premiered in New York and has been played on the National Association for American Composers and Conductors program. She is now completing a string quartet.

MIRIAM GIDEON (*Continued*)

COMPOSITIONS

ORCHESTRAL WORKS	DURATION	PUBLISHER	DATE
ALLEGRO AND ANDANTE	12 minutes	Manuscript	1940
LYRIC PIECE FOR STRING ORCHESTRA	10 "	Manuscript	1942

CHAMBER ORCHESTRA

EPIGRAMS	8 minutes	Manuscript	1941
10 instruments			

CHORAL WORKS

FOUR MADRIGALS	12 minutes	Manuscript	1943
mixed chorus a cappella			

CHAMBER MUSIC

LYRIC PIECE FOR STRING QUARTET	10 minutes	Manuscript	1942
SONATA FOR FLUTE AND PIANO	12 "	Manuscript	1943
HOUND OF HEAVEN	12 "	Manuscript	1945
baritone, oboe, string trio			
DANCES FOR TWO PIANOS		Manuscript	

HENRY FRANKLIN BELKNAP GILBERT

Born in Somerville, Massachusetts, in 1868 and died in Cambridge, Massachusetts, in 1928. He studied violin with Mollenhauer, harmony with Whiting and composition with MacDowell. In his early years he made his living by playing in small orchestras, and later he entered a business firm which sent him to Paris for a few years.

His great interest in folk music, particularly in Negro folk songs, strongly influenced his composition. He was a founder of the Wa-Wan Press and contributed articles to many magazines. His symphonic ballet "Dance in the Place Congo," based on Louisiana Creole Negro songs, was first written as an orchestral piece. He later made this into a ballet scenario and in 1918 it was performed at the Metropolitan Opera House. "Americanesque" for orchestra is based on minstrel tunes. He also wrote sketches for an operetta which he based on "Uncle Remus" tales by Joel Chandler Harris. The Boston Symphony gave the first performance of the "Comedy Overture on Negro Themes," and the Russian Symphony first presented "Salammbo's Invocation to Tanith." He was commissioned to write a work for the Litchfield County Festival, which he called "Negro Rhapsody."

COMPOSITIONS

ORCHESTRAL WORKS	PUBLISHER
SALAMMBO'S INVOCATION TO TANITH	
soprano, orchestra	
COMEDY OVERTURE ON NEGRO THEMES	H. W. Gray
THREE AMERICAN DANCES	
NEGRO RHAPSODY	H. W. Gray

HENRY FRANKLIN BELKNAP GILBERT (*Continued*)

ORCHESTRAL WORKS (*Continued*)	PUBLISHER
THE DANCE IN THE PLACE CONGO SYMPHONIC PRELUDE—from one-act opera "Phantasy in Delft"	H. W. Gray
SYMPHONIC PROLOGUE "RIDERS TO THE SEA"	G. Schirmer, Inc.
TWO EPISODES FOR ORCHESTRA LEGEND	Wa-Wan Press
NEGRO EPISODE	H. W. Gray

STAGE WORKS

THE DANCE IN THE PLACE CONGO—ballet

DON GILLIS

Born in Cameron, Missouri, in 1912. He studied theory and brass instruments with William Tracy at the Missouri Wesleyan College. His Master of Music degree was received at North Texas State Teachers College.

He taught theory and was Band Director at Texas Christian University and played and arranged music for WBAB (NBC affiliate) in Fort Worth, Texas. He joined the NBC staff as Music Production Director and is now working for Arturo Toscanini and Frank Black. His main interest is composition.

The Minneapolis Symphony, the Robin Hood Dell Orchestra and the NBC Symphony presented his Symphony No. 5 and Frank Black, Sigmund Romberg and Roy Shield have performed many of his works. NBC has broadcast his Short Overture, "Raven," "Cowtown Suite," Suite for Strings and "Night before Christmas." Mr. Gillis is preparing a sixth symphony, a piano concerto and a folk opera.

COMPOSITIONS

ORCHESTRAL WORKS	DURATION	PUBLISHER	DATE
SYMPHONIC POEM—The Raven	12 minutes	Manuscript	1937
WILLIE THE WOOLYWORM for children *narrator, orchestra*	12 "	Manuscript	1937
THOUGHTS PROVOKED ON BECOMING A PROSPECTIVE PAPA—suite	15 "	Manuscript	1939
THE PANHANDLE—suite	20 "	Manuscript	1940
PRAIRIE POEM	14 "	Manuscript	1941
SYMPHONY NO. 1—AN AMERICAN SYMPHONY	32 "	Manuscript	1941
SYMPHONY NO. 2—A SYMPHONY OF FAITH	29 "	Manuscript	1942
INTERMISSION—TEN MINUTES	10 "	Manuscript	1942
SYMPHONY NO. 3—A SYMPHONY FOR FREE MEN	26 "	Manuscript	1943
COWTOWN—suite	22 "	Manuscript	1943
SYMPHONY NO. 4	27 "	Manuscript	1944
SYMPHONY NO. 5	30 "	Manuscript	1945
TO AN UNKNOWN SOLDIER	12 "	Manuscript	1945
SHORT OVERTURE TO AN UNWRITTEN OPERA	4 "	Boosey & Hawkes	1945

DON GILLIS *(Continued)*

ORCHESTRAL WORKS *(Continued)*	DURATION	PUBLISHER	DATE
THE ALAMO—symphonic poem	14 minutes	Manuscript	1945
PERPETUAL EMOTION	2¾ "	Boosey & Hawkes	1946

CHAMBER ORCHESTRA

SEVEN SKETCHES FOR STRINGS	12 minutes	Boosey & Hawkes	1944

CHORAL WORKS

THE CRUCIFIXION—cantata for radio	28 minutes	Manuscript	1940

CHAMBER MUSIC

FIVE STRING QUARTETS	20 minutes	Manuscript	1937–44
PIANO QUINTET NO. 1	22 "	Manuscript	1938
piano, string quartet			
THREE QUINTETS FOR WOODWIND	10 "	Manuscript	1939
flute, oboe, horn, clarinet,			
bassoon			
SONATINA FOR TRUMPET QUARTET		Manuscript	1943

AURELIO GIORNI

Born in Perugia, Italy, 1895, and died in Massachusetts in 1938. He studied piano at the St. Cecilia Academy in Rome and graduated with high honors at the age of fifteen. In Berlin he continued his study of the piano with Busoni, coached with Lhevinne, Gabrilowitsch, and Da Motta, and also studied composition with Humperdinck.

He came to the United States in 1914 after touring as pianist in all the principal European cities. Joining the Elshuco Trio in 1919, he toured with it as pianist throughout the United States. He taught at the Institute of Musical Art, at the New York College of Music, the Philadelphia Conservatory, the Hartford School of Music and at the Springfield Conservatory. He was instructor in composition and counterpoint at Smith College. He received the Society for the Publication of American Music Award.

His orchestral works have been played frequently and have also been broadcast over WOR and WEAF.

COMPOSITIONS

ORCHESTRAL WORKS	DURATION	PUBLISHER	DATE
ORLANDO FURIOSO—symphonic poem	18 minutes	Manuscript	1926
MINUET AND ALLEGRO—early romantic style	15 "	Manuscript	1928
SINFONIA CONCERTANTE	30 "	Manuscript	1931
piano			
SYMPHONY IN D	29 "	Manuscript	1936

CHAMBER ORCHESTRA

MINUET AND ALLEGRO	15 minutes	Manuscript	1930
11 instruments			
PASSACAGLIA FOR STRINGS—4 parts	7 "	Manuscript	
INTERMEZZO FOR CHAMBER ORCHESTRA	6 "	Manuscript	1932
11 instruments			

CHORAL WORKS	DURATION	PUBLISHER	DATE
SIX MODAL QUATRAINS	8 minutes	Manuscript	1928
women's voices, a cappella		*for hire*	
ZODIAC TOWN	15 "	Manuscript	1929
mixed voices, a cappella		*for hire*	
THE PHANTOM LEAVES	6 "	Manuscript	1929
mixed voices, a cappella			
TWO FOUR-PART SONGS	10 "	Manuscript	1936
		for hire	

CHAMBER MUSIC			
SONATA FOR CELLO (OR VIOLA) AND			
PIANO	24 minutes	Manuscript	1924
SONATA FOR VIOLIN AND PIANO	26 "	Manuscript	1924
PIANO QUARTET	34 "	Manuscript	1926
piano, strings			
PIANO QUINTET	32 "	Manuscript	1927
piano, strings			
SONATA FOR FLUTE AND PIANO	19 "	Manuscript	1932
SONATA FOR CLARINET AND PIANO	21 "	Manuscript	1933
PIANO TRIO	30 "	Manuscript	1934
STRING QUARTET	29 "	Manuscript	1936

RICHARD FRANKO GOLDMAN

Born in New York City in 1910. He received his Bachelor of Arts degree at Columbia University, where he earned a special fellowship in fine arts and became a member of Phi Beta Kappa. He studied piano with Leopold and Adler and composition with Floridia.

He has been active as a composer, conductor, arranger, musicologist and lecturer. He is the author of *The Band's Music* (1938) a standard reference work on band repertory, and is co-author of *Landmarks of Early American Music*. His most recent book, *The Concert Band* (1946), is published by Rinehart and Co. in a series entitled "The Field of Music." His articles on music have appeared in the League of Composers' magazine, *Modern Music,* and elsewhere. He is Associate Conductor of the Goldman Band and is a leading authority on band music. He is a member of the American Bandmasters' Association, the American Musicological Society, is on the Board of Directors of the League of Composers and was formerly on the Board of Governors of the American Composers Alliance. He served as consultant to the Music Division of the Pan American Union in 1941 and to the Joint Army-Navy Committee on Welfare and Recreation from 1941 to 1943. He enlisted in the U. S. Army in 1943 and served during World War II with the Office of Strategic Services.

"The Lee Rigg," "Curtain-Raiser and Country Dance," Divertimento for Flute and Piano and other works have been broadcast over CBS, NBC and other national networks many times. His band works have been performed by all of the important bands. Performances of his other works have been given by the National Symphony, the League of Composers and by many prominent soloists.

RICHARD FRANKO GOLDMAN (*Continued*)

COMPOSITIONS

ORCHESTRAL WORKS	DURATION	PUBLISHER	DATE
THE LEE RIGG	3½ minutes	Mercury Music Corp. *score and parts for sale*	1942
LE BOBINO—suite	11 "	Manuscript	1942

CHAMBER ORCHESTRA			
HYMN FOR BRASS CHOIR *16 instruments*	3 minutes	New Music *parts for hire*	1939

BAND MUSIC			
A SENTIMENTAL JOURNEY	9 minutes	Mills Music Inc.	1941
A CURTAIN-RAISER AND COUNTRY DANCE	4½ "	E. B. Marks	1941

CHORAL WORKS			
CARE-CHARMING SLEEP—madrigal *mixed chorus a cappella*	3 minutes	Mills Music Inc.	1944

CHAMBER MUSIC			
TWO SONGS (Stevenson) *soprano, string trio*	6 minutes	Manuscript	1933
DIVERTIMENTO FOR FLUTE AND PIANO	7 "	Axelrod Inc.	1937
SONATINA FOR PIANO	12 "	Mercury Music Corp.	1942
THREE DUETS FOR CLARINETS	6 "	Mills Music Inc.	1944

RUBIN GOLDMARK

Born in New York City in 1872 and died in 1936. He attended the College of the City of New York, the University of Vienna and also the Vienna Conservatory, where he studied piano and theory with Door and the Fuchs brothers. On his return to New York he studied piano with Joseffy and composition with Dvorák. He later moved to Colorado on account of his health and there he became Director of the Colorado College Conservatory. In 1902 he returned to New York City, where he taught and lectured, and in 1924 he became Director of the Composition Department of the Juilliard Graduate School.

His compositions have been played throughout the United States, and the "Requiem" (suggested by Lincoln's Gettysburg Address) has had frequent performances. In addition to the works written for orchestra he has written many works for chamber music, choruses and songs.

COMPOSITIONS (List incomplete)

ORCHESTRAL WORKS	PUBLISHER	DATE
SAMSON—tone poem	G. Schirmer, Inc.	
NEGRO RHAPSODY	Associated Music Publishers	
HIAWATHA OVERTURE		
CALL OF THE PLAINS	Carl Fischer, Inc.	
REQUIEM	G. Schirmer, Inc.	1919

EUGENE GOOSSENS

Born in London in 1893. He studied at the Bruges Conservatory, the Liverpool College of Music and the Royal College of Music in London, where Stanford was his teacher in composition.

He played the violin in the Queens Hall Orchestra from 1911–1915, and then became an assistant conductor, which post he held until 1920. In 1921 he gave a series of six concerts with his own orchestra, and later he conducted the British National Opera Company, the Carl Rosa Company, and many symphonic orchestras, also the Russian Ballet and opera at Covent Garden. He came to the United States in 1923 to become Conductor of the newly founded Rochester Philharmonic Orchestra. He was commissioned by the Elizabeth Sprague Coolidge Foundation to write the Sextet for Strings, which was premiered in 1923 at the Berkshire Festival. In 1931 he became the Conductor of the Cincinnati Symphony Orchestra and the Cincinnati May Festival. He has also appeared as guest conductor with every major orchestra in America, and he has occasionally returned to conduct in England. Among his many works are two operas to librettos by Arnold Bennett: "Judith," written in 1925, had its first American performance in concert form in Cincinnati in 1937; and "Don Juan de Mañara" was first presented at Covent Garden, London, in 1937. One of his most recent works is the Second Symphony.

At present he is working on a large composition for chorus, soloists, ballet and orchestra based on the Apocalypse. He is a Fellow and Associate of the Royal College of Music, medallist of the Worshipful Company of Musicians, and a Chevalier of the Legion of Honor of France.

COMPOSITIONS WRITTEN IN AMERICA

ORCHESTRAL WORKS	DURATION	PUBLISHER	DATE
OBOE CONCERTO IN ONE MOVEMENT		Curwen *for hire*	1927
CONCERTINO FOR STRING ORCHESTRA OR STRING OCTET		J. & W. Chester	1928
THREE PICTURES FOR FLUTE AND STRING ORCHESTRA		J. & W. Chester *for hire*	
FANFARE FOR ANY OCCASION		Manuscript	1930
SYMPHONY NO. 1	38 minutes	Carl Fischer, Inc. *parts for hire*	1940
SYMPHONY NO. 2	40 "	Carl Fischer, Inc. *for hire*	1944
FANTASIE CONCERTO FOR PIANO AND ORCHESTRA		J. & W. Chester	

CHAMBER ORCHESTRA

THREE GREEK DANCES *small orchestra*		Curwen	1927

CHAMBER MUSIC

SEXTET FOR STRINGS, OPUS 35	17 minutes	J. & W. Chester	1923
FANTASY FOR 9 WIND INSTRUMENTS		Curwen	1923
PASTORAL AND ARLEGANAISE *flute, oboe, or violin and piano*	6 "	Curwen	1924
SONATA NO. 2 FOR VIOLIN AND PIANO	25 "	J. & W. Chester	1930

EUGENE GOOSSENS (*Continued*)

CHAMBER MUSIC (*Continued*)	PUBLISHER	DATE
SECOND STRING QUARTET	Boosey & Hawkes	
QUINTET FOR PIANO AND STRINGS	J. & W. Chester	

STAGE WORKS		
JUDITH—opera	J. & W. Chester	1925
DON JUAN DE MAÑARA—opera in 4 acts	J. & W. Chester	1935

MORTON GOULD

Born in Richmond Hill, New York, in 1913. He studied piano under Abby Whiteside and harmony and counterpoint under Jones of New York University. At the age of six he had his first composition published.

For a few years he gave concerts as well as appearing in theater and vaudeville presentations and was for a time on the Radio City Music Hall staff. Later he joined the National Broadcasting Company for orchestra, piano-solo and two-piano work. He was engaged by WOR to conduct and arrange his own programs with a large orchestra over the WOR-Mutual Network. He was commissioned by Eric Leinsdorf to write a Concerto for Orchestra for the Cleveland Symphony Orchestra. The Symphony No. 2—On Marching Tunes was commissioned by the Y.M.C.A. in celebration of its centennial and was given its first performance by the New York Philharmonic Symphony. He has also been commissioned by Paul Whiteman and by the Blue Network. A recent commission was given to him by the Ballet Russe for a work to be presented soon. He recently appeared with his orchestra in a United Artists picture, and at the present time, he is conductor of an orchestra on a coast-to-coast radio program over CBS.

His compositions have been performed by the leading symphony orchestras, and the composer has also appeared as guest conductor with many of the orchestras and musical organizations in programs of his own works. The "Lincoln Legend" was first played by Toscanini with the NBC Symphony Orchestra over a nation- and world-wide broadcast in 1942. He is at present writing a musical show for George Abbott.

COMPOSITIONS

ORCHESTRAL WORKS	DURATION		PUBLISHER	DATE
CHORALE AND FUGUE IN JAZZ 2 *pianos, orchestra*	14 minutes		Carl Fischer, Inc.	1933
SYMPHONY No. 1	30	"	Mills Music, Inc.	1936
SWING SYMPHONIETTA	10	"	Mills Music, Inc.	1936
SPIRITUALS	17	"	Mills Music, Inc. *for sale*	1941
CONCERTO FOR ORCHESTRA	18	"	Mills Music, Inc. *for hire*	1944
SYMPHONY No. 2	32	"	Mills Music, Inc. *for hire*	1944

MORTON GOULD (*Continued*)

ORCHESTRAL WORKS (*Continued*)	DURATION		PUBLISHER	DATE
CONCERTO FOR VIOLA AND ORCHESTRA	27 minutes		Mills Music, Inc.	1944
			for hire	
HARVEST	12	"	Mills Music, Inc.	1945
SYMPHONY No. 3	30	"	Chappell	
MINSTREL SHOW	8	"	Chappell	

CHAMBER ORCHESTRA

CANTATA	1 hour	Manuscript	1931
chorus, 24 instruments			
PIANO CONCERTO	20 minutes	Manuscript	1937
24 instruments			

CHORAL WORKS

OF TIME AND THE RIVER			
(Thomas Wolfe)	27 minutes	Chappell	
a cappella			

CHAMBER MUSIC

PIANO SONATA No. 1	20 minutes	Manuscript	1930
PIANO SONATA No. 2	20	"	Manuscript	1933
PIANO SONATA No. 3	11	"	Manuscript	1936
VIOLIN SUITE	20	"	Mills Music, Inc.	1945

STAGE WORKS

MUSIC FOR RADIO		Mills Music, Inc.	1937
BILLION DOLLAR BABY—musical comedy	2 hours	Mills Music, Inc.	1945

FILM MUSIC

	STUDIO		
RING OF STEEL	O.E.M.		1941
DELIGHTFULLY DANGEROUS	United Artists		1945
SAN FRANCISCO CONFERENCE	O.W.I.		1946

PERCY ALDRIDGE GRAINGER

Born in Melbourne, Australia, in 1882. He first studied music with his mother and later with Pabst at Melbourne and in Germany with Kwast and Busoni. In 1900 he went to London and gave recitals and played with the large orchestras. He was inspired by Grieg's interest in national music and he threw himself heartily into the movement for recovering English folk songs, in which he has retained a deep interest. While touring as a pianist he studied the folk music of many countries and felt that his research in native music and his associations with folk singers were the most fruitful influences in his creative career. He has collected over five hundred phonograph records of folk music from European, African, Australian and New Zealandic sources. In 1915 he came to America for his first recital and in 1917 enlisted in the army as a bandsman, playing the oboe and saxophone. After a year he became instructor at the Army Music School. For many years he was Professor of Music and head of the Department of Music at New York University.

His "English Dance" for orchestra was first performed in London in 1911. The "Marching Song of Democracy" was given at the Worcester

PERCY ALDRIDGE GRAINGER *(Continued)*

Festival in 1917 and the "Tribute to Foster" was given at the Worcester Festival in 1930. Many of his choral works and chamber-music compositions have been performed frequently in Europe, Australasia and America; his arrangements of folk tunes have been recorded by Columbia, Victor, H.M.V. and Decca.

COMPOSITIONS

ORCHESTRAL WORKS	DURATION	PUBLISHER	DATE
IN A NUTSHELL—suite	14 minutes	G. Schirmer, Inc.	1916
piano, orchestra			
THE WARRIORS—music to an imaginary ballet	18 "	B. Schott's Söhne	1916
3 pianos, orchestra			
ENGLISH DANCE	10 "	G. Schirmer, Inc.	
organ, orchestra			
TO A NORDIC PRINCESS	9 "	G. Schirmer, Inc.	1928
organ, orchestra			
YE BANKS AND BRAES O' BONNIE DOON	2½ "	Schott & Co.	1932
for school or amateur orchestra			
HARVEST HYMN	3½ "	Schott & Co.	1933
for school orchestra			
DANISH FOLKSONG SUITE	17 "	G. Schirmer, Inc.	1937

CHAMBER ORCHESTRA

THE NIGHTINGALE AND THE TWO SISTERS	4½ minutes	G. Schirmer, Inc.	1931
4 to 18 instruments			
YE BANKS AND BRAES	2½ "	Schott & Co.	1932
5 to 10 instruments			
HARVEST HYMN	3½ "	Schott & Co.	1933
3 to 20 instruments			

CHORAL WORKS

MARCHING SONG OF DEMOCRACY	10 minutes	Universal Edition	1917
mixed chorus, organ, orchestra			
TRIBUTE TO FOSTER	11 "	G. Schirmer, Inc.	
5 solo voices, mixed chorus, solo piano, musical glasses, orchestra			
KIPLING SETTINGS (16 numbers)	15 "	Schott & Co.	
mixed chorus, a cappella and with chamber orchestra			
LOVE VERSES FROM "THE SONG OF SOLOMON"	6½ "	G. Schirmer, Inc.	1931
mezzo soprano and tenor solos, chamber orchestra			

CHAMBER MUSIC

HILL-SONG NO. 1	13 minutes	Universal Edition	1923
22 instruments			
SHALLOW BROWN	6 "	G. Schirmer, Inc.	1924
2 voices, 10 or more instruments			
HILL-SONG NO. 2	7 "	Manuscript	1929
15 instruments			
SPOON RIVER	5 "	G. Schirmer, Inc.	1930
3 or more instruments			
EXAMPLE OF "FREE MUSIC" FOR STRING QUARTET	1¾ "	Manuscript	1936

BAND MUSIC

CHILDREN'S MARCH	7 minutes	G. Schirmer, Inc.	1918
piano, military band			

PARKS GRANT
(William P. Grant)

Born in Cleveland, Ohio, in 1910. He showed great interest in music at an early age and when he was fourteen he began to study composition and harmony under Davidson in Columbus, and also the organ under Mayer of Capital University. He received a diploma in theory in 1930 and a Bachelor of Music degree (with honors) in 1932 from Capital University; in 1933 he received his Master of Arts degree from Ohio State University. He studied at the Eastman School of Music with Elwell.

For three years he taught music in the public schools and wrote articles on music for leading musical magazines. He was on the faculty of the Music Department of John Tarleton Agricultural College in Texas. At present he is head of the Music Department at Northeast Junior College at Louisiana State University. In the spring of 1945 he founded the Spring Music Festival at Northeast Junior College. He won prizes and awards from the National Federation of Music Clubs, the Texas Manuscript Society (3 times), the Texas Federation of Women's Clubs and the National Composer's Congress. His special interest is writing short compositions for chamber-music combinations.

His compositions, which have been performed in many parts of the United States, include the Concert Overture, "Introspective Poem," Horn Concerto, "Night Poems," "Dream of the Ballet-Master" and other works. The Horn Concerto was broadcast over the Blue network. In preparation are a "Poem for Two Violins, Two Violas, and Cello," a Double-Bass Concerto, a "Poem for String Orchestra" and the last movement of the Symphony No. 2.

COMPOSITIONS

ORCHESTRAL WORKS	DURATION	PUBLISHER	DATE
Poème Élégiaque	15 minutes	Manuscript	1928
Minuet in D	3 "	Manuscript	1928
Overture to Shakespeare's "Macbeth"	12 "	Manuscript	1930
Symphony in D minor	45 "	Manuscript	1930–38
Symphonic Fantasia	15 "	Manuscript	1931
The Masque of the Red Death	15 "	Manuscript	1931–40
Horn Concerto	20 "	Manuscript	1940
Symphony No. 2 in A minor		Manuscript	1941
Clarinet Concerto	25 "	Manuscript	1943–45
Poem for String Orchestra		Manuscript	1945

CHORAL WORKS			
Song of the Monks (from Schiller's "William Tell") *men's voices, a cappella*	2 minutes	Manuscript	1931
Benedictus *men's voices, a cappella*	4 "	Manuscript	1933

CHAMBER MUSIC			
A Shropshire Lad—song cycle	12 minutes	Manuscript	1938–39
Night Poem, Nos. 1, 2, 3 *string quartet*	6–8 "	Manuscript	1940–42
Piano Sonata	15 "	Manuscript	1940
Poem for Horn and Organ	7 "	Manuscript	1945

PARKS GRANT (*Continued*)

STAGE WORKS	DURATION	PUBLISHER	DATE
DREAM OF THE BALLET-MASTER—ballet *string quartet, piano*	25 minutes	Manuscript	1934

JOHNNY GREEN

Born in New York City in 1908. He was educated at Horace Mann School and New York Military Academy and graduated from Harvard University, where he specialized in economics. He studied with Wasserman, Hilsberg and Spalding.

He was a conductor and musical director of commercial radio programs and made a series of special recordings with Fred Astaire. He is at present under contract to M.G.M., where he is in charge of composing and directing many film scores. He has made adaptations for other composers of film music. He has written many songs and music for operettas.

His symphonic works have been performed by some of the orchestras in England and the United States. Decca has recently recorded a new album of his songs. His music for films is listed here.

COMPOSITIONS

FILM MUSIC	STUDIO	DATE
BROADWAY RHYTHM	M.G.M.	1943
BATHING BEAUTY	M.G.M.	1943–44
WEEK END AT THE WALDORF	M.G.M.	1945
THE SAILOR TAKES A WIFE	M.G.M.	1945
EASY TO WED	M.G.M.	1945
FIESTA	M.G.M.	1945–46

RAY GREEN

Born in Cavendish, Missouri, in 1909. He studied theory, composition, piano and conducting with Bloch, Elkus, Milhaud and Monteux. He made a special study of Gregorian chant under Silva. He won a scholarship in composition at the San Francisco Conservatory of Music, a Carnegie Foundation Scholarship and the University of California George Ladd Paris Prize. He lived abroad from 1935 to 1937.

He has catalogued and prepared an index for the collection of musical instruments of the San Francisco Memorial M. H. de Young Museum. He has taught piano, theory and composition and has directed the Ray Green Madrigal Group. He was an assistant in the Music Department of the University of California and head of the Composition Department at the San Francisco Conservatory of Music. He was on the Advisory Board of the New Music Society. In 1938 he was on the staff of Bennington College as composer for "American Document," with choreography by Martha Graham. He was Director of the Federal Chorus of San Francisco in 1939.

RAY GREEN (*Continued*)

He was in the armed forces from 1943 to 1945 and conducted and directed a choral group which made broadcasts for the Bureau of Inter-American Affairs for re-broadcast to Latin American countries. In 1945 he was engaged as an instructor at the University of Denver. He was commissioned to write music for the official opening of the New York World's Fair in 1938. At present he is Chief of the Music Division of the Recreation and Entertainment Services of the Veterans Administration.

His compositions have been performed in New York City, Berkeley, San Francisco, Denver and other cities and have been broadcast over NBC and also local networks throughout the country, as well as on transcontinental hook-ups. "Sea Calm" was issued by the New Music Society Quarterly Recordings. At present he is completing a work for piano and orchestra and "Opus Two" for orchestra.

COMPOSITIONS

ORCHESTRAL WORKS	DURATION	PUBLISHER	DATE
THE BIRDS (Aristophanes)		Manuscript	1934
CONCERTINO FOR PIANO AND ORCHESTRA		Manuscript	1937
PRELUDE AND FUGUE		Manuscript	1937
JIG TUNE FOR ORCHESTRA	5 minutes	Manuscript	1944
OPUS ONE—a symphony in four movements	15 "	Manuscript	1945
PRAELUDIUM: THEME AND VARIATIONS FOR ORCHESTRA	16 "	Manuscript	1946
NEW SET—concertante viola, orchestra	15 "	Manuscript	1946

CHAMBER ORCHESTRA			
OVERTURE, MARCH AND FINALE (Iphigenia in Tauris)	10 minutes	Manuscript	1935
THREE INVENTORIES OF CASEY JONES piano, orchestra	15 "	Manuscript	1939

CHORAL WORKS			
TWO MADRIGALS (Walt Whitman)		Manuscript	1933
TWO CHORAL WORKS—based on text from 1300		Manuscript	1933
SEA CALM use of quarter tones men's voices	7 minutes	New Music	1934
HEY NONNY NO—madrigal mixed chorus, a cappella	6 "	New Music	1934
LULLAY MYN LYKING—carol of Nativity mixed chorus	12 "	Axelrod	1939

CHAMBER MUSIC			
SUITE FOR VIOLIN AND PIANO three movements		Manuscript	1929
SUITE FOR VIOLA AND PIANO five movements		Manuscript	1929
SOME PIECES FOR STRING QUARTET		Manuscript	1932
FIVE EPIGRAMMATIC ROMANCES FOR STRING QUARTET		Manuscript	1933
STRING QUARTET		Manuscript	1933
WIND QUINTET		Manuscript	1933
CHAMBER QUARTET piano, bassoon, clarinet, viola		Manuscript	1937
HYMN TUNES FOR STRING QUARTET	15 minutes	Manuscript	1944

RAY GREEN (*Continued*)

STAGE WORKS	DURATION	PUBLISHER	DATE
PERRONIK THE FOOL—puppet play in two scenes	20 minutes	Manuscript	1930
ELECTRA—incidental music *percussion and flutes*	4 "	Manuscript	1937
UNION WIVES—comedy satire based on Lysistrata theme	15 "	Manuscript	1939

CHARLES TOMLINSON GRIFFES

Born in Elmira, New York, in 1884, and died in 1920. While in high school he decided to be a musician and first studied in Berlin to be a concert pianist, but Humperdinck persuaded him to be a composer. In his early student years he was influenced by his German teachers, Rüfer and Humperdinck. In a later period of study he became more interested in the French and Russian schools, and as he began to compose more, his works showed a very modern trend.

His interest in the Orient was shown first in some of his songs. He was introduced to the Javanese music through Eva Gauthier, who encouraged him to use many Javanese melodies; she first presented many of his songs. He was interested in drawing and etching and also painted landscapes in watercolor.

On his return to America in 1908, he taught at the Hackley School in Tarrytown, where he continued to teach until he died. In 1916 he became associated with Adolph Bolm's Ballet Intime and was commissioned to write a work for it which was called "Sho-Jo," a work based on Japanese mime-play. The ballet, "The Kairn of Koridwen," was presented at the Neighborhood Playhouse in 1917, and in 1922 he was commissioned to write "Salut au Monde" (Whitman text), which was also presented by the Neighborhood Playhouse. The American Music Guild gave the first performance of the Piano Sonata in 1923. His list of works include many piano pieces and songs.

COMPOSITIONS

ORCHESTRAL WORKS

	PUBLISHER
THE LAKE AT EVENING	
THE PLEASURE DOME OF KUBLA KHAN— tone poem	G. Schirmer, Inc.
POEM FOR FLUTE AND ORCHESTRA	G. Schirmer, Inc.
FIVE OLD CHINESE AND JAPANESE SONGS *voice, orchestra*	G. Schirmer, Inc.
THREE POEMS OF FIONA MCLEOD, OPUS 11	G. Schirmer, Inc.
BACCHANALE FOR ORCHESTRA	G. Schirmer, Inc.
CLOUDS	G. Schirmer, Inc.
NOCTURNE FOR ORCHESTRA	G. Schirmer, Inc.
THE WHITE PEACOCK	G. Schirmer, Inc.
THE LAMENT OF IAN THE PROUD *voice, orchestra*	

CHARLES TOMLINSON GRIFFES (*Continued*)

CHAMBER MUSIC

THREE TONE PICTURES—suite for piano
PIANO SONATA
ROMAN SKETCHES—piano suite
TWO INDIAN SKETCHES
  string quartet

STAGE WORKS

THE KAIRN OF KORIDWEN—dance
  drama in 2 acts
SALUT AU MONDE (Whitman text)
  pageant with music
  chorus and "choral speech"
THE WHITE PEACOCK—ballet
SHO-JO—music for a Japanese mime-
  play

ELLIOT GRIFFIS

Born in Boston, Massachusetts, in 1893. He studied at Ithaca College, Yale and the New England Conservatory of Music, under Parker, Chadwick, Mason and Pattison. He was awarded a Juilliard Scholarship and a Pulitzer Prize in 1931.

In his early years he worked in a factory and with a railroad company. He studied painting and produced a large number of canvases. He taught in Grinnell College, at the Brooklyn Settlement School, the St. Louis Institute of Music and in New York City privately. In 1942–43 he was Director of the Westchester Conservatory of Music in White Plains. For two years he lived in Vienna. He has appeared frequently in recitals and over the radio. He has written many essays and several volumes of verse. Recently he has written a large number of sketches for motion-picture music and a great many songs.

"A Persian Fable" was presented at the Festival of American Music over WNYC. "Montevallo" was performed at Ithaca. Other works for orchestra and chamber music have been performed in Philadelphia, New York and other cities. WNYC broadcast the Sonata for Violin and Piano.

COMPOSITIONS

ORCHESTRAL WORKS	DURATION	PUBLISHER	DATE
A PERSIAN FABLE—ballade *English horn solo, orchestra*	5 minutes	Fleisher Music Collection *parts for hire*	1925
COLOSSUS—symphonic poem	17 "	Fleisher Music Collection *parts for hire*	1928
FIRST SYMPHONY	30 "	Manuscript	1932
PRAYERS TO THE SUN AND THE WIND— two songs for soprano and orchestra	8 "	Manuscript	1939
FANTASTIC PURSUIT—symphony			

ELLIOT GRIFFIS (*Continued*)

ORCHESTRAL WORKS (*Continued*)	DURATION	PUBLISHER	DATE
for string orchestra	22 minutes	Fleisher Collection *parts for hire*	1941
YON GREEN MOUNTAIN—suite	18 "	Manuscript	1943

CHAMBER ORCHESTRA

STRING VARIATIONS	12 minutes	Manuscript	1924
MONTEVALLO—concerto grosso *organ, piano and strings*			

CHAMBER MUSIC

STRING QUARTET NO. 1	16 minutes	Manuscript	1926
STRING QUARTET NO. 2	29 "	Manuscript	1930
SONATA FOR VIOLIN AND PIANO	25 "	The Composers Press, Inc.	1931
STRING QUARTET NO. 3	26 "	Manuscript	1937
TO THE SUN—symphonic fragment *violin, cello, piano*	6 "	Manuscript	1940
SUITE FOR TRIO *violin, cello, piano*	16 "	Oliver Ditson Co. *for hire*	1941
THE AZTEC FLUTE *flute, violin, cello, piano*	5½ "	Manuscript	1942
VARIATIONS FOR VIOLIN AND VIOLA	6 "	Manuscript	1946

STAGE WORKS

THE BLUE SCARAB—operetta	80 minutes	Manuscript	1934

FERDE GROFÉ

Born in New York City in 1892. He studied piano, violin and harmony with his mother and viola with his grandfather. He was violist in the Los Angeles Symphony Orchestra for ten years and has been pianist and violinist with theater and dance orchestras. In 1920 he became pianist and arranger for the Paul Whiteman jazz orchestra. He was also professional manager of the Remick Music Company. He continued his studies in orchestration with Pietro Floridia and became an arranger of "symphonic jazz." In 1924 he made the famous arrangement of the Gershwin "Rhapsody in Blue." For four years he was head orchestrator and librarian for the Whiteman orchestra. He made concert arrangements for Columbia and Victor. From 1939 to 1943 he was on the faculty of the Juilliard Summer School, where he taught composition and orchestration. He has been conductor for many of the leading radio shows, has been guest conductor of symphony orchestras and has participated in national educational projects for music. He received the Academy Award for the musical score of "Minstrel Man." He has written musical scores for Hollywood productions and has incorporated some of the music from his suites in them. The "Grand Canyon Suite" is being used by Walt Disney in a new feature-length cartoon.

FERDE GROFÉ (*Continued*)

His orchestral suites have been performed by major orchestras in all parts of the country and the CBS, NBC and standard symphony orchestras have broadcast all of them. They have also been played on many of the leading radio programs. "The Grand Canyon Suite" was premiered in 1931 by Paul Whiteman. His works have been recorded by Bluebird, Capitol, Decca, Columbia and Victor recordings and also in England. He is, at present, completing a "California Suite."

COMPOSITIONS

ORCHESTRAL WORKS	DURATION	PUBLISHER	DATE
MISSISSIPPI SUITE	12 minutes	Manuscript *for hire*	1925
GRAND CANYON SUITE *1st violin cadenza*	34 "	Robbins Music Co. *for hire*	1932
TABLOID SUITE	20 "	Manuscript	1933
HOLLYWOOD SUITE	35 "	Manuscript	1935
AVIATION SUITE	20 "	Manuscript	1945
CHORAL WORKS			
UNCLE SAM STANDS UP *mixed chorus, orchestra or band*	6 minutes	Manuscript	1943
CHAMBER MUSIC			
TABLE D'HOTE *flute, violin, viola*	20 minutes	Manuscript	1945

LOUIS GRUENBERG

Born in Russia in 1884. He came to America when he was a year old. He received his early education in the public schools of New York. His first piano teacher was Margulies. In 1903 he went to Berlin to become the pupil of Busoni in both composition and piano. He also studied as a master pupil at the Vienna Conservatory.

After his début with the Berlin Philharmonic Orchestra, he toured all over Europe as a pianist; he gave up concertizing, however, in order to devote himself to composition. He has taught piano and composition, lectured on music, and, for several years, was head of the Department of Composition at the Chicago College of Music. During an early period of his composing, he gave great study to the subject of jazz as he felt it had a definite place in the field of classic composition. His "Jazz Suite for Orchestra," "Daniel Jazz," "Jazzettes," "Jazz Berries" and "Jazz Epigrams" were written at this time. He helped to organize the League of Composers and was an active member for many years. He was also President of the United States Section of the I.S.C.M. and a member of the I.S.C.M. European jury.

"The Hill of Dreams," a symphonic poem, won the Flagler Prize in 1910 and was performed by the New York Symphony Orchestra. He won prizes

LOUIS GRUENBERG (*Continued*)

also for a symphonic work (Symphony No. 1) from the Victor Company and one for the Quintet from the Lake Placid Club. The Juilliard Foundation Award for its annual publication of an American work was given to "Enchanted Isle," which was played by the Boston Symphony Orchestra at the Worcester Festival and by the orchestras of Chicago, New York, Baltimore, Los Angeles and Washington. "Jack and the Beanstalk," an opera commissioned by the Juilliard School, has had repeated performances in several cities since it was first presented in New York. "Daniel Jazz" was chosen to represent American music at the Venice Festival of the I.S.C.M. The opera "Emperor Jones" was presented frequently at the Metropolitan Opera House in 1932 and 1933 and has also been played in Chicago, Los Angeles, San Francisco and Boston. The David Bispham Medal was awarded to him for this work. Excerpts from the opera have been recorded by Victor. In 1937, the Columbia Broadcasting System commissioned him to write "Green Mansions," a one-act opera for radio. In 1944 he was commissioned by Heifetz to write a Violin Concerto, which has been played with the Philadelphia Orchestra and has been broadcast. All of his major works have had frequent performances in Europe and in America. At present he is completing several orchestral works.

COMPOSITIONS

ORCHESTRAL WORKS	DURATION	PUBLISHER	DATE
VAGABONDIA	20 minutes	Manuscript	1920
JAZZ-SUITE	18 "	Cos Cob Press	1925
SYMPHONY No. 1	45 "	Universal Edition	1926
ENCHANTED ISLE	16 "	C. C. Birchard & Co.	1927
NINE MOODS	11 "	Cos Cob Press	1929
SERENADE TO A BEAUTEOUS LADY	10 "	Manuscript	1939
FOUR SYMPHONIES	25–38 " ea.	Manuscript	1940–46
SECOND PIANO CONCERTO	30 "	Manuscript	1942
VIOLIN CONCERTO	38 "	Manuscript	1944
MUSIC TO AN IMAGINARY BALLET	25 "	Manuscript	1944
AMERICANA SUITE	25 "	Manuscript	1945
DANCE RHAPSODY	13 "	Manuscript	1945
violin, orchestra			
MUSIC TO AN IMAGINARY LEGEND	25 "	Manuscript	1946

CHAMBER ORCHESTRA			
DANIEL JAZZ	16 minutes	Universal Edition	1923
tenor, 8 instruments			
CREATION	20 "	Universal Edition	1924
baritone, 8 instruments			

CHAMBER MUSIC			
SECOND VIOLIN· SONATA	20 minutes	Universal Edition	1919
SUITE FOR VIOLIN AND PIANO (II)	12 "	Universal Edition	1920
INDISCRETIONS	6 "	Universal Edition	1922
string quartet			
FIRST QUINTET FOR PIANO AND STRINGS	20 "	Manuscript	1929
DIVERSATIONS	8 "	Cos Cob Press	1930
string quartet			
JAZZETTES	10 "	Manuscript	
SECOND QUINTET FOR PIANO AND STRINGS		Manuscript	1937
QUARTET FOR STRINGS		Manuscript	1937
SECOND STRING QUARTET		Manuscript	1941

LOUIS GRUENBERG (*Continued*)

STAGE WORKS	DURATION	PUBLISHER	DATE
DUMB WIFE (Anatole France)	1½ hours	Manuscript	1921
JACK AND THE BEANSTALK (John Erskine)	1½ "	Juilliard School Publication	1930
EMPEROR JONES (Eugene O'Neill)	1¼ "	Cos Cob Press	1932
QUEEN HELENA (Philip Moeller)	1½ "	Manuscript	1936
GREEN MANSIONS—nonvisual opera		Manuscript	1937

FILM MUSIC	STUDIO		
FIGHT FOR LIFE	U. S. Film Co.		1940
COMMANDOS STRIKE AT DAWN	Columbia		1942
SO ENDS OUR NIGHT	Loew-Lewin		1943
AN AMERICAN ROMANCE	MGM		1944
COUNTERATTACK	Columbia		1945

DAVID WENDEL FENTRESS GUION

Born in Ballinger, Texas, in 1895. He was educated at Polytechnic College in Forth Worth. He studied piano first in Texas and later at the Vienna Conservatory with Godowsky. He taught himself composition.

In 1915 he became Director of the Daniel Baker College School of Music at Brownwood, Texas, where he remained for two years. From 1918 to 1921 he taught at Fairmount Conservatory in Dallas, and in 1921 he joined Southern Methodist University in Dallas, where he remained until 1923. Later he taught at the Chicago College of Music. He helped to organize and is an honorary member now of the David Guion Choral and Fort Worth Harmony clubs and is a member of the Texas Teachers' Association. His interest in Negro music and in cowboy songs stems from his life in the Southwest, where he became interested in the Negro and the cowboy, and many of his larger works are based on the national idioms of that region.

Among his works which have had many performances with the major symphony orchestras, radio and concert ensembles are "Arkansas Traveler," "Turkey in the Straw," "Sheep and Goat Walking to the Pasture," "Alley Tunes" and "Southern Nights Suite." Broadcasts of his orchestral, choral and chamber works have been given over NBC, CBS and WOR. Almost all his major works have been recorded and are on sale by either Victor or Columbia.

COMPOSITIONS

ORCHESTRAL WORKS	DURATION	PUBLISHER	DATE
SOUTHERN NIGHTS SUITE	5 minutes	G. Shirmer, Inc.	1922
SHEEP AND GOAT WALKING TO THE PASTURE	5 "	G. Schirmer, Inc.	1922
ALLEY TUNES	15 "	G. Schirmer, Inc.	1926
MOTHER GOOSE SUITE	25 "	Manuscript for hire	1930
SHINGANDI—primitive African ballet	20 "	Manuscript for hire	1932
SUITE FOR ORCHESTRA	10 "	Manuscript for hire	1937

DAVID WENDEL FENTRESS GUION (*Continued*)

CHORAL WORKS	DURATION	PUBLISHER	DATE
THE BOLD VAQUERO *men's voices, boys' voices*			
RIDE COWBOY RIDE *men's voices, boys' voices*			
GREATEST MIRACLE OF ALL *mixed voices, men's voices*		G. Schirmer, Inc.	1918
THE COWBOY'S DREAM *mixed voices, men's voices, boys' voices*			
LONESOME SONG OF THE PLAINS *mixed voices, men's voices, boys' voices*			
LITTLE PICKANINNY KID *mixed voices, men's voices, boys' voices*		G. Schirmer, Inc.	1918
OH MY LAWD WHAT SHALL I DO? *men's voices*			
TEXAS MAY I NEVER WANDER *mixed voices, men's voices, boys' voices*			
OL' PAINT *mixed voices, boys' voices*			
DE OL' ARK'S A MOVERIN' *men's voices*		G. Schirmer, Inc.	1918
HOPI INDIAN CRADLE SONG *mixed voices, men's voices, women's voices*		Boosey & Co.	1918
SAIL AWAY FOR THE RIO GRANDE *men's voices, boys' voices*			
WHAT SHALL WE DO WITH A DRUNKEN SAILOR? *men's voices, boys' voices*			
HOWDY DO MIS' SPRINGTIME *men's voices*		M. Witmark & Son	1924
HOME ON THE RANGE *boys' voices, men's voices, mixed chorus*		G. Schirmer, Inc.	1931
ALL DAY ON THE PRAIRIE *boys' voices*		G. Schirmer, Inc.	1931

STAGE WORKS			
MOTHER GOOSE BALLET	25 minutes	Manuscript *for hire*	1930
COWBOY PRODUCTION AND DANCE	25 "	Manuscript	1930
SHINGANDI—primitive African ballet	20 "	Manuscript *for hire*	1932

HENRY KIMBALL HADLEY

Born in Somerville, Massachusetts, in 1874, and died in 1937. He received his first lessons in piano and composition from his father, who was in charge of the district public-school music. Emery and Chadwick were his teachers at the New England Conservatory.

Early in his career he was appointed Conductor of the Mapleson Opera Company and toured throughout the United States. In 1909 he became

HENRY KIMBALL HADLEY (*Continued*)

Conductor of the Seattle Symphony Orchestra and also conducted the San Francisco Orchestra. The New York Philharmonic Orchestra appointed him Associate Conductor in 1920. He organized the Manhattan Symphony Orchestra in 1929 with the idea of including American works on each program. He was active in founding the National Association for American Composers and Conductors, of which he was President. He appeared as Guest Conductor at the Worcester Festival, and toured in Japan and in South America. He received the Paderewski Prize in 1901 for a symphonic work, "The Four Seasons," and the National Federation of Music Clubs Prize for "The Culprit Fay" in 1909. "Bianca" was the prize-winning work for the Society of American Singers Competition in 1918.

Among his operas, "Cleopatra's Night" was in the Metropolitan Opera Company's repertoire for two seasons. His orchestral and choral music had many presentations in America and in Europe. He has written a few works for small ensemble and a great many songs which have been published and performed.

COMPOSITIONS

ORCHESTRAL WORKS	DURATION	PUBLISHER	DATE
LUCIFER—tone poem		C. C. Birchard & Co.	
THE OCEAN—tone poem		C. C. Birchard & Co.	1916
SAN FRANCISCO—suite		C. C. Birchard & Co.	
AURORA BOREALIS—overture		Carl Fischer, Inc.	1931
IN BOHEMIA—overture		G. Schirmer, Inc.	
OTHELLO—overture		G. Schirmer, Inc.	
SYMPHONY No. 4, NORTH-EAST- SOUTH- AND WEST		G. Schirmer, Inc.	
HEROD—dramatic overture		Carl Fischer, Inc.	1931
YOUTH TRIUMPHANT		Carl Fischer, Inc.	1931
ALMA MATER—overture		C. C. Birchard & Co.	1932
STREETS OF PEKIN—Chinese suite		Carl Fischer, Inc.	1932
SCHERZO DIABOLIQUE		Carl Fischer, Inc.	1934
CONCERTINO *piano*		C. C. Birchard & Co. *orch. part condensed for 2 pianos; for hire*	1937

CHORAL WORKS			
THE NEW EARTH—ode		Oliver Ditson Co. *vocal score published*	1917
THE FAIRY THORN *women's voices, orchestra*		G. Schirmer, Inc.	1917
ODE-MUSIC *4 solo voices, chorus, orchestra*	entire evening	G. Schirmer, Inc.	1917
RESURGAM *4 solo voices, chorus, orchestra*	" "	Oliver Ditson Co.	1922
MIRTIL IN ARCADIA *6 solo voices, chorus, orchestra, narrator*		C. C. Birchard & Co.	1927
BELSHAZZAR *mixed voices, orchestras*		Theodore Presser	1932

CHAMBER MUSIC			
STRING QUARTET, No. 2	30 minutes	G. Schirmer, Inc.	1934
PIANO TRIO, No. 2	25 "	Manuscript	1933
PIANO QUINTET IN A MINOR	30 "	G. Schirmer, Inc.	1920

HENRY KIMBALL HADLEY (*Continued*)

STAGE WORKS	DURATION	PUBLISHER	DATE
AZORA—3 act opera		G. Schirmer, Inc.	1915
CLEOPATRA'S NIGHT—2 act opera	1½ hours	Oliver Ditson Co.	1918
BIANCA—opera in 1 act	1¼ "	H. Flammer, Inc.	
A NIGHT IN OLD PARIS—1 act opera		Manuscript	1925

RICHARD HAGEMAN

Born in Leeuwaarden, Holland, in 1882. He comes of musical stock. His father, Maurice Hageman, was Director of the Amsterdam Conservatory and his mother was a Court singer. In his early years he studied music with his father and later went to the Brussels Conservatory.

At the age of sixteen he was recommended by the Queen of Holland to a position at the Amsterdam Royal Opera House as Assistant Conductor and after two years he was made First Conductor. In 1908 he was appointed Conductor at the Metropolitan Opera House in New York. He has also directed opera in Chicago and Los Angeles, and orchestral concerts in San Francisco, Philadelphia and Pittsburgh. Several of his works for symphony orchestra have been performed by the Los Angeles Philharmonic during the past few years.

"Caponsacchi" has had several performances at the Metropolitan Opera House and a great many performances in Germany and Austria. Many of his songs have had numerous performances and have been recorded by Victor. At present he is doing a picture score for Republic Studios.

COMPOSITIONS WRITTEN IN AMERICA

ORCHESTRAL WORKS	DURATION	PUBLISHER	DATE
OVERTURE IN A NUTSHELL			
SUITE FOR STRINGS			

CHORAL WORKS			
THE CRUCIBLE—oratorio *4 soloists, chorus, orchestra*	1 hour	G. Schirmer, Inc.	

CHAMBER MUSIC			
SUITE MINIATURE *string quartet*			

STAGE WORKS			
CAPONSACCHI—grand opera *24 singing parts, large* *orchestra, triple woodwinds*	2 hours	Society of European Stage Authors and Composers *for hire*	1931

RICHARD HAGEMAN (*Continued*)

FILM MUSIC	STUDIO	DATE
IF I WERE KING	Paramount	1938
HOTEL IMPERIAL	Paramount	1939
RULERS OF THE SEA	Paramount	1939
THIS WOMAN IS MINE	Universal	1940
PARIS CALLING	Universal	1941
LONG VOYAGE HOME	United Artists	1942
SHANGHAI GESTURE	United Artists	1942

ALEXEI HAIEFF

Born in Blagoveschensk, Russia, in 1914. He studied with Shvedoff and with Boulanger, and received a scholarship at the Juilliard Graduate School (1934–38). He was awarded a medal from the American Academy in Rome in 1942 and received the Lili Boulanger Award in 1942. In 1946, he won a Guggenheim Fellowship.

In 1946, he was commissioned by the Juilliard School of Music to write five piano pieces, and in 1945 he was commissioned by the Koussevitzky Music Foundation to write a piece for cello and piano. "Serenade" was presented by the League of Composers and at the concert of the Music Critics' Circle. The "Divertimento" was performed by the New York Little Symphony. His chamber works have been played by renowned artists. The "Cantata on a Russian Folk Text" was presented at the Library of Congress Concert in 1939.

COMPOSITIONS

ORCHESTRAL WORKS	DURATION	PUBLISHER	DATE
SYMPHONY—for full orchestra	25 minutes	Manuscript	1942

CHAMBER ORCHESTRA			
DIVERTIMENTO—for small orchestra	12 minutes	Manuscript	1944

CHORAL WORKS
A SHORT CANTATA ON A RUSSIAN FOLK TEXT
four solo voices, four string instruments

CHAMBER MUSIC			
SERENADE	15 minutes	Manuscript	1940
oboe, clarinet, bassoon, and piano			
SUITE	10 "	Manuscript	1941
violin, piano			
SONATA	16 "	Manuscript	1945
two pianos			

STAGE WORKS			
PRINCESS ZONDILDA AND HER ENTOURAGE	10 minutes	Manuscript	1946
short ballet			

EDMUND THOMAS HAINES

Born in Ottumwa, Iowa, in 1914. He returned to the serious study of music after having studied mathematics. His composition teachers were Busch, Hall, Rogers, Hanson and Harris. He received his Bachelor of Music degree from the Conservatory of Kansas City and his Master of Music and Doctorate degrees from the Eastman School of. Music. In 1946 he studied at the Berkshire Music Center under Copland.

In 1941, he joined the teaching staff of the University of Michigan School of Music, where he is at present head of the Composition Department. From 1943–45 he served in the U. S. Army. He was awarded a Pulitzer Prize for the First Symphony in 1941.

His works have been performed in Cleveland, Detroit, Kansas City, New York, Rochester, and army camps in the Southwest. CBS and NBC have broadcast his compositions over major networks. He is, at present, preparing a piano sonata, a second quartet, a second symphony and an opera.

COMPOSITIONS

ORCHESTRAL WORKS

	DURATION	PUBLISHER	DATE
LANDSCAPE	7 minutes	Manuscript	1936
POEM *viola, orchestra*	8 "	Fleisher Music Collection	1938
THREE DANCES	10 "	Fleisher Music Collection	1939
TUNE WITH VARIATIONS	6 "	Manuscript	1939
FIRST SYMPHONY	24 "	Carl Fischer, Inc. *for hire*	1941

CHAMBER ORCHESTRA

PASTORALE *flute, strings*	6 minutes	Relin	1939
SYMPHONY IN MINIATURE *16 instruments*	12 "	Fleisher Music Collection	1940
INTERLUDE *string orchestra*	8 "	Manuscript	1943
CORONACH *brass, timpani, strings*	8 "	Manuscript	1946

CHAMBER MUSIC

SONATA *violin, piano*	18 minutes	Manuscript	1936
TWO SONATINAS *piano*	12 "	Manuscript	1942
SONATINA *piano*	5 "	Manuscript	1945
QUARTET *2 violins, viola, cello*	15 "	Manuscript	1946
ECLOGUE *flute, 2 violins, cello*	5 "	Manuscript	1946
SONATA *piano*	12 "	Manuscript	1946

RICHARD HAMMOND

Born in Kent, England, in 1896. He graduated from Yale University. After studying at the Yale School of Music, he became a pupil of Boulanger in Paris.

He was the founder and Vice-President of the Composers' Music Corporation, a publishing house interested in contemporary music. He has served as a member of the Executive Board of the League of Composers, and on the board of the Franco-American Music Society. He is a contributor to *Modern Music* and other magazines devoted to music. He has been the American delegate to the I.S.C.M. Festivals in Salzburg, Venice and London. He is a resident now of California and a member of the Executive Board of the Hollywood Bowl Association.

His works have been heard on programs of various societies interested in contemporary music.

COMPOSITIONS

ORCHESTRAL WORKS	DURATION	PUBLISHER	DATE
FIVE CHINESE FAIRY TALES		Manuscript	1921
VOYAGE TO THE EAST	12 minutes	Manuscript	1926
medium voice			
THE SEA OF HEAVEN		Manuscript	1929
WEST INDIAN DANCES	23 "	Manuscript	1930
SUITE AFTER READING "THE WOMAN			
OF ANDROS"	30 "	Manuscript	1930
SINFONIETTA	11 "	Manuscript	1931
DANCE MUSIC—SUITE II		Manuscript	1937
UNTO THE HILLS—suite	25 "	Manuscript	1939
IN AN UPLAND MEADOW	5 "	Manuscript	1939
EXCURSION—suite	28 "	Manuscript	1940
PARTITA I—suite	20 "	Manuscript	1941
PARTITA II—suite	18 "	Manuscript	1942

CHAMBER ORCHESTRA			
CINQ CHANSONS GRECQUES	15 minutes	Manuscript	1928
medium voice, 15 instruments			
FIVE MADRIGALS	10 "	Manuscript	1930
voice and instruments			

CHORAL WORKS			
SUITE FOR FIVE PRIÈRES ARABES	10–15 minutes	Manuscript	1928
baritone solo, women's chorus,			
7 instruments			
SIX WOMEN'S CHORUSES		Manuscript	1928
a cappella ensemble with or			
without soloist			

CHAMBER MUSIC			
SONATA FOR OBOE AND PIANO		Manuscript	1924

STAGE WORKS			
FIESTA—ballet	25 minutes	Manuscript	1929
medium orchestra, 2 voices backstage			
CARNIVAL—ballet	20 "	Manuscript	1931
medium orchestra			
BALLET	28 "	Manuscript	1935
medium orchestra			

HOWARD HANSON

Born in Wahoo, Nebraska, in 1896. He began his musical education under his mother's guidance. He attended Luther College in Wahoo and continued his studies in music at the Institute of Musical Art in New York and at Northwestern University. The Prix de Rome was awarded to him in 1921, and he was the first composer to enter the American Academy in Rome. He remained there for three years.

At the age of twenty he was appointed Professor of Theory at the College of the Pacific in California, and three years later he was made Dean of the Conservatory of Fine Arts of that college. On his return from Rome he accepted the directorship of the Eastman School of Music in Rochester. There he inaugurated the American Composers Concerts, enlisting the services of the Rochester Philharmonic Orchestra as well as ballet corps, soloists and ensembles for the purpose of stimulating wider interest in American creative music. He received the award of the Society for the Publication of American Music and also the Eastman School Publication Award. For many years he has taken an active part in various educational activities, serving as Chairman of the Commission on Graduate Study of the National Association of Schools of Music, also as President of the Music Teachers' National Association. He is a member of the examining jury for the American Academy in Rome, and lectures frequently on music education. He has been guest conductor with many of the orchestras in the United States and Europe. He was elected to membership in the National Institute of Arts and Letters in 1935, and in 1938 he was elected a Fellow of the Royal Academy of Music in Sweden. In 1944 he was awarded the Pulitzer Prize for his Symphony No. 4, Opus 34, and in 1945 he received the Ditson Award. At present he is President of the National Music Council, and also a member of the Advisory Committee on Music of the Department of State.

The opera "Merrymount" was produced at the Metropolitan Opera House, and excerpts in concert form have been heard at the Ann Arbor Festival, also in major cities throughout the country. Many of his works have been performed by the major orchestras in the United States and in Europe, as well as at the festivals of Worcester, Ann Arbor, Bad Homburg, etc. String Quartet, Opus 23, was commissioned for the Elizabeth Sprague Coolidge Foundation (Library of Congress), and he was one of the first six Americans commissioned by CBS to write a work for radio. Excerpts from "Merrymount," "The Lament for Beowulf," the Symphonies Nos. 1 and 2 have been recorded by Victor.

COMPOSITIONS

ORCHESTRAL WORKS	PUBLISHER	DATE
SYMPHONIC RHAPSODY	Manuscript	1918
BEFORE THE DAWN—symphonic poem	Manuscript	1919
SYMPHONIC LEGEND	Manuscript	1920
EXALTATION—symphonic poem	Manuscript	1920
piano obbligato		

HOWARD HANSON (*Continued*)

ORCHESTRAL WORKS (*Continued*)	DURATION		PUBLISHER	DATE
NORDIC SYMPHONY, NO. 1	28 minutes		Eastman School of Music Publication	1922
			Carl Fischer, Inc., agents	
NORTH AND WEST—symphonic poem	18	"	Manuscript	1923
LUX AETERNA—symphonic poem	18	"	G. Schirmer, Inc.	1923
violin obbligato				
PAN AND THE PRIEST—symphonic poem	10	"	C. C. Birchard & Co.	1926
piano obbligato				
CONCERTO	18	"	Manuscript	1926
organ, orchestra				
ROMANTIC SYMPHONY NO. 2	26	"	Eastman School of Music Publication	1930
			Carl Fischer, Inc., agents	
SUITE FROM THE OPERA "MERRYMOUNT"	16	"	Harms, Inc.	1937
SYMPHONY NO. 3, OPUS 33			Eastman School of Music Publication	1937
			Carl Fischer, Inc., agents	
CONCERTO FOR ORGAN, STRINGS AND HARP	13½	"	Manuscript	1943
			Carl Fischer, Inc.	
SYMPHONY NO. 4, OPUS 34	20	"	Eastman School of Music Publication	1943
			Carl Fischer, Inc., agents	
SERENADE	6	"	Carl Fischer, Inc.	1946
flute, strings, harp				

CHORAL WORKS

THE LAMENT FOR BEOWULF	18 minutes		C. C. Birchard & Co.	1925
mixed chorus, full orchestra				
HEROIC ELEGY	16	"	Manuscript	1927
orchestra, mixed chorus obbligato				
SONGS FROM "DRUM TAPS"			J. Fischer & Bro.	1935
(text—Walt Whitman)			*vocal score*	
HYMN FOR THE PIONEERS	4½	"	J. Fischer & Bro.	1938
male voices				

CHAMBER MUSIC

QUINTET IN F MINOR, OPUS 6	30 minutes		Manuscript	1916
piano, string quartet				
CONCERTO DA CAMERA, OPUS 7	15	"	Manuscript	1917
piano, string quartet				
STRING QUARTET, OPUS 23	18	"	C. C. Birchard & Co.	1923

STAGE WORKS

CALIFORNIA FOREST PLAY OF 1920			Manuscript	1919
voices, chorus, orchestra				
MERRYMOUNT—3-act opera	2¼ hours		Harms, Inc.	1932
(libretto of Richard Stokes)				

LEIGH HARLINE

Born in Salt Lake City, Utah, in 1907. He graduated from the University of Utah, where he majored in music. He studied piano with Cornwall, Conductor of the Mormon Temple in Utah. In 1928 he went to Los Angeles, where he worked in various radio stations until 1932, when he

LEIGH HARLINE (*Continued*)

joined the Walt Disney staff for a few years. At present he is working with RKO.

In 1940 he won an Academy Award for the motion-picture score of "Pinocchio," judged the best of the year, and also the Academy Award for the best motion-picture song of the year, "When You Wish Upon a Star," from "Pinocchio." In 1941 he was commissioned by Werner Janssen to write a suite for his orchestra, called the "Civic Center Suite," which was performed in California, in South America, in Cleveland and Rochester, at New York stadium concerts and over the air. At present he is writing the score for an RKO picture and has completed songs for three film scores. He is also working on a concert overture on early American fiddle tunes. His music for films is listed here.

COMPOSITIONS

FILM MUSIC	STUDIO	PUBLISHER	DATE
SNOW WHITE (background score only)	Walt Disney		1938
PINOCCHIO songs	Walt Disney	Irving Berlin	1940
PRIDE OF THE YANKEES	Goldwyn		1942
YOU WERE NEVER LOVELIER	Columbia		1942
THE SKY'S THE LIMIT	RKO		1943
TENDER COMRADE	RKO		1943
CHINA SKY	RKO		1944
JOHNNY ANGEL	RKO		1945

SANDOR HARMATI

Born in Budapest, Hungary, in 1892 and died in New York in 1936. He was a graduate of the Budapest Royal Academy and at the age of seventeen received his degree as Professor of Music. In 1914 he came to the United States and became a member of the Letz String Quartet. He organized the Lenox String Quartet, of which he was first violinist. In 1925 he became Conductor of the Omaha Symphony Orchestra and had guest appearances as conductor with many symphonic orchestras in the United States and with the Philharmonic in Berlin and the Pas de Loup Orchestra in Paris; later he conducted the Westchester County Music Festival and the Musicians Symphony in New York.

He was one of the original members of the American Music Guild. In 1922 he won the Pulitzer Prize for his symphonic poem "Folio." In 1925 the Philadelphia Chamber Music Prize was awarded to him for a string quartet, and in 1928 he received the Juilliard Foundation Prize for an orchestral work, "Prelude to a Melodrama," which was performed by the Philadelphia Orchestra. His chamber music has had repeated performances.

SANDOR HARMATI (*Continued*)

COMPOSITIONS

ORCHESTRAL WORKS	PUBLISHER	DATE
Folio—symphonic poem		1922
Prelude to a Melodrama	C. C. Birchard & Co.	1928

CHAMBER MUSIC		
String Quartet		1924
String Quartet with Flute	Manuscript	1925

STAGE WORKS
The Jeweled Tree—
   incidental music   Manuscript

ROY HARRIS

Born in Lincoln County, Oklahoma, in 1898. He was brought up from early childhood in California and educated in the public schools of Southern California. His mother first taught him the piano. After graduating from high school he became interested in studying the clarinet. At eighteen he took up farming, then enlisted in the army during the First World War.

At the age of twenty-two he entered the University of California as a special student of philosophy and economics and then began to study music with Farwell. Bliss, Altschuler and Scalero also taught him orchestration and harmony, and in 1926 he went to Paris to study with Boulanger. From 1927 to 1929 he held two appointments for the Guggenheim Fellowship. He returned to America in 1929 and devoted himself to composing chiefly orchestral and chamber music. In 1930 and in 1931 he received the appointment of the Creative Fellowship from the Pasadena Music and Arts Association. He was head of the Composition Department of the Westminster Choir School at Princeton, New Jersey, and Director of the Princeton Festival of American Music. At present he is head of the Department of Music at Colorado College. He has contributed articles on musical subjects to various magazines and has lectured frequently.

He was commissioned by the Victor Company to write "Johnny Comes Marching Home," which was played by the major orchestras all over the United States and broadcast over CBS and NBC. The "Time Suite" was commissioned and broadcast by CBS. The League of Composers commissioned the "Songs for Occupations," which the Westminster Choir presented many times on tour in Europe and the United States. He was commissioned to write a radio piece for Stromberg Carlson, which was first presented at the Eastman School and then broadcast over NBC; a Concerto for Orchestra by the Blue Network; by Rodzinski for the New York Philharmonic Symphony; by Temple Emanu-El for a Friday evening service; by Elizabeth Sprague Coolidge, and by various artists for their concert repertories, as well as by many musical organizations.

ROY HARRIS (*Continued*)

His works have been performed frequently in all parts of the world by major orchestras and ensemble groups. He has had a great many compositions recorded by Columbia and Victor. The Fifth Symphony was recorded by the O.W.I. The first performance of the ballet "From This Earth" was given by Hanya Holm at Colorado College.

COMPOSITIONS

ORCHESTRAL WORKS

	DURATION	PUBLISHER	DATE
ANDANTE	14 minutes	Manuscript	1926
ANDANTINO	10 "	Manuscript	1931
TOCCATA	13 "	Manuscript	1931
OVERTURE	10 "	Manuscript	1931
CONCERT PIECE	14 "	Manuscript	1932
FIRST SYMPHONY	28 "	G. Schirmer, Inc. *for hire*	1933
WHEN JOHNNY COMES MARCHING HOME	8 "	G. Schirmer, Inc.	1934
SECOND SYMPHONY	28 "	G. Schirmer, Inc. *for hire*	1934
FAREWELL TO PIONEERS	8 "	G. Schirmer, Inc.	1935
TIME SUITE	19 "	G. Schirmer, Inc.	1936
THIRD SYMPHONY	18 "	G. Schirmer, Inc.	1937
FOURTH SYMPHONY (Folk Song) *chorus, orchestra*	44 "	G. Schirmer, Inc.	1939
AMERICAN CREED	10 "	Mills Music Inc. *for hire*	1940
ODE TO TRUTH	8 "	Mills Music Inc. *for hire*	1941
EVENING PIECE	4 "	Mills Music Inc.	1941
ACCELERATION	8 "	Mills Music Inc. *for hire*	1941
FIFTH SYMPHONY	30 "	Mills Music Inc. *for hire*	1942
FANFARE	4 "	Mills Music Inc. *for hire*	1942
FOLK RHYTHMS OF TODAY		Mills Music Inc. *(for band only)*	1942
MARCH IN TIME OF WAR	4½ "	Mills Music Inc.	1943
ODE TO FRIENDSHIP	6 "	Mills Music Inc. *for hire*	
CHORALE FOR ORCHESTRA	11 "	Mills Music Inc. *for hire*	
SIXTH SYMPHONY (based on Gettysburg Address)	29 "	Mills Music Inc.	1944
CONCERTO FOR PIANO AND ORCHESTRA		Manuscript	1945
MIRAGE		Manuscript	1945
MELODY		Manuscript	1945
MEMORIES OF A CHILD'S SUNDAY		Manuscript	1945
RADIO PIECE *piano, orchestra*		Manuscript	1946
THEME AND VARIATIONS ON A TYMPANI THEME OF HOWARD HANSON'S THIRD SYMPHONY		Manuscript	1946
CONCERTO FOR TWO PIANOS AND ORCHESTRA		Manuscript	1946

BAND MUSIC

CIMARRON	6 minutes	Mills Music Inc.	1941
FIRST PIANO CONCERTO WITH BAND	14 "	Mills Music Inc. *for hire*	1942

BAND MUSIC (*Continued*)

	DURATION	PUBLISHER	DATE
JOHNNY COMES MARCHING HOME	6 minutes	Mills Music Inc.	1942
FOLK RHYTHMS OF TODAY		Mills Music Inc.	1942
FANTASY FOR PIANO AND BAND	11 "	Mills Music Inc. *for hire*	1943
CONFLICT—second movement of Sixth Symphony, transcribed for band	6 "	Mills Music Inc. *for hire*	1944

CHAMBER ORCHESTRA

CHORALE FOR STRING ORCHESTRA	9 minutes	Harold Flammer, Inc.	1933
PRELUDE AND FUGUE FOR STRING ORCHESTRA	14 "	G. Schirmer, Inc.	1936
CHORALE FOR ORGAN AND BRASSES	8 "	Mills Music Inc. *for hire*	1943
TOCCATA FOR ORGAN AND BRASSES		Mills Music Inc. *for hire*	1944

CHORAL WORKS

FANTASY FOR TRIO AND CHORUS *chorus, violin, cello, piano*	15 minutes	Manuscript	1925
WALT WHITMAN SUITE *women's chorus, 2 pianos*	18 "	Manuscript	1927
CHALLENGE *chorus, orchestra*	10 "	G. Schirmer, Inc. *for hire*	1930
SONGS FOR OCCUPATIONS *8-part mixed chorus, a cappella*	15 "	G. Schirmer, Inc.	1934
SYMPHONY FOR VOICES *8-part mixed chorus, a cappella*	15 "	G. Schirmer, Inc.	1936
RAILROAD MAN'S BALLADE *chorus, orchestra*	10 "	Mills Music Inc. *for hire*	1938
FIVE SONGS OF DEMOCRACY *chorus, orchestra*	5 " each	Mills Music Inc.	1942
ROCK OF AGES *chorus, orchestra*		Mills Music Inc. *for hire*	
SUITE FOR CHORUS, STRING QUARTET AND PIANO	11 "	Mills Music Inc.	
ALLELUIA *chorus, organ, brasses*		Manuscript	1945
ISRAEL *chorus, organ*		Manuscript	1946
BLOW THE MAN DOWN *chorus, orchestra.*		Manuscript	1946

CHAMBER MUSIC

SONGS OF A RAINY DAY *string quartet*	16 minutes	Manuscript	1925
CONCERTO *piano, clarinet, string quartet*	25 "	Cos Cob Press	1927
PIANO SONATA	14 "	Cos Cob Press Arrow Music Press	1928
FIRST STRING QUARTET	28 "	Manuscript	1930
STRING SEXTET *2 violins, 2 violas, 2 cellos*	22 "	Harold Flammer, Inc.	1932
SECOND STRING QUARTET (3 variations on a theme)	20 "	G. Schirmer, Inc.	1933
TRIO *violin, cello, piano*	22 "	Modern Music	1934
PIANO QUINTET *piano, string quartet*	28 "	G. Schirmer, Inc.	1936
THIRD STRING QUARTET	50 "	Mills Music Inc. *for hire*	1937

ROY HARRIS (*Continued*)

CHAMBER MUSIC (*Continued*)	DURATION	PUBLISHER	DATE
VIOLA QUINTET *viola, string quartet*	28 minutes	Manuscript	1939
VIOLIN SONATA *violin, piano*	25 "	Mills Music Inc.	1942

STAGE WORKS			
FROM THIS EARTH—ballet in 5 scenes	25 minutes	Mills Music Inc. *for hire*	1941
WHAT SO PROUDLY WE HAIL—ballet in 5 scenes *chorus, piano, string orchestra*	25 "	Mills Music Inc. *for hire*	1942

FILM MUSIC	PRODUCER		
ONE-TENTH OF A NATION	Rockefeller Docu- mentary Film	Mills Music Inc. *for hire*	1940

FREDERIC HART

Born in Aberdeen, Washington, in 1898. He first studied music at home. Later he worked with Andersen at the American Conservatory in Chicago, where he received first honors in composition. World War I interrupted his studies and he joined the army in France. He resumed his music studies later; his teachers in composition were Wilson, Goldmark and Boulanger, and his piano teachers were Gunn, Hutcheson and Quaile. An interest in music pedagogy led him to study the Diller-Quaile School methods and in 1923 he joined the staff of that school. Since 1929 he has been a member of the music faculty at Sarah Lawrence College, and he has also lectured at Mills College.

"The Romance of Robot," a one-act opera, was presented twenty times at the Federal Music Theatre in New York City. He has also written many piano pieces and songs.

COMPOSITIONS

ORCHESTRAL WORKS	DURATION	PUBLISHER	DATE
ELEGY	7 minutes	Schirmer's Rental Library	1945

CHAMBER ORCHESTRA			
THREE PASTORALES FOR WOODWIND QUARTET AND STRING ORCHESTRA "THE HAPPY VALLEY"	20 minutes	Manuscript	1945

CHAMBER MUSIC			
STRING QUARTET No. 1	30 minutes	Manuscript	1939

FREDERIC HART (*Continued*)

STAGE WORKS	DURATION	PUBLISHER	DATE
THE WHEEL OF FORTUNE—opera in three acts *8 principals, large chorus, orchestra*	2½ hours	Manuscript	1934
THE ROMANCE OF ROBOT—opera in one act *6 principals, chorus, ballet, orchestra*	1 hour	Manuscript	1937

WELDON HART

Born in Bear Spring, Tennessee, in 1911. He graduated from Peabody College in 1933, received his Master of Music degree from the University of Michigan in 1939, and in 1946, he received his Doctorate degree from the Eastman School of Music. He studied violin with Besekersky and Rose, composition with Hanson, and orchestration with Rogers. From 1929 to 1932 he held a Juilliard Extension Scholarship in violin and for 1932–33 he held a Presser Scholarship.

He taught for a number of years at Western Kentucky State Teachers College, and since 1943, he has been on the faculty of the Eastman School of Music. He has been a member of the first violin section of the Rochester Philharmonic Orchestra. In 1945 he won first prize for orchestral compositions offered by the American Broadcasting Company through the National Composers Congress. In 1945, he was Chairman of the National Composers Congress. He is particularly interested in folk music.

"Darling Cory," the Symphony No. 1, and A Symphonic Movement (prize work of the National Composers Congress) were played by the Detroit, the Eastman-Rochester and the National Symphony Orchestras. A Symphonic Movement was broadcast over an ABC network.

COMPOSITIONS

ORCHESTRAL WORKS	DURATION	PUBLISHER	DATE
TONE POEM FOR ORCHESTRA	7 minutes	Manuscript	1933
THE DARK HILLS	8 "	Manuscript	1939
DARLING CORY	6 "	Manuscript	1944
A SYMPHONIC MOVEMENT	10 "	Manuscript	1945
SYMPHONY NO. 1	24 "	Manuscript *for hire*	1946

CHAMBER ORCHESTRA	DURATION	PUBLISHER	DATE
SINFONIETTA *16 parts*	5 minutes	Manuscript	1932

CHAMBER MUSIC	DURATION	PUBLISHER	DATE
STRING QUARTET NO. 1	20 minutes	Manuscript	1939

CHARLES HAUBIEL

Born in Delta, Ohio, in 1894. He studied piano with Ganz, Josef, and Rosina Lhevinne. He was a pupil of Rosario Scalero in composition.

For eight years he taught piano at the Institute of Musical Art, and since 1923 he has been Assistant Professor of Composition and Theory at New York University. In 1935 he organized the Composers Press for the purpose of publishing works by contemporary American composers. His symphonic work "Karma" won the first prize in the United States in the International Schubert Centennial Contest in 1929, and it has been recorded by Columbia. "Ritratti" won second prize in the Swift Symphonic Contest in 1935; its première was given by the Chicago Symphony Orchestra. "Pastoral" won honorable mention in this same Swift Symphonic Contest.

"Suite Passecaille" was first performed by the Los Angeles Symphony. Other works for chorus and chamber music have been presented in New York, and several of his works have been broadcast in the NBC Music Guild Series. "The Path of Music," a lecture-recital, was filmed for Paramount News (Educational Film).

COMPOSITIONS

ORCHESTRAL WORKS	DURATION	PUBLISHER	DATE
MARS ASCENDING	5 minutes	Manuscript	1923
KARMA: SYMPHONIC VARIATIONS	25 "	Manuscript	1928
RITRATTI	15 "	Manuscript	1929
PASTORAL	15 "	Manuscript	1930
SUITE PASSECAILLE	18 "	Manuscript	1932
VOX CATHEDRALIS	15 "	Manuscript	1934
SYMPHONY No. 1—in the form of variations	21½ "	Manuscript for hire	1937
SOLARI	40 "	Manuscript for hire	1938
MINIATURES string orchestra	10 "	Composers Press, Inc.	1939
MINIATURES symphony orchestra	11 "	Manuscript for hire	1943
NUANCES flute, string orchestra	10 "	Manuscript for hire	1944
1865 A.D.—CIVIL WAR SCENES	16 "	Manuscript for hire	1944

CHORAL WORKS			
SEA SONGS male voices, orchestra or 2 pianos	9 minutes	H. W. Gray Co.	1931
L'AMORE SPIRITUALE women's voices, orchestra or 2 pianos	30 "	Composers Press, Inc.	1932
YEOMAN'S SONG male voices, a cappella	3 "	Composers Press, Inc.	1932
VISION OF SAINT JOAN— dramatic cantata soprano, mezzo-contralto, mixed and boys' chorus, orchestra	15 "	Composers Press, Inc.	1941
SERENADE—lyric cantata solo voices, mixed chorus, orchestra	20 "	Manuscript	1943
THOU THAT DESTROYETH THE TEMPLE mixed chorus, a cappella	3 "	Boston Music Co.	1943

CHARLES HAUBIEL (*Continued*)

CHORAL WORKS (*Continued*)	DURATION	PUBLISHER	DATE
JUNGLE TALE—a musical satire *men's voices*	3½ minutes	Composers Press, Inc.	1943
FATHER ABRAHAM (Lincoln) *mixed chorus, orchestra*	5½ "	Composers Press, Inc.	1944
BOTH GRAVE AND GAY *women's voices*	13½ "	Composers Press, Inc.	1944
WHAT WONDROUS SACRIFICE IS THIS *five part, a cappella*	4¼ "	Composers Press, Inc.	1945

CHAMBER MUSIC

AMPHYCROMES—a suite for trio *piano, violin, cello*		Manuscript	1932
CRYPTICS *bassoon, piano*	8 minutes	Manuscript	1932
GAY DANCES *piano trio*	8 "	Manuscript	1932
LODANDO LA DANZA *quartet: oboe, violin, cello, piano*	15 "	Manuscript	1932
ROMANZA *piano trio*	10 "	Composers Press, Inc.	1932
PASTORALE *duo for oboe and cello*	5 "	Manuscript	1933
DUOFORMS *trio*	15 "	Manuscript	1934
ECHI CLASICI *string quartet*	10 "	Manuscript	1936
TRIO FOR FLUTE, CELLO AND PIANO	17½ "	Manuscript	1942
GOTHIC VARIATIONS *violin and piano*	16 "	Composers Press, Inc.	1943
TRIO FOR STRINGS	15 "	Manuscript	1943
SONATA FOR CELLO AND PIANO	20 "	Manuscript	1944

STAGE WORKS

BRIGANDS PREFERRED—a musical satire *solo quartet and chorus, small orchestra*	Manuscript	1932
THE PASSIONATE PILGRIM—incidental music *chamber-music ensemble*	Manuscript	1932

FILM MUSIC

SUWANEE RIVER GOES HI-HAT—short for Paramount News Pictorial	Manuscript

HERBERT HAUFRECHT

Born in New York City in 1909. He began his early piano studies with his mother. He attended the Cleveland Institute of Music, where he was a pupil in composition of Sessions, Porter and Elwell and of Loesser in ensemble playing. Later he studied with Eisenberger at the Cleveland Music School Settlement, where for several years he won a prize in piano playing. He was awarded a fellowship at the Juilliard Graduate School from 1930 to 1934 for composition, during which time he studied with Goldmark.

HERBERT HAUFRECHT *(Continued)*

He went to West Virginia as a Director of Community Music for the Resettlement Administration and while there became interested in collecting folk music. On his return to New York he became staff composer and arranger for the Federal Theatre and taught music in private schools. In 1940 he organized the Folk Festival of the Catskills, with which he is still associated. During World War II he worked in a war plant and continued to compose in his spare time. At present he is on the staff of Mills Music, Inc., as editor and arranger in the educational department.

"The Story of Ferdinand" has been played by the St. Louis Symphony and the Philharmonic and in other cities of the United States and Canada. "Three Fantastic Marches," "Overture for a Mural" and many of his works for chamber orchestra and choral groups have had performances in this country. NBC and WNYC have broadcast several of his compositions, and WNYC commissioned "Overture for a Mural," which was performed by the National Orchestral Association again in 1945. "Walkin' the Road" for band was commissioned by Leeds Music Corp.

COMPOSITIONS

ORCHESTRAL WORKS	DURATION	PUBLISHER	DATE
THE STORY OF FERDINAND	18 minutes	Leeds Music Corp.	1938
narrator, orchestra			
THREE FANTASTIC MARCHES	7 "	Manuscript	1938
OVERTURE FOR A MURAL	6 "	G. Schirmer, Inc.	1940
		for hire	

CHAMBER ORCHESTRA			
SUITE FOR STRING ORCHESTRA	16 minutes	Associated Music Publishers	1934
		for hire	
SQUARE SET FOR STRING ORCHESTRA	7 "		1941

BAND MUSIC			
WALKIN' THE ROAD	4 minutes	Leeds Music Corp.	1944
CREDO		Leeds Music Corp.	1944
band and chorus			

CHORAL WORKS			
JOHN BROWN'S BODY		Manuscript	1940
baritone solo, mixed chorus			
THE CALL FROM VILNA		Manuscript	1943
baritone solo, mixed chorus			

CHAMBER MUSIC			
SONATA FOR VIOLIN AND PIANO	18 minutes	Manuscript	1932
QUARTETINO FOR STRING QUARTET	20 "	Manuscript	1933
VARIATIONS ON AN ORIGINAL THEME	12 "	Manuscript	1935
violin, cello, piano			
MOODS FOR STRING QUARTET	15 "	Manuscript	1937
BITTER-SUITE IN OLDEN STYLE	5 "	Manuscript	1937
flute, violin, piano			
SICILIAN SUITE	6 "	3rd movement pub.	1943
piano		E. B. Marks	

HERBERT HAUFRECHT (*Continued*)

STAGE WORKS	DURATION	PUBLISHER	DATE
WHEN DAD WAS A FIREMAN—ballet	14 minutes	Manuscript	1945
8 woodwinds, 11 brass, strings			
WE'VE COME FROM THE CITY	18 "	Leeds Music Corp.	1945
single set, adults, children,			
chamber orchestra			

JOHN HAUSSERMANN

Born in Manila, Philippine Islands, in 1909. He received his elementary education in the United States and then studied music in Paris with Paul le Flem and Marcel Dupré.

In 1934, he founded the Contemporary Concert Series in Cincinnati, Ohio, which presented works of living composers.

His compositions, which have been performed in Cincinnati, Philadelphia, New York, Baltimore and Manila, include "Nocturne and Dance," "After Christmas Suite," "Pastoral Fantasy" and "Voice Concerto." "Nocturne and Dance" was also presented as a ballet. Marcel Dupré introduced the Organ Sonata in New York and has played it throughout this country and abroad. The NBC Symphony broadcast the First Symphony over an NBC nation-wide hook-up.

COMPOSITIONS

ORCHESTRAL WORKS	DURATION	PUBLISHER	DATE
NOCTURNE AND DANCE, OPUS 8	18 minutes	Boosey, Hawkes, Belwin, Inc.	1934
AFTER CHRISTMAS SUITE, OPUS 10	21 "	Boosey, Hawkes, Belwin, Inc.	1934
SYMPHONY NO. 1, OPUS 16	30 "	Manuscript *for hire*	1938
VOICE CONCERTO, OPUS 25	20 "	Boosey & Hawkes	1941
soprano, orchestra			
SYMPHONY NO. 2, OPUS 22	25 "	Manuscript *for hire*	1943

CHAMBER ORCHESTRA			
RHAPSODIC OVERTURE, OPUS 17	20 minutes	Manuscript *for hire*	1939
piano, 5 wind instruments, strings			

CHAMBER MUSIC			
QUINTET FOR FLUTE, OBOE, CLARINET, BASSOON AND HARPSICHORD, OPUS 1	16 minutes	Manuscript *for hire*	1932
TWENTY-FOUR SYMPHONIC PRELUDES FOR PIANO, OPUS 2	50 "	Maurice Sénart	1932
SONATINE FANTASTIQUE, OPUS 3	21 "	Maurice Sénart	1932
piano			
PRELUDE AND FUGUE, OPUS 4	18 "	Maurice Sénart	1933
2 pianos (4 hands); or organ and string orchestra			
PASTORAL FANTASY, OPUS 5	12 "	Maurice Sénart	1933
2 pianos (4 hands); or flute, harp and strings			

JOHN HAUSSERMANN (*Continued*)

CHAMBER MUSIC (*Continued*)	DURATION	PUBLISHER	DATE
SONATINE ROMANTIQUE, OPUS 7 *piano*	15 minutes	Maurice Sénart	1934
SUITE RUSTIQUE, OPUS 13 *flute, cello, piano*	20 "	Manuscript *for hire*	1935
QUARTET, OPUS 15 *strings*	20 "	Manuscript *for hire*	1935
SUITE GOTHIQUE, OPUS 9 *organ*	12 "	Maurice Sénart	1935
QUINTET, OPUS 11 *2 violins, viola, cello, piano*	25 "	Maurice Sénart	1935
SONATA, OPUS 19 *organ*	6 "	Manuscript	1938
DIVERTISSEMENTS, OPUS 21 *string quartet*	12 "	Manuscript	1939–45
VIOLIN SONATA, OPUS 24	22 "	Manuscript	1940

BERNHARD HEIDEN

Born in Frankfort, Germany, in 1910. He studied with Hindemith in Berlin. He won the Mendelssohn Prize for composition in 1933.

He came to the United States in 1935 and since then has been on the faculty of the Art Center Music School in Detroit, Michigan. He was a staff arranger for radio station WWJ in 1937–38, and he organized and conducted Gallery Concerts with the Detroit Chamber Orchestra, 1942–43. From 1943 to 1945, he was Assistant Bandleader of the 445th A.S.F. Band of the United States.

His works have had many performances in Detroit, Chicago, and New York. The League of Composers presented his Sonata for Violin and Piano. At the present time he is preparing a Sonata for Piano (Four Hands) and a String Quartet.

COMPOSITIONS WRITTEN IN AMERICA

ORCHESTRAL WORKS	DURATION	PUBLISHER	DATE
PRELUDE FOR ORCHESTRA	10 minutes	Manuscript	1935
SYMPHONY	18 "	Fleisher Library	1938

CHAMBER ORCHESTRA			
CONCERT MUSIC FOR 5 WIND INSTRUMENTS AND STRINGS *20 instruments*	10 minutes	Manuscript	1939

BAND MUSIC			
SOLO FOR ALTO-SAXOPHONE AND BAND	8 minutes	Manuscript	1944

CHAMBER MUSIC			
SONATA FOR SAXOPHONE AND PIANO	16 minutes	Associated Music Publishers	1937
SONATA FOR VIOLIN AND PIANO	15 "	Manuscript	1939
SONATA FOR PIANO	15 "	Manuscript	1940

BERNHARD HEIDEN (*Continued*)

STAGE WORKS	PUBLISHER	DATE
HENRY V—incidental music	Manuscript	1941
small orchestra		
THE TEMPEST—incidental music	Manuscript	1942
small orchestra		

IRWIN HEILNER

Born in New York City in 1908. He studied harmony and composition with Goldmark, counterpoint with Boulanger and Sessions, orchestration with Osses and piano with Adler and Thompson.

He is particularly interested in "swing" music and wrote the "Swing Symphony" after studying the works of George Gershwin, Louis Armstrong, Duke Ellington, Bessie Smith and others. This Symphony was broadcast by the National Orchestral Association over WNYC and has been transcribed for piano and clarinet for performance by the NBC Symphony. His Suite for Orchestra was broadcast over WABC and WNYC, and "The Traveler" was presented over WQXR. The "Boogie Woogie Rhapsody" has been recorded by Sylvia Marlowe as part of the album "From Bach to Boogie Woogie." This work was performed over WABC. He has in preparation a "Partita for Harp and Orchestra," which is scored for radio as well as concert performances. He is also adding to "The Eastern Road" song cycle, a work based on translations of classical Chinese poetry.

COMPOSITIONS

ORCHESTRAL WORKS	DURATION	PUBLISHER	DATE
SUITE FOR ORCHESTRA	15 minutes	Manuscript	1936
SWING SYMPHONY	30 "	Manuscript	1939
THE TRAVELER	2 "	Associated Music	1945
soprano or tenor, orchestra		Publishers	

CHAMBER MUSIC			
MODERN YOUTH—humorous cycle			
of songs about children	6 minutes	Manuscript	1944
voice, piano			
THE EASTERN ROAD—song cycle			
with translated Chinese texts	10 "	Manuscript	1945
voice, piano			

WALTER HELFER

Born in Lawrence, Massachusetts, in 1896. He graduated from Harvard University. He was a pupil of Respighi in Rome and of Mason in Boston, and also was the recipient of the American Academy in Rome Fellowship. He has taught Latin and French. He was Director of Music at the Deane School in Santa Barbara. He was Assistant Professor of Music at Hunter College from 1929 to 1939 and at present is Chairman of the Department of Music there. During World War I he served for two years as wireless operator in the A.E.F. He was awarded the Endicott Prize in Boston, the Paderewski Prize in 1939, and while in Rome he received the prize for composition. He is Editor of the Hunter College Choral Series.

Several of his works have been presented in Italy. His chamber music has been performed in Boston, Chicago, St. Louis and New York. An orchestral work was presented by the Chicago Symphony Orchestra. The "Prelude to Midsummer Night's Dream" has had frequent performances and a broadcast over CBS to England. He has written choral works for high school and college groups.

COMPOSITIONS

ORCHESTRAL WORKS

	DURATION	PUBLISHER	DATE
SYMPHONY ON CANADIAN AIRS	45 minutes	Manuscript	1937
CONCERT OVERTURE IN D MAJOR		Manuscript	
MUCH ADO ABOUT NOTHING	8 "	Manuscript	1944
OLD PAINT—symphonic sketch	10 "	Manuscript	1945

CHAMBER ORCHESTRA

FANTASY ON CHILDREN'S TUNES piano	12 minutes	Manuscript	1935
WATER IDYL	9 "	Manuscript	1936
PRELUDE-INTERMEZZO-FUGUE	10 "	Manuscript	1937
PRELUDE TO MIDSUMMER NIGHT'S DREAM	12 "	Carl Fischer, Inc. for hire	1939

CHORAL WORKS

O THOU WHOSE SPIRIT 2 sopranos, 2 altos		Carl Fischer, Inc.	1940
THE LORD'S PRAYER 2 sopranos, alto, timpani		Carl Fischer, Inc.	1940
SONG OF THE VOYAGEUR mixed chorus, orchestra; also 2 tenors, 2 basses or 2 sopranos, 2 altos		Carl Fischer, Inc.	1941
HOW LONG O JEHOVAH 2 sopranos, alto and solo		Carl Fischer, Inc.	1942
WYNKEN, BLYNKEN AND NOD 2 sopranos, 2 altos		M. Witmark & Sons	1943
REVEILLE 2 sopranos, alto		H. W. Gray Co., Inc.	1944

CHAMBER MUSIC

QUARTET NO. 1 strings	40 minutes	Edition S.M.R.	1923
STRING TRIO IN F	10 "	Manuscript	1928
ELEGIAC SONATA FOR PIANO		Universal Edition	1931

EVERETT HELM

Born in Minneapolis, Minnesota, in 1913. He received his Bachelor of Arts degree from Carleton College and his Master of Arts degree from Harvard University. He held the Elkan Naumburg Fellowship at Harvard, also the Paine Travelling Fellowship. He studied composition with Malipiero in Italy and Vaughan Williams in England. He received his Doctorate degree from Harvard University in 1939.

He taught at the Longy School of Music and at Mills College and was head of the Department of Music at Western College. From 1944 to 1946 he visited Latin-American countries as a Travel Grantee of the United States Department of State in connection with a book on Brazilian music which he will publish.

Entire programs of his works have been performed in Buenos Aires, Montevideo, Rio de Janeiro and have also been broadcast. The Sonata for Violin and Piano has been broadcast over CBS.

COMPOSITIONS

ORCHESTRAL WORKS	DURATION	PUBLISHER	DATE
THREE GOSPEL HYMNS	12 minutes	Boosey & Hawkes for hire	1942
KENTUCKY SONATA violin, orchestra	14 "	Manuscript for hire	1944
BRASILIANA	10 "	Manuscript	1946
SYMPHONY NO. 1	23 "	Manuscript	1946

CHAMBER ORCHESTRA			
FIVE MOVEMENTS FOR FLUTE AND STRINGS	12 minutes	Manuscript for hire	1940
SUITE FOR SMALL ORCHESTRA 10 wind instruments, strings	15 "	Manuscript for hire	1946

CHORAL WORKS			
ATTENDE DOMINE (Motet) mixed chorus, a cappella	4 minutes	Manuscript	1940
A SET OF CAROLS mixed chorus, a cappella	10 "	Manuscript	1940
THE LASS FROM THE LOW COUNTREE women's chorus, a cappella	3½ "	G. Schirmer, Inc.	1942
REQUIEM mixed chorus, orchestra	20 "	Manuscript for hire	1942
BALLAD OF THE TIMES OF MEN women's chorus, orchestra	8 "	Manuscript for hire	1943
FOR YOU, O DEMOCRACY mixed chorus, chamber orchestra	4 "	Manuscript for hire	1943

CHAMBER MUSIC			
SONATA FOR VIOLIN AND PIANO	20 minutes	Manuscript	1936
FIRST STRING QUARTET	16 "	Manuscript	1938–44
"CAMBRIDGE" SONATA piano	12 "	Manuscript	1939
THREE PASTORALS soprano, cello	8 "	Manuscript	1940
SONATA BREVIS piano	9 "	Ed. Tupy	1942
SONATA FOR VIOLA AND PIANO	12 "	Manuscript	1943

EVERETT HELM (*Continued*)

CHAMBER MUSIC (*Continued*)	DURATION	PUBLISHER	DATE
1865 QUARTET (No. 2) *2 violins, viola, cello*	12 minutes	Manuscript	1945
TRIO *violin, cello, piano*	14 "	Manuscript	1945
SONATA FOR FLUTE AND PIANO	15 "	Manuscript	1945

BERNARD HERRMANN

Born in New York City in 1911. He studied at the Juilliard Graduate School and at New York University. In 1942 he was awarded a grant by the American Academy of Arts and Letters. He received the Juilliard Foundation Publication Award for "For the Fallen." At present, he is Conductor of the Columbia Broadcasting Symphony and also presents the program "Invitation to Music."

He has written music for films and was awarded the Motion Picture Academy "Oscar" for the score to the film "All That Money Can Buy." "Welles Raises Kane" and the "Devil and Daniel Webster" have been arranged for concert performance and have been played by the St. Louis and the Philadelphia symphony orchestras and by the CBS Symphony. Many of his compositions have been played throughout the country and have been broadcast over CBS and NBC from coast to coast. Columbia, Victor and Decca have made records of his works. He is completing an opera, "Wuthering Heights."

COMPOSITIONS

ORCHESTRAL WORKS	DURATION	PUBLISHER	DATE
CURRIER AND IVES SUITE	18 minutes	Manuscript	1935
NOCTURNE AND SCHERZO	16 "	Manuscript	1936
SYMPHONY	40 "	Adler	1941
FOR THE FALLEN	8 "	Juilliard Edition	1943
THE DEVIL AND DANIEL WEBSTER SUITE	20 "	Manuscript	1944
WELLES RAISES KANE	18 "	Manuscript	1944

CHAMBER ORCHESTRA			
SINFONIETTA FOR STRING ORCHESTRA	15 minutes	New Music	1935

CHORAL WORKS			
MOBY DICK—a dramatic cantata *solo voices, male chorus, orchestra*	45 minutes	Carl Fischer, Inc.	1937
FANTASTICKS (Nicholas Breton) *mixed chorus, orchestra*	25 "	Manuscript	1942

FILM MUSIC	STUDIO		DATE

CITIZEN KANE
   ("Welles Raises Kane"—
   divertissement for orchestra)
	RKO		1940

MAGNIFICENT AMBERSONS	RKO		1941
THE DEVIL AND DANIEL WEBSTER (concert version—suite)	RKO		1941
JANE EYRE	20th Century-Fox		1943
HANGOVER SQUARE	20th Century-Fox		1944
ANNA AND THE KING OF SIAM	20th Century-Fox		1946

WERNER RICHARD HEYMANN

Born in Koenigsberg, Germany, in 1896. He studied violin and composition in Europe with Scheinpflug and Juon.

His symphonic and stage works were performed in Vienna, Paris and Berlin. Since his arrival in this country he has been chiefly engaged in writing music for motion pictures. At present he is completing the score for the Preston Sturges production, "The Sin of Harold Diddlebock," and "This is Heaven," a musical play for the stage. His music for films is listed here.

COMPOSITIONS

FILM MUSIC	STUDIO	DATE
NINOTCHKA	M. G. M.	1939
THIS THING CALLED LOVE	Columbia	1940
MY LIFE WITH CAROLINE	R. K. O.	1940
BEDTIME STORY	Columbia	1941
TO BE OR NOT TO BE	Lubitch-Korda	1942
ONE NIGHT TO REMEMBER	Columbia	1943
OUR HEARTS WERE YOUNG AND GAY	Paramount	1944
TOGETHER AGAIN	Columbia	1945
HAIL THE CONQUERING HERO	Paramount	1945

ETHEL GLENN HIER

Born in Cincinnati, Ohio, in 1889. She graduated from the Cincinnati Conservatory of Music and also studied at the Institute of Musical Art in New York. She studied piano with Thalberg and Friedberg and theory and composition with Goetschius, Kaun, Bloch, Berg and also with Malipiero in Italy.

She is actively engaged in teaching, lecturing, and playing, as well as composing.

Her Rhapsody for Violin and Piano was awarded first prize by the New York State Federation of Music Clubs. Performances of her works have been given in Cincinnati, Chicago, New York, London, and other European and American capitals. "Asolo Bells" for orchestra has been played by various orchestras. She has written a play in seven scenes, "Boyhood and Youth of Edward MacDowell," which has been performed by Junior Music Clubs throughout the country.

COMPOSITIONS

ORCHESTRAL WORKS	DURATION	PUBLISHER	DATE
CHORÉOGRAPHE	10 minutes	Manuscript for hire	1931
ASOLO BELLS	7 "	Manuscript for hire	1938
CAROLINA SUITE	14 "	Manuscript for hire	1939

ETHEL GLENN HIER (*Continued*)

CHORAL WORKS	DURATION	PUBLISHER	DATE
MOUNTAIN PREACHER *solo part, mixed chorus, orchestra*	23 minutes	Manuscript *for hire*	1940
THEN SHALL I KNOW *solo baritone, mixed chorus, organ*	15 "	Manuscript *for hire*	1945

CHAMBER MUSIC			
SUITE FOR SEXTET *flute, oboe, violin, viola,* *cello, piano*	12 minutes	Manuscript *for hire*	1925
SUITE FOR STRING QUARTET	14 "	Manuscript *for hire*	1926
RHAPSODY *violin, piano*	6 "	Manuscript	1933
SUITE FOR VOICE AND STRINGS *voice, flute, viola, cello, harp*	12 "	Manuscript *for hire*	1935

STAGE WORKS			
CHORÉOGRAPHE—ballet	10 minutes	Manuscript *for hire*	1931

EDWARD BURLINGAME HILL

Born in Cambridge, Massachusetts, in 1872 of New England ancestry. He was brought up in the atmosphere of Harvard traditions. His grandfather was President of the University and his father was Professor of Chemistry. He studied with Paine and graduated in 1894 from Harvard University with highest honors in music. Among his other teachers were Chadwick, Whiting and Widor. In 1908 he joined the faculty of Harvard as an instructor, in 1918 he was made Professor of Music, and in 1928 he became Chairman of the Division of Music. He retired in 1940. He is a member of the National Institute of Arts and Letters and a Chevalier of the Legion of Honor.

He has given the Lowell Institute Lectures on French music and has specialized in this study. These lectures were repeated at the universities of Strasbourg and Lyon. His book *Modern French Music* has been published, and he has contributed many articles on music to the *Boston Transcript* and to the *Musical Quarterly*.

The majority of his orchestral works have been performed by the Boston Symphony Orchestra and many works have been played by other major orchestras in America. Among them are the Symphonies (Nos. 1, 2 and 3), "Lilacs," Sinfonietta for Full Orchestra, Concertino for Piano and Orchestra and the "Stevensoniana Suites" (Nos. 1 and 2). The Sextet for Wind Instruments was first heard at the Elizabeth Coolidge Festival in Pittsfield, and this work, as well as other chamber works, has been played frequently.

EDWARD BURLINGAME HILL (*Continued*)

COMPOSITIONS

ORCHESTRAL WORKS

	DURATION		PUBLISHER	DATE
STEVENSONIANA SUITE No. 1, OPUS 24	15 minutes		Manuscript parts and score available	1917
LAUNCELOT AND GUINEVERE—symphonic poem			Manuscript	1920
STEVENSONIANA SUITE No. 2	14 "		G. Schirmer, Inc.	1922
LILACS—poem for orchestra	19 "		Cos Cob Press	1927
SYMPHONY No. 1, B FLAT MAJOR	18 "		Manuscript parts and score available	1928
SYMPHONY No. 2, C MAJOR	24 "		Manuscript parts and score available	1930
CONCERTINO FOR PIANO AND ORCHESTRA	12 "		G. Schirmer, Inc.	1931
SINFONIETTA FOR ORCHESTRA (in one movement)	15 "		Manuscript	1932
SINFONIETTA FOR STRING ORCHESTRA, OPUS 40	15 "		Arrow Music Press	1936
SYMPHONY No 3, G MAJOR, OPUS 41	28 "		Manuscript	1937
MUSIC FOR ENGLISH HORN AND ORCHESTRA	8 "		Manuscript score and parts available	1943

CHAMBER MUSIC

	DURATION		PUBLISHER	DATE
SONATA FOR FLUTE AND PIANO, E FLAT	16 minutes		Manuscript	1926
SONATA FOR CLARINET AND PIANO, A MAJOR	15 "		S.P.A.M.	1927
SEXTET FOR WIND INSTRUMENTS AND PIANO, B FLAT MAJOR	20 "		Manuscript	1934
STRING QUARTET, C MAJOR, OPUS 40	15 "		Manuscript	1935
QUINTET clarinet, string quartet	15 "		Manuscript score and parts available	1945

M. WOOD HILL

Born in Brooklyn, New York, in 1891. Her teachers were Rothwell and Rybner. In 1920 the first recital of her songs was given. She was awarded the national prize by the Associated Glee Clubs of America and Canada for "The Riders" for men's voices, and she also received three prizes from the National League of American Pen Women, one for her music to Yeats' poems. She was associated with the New York Music School Settlement, the Brooklyn Music School Settlement and the Hudson River Music School, which she founded. The Canadian Government commissioned "The Jolly Beggars" (Robert Burns) for the Banff Festivals.

Her works have been played both in the United States and Canada and have been broadcast over WOR, WNYC and, in London, through BBC. Several of her transcriptions of orchestral works have been performed by

M. WOOD HILL (*Continued*)

Sir Henry Wood in London and at the Elizabeth Coolidge Festivals in Pittsfield, as well as over BBC. She is completing a suite, "The Wind in the Willow."

COMPOSITIONS

ORCHESTRAL WORKS	DURATION	PUBLISHER	DATE
IMPRESSIONS—after Yeats	5 minutes	Manuscript *for hire*	1936
ADVENTURES OF PINOCCHIO—ballet suite	6 "	Manuscript *for hire*	1938
FABLES OF AESOP—suite *solo voice, orchestra*	10 "	J. Fischer & Bro.	1939
COURAGE—symphonic march	5 "	Manuscript *for hire*	1940
SCOTTISH OVERTURE	4 "	Published	1943

CHAMBER ORCHESTRA

QUINTET AND VOICE RECITING *4 solo instruments*	8 minutes	Manuscript *for hire*	1936
OLD ENGLISH SUITE	11 "	R. D. Row	1938
REACTIONS TO PROSE RHYTHMS	10 "	G. Schirmer, Inc.	1942

CHORAL WORKS

FRENCH CANADIAN FOLKSONGS *women's voices*	10 minutes	C. C. Birchard & Co.	1939
GAELIC RUNE OF HOSPITALITY *mixed chorus, a cappella*	3 "	Hall & McCreary	1941
SONG FOR COURAGE	3 "	Boston Music Co.	1944
FABLES OF AESOP *men's voices, piano*			

CHAMBER MUSIC

FOUR STRING QUARTETS		Manuscript *for hire*	1933
QUINTET VERSION OF "REACTIONS TO FIONA MACLEOD"		Manuscript	
QUINTET (poems by W. B. Yeats) *voice reciting, 4 solo instruments*		Manuscript	
TRIO *piano, horn, clarinet*		Manuscript	1937
FROM A FAR COUNTRY *string quartet*	4 minutes	Manuscript *for hire*	1937
OUT-OF-DOOR SUITE	11 "	Manuscript	1943

STAGE WORKS

THE JOLLY BEGGARS—operetta *small orchestra*		Manuscript *for hire*	1929–31
THE ADVENTURES OF PINOCCHIO— ballet *full stage production, small orchestra*		Manuscript *for hire*	1934
INTERPRETIVE SOLO DANCE *piano, percussion*		Manuscript	1937
THE ROSE AND THE RING— music play *small orchestra*	About 1 hour	Manuscript *for hire*	1941

PAUL HINDEMITH

Born in Hanau, near Frankfurt, in 1895. He studied composition with Bernhard Sekles in Frankfurt and with Arnold Mendelssohn. He also studied a number of instruments, but chose the viola as his principal instrument.

Shortly after the end of World War I he became concert master at the Frankfurt Opera House and violist in the Amar Quartet, which he founded and with which he toured Europe. In 1927 he was appointed Professor of Composition at the Hochschule in Berlin. His European works cover practically every field of composition: quartets, trios, sonatas for various instruments, works for chamber ensembles and orchestra, as well as songs, choral works and operas. In 1926 he wrote the opera "Cardillac," which was performed in Berlin and on many other German stages. His next opera, "Neues vom Tage," was written in 1929. His work, "Wir bauen eine Stadt," written in 1930, was given by many school groups in Germany and also in New York. Other notable works are "Hin und zurück" written in 1927 and the oratorio "Das Unaufhörliche" of 1931. In 1932 he wrote a complete day's program for a young people's music festival held in the small Holstein town of Plön, called "Plöner Musiktag." Among his last major works written in Europe are the Viola Concerto "Der Schwanendreher" (1935) and the "Memorial Music for Viola and String Orchestra," written in 1936 in memory of King George V of England. During these years he also was a member of a string trio with Goldberg and Feuermann. He came to the United States in 1937 at the invitation of the Elizabeth Sprague Coolidge Foundation from whom he had received a commission and toured the country as violist in performances of his own works. He is now a member of the music faculty of Yale University, where one of his varied activities is the presentation of early music on the original instruments. He is also the author of a book on composition.

The Symphony "Mathis der Maler" has been recorded by Victor and Telefunken, the latter version under the composer's direction. He also played viola in the performance of his String Trio No. 2 recorded by Columbia, which has also recorded his "Kleine Kammermusik 2."

COMPOSITIONS WRITTEN IN AMERICA

ORCHESTRAL WORKS

	DURATION	PUBLISHER	DATE
CONCERTO FOR CELLO AND ORCHESTRA	30 minutes	Manuscript	1940
SYMPHONY IN E FLAT	30 "	Manuscript	1941
CUPID AND PSYCHE OVERTURE	6 "	Associated Music Publishers	1943
SYMPHONIC METAMORPHOSIS ON THEMES BY CARL MARIA VON WEBER	18 "	Associated Music Publishers	1941
CONCERTO FOR PIANO AND ORCHESTRA		Manuscript	1945

CHAMBER ORCHESTRA

	DURATION	PUBLISHER	DATE
THEME WITH FOUR VARIATIONS (The Four Temperaments) *piano, strings*		Manuscript	1940
"HERODIADE" FOR CHAMBER ORCHESTRA	20 minutes	Manuscript	1944

PAUL HINDEMITH (*Continued*)

CHORAL WORKS	DURATION	PUBLISHER	DATE
A SONG OF MUSIC *women's chorus, piano*		Associated Music Publishers	1941
THE HARP THAT ONCE THROUGH TARA'S HALLS *mixed chorus, piano or harp, strings*		Associated Music Publishers	1941
WHEN LILACS LAST IN THE DOORYARD BLOOM'D *alto, baritone, mixed chorus, orchestra*	1 hour	Associated Music Publishers	1946

CHAMBER MUSIC			
SONATA NO. 3 FOR ORGAN		Associated Music Publishers	1940
SONATA FOR ENGLISH HORN AND PIANO		Associated Music Publishers	1942
SONATA FOR TROMBONE AND PIANO		Associated Music Publishers	1942
SONATA FOR TWO PIANOS (four hands)		Associated Music Publishers	1942
LUDUS TONALIS—12 fugues with prelude, interludes and postlude *piano*		Associated Music Publishers	1943
STRING QUARTET 1943		Associated Music Publishers	1943
NINE ENGLISH SONGS—cycle *voice, piano*		Associated Music Publishers	1942–44

DAVID JUSTIN HOLDEN

Born in White Plains, New York, in 1911. He studied at Haverford College and Harvard University. He was a pupil of Wagenaar at the Juilliard Graduate School and of Piston at Harvard University. He won two Harvard Fellowships and the Harvard George Arthur Knight Prize for a chamber-music composition.

He was an instructor in theory and history and Conductor of the Chorus and Orchestra at the Boston Conservatory of Music. At the present time, he is Assistant Professor of Music at Mt. Holyoke College. In 1946, he became Program Director of the Breck radio program, which performs familiar classics.

"Say, Paw," his rhapsody on Kentucky mountain folk tunes, was performed by the Cleveland Orchestra under the direction of Leinsdorf. His String Quartet in E was broadcast over WJZ, and his Music for Piano and Strings, which won the S.P.A.M. Publication Award in 1940, was presented over an NBC hook-up. He was given first honorable mention in the NBC Music Guild Chamber Music Contest and the second award in the Cleveland Orchestra's 25th Anniversary Composition Contest. He is now working on a Symphony in B and also writing a technical book called *A Basis for the Interpretation of Music.*

DAVID JUSTIN HOLDEN (*Continued*)

COMPOSITIONS

ORCHESTRAL WORKS	DURATION	PUBLISHER	DATE
A SYMPHONIC MOVEMENT	15 minutes	Manuscript	1942
SAY, PAW—rhapsody on Kentucky mountain folk tunes	8 "	Manuscript for hire	1942
SYMPHONY IN G	20–25 "	Manuscript for hire	1945

CHORAL WORKS			
GLORIA women's voices, a cappella	3 minutes	Manuscript for hire	1942
CANTATA ON APPALACHIAN CHRISTMAS CAROLS mezzo soprano solo, women's voices, organ or piano	10 "	Manuscript for hire	1943

CHAMBER MUSIC			
STRING QUARTET IN E	25 minutes	Manuscript for hire	1936
MUSIC FOR PIANO AND STRINGS piano, quartet, double-bass (optional)	18 "	S.P.A.M.	1938
STRING QUARTET IN D	15 "	Manuscript for hire	1945

STAGE WORKS			
WE, THE WOMEN—dance suite (choreography Gertrude Lippincott) piano or theatre orchestra	20 minutes	Manuscript	1945

MARY HOWE

Born in 1882 in Richmond, Virginia. She has made her home for many years in Washington, D. C. She studied piano with Burmeister in Germany and also with Hutcheson and Randolph. She worked with Strube in composition and received the Peabody Conservatory diploma in composition. Later she went to Paris to work with Boulanger.

From 1920 to 1935 she toured extensively in two-piano recitals with Anne Hull. She is on the Board of Directors of the National Symphony Orchestra, of Bennington College and of the MacDowell Colony and is the National Chairman of the National Federation of Music Clubs.

Her compositions have been performed in various cities in South America and in the United States and in Paris, London and other capitals in Europe. BBC in England and CBS, NBC and Canadian networks have broadcast her works. Victor has recorded "Stars" and "Allegro Inevitabile," and Columbia has recorded "Sheep May Safely Graze." She is completing at present an orchestration of "Love Song" (to the text by Rilke) and "To the Unknown Soldier" (text by Lely), as well as a symphony.

MARY HOWE (*Continued*)

COMPOSITIONS

ORCHESTRAL WORKS	DURATION	PUBLISHER	DATE
DIRGE	11 minutes	G. Schirmer, Inc.	1931
		for hire	
SAND	3 "	G. Schirmer, Inc.	1932
(arranged for chamber orchestra)		*for hire*	
AMERICAN PIECE	15 "	Manuscript	1933
CASTELLANA	14 "	Manuscript	1935
2 solo pianos, orchestra			
PAEAN	11 "	Carl Fischer, Inc.	1940
		for hire	
POTOMAC	21 "	Carl Fischer, Inc.	1940

CHAMBER ORCHESTRA

POEMA	12 minutes	Manuscript	1924
soprano, mezzo soprano,			
11 instruments			
SPRING PASTORAL	6 "	G. Schirmer, Inc.	1936
solo violin, 13 instruments			
COULENNES	10 "	Carl Fischer, Inc.	1936
12 instruments		*for hire*	
STARS AND WHIMSY	3½ "	Edition Musicus	1937
15 instruments		*for sale*	

CHORAL WORKS

CHAIN GANG SONG	9 minutes	G. Schirmer, Inc.	1925
male or mixed chorus,			
piano or orchestra			
CHAIN GANG SONG	9 "	G. Schirmer, Inc.	1936
mixed chorus, a cappella			
FIDDLER'S REEL	20 "	Manuscript	1936
alto or baritone solo, mixed chorus,			
piano or orchestra			
PROPHECY, 1792	12 "	Manuscript	1943
male chorus, piano or wind,			
brass, and percussion			

CHAMBER MUSIC

SONATA IN D	20 minutes	Manuscript	1923
violin and piano			
SUITE	20 "	Manuscript	1923
piano and string quartet			
QUATUOR	19½ "	Manuscript	1939
string quartet			
THREE PIECES AFTER EMILY DICKINSON	14 "	Manuscript	1941
string quartet			

STAGE WORKS

CARDS—ballet	22 minutes	Manuscript	1936
2 pianos, drums			

HENRY HOLDEN HUSS

Born in Newark, New Jersey, in 1862. He is a descendant of the Bohemian family of John Huss. He first studied music with his father and then went to the Munich Royal Conservatory, from which he graduated in 1885. He was a pupil of Rheinberger, Boise and Giehrl. On his return to America he toured as pianist with many of the symphonic orchestras, also playing his own Concerto for Piano. He has taught piano and theory and he has lectured at Hunter College in New York City. He received the Society for the Publication of American Music Award.

The String Quartet in B Minor won a National Federation of Music Clubs Prize and was first performed at the Bicentennial of the Federation of Music Clubs in Peterboro, New Hampshire. His chamber music has been played in New York, Cincinnati, Boston, Detroit and other cities. He has had broadcasts of his choral and chamber music.

COMPOSITIONS

ORCHESTRAL WORKS	DURATION	PUBLISHER	DATE
THE RIDE OF PAUL REVERE	30 minutes	Manuscript	1920
soprano, women's chorus, orchestra			
IN MEMORIAM 1914–1918	8 "	Manuscript	1920
LA NUIT	6 "	Manuscript	1938
INVICTUS—poem for orchestra			
in 2 parts	26 "	Manuscript	1939

CHAMBER ORCHESTRA			
ALLEGRETTO GIOCOSO	6 minutes	Manuscript	1938
string orchestra			

CHORAL WORKS			
THE 23RD PSALM	4 minutes	G. Schirmer, Inc.	1937
2 part women's chorus			
WINGED MESSENGERS OF PEACE		G. Schirmer, Inc.	1937
mixed chorus			
THE MYSTERY OF NIGHT	7 "	G. Schirmer, Inc.	1938
4 part women's chorus			
LORD MAKE MY HEART A PLACE			
WHERE ANGELS SING		G. Schirmer, Inc.	1938
mixed chorus			

CHAMBER MUSIC			
SONATA FOR VIOLA AND PIANO,			
D MINOR, OPUS 34	25 minutes	Manuscript	1915
STRING QUARTET IN B MINOR, NO. 3	23 "	S.P.A.M.	1918
		G. Schirmer, Inc.	
TRIO FOR PIANO, VIOLIN, CELLO, NO. 2	25 "	Manuscript	1921
SONATA FOR VIOLA AND PIANO	22 "	Manuscript	1922
STRING QUARTET, NO. 4		Manuscript	
SONATA FOR VIOLIN AND PIANO,			
NO. 2, D MINOR, OPUS 33	28 "	Manuscript	1937

HERBERT REYNOLDS INCH

Born in Missoula, Montana, in 1904. He graduated from the Eastman School of Music in Rochester. He studied composition with Royce and Hanson and was awarded a fellowship from the University of Rochester. Later he received the American Academy in Rome Fellowship. He holds a Doctorate degree from the University of Rochester.

From 1925 to 1928 and from 1930 to 1931, he taught theory at the Eastman School of Music. Since 1937 he has been Assistant Professor of Music at Hunter College. In 1945 he received the Ernest Bloch Award in composition for "Return to Zion," a chorus for women's voices.

Performances of his works have been given in Rochester and in other cities. His works have been included on programs of the Yaddo Festivals, the University of Wisconsin Festivals, the Rochester Festivals of American Music and the Composers' Forums of the Federal Music Project in Boston and New York.

COMPOSITIONS

ORCHESTRAL WORKS

	DURATION	PUBLISHER	DATE
VARIATIONS ON A MODAL THEME	14 minutes	Manuscript	1927
SYMPHONY	25 "	Manuscript	1932
TO SILVANUS	15 "	Manuscript	1933
CONCERTO FOR PIANO AND ORCHESTRA	30 "	Manuscript	1940
ANSWERS TO A QUESTIONNAIRE	16 "	Elkan-Vogel *score and parts for hire*	1942
NORTHWEST OVERTURE	5 "	Elkan-Vogel *score and parts for hire*	1943

CHAMBER ORCHESTRA

SUITE FOR SMALL ORCHESTRA	19 minutes	Manuscript	1929
SERENADE *5 woodwinds, 4 brasses, 5 strings*	20 "	Manuscript	1936

CHORAL WORKS

DIRGE FOR THE YEAR *mixed chorus, a cappella*	5 minutes	Manuscript	1930
SONG OF LIBERATION *women's chorus, piano*	5 "	Carl Fischer, Inc.	1943
RETURN TO ZION *women's chorus*		Carl Fischer, Inc.	1945

CHAMBER MUSIC

QUINTET *piano, string quartet*	25 minutes	Manuscript	1930
MEDITERRANEAN SKETCHES *string quartet*	15 "	Manuscript	1933
HOMILY *piano, violin, cello*	7 "	Manuscript	1934
DIVERTIMENTO *2 trumpets, 2 horns, 2 trombones, tuba*	14 "	Manuscript	1934
SONATA FOR PIANOFORTE	10 "	Manuscript	1935
STRING QUARTET	16 "	Manuscript	1936
SONATA FOR PIANO AND VIOLONCELLO	12 "	Carl Fischer, Inc.	1941

HERBERT REYNOLDS INCH (*Continued*)

CHAMBER MUSIC (*Continued*)	DURATION	PUBLISHER	DATE
FOUR BALLADS	28 minutes	Manuscript	1943
violin, piano; viola, piano;			
cello, piano; piano solo			
THREE CONVERSATIONS FOR			
STRING QUARTET	12 "	Manuscript	1944

CHARLES EDWARD IVES

Born in 1874 in Danbury, Connecticut. He is the son of a musician and teacher who had experimented over a period of years in the field of acoustics. His parent's general musical education had great influence on the boy, and it encouraged his interest in the best musical literature. At the age of twelve he began to experiment with "off-rhythms" and tried to imitate the sound of drums on the piano. He attended the Danbury public schools, the Hopkins Preparatory School at New Haven, and in 1898 he graduated from Yale University, where he studied under Horatio Parker. During the four years of training at college he continued to experiment privately; the New Haven Hyperion Theatre Orchestra was very helpful in trying out his new works.

When he was fourteen he held his first position as organist in Danbury, and he held a similar post in New Haven while studying at Yale. From 1900 to 1902 he was organist and choirmaster of the Central Presbyterian Church in New York City. In his early twenties he wrote "In the Cage," his first complete break from conventional writing. From 1906 to 1916 he wrote his major works; he stopped writing completely during the period of World War I. Since that time he has written chiefly songs. In 1922 a private edition was printed of one hundred and fourteen songs composed over a period of thirty years. Some of these have since been reprinted by New Music and by the Cos Cob Press. In 1919 he wrote *Essays Before a Sonata.* His career as a composer is only one part of his life, for he entered business in New York City after graduating from college in 1898, and from 1906 to 1930 he was active as a senior member of the firm of Ives and Myrick.

His orchestral works have been performed in Germany, France, Cuba, New York City, Washington, D. C., Los Angeles, St. Paul and other cities. A program devoted to his compositions was presented at the Columbia Festival of Contemporary Music in 1946 and was broadcast over WNYC. The Symphony No. 3 was first performed by the New York Little Symphony. Many of his works for chamber music and his song cycles have had frequent presentations in France, Hungary, Russia and the United States. There have been broadcasts of the Song Cycle with chamber orchestra from Moscow (U.S.S.R. Government Station), the "Second Orchestral Set" was broadcast over NBC and the Fourth Symphony and the First String Quartet were broadcast over CBS. "Barn Dance," "In the Night" and "General Booth Enters Heaven," as well as the Fourth Violin Sonata, were recorded by N.M.Q.R.

CHARLES EDWARD IVES (*Continued*)

COMPOSITIONS

ORCHESTRAL WORKS	DURATION	PUBLISHER	DATE
FOURTH SYMPHONY	40 minutes	New Music Publishing Co.	1916
FIRST ORCHESTRAL SET	25 "	C. C. Birchard & Co.	
THREE PLACES IN NEW ENGLAND			
SECOND ORCHESTRAL SET	abt. 15 "	Manuscript	
SYMPHONY HOLIDAYS	50 "	New Music Publishing Co.	
OVERTURE NO. 3	15 "	Manuscript	

CHAMBER ORCHESTRA			
TONE ROADS NO. 3	8 minutes	Manuscript	1915
12 or more instruments			
SCHERZO NO. 2	10 "	Manuscript	
woodwinds, strings			
SONG CYCLE NO. 4	15 "	Manuscript	1916
with small chamber orchestra			

CHORAL WORKS			
AN ELECTION	6 minutes	New Music Publishing Co.	1921
chorus, orchestra		*piano arrangement*	
THE MASSES	12 "	New Music Publishing Co.	
chorus, orchestra		*in part*	
LINCOLN—THE GREAT COMMONER	5 "	New Music Publishing Co.	
(Markham)			
chorus, orchestra			

CHAMBER MUSIC			
FOURTH VIOLIN AND PIANO SONATA	10 minutes	Arrow Music Press	1916
STRING QUARTET NO. 2	25 "	Manuscript	
AESCHYLUS AND SOPHOCLES	6 "	New Music Publishing Co.	1922
voice, string quartet, piano			

FREDERICK JACOBI

Born in San Francisco, California, in 1891. He has lived abroad and in the eastern states for many years. He was a pupil of Gallico and Joseffy and later studied composition with Goldmark and Bloch. In Berlin he attended the Hochschule für Musik where Paul Juon was his teacher.

During the years 1913–17 he was Assistant Conductor at the Metropolitan Opera House. He returned to the West for a few years and became very much interested in the music of the Pueblo Indians of New Mexico and Arizona, and he has gathered a great deal of material about them. Since 1936 he has been teaching composition at the Juilliard Graduate School in New York. He was lecturer at the University of California in Berkeley during the summers of 1940 and 1941; since 1941 lecturer at the Julius Hartt Musical Foundation, Hartford, Connecticut. He is an active mem-

FREDERICK JACOBI (*Continued*)

ber of the League of Composers. He received honorable mention in the Elizabeth Sprague Coolidge Competition of 1924, and twice received the Award of the Society for the Publication of American Music. The American Opera Society awarded him the David Bispham Memorial Medal for his opera "The Prodigal Son."

His String Quartet based on American Indian themes was selected to represent American Music for the International Festival of Contemporary Music at Zürich, and it has also been played in many cities of Europe and in the United States. Many of his orchestral works were performed by orchestras in Boston, San Francisco, Philadelphia, Cleveland, Rochester, Hartford, Chautauqua and New York, as well as at the Worcester Festival. In Europe his works were played by the Colonne Orchestra in Paris and by orchestras in Poland and Denmark, and his Piano Concerto was broadcast in Luxembourg. The "Friday Evening Service," commissioned by Temple Emanu-El of New York, has been given by the leading synagogues in San Francisco, Philadelphia, Los Angeles and elsewhere. "From the Prophet Nehemiah," written for the League of Composers, was performed at the League's birthday concert in 1942. Many articles and reviews from his pen have appeared in American and European magazines, and he has been a frequent contributor to the magazine *Modern Music*. The Scherzo for Five Wind Instruments has been recorded by N.M.Q.R.

COMPOSITIONS

ORCHESTRAL WORKS

	DURATION	PUBLISHER	DATE
The Eve of Saint Agnes	25 minutes	Manuscript	1919
Symphony	22 "	Manuscript	1922
Two Assyrian Prayers	12 "	Manuscript	1923
soprano or tenor			
Indian Dances	18 "	Universal Edition	1928
		C. C. Birchard & Co.	
Concerto for Violoncello and			
Orchestra	18 "	Universal Edition	1932
Concerto for Piano and Orchestra	26 "	Manuscript	1935
Concerto for Violin and Orchestra		Manuscript	1937
Ode	12 "	G. Schirmer, Inc.	1941
		for hire	
Four Dances from			
"The Prodigal Son"	18 "	G. Schirmer, Inc.	1945
		for hire	

CHAMBER ORCHESTRA

Two Assyrian Prayers	12 minutes	Manuscript	1923
soprano or tenor, 18 instruments			
Rhapsody	8 "	Elkan-Vogel	1940
harp and string orchestra			
Night Piece	5 "	Boosey & Hawkes	1941–1942
flute and small orchestra			

CHORAL WORKS

Friday Evening Service	20 minutes	Bloch Publishing Co.	1930
baritone solo, mixed chorus,			
a cappella			

FREDERICK JACOBI (*Continued*)

CHORAL WORKS (*Continued*)	DURATION	PUBLISHER	DATE
HYMN (Saadia)	5 minutes	Bloch Publishing Co.	1942
men's chorus			
(arranged for mixed chorus			
by C. Vinaver)	5 "	Bloch Publishing Co.	1942
AHAVAS OLOM		Bloch Publishing Co.	1945
tenor solo, mixed chorus, organ			

CHAMBER MUSIC

STRING QUARTET	18 minutes	S.P.A.M.	1924
based on Indian themes		G. Schirmer, Inc.	
		Universal Edition	
STRING QUARTET NO. 2	23 "	S.P.A.M.	1933
		J. Fischer & Bro.	
SCHERZO FOR WIND INSTRUMENTS	5 "	Carl Fischer, Inc.	1936
HAGIOGRAPHA	26 "	Arrow Press	1939
string quartet and piano			
FROM THE PROPHET NEHEMIAH	15 "	Manuscript	1942
two pianos and voice			
FANTASY SONATA FOR PIANO	9 "	Manuscript	1945
MUSIC FOR MONTICELLO	20 "	Manuscript	1945
trio for flute, cello, piano			
STRING QUARTET NO. 3	22 "	Manuscript	1945

STAGE WORKS

THE PRODIGAL SON—opera in 3 acts,			
full orchestra text by Herman			
Voaden suggested by 4 early			
American prints	2½ hours	Manuscript	1944

DOROTHY JAMES

Born in Chicago, Illinois, in 1901. She studied composition with Weidig, from whom she received two scholarships. She has been a pupil of Gruenberg, Krenek, and Delamarter and also a student in piano and theory at the Chicago Musical College. At the American Conservatory of Music she received a Master's degree in theory and composition. She won first prizes in the Mu Phi Epsilon Honorary Musical Sorority composition contests of 1926, 1930, and 1932.

She is Assistant Professor of Music Education at the Michigan State Normal College, Ypsilanti, where she is also Chairman of the Music Research Committee, and a visiting teacher of composition and orchestration at the University of Michigan. She was President of the Michigan Composers Club and Chairman of the American Composers Committee and of the Michigan Federation of Music Clubs. She was commissioned by the University Musical Society for youth cantatas and by the Philadelphia Symphony Orchestra.

Her works have received many performances in Detroit, Michigan, Rochester, Chicago, Ann Arbor and other cities. Some of her music has been broadcast over local stations. She is now completing a work for mixed chorus and orchestra.

DOROTHY JAMES *(Continued)*

COMPOSITIONS

ORCHESTRAL WORKS	DURATION	PUBLISHER	DATE
SYMPHONIC FRAGMENTS	10 minutes	Manuscript	1931
ELEGY FOR THE LATELY DEAD	8 "	Manuscript	1938

CHAMBER ORCHESTRA

THREE PASTORALES	12 minutes	Manuscript	1933–38
clarinet solo, harp and strings			
SUITE FOR SMALL ORCHESTRA	10 "	Manuscript	1940
6 wind instruments, strings			

CHORAL WORKS

CHRISTMAS NIGHT	2 minutes	H. T. Fitzsimons	1933
mixed chorus a cappella			
THE JUMBLIES	20 "	H. T. Fitzsimons	1934
youth chorus and orchestra,			
2 and 4 part treble voices,			
also piano accompaniment			
THE LITTLE JESUS CAME TO TOWN	3 "	H. T. Fitzsimons	1935
mixed chorus a cappella			
PAUL BUNYAN	25 "	Manuscript	1938
baritone solo, youth chorus,			
orchestra			
NIOBE	12 "	Manuscript	1941
women's voices, flute, strings,			
piano, full orchestra			
MARY'S LULLABY	4 "	H. T. Fitzsimons	1942
women's voices a cappella			

CHAMBER MUSIC

FOUR PRELUDES FROM THE CHINESE	15 minutes	Manuscript	1924
contralto, string quintet			
RHAPSODY	8 "	Manuscript	1930
violin, cello, piano			
STRING QUARTET IN ONE MOVEMENT	10 "	Manuscript	1932
RECITATIVE AND AIR	8 "	Manuscript	1943
viola, 2 violins, 2 cellos			

STAGE WORKS

AS YOU LIKE IT—incidental music		Manuscript	1927
small orchestra			
PAOLO AND FRANCESCA—opera in 3 acts		Manuscript	1932
5 principals, chorus, orchestra			

PHILIP JAMES

Born in Jersey City, New Jersey, in 1890. He was educated in New York. He attended the College of the City of New York. Among his teachers were Norris, Goldmark, Schenck and Scalero.

During the first World War he served in the infantry and after the armistice was appointed commanding officer and Bandmaster of the A.E.F. General Headquarters Band. He has been conductor and guest conductor of many leading orchestras in the United States and for seven years has

PHILIP JAMES (*Continued*)

conducted the Bamberger Little Symphony Orchestra of WOR. He has been instructor in music at Columbia University. He is Professor of Music and Chairman of the Department of Music of New York University. In 1927 he received the first prize offered by the *Homiletic Review* for a hymn tune, and in 1932 he was the winner of one of the National Broadcasting Company's orchestral awards for his satirical suite for orchestra, "Station WGZBX." In 1937 he obtained honorable mention by the Philharmonic Symphony Society of New York for the overture "Bret Harte" and was also given the Juilliard School of Music Publication Award. He is now President of the S.P.A.M.

His works, including "Station WGZBX," "Overture—Bret Harte" and "Overture in Olden Style on French Noels," have been given numerous performances by leading orchestras and have also been heard over the radio.

COMPOSITIONS

ORCHESTRAL WORKS

	DURATION	PUBLISHER	DATE
OVERTURE—BRET HARTE	8 minutes	Manuscript	1925
OVERTURE IN OLDEN STYLE ON FRENCH NOELS	12 "	C. C. Birchard & Co.	1926
SONGS OF THE NIGHT	15 "	Manuscript	1930
STATION WGZBX—a satirical suite for orchestra	15 "	Galaxy Music Corp. for hire	1931
OVERTURE—BRET HARTE (NO. 3)	12 "	Galaxy Music Corp. for hire	1934
GWALLIA—rhapsody	25 "	Manuscript	1936
BRENNAN ON THE MOOR	4 "	Manuscript	1940
SEA SKETCHES bass-baritone, orchestra	32 "	H. W. Gray Co., Inc.	1941
FESTAL MARCH "PERSTARE ET PRAESTAN"	5 "	Leeds Music Corp.	1942
FIRST SYMPHONY	38 "	Manuscript	1943

CHAMBER ORCHESTRA

SUITE FOR CHAMBER ORCHESTRA *11 instruments*	32 minutes	Manuscript	1924
KAMMERSYMPHONIE *11 instruments*	30 "	Manuscript	1926
SUITE FOR STRING ORCHESTRA	17 "	Juilliard School	1934
SINFONIETTA *17 instruments*	20 "	Manuscript	1943
SECOND SUITE FOR STRING ORCHESTRA	12 "	Carl Fischer, Inc.	1943

BAND MUSIC

E.F.G. OVERTURE FOR BAND	14 minutes	Leeds Music Corp.	1944

CHORAL WORKS

NIGHTINGALE OF BETHLEHEM *mixed chorus, orchestra*	30 minutes	H. W. Gray Co., Inc.	1917
THE NUN *women's chorus, orchestra*	20 "	H. W. Gray Co., Inc.	1922
A SONG OF THE FUTURE *13 part mixed chorus, a cappella*	10 "	H. W. Gray Co., Inc.	1922
LIGHT OF GOD *mixed chorus, orchestra*	25 "	H. W. Gray Co., Inc.	1928
MISSA IMAGINUM—Mass of the Pictures *mixed chorus, orchestra*	45 "	H. W. Gray Co., Inc.	1929

PHILIP JAMES (*Continued*)

CHORAL WORKS (*Continued*)	DURATION	PUBLISHER	DATE
STABAT MATER SPECIOSA	1 hour	H. W. Gray Co., Inc.	1930
mixed chorus, orchestra			
GENERAL WILLIAM BOOTH ENTERS			
INTO HEAVEN	14 minutes	Witmark Educational	1932
tenor solo, male voices,		Publications	
chamber orchestra			
THE TRIUMPH OF ISRAEL	1 hour	Manuscript	1933
soli, mixed chorus, orchestra			
PSALM 150	7 minutes	H. W. Gray Co., Inc.	1940
mixed chorus, orchestra			
WORLD OF TOMORROW	20 "	H. W. Gray Co., Inc.	1941
mixed chorus, orchestra			
PSALM 117	4 "	H. W. Gray Co., Inc.	1944
mixed chorus			
SHIRAT HA-YAM	40 "	H. W. Gray Co., Inc.	1944
mixed chorus, orchestra			

CHAMBER MUSIC			
STRING QUARTET	40 minutes	Manuscript	1926
FIRST ORGAN SONATA	25 "	H. W. Gray Co., Inc.	1929
QUINTET FOR WOODWIND	15 "	Carl Fischer, Inc.	1936
flute, oboe, clarinet, bassoon, horn			
PIANO QUARTET	30 "	Manuscript	1937
piano, violin, viola, cello			

STAGE WORKS			
JUDITH—ballet with narrator	1 hour	Manuscript	1927
chamber orchestra			
INCIDENTAL MUSIC FOR PLAY, "ARMS			
FOR VENUS"		Manuscript	1936
small orchestra			
INCIDENTAL MUSIC TO GOETHE'S			
"IPHIGENIA IN TAURIS"		Manuscript	1937
large orchestra			
FOUNDED FOR FREEDOM (Masque)	49 minutes	Manuscript	1942

WERNER JANSSEN

Born in 1900 in New York City. He graduated from Dartmouth College and studied music with Converse, Chadwick, and Friedheim. Fellowships have been granted him by the Juilliard Foundation and by the American Academy in Rome in 1930.

He was the first native New Yorker to be engaged to conduct the New York Philharmonic, in 1934–35, and he also conducted the symphonic orchestras of Philadelphia, Cleveland, Rochester, St. Louis, Chicago, Baltimore, Detroit, Hollywood Bowl and many of the major European orchestras. For his interpretations of the Sibelius symphonies he was knighted in Finland. He has been musical director and conductor for a series of broadcasts and founded the Janssen Symphony of Los Angeles in 1940.

"New Year's Eve in New York" has had performances by the symphonic orchestras in Rochester, Cleveland, New York Stadium, Berlin, Budapest, Riga and other cities. "Obsequies of a Saxophone" was first presented at

WERNER JANSSEN (*Continued*)

the Elizabeth Coolidge Festival in Washington, D. C. "Louisiana Symphony" was presented by the Augusteo Orchestra in Rome, by the Berlin Philharmonic and in Russia. There have been numerous performances of his quartets in Europe and in America.

COMPOSITIONS

ORCHESTRAL WORKS	DURATION	PUBLISHER	DATE
NEW YEAR'S EVE IN NEW YORK	18 minutes	C. C. Birchard & Co. *large and small score*	1930
LOUISIANA SYMPHONY	25 "	Manuscript *for hire*	1932
DIXIE FUGUE	8 "	Ernst Eulenburg	1932
FOSTER SUITE	10 "	C. C. Birchard & Co.	1937
CHAMBER ORCHESTRA			
OBSEQUIES OF A SAXOPHONE *6 wind instruments, snare drum*	10 minutes	Manuscript *for hire*	1930
CHAMBER MUSIC			
KALEIDOSCOPE *string quartet*	10 minutes	Manuscript	1932
FANTASY *string quartet*	10 "	Manuscript	1934
STRING QUARTET NO. 1	20 "	Manuscript	1934
STRING QUARTET NO. 2	25 "	Manuscript	1935
FILM MUSIC	STUDIO		
SYMPHONIC SCORE FOR "THE GENERAL DIED AT DAWN" *large orchestra*	Paramount		1936

HORACE JOHNSON

Born in Waltham, Massachusetts, in 1893. He studied composition with Crist and Marshall. For four years he lived abroad, studying in Italy, France and England.

He has been Associate Editor of the *Musical Observer*, Contributing Editor of the *Etude* and the *Musician,* as well as Music Editor of the *Delineator.* For three years he served on the staff of *Musical America,* and for nine years was Managing Editor of the *Musical Courier.* He was Director of the New York City W.P.A. Music Project from 1939–1941. Many of his songs and piano works have been published in the United States and in England.

Among those of his works frequently performed are "Imagery," "Astarte," "Streets of Florence" and "In the American Manner," which have been heard in England, Canada and Mexico, also in Boston, St. Louis, Cincinnati, Detroit, Baltimore, New York and other cities in America. His com-

HORACE JOHNSON (*Continued*)

positions have been broadcast by the National Broadcasting Company, Mutual Broadcasting System and by local radio stations. He is now living in Wingdale, New York, where he is President of the Wingdale Civic Association.

COMPOSITIONS

ORCHESTRAL WORKS	DURATION	PUBLISHER	DATE
IMAGERY—orchestral suite	14 minutes	J. Fischer & Bro.	1924
ASTARTE—tone poem	25 "	Boosey & Hawkes *for hire*	1929
STREETS OF FLORENCE—orchestral suite	12 "	Carl Fischer, Inc. *for hire*	1930
IN THE AMERICAN MANNER	5 "	G. Schirmer, Inc. *piano arr. published orch. score ms.*	1932
THREE-FOUR—symphonic waltz	5 "	Carl Fischer, Inc. *for hire*	1943
MUSIC FOR STRINGS—symphonic work	11 "	Carl Fischer, Inc. *for hire*	1945

CHAMBER ORCHESTRA			
JOYANCE	10 minutes	G. Schirmer, Inc. *for hire violin solo published score in ms.*	1937

CHORAL WORKS			
BABE OF BETHLEHEM mixed voices	5 minutes	G. Ricordi & Co.	1929

CHAMBER MUSIC			
TO MY LADY—song cycle	8 minutes	Manuscript	1927

HUNTER JOHNSON

Born in Benson, North Carolina, in 1906. He attended the University of North Carolina for two years. He entered the Eastman School of Music in Rochester, where he won a scholarship in composition and, in 1929, obtained a degree in music.

In 1933 he was awarded the Prix de Rome and spent two years in Europe. In 1941 he won a Guggenheim Fellowship. Since 1944 he has been Chairman of the Department of Theory at the University of Manitoba in Winnipeg, Canada.

His works have been played in New York, Ithaca, Raleigh and in other cities. The two ballets, "Letter to the World" and "Deaths and Entrances," both written in collaboration with Martha Graham, have had a great many performances. At present he is composing an Orchestral Concerto and arranging a Suite from "Letter to the World."

COMPOSITIONS

ORCHESTRAL WORKS	DURATION	PUBLISHER	DATE
PRELUDE	6 minutes	Manuscript	1929
SYMPHONY No. 1	30 "	Manuscript	1931
ANDANTE FOR FLUTE AND STRINGS	6 "	Manuscript	1938
ADAGIO FOR STRINGS	8 "	Manuscript	1940
FOR AN UNKNOWN SOLDIER	7 "	Valley Press	1944
flute, orchestra			

CHAMBER ORCHESTRA			
CONCERTO FOR PIANO AND SMALL ORCHESTRA	20 minutes	Manuscript	1936
23 instruments			

CHAMBER MUSIC			
PIANO SONATA	17 minutes	Manuscript	1936
ELEGY FOR CLARINET AND STRINGS	10 "	Manuscript	1936
6 instruments			
SERENADE FOR FLUTE AND CLARINET	6 "	Valley Press	1937

STAGE WORKS			
SOLDIER'S LEAVE	11 minutes	Manuscript	1939
2 pianos			
LETTER TO THE WORLD—ballet	44 "	Manuscript	1940
13 instruments			
DEATHS AND ENTRANCES—ballet	40 "	Manuscript	1943
13 instruments			

CHARLES JONES

Born in Tamworth, Canada, in 1910. He began his musical training studying the violin. He came to the United States in 1928, where he won a fellowship from the Graduate School of Juilliard and continued his studies in composition with Wagenaar. He also studied with Copland at the first summer session of the Berkshire School. The Juilliard Extension Division sent him to California to do special work, and while there, he conducted two of his own works with the San Francisco Symphony.

His works have been performed throughout the country under the direction of Janssen, Goldschmann, Kindler and under his own direction. The "Three Pieces for Piano" and the "Eight Dedications for Piano" were played on the 1944 and 1945 WNYC American Festival. The Sinfonietta and the Columbia Symphony have broadcast his Suite for Small Orchestra over WOR and WABC. The Society for the Publication of American Music has chosen his Violin Sonatina for publication. Recent performances include "Five Melodies for Orchestra" by the San Francisco Orchestra and the String Quartet No. 2 by the Pro Arte Quartet.

CHARLES JONES (*Continued*)

COMPOSITIONS

ORCHESTRAL WORKS	DURATION	PUBLISHER	DATE
SYMPHONY (in two parts)	18 minutes	Manuscript	1939
GALUP	4 "	Manuscript	1940
OVERTURE	4 "	Leeds-Am Rus *for hire*	1942
FIVE MELODIES FOR ORCHESTRA	17 "	Manuscript	1945

CHAMBER ORCHESTRA			
SUITE FOR SMALL ORCHESTRA *11 instruments*	13 minutes	Carl Fischer, Inc. *for hire*	1937
SUITE FOR STRINGS	12 "	Carl Fischer, Inc. *for hire*	1937
COWBOY SONG *oboe solo, percussion, strings*	4 "	Manuscript	1941

CHORAL WORKS			
DOWN WITH DRINK—sequence of American temperance songs *women's voices, piano, percussion*	15 minutes	Manuscript	1943

CHAMBER MUSIC			
TWO STRING QUARTETS	15–18 minutes	Manuscript	1936–44
SONATINA FOR VIOLIN AND PIANO	8 "	S.P.A.M. G. Schirmer, Inc.	1942
SUITE FOR VIOLIN AND PIANO	17 "	Manuscript	1945
PIANO SONATA	15 "	Manuscript	1946

STAGE WORKS			
DOWN WITH DRINK—ballet			1943

WERNER JOSTEN

Born in Elberfeld, Germany, in 1888. He studied harmony and counterpoint in Munich with Siegel and later went to Geneva to work with Jacques-Dalcroze. After several years in Paris he returned to Munich, where he was appointed Assistant Conductor at the Munich Opera House. In 1921 he moved to America. He received the Publication Award from the Juilliard Music Foundation in 1931 and 1938. Since 1923 he has been a member of the faculty of Smith College at Northampton, where he is Professor of Music and also conducts the Smith College Orchestra. His interest in the subject of early opera led him, with the help of the Smith College Music Department, to produce several important revivals of ancient works. Several of these productions were later repeated in New York City.

Performances of many of his orchestral works have been given in Philadelphia, Boston, New York, Cincinnati, Cleveland, Chicago, Rochester and other cities of the United States. "Ode for St. Cecilia's Day" was first presented at the Worcester Festival; many of his choral and chamber works have had frequent performances in America. A stage production of "Joseph and

WERNER JOSTEN (*Continued*)

His Brethren" was given with the Juilliard School. The "Concerto Sacro I" was broadcast by the Philadelphia Orchestra over the CBS. His Sonata for Violin and Piano was performed at the I.S.C.M. Festival in London in 1938.

COMPOSITIONS

ORCHESTRAL WORKS

	DURATION	PUBLISHER	DATE
CONCERTO SACRO I *string orchestra, piano*	22 minutes	C. C. Birchard & Co.	1927
CONCERTO SACRO II *string orchestra, piano*	18 "	C. C. Birchard & Co.	1927
JUNGLE	14 "	Universal Edition	1928
A UNE MADONE—Baudelaire *tenor solo, orchestra*	12 "	Manuscript	1929
JOSEPH AND HIS BRETHREN— concert suite	18 "	Associated Music Publishers *manuscript for hire*	1932
ENDYMION—concert suite	12 "	Associated Music Publishers *manuscript for hire*	1933
SERENADE FOR ORCHESTRA	17 "	Associated Music Publishers *manuscript for hire*	1934
SYMPHONY FOR STRINGS	18 "	Associated Music Publishers *manuscript for hire*	1935
SYMPHONY IN F	17 "	Affiliated Music Corp.	1936

CHAMBER ORCHESTRA

CANZONA SERIA FOR LOW STRINGS	15 minutes	Associated Music Publishers	1940

CHORAL WORKS

CRUCIFIXION *bass solo, mixed chorus, a cappella*	15 minutes	G. Schirmer, Inc.	1915
HYMNUS TO THE QUENE OF PARADYS *alto solo, women's voices, strings, organ*	5 "	G. Schirmer, Inc.	1921
INDIAN SERENADE—Shelley *tenor solo, orchestra*	5 "	Manuscript	1922
ODE FOR ST. CECILIA'S DAY *soprano and baritone soli, mixed chorus, orchestra*	25 "	G. Schirmer, Inc.	1925

CHAMBER MUSIC

STRING QUARTET	18 minutes	Manuscript	1934
SONATA FOR VIOLIN AND PIANO	12 "	Manuscript	1936
SONATA FOR PIANO	13 "	Manuscript	1937
SONATA FOR CELLO AND PIANO	15 "	Associated Music Publishers	1938
SONATINA FOR VIOLIN AND PIANO	12 "	Associated Music Publishers	1939
TRIO FOR FLUTE, CLARINET, AND BASSOON	12 "	Arrow Music Press	1940
JUNGLE *arranged for two pianos, 4 hands*	14 "	Associated Music Publishers	1940
TRIO FOR OBOE, CLARINET AND BASSOON	15 "	Manuscript	1941
TRIO FOR VIOLIN, VIOLA AND CELLO	15 "	Manuscript	1942

WERNER JOSTEN *(Continued)*

CHAMBER MUSIC (*Continued*)	DURATION	PUBLISHER	DATE
TRIO FOR FLUTE, CELLO (OR BASSOON) AND PIANO	15 minutes	Manuscript	1943
SONATA FOR HORN AND PIANO	12 "	Manuscript	1944
SONATA FOR VIOLIN AND PIANO	12 "	Manuscript	1945

STAGE WORKS

JUNGLE—ballet *full orchestra*	14 minutes	Universal Edition	1928
BATOUALA—ballet *chorus, orchestra*	1 hour	Manuscript	1931
JOSEPH AND HIS BRETHREN—ballet	35 minutes	Associated Music Publishers *manuscript for hire*	1932
ENDYMION—ballet	25 "	Associated Music Publishers *manuscript for hire*	1933

ULYSSES SIMPSON KAY

Born in Tucson, Arizona, in 1917. He studied public-school music at the University of Arizona and composition with Bernard Rogers and Howard Hanson at the Eastman School of Music. He studied with Paul Hindemith at the Berkshire Music Center and at the Yale Music School. He won a composition contest sponsored by Phi Mu Alpha, Sinfonia Fraternity.

From 1941 to 1945, he was in the U. S. Navy. He was awarded the Ditson Fellowship (Columbia University) for one year of post-war creative work. In 1946, he received an award from the American Broadcasting Company. He is especially interested in composing music for high-school and college groups.

The Rochester Civic Orchestra performed his Oboe Concerto and his Sinfonietta, which was also broadcast over NBC. "Of New Horizons" was played by the New York Philharmonic, and the Cleveland Philharmonic did his "Five Mosaics," a chamber work. The League of Composers presented his Piano Sonata in C and the Sonatina for Violin and Piano.

COMPOSITIONS

ORCHESTRAL WORKS	DURATION	PUBLISHER	DATE
SINFONIETTA	9–11 minutes	Manuscript for hire	1939
CONCERTO FOR OBOE	10 "	Manuscript for hire	1940
OF NEW HORIZONS	8 "	Manuscript for hire	1944
A SHORT OVERTURE		Manuscript	1946

CHAMBER ORCHESTRA

FIVE MOSAICS *6 wind instruments, percussion,* *piano, strings*	4 minutes	Manuscript for hire	1940

ULYSSES SIMPSON KAY (*Continued*)

BAND MUSIC	DURATION	PUBLISHER	DATE
EVOCATION	6–8 minutes	Manuscript	1944
concert band		*for hire*	

CHORAL WORKS

FOUR PIECES FOR MALE CHORUS	5–6 minutes	Manuscript	1941
a cappella			
COME AWAY, COME AWAY, DEATH	3 "	Manuscript	1943
AS JOSEPH WAS A-WALKING	3 "	Manuscript	1943
DEDICATION		Manuscript	1946
mixed chorus a cappella			

CHAMBER MUSIC

PIANO SONATA	8 minutes	Manuscript	1940
FLUTE QUINTET	10 "	Manuscript	1942
flute and string quartet			
SUITE IN B	12 "	Manuscript	1942
oboe and piano			
SUITE FOR BRASS CHOIR	8 "	Manuscript	1942
4 trumpets, 4 horns,			
3 trombones, tuba			

STAGE WORKS

DANSE CALINDA—ballet	18 minutes	Manuscript	1941

HOMER KELLER

Born in Oxnard, California, in 1915. He attended the public schools of Southern California and in 1934, he entered the Eastman School of Music where he studied with Hanson and Rogers. He received his Master of Music degree in 1938. From 1938 to 1941, he was on the faculty of Fort Hays Kansas State College, and .later he taught at the Music School of Indiana University. He entered the army in 1942 and was Band Director for the air forces in the South Pacific. In Manila he was a music instructor at the Philippine Institute and the De La Salle College for the armed forces. In 1946, he returned to the United States and is at present at the Eastman School of Music.

While in the army, he composed "The Raider" for men's choir and brass accompaniment and a Fantasy and Fugue for Organ. Both of these works were performed in Washington. His Symphony No. 1 was awarded the Henry Hadley Foundation Award and was performed by the New York Philharmonic in 1940. His Chamber Symphony was played at the Annual Festival of American Music in Rochester and was broadcast over an NBC network. The Serenade for Clarinet and Strings was recorded by Victor and was performed by the Manila Symphony in 1945. He is now completing a Symphony No. 2, a commissioned choral work with orchestral accompaniment and a Piano Sonata.

HOMER KELLER (*Continued*)

COMPOSITIONS

ORCHESTRAL WORKS	DURATION	PUBLISHER	DATE
SERENADE FOR CLARINET AND STRINGS	5 minutes	Eastman School of Music Publication Carl Fischer, agent	1937
SYMPHONY No. 1 IN A MINOR	23 "	Manuscript	1939
CHAMBER SYMPHONY	12 "	Manuscript	1941

CHORAL WORKS			
THE RAIDER men's chorus, brass	2½ minutes	Manuscript	1943

CHAMBER MUSIC			
STRING QUARTET IN ONE MOVEMENT	7 minutes	Manuscript	1935
SONATINA FOR PIANO	5 "	Manuscript	1937
STRING QUARTET No. 2	15 "	Manuscript	1937
SONATA bassoon, piano	9 "	Manuscript	1941

EDGAR STILLMAN KELLEY

Born in Sparta, Wisconsin, in 1857, and died in 1944. He studied composition at the Stuttgart Conservatory and graduated in 1880. He held positions in San Francisco for many years as music critic, teacher and organist. In 1890, he moved to New York and became an instructor in composition and lecturer on music at the New York University. In 1901–02, he was acting Professor of Theory at Yale University. He became Dean of Composition at Cincinnati Conservatory, and in 1910 he held a fellowship of composition at Western College. He was a member of the National Institute of Arts and Letters.

His works have been performed at many festivals in the United States and by the major symphonic orchestras. His chamber music has been played frequently in Europe and America and also broadcast over NBC. The "Pit and the Pendulum" received the first award of the National Federation of Music Clubs.

COMPOSITIONS

ORCHESTRAL WORKS	DURATION	PUBLISHER	DATE
ALADDIN—Chinese symphonic suite		C. C. Birchard & Co.	1915
ALICE IN WONDERLAND—symphonic suite	30 minutes	Oliver Ditson Co.	1922
NEW ENGLAND SYMPHONY		C. C. Birchard & Co.	1922
PIT AND THE PENDULUM—symphonic suite		S.P.A.M.	1930
GULLIVER—symphony		Affiliated Music Corporation	

EDGAR STILLMAN KELLEY (*Continued*)

ORCHESTRAL WORKS (*Continued*)	DURATION	PUBLISHER	DATE
SYMPHONIC MUSIC TO THE PLAY OF MACBETH—single numbers for concert			
SYMPHONIC MUSIC TO THE PLAY OF BEN HUR			
ISRAFEL *voice, orchestra*			
ELDORADO *voice, orchestra*			

CHORAL WORKS

PILGRIM'S PROGRESS	2 hours		1918
ALICE IN WONDERLAND *chorus, 20 mimes*	20 minutes		

CHAMBER MUSIC

QUINTET FOR STRING QUARTET AND PIANO	35 minutes		
STRING QUARTET	30 "		

STAGE WORKS

LYRIC OPERA PURITANIA	2 hours		
ALICE IN WONDERLAND—pantomime		Manuscript	

KENT WHEELER KENNAN

Born in Milwaukee, Wisconsin, in 1913. He studied piano and organ, attended the University of Michigan and received his Bachelor and Master of Arts degrees from the Eastman School of Music. He won the Prix de Rome and studied in Europe for three years.

Before he enlisted in the Army Air Corps, he taught theory and piano at Kent State University and composition and theory at the University of Texas. In 1944, he was appointed Warrant Officer Bandleader.

His "Night Soliloquy" was given major performances by the Detroit Symphony, Philadelphia Orchestra, National Symphony, NBC Symphony, New York Philharmonic Orchestra, and the Rochester Philharmonic Orchestra; it was also recorded by RCA Victor. His Andante and other compositions have had broadcasts over major networks.

COMPOSITIONS

ORCHESTRAL WORKS	DURATION	PUBLISHER	DATE
NIGHT SOLILOQUY *flute, orchestra*	3½ minutes	Carl Fischer, Inc.	1936
DANCE DIVERTIMENTO	10 "		1938
PROMENADE		Carl Fischer, Inc.	
LAMENT		Manuscript	
AIR DE BALLET		Manuscript	
JIG		Manuscript	

KENT WHEELER KENNAN (*Continued*)

ORCHESTRAL WORKS (*Continued*)	DURATION	PUBLISHER	DATE
SYMPHONY	28 minutes	Manuscript	1939
ANDANTE	5 "	Manuscript	1939
oboe, orchestra			
CONCERTINO	13 "	Manuscript	1942
piano, orchestra			

CHORAL WORKS			
BLESSED ARE THEY THAT MOURN	10 minutes	G. Schirmer, Inc	1939
mixed chorus, orchestra		(with piano accompaniment) *score for hire*	
THE UNKNOWN WARRIOR SPEAKS	3 "	H. W. Gray Co., Inc.	1944
male chorus, a cappella			

CHAMBER MUSIC			
QUINTET FOR PIANO AND STRINGS	22 minutes	G. Schirmer, Inc.	1936
PIANO SONATA (one movement)	7 "	Manuscript	1942

MARSHALL RUTGERS KERNOCHAN

Born in New York City in 1880. He studied with Iwan Knorr in Germany and with Percy Goetschius at the Institute of Musical Art in New York. He is a member of the Board of Governors of "The Bohemians" and of the Board of Directors of Musical Foundation, Inc.

The "Foolish Virgin," a cantata, was performed in New York City and was broadcast over WOR by the Sinfonietta. He has written many concert songs and compositions for chorus.

COMPOSITIONS

CHORAL WORKS	DURATION	PUBLISHER	DATE
THE FOOLISH VIRGIN	30 minutes	Galaxy Music Corp.	1915
soprano, contralto, baritone solo, women's chorus, orchestra			
THE SLEEP OF SUMMER	6 "	Galaxy Music Corp.	1915
women's chorus, string orchestra, piano			

HARRISON KERR

Born in Cleveland, Ohio, in 1899. He studied first with James Hotchkiss Rogers and later in France with Nadia Boulanger and Isidore Philipp.

He has been active in the field of contemporary music besides composing and teaching. He was editor of *Trend,* a magazine of contemporary arts, and has written many articles for various publications. He has served on

HARRISON KERR (*Continued*)

the editorial boards of New Music Edition and New Music Recordings. At present, he is Secretary of the American Composers Alliance, Executive Secretary of the American Music Center, Secretary of the National Music League, and a member of the Executive Committee of the National Music Council.

His works have had major performances in a number of cities in the United States and in France and Germany. Nearly all of his chamber music has been broadcast over WNYC and several works have received network broadcasts by NBC. The "Dance Sonata" was commissioned by the Bennington School of the Dance and has had many performances throughout the United States. New Music Recordings recorded the Trio for Clarinet, Violoncello, and Piano and the Study for Violoncello, Unaccompanied.

COMPOSITIONS

ORCHESTRAL WORKS

	DURATION	PUBLISHER	DATE
SYMPHONY No. 1 (one movement)	15 minutes	Arrow Music Press	1928–39
CONTRAPUNTAL SUITE	12 "	Manuscript for hire	1936
SYMPHONY No. 2	32 "	Manuscript for hire	1937
DANCE SUITE	15 "	Manuscript for hire	1933
SYMPHONY No. 3	30 "	Manuscript for hire	1945

CHAMBER ORCHESTRA

THREE SONGS WITH CHAMBER ORCHESTRA high or medium voice, 11 instruments	6 minutes	Manuscript for hire	1928
MOVEMENT FOR STRING ORCHESTRA	8 "	Manuscript for hire	1936

CHORAL WORKS

WINK OF ETERNITY mixed choir, orchestra	7 minutes	Manuscript	1937

CHAMBER MUSIC

SONATA No. 1 FOR PIANO	15 minutes	Manuscript	1929
NOTATIONS ON A SENSITIZED PLATE high or medium voice, string quartet, clarinet, piano	5½ "	New Music Edition	1935
TRIO FOR CLARINET, VIOLONCELLO AND PIANO	11 "	New Music Edition	1936
STRING QUARTET	20 "	Arrow Music Press	1937
TRIO FOR VIOLIN, VIOLONCELLO AND PIANO	15 "	Manuscript	1938
SUITE FOR FLUTE AND PIANO	9 "	Arrow Music Press	1941
SONATA No. 2 FOR PIANO	15 "	Manuscript	1943

STAGE WORKS

DANCE SONATA group of dancers, 2 pianos, percussion (also orchestrated for large orchestra)	15 minutes	Manuscript	1938

GEORGE KLEINSINGER

Born in San Bernardino, California, in 1914. He received his Bachelor of Music degree from New York University, after leaving dental school in order to further his musical studies. He was awarded the Juilliard Fellowship in composition and won the National Theater Prize for his opera, "Life in a Day of a Secretary."

Major performances and broadcasts have been given of the cantata "I Hear America Singing," which has been recorded by RCA Victor. "Tubby the Tuba" has been played frequently by leading orchestras, broadcast over major networks, has been recorded by Cosmo and is soon to be made into a motion picture. He has been given several commissions to write children's symphonic albums. In 1946 the "Fantasy for Violin" had its première by the National Orchestral Association. Other works have had numerous broadcasts over CBS, NBC and other networks. He has been commissioned to write a cello concerto, and he is completing a tone poem, "Jesse James," based on the famous "thriller" legend.

COMPOSITIONS

ORCHESTRAL WORKS

	DURATION	PUBLISHER	DATE
A WESTERN RHAPSODY	8 minutes	E. B. Marks	1942
SCHERZO FOR ORCHESTRA	6 "	Manuscript	1944
OVERTURE ON AMERICAN FOLK THEMES	6 "	Mills Music Inc.	1945
FANTASY FOR VIOLIN AND ORCHESTRA	15 "	Manuscript	1945
SYMPHONY NO. 1	20 "	Manuscript	1946

CHAMBER ORCHESTRA

JACK AND HOMER THE HORSE *with narrator*	12 minutes	Manuscript	1942
TUBBY THE TUBA *with narrator*	10 "	Manuscript	1943
PEEPO THE PICCOLO *with narrator*	12 "	Manuscript	1945

CHORAL WORKS

I HEAR AMERICA SINGING *baritone, mixed chorus, orchestra*	20 minutes	E. B. Marks	1940
FAREWELL TO A HERO *baritone, mixed chorus, orchestra*	13 "	Boosey & Hawkes	1941
SONG FOR PIONEERS *mixed chorus, piano*	6 "	Edwin Morris	1941

CHAMBER MUSIC

STRING QUARTET	18 minutes	Manuscript	1940

STAGE WORKS

LIFE IN A DAY OF A SECRETARY *12 voices, piano or orchestra*	39 minutes	Manuscript	1939
VICTORY AGAINST HEAVEN *8 singers, 2 pianos, 2 sets*	30 "	Manuscript	1941
BROOKLYN CANTATA *12 voices, piano or orchestra, one set*	12 "	Leeds Music	1942

ELLIS B. KOHS

Born in Chicago, Illinois, in 1916. He studied at the San Francisco Conservatory of Music, the Institute of Musical Art, Harvard University and the University of Chicago where he received his Master of Arts degree. His teachers were Bricken, Wagenaar and Piston. He won the Juilliard Fellowship in 1938–39, and the Ditson Post-War Fellowship (Columbia University) in 1944. He was a lecturer in music at the University of Wisconsin until he entered the U. S. Army, where he became a bandleader in 1943.

The Passacaglia for Organ and Strings was performed by the Boston Symphony at Harvard University in 1946 and also broadcast over the CBS network. Other compositions have been played in California, Boston, Washington, D. C., and New York.

COMPOSITIONS

ORCHESTRAL WORKS	DURATION	PUBLISHER	DATE
CONCERTO FOR ORCHESTRA	12 minutes	Manuscript (rental)	1941
LIFE WITH UNCLE (Sam)	9 "	Manuscript (rental)	1943
CONCERTO FOR PIANO AND ORCHESTRA	16 "	Manuscript (rental)	1945
CHAMBER ORCHESTRA			
NIGHT WATCH—a dialog for flute, horn and tympani	5 minutes	Manuscript (rental)	1944
CHORAL WORKS			
THE AUTOMATIC PISTOL men's voices, a cappella	4 minutes	Manuscript (rental)	1943
CHAMBER MUSIC			
STRING QUARTET	28 minutes	Manuscript (rental)	1941
SONATINA FOR BASSOON AND PIANO	10 "	Manuscript (rental)	1945

ERICH WOLFGANG KORNGOLD

Born in Brno, Moravia, in 1897. His teachers were Fuchs and Zemlinsky in Vienna.

He began to compose at the age of seven. His pantomime, "The Snowman," written at the age of eleven, was given at the Vienna Opera in 1910, conducted by Franz Schalk. He has also written several works for piano, chamber ensembles and orchestra and a number of operas. He conducted concerts of his own and other works in most of the musical centers of the Continent and appeared as guest conductor of his operas in Vienna and Hamburg. In 1923 he first devoted himself to the adaptation of stage works by Johann Strauss, and in 1929 he began to collaborate with Max Reinhardt. In 1930 he became professor at the Staatsakademie für Musik

ERICH WOLFGANG KORNGOLD (*Continued*)

in Vienna. In 1934 he was called to Hollywood to arrange Mendelssohn's music for Max Reinhardt's production of "A Midsummer Night's Dream." Since then he has composed the music for about eighteen pictures and has two Academy Awards to his credit. In 1942 and 1944 he conducted Johann Strauss' "Die Fledermaus" and Offenbach's "La Belle Hélène" for the New Opera Company in New York.

His opera, "Die Tote Stadt," had its first performance in 1920 simultaneously in Hamburg, Cologne and Vienna. Since then it has been given on more than seventy stages, including that of the Metropolitan Opera House, New York. "Das Wunder der Heliane" (1928) has been given in Hamburg, Vienna, Breslau, Berlin and elsewhere in Germany. Excerpts from these two operas have been recorded by Odeon and Parlophone. "The Silent Serenade," a comedy with music, is to be produced by the New Opera Company.

COMPOSITIONS WRITTEN IN AMERICA

ORCHESTRAL WORKS	PUBLISHER	DATE
TOMORROW, OPUS 33—symphonic poem, from motion picture, "The Constant Nymph"	M. Witmark & Sons	1942
alto solo, soprano and altos, orchestra		
VIOLIN CONCERTO IN D MAJOR, OPUS 35	Manuscript	1945

CHORAL WORKS		
PSALM, OPUS 30	Manuscript	1941
solo, mixed chorus, orchestra		
PRAYER, OPUS 32	Manuscript	1942
tenor solo, women's chorus, piano, organ		

CHAMBER MUSIC		
STRING QUARTET No. 2 IN E FLAT MAJOR, OPUS 26	M. Witmark & Sons	1935
STRING QUARTET No. 3, OPUS 34 IN D MAJOR	Manuscript	1935
THE ETERNAL, OPUS 27—song cycle	M. Witmark & Sons	1935

STAGE WORKS		
THE SILENT SERENADE—comedy with music		1946

FILM MUSIC	STUDIO		
ANTHONY ADVERSE	Warner Bros.		1936
ADVENTURES OF ROBIN HOOD	Warner Bros.		1938
(concert version—symphonic suite)		M. Witmark & Sons	
JUAREZ	Warner Bros.		1939
PRIVATE LIVES OF ELIZABETH AND ESSEX	Warner Bros.		1939
KINGS ROW	Warner Bros.		1941
THE CONSTANT NYMPH	Warner Bros.		1942
(concert version—"Tomorrow," symphonic suite)		M. Witmark & Sons.	
DEVOTION	Warner Bros.		1943
OF HUMAN BONDAGE	Warner Bros.		1945
ESCAPE ME NEVER	Warner Bros.		1946

BORIS KOUTZEN

Born in Uman, South Russia, in 1901. He began to study the violin with his father. At the age of seventeen he won a competition for a position as violinist with the State Opera House. Later he played in the Moscow Symphony Orchestra under Serge Koussevitzky. During this period he became a pupil of Glière at the Moscow Conservatory and while there composed several works which have been performed on various occasions.

He went to Berlin in 1922 and was active there as a violinist. In 1924 he came to the United States and became a member of the Philadelphia Orchestra. He was head of the Violin Department of the Philadelphia Conservatory of Music and taught at Vassar College.

He was awarded the Juilliard Publication Award for the symphonic poem "Valley Forge" and the S.P.A.M. Award for the Second String Quartet. He won the first prize in the ACA-BMI Competition for the "Music for Saxophone, Bassoon and Cello."

His compositions have been performed by major orchestras in Cleveland, Chicago, Philadelphia, New York and San Francisco. They have also been broadcast many times over CBS, NBC and MBS networks. Columbia Recordings has recorded the Second String Quartet. He is at present completing a Concerto for Violin and Orchestra.

COMPOSITIONS

ORCHESTRAL WORKS

	DURATION	PUBLISHER	DATE
SOLITUDE—poem-nocturne	11 minutes	score and parts for hire	1927
SYMPHONIC MOVEMENT FOR VIOLIN AND ORCHESTRA	12 "	La Sirène Musicale orch. parts for hire	1929
VALLEY FORGE—symphonic poem	10 "	Juilliard publication	1931
SYMPHONY		Manuscript	1937
FROM THE AMERICAN FOLKLORE— concert overture	8 "	score and parts for hire	1943

CHAMBER ORCHESTRA

CONCERTO FOR FIVE SOLO INSTRUMENTS AND STRING ORCHESTRA flute, clarinet, bassoon, horn, cello solo	12 minutes	score and parts for hire	1934

CHAMBER MUSIC

STRING QUARTET IN B FLAT MAJOR	29 minutes	Manuscript	1922
SONATA FOR PIANO AND VIOLIN	24 "	Manuscript	1928
SONATINA FOR PIANO	12 "	La Sirène Musicale	1931
TRIO FOR FLUTE, CELLO AND HARP	14 "	Manuscript	1933
SECOND STRING QUARTET	20 "	Society for Publication of American Music	1936
MUSIC FOR SAXOPHONE, BASSOON AND CELLO	4 "	B. M. I. (in preparation)	1940
CONCERT PIECE FOR CELLO AND STRING QUARTET (also string orchestra)	12 "	Manuscript	1940
DUO CONCERTANTE FOR VIOLIN AND PIANO	12 "	Manuscript	1943
THIRD STRING QUARTET	18 "	Manuscript	1944

BORIS KOUTZEN (*Continued*)

CHAMBER MUSIC (*Continued*)	DURATION	PUBLISHER	DATE
SONATINA FOR TWO PIANOS	8 minutes	Manuscript	1944

STAGE WORKS

ONE ACT OPERA	55 minutes	Manuscript	
5 *principals, large orchestra,* *no chorus*			

A. WALTER KRAMER

Born in New York City in 1890. He first studied violin with his father and later with Hauser and Arnold. For a short period he studied the piano. In composition he is chiefly self-taught.

For many years he held the positions of Music Critic and Editor-in-Chief of *Musical America*. In 1936 he became Managing Director and Vice-President of the Galaxy Music Corporation. He was a founder, and from 1934 to 1940 President, of the Society for the Publication of American Music. He is one of the members of the Board of Directors of the United States Section of the I.S.C.M., a Composer-Member of the League of Composers and a member of the national musical fraternity, Sinfonia (Phi Mu Alpha).

"Two Symphonic Sketches" has been performed by the symphony orchestras in New York, Cincinnati, St. Louis, Minneapolis and Los Angeles, and Symphonic Rhapsody in F Minor for violin and orchestra, at the New York Stadium Concerts. "In Normandy" has been heard in New York, Baltimore and other cities. A recent performance of his orchestral version of the Bach Chaconne was given by the Cincinnati Symphony under Eugene Goossens in the winter of 1945. This work has been performed by most of the leading symphony orchestras of this country, including the New York Philharmonic Symphony, the Cleveland and the Detroit. His compositions in the shorter forms, songs and choruses and chamber music, have been presented too often to enumerate.

COMPOSITIONS

ORCHESTRAL WORKS	DURATION	PUBLISHER	DATE
TWO SYMPHONIC SKETCHES, OPUS 37A	10 minutes	Manuscript *for hire*	1915
SYMPHONIC RHAPSODY IN F MINOR, OPUS 35 *violin, orchestra*	17 "	Carl Fischer, Inc. *orch. reduced for piano;* *orch. score and parts in* *manuscript for hire*	1915

CHORAL WORKS

IN NORMANDY (A Rococo Romance), OPUS 49—cycle in four movements *soprano solo, chorus of women's* *voices, orchestra or piano*	16 minutes	J. Fischer & Bro. *edition with piano;* *orch. score and parts* *for hire*	1924

A. WALTER KRAMER (*Continued*)

CHAMBER MUSIC	DURATION	PUBLISHER	DATE
INTERLUDE FOR A DRAMA, OPUS 46, No. 1 *medium voice without words, oboe, viola, cello, piano*	3 minutes	G. Ricordi & Co.	1921

ERNST KRENEK

Born in Vienna, Austria, in 1900. He studied composition and piano at the State Academies for Music in Vienna and Berlin, philosophy and musicology at the University of Vienna.

From 1925 to 1928 he was Assistant to the Director of the opera houses in Kassel and Wiesbaden, and from 1933 to 1937 he was President of the Austrian Association of Playwrights and Dramatic Composers. He came to the United States in 1938, and in 1939 he became Professor of Music at Vassar College, which post he held until 1942. At present he is head of the Department of Music and Dean of the School of Fine Arts at Hamline University, St. Paul, Minnesota. He is a member of the Advisory Council of Princeton University and the Chairman of the Twin Cities Chapter of the International Society for Contemporary Music. He appeared as lecturer at more than fifty universities and colleges and as guest speaker at national conventions of many organizations. His books include *Music Here and Now* and *Studies in Counterpoint*. He is also the author of over four hundred articles and essays in various languages.

His works in all media have had frequent performances by leading organizations in Europe and in this country. His most famous opera "Jonny spielt auf," was presented by many European theaters and at the Metropolitan Opera House, New York. Eleven Short Piano Pieces have been recorded by Columbia with the composer as pianist.

COMPOSITIONS WRITTEN IN AMERICA

ORCHESTRAL WORKS	DURATION	PUBLISHER	DATE
SYMPHONIC PIECE FOR STRING ORCHESTRA, OPUS 86	11 minutes	Manuscript Fleisher Collection	1939
VARIATIONS, "I WONDER AS I WANDER", OPUS 94	16 "	Manuscript *Blueprint available*	1942
TRICKS AND TRIFLES	12 "	Manuscript	1945
SYMPHONIC ELEGY *string orchestra*	12 "	Elkan-Vogel	1946
THIRD PIANO CONCERTO *piano, orchestra*	15 "	Manuscript *Blueprint available*	1946

CHAMBER ORCHESTRA	DURATION	PUBLISHER	DATE
LITTLE CONCERTO FOR PIANO, ORGAN AND CHAMBER ORCHESTRA, OPUS 88	10 minutes	Manuscript *Blueprint available*	1940

ERNST KRENEK (*Continued*)

CHORAL WORKS

	DURATION	PUBLISHER	DATE
Two Choruses on Elizabethan Poems, Opus 87	6 minutes	Manuscript	1939
soprano, alto		*Blueprint available*	
Proprium Missae, Opus 89	15 "	Manuscript	1940
(in the style of the 16th century)		*Blueprint available*	
soprano, alto			
Lamentatio Jeremiae Prophetae, Opus 93	50 "	Manuscript	1942
soprano, alto, tenor, bass		*Blueprint available*	
Cantata for Wartime, Opus 95	12 "	Manuscript	1943
soprano, alto with orchestra		*Blueprint available*	
Five Prayers (John Donne)	17 "	Manuscript	1944
soprano, alto		*Blueprint available*	
The Santa Fe Time Table	20 "	Manuscript	1945
		Blueprint available	

CHAMBER MUSIC

	DURATION	PUBLISHER	DATE
Suite for Cello Solo, Opus 84	5 minutes	G. Schirmer, Inc.	1939
Sonata for Organ, Opus 92	10 "	H. W. Gray Co., Inc.	1941
Sonata for Viola Solo, Opus 92, No. 3	5 "	Manuscript	1942
		Blueprint available	
Sonatina for Flute and Clarinet (or Viola), Opus 92, No. 2	4 "	Manuscript	1942
		Blueprint available	
Third Piano Sonata, Opus 92, No. 4	18 "	Associated Music Publishers	1943
Seventh String Quartet, Opus 96	17 "	Manuscript	1944
		Blueprint available	
The Ballad of the Railroads— song cycle, English	25 "	Manuscript	1944
		Blueprint available	
Sonata for Violin and Piano	14 "	Manuscript	1945
		Blueprint available	
Trio for Violin, Clarinet and Piano	9 "	Manuscript	1946
		Blueprint available	

STAGE WORKS

	DURATION	PUBLISHER	DATE
Tarquin—full length English words		Manuscript	1940
4 singers, 3 actors, 6 instruments		*Blueprint available*	
What Price Confidence?—chamber opera in 9 scenes	45 minutes	Manuscript	1946
4 singers, piano		*Blueprint available*	

ARTHUR KREUTZ

Born in La Crosse, Wisconsin, in 1906. He received his Bachelor of Science and his Bachelor of Music degrees from the University of Wisconsin and his Master of Arts degree from Teachers College, Columbia University. He also received a diploma in violin from the Royal Conservatory in Belgium, where he won the Premier Prix with the greatest honors.

He was an instructor at Teachers College and an Assistant Professor at the

ARTHUR KREUTZ (*Continued*)

University of Texas, where he conducted the University Opera Company and Symphony. He was also Conductor of the Madison Federal Symphony and Guest Conductor of the Milwaukee, New York, and Wisconsin Philharmonic symphonies. He won the Prix de Rome in composition in 1940 and was made a Fellow of the American Academy in Rome in 1942. In 1941, he received the Publication Award from the National Association of American Composers and Conductors. He was awarded two Guggenheim Fellowships in composition in 1944 and 1945 and also won the BMI-ACA Award in 1945.

His compositions have had many performances throughout the United States by leading orchestras. "Music for Symphony Orchestra" was broadcast over an NBC network by the NBC Symphony, the "American Dances" was played by the Sinfonietta over WOR and "Winter of the Blue Snow" was heard over WNYC. He also wrote the film music for "Salvage," a production of the Office of War Information.

COMPOSITIONS

ORCHESTRAL WORKS	DURATION	PUBLISHER	DATE
MUSIC FOR SYMPHONY ORCHESTRA	19 minutes	Manuscript for hire	1940
PAUL BUNYAN	12 "	Carl Fischer, Inc. for hire	1940
WINTER OF THE BLUE SNOW (from Paul Bunyan)	5 "	Carl Fischer, Inc.	1941
VIOLIN CONCERTO	17 "	Associated Music Publishers for hire	1942
TRIUMPHAL OVERTURE	10 "	Manuscript for hire	1944
SYMPHONIC BLUES	5 "	Broadcast Music Inc.	1945
SYMPHONY NO. 1	25 "	Manuscript	1945

CHAMBER ORCHESTRA			
AMERICAN DANCES 8 winds, strings	14 minutes	Manuscript for hire	1941
LAND BE BRIGHT for dance, 11 instruments	13 "	Manuscript for hire	1942
THREE SHAKESPEARIAN LOVE LYRICS soprano, 8 instruments	6 "	Manuscript	1943
FOUR POEMS (Robert Burns) soprano, 8 instruments	7 "	Associated Music Publishers	1944
CONCERTINO FOR OBOE, FRENCH HORN AND STRING ORCHESTRA	15 "	Manuscript	1946

FILM MUSIC			
SALVAGE (for concert use: MARCH)		Manuscript Gov't War Film for hire	1942

GAIL KUBIK

Born in South Coffeyville, Oklahoma, in 1914. He attended the Eastman School of Music and the American Conservatory as a scholarship student. He studied at the Harvard Graduate School. He was violin soloist with the Illinois Symphony, the Rochester and the New York Civic orchestras from 1936 to 1938. He taught at Teachers College, Columbia University, from 1938 to 1940. In 1940 he was a staff composer for NBC in New York, and from 1942 to 1943 he was Director of Music for the O.W.I., Bureau of Motion Pictures. From 1943 to 1945 he served in the army as composer and conductor for Air Force films and radio.

He received the Sinfonia National Award in 1934, and in 1936 NBC presented an entire program of his works. He held MacDowell Colony Fellowships in 1937 and 1938. In 1941 he won the Chicago Symphony Golden Jubilee Award and the Jascha Heifetz Violin Concerto Award. He received a citation for musical direction of important Government films, including "The World at War," by the National Association of Composers and Conductors. The Society for the Publication of American Music Award was given to him in 1943, as well as an award of a Guggenheim Post-War Fellowship. He has contributed articles to various professional journals. He has been commissioned by CBS to write "Whoopee-Ti-Yi-Yo," and also by BBC in London to write "Camptown Races."

His orchestral and chamber music has been performed frequently in many cities and has been broadcast over CBS, NBC and BBC. "Daniel Drew" was premiered at the Library of Congress under the direction of Boulanger in 1939 and has been repeated many times. The "Wartime Litany" was written for and performed by the chorus of the Army Music School in Washington in 1944. "Memphis Belle," a wartime episode, was recorded for the O.W.I. and was broadcast to the occupied countries and to the South Pacific. At present he is preparing an Overture for Orchestra, a Symphony, a Piano Concerto and a Symphonietta for Band.

COMPOSITIONS

ORCHESTRAL WORKS	DURATION	PUBLISHER	DATE
VARIATIONS ON A 13TH CENTURY TROUBADOUR SONG	12 minutes	Manuscript for hire	1935
SCHERZO	8 "	Manuscript for hire	1940
MEN AND SHIPS—film music suite	20 "	Manuscript for hire	1940
CONCERTO FOR VIOLIN AND ORCHESTRA	22 "	G. Schirmer, Inc. for hire	1940
MEMPHIS BELLE—a wartime episode for orchestra and narrator	23 "	G. Schirmer, Inc. for hire	1944
THE ERIE CANAL	3 "	G. Schirmer, Inc. for hire	1944

CHAMBER ORCHESTRA			
PUCK—a Christmas score for speaker, string quartet, woodwind quartet, horn, trumpet	7–8 minutes	Manuscript for hire	1940

GAIL KUBIK *(Continued)*

CHAMBER ORCHESTRA *(Continued)*	DURATION	PUBLISHER	DATE
PARATROOPS—film music suite for small orchestra	10 minutes	G. Schirmer, Inc. *for hire*	
GAVOTTE FOR STRING ORCHESTRA	3½ "	Mercury Music Corp.	1942
THREE AMERICAN FOLK SONGS— suite for small orchestra	12–13 "	G. Schirmer, Inc. *for hire*	1945
TOCCATA FOR ORGAN AND STRINGS	4 "	Manuscript *for hire*	1946

BAND MUSIC

STEWBALL—variations for band (also transcription for orchestra)	15 minutes	G. Schirmer, Inc. *orchestra manuscript for hire*	1941
FANFARE AND MARCH FOR BAND	6 "	G. Schirmer, Inc.	1946
OVERTURE FOR BAND (also transcription for orchestra)	5 "	Leeds Music Corp. *orchestra manuscript for hire*	1946

CHORAL WORKS

IN PRAISE OF JOHNNY APPLESEED (Vachel Lindsay) *baritone, mixed chorus, large orchestra*	35–40 minutes	Manuscript *for hire*	1937
DANIEL DREW (Rosemary & Stephen Benét) *soprano, alto, tenor, bass, solo cello, solo string bass*	3 "	Arrow Music Press	1938
A WARTIME LITANY (Episcopal Service) *men's chorus, brass, percussion*	15 "	Manuscript *for hire*	1943

CHAMBER MUSIC

TWO SKETCHES *string quartet*	9 minutes	Manuscript	1932
TRIVIALITIES *string quartet, flute, horn*	5 "	Manuscript	1934
TRIO *violin, cello, piano*	3 "	Manuscript	1934
SLOW PIECE *string quartet*	6 "	Manuscript	1938
SONATINA *piano*	8 "	Mercury Music Corp.	1941
SUITE FOR 3 RECORDERS *soprano, alto, tenor recorders*	7 "	Hargail Music Press	1941
LITTLE SUITE *flute, 2 B flat clarinets*	7 "	Hargail Music Press	1941
DANCE SUITE *piano*	10 "	Hargail Music Press	1941
SONATINA *violin, piano*	9 "	S.P.A.M. (G. Schirmer, Inc.)	1942

STAGE WORKS

INCIDENTAL MUSIC FOR "THEY WALK ALONE"	5 minutes		1941
FRANKIE AND JOHNNIE—ballet sequence *dance-band and folk singer*			1946
A MIRROR FOR THE SKY—folk opera in 2 acts, 15 scenes	2 hours	Manuscript	1946

GAIL KUBIK (*Continued*)

FILM MUSIC	PUBLISHER	DATE
MEN AND SHIPS (concert version—suite)	U. S. Maritime Commission	1940
THE WORLD AT WAR	O. W. I.	1942
PARATROOPS (concert version—suite)	O. W. I.	1942
DOVER	O. W. I.	1942
EARTHQUAKERS	Produced by	1943
MEMPHIS BELLE	Army Air Forces	1943
AIR PATTERN PACIFIC	1st Motion Picture	1944
THUNDERBOLT	Unit	1945

EDWARD KURTZ

Born in New Castle, Pennsylvania, in 1881. He became a student at the Pittsburgh Conservatory and the Cincinnati and Detroit conservatories. He studied violin with Ysaye and composition with Clapp, Stillman-Kelley and Goetschius. He received his Master of Arts degree from the State University of Iowa.

In his early years he was a member of the Pittsburgh Orchestra under Emil Paur; later he conducted various orchestras in the West, and then he became interested in teaching and in problems of school music. He has been Guest Conductor of the Cincinnati Symphony Orchestra, the Cleveland Symphony Orchestra and the Sioux City Symphony. He is at the head of the Music Department of Iowa State Teachers College. In 1935 he won an award in the State Composition Contest sponsored by the American Federation of Music Clubs, and in 1936 he won all three divisions of this contest—ensemble, organ, and voice. He is the author of several books on the violin.

The March in D has been played by the Cincinnati, Cleveland, St. Louis, Minneapolis Symphony and other orchestras. The Scherzo from the Symphony in A Minor has been performed by the Rochester Philharmonic, and the "Andante Sostenuto," by the Iowa Teachers Symphony Orchestra. The Symphony No. 3 in C Minor was performed by the Rochester Philharmonic and the State University of Iowa Symphony Orchestra.

COMPOSITIONS

ORCHESTRAL WORKS	DURATION	PUBLISHER	DATE
MARCH IN D	9 minutes	Carl Fischer, Inc. *for hire*	1919
PARTHENOPE—tone poem *violin, orchestra*	10 "	Manuscript	1922
SYMPHONY NO. 1 IN A MINOR	30 "	Manuscript	1927
THE DAMEON LOVER—tone poem	12 "	Manuscript	1933
SYMPHONY NO 2 IN C MAJOR	25 "	Manuscript	1937
SYMPHONY NO. 3 IN C MINOR	25 "	Manuscript	1939
SYMPHONY NO. 5 IN G MAJOR	25 "	Manuscript	1943
SYMPHONY NO. 4 IN D MAJOR	25 "	Manuscript	1944

EDWARD KURTZ (*Continued*)

CHAMBER MUSIC	DURATION	PUBLISHER	DATE
FROM THE WEST—suite *string quartet*	15 minutes	Manuscript	1928
STRING QUARTET C MINOR *sonata form*	30 "	Manuscript	1932

IVAN SHED LANGSTROTH

Born in Alameda, California, in 1887. He studied in Berlin at the Königliche Akademie für Musik and the Königliche Akademie der Kunste. He studied piano with Lhevinne and he was given a scholarship for Master Class in Composition with Humperdinck.

He was Kappelmeister in Kiel, Germany; organist and choirmaster at the American Church in Berlin; Professor of Composition and Theory at the Neues Wiener Conservatorium in Vienna and at the Austro-American International Conservatory of Music in Austria. In New York he taught at the Chatham Square Music School, at New York City College and at Brooklyn College. He received the Haussermann First Prize for his Phantasy and Fugue in G Minor for organ.

His compositions have been performed in New York, Philadelphia, Los Angeles, San Francisco, Washington, D. C., and throughout Europe. The Introduction and Fugue, Op. 12, was broadcast by the Sinfonietta over WOR. At present he is writing a symphony.

COMPOSITIONS

ORCHESTRAL WORKS	DURATION	PUBLISHER	DATE
PIANO CONCERTO, C MINOR, OPUS 1	25 minutes	Manuscript	1915
INDIAN ROMANCE, OPUS 4	10 "	Manuscript	1915
DIDO, OPUS 9—dramatic aria *soprano, orchestra*	11 "	W. Hansen	1919
SCHERZO	8 "	Manuscript	1931

CHAMBER ORCHESTRA			
TOCCATA AND FUGUE (arranged from Opus 16) *2 oboes, 2 horns, strings, piano*	7 minutes	Manuscript	1945

CHORAL WORKS			
MASS, E FLAT MAJOR, OPUS 23 *soli, boys' choir, a cappella*	35 minutes	Manuscript	1938
O SALUTARIS, OPUS 24 A AND B *mixed choir, a cappella, or with organ accompaniment*	5 "	Manuscript	1940
MOTET "SALUTARIS," OPUS 24C *mixed choir, a cappella*	2 "	H. W. Gray Co., Inc.	1941
MOTET "TANTUM ERGO," OPUS 24D *mixed choir, a cappella*	2 "	H. W. Gray Co., Inc.	1941
THREE AMERICAN INDIAN SONGS, OPUS 24E *women's chorus, 2 horns, 2 trumpets, 2 kettledrums*	5 "	H. W. Gray Co., Inc.	1941

IVAN SHED LANGSTROTH *(Continued)*

CHAMBER MUSIC

	DURATION	PUBLISHER	DATE
STRING QUARTET, E MAJOR, OPUS 2	15 minutes	Manuscript	1914
THIRTEEN VARIATIONS ON A THEME BY FIORILLO, OPUS 10 *violin, piano*	15 "	Manuscript	1920
INTRODUCTION AND FUGUE ON A THEME BY PAUL JUON, OPUS 12 *string quartet*	7 "	Manuscript	1927
STRING TRIO, A MAJOR, OPUS 17	15 "	Manuscript	1932
STRING QUARTET, F SHARP MINOR, OPUS 21	15 "	Manuscript	1935
FOUR PIECES FOR STRING QUARTET, OPUS 20	12 "	Manuscript	1936
SONATINA, OPUS 26A *clarinet, bassoon*	7 "	Manuscript	1944
SONATINA, OPUS 26B *piano*	6 "	Manuscript	1944
PIANO SONATA, E FLAT MAJOR, OPUS 25	15 "	Manuscript	1945
STRING TRIO IN A, OPUS 27A *violin, viola, cello*	12 "	Manuscript	1945

BEATRICE LAUFER

Born in New York City in 1916. She attended the Chatham Square Music School and the Juilliard School of Music. She has also studied with Nathan Novick and Marion Bauer.

The Eastman-Rochester Symphony performed her Symphony No. 1, and the League of Composers presented a group of her songs. WNYC broadcast her compositions at the American Festival in 1944. At present she is preparing a Rhapsody for Orchestra and a Second Symphony.

COMPOSITIONS

ORCHESTRAL WORKS

	DURATION	PUBLISHER	DATE
SYMPHONY NO. 1	17 minutes	Manuscript	1944
DANCE FROLIC	7 "	Manuscript	1945
DANCE FESTIVAL	4 "	Manuscript	1945

CHORAL WORKS

	DURATION	PUBLISHER	DATE
EVOLUTION *mixed chorus, a cappella*	2 minutes	Manuscript	1943
PEOPLE OF UNREST *mixed chorus, a cappella*	3 "	Manuscript	1943
DO YOU FEAR THE WIND? *mixed chorus, a cappella*	2 "	Manuscript	1943
SERGEANT'S PRAYER *baritone solo, mixed chorus, piano or orchestra*	3 "	Manuscript	1943
NEW ORLEANS *women's voices, a cappella*	2½ "	Manuscript	1945
WHAT IS TO COME WE KNOW NOT *women's voices, a cappella*	3½ "	Manuscript	1945

WESLEY LA VIOLETTE

Born in St. James, Minnesota, in 1894. He was brought up in Spokane, Washington, and graduated from the School of Music of Northwestern University in 1917. He received the degrees of Doctor of Music and Master of Music from the Chicago Musical College. During World War I he served with the army in France.

He was a member of the faculty of the Chicago Musical College for ten years as head of the Theory Department. Later he served as Dean of the college. At present he is head of the Theory Department in the School of Music at De Paul University, Chicago, and Director of the De Paul University Press, which was recently established for the publication of American music. He was President of the Chicago Section of the I.S.C.M. In 1930 he received the David Bispham Memorial Medal for his grand opera "Shylock" played by the Chicago American Opera Society. He lectures on contemporary music, aesthetics and philosophy.

Many of his works, among them "Requiem" and "Penetrella," have been presented in the leading cities of the United States and also in Europe. "The Broken Vine" was chosen for the second Pacific Festival of American Music at San Jose. His chamber music has been played frequently and broadcast over WGN (Chicago). In 1934–35 he gave a six months' series of radio lectures on "Current Music in Chicago" over WGN.

COMPOSITIONS

ORCHESTRAL WORKS

	DURATION	PUBLISHER	DATE
REQUIEM	15 minutes	Manuscript	1925
PENETRELLA	9 "	Manuscript	1928
18 part string orchestra		*for hire*	
OSIRIS	19 "	Manuscript	1929
		for hire	
DEDICATIONS—concerto for violin	20 "	Manuscript	1929
		for hire	
NOCTURNE	9 "	Manuscript	1932
		for hire	
ODE TO AN IMMORTAL	12 "	Manuscript	1934
		for hire	
COLLEGIANA	11 "	Manuscript	1936
		for hire	
SYMPHONY	35 "	Manuscript	1936
		for hire	
CHORALE	6 "	Manuscript	1936
		for hire	
PIANO CONCERTO		Manuscript	1937
DOUBLE CONCERTO		Manuscript	1937
string quartet and orchestra			
SAN FRANCISCO OVERTURE	12 "	Manuscript	1939
VIOLIN CONCERTO No. 2	25 "	Manuscript	1939
COMMEMORATION ODE	15 "	Manuscript	1939
SECOND SYMPHONY (Children)	8 "	Manuscript	1939
PRELUDE AND ARIA	10 "	Manuscript	1942
FOURTH SYMPHONY (Band)	12 "	Manuscript	1942

CHAMBER ORCHESTRA

SPOOK HOUR—scherzino	5 minutes	Manuscript	1931
		for hire	

WESLEY LA VIOLETTE (*Continued*)

CHAMBER ORCHESTRA (*Continued*)	DURATION	PUBLISHER	DATE
NOCTURNE	9 minutes	Manuscript for hire	1932
LARGO LYRICO string orchestra	5 "	Delkas	1941

CHORAL WORKS

THE BROKEN VINE tenor solo, mixed chorus, organ	20 minutes	Gamble Hinged Music Co.	1921
ANIMA MUNDI—festival tenor solo, mixed chorus, a cappella	30 "	Manuscript	1933

CHAMBER MUSIC

STRING QUARTET NO. 1	23 minutes	Schneider	1926
PIANO QUINTET	25 "	Schneider	1927
SONATINA two violins alone	10 "	Manuscript	1931
FIVE SONGS FOR VOICE AND STRING QUARTET	12 "	Manuscript	1931
STRING QUARTET NO. 2	19 "	Manuscript	1933
OCTET oboe, clarinet, bassoon, horn, violin, viola, cello, bass	20 "	Manuscript	1934
SONATA violin, piano	25 "	De Paul University Press	1934
STRING QUARTET NO. 3	28 "	Manuscript	1936
SONATA FOR VIOLIN, NO. 2		Manuscript	1937
THREE PIECES FOR STRING QUARTET		Manuscript	1937
FLUTE SONATA	10 "	Manuscript	1942
FLUTE QUINTET flute, string quartet	25 "	Manuscript	1943
SERENADE flute, string quartet	12 "	Manuscript	1945

STAGE WORKS

SHYLOCK (Shakespeare)—opera in 3 acts	2 hours	Manuscript	1929

DAI-KEONG LEE

Born in Honolulu, Hawaii, in 1915. He studied medicine at the University of Hawaii. After the first performance of his composition, "Valse Pensieroso," by the Honolulu Symphony, he decided to study music and came to New York City in 1937. He was a scholarship pupil of Sessions and was later awarded a fellowship at the Juilliard Graduate School to study composition with Jacobi. He received another scholarship to study with Copland. In 1941, he won honorable mention in a Prix de Rome competition.

He enlisted in the U. S. Army in 1942, and while overseas he was invited to conduct many major orchestras, especially in Australia, where he broadcast his own works, as well as many works by contemporary American composers. In 1945, following his discharge from the Army, he was awarded a Guggenheim Fellowship. He was commissioned by the Interracial Singers

DAI-KEONG LEE (*Continued*)

to write a choral work, "East and West," which was performed in 1946.

He has had major performances by the Cincinnati Symphony Orchestra, the Minneapolis Symphony Orchestra, the New York Philharmonic Symphony and the San Francisco Symphony Orchestra. The Introduction and Allegro for Strings and the "Golden Gate Overture for Chamber Orchestra" were commissioned by CBS and were broadcast on the CBS American Music Festival and British-American Festival. ABC and NBC have also presented his works. The "Prelude and Hula" was recorded by Victor. At present he is preparing a ballet score.

COMPOSITIONS

ORCHESTRAL WORKS	DURATION	PUBLISHER	DATE
PRELUDE AND HULA	9½ minutes	Mills Music Inc.	1939
HAWAIIAN FESTIVAL OVERTURE	7 "	G. Schirmer, Inc. *for hire*	1940
RENASCENCE	14 "	G. Schirmer, Inc. *for hire*	1945
SYMPHONY NO. 1	20 "	G. Schirmer, Inc. *for hire*	1946
A TROPICAL OVERTURE	8 "	G. Schirmer, Inc.	1946
CHAMBER ORCHESTRA			
INTRODUCTION AND ALLEGRO *strings*	8 minutes	Sprague-Coleman	1941
GOLDEN GATE OVERTURE	5 "	Mills Music Inc.	1942
CHORAL WORKS			
THE RETURN *soprano, alto, tenor, bass, piano*	3 minutes	Mills Music Inc.	1942
NORTH LABRADOR *soprano, alto, tenor, bass, piano*	3 "	Mills Music Inc.	1942
EAST AND WEST		Manuscript	1946
FILM MUSIC			
LETTER FROM AUSTRALIA		Dept. of Information of Commonwealth of Australia	1945

CLAIR LEONARD

Born in Newton, Massachusetts, in 1901. He graduated from Harvard University and received the Elkan Naumburg and the Paine fellowships. He later studied with Boulanger. At present he is Associate Professor of Music at Vassar College. His chief interest is in choral music.

Among his compositions, "My Country Right or Left" and "Dance of Death," two musical plays, have been given at the Vassar Experimental Theatre and in New York City at the Adelphi Theatre. Other works have

CLAIR LEONARD (*Continued*)

been on the programs of numerous college music clubs, faculty concerts, etc., and in St. Thomas Church, New York, St. Luke's Church, Baltimore, St. Mark's Church, San Antonio, etc.

COMPOSITIONS

ORCHESTRAL WORKS	DURATION	PUBLISHER	DATE
CONCERTO FOR PIANO AND ORCHESTRA	20 minutes	Manuscript	1933
SYMPHONY IN D	20 "	Manuscript	1940

CHAMBER ORCHESTRA			
TWO VARIATIONS ON "KOMM SÜSSER TOD"	5 minutes	Manuscript	1936
violin solo, string orchestra			

CHORAL WORKS			
PSALM	5 minutes	Manuscript	1930
men's voices, piano 4 hands			
ONE EVENING	3 "	H. W. Gray Co., Inc.	1930
unison singing with piano			
RHUMBA	7 "	Manuscript	1935
mixed chorus, piano or orchestra			
PATTERFUGUE	4 "	Boston Music Co.	1939
women's voices, a cappella			
PRIÈRE POUR LA PAIX	3 "	Boston Music Co.	1940
mixed chorus, organ			
MISSA SANCTI ALBANI (Episcopal Communion)	20 "	H. W. Gray Co., Inc.	1940
mixed, men's or women's chorus, organ			
VERSES FROM GITANJALI (Tagore)	7 "	Manuscript	1941
men's voices, a cappella			
SONG OF THE UNIVERSAL (Whitman)	20 "	Vassar College	1941
soprano solo, mixed chorus, brass, percussion and organ			
IF I SPEAK WITH THE TONGUES OF MEN	5 "	Composers' Press	1942
mixed chorus, a cappella			
PSALM 121	4 "	Manuscript	1943
mixed chorus, organ			
TE DEUM LAUDAMUS (for V-E Day)	5 "	Manuscript	1945
men's or women's voices, organ			

CHAMBER MUSIC			
SONATA FOR PIANO AND VIOLIN	20 minutes	Manuscript	1930
FOUR LITTLE SONATAS FOR PIANO	17 "	Manuscript	1931
TOMBEAUX—song cycle	10 "	Manuscript	1931
soprano, piano			
THE GRANDSONS	20 "	Manuscript	1943
baritone, 4 trombones, piano			
FIVE PIECES FOR ORGAN—suite	17 "	Manuscript	1945

STAGE WORKS			
MUSIC FOR "MY COUNTRY RIGHT OR LEFT"	1¼ hours	Vassar College Publication	1935
solos, choruses, dances, piano			
MUSIC FOR THE "DANCE OF DEATH"	1½ "	Manuscript	1935
solos, choruses, dances, 25 piece theatre jazz orchestra			
MURDER IN THE CATHEDRAL (T. S. Eliot)	1 hour	Manuscript	1941
choruses and Hammond organ			

JOHN AYRES LESSARD

Born in San Francisco, California, in 1920. He attended the École Normale de Musique in Paris and the Longy School of Music, receiving degrees from both institutions; he is also a pupil of Nadia Boulanger. He was awarded two Cabot Fellowships from Harvard University in 1940 and 1941, the Ditson Fellowship (Columbia University) in 1945 and the Guggenheim Fellowship in 1946. He served in the U. S. Army from 1942 to 1945.

The League of Composers presented the Sonata No. I for piano. The Violin Concerto and the Sonata No. II for piano were performed at Radcliffe College and Times Hall. The Sonata No. I for piano was broadcast over a Los Angeles station.

COMPOSITIONS

ORCHESTRAL WORKS	DURATION	PUBLISHER	DATE
VIOLIN CONCERTO	25 minutes	Manuscript	1941
OVERTURE	9½ "	Manuscript	1946
BOX HILL OVERTURE	9½ "	Manuscript	1946
CANTILENA	5½ "	Manuscript	1946
oboe solo, string orchestra			

CHAMBER MUSIC			
SONATA No. I	20 minutes	Manuscript	1940
piano			
QUINTET	40 "	Manuscript	1943
violin, viola, cello, flute, clarinet			
SONATA No. II	25 "	Manuscript	1945
piano			

OSCAR LEVANT

Born in Pittsburgh, Pennsylvania, in 1906. He studied piano with Stojowski and composition with Schoenberg and Schillinger. For several years he was a pianist for jazz bands, appearing as soloist for the all-Gershwin programs at the New York Stadium and at the Hollywood Bowl. He wrote successful popular songs before he turned to more serious composition. He has been on the "Information Please" program for many years.

His Piano Concerto has been played with many of the major orchestras and broadcast over NBC. "Overture 1912" and "Dirge" were first presented by the Boston Symphony Orchestra. The Nocturne for Symphony Orchestra has had frequent performances, also the Sinfonietta and chamber music. He has written a book called *A Smattering of Ignorance*.

COMPOSITIONS

ORCHESTRAL WORKS	DURATION	PUBLISHER	DATE
PIANO CONCERTO	32 minutes	Manuscript	1936
NOCTURNE	14 "	Published	1936
SUITE	20 "	Manuscript	

OSCAR LEVANT (*Continued*)

CHAMBER MUSIC	DURATION	PUBLISHER	DATE
PIANO SONATINA	10 minutes	Robbins Music Corp.	1931
SINFONIETTA			1934
STRING QUARTET	29 "	Manuscript	1937
SONATINA FOR PIANO			1937

FILM MUSIC	STUDIO		
IN PERSON	R.K.O.		1935
CHARLIE CHAN AT THE OPERA	Fox		1936
NOTHING SACRED	Selznick		1937

ERNST LEVY

Born in Basel, Switzerland, in 1895. He studied at the Conservatory and at the University of Basel. His teacher in piano and composition was Hans Huber. Later on he continued his studies in Paris.

From 1916 to 1920 he conducted the Master Class for Piano at the Basel Conservatory. While in Paris he founded and conducted the Choeur Philharmonique de Paris. He came to the United States in 1941, and from that time until 1945 he was a member of the faculty of the New England Conservatory of Music in Boston. In 1945 he joined the music faculty of Bennington College, Vermont. He appeared as soloist with major European orchestras and with the Boston Symphony Orchestra. He is the author of a French-German dictionary of musical terms and of musicological articles in various periodicals. A book, *Harmonic Knowledge,* is still in manuscript.

His Ninth Symphony has been performed in New York by the National Orchestral Association and the Dessoff Choirs.

COMPOSITIONS WRITTEN IN AMERICA

ORCHESTRAL WORKS	DURATION	PUBLISHER	DATE
TENTH SYMPHONY, "FRANCE"	1 hour	Manuscript	1944

CHORAL WORKS			
SO I RETURNED—cantata *women's chorus, 4 part* *accompaniment*	15 minutes	Manuscript	1945
KADDISH *tenor solo, mixed chorus, organ*	6 "	Manuscript	1946

H. MERRILLS LEWIS

Born in Meriden, Connecticut, in 1908. He studied at the Yale School of Music with Smith and Donovan. In 1931 he won the prize in composition for an orchestral suite and was awarded a prize for a choral work. In the following year he received a fellowship in composition at the Juilliard Graduate School, where he studied under Goldmark.

At present he teaches theory and composition at Furman University in Greenville, South Carolina; he organized the Bach Choir and Orchestra of Greenville, which he also conducts.

His works have been performed in Boston, New Haven, New York, Atlanta, Greenville, Rochester and also at the Yaddo Festival of American Composers.

COMPOSITIONS

ORCHESTRAL WORKS	DURATION	PUBLISHER	DATE
KING OF ELFLAND'S DAUGHTER—suite	40 minutes	Manuscript	1932
SYMPHONY IN A	35 "	Manuscript	1936
LEGEND OF THE LOW COUNTRY	15 "	Manuscript	1940
TWO MINIATURES FOR ORCHESTRA	6 "	Manuscript	1941

CHAMBER ORCHESTRA			
TWO PRELUDES ON SOUTHERN FOLK HYMN TUNES	11 minutes	Manuscript	1938
CONCERTINO FOR OBOE AND VIOLA WITH STRING ORCHESTRA	10 "	Manuscript	1939

CHORAL WORKS			
HARPER OF CHAO *women's voices, small orchestra*	8 minutes	Manuscript	1933
WOOD WITCHERY *mixed chorus, piano*	10 "	Manuscript	1933
LAKE SONG *women's voices, piano*	6 "	Manuscript	1936
THIS IS AMERICA *mixed chorus, orchestra*	14 "	H. W. Gray Co., Inc.	1941
THE LAMB *a cappella*	4 "	Galaxy Music Corp.	1941

CHAMBER MUSIC			
SONATA (two movements)	10 minutes	Manuscript	1931
SONATA IN B MINOR *violin, piano*	25 "	Manuscript	1934
TWO SONGS *soprano, string quartet*	11 "	Manuscript	1934
TWO SONGS *alto, string quartet*	12 "	Manuscript	1935
TWO MINIATURES FOR FOUR HANDS *piano, 4 hands*	6 "	Manuscript	1939
NIGHT MUSIC FOR '43 *baritone, violin, cello, oboe, horn, piano*	6 "	Manuscript	1943
LYRIC PIECE FOR TRIO *piano, violin, cello*	4 "	Manuscript	1944

GODDARD LIEBERSON

Born in Hanley, Staffordshire, England, in 1911. He came to the United States early in his childhood. He first studied with George McKay at the University of Washington. For two years he was a pupil of Bernard Rogers at the Eastman School of Music. In theoretical knowledge he is mainly self-taught.

He has taught at the Harley School, Rochester, has written musical criticism for the *Rochester Journal* and *Modern Music* and has also lectured. Since 1939 he has been associated with the Columbia Recording Corporation and is now Director of the Masterworks and Educational departments. He has also written articles and criticisms for the *New York Herald Tribune, B.B.C. Listener* in London, *Town and Country* and notes.

"Five Modern Painters" has been given by the Rochester Philharmonic. "Homage to Handel" and "Satire in Tango Rhythm" have been heard in New York.

COMPOSITIONS

ORCHESTRAL WORKS

	DURATION	PUBLISHER	DATE
FIVE MODERN PAINTERS—suite	20 minutes	Manuscript	1929
TWO CHASING DANCES	16 "	Manuscript	1929
TANGO	14 "	Manuscript	1935
piano solo, orchestra			
HOMAGE TO HANDEL—suite	23 "	Manuscript	1937
string orchestra			
SYMPHONY		Manuscript	1937

CHAMBER ORCHESTRA

SUITE	25 minutes	Manuscript	1928
20 instruments			

CHORAL WORKS

THREE CHINESE POEMS	16 minutes	Manuscript	1936
mixed chorus, a cappella			

CHAMBER MUSIC

SONATA FOR QUINTET	17 minutes	Manuscript	1934
oboe, bassoon, viola, cello, piano			
SONATA FOR STRING QUARTET	30 "	Manuscript	1937

STAGE WORKS

ALICE IN WONDERLAND (puppet show)—incidental music	30 minutes	Manuscript	1936
9 piece orchestra			

NORMAND LOCKWOOD

Born in New York City in 1906. His early musical studies were at the University of Michigan School of Music. Later he studied with Respighi and with Boulanger. He received the Prix de Rome for 1929–1932 and the Guggenheim Fellowship 1943–1945. He was awarded the Swift Orchestra

NORMAND LOCKWOOD (*Continued*)

Prize in 1934 and G. Schirmer World's Fair Prize for unaccompanied chorus for high-school voices, which was called "Out of the Cradle Endlessly Rocking" (Whitman text). He was commissioned by Elizabeth Sprague Coolidge to write a Trio for Flute, Viola and Harp in 1939. In 1945 he was commissioned by the Alice M. Ditson Fund (Columbia University) for a chamber opera, "The Scarecrow," which was presented at the Brander Matthews Theater. The String Quartet No. 2 received the S.P.A.M. Award in 1946.

He was a member of the faculty of Oberlin College from 1932 to 1943 and has been associated with the Department of Music of Columbia University since 1945. He is Chairman of the 1946 Yaddo Music Committee. He is a Composer-Member of the League of Composers, the National Association of American Composers and Conductors and the Forum Group of the I.S.C.M.

His orchestral works have been played by the Chicago Symphony and the Cleveland Symphony orchestras. Many of his works for chamber music and chorus have been presented by ensemble groups in New York, Los Angeles, Princeton and on tour, and his songs and piano pieces are in the repertoire of many artists throughout the country. He has written a group of works for radio orchestra with voice, which include special arrangements of American folk songs and are frequently programmed.

COMPOSITIONS

ORCHESTRAL WORKS	DURATION	PUBLISHER	DATE
SYMPHONY	25 minutes	Manuscript *for hire*	1941
MARY, WHO STOOD IN SORROW (Stabat Mater) *soprano, orchestra*	10 "	Manuscript *for hire*	1946

CHAMBER ORCHESTRA

MOBY DICK			1946

CHORAL WORKS

DRUM TAPS *with orchestra*	1 hour	Manuscript	1930
REQUIEM—WHEN LILACS LAST IN THE DOORYARD BLOOM'D *tenor solo, with orchestra*	35 minutes	Manuscript	1931
FRAGMENTS FROM SAPPHO *girls' voices, a cappella*		Manuscript	1933
DIRGE FOR TWO VETERANS *mixed chorus, a cappella*		M. Witmark & Sons	1934
INSCRIPTIONS FROM THE CATACOMBS *mixed chorus, a cappella*		Manuscript	1935
SWEET AND LOW *mixed chorus, a cappella*		Galaxy Music Corp.	1935
THE HOUND OF HEAVEN *tenor solo, orchestra*	1 hour	Galaxy Music Corp. *manuscript for hire*	1937
PSALMUS CL		Manuscript	1937
GIVE ME THE SPLENDID SILENT SUN *mixed chorus, a cappella*		Manuscript	1937
THREE CAPRI SONGS		Manuscript	1937

NORMAND LOCKWOOD (*Continued*)

CHORAL WORKS (*Continued*)	DURATION	PUBLISHER	DATE
girls' voices, a cappella			
OUT OF MAY'S SHOWS SELECTED		Manuscript	1937
girls' voices, a cappella			
MONOTONE		Oberlin Series	1937
mixed chorus, a cappella			
GIFTS OF THE FIRST CHRISTMAS	12 minutes	Manuscript	1939
women's chorus, piano		*for hire*	

CHAMBER MUSIC			
SONATA FOR THREE CELLOS	10 minutes	Manuscript	1934
DICHROMATIC VARIATION FOR PIANO	14 "	Manuscript	1935
SIX STRING QUARTETS		Manuscript	1937
QUINTET		Manuscript	1940
piano, string quartet			
TEN SONGS FROM JAMES JOYCE'S			
"CHAMBER MUSIC"			
soprano, string quartet			
TRIO FOR FLUTE, VIOLA AND HARP		Manuscript	1940
THREE NUMBERS FOR WOODWIND QUARTET		Manuscript	
SONATA FOR PIANO		Manuscript	1944
SERENADES FOR STRING QUARTET		Manuscript	1945

STAGE WORKS			
THE SCARECROW—chamber opera	2 hours	Manuscript	1945
8 principal singers, mixed			
chorus, small orchestra			

CHARLES MARTIN LOEFFLER

Born in Mulhouse, Alsace, in 1861 and died in Massachusetts in 1935. His early years were spent in the Province of Kiev, Russia, where his father worked for the government. At the age of eight he began violin lessons with a member of the Russian Imperial Orchestra. His early years in Russia remained clearly in his memory throughout his life. At the age of sixty he wrote an orchestral poem called "Memories of My Childhood— Life in a Russian Village" and based the work on old Russian folk songs and dances. After several years in Hungary and Switzerland he decided to become a professional violinist and studied with Joachim in Berlin and later in Paris. His experiences as violinist finally brought him to America, where he joined Leopold Damrosch's orchestra and also played in small ensemble groups. In 1883 he became a member of the Boston Symphony Orchestra and was first violinist until he resigned in 1903 in order to have more time for his own quartet and also to compose.

He was awarded first prize by the Chicago North Shore Music Festival in 1924 for an orchestral work. He was commissioned by the Elizabeth Coolidge Foundation (Library of Congress) to write a work for the opening of the Library of Congress Music Auditorium, which he called "The Canticle of the Sun;" he also wrote the dedication music for Severance Hall in Cleveland called "Evocation." He was made an officer of the

CHARLES MARTIN LOEFFLER (*Continued*)

French Academy and Chevalier in the French Legion of Honor. He was a member of the American Academy of Arts and Letters. In 1919 he received the Gold Medal of the National Institute of Arts and Letters. One of his last works was another commission from Mrs. Elizabeth Sprague Coolidge, for which he wrote a Partita for Flute, Violin and Piano.

His works have had performances in Europe and in America by the major symphony orchestras and by choral and chamber-music organizations.

COMPOSITIONS (list incomplete)

ORCHESTRAL WORKS	PUBLISHER	DATE
SUITE FOR VIOLIN AND ORCHESTRA		1891
FANTASTIC CONCERTO FOR CELLO AND ORCHESTRA		1894
EVOCATION *speaking voice, women's chorus, orchestra*	Juilliard Publication	
POEM *orchestra*	G. Schirmer, Inc.	
MEMORIES OF MY CHILDHOOD—poem for orchestra	G. Schirmer, Inc.	
BEAT, BEAT DRUMS	C. C. Birchard & Co.	
FIVE IRISH FANTASIES *voice, orchestra*	G. Schirmer, Inc.	

CHORAL WORKS

FOR ONE WHO FELL IN BATTLE
*eight part mixed chorus,
a cappella*
BY THE RIVERS OF BABYLON
women's chorus

CHAMBER MUSIC

TWO RHAPSODIES FOR OBOE,
VIOLA AND PIANO
PARTITA FOR FLUTE, VIOLIN
AND PIANO

NIKOLAI LOPATNIKOFF

Born in Revel, Russia, in 1903. He entered the Conservatory of Petrograd at the age of eleven. In 1918 his family moved to Finland, and he continued his studies at the Conservatory in Helsingfors. He completed his musical studies under Ernst Toch in Berlin. In 1945 he received a Guggenheim Fellowship.

During his residence in Berlin he was active as composer, pianist and teacher and also served as a member of the board of the I.S.C.M. He left Germany in 1933, and, after a period of concertizing, he settled in London, where he remained until 1939, when he came to the United States. He was on the teaching staff of the Hartt Musical Foundation in Hartford, Con-

NIKOLAI LOPATNIKOFF *(Continued)*

necticut, and for two years he was head of the Theory Department of the Westchester Conservatory in White Plains, New York. At present he is Assistant Professor for Composition and Theory in the Music Department of the Carnegie Institute of Technology in Pittsburgh. In 1929 he won the Belaieff Prize in Paris for his Second String Quartet, and in 1930 his First Symphony won the prize of the Reichs-Rundfunk Gesellschaft. He won the prize in the 25th Anniversary Competition of the Cleveland Orchestra for his "Opus Sinfonicum." In 1944 he won the Koussevitzky Music Foundation Award, a commission to write a Concertino for Orchestra.

His orchestral works were performed at I.S.C.M. Festivals in Vienna, 1932, and Berkeley, 1942, in many cities in Europe, and in this country by the Boston Symphony Orchestra, the New York Philharmonic and the orchestras in Philadelphia, Cleveland, Detroit, Washington, Baltimore and Hartford. His music has been broadcast over the NBC, CBS and Mutual networks and in a League of Composers broadcast over CBS.

COMPOSITIONS WRITTEN IN AMERICA

ORCHESTRAL WORKS	DURATION	PUBLISHER	DATE
SYMPHONY NO. 2, OPUS 24	25 minutes	Manuscript for hire	1939
CONCERTO FOR VIOLIN AND ORCHESTRA, OPUS 26	22 "	Manuscript for sale	1941
SYMPHONIETTA, OPUS 27	17 "	Manuscript for hire	1942
OPUS SINFONICUM	12 "	Manuscript for hire	1943
CONCERTINO, OPUS 30	13 "	Manuscript	1944
CHAMBER MUSIC			
SONATA FOR PIANO	15 minutes	Manuscript	1944
VARIATIONS AND EPILOGUE cello, piano	17 "	Manuscript	1946

ARTHUR-VINCENT LOURIÉ

Born in St. Petersburg, Russia, in 1892. He studied at the Conservatory in his native city.

From 1918 to 1921 he was Chief of the Music Department of the Commissariat for Public Instruction of Soviet Russia. In 1923 he settled in Paris, devoting himself chiefly to the composition of religious music. He came to this country in 1941 and lives in New York City.

His works have been performed in Leningrad, Moscow, Berlin, Paris and London, as well as by the major orchestras in New York, Boston and Philadelphia.

ARTHUR-VINCENT LOURIÉ (*Continued*)

COMPOSITIONS WRITTEN IN AMERICA

ORCHESTRAL WORKS

	DURATION	PUBLISHER	DATE
The Feast During the Plague— symphonic suite *soprano solo, mixed chorus*	26 minutes	G. Schirmer, Inc.	1943

CHORAL WORKS

	DURATION	PUBLISHER	DATE
De Ordinatione Angelorum—motet *mixed chorus, 5 brass instruments*	10 minutes	The Thomist Vol. V 1943	1942

STAGE WORKS

	DURATION	PUBLISHER	DATE
The Feast During the Plague— opera-ballet	1 hour	Edition Russe	1931–43

ERNEST VIVIANI LUBIN

Born in New York City in 1916. He was given a scholarship by the Manhattan School of Music to study composition with Louise Talma. He was also a pupil of Nadia Boulanger, Quincy Porter and Roger Sessions. In 1938 he won the Bearns Prize.

He has contributed articles to the *New York Times*. He orchestrated "Sing Out, Sweet Land" for the Theater Guild production and worked with Martha Graham and other dancers.

The "Three Pieces for Strings" and the "Suite in the Olden Style for String Orchestra" were broadcast by the WOR Sinfonietta. The WQXR Orchestra and the National Orchestral Association have played his compositions over WQXR and WNYC. NBC has also broadcast these works. His music was presented at the Yaddo Festivals.

COMPOSITIONS

ORCHESTRAL WORKS

	DURATION	PUBLISHER	DATE
Variations on a Theme by Stephen Foster	12 minutes	Manuscript *for hire*	1942

CHAMBER ORCHESTRA

	DURATION	PUBLISHER	DATE
Three Pieces for Strings	6 minutes	Manuscript *parts for hire*	
Suite in the Olden Style for String Orchestra	5 "	Gornston	1937

CHAMBER MUSIC

	DURATION	PUBLISHER	DATE
Songs of Innocence—song cycle	10 minutes	G. Schirmer, Inc.	1944

OTTO LUENING

Born in Milwaukee, Wisconsin, in 1900. He studied at the State Academy of Music in Munich, Germany, from 1914 to 1917 and at the Municipal Conservatory in Zurich, Switzerland, from 1917 to 1920. He was a pupil of Andreae and Jarnach, and he also attended the University of Zurich from 1919 to 1920. With Busoni he studied privately. He held the Guggenheim Fellowship from 1930 to 1932 and was awarded the David Bispham Medal for American opera in 1933.

He has given concerts as flutist and accompanist in Germany, Switzerland, the United States and Canada. Between 1915 and 1920 he served as flutist and conductor of opera, symphony and light opera in Munich and Zurich. He conducted the first all-American opera performance in Chicago in 1922. From 1925 to 1928 he was coach and executive director of the Opera Department of the Eastman School of Music and Assistant Conductor and Conductor of the Rochester American Opera Company. He was Associate Professor at the University of Arizona from 1932 to 1934, and in 1934 he joined the faculty of Bennington College, Vermont, as Chairman of the Music Department. He is now at Columbia University.

His compositions have been performed in many cities in the United States and also in Canada, Europe and South America; and several have been broadcast by the Columbia and National Broadcasting companies as well as local stations. "Songs" and the Suite for Voice and Flute have been recorded by N.M.Q.R.

COMPOSITIONS

ORCHESTRAL WORKS

	DURATION	PUBLISHER	DATE
SYMPHONIC POEM, OPUS 5	18 minutes	Manuscript	1921
CONCERTINO, OPUS 16	15 "	for hire	1923
flute solo, harp, celeste, strings			
SYMPHONIC POEM, OPUS 15	14 "	for hire	1924
AMERICANA, OPUS 28	10 "	Manuscript	1936
DIVERTIMENTO, OPUS 23	20 "	Manuscript	1936
DIRGE, OPUS 29	7 "	Manuscript	1936
TWO SYMPHONIC INTERLUDES, OPUS 35	8 "	Edition Musicus	1936
SUITE FOR STRING ORCHESTRA	10 "	Boosey & Hawkes	1937
TWO FANTASIAS FOR ORCHESTRA	12 & 8 "	Manuscript	1945–46

CHAMBER ORCHESTRA

CONCERTINO, OPUS 13	15 minutes	Affiliated Music Corp.	1923
flute, harp, celeste, strings		for hire	
THREE SONGS, OPUS 19	10 "	Manuscript	1927
soprano, orchestra			
SERENADE, OPUS 18	7 "	Manuscript	1927
3 horns, strings			
SYMPHONIETTA, OPUS 31		Manuscript	1933
PRELUDE TO A HYMN TUNE, OPUS 37	12 "	Edition Musicus	1937
11 instruments, piano			
SUITE FOR STRINGS	10 "	Boosey & Hawkes	
FANTASIA BREVIS FOR STRINGS	4 "	Manuscript	1939
		for hire	

CHORAL WORKS

TWO CHORUSES (after Byron), OPUS 20	7 minutes	Manuscript	1928
women's voices, a cappella			
CHRIST IS ARISEN, OPUS 21	5 "	Manuscript	1929
mixed chorus, organ, strings ad lib.			

OTTO LUENING (*Continued*)

CHORAL WORKS (*Continued*)	DURATION	PUBLISHER	DATE
WHEN IN THE LANGUOR OF EVENING *soprano, mixed chorus, piano,* *strings, 4 winds ad lib.*	5 minutes	Manuscript	1939

CHAMBER MUSIC

	DURATION	PUBLISHER	DATE
SONATA FOR VIOLIN AND PIANO, OPUS 1	12 minutes	Manuscript	1918
SEXTET, OPUS 2 *flute, clarinet, horn, violin, viola, cello*	10 "	Manuscript	1919
SONATA FOR FLUTE AND PIANO, OPUS 3	7 "	Manuscript	1919
STRING QUARTET, OPUS 4 *clarinet obbligato*	40 "	Manuscript	1920
TRIO FOR PIANO, VIOLIN AND CELLO, OPUS 7	18 "	Manuscript	1922
SECOND SONATA FOR VIOLIN AND PIANO, OPUS 9	20 "	Manuscript	1922
THE SOUNDLESS SONG, OPUS 11 *soprano, string quartet, piano, flute,* *clarinet*	25 "	Manuscript	1922
SONATA FOR VIOLONCELLO SOLO, OPUS 12	10 "	Manuscript	1923
TRIO FOR FLUTE, VIOLIN AND SOPRANO, OPUS 13	12 "	Manuscript	1923
SECOND STRING QUARTET, OPUS 14	20 "	Manuscript	1924
THIRD STRING QUARTET, OPUS 20	30 "	Manuscript	1928
SONATA FOR PIANO, OPUS 22	8 "	Manuscript	1929
FANTASIA BREVIS FOR STRING TRIO, OPUS 34	10 "	Manuscript	1936
SHORT SUITE FOR STRING TRIO		Manuscript	1937
SHORT SONATA FOR FLUTE AND PIANO	9 "	Manuscript	1939
SUITE FOR SOPRANO AND FLUTE	9 "	Manuscript	1939
FUGUING TUNE FOR FLUTE, OBOE, CLARINET, BASSOON, HORN	6 "	Associated Music Publishers	1941
THIRD VIOLIN SONATA WITH PIANO	18 "	Manuscript	1945

STAGE WORKS

	DURATION	PUBLISHER	DATE
MUSIC SETTING FOR "SISTER BEATRICE" (Maeterlinck), OPUS 17 *cast, alto solo, chorus, organ*	45 minutes	Manuscript	1925
EVANGELINE—opera in 4 acts, OPUS 30 *soloists, orchestra, chorus*	2½ hours	Manuscript *also possible in con-* *densed version*	1932

HUGH FREDERICK MacCOLL

Born in Pawtucket, Rhode Island, in 1885. He studied violin, piano and organ in his home city. From 1897 to 1903 he attended St. Paul's School in Concord, New Hampshire, where he was a pupil of Knox and served unofficially as assistant organist. From 1903 until 1907 he specialized in music at Harvard College, where he received the degree of Bachelor of Arts magna cum laude. He is a charter member of the University Glee Club of Providence and from its organization in 1911 until 1916 was its accompanist. He is a Trustee of the New England Conservatory of Music and a member of the visiting committee in the Department of Music of Brown University.

HUGH FREDERICK MacCOLL (*Continued*)

He has been active in business since 1907 and is now the senior partner of MacColl, Fraser and Co., investment bankers of Providence.

Among his works, which have been performed by the Providence Symphony, Boston Symphony and Rochester Civic Symphony orchestras, are "Arabs," "Ballad for Orchestra and Piano" and "Romantic Suite." Several of his works have also received broadcasts over WNYC, WMCA, WEAF and WEAN.

COMPOSITIONS

ORCHESTRAL WORKS	DURATION	PUBLISHER	DATE
ARABS—symphonic illustration	8 minutes	Axelrod Publications	1932
BALLAD	20 "	Fleisher Collection	1934
piano, orchestra			
ROMANTIC SUITE IN THE FORM OF			
VARIATIONS	25 "	Fleisher Collection	1935
NOEL—pedal points and variations	20 "	Fleisher Collection	1940

CHORAL WORKS			
TWO DRAMATIC SONGS FOR SOPRANO			
AND ORCHESTRA	12 minutes	Manuscript	1938
TWO KEATS SONGS	8 "	Manuscript	1939
mixed chorus, string orchestra			
SIX LYRIC SKETCHES	15 "	Manuscript	1940
soprano, orchestra			
FUGALITIES	15 "	Manuscript	1943
women's chorus, a cappella			
SUN STAND THOU STILL	12 "	Manuscript	1944
women's chorus, piano			

CHAMBER MUSIC			
SAHARA SUITE	30 minutes	Manuscript	1927
2 pianos (4 hands)			
STRING QUARTET IN F	35 "	Manuscript	1928
MARTHA—SUITE	20 "	Manuscript	1930
2 pianos (4 hands)			
VARIATIONS ON AN ORIGINAL THEME			
IN F	20 "	Manuscript	1934
piano			
TRIO IN E MINOR	45 "	Manuscript	1935
piano, violin, cello			
SONATA FOR VIOLIN, CELLO AND PIANO	20 "	Manuscript	1938
SECOND STRING QUARTET IN C	25 "	Manuscript	1945

QUINTO MAGANINI

Born in Fairfield, California, in 1897. He was educated in California and attended the University of California; he later studied in Paris. His teachers were Barrère and Boulanger. In 1925 and 1926 he attended the American Conservatory at Fontainebleau. In 1927 he received the Pulitzer Award and in 1928–29, the Guggenheim Fellowship.

QUINTO MAGANINI (*Continued*)

His early career began as a flutist with the San Francisco Symphony. In 1930 he was made Conductor of the New York Sinfonietta. He founded the Maganini Chamber Symphony in 1932 and toured extensively with it. He was Conductor of the Silvermine Music Festival and conducted in Stamford, Norwalk and Greenwich. He taught counterpoint and orchestration at Columbia University and has lectured on music in various educational institutions throughout the country. He was an editor for Carl Fischer, Inc., and for Edition Musicus and is now President of the latter organization. He is also President of Kingsbury Machine Works, which received citations during the war for its contributions to coast-guard materiel. He was commissioned by CBS for the School of the Air, and "An Ancient Greek Melody" was presented by the CBS Orchestra. He received the David Bispham Award for "The Argonauts."

Many of his orchestral works have been performed in New York, San Francisco, San Antonio, Chautauqua and other cities. His chamber music and choral works have had frequent performances in the United States, and "Songs of the Chinese" has also been given in Paris. Many of his works for the flute are in the concert repertoire of leading flutists. The work "Tennessee's Partner" was broadcast over WOR and nationally. The Schola Cantorum presented "Gallegada."

COMPOSITIONS

ORCHESTRAL WORKS

	DURATION	PUBLISHER	DATE
TUOLUMNE—a Californian rhapsody *trumpet, orchestra*	14 minutes	Edition Musicus— New York *score and parts published*	1920
SOUTH WIND—an orchestral fancy	18 "	Edition Musicus— New York *score published, parts for hire*	1922
CUBAN RHAPSODY	8 "	J. Fischer & Bro. *full score, parts and transcription for piano solo*	1925
AN ORNITHOLOGICAL SUITE (three movements)	15 "	Edition Musicus— New York *full score and parts*	1928
ZAMBOANGA—a South Seas bacchanale	9 "	Carl Fischer, Inc. *score and parts*	1937
THE ROYAL LADIES SUITE (3 movements)	18 "	Edition Musicus— New York *score and parts*	1938
AT THE SETTING OF THE SUN	8½ "	Edition Musicus— New York *score and parts*	1939
AMERICANESE—suite on three early American pieces	11 "	Edition Musicus— New York *score and parts*	1940
FRANCE FOREVER	12 "	Manuscript	1943
MOONLIGHT ON THE PAINTED DESERT from "Western Sketches"	5 "	Edition Musicus— New York *score and parts*	1944

ORCHESTRAL WORKS (*Continued*)

	DURATION	PUBLISHER	DATE
AN ANCIENT GREEK MELODY	5 minutes	Edition Musicus New York *score and parts*	1945
PEACEFUL LAND	6 "	Manuscript	1945

CHAMBER ORCHESTRA

	DURATION	PUBLISHER	DATE
CONCERTO IN D MINOR—after Dante (three movements) *strings*	22 minutes	Edition Musicus— New York *score and parts*	1929
NOCTURNE *strings*	7 "	Edition Musicus— New York *score and parts*	1929
AN ORNITHOLOGICAL SUITE *18 instruments*	17 "	Edition Musicus— New York	1930
SYLVAN SYMPHONY (four movements) *13 instruments*	17 "	Edition Musicus— New York *score and parts*	1932
THREE PIECES FOR SMALL ORCHESTRA		Carl Fischer, Inc. *score and parts*	1936
LAKE AT SUNSET	6 "		
MILADY'S FAN	4½ "		
VENETIAN DOLL *17 instruments*	4 "		
LADIES OF THE BALLET SUITE (4 movements) *string orchestra*	11 "	Edition Musicus— New York *score and parts*	1938

CHORAL WORKS

	DURATION	PUBLISHER	DATE
SONGS OF THE CHINESE (three movements) *women's voices, 2 pianos, percussion*	15 minutes	J. Fischer & Bro.	1925
FOUR ORCHESTRAL SONGS *tenor, orchestra*	20 "	Edition Musicus— New York	1927
CATHEDRAL AT SENS—CONCERTO DA CHIESA *solo violoncello, mixed choir, orchestra*	19 "	Edition Musicus *score published parts for hire*	1935
GALLEGADA *dancer, 7 wind instruments, chorus*	5 "	Manuscript	1946

BAND MUSIC

	DURATION	PUBLISHER	DATE
SYMPHONIC MARCH REVIEW OF THE ALLIED AFRICAN COMMAND *symphonic band*	7 minutes	Edition Musicus— New York *score and parts*	1944

CHAMBER MUSIC

	DURATION	PUBLISHER	DATE
REALM OF DOLLS (three movements) *quartet for four flutes*	12 minutes	Carl Fischer, Inc.	1922
SONATE CAULOISE (three movements) *flute, piano*	14 "	Carl Fischer, Inc.	1929
NOCTURNE *string quartet*	7 "	Edition Musicus— New York	1929
SONATA DA CAMERA (three movements) *violin, piano*	24 "	Manuscript	1935
GAETA *flute, English horn and tambourine*	4 "	Manuscript	1940
MEDEOVALE *brass quartet*	6½ "	Edition Musicus— New York *score and parts published*	1940

QUINTO MAGANINI (*Continued*)

STAGE WORKS	DURATION	PUBLISHER	DATE
EVEN HOURS—ballet in five episodes *2 solo dancers, mixed dance* *ensemble, full orchestra*	22 minutes	Edition Musicus— New York *transcription for* *piano published*	1928
THE ARGONAUTS—a California tetralogy *large cast, chorus, full orchestra*	3¾ hours	Edition Musicus— New York *piano vocal score* *published; orch.* *score manuscript*	1934

MORRIS MAMORSKY

Born in Ansonia, Connecticut, in 1910. He received his Bachelor of Music degree from the Yale University School of Music in 1937. He was composer for the Bennington School of Dance (summer 1937–8) and Music Director of the Humphrey-Weidman Dance Group (1937–8). Since 1940 he has been a staff composer-conductor for the National Broadcasting Company in New York and has written the music for many of the dramatic series heard over WEAF. He has also composed music for short-wave broadcasts for the Office of Inter-American Affairs. He is now writing music for the Eternal Light Program. An article, "Composing for Radio," was published in *Music for Radio*. The Concerto for Piano and Orchestra was awarded the Paderewski Fund Prize in 1939.

His compositions have been performed by many of the orchestras in the East. The Nocturne and Scherzo, "Blues and Dance" and Introduction and Allegro have been broadcast over NBC networks.

COMPOSITIONS

ORCHESTRAL WORKS	DURATION	PUBLISHER	DATE
CONCERTO FOR PIANO AND ORCHESTRA	30 minutes	Manuscript	1938
SYMPHONY NO. 1	25 "	Manuscript	1940
THE BLUEBIRD (7 scenes from Maeterlinck)	15 "	Manuscript	1945

CHAMBER ORCHESTRA			
PASSACAGLIA FOR STRINGS	10 minutes	Manuscript	1939
NOCTURNE AND SCHERZO *string orchestra*	6 "	Manuscript	1944
BLUES AND DANCE *string orchestra*	8 "	Manuscript	1945
INTRODUCTION AND ALLEGRO *solo trumpet*	5 "	Manuscript	1945

CHAMBER MUSIC			
SUITE IN SWING *violin, piano*	15 minutes	Manuscript	1939
STRING QUARTET NO. 1	15 "	Manuscript	1945
SILENCES OF THE NIGHT—suite *piano*	15 "	Manuscript	1945

MORRIS MAMORSKY (*Continued*)

STAGE WORKS	DURATION	PUBLISHER	DATE
BOURGEOIS GENTILHOMME (Molière) *small string orchestra*	2 hours	Manuscript	1937
AMERICAN HOLIDAY—dance *piano, percussion*	19 minutes	Manuscript	1938
DIVINE COMEDY (Owen Dodson) *chamber orchestra*	2 hours	Manuscript	1938
TWELVE DANCING PRINCESSES—operetta *chamber orchestra*	1 hour	Manuscript	1939

LEOPOLD DAMROSCH MANNES

Born in New York City in 1899. He graduated from Harvard University and studied piano with Maier, Cortot and Quaile. He was a pupil of Scalero, Schreyer and Goetschius in composition. He has won the Walter Scott Foundation Piano Scholarship, the Pulitzer Scholarship and the Guggenheim Fellowship. He is associate director and teacher of composition and lecturer at the Mannes Music School. Besides his career in music, he has had an active interest in photographic research and photographic chemistry. For ten years he has been on the staff of the Eastman Kodak Company, where, with Godowsky, he has developed the Kodachrome process of color photography.

His Suite for Two Pianos has been presented often, and his String Quartet has been played on tours in America and abroad.

COMPOSITIONS

ORCHESTRAL WORKS	DURATION	PUBLISHER	DATE
SUITE—3 short pieces	8 minutes	Manuscript	1926

CHORAL WORKS			
TWO MADRIGALS	6 minutes	Manuscript	1926

CHAMBER MUSIC			
SUITE FOR 2 PIANOS	10 minutes	Maurice Sénart	1924
STRING QUARTET	30 "	Manuscript	1927

STAGE WORKS			
INCIDENTAL MUSIC FOR CHILDREN'S PERFORMANCE OF SHAKESPEARE'S "THE TEMPEST"	20 minutes	Manuscript	1930

MARCELLE de MANZIARLY

Born in Kharkov, Russia, in 1900. She has made her home in Paris and studied music with Nadia Boulanger. She came to the United States in 1941 and has lived in New York recently.

In 1933 her Concertino for Piano and Orchestra was performed at the I.S.C.M. Festival in Amsterdam. Her String Quartet was first performed in 1943 at the Museum of Modern Art, New York, and it was broadcast over station WEAF, New York. Other chamber-music works have been performed in New York and Hartford and broadcast over station WNYC, New York, and WTIC, Hartford.

COMPOSITIONS WRITTEN IN AMERICA

ORCHESTRAL WORKS	DURATION	PUBLISHER	DATE
SONATE POUR NOTRE DAME DE PARIS	12 minutes	Manuscript	1945
CHAMBER MUSIC			
STRING QUARTET	18 minutes	Manuscript	1943
SONATA FOR TWO PIANOS	12 "	Manuscript	1946

BOHUSLAV MARTINŮ

Born in Polička, Czechoslovakia, in 1890. He began to study the violin at the age of six and later on continued his studies at the Prague Conservatory, where he also studied composition under Josef Suk.

He began to appear in concerts at the age of eight, and, after completing his studies, in 1913, he became a member of the Czech Philharmonic Orchestra in Prague. He started composing at the age of ten and has since written more than a hundred works. In 1923 he went to Paris, intending to stay only a few months. However, he remained for seventeen years, leaving only after the fall of France. After spending several months in Aix-en-Provence he arrived in New York in March, 1941. In the summer of 1942 he became a member of the faculty of the Berkshire Music Center.

In 1932 he won the Elizabeth Sprague Coolidge Prize for his String Sextet. In 1938 he was commissioned to write "Tre Ricercari" for the Venice Music Festival. In 1940 he wrote a "Field Mass" and a "Military March" for the Czechoslovak army volunteers in France. His First Symphony was commissioned by the Koussevitzky Music Foundation in 1942. Several of his works had their first performance at Festivals for Contemporary Music (Prague, 1925; Venice, 1935 and 1938), and his Madrigal Sonata was first heard at the Jubilee Concert of the League of Composers, New York, in 1942. His works have been widely performed by leading orchestras and chamber-music groups in Europe, notably in Prague, Paris, Berlin, Geneva, Basel and London. In this country his works have had many performances

BOHUSLAV MARTINŮ *(Continued)*

by the New York Philharmonic and the Boston Symphony Orchestra, as well as in Cleveland, Philadelphia, Chicago, Los Angeles, Rochester, Pittsburgh and Washington, and also over the Mutual and Columbia networks. His Duo for Violin and Cello has been recorded by French Columbia and the Sonata for Flute, Violin and Piano, by the French Gramophone Company.

COMPOSITIONS WRITTEN IN AMERICA

ORCHESTRAL WORKS	DURATION	PUBLISHER	DATE
SYMPHONY No. 1	34 minutes	Boosey & Hawkes	1942
SYMPHONY No. 2	28 "	Boosey & Hawkes	1943
CONCERTO FOR VIOLIN AND ORCHESTRA	25 "	Manuscript	1943
CONCERTO FOR TWO PIANOS AND ORCHESTRA	26 "	Manuscript	1943
MEMORIAL TO LIDICE	7 "	Manuscript	1943
SUITE CONCERTANTE *violin, orchestra*		Associated Music Publishers	1944
SYMPHONY No. 3	30 "	Manuscript	1944
SYMPHONY No. 4	30 "	Boosey & Hawkes	1945
CONCERTO FOR CELLO AND ORCHESTRA	28 "	Manuscript	1945
THUNDERBOLT-P45	8 "	Boosey & Hawkes	1945
SYMPHONY No. 5		Manuscript	1946

CHAMBER MUSIC			
SONATA FOR CELLO AND PIANO, No. 2		Associated Music Publishers	1941
MADRIGAL SONATA *flute, violin, piano*		Associated Music Publishers	1942
SONATA FOR VIOLIN AND PIANO, No. 3		Associated Music Publishers	
PIANO QUARTET		Associated Music Publishers	1942
TRIO FOR FLUTE, CELLO, PIANO		Associated Music Publishers	1944
QUINTET FOR STRINGS AND PIANO		Associated Music Publishers	1944
SONATA FOR FLUTE AND PIANO		Associated Music Publishers	1945

DANIEL GREGORY MASON

Born in Brookline, Massachusetts, in 1873. He is a descendant of one of the early American families. The piano house of Mason and Hamlin was founded by his father. His family included several renowned composers and educators. While at Harvard University he studied with Paine, and after graduating he continued his studies with Chadwick, Goetschius and later, in Paris, with D'Indy.

In 1909 he was appointed to the music faculty of Columbia University and in 1929 he was made the MacDowell Professor of Music. As a critic and

DANIEL GREGORY MASON (*Continued*)

historian of music he is the author of a series of books, including *Beethoven and His Forerunners, The Romantic Composers, Contemporary Composers, From Grieg to Brahms.* There are also several analytical books, one on orchestral instruments and another entitled *The Dilemma of American Music.* He received awards from the Juilliard School Foundation and the Society for the Publication of American Music.

His major works have been played by all the leading orchestras in the United States and at many festivals, too great a number to list. His chamber works have been performed by various musical ensembles on their tours in America and in Europe; they have also been broadcast. Concerts devoted entirely to his works have been heard in Europe and in North and South America. There is a Victor record of his "Negro Quartet." Broadcasts of his compositions have been given over WQXR, WNYC, by the NBC and other major networks.

COMPOSITIONS

ORCHESTRAL WORKS

	DURATION	PUBLISHER	DATE
SYMPHONY NO. 1 IN C MINOR, OPUS 11	38 minutes	Universal Edition	1916
RUSSIANS, OPUS 18	16 "	G. Schirmer, Inc.	1918
baritone, orchestra		*for hire*	
PRELUDE AND FUGUE, OPUS 20	12 "	J. Fischer & Bro.	1920
piano, orchestra			
CHANTICLEER OVERTURE, OPUS 27	12 "	C. C. Birchard & Co.	1928
SYMPHONY NO. 2 IN A MAJOR, OPUS 30	30 "	Manuscript	1929
SUITE AFTER ENGLISH FOLK SONGS,			
OPUS 22	22 "	G. Schirmer, Inc.	1934
SYMPHONY NO. 3 (Lincoln), OPUS 35	30 "	Juilliard	1936

CHAMBER ORCHESTRA

	DURATION	PUBLISHER	DATE
LOVE SONGS FOR SOPRANO AND			
ORCHESTRA	17 minutes	Manuscript	1936
PRELUDE AND FUGUE FOR STRING			
ORCHESTRA, OPUS 37	8 "	Manuscript	1939

CHORAL WORKS

	DURATION	PUBLISHER	DATE
SONGS OF THE COUNTRYSIDE, OPUS 23	21 minutes	G. Ricordi & Co.	1923
soprano, baritone, chorus			

CHAMBER MUSIC

	DURATION	PUBLISHER	DATE
VIOLIN SONATA, OPUS 5	24 minutes	G. Schirmer	1913–44
INTERMEZZO, OPUS 17	10 "	Weaner-Levant	1916–37
string quartet			
STRING QUARTET ON NEGRO THEMES,			
OPUS 19	27 "	S.P.A.M.	1919
THREE PIECES, OPUS 13	10 "	S.P.A.M.	1922
flute, harp, string quartet			
SONATA FOR CLARINET AND PIANO,			
OPUS 14	23 "	S.P.A.M.	1923
VARIATIONS ON A THEME OF JOHN			
POWELL FOR STRING QUARTET,			
OPUS 24	13 "	Carl Fischer, Inc.	1926

DANIEL GREGORY MASON (*Continued*)

CHAMBER MUSIC (*Continued*)	DURATION	PUBLISHER	DATE
DIVERTIMENTO FOR FIVE WINDS,			
OPUS 26	14 minutes	Witmark	1927
flute, oboe, horn, clarinet, bassoon			
FANNY BLAIR—FOLK SONG FANTASY			
FOR STRING QUARTET, OPUS 28	12 "	Carl Fischer, Inc.	1929
SERENADE FOR STRING QUARTET,			
OPUS 31	20 "	S.P.A.M.	1932
SENTIMENTAL SKETCHES, OPUS 34—			
4 short pieces	7½ "	J. Fischer & Bro.	1935
violin, cello, piano			
VARIATIONS ON A QUIET THEME,			
OPUS 40	10 "	Manuscript	1939
string quartet			

ROBERT GUYN McBRIDE

Born in Tucson, Arizona, in 1911. At ten years of age he played the clarinet, and at a very early age he began playing the oboe, saxophone and piano in school bands, local theater orchestras and jazz bands. His first composition, "March for a Band," written while still at school, was played at the annual high-school band concert. In 1933 he received his degree of Bachelor of Music from the University of Arizona, specializing in public-school music, and two years later received his Master's degree in composition. He studied singing and gave recitals of his own compositions while still at college.

In 1935 he gave a demonstration in composition for the National Teachers Convention, and that fall he joined the faculty at Bennington College as instructor of music. He taught at the Concord Summer School of Music in 1937 and at the Bennington Summer School of Arts in 1940 and 1941. In 1941 he toured Central and South America as a clarinetist in a woodwind quintet under the auspices of the League of Composers. He has given numerous woodwind recitals at colleges for the American Association of Colleges. In 1936 he received the League of Composers' commission in the American Composers Series, for which he wrote "Go Choruses," based on the adventures in a jazz band. This work was broadcast by CBS. He received the Guggenheim Fellowship in 1937. He won the American Academy of Arts and Letters and the National Institute of Arts and Letters Award in 1942. He also won the Composers Press Award for "Jam Session" in 1943.

He has played his own works at the Yaddo Festival of American Music, at the League of Composers' concerts and the New School for Social Research. His orchestral compositions have been played by the New York Philharmonic Chamber Orchestra and the Rochester Philharmonic, as well as in Chicago, Buffalo, San Francisco and other cities; they have also been broadcast. He is at present completing a composition for band and a composition for violin and piano.

ROBERT GUYN McBRIDE (*Continued*)

COMPOSITIONS

ORCHESTRAL WORKS	DURATION	PUBLISHER	DATE
MEXICAN RHAPSODY	12 minutes	Eastman School Series	1934
		Carl Fischer, Inc.	
PRELUDE TO A TRAGEDY	8 "	Manuscript	1935
SWING STUFF	4 "	Manuscript	1938
clarinet, orchestra		*published for clarinet*	
		and piano, Gornston	
PUNCH AND THE JUDY SUITE	10 "	Manuscript	1941
STRAWBERRY JAM (Home-Made)	5 "	Manuscript	1941
STUFF IN G	4 "	Manuscript	1942
SIDE SHOW (Fugato #2)	3 "	Manuscript	1944
arranged for band		*published*	
		by Gornston	
POPOVER	4 "	Manuscript	1945
clarinet, orchestra		*published for clarinet*	
		and piano, Gornston	

CHAMBER ORCHESTRA			
FUGATO ON A WELL-KNOWN THEME	4 minutes	Carl Fischer, Inc.	1935
25 instruments		*for hire*	
WORKOUT	15 "	Manuscript	1936
15 instruments			

BAND MUSIC			
LONELY LANDSCAPE	5 minutes	Leeds	1944
SHERLOCK HOLMES SUITE	6 "	Gornston	1945

CHORAL WORKS			
SIR PATRICK SPENCE	5 minutes	Manuscript	1932
men's voices			
HOT STUFF WE HOPE	4 "	Carl Fischer, Inc.	1938
men's voices, piano,			
clarinet obbligato			

CHAMBER MUSIC			
DEPRESSION—sonata	15 minutes	Manuscript	1934
violin, piano			
DANCE SUITE	12 "	Manuscript	1935
piano			
WORKOUT	15 "	Manuscript	1936
oboe, piano			
PRELUDE AND FUGUE	5 "	Manuscript	1936
string quartet			
OBOE QUINTET	4 "	G. Schirmer, Inc.	1937
oboe, string quartet			
WISE APPLE FIVE (called "Wise			
Apples" when accompanied			
by piano)	5 "	Manuscript	1940
4 strings, clarinet		*published for clarinet*	
		and piano, Gornston	
JAM SESSION	3½ "	Composers Press	1941
flute, oboe, clarinet, horn, bassoon			

ROBERT GUYN McBRIDE (*Continued*)

STAGE WORKS	DURATION	PUBLISHER	DATE
SHOW PIECE—ballet	30 minutes	Manuscript	1937
20 dancers, full orchestra			
TURANDOT—incidental music		Manuscript	1941
10 instruments, elaborate production			
PUNCH AND THE JUDY	30 "	Manuscript	1941
1 or 2 pianos, 10 dancers			
FURLOUGH	5 "	Manuscript	1945
2 dancers, piano			

FILM MUSIC

SHORT SUBJECTS FOR RKO PATHÉ			1944–45

FRANCES McCOLLIN

Born in Philadelphia, Pennsylvania, in 1892. She received her education at the Pennsylvania Institute for the Blind, Overbrook, Pennsylvania, and also at Miss Wright's School, Bryn Mawr, Pennsylvania, and was a pupil in composition of Gilchrist and Matthews.

She has won three awards from the National Federation of Music Clubs and sixteen national prizes in music. She has lectured frequently on music. She has had many of her compositions published.

Her orchestral compositions have been performed by the Philadelphia Orchestra, the Indianapolis Symphony Orchestra, the Warsaw (Poland) Philharmonic Orchestra, the Robin Hood Dell Orchestra of Philadelphia, the People's Symphony Orchestra of Boston, the Wallenstein Sinfonietta, the Philadelphia Chamber String Sinfonietta and the Vancouver (B. C.) Symphony Orchestra.

COMPOSITIONS

ORCHESTRAL WORKS	DURATION	PUBLISHER	DATE
PAVANE	6 minutes	Manuscript	1932
SUITE IN F		Manuscript	1934
ALL GLORY, LAUD AND HONOR—			
choral prelude	3 "	G. Ricordi & Co.	1936
NOW ALL THE WOODS ARE SLEEPING—			
choral prelude	3 "	G. Ricordi & Co.	1936
SUBURBAN SKETCHES		Manuscript	1936
CHRISTMAS FANTASIA		Manuscript	1938
NURSERY RHYME SUITE	10 "	Manuscript	1939
CHRISTMAS POEM	10 "	Manuscript	1940
NOCTURNE	12 "	Manuscript	1940
MADRIGAL FOR FLUTE AND ORCHESTRA	10 "	Manuscript	1941
VARIATIONS ON AN ORIGINAL THEME			
for PIANO AND ORCHESTRA	13 "	Manuscript	1942

STRING ORCHESTRA			
ADAGIO	7 minutes	Carl Fischer, Inc.	1927
SCHERZO	7 "	Manuscript	1929
PRAYER	3 "	Manuscript	1930
SUITE FOR STRINGS	15 "	Manuscript	1941

FRANCES McCOLLIN (*Continued*)

CHORAL WORKS

	DURATION	PUBLISHER	DATE
THE SINGING LEAVES *soprano, tenor, bass, women's* *chorus, piano*	15 minutes	Charles Ditson	1917
THE SLEEPING BEAUTY *soprano, tenor, women's* *chorus, piano*	15 "	Charles Ditson	1917
NIGHT BEFORE CHRISTMAS *mezzo-soprano, women's chorus,* *piano*	12 "	Arthur P. Schmidt Co.	1922
SPRING IN HEAVEN *women's voices, piano*	8 "	Theodore Presser Co.	1929
GOING UP TO LONDON *women's chorus, flute, piano*	12 "	Carl Fischer, Inc.	1931
THE TRUE GOD *mixed chorus, a cappella*	15 "	Charles Ditson	1937
RING OUT WILD BELLS *mixed chorus, orchestra*	6 "	Manuscript	1938
HOW LIVING ARE THE DEAD *mixed chorus, harp, organ*	8 "	Charles Ditson	1941
HOW FIRM A FOUNDATION *soprano, alto, mixed chorus, organ*	10 "	Manuscript	1941

CHAMBER MUSIC

STRING QUARTET IN F	20 minutes	Manuscript	1920
QUINTET FOR PIANO AND STRINGS	20 "	Manuscript	1927
SEXTET FOR STRINGS	16 "	Manuscript	1932
FANTASIA FOR STRING QUARTET	20 "	Manuscript	1936
DIVERSION FOR FIVE WIND INSTRUMENTS	5 "	Manuscript	1943

STAGE WORKS

KING CHRISTMAS—children's opera with small orchestra		G. Schirmer, Inc.	1926

FILM MUSIC

THE THREE BEARS		Manuscript	1940

HARL McDONALD

Born near Boulder, Colorado, in 1899. He received his early musical training from his mother. He started to compose when he was seven and learned to play a number of instruments. Later he worked with other teachers and studied also in Germany.

He has been organist and choirmaster and given piano recitals in various cities of the United States; he has also toured as accompanist for vocalists and violinists. He has taught composition and piano. At the present time he is Chairman of the Department of Music of the University of Pennsylvania. From 1930 to 1933 he did research work under a Rockefeller grant, collaborating with two electrical engineers and a physicist. This work included instrumental and vocal tone, new scale divisions and resultant harmonies, and the recording and transmission of tone. In recogni-

HARL McDONALD (*Continued*)

tion of this research he was made a member of Sigma Xi. Since 1939 he has been manager of the Philadelphia Orchestra.

His works have been performed in many cities in the United States, as well as in Berlin, London and Wiesbaden. A number of his works, performed by the Philadelphia Orchestra, were recorded by Victor.

COMPOSITIONS

ORCHESTRAL WORKS

	DURATION	PUBLISHER	DATE
Mojave—symphonic fantasy	20 minutes	Manuscript	1922
Festival of the Workers—suite	12 "	Elkan-Vogel Co., Inc.	1932
Santa Fé Trail, Symphony No. 1	22 "	Elkan-Vogel Co., Inc.	1934
Symphony, No. 2 (Rhumba)	32 "	Elkan-Vogel Co., Inc.	1935
Three Poems on Traditional Aramaic and Hebrew Themes	11 "	Elkan-Vogel Co., Inc.	1935
Concerto for Two Pianos and Orchestra	23 "	Elkan-Vogel Co., Inc.	1936
Symphony No. 3—tragic cycle *solo soprano, mixed chorus, orchestra*	33 "	Elkan-Vogel Co., Inc.	1936
Symphony No. 4	25 "	Elkan-Vogel Co., Inc.	1937
San Juan Capistrano—two nocturnes	8½ "	Elkan-Vogel Co., Inc.	1938
The Legend of the Arkansas Traveller	4 "	Elkan-Vogel Co., Inc.	1939
Chameleon Variations	27 "	Elkan-Vogel Co., Inc.	1940
From Childhood—suite *harp, orchestra*	23 "	Elkan-Vogel Co., Inc.	1940
My Country at War—symphonic suite	26 "	Elkan-Vogel Co., Inc.	1943
Concerto for Violin and Orchestra	21 "	Elkan-Vogel Co., Inc.	1943

CHORAL WORKS

Missa Patriem *double chorus, a cappella*		Manuscript *for hire*	1937
The Breadth and Extent of Man's Empire *mixed chorus*		Elkan-Vogel Co., Inc.	1938
Songs of Conquest (4 movements) *mixed chorus*	4½ minutes	Elkan-Vogel Co., Inc.	1938
Come Quickly, Lord, and Take My Soul to Rest *mixed chorus*		Elkan-Vogel Co., Inc.	1939
Lament for the Stolen *women's chorus, orchestra*	21 "	Elkan-Vogel Co., Inc.	1939
The Sea *mixed chorus, string orchestra*		Elkan-Vogel Co., Inc.	1939
Dirge for Two Veterans *women's chorus, orchestra*	11 "	Elkan-Vogel Co., Inc.	1940
Wind in the Palm Trees *women's voices, string orchestra*		Elkan-Vogel Co., Inc.	1940
Evening *women's voices*		Elkan-Vogel Co., Inc.	1940
The Lover's Lament (English Drinking Song) *men's voices*		Elkan-Vogel Co., Inc.	1941
Pioneers, O Pioneers (4 movements) *mixed chorus*		Elkan-Vogel Co., Inc.	1941
Day Break *high voice, orchestra*	2 "	Elkan-Vogel Co., Inc.	1941
Song of Free Nations *soprano, orchestra*	2½ "	Elkan-Vogel Co., Inc.	1945

HARL McDONALD (*Continued*)

CHAMBER MUSIC	DURATION	PUBLISHER	DATE
TRIO IN G MINOR	15 minutes	Elkan-Vogel Co., Inc.	1931
piano, violin, cello			
FANTASY FOR STRING QUARTET	14 "	Manuscript	1932
TRIO NO. 2	20 "	Manuscript	1932
QUARTET ON NEGRO THEMES	18 "	Manuscript	1933

GEORGE FREDERICK McKAY

Born in Harrington, Washington, 1899. He began his early musical education at the University of Washington, Seattle, under Wood and later studied with Palmgren and Sinding at the Eastman School, from which he graduated in 1923. In 1925, at the first American Composers' Concert in Rochester, in a national competition, his Sinfonietta No. 1 was selected for performance.

He is now Professor of Music at the University of Washington. Many of his works which reflect the regional background of the Pacific Northwest have been performed by the symphony societies of Seattle, Tacoma, Boston, Rochester and other cities. The music to "Bury the Dead" was given many times at the Repertory Playhouse, Seattle, and "Epoch," a dance drama in Four American Phases, for full orchestra—was presented at the University of Washington with the composer conducting. The NBC has given broadcasts of his works. His Quintet for Woodwinds, also broadcast, received honorable mention in a competition of the NBC. He won first prize in the American Guild of Organists Competition, 1939, and honorable mention in the Jascha Heifetz Award Competition in 1941.

COMPOSITIONS

ORCHESTRAL WORKS	DURATION	PUBLISHER	DATE
SINFONIETTA NO. 1	15 minutes	Carl Fischer, Inc.	1925
SINFONIETTA NO. 2	24 "	Manuscript	1929
A PRAIRIE PORTRAIT	10 "	Manuscript	1932
SINFONIETTA NO. 3	11 "	Manuscript	1933
SYMPHONY (EVOCATION)	26 "	Manuscript	1935–45
SYMPHONIE MINIATURE	14 "	C. C. Birchard & Co.	1937
CONCERTO FOR VIOLIN	23 "	Manuscript	1940
TO A LIBERATOR	10 "	Boosey & Hawkes	1940
		for hire	
CONCERTO FOR CELLO	15 "	Manuscript	1942
SINFONIETTA NO. 4	14 "	University of Washington Press	1942
SUITE ON FIDDLERS' TUNES	15 "	J. Fischer & Bro.	1943
VARIATIONS—"There's A Great Day Coming"	5 "	Manuscript	1943
SUITE ON NORTHWEST INDIAN SONGS AND DANCE	12 "	Manuscript	1945

GEORGE FREDERICK McKAY (*Continued*)

	DURATION	PUBLISHER	DATE
CHAMBER ORCHESTRA			
THREE LYRIC SOLILOQUIES	10 minutes	Manuscript	1928
12 instruments			
SONATINE FOR CLARINET AND STRING ORCHESTRA	10 "	Manuscript	1929
FANTASY ON A WESTERN FOLKSONG	12 "	Boosey & Hawkes	1931–36
10 instruments		*for hire*	
A LANIER PASTORALE	12 "	Manuscript	1935
women's voices, 15 instruments			
VARIANTS ON A TEXAS TUNE	11 "	Manuscript	1937
14 instruments			
PASTORAL SOLILOQUY FOR OBOE AND SMALL ORCHESTRA	5 "	Manuscript	1941
9 instruments			
STRING ORCHESTRA			
MOODS FANTASTIC AND LYRIC	15 minutes	Manuscript	1933
INTROSPECTIVE POEM	7 "	Manuscript	1938
PORT ROYAL, 1861	8 "	C. C. Birchard & Co.	1939
(Suite on Negro Folksongs)			
SUITE ON CHILDREN'S THEMES	10 "	Manuscript	1942
CHORAL WORKS			
IN GREEN WAYS—choral cycle	10 minutes	Manuscript	1932
women's chorus, flute and string quartet			
HERTHA	5 "	Manuscript	1935
mixed chorus, orchestra			
CHORAL RHAPSODY (Pioneers)	12 "	C. C. Birchard & Co.	1939
mixed chorus, orchestra			
THE SEER—choral rhapsody No. 2	12 "	J. Fischer & Bro.	1944
mixed chorus, piano			
LINCOLN LYRICS (Edwin Markham)—choral suite	25 "	C. C. Birchard & Co.	1945
mixed chorus, orchestra			
ALL IN FUN—14 nonsense songs	15 "	C. C. Birchard & Co.	1945
mixed chorus, piano			
CHAMBER MUSIC			
AN APRIL POEM	5 minutes	Manuscript	1927
flute, string quartet, piano			
QUINTET	10 "	Manuscript	1930
flute, oboe, clarinet, horn, bassoon			
TRIO	13 "	Manuscript	1931
violin, cello, piano			
QUARTETS NOS. 1, 2	15, 10 "	Manuscript	1935–37
string quartet			
QUINTET—AMERICAN STREET SCENES	15 "	Manuscript	1935
clarinet, trumpet, saxophone, bassoon, piano			
SONATA NO. 1	11 "	White-Smith	1937
organ			
QUINTET	12 "	Manuscript	1938
piano and string quartet			
SONATA NO. 2	11 "	Manuscript	1940
organ			
BENEDICTIONS—suite	12 "	Carl Fischer, Inc.	1944
organ			
SYMPHONIC BAND			
BURLESQUE MARCH	3 minutes	Manuscript	1925
BRAVURA PRELUDE	3 "	Associated Music Publishers	1936
brass ensemble			

GEORGE FREDERICK McKAY (*Continued*)

MUSIC FOR STAGE	DURATION	PUBLISHER	DATE
EPOCH—a choreographic drama (in Four American Phases)	1 hour	Manuscript	1935

CARL McKINLEY

Born in Yarmouth, Maine, in 1895. He received his Bachelor of Music degree from Knox Conservatory and his Bachelor of Arts degree from Harvard University, with special honors in music. While at Harvard, he won the Francis Boott Prize for his motet, "The Man of Galilee." He was awarded a Harvard fellowship, which enabled him to study composition with Rubin Goldmark and organ with Gaston M. Dethier. In 1927 and 1928 he was the recipient of two Guggenheim Fellowships. He studied with Nadia Boulanger in Paris and then became coach and stage assistant at the Munich Opera.

He has been active as a church organist, choirmaster and teacher. He was organist of the Capitol Theater in New York City in 1923, and while there, he became Assistant Conductor of the Capitol Orchestra. When he returned from Europe in 1929, he became an instructor at the New England Conservatory of Music, a position which he now holds; he is also on the faculty of the Organ School of the Conservatory.

The "Blue Flower," a symphonic poem which won the Flagler Prize in 1921, was performed by the Chicago Symphony and the New York Philharmonic orchestras. His other works, including "Masquerade" (an American rhapsody), Variations and Fugue and the String Quartet, have been played by leading symphonic organizations in the United States and in various cities in Germany.

COMPOSITIONS

ORCHESTRAL WORKS	DURATION	PUBLISHER	DATE
INDIAN SUMMER IDYL	8 minutes	Manuscript	1917
THE BLUE FLOWER—symphonic poem	15 "	Manuscript	1920
MASQUERADE—an American rhapsody	10 "	J. Fischer & Bro.	1925
CHORALE, VARIATIONS AND FUGUE	16 "	Manuscript	1941

CHORAL WORKS			
THE MAN OF GALILEE mixed chorus, organ	10 minutes	Manuscript	1917

CHAMBER MUSIC			
SUITE FOR FIVE WIND INSTRUMENTS flute, oboe, clarinet, horn, bassoon	10 minutes	Manuscript	1935
STRING QUARTET IN ONE MOVEMENT	15 "	Manuscript	1942

COLIN McPHEE

Born in Montreal, Canada, in 1901. He first studied composition in Baltimore with Strube, then in Paris with Le Flem and later with Varese in New York. His piano teachers were Friedheim and Phillipp. He lived in Bali most of the 1930's, studying music of Bali and Java, and has published monographs in Java on music, including articles on puppet-shows of Bali, its music and religious significance. His book, *A House in Bali,* is published by Asia Press (1946). He returned to New York in 1939 and has conducted a column for the League of Composers' publication, *Modern Music,* and a column on jazz for the magazine *Mademoiselle.* He received a Guggenheim Award for two successive years.

He was commissioned by the League of Composers in the American Composers Series to write a choral work, which was first presented with the Princeton Glee Club. The Concerto for Piano and Orchestra was performed by the Toronto Symphony. "Sea Shanty Suite" has had several performances, including those by the Schola Cantorum and the Columbia University Glee Club. The chamber music has been played in New York, Rochester and Boston, also with the Pan American Association of Composers and the League of Composers. The music for the film "H2O" was first heard at the Copland-Sessions Concerts. "Tabuh-Tabuhan" has been performed frequently by Chavez with the Mexican Symphony. "Balinese Ceremonial Music" was recorded by G. Schirmer. "Iroquois Eclogue" and "Iroquois Dances" were recorded for Pan American Union and broadcast to Latin-American countries.

COMPOSITIONS

ORCHESTRAL WORKS	DURATION	PUBLISHER	DATE
CONCERTO FOR PIANO AND ORCHESTRA	30 minutes	Manuscript	1923
SARABANDE	7 "	Manuscript	1927
SYMPHONY IN ONE MOVEMENT	20 "	Manuscript	1930
BALI	20 "	Manuscript	1936
TABUH-TABUHAN *2 pianos, orchestra*	20 "	Manuscript	1936
IROQUOIS ECLOGUE (based on Iroquois melodies)	6 "	Manuscript	1944
FOUR IROQUOIS DANCES (based on Iroquois melodies)	8 "	New Music	1944

CHAMBER ORCHESTRA			
CONCERTO FOR PIANO AND WIND OCTET	16 minutes	New Music	1929

CHORAL WORKS			
SEA SHANTY SUITE *baritone solo, men's chorus,* *2 pianos, 2 sets timpani*	20 minutes	Edwin F. Kalmus	1929
FROM THE REVELATION OF ST. JOHN THE DIVINE *men's chorus, 3 trumpets,* *2 pianos, 2 timpani*	15 "	Manuscript	1935

CHAMBER MUSIC			
SONATINA *2 flutes, clarinet, trumpet, piano*	11 minutes	Manuscript	1925
BALINESE CEREMONIAL MUSIC *2 pianos*	10 "	G. Schirmer, Inc.	1942

COLIN McPHEE (*Continued*)

STAGE WORKS	DATE
MUSIC TO EMPEROR JONES	1941

FILM MUSIC

MECHANICAL PRINCIPLES	1931
H₂O	1931

JACQUES de MENASCE

Born in Bad Ischl, Austria, in 1905. He studied at the State Academy for Music in Vienna. His teachers in composition were Josef Marx, Alban Berg and Paul Pisk. His piano teachers were Emil von Sauer and Paul Weingarten.

His first concert appearance as pianist was in 1933 at the Salzburg Festival. Extensive Continental tours followed, including appearances on major radio stations. He came to the United States in 1941 and lives in New York City. Besides his activities as a concert pianist, he has contributed articles to *Modern Music, The Etude,* and *Tomorrow.* He is a composer-member of the League of Composers and of the I.S.C.M. Committee.

Some of his works were performed at the I.S.C.M. Festivals in Basel in 1941 and in Berkeley in 1942. Other performances of his works took place in Brno, Budapest, Vienna, Rotterdam, Geneva, Lausanne, New York and Chicago. His music was broadcast by stations in Luxembourg, Zürich, Lausanne, Havana and New York. CBS broadcast the first performance of his Piano Concerto, No. 2.

COMPOSITIONS WRITTEN IN AMERICA

CHAMBER MUSIC	DURATION	PUBLISHER	DATE
POUR UNE PRINCESSE—song cycle	8 minutes	A. Henn	1941
SONATINA, No. 2	7 "	Mercury Music Corp.	1942
piano			
THIRD SONATINA FOR PIANO	8 "	Manuscript	1946

STAGE WORKS			
THE FATE OF MY PEOPLE	15 minutes	Manuscript	1945
solo dancer, piano			

PETER MENNIN

Born in Erie, Pennsylvania, in 1923. He attended Oberlin Conservatory. After his discharge from the Air Force, he continued his studies at the Eastman School of Music. He was a pupil of Hanson and Rogers, and he

PETER MENNIN *(Continued)*

received his Bachelor of Music and his Master of Music degrees and a fellowship in orchestration from the Eastman School.

In 1945, he won the first annual George Gershwin Memorial Award for the Allegro movement of the Second Symphony and also the Joseph H. Bearns Prize (Columbia University) for the Second Symphony. He was awarded a grant by the American Academy of Arts and Letters and the National Institute of Arts and Letters in 1946 for his "Folk Overture."

His compositions, which were performed by the National Symphony, the New York Philharmonic and the Rochester Symphony orchestras, include the First and Second Symphonies, the Concertino for Flute and the "Folk Overture." The Concertino for Flute was broadcast over a Rochester radio station, and the "Folk Overture" was heard over a CBS network. At the present time, he is completing a Violin Concerto commissioned by Roman Totenberg.

COMPOSITIONS

ORCHESTRAL WORKS	DURATION	PUBLISHER	DATE
FIRST SYMPHONY	45 minutes	Manuscript	1942
SECOND SYMPHONY	26 "	Harms, Inc.	1944
FOLK OVERTURE	8 "	Hargail Music Press	1945
THIRD SYMPHONY	20 "	Hargail Music Press	1946
CHAMBER ORCHESTRA			
CONCERTINO FOR FLUTE, STRINGS AND PERCUSSION	11 minutes	Hargail Music Press	1945
CHAMBER MUSIC			
PIANO SONATA	12 minutes	Manuscript	1941
STRING QUARTET	40 "	Manuscript	1941

GIAN CARLO MENOTTI

Born in Cadegliano, Italy, in 1911. He started his music studies with his mother. He came to America in 1928 to study composition at the Curtis Institute of Music with Rosario Scalero.

He is particularly interested in opera and writes his own librettos as well as the music. His first opera, "Amelia Goes to the Ball," was premiered by Fritz Reiner and was also performed by the Metropolitan Opera. NBC commissioned him to write "The Old Maid and the Thief," a radio opera, which was played by the NBC Symphony. "The Island God" had its première at the Metropolitan Opera House. "The Medium," commissioned by the Ditson Fund, was heard at the 1946 Columbia University Music Festival and was broadcast over WNYC. In 1946, he was awarded a Guggenheim Fellowship. He has recently become a member of the faculty of the Curtis Institute.

GIAN CARLO MENOTTI (*Continued*)

"Sebastian," a commissioned ballet, was presented by the Ballet International. The Piano Concerto in F was played by the Boston Symphony. At the present time, he is working on a commissioned ballet based on a work of Marcel Proust.

COMPOSITIONS

ORCHESTRAL WORKS	PUBLISHER	DATE
PIANO CONCERTO IN F	G. Ricordi & Co.	

CHAMBER MUSIC		
TRIO FOR A HOUSE WARMING PARTY *piano, cello, flute*	Manuscript	1936

STAGE WORKS		
AMELIA GOES TO THE BALL—opera buffa in one act	Manuscript	
THE OLD MAID AND THE THIEF—radio opera in one act	Manuscript	
THE ISLAND GOD—tragic opera in one act	G. Ricordi & Co.	
SEBASTIAN—ballet	G. Ricordi & Co.	

MICHEL MICHELET

Born in Kieff, Russia, in 1894. He studied composition with Reger and Glière. He was Professor at the Kieff and Vienna conservatories and has appeared as cellist, pianist and conductor in concerts throughout Russia and Europe.

He has written many symphonic and chamber works; since 1928, he has composed mainly for motion pictures. Since he came to the United States in 1941, he has written several scores for Hollywood productions. The score for "Voice in the Wind" was selected by the Academy of Motion Pictures for having the best dramatic scoring. "Abraham Lincoln Collects a Dividend," a war ballad, was produced by the Writers Mobilization in coöperation with the Office of War Information. His music for films and concert arrangements are listed here.

COMPOSITIONS

FILM MUSIC	STUDIO	PUBLISHER	DATE
VOICE IN THE WIND	United Artists		1944
THE HAIRY APE	United Artists		1945
(concert version—Czech Lullaby for violin and piano)		Theodore Presser Co.	
DIARY OF A CHAMBERMAID	United Artists		1945

DARIUS MILHAUD

Born in 1892 at Aix-en-Provence, France. At the age of two he began picking out on the piano notes of songs he had heard in the street, and at the age of six he began to study the violin. He gave his first concert in public at the age of ten. Following the completion of his studies at the Lycée, where he specialized in Latin, Greek and philosophy, he entered the Paris Conservatory, where he studied composition, history of music, conducting and violin.

His first work performed in public was a Sonata for Piano and Violin, and shortly after he won his first prize in composition. In 1917 he joined the French Legation in Brazil, where Paul Claudel was minister, and lived there for two years. On his return to France he founded the Group of Six. In 1922 he went to the United States as conductor and pianist and lectured in the universities. He went on another tour to Russia later, also concertizing and giving lectures. He is a Chevalier of the Legion of Honor of France; he was made a member of the Higher Council Boards of both the French National Radio and the Paris Conservatory and was on a committee of the Opéra Comique of Paris. In 1940 he came to America and became a member of the music faculty at Mills College. In 1943 he was made an honorary associate of the National Institute of Arts and Letters of New York.

He has been commissioned by the Elizabeth Sprague Coolidge Foundation (Library of Congress) and the League of Composers, as well as by the French Ministry of Fine Arts, also by the St. Louis Symphony Orchestra and the Chicago Symphony Orchestra for their anniversaries. His works are on the programs of all the leading orchestras and chamber-music societies in America and in Europe and have been frequently broadcast. His opera "Christophe Colomb" was presented in Berlin, and the opera "Maximilien" was given in Paris. Many of his operas and ballets have been given in other cities in Europe.

COMPOSITIONS WRITTEN IN AMERICA

ORCHESTRAL WORKS	DURATION		PUBLISHER	DATE
Opus Americanum No. 2—ballet suite	30 minutes		Elkan-Vogel *for hire*	1940
Four Chansons de Ronsard *soprano, orchestra*	10	"	Boosey & Hawkes	1941
Concerto No. 2 *piano, orchestra*	18	"	Boosey & Hawkes	1941
Four Sketches for Orchestra	10	"	Mercury Music Corp.	1941
Concerto for Two Pianos and Orchestra	20	"	Elkan-Vogel *for hire*	1941
Concerto for Clarinet and Orchestra	20	"	Elkan-Vogel	1941
Suite for Harmonica and Orchestra *(also for harmonica & piano, violin & orchestra, or violin & piano)*	17	"	Boosey & Hawkes	1942
Fanfare de la Liberté	3	"	Manuscript	1942
Cain and Abel *narrator, orchestra*	4	"	Manuscript	1944
Air (from the viola sonata) *viola, orchestra*	3	"	Manuscript	1944

DARIUS MILHAUD (*Continued*)

ORCHESTRAL WORKS (*Continued*)

	DURATION	PUBLISHER	DATE
LA MUSE MÉNAGÈRE (orchestral version)	25 minutes	Elkan-Vogel (*piano version only*)	1944
SYMPHONY No. 2	30 "	Manuscript	1944
SUITE FRANÇAISE full orchestra, or symphonic band, or piano, 4 hands	18 "	Leeds Music Corp. (*for band*)	1944
LE BAL MARTINIQUAIS (*also for 2 pianos*)	8 "	Delkas Music Pub. Co.	1944
INTRODUCTION AND MARCHE-FÊTE DE LA VICTOIRE—completion of "Suite Française" for use as ballet music	5 "	Manuscript	1945
CONCERTO No. 2 cello, orchestra	20 "	Associated Music Publishers	1945
CONCERTO No. 2 violin, orchestra	20 "	Associated Music Publishers	1946
THIRD SYMPHONY WITH CHOIR			1946

CHAMBER ORCHESTRA

MILLS FANFARE string orchestra	1 minute	Manuscript	1941

CHORAL WORKS

BORECHU-SHEMA (Hebrew and English text) solo voice, chorus, organ	3 minutes	Manuscript	1944
KADDISH (Hebrew and French text) solo voice, chorus ad lib., organ	5 "	Manuscript	1945
SIX SONNETS ECRITS AU SECRET (by Jean Cassou)	18 "	Manuscript	1946

CHAMBER MUSIC

STRING QUARTET No. 10 (Birthday Quartet)	18 minutes	Manuscript	1940
SONATINA 2 violins	4 "	Manuscript	1940
STRING TRIO violin, viola, cello	3 "	Manuscript	1940
SONATINA violin, viola	6 "	Manuscript	1941
STRING QUARTET No. 11	18 "	Manuscript	1942
RÈVES—song cycle voice, piano	6 "	Heugel	1942
LA LIBERTADORA—dance suite 2 pianos	7 "	Manuscript	1943
SONGES—suite 2 pianos	4 "	Deiss-Elkan-Vogel	1943
SONATA ON ANONYMOUS THEMES OF THE 18TH CENTURY viola, piano	12 "	Heugel	1944
SONATA viola, piano	17 "	Heugel	1944
LA MUSE MÉNAGÈRE—piano suite	25 "	Elkan-Vogel	1944
STRING QUARTET No. 12	15 "	Manuscript	1945
SONATA violin, harpsichord	14 "	Elkan-Vogel	1945
DUO 2 violins	5 "	Manuscript	1945
QUATRE CHANTS DE MISÈRE—song cycle	9 "	Manuscript	1946

STAGE WORKS

L'ANNONCE FAITE À MARIE (text by Paul Claudel)—incidental music, new version	30 minutes	Manuscript	1942

DARIUS MILHAUD *(Continued)*

STAGE WORKS *(Continued)*	DURATION	PUBLISHER	DATE
BOLIVAR—opera in 3 acts, 10 scenes	3 hours, 20 minutes	Manuscript	1943
JEUX DE PRINTEMPS—ballet *full orchestra, or chamber orchestra, or piano, 4 hands*	25 "	Manuscript	1944
THE BELLS—ballet	32 "	Manuscript	1945

FILM MUSIC	STUDIO		
THE PRIVATE AFFAIRS OF BEL AMI	Enterprise		1947

CHARLES BORROMEO MILLS

Born in Asheville, North Carolina, in 1914. He was self-taught until 1933, when he came to New York and studied with Copland, Garfield, Harris and Sessions. He has contributed articles to the League of Composers' magazine, *Modern Music,* and to other publications. He has taught theory and composition. The Third String Quartet in F Sharp Minor was awarded the Roth String Quartet Prize.

His compositions have had performances in many cities of the United States and frequently in South America. The League of Composers presented the Piano Sonata in A Minor, which was also broadcast over WNYC. The Sonata for Cello and Piano was premiered on the WNYC American Music Festival. The Chamber Concerto for Ten Instruments and the "John Brown Music for Dance" were both commissioned and were played in Detroit and New York. He is completing a Thirteenth Piano Sonatine in E Flat Minor and a Third Symphony in D Minor, Opus 55.

COMPOSITIONS

ORCHESTRAL WORKS	DURATION	PUBLISHER	DATE
SLOW MOVEMENT FOR STRING ORCHESTRA	7 minutes	Manuscript	1935
CONCERTINO FOR FLUTE AND ORCHESTRA	18 "	Manuscript	1939
FESTIVAL OVERTURE FOR CHORUS AND ORCHESTRA	10 "	Manuscript	1940
FIRST SYMPHONY IN E MINOR	25 "	Manuscript	1940
SECOND SYMPHONY IN C MAJOR	30 "	Manuscript	1942

CHAMBER ORCHESTRA			
CHAMBER SYMPHONY FOR ELEVEN INSTRUMENTS	15 minutes	Manuscript	1939
CHAMBER CONCERTO FOR TEN INSTRUMENTS	18 "	Manuscript	1942

CHORAL WORKS			
ARS POETICA *mixed chorus, a cappella*	5 minutes	Manuscript	1940
THE DARK NIGHT *women's chorus, string orchestra*	10 "	Manuscript	1945

CHARLES BORROMEO MILLS (*Continued*)

CHAMBER MUSIC	DURATION	PUBLISHER	DATE
PIANO TRIO IN D MINOR	20 minutes	Manuscript	1941
CHAMBER CONCERTANTE FOR WIND QUINTETTE	15 "	Manuscript	1941
THIRD STRING QUARTET IN F SHARP MINOR	19 "	Manuscript	1943
FOURTH SUITE IN D MAJOR *piano*	20 "	Manuscript	1946
FORTY PENITENTIAL PRELUDES FOR PIANO	1 hour	Manuscript	1946
DUO PICCOLO FOR VIOLINS SOLI	12 minutes	Manuscript	1946
SERENADE FOR FLUTE, HORN AND PIANO	8 "	Manuscript	1946
SONATA FOR ENGLISH HORN AND PIANO	30 "	Manuscript	1946

STAGE WORKS			
JOHN BROWN—music for dance *wind quintet, piano, and snare drum*	20 minutes	Manuscript	1945

CYRIL JOHN MOCKRIDGE

Born in London, England, in 1896. He studied at the Royal Academy of Music in London. He came to America in 1922 and made piano arrangements for the Rodgers and Hart musical shows. His scores include "Garrick Gaieties," "Girl Friend," "Peggy-Ann," "Chee-Chee" and "Present Arms." Since 1931, he has been a composer for the Fox Film Corporation. He wrote the music for the early Shirley Temple and Will Rogers pictures. At present, he is working on the score of "Claudia and David." His music for films is listed here.

COMPOSITIONS

FILM MUSIC	STUDIO
THE DARK CORNER	20th Century-Fox
SENTIMENTAL JOURNEY	20th Century-Fox
THE RICKENBACKER STORY	20th Century-Fox
THUNDERHEAD	20th Century-Fox
THE EVE OF ST. MARK	20th Century-Fox
THE SULLIVANS	20th Century-Fox
HAPPY LAND	20th Century-Fox
HOLY MATRIMONY	20th Century-Fox
TONIGHT WE RAID CALAIS	20th Century-Fox
THE OX-BOW INCIDENT	20th Century-Fox
RINGS ON HER FINGERS	20th Century-Fox

ITALO MONTEMEZZI

Born in Vigasio, near Verona, Italy, in 1875. He studied the piano in his early youth without intending to become a musician; he was trained to become an engineer, but gave up that career and turned to music. He

ITALO MONTEMEZZI (*Continued*)

studied at the Conservatory of Milan, and, upon his graduation in 1900, he wrote a work which was performed at the Conservatory under the direction of Arturo Toscanini.

His first opera was "Bianca," followed by "Giovanni Gallurese," which Serafin conducted in Italy and New York. "L'Amore dei Tre Re" was first performed in Milan in 1913 and then in Paris, Prague and other cities in Europe, as well as in South America and Australia. Since 1914 it has been in the repertory of the Metropolitan Opera Company and has been presented in many cities in the United States. Other works include the operas "Héllera," "La Nave" and "La Notte di Zoraima"; a symphonic poem, "Paolo e Virginia," and a cantata. In 1939 he came to the United States and now lives in California. His one-act opera, "L'Incantesimo," composed in this country, was first heard in 1943 over the NBC network, performed by the NBC Orchestra under the composer's direction.

COMPOSITIONS WRITTEN IN AMERICA

ORCHESTRAL WORKS	DURATION	PUBLISHER	DATE
ITALIA MIA! NULLA FERMERÀ IL TUO CANTO!—symphonic poem	17 minutes	Manuscript	1944
STAGE WORKS			
L'INCANTESIMO—one act opera *full orchestra*		Manuscript	1943

DOUGLAS STUART MOORE

Born in Cutchogue, New York, in 1893. He studied at Yale and received his degree of Bachelor of Arts in 1915 and of Bachelor of Music in 1917. He was a pupil in composition of Parker and Bloch and of D'Indy at the Schola Cantorum in Paris. He won the Pulitzer Scholarship in 1924 and in 1933 received a Guggenheim Fellowship.

He became executive officer of the Department of Music, Columbia University, in 1940, and was appointed MacDowell Professor of Music in 1945. He won the Eastman School Publication Award and the S.P.A.M. Publication Award. In 1941 he was elected a member of the National Institute of Arts and Letters and in 1946 he became President of this organization. He is at present Secretary of the Advisory Board of the Ditson Fund. His books include *Listening to Music* and *From Madrigal to Modern Music;* he has also contributed to magazines and reviews.

His works have had numerous performances in the United States, Canada and Cuba and over the NBC network. He appeared as Guest Conductor with the Cleveland, Manhattan and Philharmonic Orchestras. The opera "The Devil and Daniel Webster" was presented in New York, San Francisco, Los Angeles, and at the Chautauqua and Worcester festivals.

DOUGLAS STUART MOORE (*Continued*)

COMPOSITIONS

ORCHESTRAL WORKS

	DURATION	PUBLISHER	DATE
FOUR MUSEUM PIECES	12 minutes	Manuscript	1922
PAGEANT OF P. T. BARNUM	18 "	C. C. Birchard & Co.	1924
MOBY DICK	20 "	Manuscript	1928
A SYMPHONY OF AUTUMN	22 "	G. Schirmer, Inc. for hire	1930
OVERTURE ON AN AMERICAN TUNE	8 "	Manuscript	1931
SUITE FROM "POWER AND THE LAND"	13 "	Manuscript	1941
SUITE FROM "YOUTH GETS A BREAK"	12 "	Manuscript	1941
VILLAGE MUSIC	12 "	Music Press	1942
IN MEMORIAM	11 "	Elkan-Vogel	1943
SYMPHONY NO. 2 IN A MAJOR	22 "	G. Schirmer, Inc.	1945

CHORAL WORKS

GOD REST YOU MERRY GENTLEMEN a cappella	4 minutes	Carl Fischer, Inc.	1932
SIMON LEGREE (Vachel Lindsay) men's chorus, piano	10 "	Carl Fischer, Inc.	1937
PERHAPS TO DREAM (S. V. Benét) women's chorus, a cappella	3 "	Carl Fischer, Inc.	1937
DEDICATION (Archibald MacLeish) mixed chorus, a cappella	4 "	Arrow Press	1938
PRAYER FOR ENGLAND (W. R. Benét) men's chorus, piano	3 "	Boosey & Hawkes	1941
PRAYER FOR THE UNITED NATIONS (S. V. Benét) alto solo, chorus, orchestra or piano	8 "	H. W. Gray Co., Inc.	1943

CHAMBER MUSIC

BALLADE OF WILLIAM SYCAMORE baritone, flute, trombone, piano	8 minutes	Manuscript	1926
SONATA FOR VIOLIN AND PIANO	12 "	Manuscript	1929
QUARTET FOR STRINGS	15 "	S.P.A.M.	1933
QUINTET woodwinds and horn	12 "	Manuscript	1942
DOWN EAST SUITE violin and piano	12 "	Carl Fischer, Inc.	1944
QUINTET FOR CLARINET AND STRINGS	15 "		1946

STAGE WORKS

TWELFTH NIGHT—incidental music		Manuscript	1925
MUCH ADO ABOUT NOTHING— incidental music		Manuscript	1927
THE ROAD TO ROME (R. E. Sherwood)— incidental music		Brady & Wiman	1927
WHITE WINGS—chamber opera orchestra of 30	2 hours	Manuscript	1935
THE HEADLESS HORSEMAN—operetta orchestra of 25	1 hour	E. C. Schirmer Music Co.	1936
THE DEVIL AND DANIEL WEBSTER (S. V. Benét)—opera orchestra of 45 or 20	1 "	Boosey & Hawkes	1938

FILM MUSIC

	STUDIO		
POWER AND THE LAND—documentary concert version—suite	U. S. Gov't. Rural Electrification Adm.		1940
YOUTH GETS A BREAK—documentary concert version—suite	U. S. Gov't. N.Y.A.		1940

DOUGLAS STUART MOORE (*Continued*)

FILM MUSIC (*Continued*)	STUDIO	DATE
BIP GOES TO TOWN—documentary	U. S. Gov't. Rural Electrification Adm.	1941

JEROME MOROSS

Born in Brooklyn, New York, in 1913. He studied at New York University and was a Fellow at the Juilliard School of Music. He has been a composer, orchestrator and pianist for the theater, radio and films. He received a CBS commission to write "A Tall Story," which was performed over a CBS network. His compositions have been performed in Chicago, Los Angeles, New York and Seattle, and the "Biguine" was heard over an NBC network. At present he is completing a series of "Choral Ballets" and a Second Symphony.

COMPOSITIONS

ORCHESTRAL WORKS	DURATION	PUBLISHER	DATE
PAEANS	5 minutes	New Music	1931
BIGUINE	5 "	New Music	1934
A TALL STORY	9 "	Manuscript	1938
SYMPHONY	22 "	Manuscript	1942
THE WOLF WALTZES from "Riding Hood"	8 "	Manuscript	1945

CHAMBER ORCHESTRA			
THOSE EVERLASTING BLUES *low voice, 18 instruments*	5 minutes	Manuscript	1932
SUITE FOR CHAMBER ORCHESTRA *18 instruments*	15 "	New Music	1934

CHORAL WORKS			
THE ECCENTRICITIES OF DAVY CROCKETT *baritone, mixed chorus, orchestra*	50 minutes	Manuscript	1946
WILLIE THE WEEPER *tenor solo, mixed chorus, orchestra*	45 "	Manuscript	1946

STAGE WORKS			
AMERICAN PATTERN—ballet *orchestra*	30 minutes	Manuscript	1936
FRANKIE AND JOHNNY—ballet *women's trio, orchestra*	30 "	Chappell	1938
SUSANNA AND THE ELDERS—ballet *soprano, baritone, chorus, orchestra*	20 "	Manuscript	1940
WILLIE THE WEEPER—ballet *tenor, chorus, orchestra*	45 "	Manuscript	1945
THE ECCENTRICITIES OF DAVY CROCKETT—ballet *soprano, alto, baritone, chorus, orchestra*	40 "	Manuscript	1945
RIDING HOOD—ballet *mezzo soprano, tenor, chorus, orchestra*	30 "	Manuscript	1946

HAROLD MORRIS

Born in San Antonio, Texas, in 1890. He was educated at the University of Texas at Austin. His studies in music began while he was at high school and continued through his college years. At the Cincinnati Conservatory of Music he received the highest honors in graduate and postgraduate work.

For many years he was a member of the faculty of the Juilliard Institute of Musical Art. Since 1939 he has been on the faculty of Teachers College, Columbia University. He has also lectured at the Rice Institute of Houston, Texas, and at Duke University. He has toured as a pianist in the United States and Canada and was soloist in his own Piano Concerto with the Boston Symphony Orchestra in New York and Boston. The Juilliard Publication Award was given to him for his Piano Concerto. The Violin and Piano Sonata was chosen by the Curtis Institute as a representative American work for performance at the American Embassy in London for the King's Jubilee. He received the New York State and national awards of the National Federation of Music Clubs for his Violin Concerto, the Publication Award of the National Association for American Composers and Conductors for the Piano Sonata No. 4, the Philadelphia Music Guild Award for his Suite for Orchestra, the Award of Merit of the National Association for American Composers and Conductors for service to American music in 1938–1939. His Piano Sonata No. 3 won a prize of the Fellowship of American Composers in 1946. He is a member of the United States Section of the I.S.C.M., a composer-member of the League of Composers, an honorary life member of the Texas Music Teachers Association, a life member of the National Association for American Composers and Conductors.

His orchestral works have been played by the orchestras in Boston, New York, Cincinnati, Los Angeles, Rochester, Indianapolis and St. Louis; his chamber music has been frequently performed in America and Europe, and his works have been broadcast over the major networks. He has written a great many piano works not listed here.

COMPOSITIONS

ORCHESTRAL WORKS

	DURATION	PUBLISHER	DATE
POEM—after Tagore's "Gitanjali"	16 minutes	Manuscript	1915
CONCERTO FOR PIANO AND ORCHESTRA	27 "	Juilliard Publication Award (C. C. Birchard & Co.)	1927
SYMPHONY No. 1—after Browning's "Prospice"	31 "	Affiliated Music Corp. Edition Musicus	1936
PASSACAGLIA AND FUGUE FOR ORCHESTRA	20 "	Manuscript	1936
SUITE FOR ORCHESTRA	15 "	Manuscript	1937
CONCERTO FOR VIOLIN AND ORCHESTRA	26 "	Manuscript	1938
AMERICAN EPIC *orchestra*	11 "	Manuscript	1942
SYMPHONY No. 2, "VICTORY"	27 "	Manuscript	1943
OVERTURE HEROIC	13 "	Manuscript	1943
SYMPHONY No. 3	30 "	Manuscript	1946

CHAMBER ORCHESTRA

	DURATION	PUBLISHER	DATE
"DUM-A-LUM"—variations on the Negro Spiritual *11 instruments*	14 minutes	Manuscript	1925

HAROLD MORRIS (*Continued*)

CHAMBER ORCHESTRA (*Continued*)	DURATION	PUBLISHER	DATE
SUITE FOR PIANO AND STRINGS	14 minutes	Manuscript	1940
SUITE FOR STRINGS	13 "	Manuscript	1941

CHAMBER MUSIC

	DURATION	PUBLISHER	DATE
PIANO SONATA No. 2	20 minutes	Manuscript	1915
TRIO No. 1 FOR PIANO, VIOLIN AND CELLO	15 "	Manuscript	1917
SONATA FOR PIANO AND VIOLIN	25 "	Manuscript	1919
PIANO SONATA No. 3—one movement	20 "	Manuscript	1920
STRING QUARTET No. 1	21 "	Manuscript	1928
QUINTET FOR PIANO AND STRINGS, No. 1	28 "	Manuscript	1929
SET OF SIX FOR PIANO	15 "	Manuscript	1931
PROLOGUE AND SCHERZO FOR FLUTE, VIOLIN, CELLO AND PIANO	12 "	Manuscript	1935
TRIO No. 2 FOR PIANO, VIOLIN AND CELLO	20 "	Manuscript	1937
STRING QUARTET No. 2	17 "	Manuscript	1937
PIANO SONATA No. 4	14 "	Composers Press	1939
QUINTET No. 2 FOR PIANO AND STRINGS	20 "	Manuscript	1940
RHAPSODY FOR FLUTE, CELLO AND PIANO	15 "	Manuscript	1944

OTTO MUELLER

Born in Voehl-Cassel, Germany, in 1870. He studied at the Conservatory of Music in Leipzig. He was first violinist of the opera orchestra in Kieff, Russia, and also with opera and symphony orchestras in Germany. He came to the United States in 1908 and became first violinist in the Philadelphia Symphony Orchestra, a position which he held until he retired in 1926.

In 1945, his "Scherzo Polyphonic" won first prize in the Broadcast Music, Inc., Contest. His symphonic poem, "Atlantic," the carnival overture, "Schlaraffiada," and the "Introduction and Scherzo Grotesque" have been performed by the Philadelphia Orchestra.

COMPOSITIONS

ORCHESTRAL WORKS	DURATION	PUBLISHER	DATE
SCHLARAFFIADA—CARNIVAL OVERTURE	12 minutes	Manuscript	1921
VIOLIN CONCERTO No. 2 IN G MINOR	18 "	Manuscript	1925
SYMPHONY No. 2 IN D MAJOR	24 "	Manuscript	1930
LA CHASSE—OVERTURE CHARACTERISTIC horn solo, orchestra	9 "	Manuscript	1931
INTRODUCTION AND SCHERZO GROTESQUE	11 "	Manuscript	1932

CHAMBER ORCHESTRA

	DURATION	PUBLISHER	DATE
ROSENDALE SUITE flute, oboe, horn, strings	14 minutes	Manuscript	1928

OTTO MUELLER (*Continued*)

CHORAL WORKS	DURATION	PUBLISHER	DATE
SONG OF THE HEROES *alto solo, men's chorus, orchestra*	28 minutes	Manuscript	1935
THE ROLLING DRUMS *mixed chorus, orchestra, baritone solo*	26 "	Manuscript	1938

CHAMBER MUSIC			
STRING QUARTETTE NO. 2	16 minutes	Manuscript	1915

NICHOLAS NABOKOFF

Born in St. Petersburg, Russia, in 1902. He studied with Rebikoff and with Juon, and later in Berlin with Busoni. He came to America in 1933. He became a member of the faculty of Wells College in 1938, and in 1944 he was elected a member of the faculty of the Peabody Conservatory of Music. The Barnes Foundation in Pennsylvania awarded a scholarship to him.

He collaborated with Balanchine on a book on classical ballet and music. He translated a history of Russian music for the Council of Learned Societies of America. During World War II, he was a Colonel with the American Military Government in Germany (Morale Division).

"Union Pacific" was presented by the Ballet Russe de Monte Carlo frequently in their repertoire in 1935. The "Sinfonia Biblica" was performed by the Philharmonic Symphony Orchestra. "Job" was presented by the Schola Cantorum and at the Worcester Festival. "Samson Agonistes" was first produced at Wells College in 1938. He has had performances of his orchestral and his chamber music in Paris, London, Berlin, Brussels, Amsterdam and Geneva and also in many cities in the United States. "America Was Promises," a choral work written for radio with a text by MacLeish, was broadcast over WABC in 1940. At present he is completing a concert piece for cello, a ballet, "Don Quixote," and a piano concerto.

COMPOSITIONS WRITTEN IN AMERICA

ORCHESTRAL WORKS	PUBLISHER	DATE
SUITE FROM "VIE DE POLICHINELLE"	Edition Russe de Musique	1934
LE FIANCÉ	Edition Russe de Musique	1934
SINFONIA BIBLICA	Manuscript	1940
SYMPHONIC SUITE OF MARCHES	Edition Russe de Musique	1945

CHORAL WORKS		
COLLECTIONNEUR D'ECHOS *soprano, bass, 9 per- cussion instruments*	Edition Russe de Musique	1933
"JOB" *soli, chorus, orchestra*	Edition Russe de Musique	1933
"AMERICA WAS PROMISES" (Archibald MacLeish) *written for radio*	Edition Russe de Musique	

NICHOLAS NABOKOFF (*Continued*)

CHAMBER MUSIC	PUBLISHER	DATE
QUARTETTE	Edition Russe de Musique	
SONATA *piano*	Edition Russe de Musique	
CANTANTE	Edition Russe de Musique	

STAGE WORKS		
PETITE CATHERINE	Edition Russe de Musique	
UNION PACIFIC—ballet	Edition Russe de Musique	1934
SAMSON AGONISTES—incidental music for Milton's play	Edition Russe de Musique	1938
THE LAST FLOWER—ballet	Edition Russe de Musique	1941
APHRODITE—ballet	Edition Russe de Musique	

CHARLES NAGINSKI

Born in Cairo, Egypt, in 1909 and died in 1940. At the age of eight he began to study the piano with his father; later he had other teachers. At ten, without any training in theory or composition, he commenced to compose. From 1928 to 1933 he held a fellowship in composition at the Juilliard Graduate School, where he studied with Goldmark.

In 1937 he was commissioned by the League of Composers to write a chamber-music work for the American Composers Series to be broadcast over WOR.

His chamber works have been presented by various string quartets. The "Orchestral Poem" was performed by the Juilliard Graduate School Orchestra. String Quartet No. 1 was broadcast over WABC. "Nonsense Alphabet Suite" was recorded by Columbia and Sinfonietta for Chamber Orchestra by Yaddo.

COMPOSITIONS

ORCHESTRAL WORKS	DURATION	PUBLISHER	DATE
SUITE FOR ORCHESTRA	8 minutes	Manuscript *for hire*	1931
SYMPHONY No. 1	20 "	Manuscript *for hire*	1935
"1936"—orchestral poem	7 "	Manuscript *for hire*	1936
SYMPHONY No. 2		Manuscript	1937
SINFONIETTA		Manuscript	1937
NONSENSE ALPHABET SUITE		Manuscript	1940

CHARLES NAGINSKI *(Continued)*

CHAMBER ORCHESTRA	DURATION	PUBLISHER	DATE
THREE MOVEMENTS FOR CHAMBER ORCHESTRA *20 instruments*	8 minutes	Manuscript	1937
FOUR SONGS WITH CHAMBER ORCHESTRA *soprano, 20 instruments*	10 "	Manuscript	
MOVEMENT FOR STRINGS		Manuscript	
SINFONIETTA FOR CHAMBER ORCHESTRA		Manuscript	1940

CHAMBER MUSIC			
STRING QUARTET NO. 1 IN F MINOR	18 minutes	Manuscript	1933
STRING QUARTET NO. 2 IN A MINOR	15 "	Manuscript	1933
SONATINA FOR PIANO		Manuscript	1937

ALFRED NEWMAN

Born in New Haven, Connecticut, in 1901. He began to study the piano at the age of seven and made his first public appearance when he was eight years old, playing a Beethoven Sonata. In 1911 he moved to New York, where he studied with Goldmark, Paderewski, Stojowski and Wedge. He won two gold medals for piano and composition from the Foranda Conservatory. At an early age he gave recitals in Boston, New York and Philadelphia and on two occasions was soloist with the New Haven Symphony under Horatio Parker. At sixteen he became Musical Director of the first George White Scandals, and before going to Hollywood, he conducted many of the Gershwin shows. He has been a guest conductor of the Cincinnati Symphony, the Los Angeles Philharmonic and the Hollywood Bowl orchestras and of the American Orchestral Association. Since 1939 he has been composing film music for 20th-Century Fox and at present is Musical Director of the studio.

He won the Academy Award in 1943 for the score of "Song of Bernadette." Besides composing for motion pictures, he has written a Piano Quintet, a Piano Sonata and several orchestral suites. His music for films and concert arrangements are listed here.

COMPOSITIONS

FILM MUSIC	STUDIO	PUBLISHER	DATE
STREET SCENE	Samuel Goldwyn		1931
concert version—Street Scene		Robbins Music Corp.	
HURRICANE	Samuel Goldwyn		1937
THE RAINS CAME	20th Century-Fox		1939
WUTHERING HEIGHTS	Samuel Goldwyn		1939
GUNGA DIN	RKO		1939
HOW GREEN WAS MY VALLEY	20th Century-Fox		1941
SONG OF BERNADETTE	20th Century-Fox		1943
KEYS OF THE KINGDOM	20th Century-Fox		1944
LEAVE HER TO HEAVEN	20th Century-Fox		1945
DRAGONWYCK	20th Century-Fox		1945
THE RAZOR'S EDGE	20th Century-Fox		1946

PAUL NORDOFF

Born in Philadelphia, Pennsylvania, in 1909. He began his musical education when he was eight years old. In 1923 he entered the Philadelphia Conservatory of Music, where he studied piano with Ezerman and later with Samaroff; he also studied ensemble playing, harmony and composition. In 1929 he entered the Juilliard School and was awarded a fellowship in piano with Mme. Samaroff and in composition with Goldmark. He won the Bearns Prize from Columbia University in 1933, and in that same year and again in 1935 he was awarded the Guggenheim Fellowship. In 1940 he won the Pulitzer Award.

He has specialized in contemporary piano music and has lectured in many cities. During 1936 and 1937 he did research in Honolulu for the preparation of an opera with a Polynesian setting. From 1938 to 1943 he was appointed the head of the Composition Department of the Philadelphia Conservatory of Music. He is now Assistant Professor of Music at Michigan State College.

The ballets for Martha Graham, "Every Soul is a Circus" and "Salem Shore," were presented in New York and on tour throughout the United States. "Tallyho," written for Agnes DeMille, was presented by the Ballet Theater in the season of 1944–45. His major compositions have been performed by many of the leading symphonic orchestras and his chamber music has been presented frequently. He was commissioned by the League of Composers in the American Composers Series. At present he is writing a commissioned work for violin, piano and orchestra, a new symphony and a song cycle, "Songs for the Dead."

COMPOSITIONS

ORCHESTRAL WORKS	DURATION	PUBLISHER	DATE
PRELUDE AND THREE FUGUES	8 minutes	Manuscript	1932
FIRST PIANO CONCERTO	28 "	Manuscript	1934
SECOND PIANO CONCERTO	32 "	Manuscript	1936
SUITE	14 "	Manuscript	1939
VIOLIN CONCERTO	29 "	Manuscript	1940

CHAMBER ORCHESTRA			
PRELUDE AND THREE FUGUES	8 minutes	Manuscript	1936
SUITE	14 "	Manuscript	1939

CHORAL WORKS			
SECULAR MASS *mixed chorus, orchestra*	40 minutes	Manuscript	1934

CHAMBER MUSIC			
STRING QUARTET IN E MINOR	20 minutes	Manuscript	1932
THE PATH OF LOVE—song cycle (15 songs) *tenor and piano*		Manuscript	1943
SONGS FOR PILGRIMS—song cycle *soprano, contralto and piano*		Manuscript	1943

STAGE WORKS			
ROMEO AND JULIET—incidental music *flute, violin, harp, cello*		Manuscript	1935

PAUL NORDOFF (*Continued*)

STAGE WORKS (*Continued*)	DURATION	PUBLISHER	DATE
MR. FORTUNE—opera in 2 acts	2 hours	Manuscript	1937
ballet, soloists, orchestra			
EVERY SOUL IS A CIRCUS		Manuscript	1938
11 instruments			
SALEM SHORE		Manuscript	1944
clarinet, oboe, piano, cello			
THE SUN—work for speaking chorus	75 minutes	Manuscript	1945
solo speaker, Eurhythmists, soprano,			
contralto, instruments			

ALEX NORTH

Born in Chester, Pennsylvania, in 1910. He studied piano with George Boyle. He received a scholarship at the Institute of Musical Art and in 1933 he went to the Moscow Conservatory to continue his studies. He returned to the United States in 1937 and studied with Aaron Copland and Ernst Toch.

While in Moscow, he became Music Director of the German Theater Group as well as Music Director for the Latvian State Theater. He was a member of the Union of Soviet Composers and received several commissions from them. In the United States, he was Music Director for the Anna Sokolow Dance Company. He has been a Captain in the U. S. Army and has organized programs for recreational and therapeutic purposes for hospitalized veterans.

The Rhapsody for Orchestra and Piano was broadcast over WOR. He wrote film music for the Office of War Information. The "Yank and Christopher Columbus" was recorded by Keynote Recordings. He recently completed a work for clarinet and orchestra, commissioned by Benny Goodman.

COMPOSITIONS

ORCHESTRAL WORKS	DURATION	PUBLISHER	DATE
QUEST	15 minutes	Manuscript for hire	1938
RHAPSODY FOR ORCHESTRA AND PIANO	13 "	Manuscript	1939
YANK AND CHRISTOPHER COLUMBUS	12 "	Manuscript	1942
CONCERT SUITE FOR CLARINET AND ORCHESTRA	16 "	Manuscript	1945

CHAMBER ORCHESTRA			
SLAUGHTER OF THE INNOCENTS	8 minutes	Manuscript	1937
with guitar solo			
AMERICAN LYRIC	10 "	Manuscript	1938
GOLDEN FLEECE	18 "	Manuscript	1940

ALEX NORTH (*Continued*)

CHORAL WORKS	DURATION	PUBLISHER	DATE
NEGRO MOTHER	8 minutes	Manuscript	1940
contralto, chorus			
BALLAD OF VALLEY FORGE	6 "	E. B. Marks Corp.	1941
baritone, chorus			
RHAPSODY, U.S.A.	5 "	Manuscript	1942
MORNING STAR—cantata	15 "		

CHAMBER MUSIC			
SUITE FOR FLUTE, CLARINET, BASSOON	8 minutes	Manuscript	1938
SUITE FOR STRING QUARTET	9 "	Manuscript	1939
WOODWIND QUINTET	9 "	Manuscript	1942

STAGE WORKS			
DOG BENEATH THE SKIN—songs and incidental music	1 hour	Manuscript	1937
LIFE AND DEATH OF AN AMERICAN—incidental music	2 hours	Manuscript	1939
HITHER AND THITHER OF DANNY DITHER—children's opera	2½ "	E. B. Marks Corp.	1942
INTERSECTION—ballet	12 minutes		
DESIGN FOR FIVE—ballet	10 "		

FILM MUSIC	STUDIO		
PEOPLE OF THE CUMBERLAND	Frontier Films		1938
A BETTER TOMORROW	Office of War Information		1944
LIBRARY OF CONGRESS	Office of War Information		1945
CITY PASTORALE—documentary	State Department		
RURAL NURSE—documentary	Willard Pictures		

LIONEL NOWAK

Born in Cleveland, Ohio, in 1911. He studied with Elwell, Porter and Sessions. He has won awards as a pianist.

He was a professor at Fenn College and Converse College. He was pianist and composer for the Humphrey-Weidman Dance Company. At present he is a traveling artist for the American Association of Colleges. He has been represented on programs of the Yaddo Festivals and the League of Composers. He is especially interested in music for the dance, and his ballets have been presented frequently in the United States.

COMPOSITIONS

ORCHESTRAL WORKS	DURATION	PUBLISHER	DATE
SUITE IN C	11 minutes	Manuscript	1936
CONCERTINO FOR PIANO AND ORCHESTRA	18 "	Manuscript	1944

CHAMBER MUSIC			
STRING QUARTET	20 minutes	Manuscript	1938

LIONEL NOWAK (*Continued*)

CHAMBER MUSIC (*Continued*)	DURATION	PUBLISHER	DATE
SONATA *violin alone*	13 minutes	Manuscript	1940
SUITE FOR FLUTE AND PIANO	9 "	Manuscript	1941
STRING TRIO	11 "	Manuscript	1942
QUARTET FOR WINDS	12 "	Manuscript	1944
SONATINA FOR VIOLIN AND PIANO	12 "	Manuscript	1944

STAGE WORKS

	DURATION	PUBLISHER	DATE
SQUARE DANCES *piano*	18 minutes	Manuscript	1939
ON MY MOTHER'S SIDE *piano*	27 "	Manuscript	1939
MEXICAN SUITE *piano*	25 "	Manuscript	1940
LAND OF ING *piano, voice, percussion*	18 "	Manuscript	1942
HERITAGE FOR TOMORROW *piano, voice, percussion*	27 "	Manuscript	1943
HOUSE DIVIDED *piano*	32 "	Manuscript	1945
DANCING FEET *piano, voice, percussion*	17 "	Manuscript	1945

UNO NYMAN

Born in Linkohing, Sweden, in 1879. He received his early musical training from an uncle who was concertmaster of the Royal Orchestra in Stockholm. At the age of seventeen he came to the United States and graduated from the University of Pennsylvania. He has since resided in Milwaukee. A composition for voice, viola, and piano was awarded first prize by the Civic Music Association of Milwaukee.

Since boyhood he has played in chamber-music organizations as violinist and violist; many of his compositions are written for strings.

His works have been heard in Milwaukee and Chicago.

COMPOSITIONS

ORCHESTRAL WORKS	DURATION	PUBLISHER	DATE
PHANTASIE	15 minutes	Manuscript	1935
IN MEMORIAM *string orchestra*	10 "	Manuscript *score and parts*	1936
SYMPHONY IN B	30 "	Manuscript *no parts*	1941
ALLEGRO GIOCOSO	5 "	Manuscript	1945
HIGHLIGHT AND TWILIGHT	7 "	Manuscript	1945

CHAMBER ORCHESTRA

	DURATION	PUBLISHER	DATE
MIRAGE *11 instruments, piano*	12 minutes	Manuscript *score and parts*	1926

UNO NYMAN (*Continued*)

CHAMBER MUSIC	DURATION	PUBLISHER	DATE
VIOLIN SONATA	30 minutes	Manuscript	1921
violin, piano			
MEMORIES WITH THE DUSK RETURN	8 "	Manuscript	1923
(poem by Li Po, 702–762)			
voice, 5 strings, piano,			
clarinet, flute			
PHANTASIE	10 "	Manuscript	1928
string quartet			
CELLO SONATA	35 "	Manuscript	1929
cello, piano			
QUARTET	25 "	Manuscript	1930
4 celli			
CELLO PHANTASIE	15 "	Manuscript	1931
solo cello, string quartet, piano			
PIANO TRIO	30 "	Manuscript	1933
TWO TRIOS		Manuscript	1933
2 violins, piano			
QUINTET	20 "	Manuscript	1934
strings, flute			
ARCTIC SUITE	20 "	Manuscript	1934
quintet for woodwinds			
PIANO QUINTET	30 "	Manuscript	1935
TRIO	25 "	Manuscript	1935
violin, viola, clarinet			
SIX QUARTETS		Manuscript	1936
TWO STRING QUARTETS	30 "	Manuscript	1939–45
QUARTET	30 "	Manuscript	
2 violins, cello, clarinet			
VIOLA SONATA	35 "	Manuscript	1941
TRIO	35 "	Manuscript	1944
viola, 2 celli			

LEO ORNSTEIN

Born in Kremenchough, Russia, in 1895. He came to America at the age of twelve. His musical education began in Russia at the Petrograd Conservatory with Glazounov, where he was regarded as a child prodigy. In 1905 he and his family fled from the Russian Revolution and came to America. His talent was quickly recognized on his arrival in New York, and he became a student at the Institute of Musical Art, studying piano with Bertha Tapper.

In 1911 he made his début as a concert pianist. His early compositions, written when a very young boy, were quite conventional, but in 1914, after a concert tour in Europe, he returned to America with works he had written in a new form. He was soon hailed as one of the forerunners of the modern movement in music, and his compositions, especially "Wild Men's Dance," "Dwarf Suite" and "Impressions of Notre Dame," created violent discussions between conservative and radical musicians. He continued to tour as a pianist in recitals and with the leading orchestras in America and in Europe. In recent years he has also lectured and taught piano. One

LEO ORNSTEIN (*Continued*)

of his great interests is the study of agriculture. He was a member of the faculty at the Philadelphia Musical Academy and he is now Director and head of the Piano Department of the Ornstein School of Music. He is also a member of the special faculty of Temple University. He received the first prize in the National Anthem Contest and was commissioned by the League of Composers to write an orchestral work which was performed by the St. Louis Symphony, called "Nocturne and Dance of Fates."

The Piano Concerto, as well as the "Lysistrata Suite," has been presented by the orchestras in New York, Philadelphia, Chicago and other cities. His chamber music has had many performances in America and in Europe, also at the Elizabeth Coolidge Festival in Paris, the Contemporary Music Society in Philadelphia and at the League of Composers' concerts.

COMPOSITIONS

ORCHESTRAL WORKS	DURATION	PUBLISHER	DATE
THE FOG—symphonic poem	14 minutes	Manuscript	1915
CONCERTO FOR PIANO	35 "	Manuscript *for hire*	1923
TWO NOCTURNES	12 "	Manuscript	1924
FIVE SONGS FOR VOICE AND ORCHESTRA	15 "	Manuscript	1929
LYSISTRATA SUITE	20 "	Manuscript *for hire*	1930
SYMPHONY		Manuscript	
NOCTURNE AND DANCE OF THE FATES	13 "	Manuscript *for hire*	1936

CHAMBER ORCHESTRA			
INCIDENTAL MUSIC TO LYSISTRATA *12 instruments*	20 minutes	Manuscript *for hire*	1930

CHORAL WORKS			
THREE RUSSIAN CHORUSES *a cappella*	14 minutes	Breitkopf & Härtel	

CHAMBER MUSIC			
TWO CELLO SONATAS		Carl Fischer, Inc.	
TWO VIOLIN SONATAS		Carl Fischer, Inc. Breitkopf & Härtel	
QUINTET *piano, string quartet*	25 minutes	Manuscript *for hire*	1929
QUARTET	35 "	Manuscript	1929

STAGE WORKS			
PANTOMIME BALLET *full orchestra*	30 minutes	Manuscript	1930
LIMA BEANS—pantomime *contralto, baritone, tenor, chamber orchestra, puppets*	18 "	Manuscript	1931

ROBERT PALMER

Born in Syracuse, New York, in 1915. He studied at the Eastman School of Music with Hanson and Rogers, later with Harris and at the Berkshire Music Center with Copland.

He taught composition and theory at the University of Kansas. At present he is on the faculty of the Music Department at Cornell University. He received honorable mention in the National Composers Congress Contest for the Sonata for Two Pianos. In 1946 he was awarded a grant from the American Academy of Arts and Letters and the National Institute of Arts and Letters. He is particularly interested in chamber music and the orchestra.

The Concerto for Small Orchestra, which was commissioned by the Columbia Broadcasting Company and the League of Composers, was performed in New York, San Francisco, Washington, D. C., and over a CBS network. The League of Composers also presented the First String Quartet, and this work and the Three Preludes for Piano were broadcast over WNYC. His compositions have been represented at the Columbia, Cornell and Yaddo Festivals. He was commissioned by the Koussevitzky Music Foundation to write the Second String Quartet and by Dimitri Mitropoulos to write the Symphonic Variations for Large Orchestra. In preparation are a Second and a Third Piano Sonata, a Sonata for Viola and Piano, a String Quartet and a Concerto for Two Pianos, Double Stringed Orchestra and Tympani.

COMPOSITIONS

ORCHESTRAL WORKS	DURATION	PUBLISHER	DATE
CONCERTO FOR ORCHESTRA	28 minutes	Manuscript	1943
"K.19"—an elegy for Thomas Wolfe	9 "	Manuscript	1945
SYMPHONIC VARIATIONS FOR LARGE ORCHESTRA	15 "	Manuscript	1946
VARIATIONS, CHORALE AND FUGUE	15 "	Manuscript	

CHAMBER ORCHESTRA			
POEM FOR VIOLIN AND CHAMBER ORCHESTRA *22 instruments*	5 minutes	Manuscript	1938
CONCERTO FOR SMALL ORCHESTRA *24 instruments*	13 "	Blueprint	1940

CHORAL WORKS			
ABRAHAM LINCOLN WALKS AT MIDNIGHT (Vachel Lindsay) *mixed chorus, orchestra*	15 minutes	Blueprint	1945

CHAMBER MUSIC			
FIRST STRING TRIO *violin, viola, cello*	14 minutes	Manuscript	1937
PIANO SONATA	17 "	Photostat	1938
FIRST STRING QUARTET	25 "	Photostat	1939
SECOND STRING TRIO *violin, viola, cello*	19 "	Blueprint	1942
SONATA FOR VIOLIN AND PIANO	24 "	Blueprint	1942
CONCERTO FOR FIVE INSTRUMENTS *flute, violin, clarinet in B flat,* *English horn, cello*	12 "	Blueprint	1943

ROBERT PALMER (*Continued*)

CHAMBER MUSIC (*Continued*)	DURATION	PUBLISHER	DATE
SECOND STRING QUARTET	38 minutes	Blueprint	1943
SONATA FOR TWO PIANOS	18 "	Blueprint	1944
QUARTET FOR PIANO AND STRINGS	17 "	Blueprint	1945

STAGE WORKS

IRISH LEGEND—dance score *13 instruments*	11 minutes	Manuscript	1944

HARRY PARTCH

Born in Oakland, California, in 1901. He was brought up in Arizona. He received his education in musical theory through his studies in the public libraries. In 1923 he began to develop new theories, and his investigations led him to build a group of instruments all built for or adapted to a 43-tone-to-the-octave scale. Between 1930 and 1946 he completed an Adapted Viola, the "Ptolemy" (reed organ with special keyboard), several Adapted Electric Guitars, Chromelodeons, a Kithara and a Harmonic Canon; other instruments are still under construction. He received a grant from the Carnegie Corporation of New York in 1934 and two Guggenheim Fellowships in 1943 and 1944. He became Research Associate at the University of Wisconsin in 1945.

Programs devoted to his compositions, in which he himself played and also chanted, were presented at the Carnegie Chamber Hall by the League of Composers, at the Brander Matthews Theater (Columbia University) and at the University of Wisconsin Festival. He is at present working on a book on theory, *Genesis of a Music*.

COMPOSITIONS

	DURATION	DATE
SEVENTEEN LYRICS (by Li Po)	1 hour	1930–33
MONOPHONIC CYCLE	1½ "	
BARSTOW-HITCHHIKER INSCRIPTIONS		1931–32
Y.D. FANTASY		1941
SAN FRANCISCO NEWSBOY CRIES		1942
LETTER FROM HOBO PABLO		1943
DARK BROTHER (Thomas Wolfe)		1943
TWO PSALMS—23RD AND 137TH		1943
U.S. HIGHBALL—ACCOUNT OF HOBO TRIP		1944
TWO EXCERPTS FROM JAMES JOYCE		1944
ACCOUNT OF THE NORMANDY INVASION by American Glider Pilot (setting of a transcription record)	15 minutes	1945

NOTE: Instruments all built for, or adapted to, a 43-tone-to-the-octave just scale: Adapted Viola; "Ptolemy" (reed organ with special keyboard); Adapted Guitar; Chromelodeon (reed organ); Kithara; Double Canon; Adapted Electric Guitar; Adapted Electric Guitar II; Harmonic Canon; Chromelodeon II; Chromelodeon III (with special keyboard —now under construction).

FRANK PATTERSON

Born in Philadelphia, Pennsylvania, in 1871. He studied the violin with
Stoll and Schmidt, composition with Clark and the bassoon with Fach.
He later attended the Munich Conservatory of Music. He has received the
Bispham Memorial Medal and the National Federation of Music Clubs
Medal. An early work, "Beggar's Love," won the Chamber Opera Guild
Prize; "The Echo" was selected for publication by the Opera in Our Lan-
guage Foundation and was produced by the National Federation of Music
Clubs.

He was formerly a member of the Los Angeles Symphony Orchestra, playing the viola. From 1911 to 1933 he was on the staff of the *Musical Courier.*
His special interests are the stage and theoretical research. He is the author
of *The Leit-Motives of the Nibelungen Ring, The Perfect Modernist, Practical Instrumentation,* and *How to Write a Good Tune.*

The overture to his opera "Mountain Blood" has been given by the Cleveland, Rochester and San Diego orchestras, and "Beggar's Love" was performed in Los Angeles, San Diego and New York City.

COMPOSITIONS

ORCHESTRAL WORKS	DURATION	PUBLISHER	DATE
BACCHANALE—from "THE ECHO"	6 minutes	G. Schirmer, Inc.	1920
OVERTURE TO OPERA "MOUNTAIN BLOOD"	12 "	Manuscript	1925

STAGE WORKS			
BEGGAR'S LOVE—chamber opera *soprano, tenor, baritone, no chorus, string trio or chamber orchestra*	40 minutes	C. C. Birchard & Co.	1918
THE ECHO—one-act opera *soprano, alto, tenor, baritone, chorus*	1¼ hours	G. Schirmer, Inc.	1920
MOUNTAIN BLOOD—opera in 3 acts *chorus, orchestra*	2½ "	Manuscript	1925

VINCENT PERSICHETTI

Born in Philadelphia, Pennsylvania, in 1915. He received his early musical
training at Combs College of Music, where he studied composition with
Russell King Miller. He graduated from Curtis Institute of Music, where
he studied with Fritz Reiner. He was awarded scholarships to study with
Madame Olga Samaroff and Paul Nordoff at the Philadelphia Conservatory
of Music, where he received his degrees of Master and Doctor of Music.
He later studied with Roy Harris at Colorado College.

He was head of the Composition Department at Combs College from
1939 to 1942. At present, he is head of the Composition Department and
special instructor for post-graduate students at the Philadelphia Conservatory. Since he was sixteen years of age, he has held a position as church

VINCENT PERSICHETTI (*Continued*)

organist and music director in Philadelphia. He won the Juilliard Publication Award for his "Dance Overture" and received first prize from the Colorado College of Fine Arts for his Third Piano Sonata. In 1945 he was awarded the Blue Network Prize for Chamber Music for the Second String Quartet.

His compositions have been performed many times in Philadelphia, Rochester, New York, Washington, D. C., and Colorado Springs. The League of Composers presented his "Poems for Piano" over a CBS network. Major networks and local stations have broadcast several of his works. He is now completing a Third Symphony.

COMPOSITIONS

ORCHESTRAL WORKS	DURATION	PUBLISHER	DATE
CONCERTINO FOR PIANO AND ORCHESTRA	9 minutes	Fleisher Collection	1941
FIRST SYMPHONY	18 "	Black and White Reproduction	1942
SECOND SYMPHONY	22 "	Black and White Reproduction	1942
DANCE OVERTURE	8 "	Juilliard Edition	1942
FABLES FOR NARRATOR AND ORCHESTRA	22 "	Black and White Reproduction	1943
CHAMBER ORCHESTRA			
SUITE FOR CHAMBER ORCHESTRA *13 or more instruments*	10 minutes	Manuscript	1939
THE HOLLOW MEN *trumpet, string orchestra 18 or more instruments*	8 "	Black and White Reproduction	1944
CHORAL WORKS			
MAGNIFICAT *mixed chorus, piano*	6 minutes	Black and White Reproduction	1940
CHAMBER MUSIC			
FIRST STRING QUARTET	14 minutes	Black and White Reproduction	1939
FIRST PIANO SONATA	15 "	Manuscript	1939
SECOND PIANO SONATA	10 "	Manuscript	1939
POEMS FOR PIANO, BOOKS I, II	40 "	Black and White Reproduction	1939–41
QUINTET FOR PIANO AND STRINGS	18 "	Manuscript	1940
SUITE FOR VIOLIN AND CELLO	6 "	Black and White Reproduction	1940
SONATA FOR SOLO VIOLIN	8 "	Black and White Reproduction	1940
SONATA FOR TWO PIANOS	13 "	Black and White Reproduction	1940
SONATINE FOR ORGAN *pedals alone*	5 "	Black and White Reproduction	1940
FIRST SONATINE FOR PIANO	5 "	Black and White Reproduction	1940
SONATA FOR VIOLIN AND PIANO	10 "	Black and White Reproduction	1941
TRIO FOR VIOLIN, CELLO AND PIANO	13 "	Black and White Reproduction	1941

VINCENT PERSICHETTI (*Continued*)

CHAMBER MUSIC (*Continued*)	DURATION		PUBLISHER	DATE
PASTORAL QUINTET FOR WIND INSTRUMENTS *flute, oboe, clarinet, horn, bassoon*	6 minutes		Black and White Reproduction	1943
THIRD PIANO SONATA	13	"	Elkan-Vogel	1943
SECOND STRING QUARTET	17	"	Black and White Reproduction	1944

STAGE WORKS				
PRELUDE *solo dancer, piano*	4 minutes		Manuscript	1940
THEN ONE DAY *three dancers, piano*	10	"	Black and White Reproduction	1944

BURRILL PHILLIPS

Born in Omaha, Nebraska, in 1907. He received his early training in composition from Stringham in Denver. Later he was awarded a Juilliard Extension Scholarship. In 1931 he entered the Eastman School of Music in Rochester and studied composition and orchestration under Royce, Rogers and Hanson. He was awarded the degree of Master of Music in 1933 and the Eastman School of Music Teaching Fellowship for 1932–33. That same year he joined the faculty of the Eastman School in the Department of Theory and Composition. He was awarded a Guggenheim Fellowship in 1942 and received an award from the American Academy of Arts and Letters in 1944. He was commissioned by the League of Composers to write Scherzo for Orchestra for the City Center Orchestra in 1944 and, in the same year, was commissioned to write an orchestral work for the Koussevitzky Music Foundation.

His compositions have had major performances in New York, Pittsburgh and Rochester. The "Three Informalities" and the Scherzo for Orchestra were presented on the American Music Festival over WNYC in 1945. The Violin Sonata was also presented over WNYC. RCA Victor has recorded the "Concertpiece for Bassoon and Strings" and "Selections from McGuffey's Reader." He is completing at the present time an overture, "Tom Paine," a Symphony No. 1, a Duo Cantata and a Concerto Grosso.

COMPOSITIONS

ORCHESTRAL WORKS	DURATION		PUBLISHER	DATE
GROTESQUE DANCE—for projected ballet	5 minutes		Manuscript	1932
SELECTIONS FROM McGUFFEY'S READER	17	"	Eastman School Publication	1934
COURTHOUSE SQUARE	12	"	Manuscript	1936
CONCERTO FOR PIANO AND ORCHESTRA	23	"	Manuscript *for hire* Elkan-Vogel	1943
SCHERZO FOR ORCHESTRA	10	"	Manuscript *for hire* Elkan-Vogel	1944

BURRILL PHILLIPS (*Continued*)

CHAMBER ORCHESTRA	DURATION	PUBLISHER	DATE
SYMPHONY CONCERTANTE	15 minutes	Manuscript	1936
MUSIC FOR STRINGS	15 "	Manuscript	1940
CONCERTPIECE FOR BASSOON AND STRINGS	4 "	Eastman School Publication Carl Fischer, Inc.	1940

CHORAL WORKS

OH ANGEL	4 minutes	Manuscript	1939
mixed chorus, a cappella			
DECLARATIVES	12 "	Elkan-Vogel	1943
women's voices, small orchestra			

CHAMBER MUSIC

A SET OF INFORMALITIES—piano suite		Manuscript	1936
TRIO FOR TRUMPETS	5 minutes	Manuscript	1937
CONCERTO FOR PIANO		Manuscript	1937
STRING QUARTET NO. 1	14 "	Manuscript	1939
NINE BY NINE—sonata for piano	17 "	Manuscript	1942
VIOLIN SONATA	10 "	G. Schirmer, Inc.	1942
violin and piano			
GO 'WAY FROM MY WINDOW—trio cantata	12 "	Manuscript	1946
mezzo-soprano, baritone, piano			
SONATA FOR CELLO AND PIANO	15 "	Manuscript	1946

STAGE WORKS

PRINCESS AND PUPPET—ballet	40 minutes	Manuscript	1933
6 solo parts, ensemble, full orchestra			
PLAY BALL—ballet	17 "	Manuscript	1938
ballet company, full orchestra			
THREE SATIRIC FRAGMENTS	7 "	Manuscript	1939
solo dancer, full orchestra			
STEP INTO MY PARLOR	12 "	Manuscript	1941
6 dancers, orchestra			

SOLOMON PIMSLEUR

Born in Paris, France, in 1900. He came to the United States when he was three years old. He is a graduate of Columbia University, where he studied composition with Mason. He studied piano with Hochmann, Fibisch and Schoen, orchestration with Arnold and organ and fugue-writing with Frank Ward. Upon receiving a Juilliard Fellowship he studied with Goldmark, and in 1929 he went to Salzburg to study orchestration and conducting with Baumgartner.

He lives in New York City and is a teacher of piano, harmony, theory and composition. He is at present working at his Fifth String Quartet and a "Symphony to Terror and Despair."

His Symphonic Ballade has been given by the New York Philharmonic, the Municipal Symphony Orchestra, Brooklyn, and the City Symphony Orchestra of Philadelphia. "Meditative Nocturne" has been heard in New York, Brooklyn, San Diego and other cities. The tone poem, "The Miracle of Life and the Mystery of Death," was played in Philadelphia. The "Fugal

SOLOMON PIMSLEUR (*Continued*)

Fantasia" was presented by the Eastman-Rochester Symphony Orchestra. His Third String Quartet was performed and broadcast at the New York World's Fair in 1940, and some of his works have been heard over WOR.

COMPOSITIONS

ORCHESTRAL WORKS	DURATION	PUBLISHER	DATE
SYMPHONIC BALLADE, B FLAT MINOR, OPUS 18, No. 5	12 minutes	Manuscript	1924
MEDITATIVE NOCTURNE, F MINOR, OPUS 22	13 "	Manuscript	1924
NEO-CLASSIC OVERTURE, A MINOR, OPUS 24	13 "	Manuscript	1927
SYMPHONY TO DISILLUSIONMENT, B FLAT MAJOR, OPUS 25		Manuscript	1928
MIRACLE OF LIFE AND THE MYSTERY OF DEATH, A MAJOR, OPUS 32— tone poem		Manuscript	1932
SYMPHONIC SUITE, OPUS 33		Manuscript	1935
SYMPHONIC ODE AND PERORATION, OPUS 35		Manuscript	1936
FOUR DRAMAS IN A CYCLE OF SYMPHONIES, OPUS 40, 42, 48, 50	whole evening	Manuscript	1931–45

CHAMBER ORCHESTRA			
IMPETUOUS TOCCATA AND FUGAL FANTASIA, OPUS 18		Manuscript	1930
PARTITA, OPUS 30 *violin, viola soli, string orchestra*	35 minutes	Manuscript	1933
RHAPSODIC SUITE, OPUS 41 *violin, piano*		Manuscript	1938
STATUESQUE SONATA, OPUS 47 *woodwind, harp*	25 "	Manuscript	1942

CHORAL WORKS			
VOCAL QUARTETS, OPUS 21		Manuscript	1927
SONNET-TABLEAU (Keats), OPUS 23 *chorus, string orchestra*		Manuscript	1928
ORATORIO—HAST THOU CONQUERED, O GALILEAN, OPUS 31 (Swinburne) *large mixed chorus, orchestra*	3 hours	Manuscript	1933
FIGHT AGAINST WAR AND FASCISM, OPUS 37—a cantata *mixed chorus, piano*	30 minutes	Manuscript	1936
ANTHEM FOR DOOMED YOUTH, OPUS 38, No. 2 *men's voices, harmonium*	10 "	Manuscript	1937
PAGEANT OF WAR SONNETS, OPUS 51—oratorio	2 hours	Manuscript	1943–45

CHAMBER MUSIC			
FOUR STRING QUARTETS, OPUS 12, 13, 28, 54	30 minutes each	Manuscript	
MOODY SONATA FOR CELLO, OPUS 8	25 minutes	Manuscript *parts available*	1922
FIERY SONATA FOR TRIO, OPUS 19	45 "	Manuscript	1925
VERSION FOR QUINTET, OPUS 20	45 "	Manuscript	1926

SOLOMON PIMSLEUR (*Continued*)

CHAMBER MUSIC (*Continued*)	DURATION	PUBLISHER	DATE
PARTITA, OPUS 29	35 minutes	Manuscript	1931
violin, viola, piano		*parts available*	
IMPETUOUS SONATA, OPUS 15	45 "	Manuscript	1921–35
violin, piano			
STATUESQUE SONATA, OPUS 46			
oboe, bassoon, piano			

PAUL AMADEUS PISK

Born in Vienna, Austria, in 1893. He studied musicology at the University of Vienna and conducting at the Vienna Conservatory of Music. His teachers in composition were Franz Schreker and Arnold Schoenberg.

In 1912 and 1913 he conducted in many of the German opera houses, and in 1920 he conducted the Chamber Opera in Vienna. From 1922 to 1934 he held various positions in Vienna: he conducted the Singverein der Kunststelle, a mixed chorus; he was head of the Music Department of the Volkshochschule, and for a short time he taught theory at the New Vienna Conservatory. He also appeared as Guest Conductor with the Vienna Philharmonic Orchestra, the Vienna Symphony Orchestra and with orchestras of various European broadcasting stations. In 1925 he received the Prize of the City of Vienna for composition. He taught theory at the Austro-American Conservatory in Mondsee near Salzburg from 1931 to 1933. In 1936 he came to the United States. In 1937 he appeared as Guest Conductor under the auspices of the Federal Music Project, New York, and was Musical Director at Camp Oquago, New York. Since 1937 he has been head of the Piano Department and Professor of Theory at the University of Redlands, California. In 1939 he conducted the Meistersinger, a mixed chorus, of San Bernardino, California. He is an examiner for the California State Music Teachers' Association, of which he is an honorary member. In the summer of 1945 he gave a course in musicology at the University of Texas in Austin. He is also active as an editor, writer on music, pianist and accompanist.

His works have been performed at the International Music Festivals in Salzburg (1922 and 1923), Prague (1925) and Vienna (1928), the Festivals in Düsseldorf (1922) and Schwerin (1927), at the Yaddo Festival of 1941, and also by orchestras in Germany, Austria, Paris, Stockholm and New York. His works were broadcast by a number of European stations and by several stations in New York and Los Angeles.

COMPOSITIONS WRITTEN IN AMERICA

ORCHESTRAL WORKS	DURATION	PUBLISHER	DATE
PASSACAGLIA FOR ORCHESTRA	8 minutes	Manuscript	1944

PAUL AMADEUS PISK (*Continued*)

CHAMBER ORCHESTRA	DURATION	PUBLISHER	DATE
MUSIC FOR STRING ORCHESTRA	10 minutes	Manuscript	1936
strings		*for hire*	
SUITE ON AMERICAN FOLKSONGS	10 "	Manuscript	1944
24 instruments			

CHORAL WORKS			
THE STORM—cantata	20 minutes	Manuscript	1943
2 soloists, mixed chorus, organ			

CHAMBER MUSIC			
WOODWIND QUARTET	10 minutes	Manuscript	1945

WALTER PISTON

Born in Rockland, Maine, in 1894. He is of Italian descent. He first specialized in the study of drawing and painting and graduated from the Massachusetts School of Art in 1916. At Harvard University, where he later pursued his musical studies, he received a Bachelor of Arts degree, summa cum laude, in 1924. He studied composition in Paris with Boulanger, piano with Shaw in Boston and violin with Fiumara, Theodorowicz and Winternitz. He was awarded the John Knowles Paine and the Guggenheim fellowships. For several seasons he conducted the Pierian Sodality Orchestra at Harvard University.

He is now Professor of Music at Harvard University. The League of Composers commissioned him to write an orchestral work in the American Composers Series, which was presented in Cleveland, also a Quintet for Flute and String Quartet, which was presented at Town Hall at the League's 20th Anniversary Program. The Elizabeth Sprague Coolidge Foundation (Library of Congress) commissioned his Partita for Violin, Viola and Organ and the Alice M. Ditson Fund (Columbia University) commissioned the Symphony No. 2, which was performed by the Washington National, the Boston and the New York Philharmonic symphonies. This Symphony received the New York Critics' Circle Award for symphonic music for the season 1944–45. His book, *Harmony*, was published in 1940 (W. W. Norton) and has been widely used by the U. S. Armed Forces Institute.

His works have had major performances throughout the United States, at the Library of Congress, at the Yaddo Festivals and at the Pan American Festival. "The Incredible Flutist," a suite from the ballet, was played in Moscow in 1943 in honor of the United States Independence Day; it was also performed in London and in many other cities. CBS, NBC, Blue Network and Mutual, as well as local stations, have broadcast many of his orchestral and chamber compositions. Many of the chamber works are in the repertory of reknowned artists.

WALTER PISTON *(Continued)*

COMPOSITIONS

ORCHESTRAL WORKS	DURATION	PUBLISHER	DATE
SYMPHONIC PIECE	8 minutes	Manuscript	1927
SUITE FOR ORCHESTRA	15 "	Cos Cob Press *score for sale* *parts for hire*	1929
CONCERTO FOR ORCHESTRA	14 "	Cos Cob Press	1933
PRELUDE AND FUGUE FOR ORCHESTRA	13 "	Cos Cob Press	1934
SYMPHONY NO. 1	27 "	G. Schirmer, Inc. *score for sale* *parts for hire*	1937
SUITE FROM THE BALLET "THE INCREDIBLE FLUTIST"	17 "	Arrow Music Press *score for sale* *parts for hire*	1938
CONCERTO FOR VIOLIN AND ORCHESTRA	23 "	Manuscript Arrow Music Press, agent	1939
SYMPHONY NO. 2	26 "	Arrow Music Press *score for sale* *parts for hire*	1943
PRELUDE AND ALLEGRO FOR ORGAN AND STRINGS	9 "	Arrow Music Press *score for sale* *parts for hire*	1943
FANFARE FOR THE FIGHTING FRENCH	2 "	Boosey & Hawkes	1943
FUGUE ON A VICTORY TUNE	4 "	Manuscript Arrow Music Press, agent	1944

CHAMBER ORCHESTRA

CONCERTINO FOR PIANOFORTE AND CHAMBER ORCHESTRA *24 instruments*	14 minutes	Manuscript	1937
SINFONIETTA *25 instruments*	17 "	Boosey & Hawkes	1941

CHORAL WORKS

CARNIVAL SONG *men's chorus and brass instruments* *11 instruments*	6 minutes	Arrow Music Press	1938

CHAMBER MUSIC

THREE PIECES FOR FLUTE, CLARINET AND BASSOON	12 minutes	New Music	1926
SONATA FOR FLUTE AND PIANO	10 "	Cos Cob Press	1930
SUITE FOR OBOE AND PIANO	10 "	E. C. Schirmer Music Co.	1931
STRING QUARTET NO. 1	20 "	Cos Cob Press	1933
STRING QUARTET NO. 2	20 "	Manuscript	1935
TRIO FOR VIOLIN, CELLO AND PIANOFORTE	17 "	Manuscript	1935
SONATA FOR VIOLIN AND PIANO	20 "	Arrow Music Press	1939
QUINTET FOR FLUTE AND STRING QUARTET	17 "	Arrow Music Press	1942
PARTITA FOR VIOLIN, VIOLA AND ORGAN	16 "	Manuscript	1944
SONATINA FOR VIOLIN AND HARPSICHORD	13 "	Manuscript	1945
DIVERTIMENTO FOR NINE INSTRUMENTS	13 "	Broadcast Music, Inc.	1946

STAGE WORKS

THE INCREDIBLE FLUTIST—ballet *little scenery required* *full symphony orchestra*	30 minutes	Manuscript	1938

QUINCY PORTER

Born in New Haven, Connecticut, in 1897. He is a descendant of early American pioneers. His father was a minister and professor at the Yale Divinity School. He graduated from Yale College in 1919 and from the Yale School of Music in 1921, where he studied with Parker and Smith. While at Yale he won two prizes in composition. He continued his work in Paris with D'Indy and Capet and on his return to America became a pupil of Bloch, whom he assisted at the Cleveland Institute of Music. Later he headed the Department of Theory. In 1928 he returned to Paris, where for two years he held a Guggenheim Fellowship.

Shortly after his return to the United States he joined the music faculty at Vassar College where he became Professor of Music and Conductor of the Vassar Orchestra. He left Vassar in 1938 to become Dean of the New England Conservatory of Music, and in 1942 he became Director of the Conservatory. He received the Coolidge Medal for chamber music in 1943. He was elected to membership in the National Institute of Arts and Letters in 1943. He is a viola player and has written a great deal for string ensemble.

He was commissioned by the Elizabeth Sprague Coolidge Foundation (Library of Congress), by the League of Composers in 1935, and in 1938 by CBS. Among his larger works are the "Ukrainian Suite" for string orchestra which has had several performances by the New York Philharmonic Chamber Orchestra, the Rochester Philharmonic and others. The Suite in C Minor and the "Poem and Dance" have been played in Rochester, Cleveland and Brooklyn. The First Symphony, given its première by the Philharmonic, won honorable mention in the 1937 Philharmonic Symphony Competition. His chamber music has been heard frequently in Europe and America, as well as at the Westminster, the Elizabeth Coolidge, and the Yaddo festivals. The orchestral Suite in C Minor was broadcast over WOR.

Music for "Antony and Cleopatra" was recorded at the Yaddo Festival, Suite for Viola Alone was recorded by the Modern Music Recordings, and the String Quartet No. 3 was recorded by Columbia.

COMPOSITIONS

ORCHESTRAL WORKS

	DURATION	PUBLISHER	DATE
UKRAINIAN SUITE FOR STRINGS	11 minutes	C. C. Birchard & Co.	1925
SUITE IN C MINOR	12 "	Manuscript	1926
POEM AND DANCE	10 "	Manuscript	1932
SYMPHONY NO. 1	26 "	Manuscript	1934
TWO DANCES FOR RADIO	13 "	Manuscript	1938
MUSIC FOR STRINGS	9 "	Music Press	1941
A MOVING TIDE	3 "	Manuscript	1944

CHAMBER ORCHESTRA

	DURATION	PUBLISHER	DATE
SUITE FROM MUSIC FOR "ANTONY AND CLEOPATRA"	11 minutes	Manuscript	1937
DANCE IN THREE TIME	8 "	Manuscript	1937
FANTASY ON A PASTORAL THEME *organ, string orchestra*	8 "	Manuscript	1943

QUINCY PORTER (*Continued*)

CHAMBER MUSIC	DURATION	PUBLISHER	DATE
STRING QUARTET NO. 1, IN E MINOR	16 minutes	Manuscript	1923
STRING QUARTET NO. 2, IN G MINOR	17 "	Manuscript	1925
SONATA FOR VIOLIN AND PIANO, NO. 1	15 "	Manuscript	1926
IN MONASTERIO	9 "	Manuscript	1927
string quartet			
LITTLE SUITE	6½ "	Manuscript	1928
flute, violin, viola			
SONATA FOR VIOLIN AND PIANO, NO. 2	17 "	S.P.A.M.	1929
		G. Schirmer, Inc.	
		sales agent	
QUINTET FOR CLARINET AND STRINGS	14 "	Manuscript	1929
SONATA FOR PIANO	15 "	Manuscript	1930
STRING QUARTET NO. 3	17 "	S.P.A.M.	1930
		G. Schirmer, Inc.	
		sales agent	
STRING QUARTET NO. 4	15½ "	Manuscript	1931
STRING QUARTET NO. 5	17 "	Manuscript	1935
STRING QUARTET NO. 6	19 "	Manuscript	1936
QUINTET IN ONE MOVEMENT—			
on a theme of childhood	5½ "	"Musicology"	1940
flute and strings			
STRING QUARTET NO. 7	17 "	Manuscript	1943
SONATA FOR HORN AND PIANO	15 "	N.A.S.M.	1945
SONATA FOR HORN (OR CELLO)			
AND PIANO	16 "	Gamble Hinged	1946
		Music Co.	

STAGE WORKS

	DURATION	PUBLISHER	DATE
INCIDENTAL MUSIC TO "SWEENEY AGONISTES" (T. S. ELIOT) AND "3 GREEK MIMES" *string quartet, voices, percussion*		Manuscript	1933
INCIDENTAL MUSIC FOR "ANTONY AND CLEOPATRA" (SHAKESPEARE) *flute, 2 trumpets, percussion, strings, piano*	30 minutes	Manuscript	1935

JOHN POWELL

Born in Richmond, Virginia, in 1882. His musical education began with Hahr in Richmond, and he continued his studies in Vienna with Leschetizky and Navratil. After receiving his degree of Bachelor of Arts from the University of Virginia, he began his musical career as a pianist, touring throughout the United States and Europe in recitals and appearing as soloist with the major orchestras. His English ancestry and Southern parentage gave him a great interest in the Anglo-Saxon basis of American folk music. For many years he has collected American folk songs and done research in this field. He is a member of the American Institute of Arts and Letters and also of the Société Astronomique de France.

He was commissioned to write a symphony by the National Federation of Music Clubs and asked to make use of American folk tunes in this work. Among the orchestral works, "Rhapsodie Nègre," overture "In Old Virginia" and "Natchez on the Hill" are widely known all over America

JOHN POWELL (*Continued*)

and Europe. "At the Fair," for chamber orchestra, and other works for small ensemble have been played too often to list performances. Many of his works are in the repertoire of eminent artists, and he frequently is soloist with the orchestras in his own compositions. The Sonata in A Flat has been presented at the Berkshire Festival and on many other occasions; it has also been broadcast over NBC. WOR, NBC and local stations have broadcast his works.

COMPOSITIONS

ORCHESTRAL WORKS

	DURATION	PUBLISHER	DATE
RHAPSODIE NÈGRE *piano*	14 minutes	G. Schirmer, Inc.	1918
IN OLD VIRGINIA—overture	12 "	G. Schirmer, Inc.	1921
NATCHEZ ON THE HILL	7 "	G. Schirmer, Inc.	1932
A SET OF THREE	19 "	G. Schirmer, Inc.	1935
SYMPHONY IN A		Affiliated Music Corp.	1937
PIANO CONCERTO		Manuscript	
CONCERTO IN E *violin*	35 "	Manuscript *for hire*	

CHAMBER ORCHESTRA

AT THE FAIR—suite		G. Schirmer, Inc.	1925

CHORAL WORKS

THE BABE OF BETHLEHEM—folk carol *mixed chorus, a cappella*		J. Fischer & Bro.	1934
FOLK HYMNS (from Twelve Folk Hymns)		J. Fischer & Bro.	1934
SOLDIER, SOLDIER—folk song *a cappella, soprano and baritone solo*		J. Fischer & Bro.	1936

CHAMBER MUSIC

SONATA VIRGINIANESQUE *violin, piano*	21 minutes	G. Schirmer, Inc.	1919
SONATA IN A FLAT *violin, piano*	24 "	G. Schirmer, Inc.	1928
STRING QUARTET	20 "	Manuscript	
SONATA NOBLE *piano*	25 "	G. Schirmer, Inc.	

LAURENCE POWELL

Born in Birmingham, England, in 1899. He received his training under Granville Bantock. He won the Martineau Medal for theory at the Midland Institute and also a scholarship for composition at Birmingham University, from which he graduated in 1922. He received a degree of Bachelor of Music and first honors.

In England he often appeared as guest conductor in programs of his own works. Coming to the United States in 1923, he became music critic on the

LAURENCE POWELL (*Continued*)

Boston Transcript under Parker. From 1924 to 1926 he was instructor in theory at the University of Wisconsin, and while there he received a Master of Arts degree. From 1926 to 1934 he was at the University of Arkansas as Associate Professor of Theory. Since 1935 he has been head of the Music Department at Little Rock Junior College, where he organized and became Conductor of the Little Rock Symphony Orchestra. In 1936 he organized and directed the Arkansas State Centennial Music Festival. In 1939–41, he was Conductor of the Grand Rapids, Michigan, W.P.A. Symphony. Since 1941 he has been organist and choirmaster at the Cathedral in Grand Rapids. He has contributed articles to various music journals. He is greatly interested in Celtic and Icelandic subjects and American folk music.

His works have received performances in England and the United States and have been broadcast by the BBC, CBS and MBS. At present, he is preparing a Gregorian Suite for Orchestra.

COMPOSITIONS

ORCHESTRAL WORKS	DURATION	PUBLISHER	DATE
THE OGRE OF THE NORTHERN FASTNESS—suite	15 minutes	Manuscript	1921
SYMPHONY NO. 1	40 "	Fleisher Collection for hire	1929
KELTIC LEGEND	12 "	Fleisher Collection for hire	1930
DEIRDRE OF THE SORROWS— romantic prelude	10 "	Fleisher Collection for hire	1932
COUNTY FAIR—suite in 7 movements	15 "	C. C. Birchard & Co.	1935
THEME AND THIRTEEN VARIATIONS	40 "	Fleisher Collection for hire	1937
DUO CONCERTANTE FOR RECORDERS AND ORCHESTRA soprano and alto recorders	12 "	Manuscript	1941
SYMPHONY NO. 2	22 "	Manuscript	1943
CHAMBER ORCHESTRA			
CHARIVARI—suite for small orchestra	12 minutes	Fleisher Collection for hire	1925
SUITE FOR STRING ORCHESTRA 3 movements	30 "	Fleisher Collection for hire	1931
PICNIC—an Arkansas pastoral for strings	7 "	Fleisher Collection for hire	1936
CHORAL WORKS			
HALCYONE—dramatic poem soli, chorus, orchestra	20 minutes	C. C. Birchard & Co.	1923
ALLELUYA—sacred cantata soli, chorus, orchestra	30 "	Manuscript	1926
THE SEASONS (Blake Poems) a cappella	20 "	J. Williams, Ltd.	1928
MASS IN HONOR OF ST. LAURENCE	12 "	J. Fischer	1941
MASS IN HONOR OF ST. ANDREW	25 "	Manuscript	1942
A SONG OF PEACE	20 "	Manuscript	1943
LORD ULLIN'S DAUGHTER	6 "	Manuscript	1944
CHAMBER MUSIC			
QUARTET FOR PIANO AND STRINGS	12 "	Manuscript	1933
QUARTET FOR MIXED CLARINETS	8 "	Carl Fischer, Inc.	1936

SERGEI RACHMANINOFF

Born in Onega (province of Novgorod), Russia, in 1873 and died in California in 1943. His mother was his first music teacher. When he was nine years old he entered the Petrograd Conservatory, and at thirteen he began to study at the Moscow Conservatory, where Arensky and Taneiev were his teachers in theory. He graduated in 1891, winning the Gold Medal for his opera "Aleko."

In Europe he wrote a great many works for piano solo, songs, several piano concertos, symphonies and other orchestral works. In 1898 he was invited by the London Philharmonic Orchestra to direct a concert of his works. He was Conductor of Opera at the Imperial Grand Theatre, Moscow, from 1905 to 1906 and then moved to Dresden. For his first visit to the United States, in 1909, he wrote the Piano Concerto No. 3, which was conducted in New York by Damrosch. He also appeared as conductor and pianist in Boston. He spent the next seven years, from 1910 to 1917, in Moscow, was Vice-President of the Imperial Russian Musical Society and, from 1911 to 1913, Conductor of the Philharmonic Concerts. During World War I he gave concerts for various charities and also served as Inspector of Music at the Nobility High School for Girls. Upon the death of Scriabin in 1915, he went on a concert tour playing programs devoted entirely to the music of this composer. This tour was the real beginning of his career as a concert pianist. He left Russia in 1917, going first on a concert tour through the Scandinavian countries and later visiting the United States again. In 1918 the conductorship of the Boston Symphony Orchestra was offered to him, a position which he refused as he had determined to concentrate on a pianist's career. From then until his death he divided his time between America and Europe.

His Symphony No. 2 has been recorded by Columbia and Victor, his Symphony No. 3, all four piano concertos and the "Rhapsody on a Theme by Paganini" by Victor, and there are many recordings of his Preludes and other shorter works, the composer being the soloist in many of the recorded piano works.

COMPOSITIONS WRITTEN AFTER LEAVING RUSSIA

ORCHESTRAL WORKS	PUBLISHER	DATE
PIANO CONCERTO NO. 4 IN G MINOR, OP. 40	Charles Foley	1926/1941
VARIATIONS ON A THEME BY CORELLI, OP. 42	Charles Foley	1931
RHAPSODY ON A THEME BY PAGANINI, OP. 43 *piano, orchestra*	Charles Foley	1934
SYMPHONY NO. 3 IN A MINOR, OP. 44	Charles Foley	1936
SYMPHONIC DANCES, OP. 45	Charles Foley	1940

CHORAL WORKS		
THREE RUSSIAN FOLKSONGS, OP. 41 *chorus, orchestra*	Charles Foley	1926

DAVID RAKSIN

Born in Philadelphia, Pennsylvania, in 1912. Before studying music seriously, he played in dance bands and radio stations and arranged music for them. Later he studied with Freed, Happich, McDonald and Schoenberg. He won music prizes from the University of Pennsylvania.

He has arranged radio programs and musical shows in New York and London and has composed music for cartoons and documentaries and also Army, Navy and O.W.I. films. He helped to organize and has worked with the New Music Forum of Los Angeles and the Musicians' Congress.

Many of his film scores have been arranged for concert and have been performed by leading orchestras. An excerpt from the score of "Laura" has been recorded by RCA Victor and was performed at the Hollywood Bowl. It was also released as a "popular" song. At present he is re-orchestrating the music from "Feather in Your Hat" and preparing a Litany from "Main Street Today." His music for films and concert arrangements are listed here.

COMPOSITIONS

FILM MUSIC	STUDIO	PUBLISHER	DATE
STORM WARNING (documentary)	Paul Barnford		1941
concert version—suite		Manuscript	
DR. RENAULT'S SECRET	20th Century-Fox		1941
THE UNDYING MONSTER	20th Century-Fox		1942
THE MEN IN HER LIFE	Columbia		1942
CITY WITHOUT MEN	Columbia		1942
TAMPICO	20th Century-Fox		1943
MAIN STREET TODAY	M.G.M.		1943
concert version untitled		Manuscript	
LAURA	20th Century-Fox		1944
concert version—excerpts		Manuscript	
FALLEN ANGEL	20th Century-Fox		1945
SMOKY	20th Century-Fox		1945
THE SECRET LIFE OF WALTER MITTY	Goldwyn		1947

EDA RAPOPORT

Born in Dwinsk, Russia, in 1900. She came to America in 1908. She studied piano at the Peabody Institute of Music in Baltimore, where she received a three-year, free scholarship. She was also a pupil of Gallico, Lambert and Stasny. She attended the Institute of Musical Art and studied composition with Goetschius; she later studied with Copland, Piston and Schoenberg.

Three of her major works, the "Mathmid" (a symphonic tone poem), the "Three Symphonic Dances" and the Suite for String Orchestra, have been performed by leading orchestras in New York and Rochester. Her chamber compositions have been played in Boston and New York. WNYC has broadcast the "Mathmid," the "Midrash," the Piano Sonata No. 1, the Sonata for Violin and Piano No. 1 and the "Valce Pathétique" (from the

EDA RAPOPORT (*Continued*)

"Three Symphonic Dances"). The Cello Concerto was heard over a nation-wide hook-up. She is now completing a symphony in one movement and an opera-fantasy based on a Grimms' fairy tale, called "The Fisherman and His Wife."

COMPOSITIONS

ORCHESTRAL WORKS	DURATION	PUBLISHER	DATE
THE MATHMID—symphonic tone poem	12 minutes	Manuscript	1934
THREE SYMPHONIC DANCES	14 "	Manuscript	1935
CONCERTO FOR PIANO AND ORCHESTRA	15 "	Manuscript	1938
CONCERTO FOR VIOLIN AND ORCHESTRA	15 "	Manuscript	1942
SUITE FOR ORCHESTRA	10 "	Manuscript	1943

CHAMBER ORCHESTRA

LAMENTATIONS FOR VIOLONCELLO AND CHAMBER ORCHESTRA (based on Hebrew themes)	10 minutes	Manuscript	1933
or for cello and piano		El Cantor Music Co.	
THE RAVEN (Edgar Allan Poe) *tenor, string orchestra*	10 "	Weaner-Levant	1936
ISRAFEL (Edgar Allan Poe) *flute, harp, string orchestra*	8 "	Manuscript	1936
SUITE FOR STRINGS	12 "	Manuscript	1940
ADAGIO FOR STRINGS	7 "	Manuscript	1941
REVOLT IN THE WARSAW GHETTO *string orchestra*	8 "	Manuscript	1944

CHORAL WORKS

CANTATA—The Song of Songs *soprano, tenor, flute, cello, piano*	12 minutes	Manuscript	1937
CHORAL SUITE *a cappella*	9 "	Manuscript	1939
PSALM 98 *women's voices, organ*	8 "	Manuscript	1944
WELCOME QUEEN SABBATH *mixed chorus, piano*	8 "	Manuscript	1944

CHAMBER MUSIC

TWO TRIOS *violin, cello, piano*	12–15 minutes	Manuscript	1933–42
SONATAS NOS. 1, 2 *violin, piano*	12–14 "	Manuscript	1933–41
QUARTET FOR FLUTE, VIOLIN, CELLO, PIANO	12 "	Manuscript	1933
STRING QUARTET NO. 1 (on Hebrew themes)	15 "	Transcontinental Music Publishers	1934
PASTORAL STRING QUARTET WITH VOICE *soprano*	15 "	Manuscript	1934
STRING QUARTET IN G NO. 2	14 "	Weaner-Levant	1935
QUINTET *piano, strings*	15 "	Manuscript	1935
QUARTET FOR VIOLIN, CELLO, CLARINET, HARP	12 "	Manuscript	1935
SONATA FOR VIOLONCELLO AND PIANO	14 "	Manuscript	1936
PIANO SONATAS NOS. 1, 2, 3	9–10 "	Manuscript	1937–45
STRING TRIO *violin, viola, cello*	10 "	Manuscript	1939
STRING QUARTET NO. 3	14 "	Manuscript	1940

EDA RAPOPORT (*Continued*)

CHAMBER MUSIC (*Continued*)	DURATION	PUBLISHER	DATE
PIANO QUARTET *piano, strings*	14 minutes	Manuscript	1940
SUITE FOR TWO PIANOS	12 "	Independent Music Publishers	1941
QUINTET FOR FLUTE AND STRINGS	14 "	Manuscript	1944

STAGE WORKS

G.I. JOE—one act opera in 3 scenes *soprano, tenor, baritone, bass, chorus, dancers, medium size orchestra*	75 minutes	Manuscript	1945

KAROL RATHAUS

Born in Tarnopol, Poland, in 1895. He studied music with Schreker in Vienna and Berlin and in 1922 graduated from the University of Vienna.

After an active career in Europe, he came to the United States in 1938 and now lives in Flushing, Long Island. He is Associate Professor and Chairman of the Department of Music at Queens College. He has served on the Board of Directors as Vice-President of the I.S.C.M. and on the Composer-Members Committee of the League of Composers. He is a member of the Polish Academy of Science and Art (Music Committee) in New York.

His "Polonaise Symphonique," commissioned by the New York Philharmonic Symphony Orchestra, together with the Trio for Violin, Clarinet and Piano, has been recorded by the Office of War Information for overseas broadcasts. Many of his works have had their first performance at music festivals, e.g. Frankfurt, 1924, Donaueschingen, 1926, and at the Festivals of the I.S.C.M. in Liége, 1930, London, 1938, and San Francisco, 1942. His stage works were first performed at the Berlin Staatsoper and at Covent Garden, London. He wrote incidental music for several plays produced by Granowski and for "Uriel Acosta" given by the Habimah Players. His orchestral and chamber-music works have had many performances in Europe and in North and South America. His music for European films includes "Karamasoff" (Berlin, 1931), "Amok" (Paris, 1934) and "Broken Blossoms" (London, 1936).

COMPOSITIONS WRITTEN IN AMERICA

ORCHESTRAL WORKS	DURATION	PUBLISHER	DATE
CONCERTO FOR PIANO AND ORCHESTRA, Opus 45	23 minutes	Manuscript	1938
ADAGIO FOR STRINGS	10 "	Boosey & Hawkes	1941
NOCTURNO JACOBS DREAM, Opus 44	10 "	Manuscript	
THIRD SYMPHONY, Opus 50	35 "	Associated Music Publishers	1942

KAROL RATHAUS (*Continued*)

ORCHESTRAL WORKS (*Continued*)	DURATION	PUBLISHER	DATE
POLONAISE SYMPHONIQUE, OPUS 52	6 minutes	Associated Music Publishers	1944
VISION DRAMATIQUE, OPUS 55	14 "	Manuscript	1945

CHORAL WORKS

XXIII PSALM, OPUS 54C *tenor solo, women's chorus,* *orchestra or piano*	8 minutes	Manuscript	1945

CHAMBER MUSIC

SONATA FOR PIANO, NO. 4, OPUS 58	20 minutes	Manuscript	1946

STAGE WORKS

HERODES AND MARIAMNE—incidental music		1938

FILM MUSIC	STUDIO	
LET US LIVE	Columbia	1939
JAGUAS	Documentary Film for the Viking Fund	1942
HISTADRUTH	Documentary Film for the Palestine Labor Union	1945

GARDNER READ

Born in Evanston, Illinois, in 1913. At the age of fifteen he began to study the piano, harmony, musical appreciation, theory and composition with various local teachers and continued his studies at the Northwestern University School of Music. For outstanding work in composition in 1932, he was awarded a scholarship at the National Music Camp at Interlochen, Michigan, and later he received a scholarship at the Eastman School of Music, where he spent four years, graduating in 1936 with the degree of Bachelor of Music. In 1937 he received a degree of Master of Music in composition and theory. At the MacDowell Colony at Peterboro, New Hampshire, he completed his first symphony and this work brought him the first prize in an American orchestral contest sponsored by the Philharmonic Society of New York.

During the summer of 1938 he received the Cromwell Fellowship for travel and studied with Pizzetti, later with Sibelius, and traveled through Europe and the Near East. In 1940 he served as Professor of Composition at the National Music Camp, and in 1941 he received a fellowship to study with Copland at the Berkshire Music Center. He was appointed to the faculty of the St. Louis Institute of Music, then became head of the Composition Department of the Kansas City Conservatory of Music, and is now head of the Theory Department at the Cleveland Institute of Music.

Many of his works have been presented by the Philharmonic, Boston,

GARDNER READ (*Continued*)

Chicago, Pittsburgh, Rochester and St. Louis Symphony orchestras. His chamber music has been performed frequently by the smaller orchestras. His compositions have been heard over WNYC, NBC, WQXR, WHAN, WJZ and other stations. He is now completing a ballet called "The Temptation of St. Anthony."

COMPOSITIONS

ORCHESTRAL WORKS

	DURATION	PUBLISHER	DATE
THE LOTUS-EATERS, OPUS 19	15 minutes	Manuscript	1932
THE PAINTED DESERT, OPUS 22	26 "	Manuscript	1933
SKETCHES OF THE CITY, OPUS 26	15 "	Edwin F. Kalmus	1933
FANTASY FOR VIOLIN AND ORCHESTRA, OPUS 38	10 "	Associated Music Publishers	1935
SYMPHONY No. 1, OPUS 30	38 "	Edition Musicus	1936
PRELUDE AND TOCCATA, OPUS 43	7 "	Edwin F. Kalmus	1937
PASSACAGLIA AND FUGUE, OPUS 34A	12 "	Manuscript *for hire*	1938
SONGS FOR A RAINY NIGHT, OPUS 48 *baritone, orchestra*	9 "	Manuscript *for hire*	1940
PAN E DAGNI, OPUS 53	10 "	Associated Music Publishers	1940
THREE SATIRICAL SARCASMS, OPUS 29A	6 "	Manuscript *for hire*	1941
NIGHT-FLIGHT, OPUS 44	7 "	E. B. Marks	1942
SYMPHONY No. 2, OPUS 45	25 "	Associated Music Publishers	1942
FIRST OVERTURE, OPUS 58	8 "	Manuscript *for hire*	1943
DANCE OF THE LOCOMOTIVES, OPUS 57A	4 "	Manuscript *for hire*	1944
CONCERTO FOR VIOLONCELLO AND ORCHESTRA	25 "	Associated Music Publishers	1945

CHAMBER ORCHESTRA

FOUR NOCTURNES, OPUS 23 *contralto, 30 instruments*	11 minutes	Manuscript *for hire*	1934
FROM A LUTE OF JADE, OPUS 36 *mezzo soprano, 38 instruments*	8 "	Composers Press, Inc.	1936
SUITE FOR STRING ORCHESTRA, OPUS 33A *32–76 instruments*	13 "	Galaxy Music Publishers	1937
PETITE PASTORALE, OPUS 40A *24 instruments*	2 "	Manuscript *for hire*	1940
AMERICAN CIRCLE, OPUS 52A *46 instruments*	4 "	Manuscript *for hire*	1941

CHORAL WORKS

WHERE CORALS LIE, OPUS 49 *mixed chorus, two-piano*	6 minutes	Fitzsimons	1937
THE GOLDEN JOURNEY TO SAMARKAND, OPUS 41 *solos, mixed chorus, orchestra*	26 "	Manuscript *for hire*	1939
TO A SKYLARK, OPUS 51 *mixed chorus, a cappella*	6 "	Associated Music Publishers	1939

CHAMBER MUSIC

MOUNTAIN SKETCHES, OPUS 11 **piano**	15 minutes	Manuscript	1932

GARDNER READ (*Continued*)

CHAMBER MUSIC (*Continued*)	DURATION	PUBLISHER	DATE
SONATA IN A MINOR, OPUS 27 *piano*	24 minutes	Manuscript	1935
SUITE FOR STRING QUARTET, OPUS 33	13 "	Galaxy	1935
PIANO QUINTET, OPUS 47 *piano, string quartet*	24 "	Manuscript *for hire*	1945
SONATA DA CHIESA *piano*	11 "	Manuscript *for hire*	1945

H. OWEN REED

Born in Odessa, Missouri, in 1910. He studied music at the University of Missouri and at the Louisiana State University, where he received his Bachelor of Music, Bachelor of Arts and Master of Music degrees. He attended the Eastman School of Music, where he studied with Hanson, Rogers and White. In 1939, he received his Doctor of Music degree in composition. At the Berkshire Music Center, he studied with Aaron Copland, Stanley Chappel and Bohuslav Martinů.

At present, he is Associate Professor of Music and Chairman of the Theory Department at Michigan State College. He has written two textbooks, *A Workbook in the Fundamentals of Music* and *A Workbook in Harmony*.

His works, which have been performed by various college orchestras throughout the country, also by the Lansing Symphony Orchestra and the Rochester Philharmonic, include "Masque of the Red Death," Overture, Symphony No. 1 and a "Psalm of Praise." The Symphony was broadcast over an affiliated station of the Blue Network of NBC. A Michigan broadcasting station played the Overture. He is at present completing a "Spiritual" for symphonic band.

COMPOSITIONS

ORCHESTRAL WORKS	DURATION	PUBLISHER	DATE
EVANGELINE	15 minutes	Blueprint	1938
SYMPHONY No. 1	20 "	Blueprint	1939
OVERTURE	6 "	Blueprint	1940
SYMPHONIC DANCE	3 "	Blueprint	1942

CHORAL WORKS			
A PSALM OF PRAISE *7 part mixed chorus, a cappella*	3 minutes	Blueprint	1939
OUR COUNTRY *mixed chorus, orchestra*	3 "	Blueprint	1942

CHAMBER MUSIC			
PIANO SONATA	9 minutes	Manuscript	1934
STRING QUARTET	15 "	Blueprint	1937
A PSALM OF PRAISE *solo soprano, 2 flutes, oboe, 2 clarinets, bassoon, horn*	3 "	Manuscript	1939

H. OWEN REED (*Continued*)

STAGE WORKS	PUBLISHER	DATE
THE MASQUE OF THE RED DEATH—		
ballet-pantomime	Photostat	1936
small orchestra, ballet and pantomime cast		

ALOIS REISER

Born in Prague, Czechoslovakia, in 1889. He graduated from the Conservatory at Prague, where he studied with Dvořák. In 1905 he came to America and took up his residence in New York. In 1936 he received the second prize in the NBC Music Guild Competition. The String Quartet in E Minor received the Elizabeth Sprague Coolidge Prize and the String Quartet in C Major won the NBC Prize. The Trio for Violin, Cello and Piano was awarded the Pittsburgh Art Society Prize, the Prelude to the opera "Gobi" was awarded a prize, and the Concerto for Cello and Orchestra, Op. 15, received the Hollywood Bowl Award and he won a Coolidge Berkshire Prize.

His orchestral works have been played in New York City, Los Angeles and Philadelphia, as well as in Prague. The String Quartet in E Minor was first given at the Elizabeth Sprague Coolidge Festival in Pittsfield. His chamber works have been played here and abroad.

COMPOSITIONS

ORCHESTRAL WORKS	DURATION	PUBLISHER	DATE
FROM MOUNT RAINIER	10 minutes	G. Schirmer, Inc.	1926
SLAVIC RHAPSODY	30 "	Manuscript	1927
EREHWON	17 "	Manuscript	1931
CONCERTO, OPUS 15	35 "	Manuscript	1932
cello and orchestra			

CHAMBER ORCHESTRA			
CONCERTO FOR CELLO AND ORCHESTRA, OPUS 5	35 minutes	Manuscript	1916
LITTLE COQUETTE	3 "	Carl Fischer, Inc.	1918
SPANISH SERENADE	4 "	Carl Fischer, Inc.	1918
APPASSIONATE D'AMOUR	4 "	G. Schirmer, Inc.	1926
ENTRE NOUS	3 "	G. Schirmer, Inc.	1926
CHINK WALK	5 "	Carl Fischer, Inc.	
BALANESE SUITE	40 "	Sam Fox Publishing Co.	
IGOROTTAN SUITE	35 "	Sam Fox Publishing Co.	

CHAMBER MUSIC			
STRING QUARTET IN E MINOR	40 minutes	G. Schirmer, Inc.	1916
STRING QUARTET IN C MAJOR	45 "	Manuscript	1930
SONATA FOR VIOLIN AND PIANO, OPUS 17	30 "	Manuscript	1932
TRIO IN F MAJOR	40 "	Manuscript	1941
violin, cello, piano			

STAGE WORKS			
GOBI—grand opera	3¾ hours	Manuscript	1919
DAPHNE—light opera in two acts	2½ "	Manuscript	1945

WALLINGFORD RIEGGER

Born in Albany, Georgia, in 1885. He graduated as a cellist from the Institute of Musical Art in 1907. He studied composition with Goetschius. Later he studied counterpoint at the Berlin Hochschule and was a pupil of Stillman-Kelley in composition and orchestration. In Berlin he conducted the Bluthner Orchestra and in southern Germany, operas. On his return to America, he became head of the cello and theory departments at Drake University. He also taught at the Institute of Musical Art, Ithaca Conservatory, Teachers College, the New School for Social Research; he is at the present time on the faculty of the Metropolitan Music School in New York.

He received the Paderewski Award in 1921, the Elizabeth Coolidge Prize in 1924. He has also been the recipient of the Society for the Publication of American Music award. He also received honorable mention at the Lewisohn Stadium concerts and from the National Composers Clinic and Chamber Music Guild in Washington. He was appointed an advisory member of the first Yaddo Music Festival and was a member of the Executive Board of the Pan American Association of Composers. At present he is on the editorial board of New Music Editions and New Music Recordings. He has arranged many choral works and has lectured extensively on the twelve-tone system and on modern music.

The major orchestral works have been played at the New York Stadium and in many cities throughout the country. Other works for chamber orchestra and small ensemble have been performed at the Elizabeth Coolidge and Yaddo festivals, and by the Pan American Association, the League of Composers, New Music Society and also in the Rochester series of American Composers Concerts. Works written for dance groups have been presented on the stage in many cities in the United States. He has had many broadcasts over various networks in the United States and in Europe. He is completing at present a Sonata for Violin and Piano.

COMPOSITIONS

ORCHESTRAL WORKS	DURATION	PUBLISHER	DATE
American Polonaise (Triple Jazz)	8 minutes	Manuscript	1923
Rhapsody	12 "	Manuscript	1925
Fantasy and Fugue	20 "	Manuscript	1931
organ (2 players), orchestra			
Dance Suite	18 "	Manuscript	1937
(also for Band)			
Consummation	10 "	Manuscript	1938
Canon and Fugue for Strings	8 "	H. Flammer, Inc.	1939
Passacaglia and Fugue	8 "	Manuscript	1942
(also for Band)			
Funeral March	8 "	Leeds	1943
(also for Band)			
Symphony	25 "	Manuscript	1944

CHAMBER ORCHESTRA			
La Belle Dame Sans Merci	15 minutes	Manuscript	1924
4 solo voices, 8 instruments			

WALLINGFORD RIEGGER (*Continued*)

CHAMBER ORCHESTRA (*Continued*)	DURATION	PUBLISHER	DATE
STUDY IN SONORITY *10 violins or any multiple of 10*	9 minutes	G. Schirmer, Inc.	1927
DICHOTOMY *14 instruments*	12	New Music	1932
SCHERZO *(also for 2 pianos)*	7 "	Manuscript	1937
NEW DANCE *piano, 12 instruments*	5 "	Manuscript	1944

CHORAL WORKS

ETERNITY *2 sopranos, alto, bass, flute, 2 horns*	4½ minutes	H. Flammer, Inc.	1942
FROM SOME FAR SHORE *soprano, alto, tenor, bass, piano*	5½ "	Manuscript	1943
EASTER PASSACAGLIA *soprano, alto, tenor, bass, piano*	4 "	H. Flammer, Inc.	1944

CHAMBER MUSIC

THREE CANONS FOR WOODWINDS	10 minutes	New Music	1930
TRIO IN B MINOR *piano, violin, cello*	30 "	S.P.A.M.	1931
DIVERTISSEMENT *flute, harp, cello*	15 "	Manuscript	1933
DANCE SUITE (New Dance-Arrow) *2 pianos*	18 "	Manuscript	1937
STRING QUARTET	17 "	Manuscript	1940
DUOS FOR THREE WOODWINDS *flute, oboe, clarinet*	20 "	New Music	1943
NEW AND OLD—a suite of 12 pieces for piano	20 "	Boosey & Hawkes	1945

STAGE WORKS

FRENETIC RHYTHMS *voice, piano, 3 woodwinds*	18 minutes	Manuscript	1932
BACCHANALE *piano 4 hands*	6 "	Manuscript	1932
NEW DANCE *full orchestra*	40 "	Manuscript	1935
THEATRE PIECE *piano 4 hands, drums, etc.* *with small orchestra*	40 "	Manuscript	1935
WITH MY RED FIRES *chamber orchestra*	40 "	Manuscript	1936
CHRONICLE *piano, 6 instruments*	40 "	Manuscript	1936
CANDIDE *chamber orchestra*	40 "	Manuscript	1936
CASE HISTORY *piano 4 hands*	10 "	Manuscript	1937
TREND *piano and 6 instruments*	40 "	Manuscript	1937
TROJAN INCIDENT *chamber orchestra*	50 "	Manuscript	1937

VITTORIO RIETI

Born in Alexandria, Egypt, in 1898, of Italian parents. He studied music in Milan with Frugatta and in Rome with Respighi.

After the First World War he destroyed all his early compositions and made a fresh start. Between 1925 and 1940 he divided his time between France and Italy. In Paris he was one of the most active committee members of the musical society "Sérénade" (1931 to 1939). He wrote all the incidental music for plays presented by the Louis Jouvet Theatre between 1936 and 1939. During this period he also conducted several performances of his own music in Paris, London, Brussels, Vienna, Rome, Venice and elsewhere. He came to the United States in 1940 and lives in New York City.

He first came to the attention of the musical world in 1924 when Casella conducted his Woodwind Concerto at the Prague International Festival. His ballets "Baraban" and "The Ball" were given by Diaghilev in Paris, London and Monte Carlo. His chamber opera, "Teresa nel Bosco," was first given at the Venice International Festival in 1934, conducted by Hermann Scherchen. The "Concerto du Loup" was heard at the I.S.C.M. Festival in San Francisco in 1943. American performances include his ballet "Waltz Academy" at the Ballet Theatre, Boston, the ballet "Night Shadow" by the Monte Carlo Ballet, New York, and the "Sinfonia Tripartita" by the NBC Orchestra under Arturo Toscanini. His orchestral and chamber-music works have had numerous performances in Europe and in this country. His String Quartet No. 1 has been recorded by the Gramophone Company, London.

COMPOSITIONS WRITTEN IN AMERICA

ORCHESTRAL WORKS	DURATION	PUBLISHER	DATE
SINFONIA TRIPARTITA (FOURTH SYMPHONY)	15 minutes	Associated Music Publishers	1944
CHAMBER MUSIC			
STRING QUARTET No. 2	15 minutes	Manuscript	1941
SECOND AVENUE WALTZES FOR TWO PIANOS	17 "	Manuscript	1942
CHESS SERENADE FOR TWO PIANOS	13 "	Manuscript	1945
PARTITA FOR HARPSICHORD AND SIX INSTRUMENTS	18 "	Manuscript	1945
STAGE WORKS			
THE NIGHT SHADOW—ballet	25 minutes	Manuscript	1941
WALTZ ACADEMY—ballet	25 "	Manuscript	1944
OEDIPUS—ballet	30 "	Manuscript	1944

LEROY ROBERTSON

Born in Fountain Green, Utah, in 1896. He graduated from the New England Conservatory, where he studied with Chadwick, Converse, Keller and Stevens. Later he was a student of Bloch and Leichtentritt. He received his Master of Arts degree from Brigham Young University.

He has been on the faculty of Brigham Young University since 1925, where he is now Professor of Music. The Overture in E Minor won the Endicott Prize in 1923, the Piano Quartet won the Society for the Publication of American Music Award in 1936, the String Quartet was chosen for the New York Music Critics' Circle in 1944 and the Rhapsody for Piano and Orchestra won an award from the Utah Institute of Fine Arts. He is a Fellow in the Utah Academy of Science, Arts, and Letters and is a member of the National Association for American Composers and Conductors. He was given an initial Academy Award for achievement in art in 1941.

His compositions have been performed in Chicago, Ann Arbor, Cleveland, Colorado Springs, Indianapolis, Provo and Salt Lake City by leading orchestras and chamber groups. The Quartet in A Minor was broadcast over WQXR and the "Lord's Prayer" is sung frequently over a CBS network. He is, at present, preparing a Concerto for Violin and Orchestra and an oratorio with text from the Book of Mormon.

COMPOSITIONS

ORCHESTRAL WORKS	DURATION	PUBLISHER	DATE
OVERTURE IN E MINOR	6½ minutes	Manuscript	1924
TRILOGY	36 "	Manuscript	1940
PRELUDE, SCHERZO, RICERCARE	20 "	Elkan-Vogel *for hire*	1941
RHAPSODY *piano, orchestra*	18 "	Carl Fischer Inc. *for hire*	1944
PUNCH AND JUDY—overture	7 "	Manuscript	1945
CHORAL WORKS			
LORD'S PRAYER	4 minutes	Galaxy Music Corp.	1939
CHAMBER MUSIC			
QUINTET IN A MINOR *piano, string quartet*	17½ minutes	G. Schirmer, Inc.	1933
QUARTET IN E MINOR *string quartet*	25 "	Manuscript	1940
AMERICAN SERENADE *string quartet*	15½ "	Manuscript	1944

EARL ROBINSON

Born in Seattle, Washington, in 1910. He received his Bachelor of Music degree from the University of Washington. While still in college, he conducted his "Symphonic Fragment" and "Rhapsody in Brass."

During his travels across the country, he became interested in native

American folk songs and recorded some for the Library of Congress. He was musical director of a small theater group and joined the W.P.A. Federal Theater Project, for which he wrote the music to "Processional" and "Life and Death of an American." "Ballad for Americans" was written for the production "Sing for Your Supper," and, after its première over CBS in 1939, he was awarded a Guggenheim Fellowship to write a musical play based on Sandburg's "The People, Yes." He worked at Warner Brothers and later worked at Paramount Studios on the film score of "California." He wrote the ballad for the 20th Century-Fox production, "A Walk in the Sun." He was a studio writer-composer for a major broadcasting company.

His compositions have had major performances throughout the country and have been broadcast over ABC, CBS and other networks from coast to coast. Decca Records has recorded the "Ballad for Americans," "The House I Live In" and "The Lonesome Train." At present he is preparing a musical show for Broadway, a new cantata on atomic power and a string quartet.

COMPOSITIONS

CHAMBER ORCHESTRA	DURATION	PUBLISHER	DATE
RHAPSODY IN BRASS	7 minutes	Manuscript	1932
for trumpets and trombones			
SYMPHONIC FRAGMENT	9 "	Manuscript	1933
16 instruments			

CHORAL WORKS			
BALLAD FOR AMERICANS	11 minutes	Robbins Music Corp.	1939
mixed chorus, orchestra			
IN THE FOLDED AND QUIET YESTERDAYS	8 "	Manuscript	1940
mixed chorus, orchestra			
TOWER OF BABEL	18 "	Manuscript	1941
mixed chorus, orchestra			
BATTLE HYMN	15 "	Chappell	1942
mixed chorus, orchestra			
THE LONESOME TRAIN	25 "	Sun Music Co.	1943
mixed chorus, orchestra			
THE TOWN CRIER	12 "	Manuscript	1945
mixed chorus, orchestra			

STAGE WORKS			
IN THE FOLDED AND QUIET YESTERDAYS (written for stage production of "The People, Yes") *soloists, mixed chorus, orchestra*	8 minutes	Manuscript	1940
TOWER OF BABEL (written for stage production of "The People, Yes") *soloists, mixed chorus, moderate size orchestra*	18 "	Manuscript	1941

FILM MUSIC	STUDIO		
WALK IN THE SUN—ballad	20th Century-Fox	Manuscript	1940
CALIFORNIA—songs and background music	Paramount	Famous Music, Inc.	1945

BERNARD ROGERS

Born in New York City, N. Y., in 1893. He attended the Institute of Musical Art in New York City. He was also a pupil of Bloch in Cleveland. The Eastman School Publication was awarded to him and he was the recipient of a Pulitzer Scholarship and a Guggenheim Fellowship. He received the Bispham Medal for his opera "The Marriage of Aude." He is now teaching composition at the Eastman School of Music, Rochester.

His orchestral compositions "Adonais," the "Prelude to Hamlet," "Five Fairy Tales," "Three Japanese Dances" and other works have been heard with the symphonic orchestras in New York, Rochester, Boston, Chicago and Philadelphia. The chamber music has been played in many cities, also on the League of Composers' programs. "Dance of Salome," "Two American Frescoes" and other works have been played by the major symphony orchestras in many cities in the United States. "The Passion" was presented at the Cincinnati May Festival in 1944. The Fantasy for Flute, Viola and Orchestra was presented in Zurich, Switzerland. "The Warrior" (text by Norman Corwin) received the Alice M. Ditson Fund Award (Columbia University) in 1945 and was presented by the Metropolitan Opera Company.

The League of Composers commissioned "Invasion," which was presented by the Philharmonic Orchestra and over CBS. "Characters from Hans Andersen" and "Flute Soliloquy" were broadcast over NBC. His chamber music has been played in many cities and broadcast. Victor has recorded the "Soliloquy for Flute and String Orchestra" and "Five Fairy Tales."

COMPOSITIONS

ORCHESTRAL WORKS	DURATION	PUBLISHER	DATE
To the Fallen—dirge	7 minutes	Manuscript	1915
The Faithful—overture	12 "	Manuscript	1918
Japanese Landscapes	18 "	Manuscript	1925
Adonais—poem	12 "	Manuscript	1927
Prelude to Hamlet	14 "	Manuscript	1928
Symphony No. 2	28 "	Manuscript	1929
Two American Frescoes	11 "	Manuscript	1931
Three Japanese Dances	12 "	Manuscript	1933
mezzo soprano, orchestra			
Five Fairy Tales	12 "	C. C. Birchard & Co.	1934
Symphony No. 3	40 "	Manuscript	1936
The Supper at Emmaus	8 "	Manuscript	1937
Soliloquy for Bassoon and Strings	6 "	Manuscript	1938
Fantasy for Flute, Viola and Orchestra	8 "	Manuscript	1938
Dance of Salome	10 "	Manuscript	1939
The Colours of War	6 "	Manuscript	1939
The Song of the Nightingale	19 "	Manuscript	1939
Sailors of Toulon	8 "	Manuscript	1940
Invasion	5 "	Manuscript	1943
Symphony, No. 4	31 "	Manuscript	1945
Amphitryon—overture			

CHAMBER ORCHESTRA

Soliloquy	6 minutes	C. C. Birchard & Co.	1922
flute, string orchestra			

BERNARD ROGERS (*Continued*)

CHAMBER ORCHESTRA (*Continued*)	DURATION	PUBLISHER	DATE
PASTORALE	9 minutes	Manuscript	1928
11 instruments			
RHAPSODY NOCTURNE	10 "	Manuscript	1928
small orchestra			
THE PLAINS	10 "	Manuscript	1940
small orchestra			
CHARACTERS FROM HANS ANDERSEN	8 "	Elkan-Vogel	1944
small orchestra			

CHORAL WORKS

	DURATION	PUBLISHER	DATE
THE RAISING OF LAZARUS	25 minutes	C. C. Birchard & Co.	1928
solo voices, chorus, orchestra			
THE EXODUS—sacred poem	28 "	C. C. Birchard & Co.	1932
solo voices, chorus, orchestra			
THE PASSION	65 "	Elkan-Vogel	1943
soloists, mixed chorus,			
large orchestra			
RESPONSE TO SILENT PRAYER	5 "	Manuscript	1945

CHAMBER MUSIC

	DURATION	PUBLISHER	DATE
STRING QUARTET IN D MINOR	30 minutes	Manuscript	1927

STAGE WORKS

	DURATION	PUBLISHER	DATE
THE MARRIAGE OF AUDE—grand opera	1 hour	Manuscript	1931
large orchestra			
THE WARRIOR—opera			1946

FILM MUSIC

MUSIC FOR AN INDUSTRIAL FILM		Manuscript	
		Eastman Kodak Co.	

MIKLOS ROZSA

Born in Budapest, Hungary, in 1907. He studied composition and musicology at the Leipzig Conservatory and University and also studied conducting at Trinity College of Music in London. He arrived in this country in 1940 and is now Professor of Composition at the University of Southern California. He is also a composer of film music. In 1945 he received an Academy Award for the best dramatic score in motion pictures. The Society of American Composers and Conductors awarded him a citation of merit for the Serenade for Chamber Orchestra.

His major compositions have been performed by leading orchestras from coast to coast. "Jungle Book" and the "Spellbound" suite have been arranged for concert and have been presented by the Los Angeles Philharmonic Orchestra. He is at present writing a motet for mixed choir based on Ecclesiastes. He is also preparing the music and conducting the orchestra in a motion picture based on the music and life of Rimsky-Korsakoff.

MIKLOS ROZSA (*Continued*)

COMPOSITIONS WRITTEN IN AMERICA

ORCHESTRAL WORKS

	DURATION	PUBLISHER	DATE
THE THIEF OF BAGDAD—suite	15 minutes	Manuscript *for hire*	1940
THE JUNGLE BOOK—suite	28 "	Manuscript *for hire*	1942
CONCERTO FOR STRING ORCHESTRA, OPUS 17	19 "	Delkas Music Publishing Co.	1943
THE SPELLBOUND SUITE	25 "	Chappell & Co.	1945

CHAMBER ORCHESTRA

TWO SONGS: INVOCATION and BEASTS OF BURDEN, OPUS 16A AND B *contralto, piano*		Delkas Music Publishing Co.	1940

CHORAL WORKS

LULLABY, OPUS 18A *women's chorus, a cappella*	4 minutes	Associated Music Publishers	1944
MADRIGAL OF SPRING, OPUS 18B *women's chorus, a cappella*	4 "	Associated Music Publishers	1944
FOR EVERYTHING THERE IS A SEASON—motet *mixed chorus, a cappella*	12 "	Manuscript	1946

CHAMBER MUSIC

SONATA FOR TWO VIOLINS, OPUS 15	15 minutes	Associated Music Publishers	1940

FILM MUSIC

	STUDIO		
THE THIEF OF BAGDAD concert version—suite	Korda	Manuscript *for hire*	1940
THE JUNGLE BOOK concert version—suite *narrator and orchestra*	Korda	Manuscript	1942
JACARE	United Artists		1943
FIVE GRAVES TO CAIRO	Paramount		1944
SONG TO REMEMBER *adaptation from Chopin*	Columbia Pictures		1945
DOUBLE INDEMNITY	Paramount		1945
SPELLBOUND concert version—suite	Selznick	Chappell & Co.	1945
THE LOST WEEKEND	Paramount		1945
STRANGE LOVE OF MARTHA IVERS concert version—song	Paramount	Famous Music Publishers	1946

BERYL RUBINSTEIN

Born in Athens, Georgia, in 1898. He studied piano with his father and later with Lambert. As a child pianist he toured the United States from 1905 to 1911, and at the age of thirteen made his début with the Metropolitan Opera Orchestra. From 1911 to 1916 he studied in Europe with Da Motta and Busoni. He made his first appearance in London in 1925. He is

BERYL RUBINSTEIN *(Continued)*

a member of Phi Mu Alpha and of Delta Omicron. From 1921 to 1929 he was on the faculty of the Cleveland Institute of Music, as head of the Piano Department and later as dean. In 1932 he became the Director of the Institute. He has appeared as soloist with many orchestras, including the New York Philharmonic, Cleveland, Detroit, Philadelphia and San Francisco organizations. He served in the U. S. Army for two years as Captain in recreational work in Africa and Sicily.

Scherzo and Concerto were presented by the Cleveland and Chautauqua orchestras. His Concerto in C was given on the air over WEAF. Some of his compositions have been presented in New York, Los Angeles and Pittsburgh and have had broadcasts over many networks. Victor and Columbia have recorded his works.

COMPOSITIONS

ORCHESTRAL WORKS	DURATION	PUBLISHER	DATE
SCHERZO	15 minutes	Manuscript	1927
CONCERTO FOR PIANO AND ORCHESTRA	30 "	Juilliard Foundation	1935

CHORAL WORKS			
PRAYER OF PRAISE *men's voices, a cappella*	5 minutes	Carl Fischer, Inc.	1932

CHAMBER MUSIC			
PASSEPIED *string quartet*	6 minutes	Carl Fischer, Inc.	1924
QUARTET IN D FLAT *string quartet*	25 "	Manuscript	1933
SUITE FOR TWO PIANOS	20 "	G. Schirmer, Inc.	1938
SONATA FOR FLUTE AND PIANO	18 "	Manuscript	

STAGE WORKS			
SLEEPING BEAUTY—opera *soloists, chorus, orchestra*	2 hours	Manuscript	1937
LETTER FROM THE FRONT *narrator, baritone soloist, chorus, orchestra*	15 minutes	Edward Marks, Inc.	1943

CARL RUGGLES

Born in Marion, Massachusetts, in 1876. For many years he has made his home in Arlington, Vermont. He studied with Claus, Spalding and Timner and also followed some music courses at Harvard University. The Winona Symphony Orchestra, which at one time he conducted, was also founded by him. He was formerly a member of the International Composers Guild and was also active in the Pan American Association of Composers. He gives a part of his time to painting and he is also adept as a craftsman.

"Men and Mountains" was performed by the New York Philharmonic,

CARL RUGGLES (*Continued*)

as well as in San Francisco, Boston, Havana and Paris. "Portals" was performed in Boston, San Francisco, Havana, Paris, Budapest, Berlin, Madrid, as well as in New York by the Conductorless Orchestra and in 1946 on a League of Composers' program by Joseph Barone. The "Sun Treader" was played at the Festival of the I.S.C.M. in Barcelona, also in Paris and Berlin; it has been broadcast from Spain. The choral and chamber works have been included on several programs of the American Association of Composers, the International Composers Guild, the International Society for New Music and the New School for Social Research. "Evocations" has had numerous performances. "Men and Mountains" and "Men and Angels" have been recorded by N.M.Q.R.

COMPOSITIONS

ORCHESTRAL WORKS	PUBLISHER	DATE
MEN AND ANGELS	Curwen	1920
MEN AND MOUNTAINS		1924–44
PORTALS	New Music	1926–45
string orchestra		
SUN TREADER	New Music	1933
ORGANUM	Manuscript	1945

CHAMBER ORCHESTRA		
ANGELS—2nd movement of		
"Men and Angels"	Curwen	
6 trumpets		
MEN AND MOUNTAINS	New Music	
21 instruments		
PORTALS	New Music	
13 strings		
VOX CLAMANS IN DESERTO	Manuscript	
solo voice, chamber orchestra		

CHAMBER MUSIC		
POLYPHONIC COMPOSITION FOR		
THREE PIANOS	Manuscript	
EVOCATIONS—suite	New Music	1945
4 chants for piano		

LOUIS VICTOR SAAR

Born in Rotterdam, Holland, in 1868 and died in 1937. He graduated from Strasbourg University and attended the Royal Academy of Music in Munich. He was a pupil of Rheinberger and Abel and later of Brahms. His studies included piano composition and theory. He was awarded the Mendelssohn Composition Prize for a piano suite and songs and the National Federation of Music Clubs Prize.

He was accompanist for the Metropolitan Opera Company and gave piano concerts and recitals. At the National Conservatory and at the Col-

LOUIS VICTOR SAAR (*Continued*)

lege of Music, New York, he taught theory and composition; he also taught at the Cincinnati College of Music. In 1917 he joined the Chicago Musical College. He wrote musical criticism for newspapers in St. Louis.

Among the compositions which have been widely heard in the United States and abroad are "Rococo Suite," "Gondoliera" and the Sonata in G.

COMPOSITIONS

ORCHESTRAL WORKS	DURATION	PUBLISHER	DATE
Rococo—suite, OPUS 27	15 minutes	G. Schirmer, Inc.	1915
FROM THE MOUNTAIN KINGDOM OF THE GREAT NORTH WEST—suite	20 "	F. E. C. Leuckart	1922
ALONG THE COLUMBIA RIVER—suite	10–12 "	Manuscript	1924
OLD GERMAN MASTERS—suite	20 "	G. Schirmer, Inc.	1930
string orchestra			
OVERTURE IN A (Telemann)	10 "	Manuscript	1936

CHAMBER ORCHESTRA			
Rococo—suite, OPUS 27		G. Schirmer, Inc.	
for chamber orchestra			
GONDOLIERA		Carl Fischer, Inc.	
violin, string orchestra			
CHANSON D'AMOUR		Carl Fischer, Inc.	
EN BERCEAU		Theodore Presser Co.	

CHORAL WORKS			
THE 128TH PSALM	15 minutes	G. Schirmer, Inc.	
mixed or women's chorus, orchestra			
DAS HOHELIED DER DEUTSCHEN KUNST	12 "	Manuscript	
mixed chorus, orchestra			
THE NIGHTINGALES, OPUS 137	10 "	E. C. Schirmer	1931
oboe or flute solo			
NACHTGESANG, OPUS 44	12 "	Siegel-Kistner, Leipzig	
flute solo			
AVE MARIA, OPUS 136	10 "	Reilly & McLaughlin	
10 voice mixed chorus, a cappella			

CHAMBER MUSIC			
SONATA IN G MAJOR, OPUS 44		Siegel-Kistner, Leipzig	
piano, violin			
QUARTET, OPUS 39		Manuscript	
piano, violin, viola, cello			
TRIO A MAJOR, OPUS 97		Manuscript	
piano, violin, cello			
SONATA, OPUS 121	20 minutes	Manuscript	1926
piano, cello			
SONATINA, OPUS 142	20 "	Manuscript	1934
violin, piano			
QUARTETTINO, OPUS 145	25 "	Manuscript	1936
violin, viola, cello, piano			

CARLOS SALZEDO

Born in Arcachon, Gironde, France, in 1885. He has made his home in New York for many years. After graduating from the Paris Conservatory with honors in harp and piano, he toured extensively in Europe and America, giving harp recitals and appearing as soloist with all the symphony orchestras. With Edgar Varese he founded the International Composers Guild in 1921. He has been active as President of the National Association of Harpists and Editor of *Eolus*. He organized and is head of the Harp Department of the Curtis Institute of Music and of the Salzedo Harp Ensemble—a group which often tours with him. He was a member of the board of the United States Section of the I.S.C.M. and of Pro Musica. He received the Award from the Society for the Publication of American Music. At Camden, Maine, he has developed a summer colony of harpists who come there to study with him.

"The Enchanted Isle" has been performed by many of the orchestras in the United States, including those of Chicago, Boston, Philadelphia, Cleveland, Detroit, Baltimore and Syracuse. Works for chamber orchestra and chamber music have had repeated performances at the Elizabeth Coolidge Festivals and by the Pan American Association of Composers, the International Composers Guild and other societies. "Short Stories in Music" has been played throughout the United States in concerts and numerous broadcasts. "Scintillation" has been broadcast over WABC. Other broadcasts of his works have been given over WOR, WEAF and WJZ. "Chansons dans la Nuit" and the Concerto for Harp and Woodwinds are recorded by Columbia and "Short Stories in Music" and "Scintillation" by the Victor Company. His *Book on the Art of Modulating* (in collaboration with Lucile Lawrence) has been published by Schirmer.

COMPOSITIONS

ORCHESTRAL WORKS	DURATION	PUBLISHER	DATE
THE ENCHANTED ISLE *with harp principal*	13 minutes	Manuscript	1918

CHAMBER ORCHESTRA			
THREE POEMS BY SARA YARROW *soprano, 6 harps, 3 wind instruments*	15 minutes	Manuscript	1919
CONCERTO *harp, 7 wind instruments*	17 "	Manuscript	1926
PRÉAMBULE ET JEUX *harp, 4 winds, 5 string instruments*	9 "	Manuscript	1929

CHAMBER MUSIC			
BOLMIMERIE *7 harps*	12 minutes	Manuscript	1919
FOUR PRELUDES TO THE AFTERNOON OF A TELEPHONE *2 harps*	15 "	Manuscript	1921
SONATA FOR HARP AND PIANO	12 "	G. Schirmer, Inc.	1922
THREE POEMS BY MALLARMÉ *soprano, harp, piano*	9 "	Manuscript	1924
PENTACLE *2 harps*	17 "	Manuscript	1928
PANORAMA—Suite for Harp Solo *4 parts*		Manuscript	1937

LAZARE SAMINSKY

Born near Odessa, Russia, in 1882. He was educated at the University of St. Petersburg, where he specialized in mathematics. He studied music and composition at the Conservatory of Petrograd with Liadoff and Rimsky-Korsakoff. In 1920 he came to New York and soon after became a citizen of the United States. For many years he was a member of the Executive Board of the League of Composers. He has traveled extensively in the Caucasus and the Near East and has felt the strong influence of these countries in his own creative work. He has made a special study of Oriental folklore and Caucasian and Hebrew music. He is the author of *Music of Our Day* and *Music of the Ghetto and the Bible,* of essays on the philosophy of mathematics and of many magazine articles on various musical subjects. He has been guest conductor with many of the major orchestras in America and in Europe, and has lectured on and conducted concerts of contemporary music in South America and Canada. For a decade he has directed the annual Three Choir Festival of New York.

The First, Second, Third and Fourth symphonies have had performances in St. Petersburg, Amsterdam, New York, Paris, Vienna and Berlin. "Ausonia" was performed at the Paris Exposition and also in Florence and Cleveland. "Litanies of Women" was given in Vienna, Berlin and Milan and at the American Festival in Rochester and the International Music Festival in Venice. "Jephtha's Daughter," "The Plague's Galliard," "Songs of Three Queens," "Venice," "King Saul" and many other of his works have had numerous performances by leading choral and instrumental groups. "Pueblo, a Moon Rhapsody," a work commissioned in the League of Composers' American Series, had its première with the National Symphony Orchestra in Washington, D. C. Several of these works have been broadcast by CBS and NBC and over WOR. His "Rye Septet with Voice" was premiered at the 20th Anniversary Concert of the League of Composers in 1942. "Stilled Pageant" was presented in Buenos Aires and Toronto.

COMPOSITIONS

ORCHESTRAL WORKS	DURATION	PUBLISHER	DATE
SECOND SYMPHONY—OF THE SUMMITS	18 minutes	Maurice Sénart	1918
THIRD SYMPHONY—OF THE SEAS	20 "	Universal Edition	1924
FOURTH SYMPHONY	27 "	Universal Edition	1927
AUSONIA—ITALIAN PAGES full orchestra	16 "	Maurice Sénart	1930
FIFTH SYMPHONY—CITY OF SOLOMON AND CHRIST with chorus	30 "	Manuscript	1932
TO A NEW WORLD full orchestra	15 "	Manuscript	1932
THREE SHADOWS	10 "	J. & W. Chester	1935
PUEBLO, A MOON RHAPSODY	17 "	Manuscript	1936
STILLED PAGEANT	8 "	Maurice Sénart	1937
THE VOW—concerto piano, orchestra	15 "	Manuscript	1943
EAST AND WEST—suite violin, orchestra	18 "	Manuscript	1943

LAZARE SAMINSKY (*Continued*)

CHAMBER ORCHESTRA

	DURATION	PUBLISHER	DATE
LITANIES OF WOMEN *mezzo soprano, 10 instruments*	10 minutes	Maurice Sénart	1925
VENICE *10 instruments*	4 "	Maurice Sénart	1927
EON HOURS *4 voices, 4 instruments*	14 "	Manuscript	1935
SONGS OF THREE QUEENS *soprano solo, chamber orchestra*	10 "	Carl Fischer, Inc.	1936
CHASSIDIC SUITE *violin or cello, small orchestra*	10 "	Carl Fischer, Inc.	1937
RYE SEPTET *with voice*	12 "	Manuscript	1942

CHORAL WORKS

BY THE RIVERS OF BABYLON—PSALM 137 *soprano, baritone, mixed chorus,* *four instruments*	6 minutes	Carl Fischer, Inc.	1926
PSALM 93 *solo soprano, chorus, clarinet, piano,* *1 percussion*	6 "	Manuscript	1933
NEWFOUNDLAND AIR *chorus, piano*	5 "	C. C. Birchard & Co.	1935
REQUIEM *soli, chorus, orchestra*	20 "	Manuscript	1945

CHAMBER MUSIC

VISION; CONTE; DANCE *piano*	12 minutes	Maurice Sénart	1919
SIX SONGS OF THE RUSSIAN ORIENT *piano or small orchestra* *accompaniment*	20 "	Universal Edition	1927
CHASSIDIC SUITE *violin or cello solo, piano or harp*	10 "	Carl Fischer, Inc.	1937

STAGE WORKS

THE VISION OF ARIEL—opera ballet, one act *symphony orchestra*	30 minutes	Manuscript	1915
LAMENT OF RACHEL—one act ballet *small chorus, symphony orchestra*	30 "	Maurice Sénart *piano score for sale*	1920
THE PLAGUE'S GALLIARD—opera ballet	30 "	Maurice Sénart *piano score for sale*	1924
JEPHTHA'S DAUGHTER—opera ballet, one act *symphony orchestra*	50 "	Maurice Sénart *piano score for sale*	1928
JULIAN THE APOSTATE CAESAR— opera in 3 acts *symphony orchestra*		Manuscript	1933–38
PUEBLO—ballet *symphonic orchestra*		Manuscript	1936

ROBERT L. SANDERS

Born in Chicago, Illinois, in 1906. He studied at Bush Conservatory, Chicago. Later he went to Rome to study with Respighi, Bustini and Dobici. In Paris, De Lioncourt and Brand were his teachers. He received a fellowship of the American Academy in Rome.

ROBERT L. SANDERS (*Continued*)

He was Assistant Conductor of the Chicago Civic Orchestra from 1933 to 1936, and Conductor of the Chicago Conservatory Symphony Orchestra. While an instructor at Meadville Theological School and the University of Chicago, he taught counterpoint. He is an organist and a choirmaster and also lectures on hymnology and liturgical music. He was joint-editor of the *Unitarian Hymnal.* Since 1938 he has been Dean of the School of Music of Indiana University.

His compositions have been performed by the Orchestra dell'Augusteo, by several other musical societies in Rome and by leading orchestras in the United States. The Symphony for Concert Band was premiered in 1944 by the Goldman Band. The first performance of the Violin Concerto took place at Rochester in 1945. The ballet, "L'Agiya," was first performed in concert version at the Hollywood Bowl, and during the 1944-45 season it formed part of Martha Graham's "Tropical Review." The New York St. Cecilia Society commissioned him to write a cantata to be performed next season.

COMPOSITIONS

ORCHESTRAL WORKS	DURATION	PUBLISHER	DATE
Two Songs	10 minutes	Manuscript	1926
lyric soprano, orchestra			
Suite for Large Orchestra	20 "	Manuscript	1928
pianoforte obbligato			
Saturday Night	5 "	Carl Fischer, Inc.	1933
Concerto in A minor	23 "	Manuscript	1935
violin, orchestra			
Scenes of Poverty and Toil	22 "	Manuscript	1935
Little Symphony in G major	15 "	Manuscript	1937
BAND MUSIC			
Symphony in B flat (3 movements)	22 minutes	Manuscript *for hire*	1943
CHORAL WORKS			
Psalm XXIII	7 minutes	Manuscript	1928
mixed chorus, a cappella			
Recessional	5 "	H. W. Gray Co., Inc.	1933
mixed chorus, organ			
Chanson of the Bells of Oseney	7 "	Carl Fischer, Inc.	1938
7 part mixed chorus, a cappella			
The Mystic Trumpeter (Whitman)	30 "	Manuscript	1941
baritone solo, reader, mixed chorus, orchestra			
An American Psalm—cantata	15 "	Manuscript	1945
women's voices, small ensemble, or organ			
CHAMBER MUSIC			
Trio in C sharp minor	25 minutes	Manuscript	1926
piano, violin, cello			
Sonata in C major	22 "	Manuscript	1928
piano, violin			
Quartet in A minor	32 "	Manuscript	1929
2 violins, viola, cello			
Sonata in G minor (in one movement)	12 "	Manuscript	1932
cello, piano			
Quintet in B for Brass Instruments	14 "	Carl Fischer, Inc.	1942

ROBERT L. SANDERS (*Continued*)

CHAMBER MUSIC (*Continued*)	DURATION	PUBLISHER	DATE
TWELVE TWO-PART INVENTIONS *piano solo*	15 minutes	Manuscript	1943
MOVEMENT FOR WOODWINDS (untitled) *flute, oboe, clarinet, bassoon*	10 "	Manuscript	1943
SONATA IN FOUR MOVEMENTS, E FLAT *trombone, piano*	18 "	Manuscript	1945

STAGE WORKS

L'AGIYA—ballet *full orchestra (also arranged* *for theatre orchestra)*	21 minutes	Manuscript	1944

PEDRO SANJUAN

Born in San Sebastian, Spain, in 1887. He studied at the Madrid Conservatory and at the Schola Cantorum in Paris.

He visited the United States for the first time in 1929. In 1934 he received the National Music Prize of Spain for his "Liturgia Negra." He appeared as conductor-composer at the International Congress of Music in Barcelona in April, 1936. After spending several years in Cuba, where he founded the Havana Philharmonic Orchestra, he settled in the United States in 1941 and has made his home in California. He has appeared as guest conductor with the Symphony and Philharmonic orchestras of Madrid, the Casals Orchestra of Barcelona, the Société des Concerts in Paris, the Symphony Orchestra of Mexico, the Los Angeles Philharmonic, Hollywood Bowl and with "New Music" of San Francisco. He gave lecture-recitals at the Lyceum Français of Madrid, the Lyceum of Havana, the Cuban-Spanish Institution for Culture and the University of Southern California.

His "Sones de Castilla" was given at the I.S.C.M. Festival in Berkeley in 1942. Other works have been performed in Spain, France, Germany, Austria, Hungary, Russia, Switzerland, Portugal, the United States, Mexico, Cuba and Brazil.

COMPOSITIONS WRITTEN IN AMERICA

ORCHESTRAL WORKS	DURATION	PUBLISHER	DATE
CHANGÓ—from the Negro liturgy	8 minutes	Associated Music Publishers	1929
RITUAL DANCE	7 "	Associated Music Publishers	1942
CONCERTO IN G MAJOR *piano, orchestra*	25 "	Manuscript	1942
DESERT CARAVAN	5 "	American Composers Alliance *for hire*	1944
LA MACUMBA	6 "	Boosey & Hawkes *for hire*	1945
FIRST SYMPHONY	30 "	Manuscript	1945

PEDRO SANJUAN (*Continued*)

BAND MUSIC	DURATION	PUBLISHER	DATE
YORUBA SONG	7 minutes	Leeds Music Corp.	1943
CARIBBEAN SKETCH	9 "	Leeds Music Corp.	1944
ANTILLEAN POEM	12 "	Leeds Music Corp.	1944

CHORAL WORKS			
ERA DE NOGAL (The Walnut Shell) *mixed chorus, a cappella*	3 minutes	Associated Music Publishers	1941

ON THE HILL DIED CHRIST THE
  SAVIOR
  women's chorus, a cappella
	5 "	Associated Music
		Publishers
			1942

RITUAL *mixed chorus, a cappella*	4 "	Leeds Music Corp.	1945

CHAMBER MUSIC			

INVOCATION TO OGGUN—from
  the Negro liturgy
  voice, piano or orchestra
	5 minutes	Associated Music
		Publishers
			1941

ALLEN DWIGHT SAPP

Born in Philadelphia, Pennsylvania, in 1922. He studied theory with Happich and piano with Robert Ellmore. He graduated from Haverford School and from Harvard College, where he studied with Walter Piston and received a magna cum laude at graduation. While an undergraduate, he won the New York Philharmonic Society Competition for his Andante for Orchestra, which was also performed. He was awarded the Paine Travelling Fellowship and studied with Aaron Copland and Nadia Boulanger. In 1942, he won the Knight Prize for the Sonata for Violin and Piano.

He entered the U. S. Army in 1943, and, while overseas with the Signal Corps, he wrote several chamber-music compositions. His works were performed in London, Paris, Belgium, Luxembourg and in Munich, where he was stationed. The League of Composers and the Harvard Music Club performed his Violin Sonata. The Concertino for Piano and Small Orchestra, commissioned in 1942 for the Town Hall Award, was broadcast over Radio Diffusion Française in Paris and over the BBC in London. It has also been recorded by Radio Diffusion Française. The Andante for Orchestra and Violin Sonata have been recorded by the Carnegie Recording Company. He is now completing a symphony.

COMPOSITIONS

ORCHESTRAL WORKS	DURATION	PUBLISHER	DATE
ANDANTE	10 minutes	Manuscript	1941
CONCERTINO *piano*	15 "	Manuscript	1942

CHAMBER MUSIC			
SONATA *violin, piano*	15 minutes	Manuscript	1942
SONATINA FOR PIANO	14 "	Manuscript	1946
SONATA FOR PIANO—four hands	13 "	Manuscript	1946

ERNEST SCHELLING

Born in Belvedere, New Jersey, in 1876 and died in 1939. He made his first public appearance at the Philadelphia Academy of Music at the age of four and was hailed at once as a musical prodigy. Two years later he went to Paris to study with Mathias. Among his other teachers were Moszkowski, Huber, Leschetizky and Barth; in his later years he worked with Paderewski.

He began touring in America and in Europe, giving recitals and making appearances with the major orchestras very early in his career, which, however, was interrupted by the war. He entered the war college, taking intensive training at the officers' camp and later was detailed to France. At the close of the war he had been promoted to the rank of Major in the army. He then proceeded to organize the children's and junior orchestral concerts with the New York Philharmonic Orchestra, which he conducted for many years. He was also guest conductor of many of the orchestras in the United States and in Europe and Conductor of the Baltimore Symphony Orchestra.

"Impressions from an Artist's Life," the Concerto for Violin and Piano and "A Victory Ball" (to the text of Noyes' poem and written as a satire against war following World War I) have been presented many times with the orchestras in the United States as well as in Europe. "Morocco," based on impressions which he received during a trip through the desert, has been heard in New York, Philadelphia and Chicago. "A Victory Ball" has been recorded by Victor and Nocturne, by Gramophone.

COMPOSITIONS

ORCHESTRAL WORKS	DURATION	PUBLISHER	DATE
IMPRESSIONS FROM AN ARTIST'S LIFE *piano*	40 minutes	F. E. C. Leuckart, Leipzig Carl Fischer, Inc.	1915
CONCERTO FOR VIOLIN AND PIANO	20 "	F. E. C. Leuckart, Leipzig Carl Fischer, Inc.	1916
A VICTORY BALL	13 "	F. E. C. Leuckart, Leipzig Carl Fischer, Inc.	1923
MOROCCO—symphonic tableau	22 "	Carl Fischer, Inc.	1927

CHAMBER MUSIC			
DIVERTIMENTO FOR STRINGS WITH PIANO OBBLIGATO	30 minutes	F. E. C. Leuckart, Leipzig Carl Fischer, Inc.	1925
SONATA FOR VIOLIN AND PIANO			

JOSEPH SCHILLINGER

Born in Kharkov, Russia, in 1895 and died in 1943. He graduated in 1918 from the St. Petersburg Imperial Conservatory of Music, where he studied composition and conducting. He directed the United Students Symphony Orchestra in Kharkov from 1918 to 1920 and the Ukraine Symphony Orchestra from 1920 to 1921. In Leningrad from 1925 to 1928 he was one of the composers for the State Academic Theatre of Drama. He was also at the State Institute of History of Arts from 1926 to 1928. For four years, from 1918 to 1922, he directed the Music Department of the Ukraine Board of Education and he was also consultant in the Music Department of the Moscow and Leningrad boards of education. From 1926 to 1928 he was Vice-President of the International Society for Modern Music at Leningrad. In the Ukraine he was Dean at the State Academy of Music, and Professor at the State Institute of Musical Education and the State Music Technicum.

He lectured at the New School for Social Research, New York University, the American Institute of the City of New York and at other educational institutions. At Teachers' College of Columbia University, he taught fine arts, music and mathematics.

His major books include the *Mathematical Basis of the Arts* and the *Schillinger System of Musical Composition*. The latter was published in 1946.

The Russian Government commissioned him to write a Symphonic Rhapsody to celebrate the first decade of the U.S.S.R. in Moscow. This work was later played in Leningrad and in Philadelphia. His orchestral and chamber works have been heard in Leningrad and Koenigsberg, also in New York City, Cleveland and other cities in the United States. Many of his works have been broadcast in Europe and in America.

COMPOSITIONS

ORCHESTRAL WORKS	DURATION	PUBLISHER	DATE
MARCH OF THE ORIENT	4 minutes	Manuscript for hire	1921
SYMPHONIC RHAPSODY *piano solo*	20 "	Manuscript for hire	1927
FIRST AIRPHONIC SUITE *solo Ether-Wave Theremin*	8 "	Manuscript for hire	1929
NORTH RUSSIAN SYMPHONY *accordion*	11 "	Manuscript for hire	1931

CHAMBER MUSIC			
SONATA FOR VIOLIN AND PIANO	15 minutes	Manuscript	1922
EXCENTRIADE—suite *piano*	8 "	Published	1924

STAGE WORKS			
MERRY GHOST (Japanese Suite) *2 male voices, 5 instruments*	15 minutes	Manuscript for hire	1926
MUSIC TO "PROFITABLE JOB" *10 instruments*	40 "	Manuscript	1926
THE PEOPLE AND THE PROPHET—ballet *piano*	35 "	Manuscript	1931

IRVING SCHLEIN

Born in New York City in 1905. He graduated from the Brooklyn College of Pharmacy, the Institute of Musical Art and the New York College of Music. He also studied at City College and the Columbia University School of Music. Later he worked with Copland, Riegger, Sessions and Harris in composition.

The Second Symphony (one movement) was first performed over NBC. The New School for Social Research presented "The Aristocrats." His chamber music has had performances in New York and on tour. Decca has recorded his arrangements of Hebrew folk songs.

COMPOSITIONS

ORCHESTRAL WORKS	DURATION	PUBLISHER	DATE
SYMPHONY NO. 2 THROUGH No. 11	20 to 45 minutes	Manuscript	1936–43
SINFONIA BREVIS *for school orchestra*	20 "	Manuscript	1938
CONCERTINO FOR PIANO AND ORCHESTRA	20 "	Manuscript	1942
EPIC OF DEMOCRACY (Whitman's poem) *chorus, baritone, orchestra*	20 "	Manuscript	1942
ODE TO VICTORY	40 "	Manuscript	1943
AMERICAN OVERTURE	18 "	Manuscript	1944
GIVE ME THE SPLENDID SILENT SUN *narrator, orchestra*	23 "	Manuscript	1945

CHAMBER MUSIC			
THREE PIECES FOR WOODWIND QUARTET	4 minutes	Manuscript	1940
CONCERTINO FOR BASSOON AND STRING QUARTET	20 "	Manuscript	1942
SONATA FOR OBOE AND PIANO	10 "	Manuscript	1942
AMERICA—suite *piano*	10 "	Manuscript	1943

BAND MUSIC			
SYMPHONY NO. 8	30 minutes	Manuscript	1943
SUMMER PIECE	7 "	Manuscript	1945
FESTIVE OVERTURE	8 "	Am-Russ	1946
SONATINA FOR BAND	10 "	Manuscript	1946

STAGE WORKS			
THE ARISTOCRATS—incidental music *chorus, solos, 2 pianos*	3 hours		1946

FILM MUSIC	STUDIO		
THE ENCHANTED FIDDLE (cartoon)	Film Highlights		1945

Works for chamber orchestra and choral works not listed here.

ARTUR SCHNABEL

Born in Lipnik, Austria, in 1882. He studied in Vienna. He lived in Germany, Italy and England until 1938 and then came to the United States, where he now lives.

In Europe, he wrote a Piano Concerto and a work for voice and orchestra which were performed in Berlin, Four String Quartets, a Quintet for Piano and Strings, and many smaller chamber works which were played in Germany, Italy, Holland, Austria and in England. His Symphony No. 1 was first performed by the Minneapolis Symphony Orchestra in 1946. Many of his chamber music works have been played in New York and in other cities. He has toured all over the world as a pianist.

COMPOSITIONS WRITTEN IN AMERICA

ORCHESTRAL WORKS	PUBLISHER	DATE
FIRST SYMPHONY	Edition Adler, Inc.	1939
SECOND SYMPHONY	Manuscript	1941–43
RHAPSODY FOR ORCHESTRA	Manuscript	1946
CHORAL WORKS		
TWO PIECES FOR MIXED CHORUS AND ORCHESTRA	Manuscript	1944
CHAMBER MUSIC		
FIFTH STRING QUARTET	Manuscript	1940
TRIO FOR PIANO, VIOLIN AND CELLO	Manuscript	1945

ARNOLD SCHOENBERG

Born in Vienna, Austria, in 1874. He began to study the violin at eight, and while still in school he composed duets and trios for string instruments. For several years he studied music by himself, teaching himself the cello and playing with amateur groups, for which he composed several string quartets. When he was twenty he studied counterpoint with Zemlinsky for several months.

He moved to Berlin in 1901 and, for a short time, he was Conductor at Wolzogen's Buntes Theatre. In 1902 he obtained the Liszt Stipendium and a position as teacher at the Stern Conservatory. He returned to Vienna in the summer of 1903 and began to teach classes in harmony and composition at the Schwarzwald-Schule; he also taught privately. In 1904 he helped to organize the Vereinigung Schaffender Tonkünstler, and this society gave the first performance of his symphonic poem "Pelleas and Melisande." In 1910 he was appointed teacher of composition at the Imperial Academy for Music, and in the following year he completed his *Harmonielehre*. In that year he also gave ten lectures on composition at the Stern Conservatory, Berlin. During that and the following three years he appeared as conductor of his own works in Amsterdam, St. Petersburg

ARNOLD SCHOENBERG (*Continued*)

and London. From 1918 to 1920 he lived in Mödling, near Vienna, where he conducted his Seminar for Composition and founded the Society for Private Musical Performances, with which he gave many concerts of modern music. In 1920-21 he lectured on theory in Amsterdam and conducted ten concerts of his own works in Holland. In 1925 he was made an honorary member of the Santa Cecilia Academy in Rome. In the same year he succeeded Busoni as Professor of a master class at the Prussian Academy of Arts in Berlin. He resigned from that position in 1933, went first to Paris and, in October of that year, came to the United States. He was welcomed by concerts of his works given by the League of Composers, New York, the Library of Congress and other organizations. He became a teacher at the Malkin Conservatory in Boston. In 1935 he was appointed Professor of Music at the University of Southern California, and in 1936 he accepted a similar position at the University of California in Los Angeles, where he is now living. He has also been active as a painter, and he wrote the librettos of two of his operas, "Die glückliche Hand" and "Moses and Aaron," as well as the words to some of his other vocal works. Theme and Variations for Band was written for and first presented by the Goldman Band.

His works have been widely performed in Europe and the United States. "Verklärte Nacht" has been recorded by Victor and "Pierrot Lunaire" by Columbia.

COMPOSITIONS WRITTEN IN AMERICA

	PUBLISHER	DATE
ORCHESTRAL WORKS		
CONCERTO FOR STRING QUARTET AND ORCHESTRA	G. Schirmer, Inc. *for hire*	1933
SUITE FOR STRING ORCHESTRA	G. Schirmer, Inc. *for hire*	1934
CONCERTO FOR VIOLIN AND ORCHESTRA, OPUS 36	G. Schirmer, Inc. *for hire* *piano score for sale*	1936
CONCERTO FOR PIANO AND ORCHESTRA, OPUS 42	G. Schirmer, Inc. *for hire* *piano score for sale*	1942
ODE TO NAPOLEON BUONAPARTE *reciter, string quartet, or string orchestra and piano*	G. Schirmer, Inc.	1943
THEME AND VARIATIONS FOR ORCHESTRA, OPUS 43B	G. Schirmer, Inc. *for hire*	1943
BAND MUSIC		
THEME AND VARIATIONS FOR BAND, OPUS 43	G. Schirmer, Inc.	1943
CHAMBER MUSIC		
FOURTH STRING QUARTET, OPUS 37	G. Schirmer, Inc.	1939

WILLIAM HOWARD SCHUMAN

Born in New York City in 1910. He attended the public schools and Columbia University, receiving his degree of Bachelor of Science in 1935 and his Master of Arts degree in 1937. He was a pupil of Persin, Haubiel and Harris. In the summer of 1935 he attended the Mozarteum Academy in Salzburg. He received a Guggenheim Fellowship in 1939-40, which was renewed the following year.

While in high school he organized his own jazz band, and soon after graduation he began to compose popular songs. It was not until he was nineteen that he showed an interest in symphonic music, and even then for a while he still continued to write and arrange popular music. He is today particularly interested in progressive education in relation to problems of art. During the summer of 1936 he was a member of the faculty of Columbia University. In the fall of 1935 he joined the music faculty of Sarah Lawrence College and became conductor of the college chorus in 1938. He succeeded the late Carl Engel as editor at G. Schirmer, Inc., and is serving as a member of their advisory board. He was appointed President of the Juilliard School of Music in 1945. He won the first Award of the Critics' Circle of New York for his Symphony No. III in 1942, the first Pulitzer Music Prize for "A Free Song" in 1943 and the Koussevitzky Music Foundation Award. He received a grant-in-aid from the Metropolitan Opera and, recently, the Composition Award of the American Academy of Arts and Letters. He won citations from the Encyclopedia Britannica and the National Association of Composers and Conductors in 1942. He was elected a Fellow of the American Academy of Arts and Letters.

The Town Hall and the League of Composers commissioned him to write a string quartet in 1939. His works have had frequent performances by all major orchestras and by choral and chamber-music groups in the United States, South America and Europe. His ballet "Undertow" was first performed by the Ballet Theatre at the Metropolitan Opera House, New York, in 1945. The Boston Symphony Orchestra gave the first performances of his "American Festival Overture," the Symphony No. III, the Symphony for Strings and "A Free Song." "Prayer in Time of War" was first presented by the Pittsburgh Symphony Orchestra, and the "William Billings Overture" by the New York Philharmonic Symphony Orchestra. His Quartettino for Four Bassoons has been recorded by N.M.Q.R., the "American Festival Overture" by Victor and the Symphony for Strings and the String Quartet No. III by Concert Hall Society, Inc. At present he is completing a Concerto for Violin and Orchestra which was commissioned by Samuel Dushkin.

COMPOSITIONS

ORCHESTRAL WORKS	* DURATION	PUBLISHER	DATE
PRELUDE AND FUGUE †	15 minutes	Manuscript	1937
SYMPHONY No. 2 †		Manuscript	1937
AMERICAN FESTIVAL OVERTURE	9 "	G. Schirmer, Inc.	1939
SYMPHONY No. 3	28 "	G. Schirmer, Inc.	1941
SYMPHONY No. 4	24 "	G. Schirmer, Inc.	1941

WILLIAM HOWARD SCHUMAN (*Continued*)

ORCHESTRAL WORKS (*Continued*)	DURATION	PUBLISHER	DATE
PRAYER IN TIME OF WAR	16 minutes	G. Schirmer, Inc.	1943
WILLIAM BILLINGS OVERTURE	8 "	G. Schirmer, Inc.	1943
SYMPHONY FOR STRINGS	17 "	G. Schirmer, Inc.	1943
SIDE SHOW FOR ORCHESTRA	7 "	G. Schirmer, Inc.	1944
CONCERTO FOR VIOLIN AND ORCHESTRA	24 "	G. Schirmer, Inc.	1946

CHAMBER ORCHESTRA

SYMPHONY No. 1 †	30 minutes	Manuscript	1935
18 instruments			
CONCERTO FOR PIANO AND SMALL ORCHESTRA	20 "	G. Schirmer, Inc.	1942

BAND MUSIC

NEWSREEL IN FIVE SHOTS	8 minutes	G. Schirmer, Inc.	1941
also arranged for orchestra			

CHORAL WORKS

FOUR CANONIC CHORUSES FOR MIXED VOICES	8 minutes	G. Schirmer, Inc.	1933
a cappella			
PIONEERS!	8 "	J. & W. Chester	1937
CHORAL ETUDE	4 "	Carl Fischer, Inc.	1937
mixed chorus, a cappella			
PROLOGUE	7 "	G. Schirmer, Inc.	1939
mixed chorus, orchestra			
PRELUDE	8 "	G. Schirmer, Inc.	1939
women's chorus, a cappella			
THIS IS OUR TIME, SECULAR CANTATA No. 1	30 "	Boosey & Hawkes	1940
mixed chorus, orchestra			
REQUIESCAT	4 "	G. Schirmer, Inc.	1942
women's chorus, piano, or mixed chorus, piano			
HOLIDAY SONG	2 "	G. Schirmer, Inc.	1942
mixed chorus, piano			
A FREE SONG, SECULAR CANTATA No. 2	16 "	G. Schirmer, Inc.	1942
mixed chorus, orchestra			
MUSIC FOR "HENRY VIII"—TE DEUM CORONATION SCENE	2 "	G. Schirmer, Inc.	1944
mixed chorus			
TRUTH SHALL DELIVER—A BALLAD OF GOOD ADVICE		Manuscript	1946
3 part male chorus, a cappella			

CHAMBER MUSIC

CANON AND FUGUE †	8 minutes	Manuscript	1934
violin, cello, piano			
CHOREOGRAPHIC POEM †		Manuscript	1934
7 instruments			
STRING QUARTET No. 1 †		Manuscript	1936
STRING QUARTET No. 2	16 "	Arrow Music Press	1937
QUARTETTINO FOR FOUR BASSOONS	4 "	Boletin Latino-Americano de Musica	1939
STRING QUARTET No. 3	20 "	Boosey & Hawkes	1939
FUGUE FOR STRINGS		Manuscript	1946

STAGE WORKS

UNDERTOW—ballet		G. Schirmer, Inc.	1945

FILM MUSIC

	STUDIO		
STEELTOWN	O.W.I.		1944

* All timings are approximate.
† Withdrawn pending revision.

PAUL SCHWARTZ

Born in Vienna, Austria, in 1907. He received his Doctor of Philosophy degree in music from the University of Vienna in 1933 and graduated from the Vienna State Academy of Music in the same year. He also studied composition privately with Ernst Krenek.

He came to the United States in 1938 and since then has been head of the Music Department of Bard College, Annandale-on-Hudson, New York. He is a member of the Forum Group of I.S.C.M. and of the National Association of American Composers and Conductors.

His String Quartet was performed in Vienna in 1936 and 1937. The Serenade for String Orchestra was commissioned and performed by the Maverick String Ensemble in Woodstock, New York, in 1941. Two of his chamber-music works were broadcast over station WNYC as part of American Music Festivals in 1942 and 1945. Other performances of his works were given in Poughkeepsie, Chicago and Akron.

COMPOSITIONS WRITTEN IN AMERICA

ORCHESTRAL WORKS	DURATION	PUBLISHER	DATE
BAROQUE SUITE	15 minutes	Manuscript	1938
SERENADE FOR STRING ORCHESTRA	15 "	Manuscript	1941
CHORAL WORKS			
TWO MOTETS FOR MALE CHORUS	5 minutes	Manuscript	1940
TWO CHORUSES FOR WOMEN'S VOICES	5 "	Manuscript	1942
CHAMBER MUSIC			
PIANO TRIO	25 minutes	Manuscript	1939
VIOLIN SONATA	16 "	Manuscript	1941
CHAMBER CONCERTO FOR TWO PIANOS	12 "	Manuscript	1944

ROGER SESSIONS

Born in Brooklyn, New York, in 1896. He comes of New England ancestry. At the age of twelve he began to compose, and at the age of fourteen he entered Harvard University, where he studied music and later became editor of the *Harvard Musical Review,* for which he wrote various articles. After graduating from Harvard, he studied under Horatio Parker at Yale University and with Ernest Bloch in Cleveland and New York. In 1917 he joined the faculty of Smith College and taught music there until 1921, when he went to the Cleveland Institute of Music as head of the Theory Department. In 1924 he went to Europe and lived in Italy and Germany for eight years. He received the Guggenheim Fellowship for 1926–27 and was awarded a two-year fellowship at the American Academy in Rome in 1928 and the Carnegie Fellowship for 1931–32. On his return to America in 1933 he taught composition in various educational institutions in Boston and New York. He became Assistant Professor of Music at Princeton Uni-

ROGER SESSIONS *(Continued)*

versity and now holds the post of Professor of Music at the University of California.

He received the Ditson Fund Commission (Columbia University) for a symphony to be performed over the radio, a commission from the Elizabeth Coolidge Foundation (Library of Congress) for a string quartet, which received its first performance at the Coolidge Festival in Washington in 1937. He received a commission from the League of Composers for a symphonic work and a commission for a duo for violin and piano from Irene Jacobi which was performed in 1942. He was commissioned to write music for "The Black Maskers" (Andreyev) for a Smith College production, and this work was later arranged for a Suite for a large orchestra. In coöperation with Aaron Copland, he organized the Copland-Sessions Concerts. He has served as President of the United States Section of the I.S.C.M. and as a member of the League of Composers' Executive Board.

The Suite from "The Black Maskers," the Symphony No. 1 and many of his compositions for chamber music have had performances in many cities in the United States as well as in London and Berlin and at the Geneva and Oxford festivals of the I.S.C.M., also at the festivals at Yaddo and Bad Homburg and the Pan American Festival in Mexico City. Works he has now in preparation are an opera, "Montezuma," Symphony No. 3, String Quartet No. 2, a Trio for Piano, Violin and Cello and "Music for Four Trombones and Tuba."

COMPOSITIONS

ORCHESTRAL WORKS

	DURATION	PUBLISHER	DATE
Suite from "The Black Maskers"	22 minutes	Cos Cob Press	1928
Symphony No. 1	23 "	Cos Cob Press	
Concerto for Violin	29 "	Edgar Stillman Kelley Society	1935
Symphony No. 2	30 "	Manuscript	1946

CHORAL WORKS

"Turn O Libertad" *mixed chorus, piano four-hands*		Manuscript	1944

CHAMBER MUSIC

Sonata for Piano	16 minutes	Schott	1928
String Quartet No. 1	30 "	Manuscript	1936
Duo for Violin and Piano		Manuscript	1942
Piano Sonata No. 2, C Major	13 "	Manuscript	1946

STAGE WORKS

The Black Maskers (Andreyev)— incidental music *30 instruments*	2 hours	Manuscript	1923

HAROLD SAMUEL SHAPERO

Born in Lynn, Massachusetts, in 1920. He studied with Boulanger, Hindemith, Krenek, Piston, Slominsky and Stravinsky. He is a graduate of Harvard University. He was awarded the Knight Prize, the Naumburg Fellowship and the Paine Fellowship from Harvard. He received the Prix de Rome in 1941 and also won the second annual Gershwin Contest. In 1946, he was given the Joseph Bearns Award from Columbia for his Symphony for Strings, and received a Guggenheim Fellowship.

The "Nine-Minute Overture," which won for him the Prix de Rome, was broadcast from coast to coast by the CBS Symphony Orchestra. The League of Composers presented his Four-Hand Piano Sonata and Sonata for Violin and Piano. Both of these works and the "Three Amateur Sonatas" were played over WNYC. At present, he is working on an orchestral composition commissioned by the Koussevitzky Music Foundation.

COMPOSITIONS

ORCHESTRAL WORKS	DURATION	PUBLISHER	DATE
NINE-MINUTE OVERTURE	9 minutes	Manuscript Fleisher Collection	1940
SERENADE IN D *string orchestra*	28 "	Manuscript	1945
SYMPHONY FOR CLASSICAL ORCHESTRA	40 "	Manuscript	1946

CHAMBER MUSIC			
THREE PIECES FOR THREE PIECES *flute, clarinet, bassoon*	13 minutes	Manuscript	1938
TRUMPET SONATA *trumpet, piano*	10 "	Manuscript	1939
STRING QUARTET	23 "	Manuscript	1940
FOUR-HAND PIANO SONATA *one piano*	15 "	Manuscript	1941
SONATA FOR VIOLIN AND PIANO	18 "	Manuscript	1942
THREE AMATEUR SONATAS *piano*	7,8,10 "	Manuscript	1944

ARTHUR SHEPHERD

Born in Paris, Idaho, in 1880. He graduated from the New England Conservatory of Music and studied piano with Dennee and Faelten, harmony with Cutter and counterpoint and composition with Goetschius and Chadwick. He received the Juilliard School Publication and the Society for Publication of American Music awards. He also won the first Paderewski Prize, and three prizes from the National Federation of Music Clubs were awarded to him.

He taught at the New England Conservatory of Music and also in Salt Lake City. He conducted the St. Cecilia Society in Boston. In 1917 he was Bandmaster of the United States Field Artillery in France. In 1920, as Assistant Conductor of the Cleveland Orchestra, he conducted the chil-

ARTHUR SHEPHERD (*Continued*)

dren's concerts and was program annotator. At Cleveland College he has lectured on music and is now Chairman of the Music Division of Western Reserve University. He was music critic for the *Cleveland Press*. In 1941 he was elected to the National Institute of Arts and Letters.

"Overture to a Drama," "Horizons," "Ouverture Joyeuse," "Choreographic Suite" and "Fantasy for Piano and Orchestra" have been heard with the symphonic orchestras in New York City, Cleveland, Boston, Philadelphia, Prague, Paris, Warsaw and other cities, as well as in South America. Many of his works have been broadcast by CBS and NBC over a coast-to-coast network. The League of Composers commissioned him to write a string quartet in the American Composers Series. He is now working on a "Fantasy on Down East Tunes for Orchestra."

COMPOSITIONS

ORCHESTRAL WORKS

	DURATION	PUBLISHER	DATE
THE FESTIVAL OF YOUTH—overture		Manuscript	1915
FANTASY FOR PIANO AND ORCHESTRA		Manuscript	1916
OVERTURE TO A DRAMA	17 minutes	C. C. Birchard & Co.	1919
HORIZONS—SYMPHONY NO. 1	41 "	C. C. Birchard & Co.	1927
CHOREOGRAPHIC SUITE	28 "	Manuscript	1931
SYMPHONY NO. 2 IN D	45 "	Manuscript	1938
FANTASIA CONCERTANTE	10 "	Manuscript	1943
HILARITAS—overture		Manuscript	
concert band			
CONCERTO FOR VIOLIN AND ORCHESTRA	15 "	Manuscript	1946

CHORAL WORKS

	DURATION	PUBLISHER	DATE
SONG OF THE SEA WIND		A. P. Schmidt	1915
women's voices, orchestra or piano			
HE CAME ALL SO STILL		A. P. Schmidt	1915
women's voices			
O JESU WHO ART GONE BEFORE—anthem		Boston Music Co.	1918
DECK THYSELF MY SOUL—response		Boston Music Co.	1918
mixed chorus, organ			
BALLAD OF TREES AND THE MASTER		C. C. Birchard & Co.	1935
mixed chorus, a cappella			
SONG OF THE PILGRIMS—cantata	28 minutes	C. C. Birchard & Co.	1937
mixed chorus, tenor solo, orchestra			
INVITATION TO THE DANCE	12 "	Manuscript	1937
(Sidonius Appolinaris)			
mixed chorus, pianoforte			
4 hands or orchestra			
GRACE FOR GARDENS		Arrow Press	1938
mixed chorus, a cappella			
BUILD THEE MORE STATELY MANSIONS		Manuscript	1938
women's voices			
PLANTING A TREE			
mixed chorus			
SLOWLY SILENTLY NOW THE MOON			
women's voices			
PSALM XLII		Manuscript	1944
chorus, orchestra			

CHAMBER MUSIC

	DURATION	PUBLISHER	DATE
TRIPTYCH	17 minutes	S.P.A.M.	1926
high voice, string quartet			

ARTHUR SHEPHERD (Continued)

CHAMBER MUSIC (Continued)	DURATION	PUBLISHER	DATE
SONATA FOR VIOLIN AND PIANO		Editions Maurice Sénart	1927
QUARTET FOR STRINGS, NO 1, G MINOR		Manuscript	1928
SONATA, NO. 2, F MINOR piano	14 minutes	Oxford University Press	1930
QUARTET FOR STRINGS, NO. 2, E MINOR		S.P.A.M.	1935
QUARTET FOR STRINGS, NO. 3, G MINOR		Manuscript	1936
QUINTET FOR PIANO AND STRINGS		J. Fischer & Bro.	1940
PRAELUDIUM FOR WIND AND STRING INSTRUMENTS flute, oboe, horn, bassoon, violin, viola, cello		Manuscript	1942
DIVERTISSEMENT FOR WIND ENSEMBLE flute, oboe, clarinet, bassoon, horn		Manuscript	1943

NATHANIEL SHILKRET

Born in New York City in 1895. At the age of twelve, he joined the Victor Herbert Orchestra. He received his Doctor of Music degree at Bethelny College, Kansas.

He has played with the Damrosch Orchestra, where he was assistant to Walter Damrosch, the New York Philharmonic, and also with Sousa, Pryor and Goldman. He was the music director and manager of Victor Recordings for twenty years. From 1926 to 1942, he conducted the Philadelphia Symphony Summer Concerts, and he has also conducted many radio programs. At present, he is an arranger of scores and conductor for Metro-Goldwyn-Mayer Studios.

His compositions, which have had many performances throughout the United States, include the "Concert for Trombone," "Ode to Victory" and "Serenade Rhapsodie for Guitar or Banjo." NBC broadcast the Quintet for Clarinet and Strings. RCA Victor recorded the "Bible Album—Genesis Suite," and is recording a "Bible Album No. 2," the Suite for Banjo and Orchestra and the "Concert Overture" for Warner Janssen.

COMPOSITIONS

ORCHESTRAL WORKS	DURATION	PUBLISHER	DATE
FOUR POEMS (Seasons) violin, orchestra		Manuscript	1924–38
SKYWARD—tone poem	8 minutes	Manuscript	1928
ODE TO VICTORY	6 "	Mills Music, Inc.	1942
CONCERTO FOR TROMBONE—3 movements	20 "	Manuscript	1942
SERENADE RHAPSODIE banjo, guitar or violin, orchestra		Manuscript	1942

CHORAL WORKS	DURATION	PUBLISHER	DATE
CREATION (Genesis Suite) narrator, without lyric, mixed choir, orchestra		Manuscript	1942
A SOPRANO'S DAY—song cycle in 4 movements voice, piano	10 minutes	Manuscript	1943

NATHANIEL SHILKRET *(Continued)*

CHAMBER MUSIC	DURATION	PUBLISHER	DATE
CLARINET QUINTET—4 movements *clarinet, strings*	26 minutes	Manuscript *3rd movement printed*	1936
CLARINET SEXTET *clarinet, piano, strings*	6 "	Manuscript	1938

STAGE WORKS

NEW YORK BALLET—12 movements *orchestra, ballet, voices*	40 minutes	Manuscript	1937

FILM MUSIC	STUDIO		
LILAC TIME (concert version—"I Dream of Lilac Time")	1st National ·	Feist	1928
WINTERSET (concert version—"Winterset")	RKO	I. Berlin	1936
MARY, QUEEN OF SCOTS	RKO	I. Berlin Manuscript	1936
THIS IS AMERICA	Pathe		1942
ODE TO VICTORY (concert version—"Ode to Victory")	MGM	Mills Music, Inc. *band arrangement printed*	1943
HOODLUM SAINT	MGM	Robbins—Manuscript	1945
ONE MAN'S NAVY (concert version—"Skyward")	MGM	Nathaniel Shilkret Music Co., Inc. *for hire*	1945
BOYS RANCH	MGM	Robbins—Manuscript	1946
FAITHFUL IN MY FASHION	MGM	Robbins—Manuscript	1946
TENTH AVENUE ANGEL	MGM	Robbins	1946

HARRINGTON SHORTALL

Born in Chicago, Illinois, in 1895. He was educated in the public and private schools of Chicago. He attended the Thacher School in Ojai, California, and received his Bachelor of Arts degree from Harvard University. During the first World War he was an ensign in the navy. He studied in Paris for one year with Boulanger. From 1940 to 1946 he taught theory at Rosary College in Illinois, and in 1946 he became a member of the faculty of the Chicago Theological Seminary.

His "Choral Memorial" won the Westminster Choir School Award in 1936 and was broadcast. Other compositions have been performed by string-quartet societies in the United States.

COMPOSITIONS

ORCHESTRAL WORKS	DURATION	PUBLISHER	DATE
SYMPHONIA BREVIS	13 minutes	Manuscript	1933
SYMPHONY ·		Manuscript	1937
SIX PIECES IN ONE	17 "	Manuscript	1944

CHAMBER ORCHESTRA

WREATH OF VARIATIONS FOR THOMAS JEFFERSON'S PROPOSED ORCHESTRA OF ARTISANS	12 minutes	Manuscript	1942

CHORAL WORKS

CHORAL MEMORIAL *mixed chorus, a cappella*	11 minutes	Manuscript	1935

HARRINGTON SHORTALL (*Continued*)

CHORAL WORKS (*Continued*)	DURATION	PUBLISHER	DATE
A Ballet Cantata—for children	10 minutes	Manuscript	1939
with piano or small orchestra			
Romans XIII	8 "	Manuscript	1940
with small orchestra			
Hymn for Uncle Sam's Nephews			
AND Nieces	5 "	Manuscript	1943
double chorus, piano or small			
orchestra			

CHAMBER MUSIC			
Song Cycle	20 minutes	Manuscript	1930
mezzo-soprano, 2 violins, cello, viola			
Opus for String Quartet	27 "	Manuscript	1931
Fantasia for String Quartet	12 "	Manuscript	1936
Ten-Minute Trio	10 "	Manuscript	1937
violin, viola, cello			
One Song from Three Poets	6 "	Manuscript	1944
mezzo-soprano, string quartet			

ELIE SIEGMEISTER

Born in New York City in 1909. He studied piano with Friedberger, harmony, counterpoint and composition with Bingham, Riegger and Boulanger, and conducting with Stoessel. He received his Bachelor of Arts degree from Columbia College. He was awarded a Juilliard Graduate School Fellowship in 1935–38.

He taught in Brooklyn College and at the New School of Social Research. He conducted the Manhattan Chorus and organized the American Ballad Singers. He was one of the founders of the American Composers Alliance. In 1945, he was an expert consultant for the U. S. Army Soldier Shows program. He was Musical Director and Conductor of the Theater Guild production, "Sing Out Sweet Land." He is especially interested in native American themes. The books that he has written include *A Treasury of American Song* (with Olin Downes), *Music Lover's Handbook* and *Work and Sing*. He conducted the music for the films "People of the Cumberland" and "Mr. Flagmaker."

The symphonic orchestras of Detroit, Philadelphia, Minneapolis and Rochester and also the NBC Symphony and Eastman Symphony have performed many of his compositions, including the "Western Suite," "Wilderness Road," "Ozark Set" and the "Walt Whitman Overture."

His recorded works include "American Folk Songs" (Victor), "Funnybone Alley" (Asch), "Ozark Set" (Columbia), "Sing Out Sweet Land" (Decca), "Songs of Early America" (Bost) and "Strange Funeral in Braddock" (New Music). He is preparing a musical folk tale, "A Tooth for Paul Revere," based on the Stephen Vincent Benét story.

COMPOSITIONS

ORCHESTRAL WORKS	DURATION	PUBLISHER	DATE
May Day	11 minutes	Manuscript	1933
Strange Funeral in Braddock	8 "	Manuscript	1933
solo voice, orchestra			

ELIE SIEGMEISTER (*Continued*)

ORCHESTRAL WORKS (*Continued*)	DURATION	PUBLISHER	DATE
AMERICAN HOLIDAY	10 minutes	American Music Center *for hire*	1933
RHAPSODY FOR ORCHESTRA	12 "	Associated Music Publishers *for hire*	1937
A WALT WHITMAN OVERTURE	10 "	Associated Music Publishers *for hire*	1939
OZARK SET	16 "	E. B. Marks	1943
WESTERN SUITE	20 "	Leeds Music Corp.	1945
WILDERNESS ROAD	5 "	Leeds Music Corp.	1945
PRAIRIE LEGEND	10 "	Leeds Music Corp. *for hire*	1945

CHAMBER ORCHESTRA

AMERICAN HOLIDAY *22 instruments*	10 minutes	American Music Center	1933
MAY DAY *24 instruments*	11 "	Manuscript	1933
DANCE TRILOGY *7 instruments*	15 "	Manuscript	1937

BAND MUSIC

PRAIRIE LEGEND *symphonic band*	10 minutes	Leeds Music Corp.	1945
WILDERNESS ROAD	5 "	Leeds Music Corp.	1945

CHORAL WORKS

JOHN HENRY	4 minutes	Carl Fischer, Inc.	1936
ABRAHAM LINCOLN WALKS AT MIDNIGHT *with orchestra*	8 "	Arrow Music Co.	1937
CHILDREN'S GAMES *mixed chorus, a cappella*	3 "	Manuscript	1940
EIGHT AMERICAN FOLKSONGS *mixed chorus, a cappella*	2–3 " each	Carl Fischer, Inc.	1940
NANCY HANKS *mixed chorus, piano*	3 "	Manuscript	1941
ANNE RUTLEDGE *mixed chorus, piano*	3 "	Manuscript	1941
PAUL BUNYAN *men's voices, piano*	2 "	Manuscript	1941
A NEW WIND A-BLOWIN'	3 "	Musette	1942
FREEDOM TRAIN *men's voices, piano*	2 "	Manuscript	1943

CHAMBER MUSIC

SONATA FOR VIOLIN AND PIANO	18 minutes	Manuscript	1931
WOODWIND QUINTET	10 "	Manuscript	1932
STRING QUARTET	20 "	Manuscript	1936
FUNNYBONE ALLEY—song cycle, 14 songs		Leeds Music Corp.	1941
AMERICAN SONATA FOR PIANO	17 "	E. B. Marks	1944

STAGE WORKS

CREATED EQUAL	2 hours	Manuscript	1938
MAID IN JAPAN	2 "	Manuscript	1938
DOODLE DANDY OF THE U.S.A.	2 "	Musette *album*	1942
THE GOLDEN DOORS—pageant	1 hour	Manuscript	1943
SING OUT SWEET LAND	2½ hours	Northern Music Co. *album*	1944

CHARLES SANFORD SKILTON

Born in Northampton, Massachusetts, in 1868 and died in 1941. His only early musical training was in the public schools, but his sister's piano teacher and her playing were a stimulus throughout his youth. Although he had no early instruction in music, during his junior year at college he wrote his first serious work to the poem "The Burial of Moses."

In 1889 he graduated from Yale University with literary honors and that year composed the Choral Odes to the performance of *Electra* given in Greek by Smith College. He went to Germany in 1891 and studied with Bargiel, Boise and Heintz. In 1893 he returned to America and became Director of Music at Salem College, Winston, where he stayed for three years. He won first prize for a women's chorus and a song at the Kansas Federation of Music Clubs, also for a violin sonata. From 1897 to 1903 he was Director of Music at the State Normal School in Trenton, New Jersey. Following this he was appointed to the position of Professor of Music at the State University in Lawrence, Kansas; he also served as Dean of the School of Fine Arts. As Haskell Institute, the Government Indian School, was near the university he became interested in their tribal melodies, which he developed into orchestral suites, operas and short instrumental pieces. He became an authority on American Indian music.

These compositions have been widely played in foreign countries as well as in America and broadcast by the NBC, Columbia, and the Ford Hour. Among the orchestras which have performed his works are the New York Philharmonic, the Los Angeles, the National Symphony and Kansas City. Many of his choral and chamber works have been played frequently. He has had works recorded by the Columbia, Victor and Edison companies and by Pathé Frères.

COMPOSITIONS

ORCHESTRAL WORKS

	DURATION	PUBLISHER	DATE
TWO INDIAN DANCES—DEER DANCE, WAR DANCE	8 minutes	Carl Fischer, Inc.	1915
SUITE PRIMEVAL	20 "	Carl Fischer, Inc.	1920
AMERICAN INDIAN FANTASIE		Manuscript	1932
cello			
OVERTURE IN E MAJOR	8 "	Manuscript	1934
cello			
GIGUE FOR STRINGED ORCHESTRA			
SUITE IN E MINOR			
FUGUE FOR FULL ORCHESTRA			

CHAMBER ORCHESTRA

TWO INDIAN DANCES	8 minutes	Carl Fischer, Inc.	1915
10 instruments			
SIOUX FLUTE SERENADE	4 "	Carl Fischer, Inc.	1920
EAST AND WEST—suite	15 "	Manuscript	1921

CHORAL WORKS

THE WITCH'S DAUGHTER—cantata	33 minutes	Carl Fischer, Inc.	1918
soprano, baritone, chorus with orchestra		vocal score	

CHORAL WORKS (*Continued*)

	DURATION	PUBLISHER	DATE
THE GUARDIAN ANGEL—oratorio *5 solo voices, chorus, children's* *chorus, organ and orchestra*	1½ hours	J. Fischer & Bro. *vocal score*	1925
SONG FOLIO—FROM FOREST AND STREAM *12 songs for treble voices, 3 parts*	30 minutes	Carl Fischer, Inc.	1930
MIDNIGHT *women's voices, 4 parts*	5 "	A. P. Schmidt Co.	
THE FOUNTAIN *women's voices, 4 parts*	4 "	A. P. Schmidt Co.	
TICONDEROGA—cantata *male chorus, orchestra*	40 "	Manuscript	1933

CHAMBER MUSIC

SONATINA FOR VIOLIN AND PIANO	15 minutes	Ogren & Uhe	1923
TWO INDIAN DANCES FOR STRING QUARTET	8 "	Published	
STRING QUARTET IN B MINOR			
SARABANDE FOR WIND INSTRUMENTS			

STAGE WORKS

MUSIC TO "ELECTRA" (Sophocles) *acting cast, women's chorus, chamber* *orchestra, 1 stage set*	2 hours	A. P. Schmidt Co.	1918
KALOPIN—Indian opera in 3 acts *two stage sets*	2½ "	Manuscript	1927
THE SUN BRIDE—Indian opera in 1 act *one stage set*	1¼ "	Manuscript	1930
MUSIC TO "MARY ROSE" (Barrie)	2½ "	Manuscript	1933
THE DAY OF GAYOMAIR—opera with prologue and two scenes *drop curtain, 2 stage sets*	2½ "	Manuscript	1936

NICOLAS SLONIMSKY

Born in Leningrad, Russia, in 1894. He began his piano studies at an early age and later studied at the St. Petersburg Conservatory. He came to the United States in 1923. From 1923 to 1925, he was on the faculty of the Eastman School of Music. He has conducted programs of American music in Paris, Berlin, Budapest, Havana and in many cities of this country. In 1941–42, he toured South America, giving lectures and concerts.

"The Prince Goes Hunting" was produced at the Eastman School of Music in 1925. He has written numerous songs and piano pieces that have been played often and many of them are published. His orchestral variations on a Brazilian folk song, "My Toy Balloon," has been performed by the Boston Pops Orchestra and has been presented in Buenos Aires, Bogota, Buffalo, Chicago and in other cities in the United States and in South America. He is the author of *Music Since 1900* (published in 1937), *Music of Latin America* (published in 1945), *The Road to Music* (published in 1946) and the *Thesaurus of Musical Scales and Melodic Patterns* (published in 1947).

NICOLAS SLONIMSKY (*Continued*)

COMPOSITIONS

ORCHESTRAL WORKS	DURATION	PUBLISHER	DATE
FOUR SIMPLE PIECES	7 minutes	Manuscript	1931
MY TOY BALLOON—variations on a Brazilian tune	6 "	Axelrod	1942

CHAMBER ORCHESTRA			
ORESTES (in the Greek enharmonic scale) *for strings, trumpet, suspended cymbal, tambourine, tam-tam*	4 minutes	Manuscript	1933
SUITE FOR WIND AND PERCUSSION INSTRUMENTS	8 "	Manuscript	1942

CHAMBER MUSIC			
STUDIES IN BLACK AND WHITE— suite for piano	15 minutes	New Music	1928
GRAVESTONES AT HANCOCK, N. H.— song cycle	10 "	Axelrod Publications	1946

STAGE WORKS			
THE PRINCE GOES HUNTING—ballet	20 minutes	Manuscript	1925

LEO SMIT

Born in Philadelphia, Pennsylvania, in 1921. He received a scholarship from the Curtis Institute of Music at the age of nine. He studied composition with Nicolas Nabokov. He made his debut as pianist in Carnegie Hall in 1939, and has concertized throughout the United States.

His works have been presented by the League of Composers and broadcast over WNYC in the American Music Festival. The Suite of Piano Pieces was played at Town Hall by the composer. He wrote the film music for "Garment Center" for the Office of War Information.

COMPOSITIONS

ORCHESTRAL WORKS	DURATION	PUBLISHER	DATE
JOAN OF ARC	22 minutes	Manuscript	1942
FIVE TRANSITIONS AND EPILOGUE	20 "	Manuscript	1945

CHAMBER ORCHESTRA			
HYMN AND TOCCATA-BREAKDOWN	8 minutes	Manuscript	1945

CHORAL WORKS			
CAROL, EPITAPH, LOVE IS A SICKNESS *a cappella*		Manuscript	1943
PSALM *a cappella*		Manuscript	1943
CAROL *mixed voices*		Manuscript	1944

<h2 style="text-align:center">LEO SMIT (Continued)</h2>

CHAMBER MUSIC	DURATION	PUBLISHER	DATE
SEXTET	15 minutes	Manuscript	1940
clarinet, bassoon, strings			
SUITE OF PIANO PIECES	13 "	Manuscript	1944
RURAL ELEGY AND ROUND	11 "	Manuscript	1945
violin, piano			

FILM MUSIC			
GARMENT CENTER		O.W.I.	1945

DAVID STANLEY SMITH

Born in Toledo, Ohio, in 1877. He graduated in 1900 as Bachelor of Arts from Yale University and took his degree of Bachelor of Music in 1903. He studied with Parker at the Yale School of Music and later went to Europe to continue his musical education. In 1903 he was appointed instructor at the Yale School of Music, in 1909 became Assistant Professor and in 1916 Professor. He was appointed Dean of the Yale School of Music, succeeding Parker, and held this position until he retired from it in 1940. He also held the Battell Professorship from 1920 until his retirement from teaching in 1946. He has conducted the New Haven Symphony for twenty-six years and also the Horatio Parker Choir; he has been a guest conductor with the New York Philharmonic Orchestra, the Boston, Cleveland and Detroit symphony orchestras. Four times he has received the Music Award for the Society for the Publication of American Music. He is a Fellow of the American Guild of Organists, an Associate Fellow of Berkeley College and Yale and a member of the National Institute of Arts and Letters.

His choral work "Rhapsody of St. Bernard" for chorus, soli, and orchestra was first presented at the Chicago North Shore Festival. His symphonies, "Fête Galante," "Impressions," "Cathedral Prelude," "1929—A Satire," and other works have had many performances by the major orchestras in this country. Other works have been given at the Chicago, Norfolk and Pittsfield festivals as well as at the National Music Teachers' Convention. The performances of his chamber works are too numerous to list.

COMPOSITIONS

ORCHESTRAL WORKS	DURATION	PUBLISHER	DATE
IMPRESSIONS—suite, OPUS 40	15 minutes	Manuscript	1916
SYMPHONY NO. 2, D MAJOR, OPUS 42	30 "	Manuscript	1917
FÊTE GALANTE, OPUS 48	11 "	Manuscript	1920
flute, orchestra			
CATHEDRAL PRELUDE, OPUS 54	15 "	Manuscript	1926
organ, orchestra			
SYMPHONY NO. 3, C MINOR, OPUS 60	30 "	Manuscript	1928
1929—A SATIRE, OPUS 66, No. 1	15 "	Manuscript	1932
SYMPHONY NO. 4, OPUS 78	35 "	Manuscript	1937
REQUIEM, FOR VIOLIN AND			
ORCHESTRA, OPUS 81	14 "	Manuscript	1939

DAVID STANLEY SMITH (*Continued*)

ORCHESTRAL WORKS (*Continued*)	DURATION	PUBLISHER	DATE
CREDO, POEM, OPUS 83	11 minutes	Manuscript	1941
FOUR PIECES FOR STRING ORCHESTRA, OPUS 89	15 "	Manuscript	1943
THE APOSTLE, POEM, OPUS 92	16 "	Manuscript	1944

CHAMBER ORCHESTRA

FLOWERS—4 pieces, OPUS 52 *10 instruments*	15 minutes	Manuscript	1924
SINFONIETTA *string orchestra*	12 "	Manuscript	1931
SONATINA *junior string orchestra*	10 "	Manuscript	1932

CHORAL WORKS

RHAPSODY OF ST. BERNARD, OPUS 38 *soli, mixed chorus, orchestra*	1¼ hours	G. Schirmer, Inc.	1915
VISION OF ISAIAH, OPUS 58—symphonic poem *soprano, tenor, chorus, orchestra*	20 minutes	Manuscript	1927
THE OCEAN, OPUS 94 *bass solo, mixed chorus, orchestra*	10 "	Manuscript	1945

CHAMBER MUSIC

SONATA PASTORALE, OPUS 43 *oboe, piano*	15 minutes	S.P.A.M.	1918
STRING QUARTET, C MAJOR, OPUS 46 (Gregorian)	18 "	S.P.A.M.	1921
SONATA, OPUS 51 *violin, piano*	25 "	S.P.A.M.	1921
QUINTET, OPUS 56 *piano, string quartet*	20 "	Oxford University Press	1927
STRING QUARTET, E FLAT, OPUS 57	25 "	Oxford University Press	1927
SONATA, OPUS 69 *violoncello, piano*	20 "	G. Schirmer, Inc.	1928
SONATA, A FLAT, OPUS 61 *piano*	20 "	Manuscript	1929
STRING QUARTET, C MAJOR, OPUS 71	30 "	S.P.A.M.	1934
STRING QUARTET, A MAJOR, OPUS 77 (one movement)	18 "	Manuscript	1936
STRING QUARTET NO. 10, OPUS 93	20 "	Manuscript	1944

LEO SOWERBY

Born in Grand Rapids, Michigan, in 1895. He was educated in Chicago and graduated from the American Conservatory in Chicago. Among his teachers were Lampert, Anderson and Grainger. In 1917 he joined the army, was appointed Bandmaster, and served in America, England and France. He received a fellowship from the American Academy in Rome and was the recipient of the Eastman School Publication and the Society for the Publication of American Music awards.

He is on the faculty of the American Conservatory in Chicago, teaching composition and orchestration; he also holds the positions of organist and

LEO SOWERBY (*Continued*)

choirmaster at the St. James Episcopal Church. He is a member of the American Institute of Arts and Letters and an honorary member of the American Bandmasters' Association. Some of his works are based on church hymns; others he has written for performance by Whiteman's band. The "Medieval Poem" is based on a hymn from the liturgy of St. James.

He was commissioned by the CBS to write a work for radio to be broadcast in 1938. His orchestral works have had many performances by the symphonic orchestras in America and in Europe, including the Concerto for Pianoforte, "Money Musk," "King Estmere" and most of the other concertos and the symphonies. Several chamber works have been played at the Elizabeth Coolidge Festivals. Victor has recorded the "Irish Washerwoman," the "Overture—Comes Autumn Time," the "Symphony for Organ" and piano works. He is now completing a symphony.

COMPOSITIONS

ORCHESTRAL WORKS

	DURATION	PUBLISHER	DATE
COMES AUTUMN TIME—overture	5 minutes	Boston Music Co.	1916
IRISH WASHERWOMAN	2 "	Boston Music Co.	1916
SET OF FOUR	18 "	C. C. Birchard & Co.	1917
CONCERTO FOR PIANO AND ORCHESTRA No. 1 IN F	30 "	Manuscript	1919
KING ESTMERE—ballad	17 "	Manuscript	1922
two solo pianofortes with orchestra			
SUITE FROM THE NORTHLAND	20 "	Boston Music Co.	1923
MONEY MUSK	3 "	C. C. Birchard & Co.	1924
MEDIEVAL POEM	16 "	Eastman School	1926
organ		Publication	
SYMPHONY No. 2	28 "	Manuscript	1927
PRAIRIE—symphonic poem	17 "	C. C. Birchard & Co.	1929
PASSACAGLIA, INTERLUDE AND FUGUE	18 "	Manuscript	1931
CONCERTO FOR PIANO AND ORCHESTRA	16 "	Manuscript	1932
CONCERTO FOR VIOLONCELLO AND ORCHESTRA IN E MINOR	30 "	Manuscript	1933
CONCERTO FOR ORGAN AND ORCHESTRA IN C	29 "	Manuscript	1937
THEME IN YELLOW	15 "	Manuscript	1938
SYMPHONY No. 3, E MINOR	35 "	Manuscript	1940
CONCERT OVERTURE	9 "	Music Press	1941
FANTASY ON HYMN TUNES	10 "	Manuscript	1943
"CLASSIC" CONCERTO FOR ORGAN AND STRING ORCHESTRA	16 "	H. W. Gray Co., Inc. *for hire*	1944
PORTRAIT—fantasy in triptych	16 "	Manuscript	1946

CHAMBER ORCHESTRA

RHAPSODY FOR CHAMBER ORCHESTRA	12 minutes	Manuscript	1923
SINFONIETTA FOR STRING ORCHESTRA	18 "	Manuscript	1934

CHORAL WORKS

VISION OF SIR LAUNFAL	35 minutes	C. C. Birchard & Co.	1926
3 solo parts, mixed chorus			
GREAT IS THE LORD—cantata	12 "	H. W. Gray Co., Inc.	1934
mixed chorus, organ			
TE DEUM IN D MINOR	8 "	H. T. Fitzsimons Co.	1936
mixed chorus, organ			
SONG FOR AMERICA	9 "	H. W. Gray Co., Inc.	1942
mixed chorus, orchestra			

LEO SOWERBY (*Continued*)

CHORAL WORKS (*Continued*)	DURATION		PUBLISHER	DATE
FORSAKEN OF MEN—cantata	65 minutes		H. W. Gray Co., Inc.	1942
mixed chorus, organ				
CANTICLE OF THE SUN	30	"	H. W. Gray Co., Inc.	1943
mixed chorus, orchestra				

CHAMBER MUSIC

	DURATION		PUBLISHER	DATE
SUITE FOR VIOLIN AND PIANO	18 minutes		Boston Music Co.	1916
SERENADE FOR STRING QUARTET	8	"	S.P.A.M.	1916
			G. Schirmer, Inc.	
QUINTET FOR FLUTE, OBOE, CLARINET, BASSOON, HORN	15	"	S.P.A.M.	1916
			G. Schirmer, Inc.	
SONATA FOR VIOLONCELLO AND PIANO	22	"	Manuscript	1921
SONATA FOR VIOLIN AND PIANO	27	"	Universal Edition	1922
STRING QUARTET NO 1 IN D MINOR	25	"	Manuscript	1923
POP GOES THE WEASEL	5	"	H. T. Fitzsimons Co.	1927
flute, oboe, clarinet, bassoon, horn				
SYMPHONY FOR ORGAN	35	"	Oxford University Press	1930
SUITE FOR ORGAN	35	"	Oxford University Press	1933
STRING QUARTET NO. 2 IN G MINOR	28	"	Manuscript	1935
SONATA FOR CLARINET AND PIANO	35	"	S.P.A.M.	1938
			G. Schirmer, Inc.	
POEM FOR VIOLA AND ORGAN	14	"	H. W. Gray Co., Inc.	1942
SONATA NO. 2 FOR VIOLIN AND PIANO	25	"	Manuscript	1944
SONATA FOR TRUMPET AND PIANO	23	"	Gamble Co.	1945

TIMOTHY MATHER SPELMAN

Born in Brooklyn, New York, in 1891. He won the Harvard Naumburg Fellowship in music and then went to Munich to study. When he returned to the United States, he gave many lecture-recitals on the development and history of opera, playing and singing selections.

He has written four operas and three ballets. "Saints' Days" has been performed in Boston, also in Paris and Rome, and has been broadcast over WJZ. His Symphony in G Minor and "Litany of the Middle Ages" were presented in Rochester and in Paris by several well-known orchestras. He is interested in writing music for large radio orchestras, and "Homesick Yankee," commissioned by WQXR, is played often on that station. At present he is completing a new ballet, an orchestral suite in B flat major and a musical work for theater.

COMPOSITIONS

ORCHESTRAL WORKS	DURATION		PUBLISHER	DATE
BARBARESQUES—suite	20 minutes		J. & W. Chester	1923
SAINTS' DAYS—symphonic suite	28	"	J. & W. Chester	1925
SYMPHONY IN G MINOR	28	"	Manuscript *for hire*	1935
HOMESICK YANKEE IN NORTH AFRICA— rhapsody	5	"	Carl Fischer, Inc.	1944
JAMBOREE—pocket ballet	5	"	Broadcast Music Inc.	1945

CHAMBER ORCHESTRA

	DURATION	PUBLISHER	DATE
ECLOGUE *10 instruments*	11 minutes	J. & W. Chester	1926
HOMESICK YANKEE IN NORTH AFRICA *strings, flute, piano, organ, clarinet*	5 "	Carl Fischer, Inc.	1945

CHORAL WORKS

LITANY OF THE MIDDLE AGES *soprano solo, women's chorus,* *orchestra*	15 minutes	J. & W. Chester	1928
PERVIGILIUM VENERIS *soprano and baritone soli,* *chorus, orchestra*	40 "	J. & W. Chester	1929
I LOVE THE JOCUND DANCE *women's chorus, piano*	4 "	Galaxy Music Corp.	1938

CHAMBER MUSIC

BARBARESQUES—suite for piano	28 minutes	J. & W. Chester	1922
FIVE WHIMSICAL SERENADES *string quartet or piano suite*	12 "	J. & W. Chester	1924
LE PAVILLON SUR L'EAU *flute, harp, strings*	10 "	J. & W. Chester	1925
PIANO SONATA IN D MINOR	23 "	J. & W. Chester	1929

STAGE WORKS

LA MAGNIFICA—1 act drama *one set, medium sized orchestra*	1 hour	J. & W. Chester	1920
THE SEA ROVERS—3 act opera *four sets, orchestra*	2½ hours	Manuscript *for hire*	1928
BABAKAN—fantastic comedy in 1 act *one set, medium sized orchestra*	1 hour	Manuscript *for hire*	1935

WILLY STAHL

Born in New York City, N. Y., in 1896. He graduated in 1913 from the Vienna Conservatory of Music, where he studied violin, piano and composition.

He has played the violin with the New York, St. Paul and Russian Symphony orchestras. In 1921 he became interested in commercial theater work and for five years was Director at the Rialto Theatre, New York City. Until 1929 he held a similar position in various other theaters in the United States. He teaches orchestration and composition, and is also engaged by various moving-picture companies. He has had several exhibits of his oil and watercolor painting in Los Angeles.

His orchestral composition "Dead Forest—Tone Poem" has been presented by the National Symphony Orchestra, New York City. In 1936 he won honorable mention in the NBC music awards for his String Quartet, which was broadcast. The "American Paraphrase for Orchestra" was heard over an NBC network. At present he is composing music for the Westinghouse radio programs.

WILLY STAHL (*Continued*)

COMPOSITIONS

ORCHESTRAL WORKS	DURATION	PUBLISHER	DATE
CONTINENTAL DIVIDE—tone poem	30 minutes	Manuscript	1922
NIAGARA FALLS—symphonic tone poem	10 "	Manuscript	1927
DEAD FOREST—tone poem	20 "	Manuscript	1932
SYMPHONY No. 1	32 "	Manuscript	1934
SYMPHONIC TRIO FOR ORCHESTRA AND TRIO	20 "	Manuscript	1936
violin, cello, piano			
TWO MOVEMENTS IN SYMPHONIC FORM	10 "	Manuscript	1939
THREE SHORT PIECES FOR ORCHESTRA	15 "	Manuscript	1940
SECOND SYMPHONY	30 "	Manuscript	1945

CHAMBER ORCHESTRA			
PERFUME SUITE	7 minutes	Manuscript	1928
A PIECE FOR STRINGS AND HARP	5 "	Manuscript	1936

CHAMBER MUSIC			
FIVE STRING QUARTETS	30 minutes each	Manuscript	1936–45
STRING TRIO	10 minutes	Manuscript	1936
violin, viola, cello			
TWO TRIOS	20 minutes each	Manuscript	1936
violin, cello, piano			

FILM MUSIC			
FANTASTIC PATROL		G. Schirmer, Inc.	1923
THELMA		Robins Engle	1924
TIMBER QUEEN		Pine & Thomas	1944
NAVY WAY		Pine & Thomas	1944
DARK MOUNTAIN		Pine & Thomas	1944

LEON STEIN

Born in Chicago, Illinois, in 1910. He studied the violin with Butler at the American Conservatory and composition and orchestration with Becker, Jones, Sowerby and La Violette. In 1931 he received the degree of Bachelor of Music from De Paul University School of Music and in 1935 a Master of Music degree. He was a member of the Chicago Civic Orchestra conducting class for several years, studying conducting with Lange and score analysis with Gunn.

Since 1931 he has been a member of the faculty of De Paul University School of Music, and at the present time he is Associate Professor of Music in the Theory Department there. He is Conductor of the De Paul Chamber Orchestra and has been a guest conductor with other orchestras. He was Conductor of the Great Lakes Concert Band at the Great Lakes Naval Training Center from 1944 to 1945. He has contributed articles to the *University of Knowledge Encyclopedia* and the *Journal of Musicology*. *An Analytic Study of Brahms Variations on a Theme by Haydn* was published in 1944 by the De Paul University Press.

LEON STEIN (*Continued*)

Some of his compositions have been performed in Chicago and in Grand Rapids, Michigan, and at De Paul University School of Music.

COMPOSITIONS

ORCHESTRAL WORKS	DURATION	PUBLISHER	DATE
PRELUDE AND FUGUE	12 minutes	Manuscript	1935
PASSACAGLIA	10 "	Manuscript	1936
VIOLIN CONCERTO IN A MINOR	30 "	Manuscript	1939
violin, orchestra			
THREE HASSIDIC DANCES	14 "	Transcontinental Music Corp.	1940
SYMPHONY No. 1 IN C	28 "	Manuscript	1940
SYMPHONY No. 2 IN E MINOR	30 "	Manuscript	1942
TRIPTYCH (on three poems of Walt Whitman)	30 "	Manuscript	1943
SAILOR'S HORNPIPE	3½ "	Manuscript	1944

CHAMBER ORCHESTRA			
SINFONIETTA FOR STRING ORCHESTRA	18 minutes	Manuscript	1938
LARGHETTO FOR STRING ORCHESTRA	5 "	Manuscript	1938

CHAMBER MUSIC			
SUITE FOR STRING QUARTET	15 minutes	Manuscript	1930
ADAGIO	5 "	Manuscript	1932
violin, cello, piano			
DANCE	6 "	Manuscript	1932
violin, cello, piano			
STRING QUARTET No. 1	25 "	Manuscript	1934
STRING QUARTET No. 2	23 "	Manuscript	1935
SONATINA FOR TWO VIOLINS	14 "	De Paul University Press	1937
QUINTET FOR WINDS	20 "	Manuscript	1937
flute, oboe, clarinet, horn, bassoon			

STAGE WORKS			
EXODUS—ballet	12 minutes	Manuscript	1939
piano			
DOUBT—ballet	20 "	Manuscript	1940
piano			

MAX STEINER

Born in Vienna, Austria. He studied at the Imperial Academy of Music under Fuchs, Graedener, Mahler and Rosé. When he was fourteen, he conducted his own first operetta, called "Beautiful Greek Girl," which was played for a year in Vienna. He wrote both symphonic and popular music which was published in Vienna. In 1904 he went to England, where he conducted at the London Opera House and in many theaters, and in 1911, he conducted in Paris. He came to America in 1914 and conducted and orchestrated many operettas and reviews. In 1929 he went to Hollywood

MAX STEINER (*Continued*)

as General Music Director for RKO Studios. He has written and conducted the musical scores for many pictures.

He received the Academy Award in 1935 for the score of "The Informer," again, in 1943, for "Now, Voyager" and a third time, in 1945, for "Since You Went Away." He was decorated by the French Government with the award of Officier de l'Academie Française; also he was awarded the Bronze Medal by the King of Belgium at the Cinema Exhibition in Brussels.

Many themes from his film scores have been arranged as song and piano pieces and have been published. His list of film scores is very long; although it is impossible to give the complete record, some of the important works are listed here.

COMPOSITIONS

FILM MUSIC	STUDIO	PUBLISHER	DATE
KING KONG	RKO		1933
THE INFORMER	RKO		1935
CHARGE OF THE LIGHT BRIGADE	Warner Bros.		1936
GONE WITH THE WIND	Selznick International Pictures		1939
FOUR WIVES	Warner Bros.		1939
concert version—Symphonie Moderne		Remick Music Corp.	
THE LETTER	Warner Bros.		1940
NOW, VOYAGER	Warner Bros.		1942
CASABLANCA	Warner Bros.		1942
SARATOGA TRUNK	Warner Bros.		1943
SINCE YOU WENT AWAY	Selznick International Pictures		1944
TOMORROW IS FOREVER	International		1945

ALEXANDER LANG STEINERT

Born in Boston, Massachusetts, in 1900. He graduated in 1922 magna cum laude in music from Harvard University. He then went to the Paris Conservatory and was a pupil of Loeffler, Gedalge, Koechlin and D'Indy. In 1927 he won the American Prix de Rome and studied three years at the American Academy in Rome.

He has appeared with the Boston Symphony Orchestra as piano soloist and has been a conductor for opera and musical comedies in many cities of the United States. He conducted modern chamber opera at the inauguration of the Fine Arts Center in Colorado Springs. He was appointed Conductor of the National Youth Orchestra of Los Angeles in 1941. He orchestrated and conducted the score for Walt Disney's production of "Bambi." In 1942 he enlisted in the Army Air Forces Motion Picture Unit and was the head of the music department; here he composed and conducted scores for documentary and training films. He was invited to compose a Rhapsody

ALEXANDER LANG STEINERT (*Continued*)

for Clarinet and Orchestra for performance and broadcast at the Hollywood Bowl.

Many of his works have been performed by the Rochester, Boston and St. Louis Symphony orchestras, as well as in Rome.

COMPOSITIONS

ORCHESTRAL WORKS	DURATION	PUBLISHER	DATE
Nuit Méridionale	12 minutes	Manuscript	1926
Leggenda Sinfonica	15 "	Universal Edition	1931
Three Poems by Shelley	7 "	Elkan-Vogel Co.	1932
soprano solo		*for hire*	
Concerto Sinfonico	14 "	Manuscript	1934
piano solo			
Air Corps Suite	9 "	Manuscript	1942
Flight Cycle	17 "	Manuscript	1944
Rhapsody for Clarinet and Orchestra	6 "	Manuscript	1945

CHORAL WORKS			
Hymn to Diana	4 minutes	Manuscript	1928
mixed chorus, a cappella			

CHAMBER MUSIC			
Sonata	15 minutes	Universal Edition	1925
violin, piano			
Trio	16 "	Universal Edition	1927
violin, cello, piano			
Sonata	10 "	Universal Edition	1929
piano solo			

FILM MUSIC	STUDIO		
The Strangler of the Swamp	PRC		1945

HALSEY STEVENS

Born in Scott, New York, in 1908. He graduated from Syracuse University, where he was a pupil of William Berwald. He also attended the University of California and studied with Ernest Bloch.

He has been on the faculties of Dakota Wesleyan University, Syracuse University and the University of Redlands (California) and was Director of the College of Music of Bradley Polytechnic Institute. The Sonatina for Piano received the Phi Mu Alpha Award in the 1943 national competition. He also won the Chamber Music Award of the National Federation of Music Clubs in 1945 for his Trio No. 2. He served in the U. S. Naval Reserve from 1943 to 1945. He is now actively engaged as a pianist, conductor, and critic.

His compositions, including the Symphony No. 1, the Trio No. 2, the Sonatina No. 1 and the Suite for Clarinet and Piano, have been performed in New York, Illinois and San Francisco. At the present time, he is working on a Trio No. 3, a "Comedy Overture" and a Concerto Grosso.

HALSEY STEVENS (*Continued*)

COMPOSITIONS

ORCHESTRAL WORKS	DURATION	PUBLISHER	DATE
CONCERTINO	21 minutes	Manuscript	1936
piano, orchestra			
SYMPHONY NO. 1	15 "	Manuscript	1945
SYMPHONY NO. 2	18ᐟ "	Manuscript	1945
SYMPHONY NO. 3	22 "	Manuscript	1946

CHAMBER ORCHESTRA

SUITE	10 minutes	Manuscript	1945

CHORAL WORKS

WHEN I AM DEAD, MY DEAREST		Arrow Music Press	1938
mixed chorus, a cappella			
OF THE HEAVENLY BODIES		Manuscript	1942
mixed chorus, a cappella			
GO, LOVELY ROSE		Manuscript	1942
mixed chorus, a cappella			

CHAMBER MUSIC

QUARTET NO. 1	13 minutes	Manuscript	1931
SEXTET	21 "	Manuscript	1936
2 violins, 2 violas, 2 cellos			
TRIO NO. 1	14 "	Manuscript	1937
piano, violin, cello			
SONATINA NO. 1	9 "	Manuscript	1937
violin, piano			
SONATINA	8½ "	Broude Bros.	1943
flute, piano			
DIVERSION ON "BEAU CHASSEUR DE LIÈVRE"	8 "	Manuscript	1943
2 violins, viola, cello			
QUARTET NO. 2	23 "	Manuscript	1944
SONATINA NO. 2	12 "	Manuscript	1944
violin, piano			
TRIO NO. 2	20 "	Manuscript	1945
piano, violin, cello			
SUITE	16 "	Manuscript	1945
clarinet, piano			
QUINTET	24 "	Manuscript	1945
flute, piano, violin, viola, cello			
QUARTET	18 "	Manuscript	1946
piano, violin, viola, cello			

WILLIAM GRANT STILL

Born in Woodville, Mississippi, in 1895. He was educated in Little Rock, Arkansas, and later at Wilberforce University and Oberlin College. His mother, who had taught in secondary schools, had a great influence upon him throughout his school and college years. Following the period he spent at Oberlin he entered the New England Conservatory of Music under George W. Chadwick.

In 1918 his musical education was interrupted, as he enlisted in the United States Navy and spent a year in the service. Several years later he

WILLIAM GRANT STILL (*Continued*)

returned to his musical studies under Edgar Varese. In 1934 he won a Guggenheim Fellowship, which was renewed for a second year. He has spent several years with the Columbia network and WOR arranging and directing programs. He has also worked in Hollywood with music for films. He won a Rosenwald Fellowship, which was renewed for a second year.

"Africa," a symphonic poem in three parts (Land of Peace, Land of Romance and Land of Superstition), has been revised at least six times. It has been played frequently in the United States. The "Afro-American Symphony" was sponsored by Stokowski and the Philadelphia Orchestra in their transcontinental tour and performed by the Chicago Symphony and the New York Philharmonic Orchestra; it has also had performances in Europe and has been broadcast over BBC. "Kaintuck!," which was commissioned by the League of Composers, has been performed by the Cincinnati Symphony Orchestra, the Rochester Philharmonic, the Los Angeles Philharmonic, the Indianapolis Symphony and other orchestras and also broadcast over NBC. "La Guiablesse" has been presented with stage in Rochester and Chicago. "Lenox Avenue" was especially commissioned for radio by CBS in its first American Composers Series. The New York World's Fair 1939–40 commissioned its theme music from him, and the Cleveland Orchestra commissioned his "Poem for Orchestra" in 1944. In 1944 he won the prize offered by the Cincinnati Symphony Orchestra in a nation-wide contest with "Festive Overture." "Ebon Chronicle" was commissioned by Paul Whiteman.

COMPOSITIONS

ORCHESTRAL WORKS	DURATION	PUBLISHER	DATE
DARKER AMERICA	17 minutes	C. C. Birchard & Co.	1924
FROM THE JOURNAL OF A WANDERER	20 "	Manuscript	1925
FROM THE BLACK BELT	12 "	Carl Fischer, Inc.	1926
AFRICA	30 "	Manuscript	1930
AFRO-AMERICAN SYMPHONY	28 "	J. Fischer & Bro.	1931
A DESERTED PLANTATION—suite		Robbins Music Corp.	1933
EBON CHRONICLE—poem for orchestra		Manuscript	1934
KAINTUCK!	13 "	Manuscript	1935
piano, orchestra			
THE BLACK MAN DANCES—suite		Manuscript	1935
DISMAL SWAMP	15 "	New Music	1936
BEYOND TOMORROW—poem for orchestra		Manuscript	1936
SYMPHONY IN G MINOR	30 "	J. Fischer & Bro.	1937
SONG OF A CITY	10 "	J. Fischer & Bro.	1939
chorus, orchestra			
CAN'TCHA LINE 'EM	3 "	Manuscript	1940
PLAIN-CHANT FOR AMERICA	10 "	J. Fischer & Bro.	1941
baritone, orchestra, organ			
OLD CALIFORNIA	10 "	Carl Fischer, Inc.	1941
IN MEMORIAM: THE COLORED SOLDIERS			
WHO DIED FOR DEMOCRACY	6 "	Delkas	1943
PAGES FROM NEGRO HISTORY	10 "	Carl Fischer, Inc.	1943
school orchestra			
FESTIVE OVERTURE	10 "	J. Fischer & Bro.	1944
POEM FOR ORCHESTRA	15 "	Delkas	1944
SYMPHONY No. 3	30 "	Manuscript	1945
ARCHAIC RITUAL	25 "	Delkas	1946

WILLIAM GRANT STILL *(Continued)*

	DURATION	PUBLISHER	DATE
BAND MUSIC			
FROM THE DELTA	5 minutes	Leeds Music Co.	1945

	DURATION	PUBLISHER	DATE
CHORAL WORKS			
AND THEY LYNCHED HIM ON A TREE	19 minutes	J. Fischer & Bro.	1940
contralto, mixed chorus, orchestra, narrator			
THOSE WHO WAIT	9 "	Manuscript	1943
bass, mezzo-soprano, mixed chorus, orchestra			
WAILING WOMAN	9 "	Manuscript	1946
soprano solo, mixed chorus			
THE VOICE OF THE LORD— a setting of Psalm 29	5 "	Witmark	1946
tenor solo, mixed chorus			

	DURATION	PUBLISHER	DATE
CHAMBER MUSIC			
CARIBBEAN MELODIES	1 hour	John Church Company	1941
mixed chorus, piano, percussion			
SUITE FOR VIOLIN AND PIANO	15 minutes	Delkas	1943
PASTORELA	11 "	Manuscript	1946
violin, piano			

	DURATION	PUBLISHER	DATE
STAGE WORKS			
LA GUIABLESSE	30 minutes	Carl Fischer	1927
one stage set, corps de ballet, 4 solo dancers, full orchestra			
SAHDJI	45 "	Manuscript	1930
one stage set, corps de ballet, chorus, bass soloist, 3 solo dancers, full orchestra			
BLUE STEEL—opera in 3 acts	2 hours	Manuscript	1935
3 stage sets, full orchestra, chorus, 5 vocal soloists			
LENOX AVENUE—ballet	35 minutes	J. Fischer & Bro.	1937
one stage set, chorus, orchestra, corps de ballet, 2 soloists (Also written for radio for orchestra, chorus and announcer)			
TROUBLED ISLAND—opera in 4 acts	2 hours	Manuscript	1938
4 stage sets, large orchestra, chorus, ballet, vocal soloists			
A BAYOU LEGEND—opera in 3 acts	2 "	Manuscript	1940
3 stage sets, full orchestra, chorus, 5 vocal soloists			
MISS SALLY'S PARTY	30 minutes	Manuscript	1940
one stage set, corps de ballet, 7 solo dancers, full orchestra			
A SOUTHERN INTERLUDE—opera in 2 acts	1 hour	Manuscript	1942
1 stage set, full orchestra, small chorus, 4 vocal soloists			

ALBERT STOESSEL

Born in St. Louis, Missouri, in 1894 and died in New York in 1943. He first studied music in his native city and later went to Berlin to study violin, conducting and composition at the Royal High School of Music with Hess, Wirth and Kretschmar. There he made his début as violinist with the orchestra and later toured in Europe. His opportunity to conduct came during World War I, when he became Bandmaster in the army and directed the School for Bandmasters in the A.E.F. in France.

In 1923 he became head of the Music Department of New York University, where he received his Master's degree. He resigned in 1930 in order to join the Juilliard Graduate School as Director of the Opera and Orchestra departments. He conducted the Bach Cantata Club, the Oratorio Society of New York, the Westchester Festival and the Worcester Music Festival. He received the American Music Award from the Society for the Publication of American Music.

The "Suite Antique" has been played in New York, Chicago, San Francisco, Rochester and at Chautauqua and the Worcester Festival. "Hispania" has had innumerable performances by the orchestras and has been broadcast. The opera "Garrick" was performed by the Juilliard Opera School, the Chautauqua Opera Association and also at the Worcester Festival. The Concerto Grosso has been played by the orchestras in Cleveland, St. Louis, Rochester, New York, Toronto and Chautauqua.

COMPOSITIONS

ORCHESTRAL WORKS	DURATION	PUBLISHER	DATE
HISPANIA SUITE	17 minutes	Carl Fischer, Inc.	1921
MINUET CRINOLINE	5 "	Published	1921
CYRANO DE BERGERAC—symphonic portrait	18 "	C. C. Birchard & Co.	1922
SONG OF THE VOLGA BOATMEN	8 "	C. C. Birchard & Co.	1925
EARLY AMERICANA—suite	11 "	C. C. Birchard & Co.	1935
CHAMBER ORCHESTRA			
SUITE ANTIQUE *13 instruments, 2 solo violins*	20 minutes	G. Schirmer, Inc.	1922
CONCERTO GROSSO *strings, piano obbligato*	22 "	J. Fischer & Bro.	1936
CHORAL WORKS			
A FESTIVAL FANFARE *mixed chorus, orchestra*	8 minutes	Manuscript	1933
HYMN TO DIANA *women's voices, orchestra*	5 "	C. C. Birchard & Co.	1933
A LOVER AND HIS LASS *women's voices, orchestra*	5 "	C. C. Birchard & Co.	1933
CHAMBER MUSIC			
SONATA *violin, piano*	20 minutes	Boston Music Co.	1921
SUITE ANTIQUE *2 violins, piano*	20 "	S.P.A.M.	1922
STAGE WORKS			
GARRICK—opera in 3 acts (book by Robert A. Simon)	2½ hours	J. Fischer & Bro.	1936

LEOPOLD STOKOWSKI

Born in 1887 of Polish origin. At the age of seven he played the violin and piano, and when he was ten he began to play the works of Bach on the organ. He was educated at the Royal College of Music in England and later continued his studies in Paris and Munich, receiving a thorough training in harmony, counterpoint, fugue and orchestration; he also studied all the instruments in the orchestra. At the age of eighteen he came to the United States.

He has traveled all over the world studying different kinds of music, particularly Arabic, Japanese, Chinese, Hindu, Javanese and Balinese, and has made a large collection of recordings from these countries and from Africa. In addition to appearing as guest conductor in the United States, Europe and Latin America, he has served as Conductor and Music Director of the Cincinnati, Philadelphia, the All-American Youth, the NBC, the New York City Symphony and the Hollywood Bowl orchestras. This year he has conducted the Philharmonic and made a tour of the United States. He is a Fellow of the Royal College of Music, London, and has received various degrees from other institutions. The Order of Polonia Restituta of Poland has been bestowed on him and he is a Chevalier of the Legion of Honor of France and an Officer of the Crown of Roumania. He has appeared on the screen in three motion pictures conducting numerous orchestral works.

He has transcribed over thirty works by Bach for orchestra, as well as many works by Brahms, Chopin, Debussy, Handel, Beethoven, Moussorgsky, Tschaikovsky, Wagner and other composers. His transcriptions have been performed and broadcast all over the world, and a very large number of them have been recorded by RCA Victor. His most recent composition "Benedicite Omnia Opera" was written for his daughter Sonia's wedding in 1946.

COMPOSITIONS

ORCHESTRAL WORKS	DURATION
PRELUDE TO EINE FESTE BURG	5 minutes
BENEDICITE	3 "
GYPSY RHAPSODY	
NEGRO RHAPSODY	11 "
PRELUDE ON TWO ANCIENT LITURGICAL MELODIES	5 "
BENEDICITE OMNIA OPERA	

HERBERT STOTHART

Born in Milwaukee, Wisconsin, in 1885. He was an instructor of musical dramatics at the University of Wisconsin from 1910 to 1915 and also taught in the public schools of Milwaukee. He was general musical conductor and

HERBERT STOTHART (*Continued*)

collaborator for the Arthur Hammerstein operettas from 1917 to 1928. He won the Academy Award in 1939 for the score of the motion picture "The Wizard of Oz" and has been a nominee for the Award each year since then. He is essentially a film composer and has numerous film scores to his credit which are not listed here. Many of his film compositions have been arranged for concert and have been performed and broadcast frequently. He was composer and conductor of the pageant "China," a tribute to Madame Chiang Kai-shek, which was presented in the Hollywood Bowl. At present he is completing a cantata, "Voices of Liberation." His music for films is listed here.

COMPOSITIONS

FILM MUSIC	STUDIO	DATE
THE ROGUE SONG	M.G.M.	1929
concert version—selection		
songs published		
VIVA VILLA	M.G.M.	1933
DAVID COPPERFIELD	M.G.M.	1934
MUTINY ON THE BOUNTY	M.G.M.	1935
THE WIZARD OF OZ	M.G.M.	1939
DRAGON SEED	M.G.M.	1944
THE PICTURE OF DORIAN GRAY	M.G.M.	1945
NATIONAL VELVET	M.G.M.	1945
THE GREEN YEARS	M.G.M.	1946
THE YEARLING	M.G.M.	1946

GERALD STRANG

Born in Claresholm, Canada, in 1908. He received a Bachelor of Arts degree from Stanford University in 1928. He then attended the universities of California and of Southern California for graduate study in music.

He is specially interested in chamber music and comparative musicology. He has written articles on music, taught and lectured in the West. In 1933 he founded and directed the New Music Workshops and in 1936 became Director of the New Music Society of California. He was managing editor of the New Music Edition from 1935 to 1940. He was assistant to Schoenberg at the University of California in Los Angeles from 1936 to 1938 and then taught theory at the Long Beach City College in California until 1942. From 1943 to 1945 he was an engineer at the Douglas Aircraft Company.

His works have been presented in Los Angeles and other cities in the West and also in Rome, Berlin, Havana and Buenos Aires. He is at present completing a Second Symphony.

COMPOSITIONS

ORCHESTRAL WORKS	DURATION	PUBLISHER	DATE
INTERMEZZO—2nd movement of symphony	2 minutes	New Music	1935
SYMPHONY	25 "	Manuscript	1942
1943	6 "	Manuscript	1942

GERALD STRANG (*Continued*)

ORCHESTRAL WORKS (*Continued*)	DURATION	PUBLISHER	DATE
CANZONET	4 minutes	Manuscript	1942
string orchestra, string quintet,			
or string quartet			

CHORAL WORKS

VANZETTI IN THE DEATH HOUSE		Manuscript	1937
baritone, mixed chorus, small			
orchestra			

CHAMBER MUSIC

SONATINA FOR CLARINET ALONE	4½ minutes	New Music	1932
QUINTET	12 "	Manuscript	1933
clarinet, string quartet			
FIVE PIECES FOR FLUTE AND CLARINET		Manuscript	1933
THREE PIECES FOR FLUTE AND PIANO		New Music	1933
THREE PIECES FOR FLUTE OR OBOE			
AND CLARINET		Manuscript	1933
STRING QUARTET	15 "	Manuscript	1934
PERCUSSION MUSIC FOR THREE PLAYERS		New Music	1935

IGOR STRAVINSKY

Born in Oranienbaum, near St. Petersburg, in 1882. His father was a leading bass at the Maryinsky Theatre and brought him at an early age under theatrical influence. He began to study the piano at the age of nine under a pupil of Rubinstein. However, upon the completion of his classical education he entered St. Petersburg University to study law. In 1902 Rimsky-Korsakoff heard a few of his compositions and immediately took him as a pupil. Upon his graduation in 1905, he decided to drop the legal profession in favor of music.

His first major work was a symphony which he completed in 1907 and dedicated to his teacher. His next large work was "Feu d'Artifice." This attracted the interest of Diaghilev, who commissioned him to write a ballet on an old Russian legend, "L'Oiseau de Feu," performed for the first time at the Paris Opera in 1910. Other ballets followed: "Petrouchka" in 1911, "Le Sacre du Printemps" in 1913 and "Le Chant du Rossignol" in 1917, the last of his ballets for Diaghilev. He settled in Paris in 1917 and wrote a number of instrumental and vocal works, such as "Renard," "Les Noces," "Histoire du Soldat," Concerto for Piano and Orchestra and "Oedipus Rex." In 1923 he made his début as a conductor in the first performance of his Octet for Wind Instruments at the Paris Opera House. During the next two years he toured Europe, conducting his own works and playing the solo part in his Piano Concerto. He visited the United States for the first time in 1925, upon the invitation of the New York Philharmonic Society, to conduct three concerts of his own music. During the following years he returned for several visits and also continued his European tours. He completed his "Capriccio" in 1929, and in 1930 he finished the "Symphonie

IGOR STRAVINSKY (*Continued*)

de Psaumes," celebrating the fiftieth anniversary of the Boston Symphony Orchestra. The "Duo Concertant" was first performed in Berlin in 1932. The ballet "Persephone" was introduced at the Paris Opera in 1934, and later in the same year the composer conducted it at a BBC concert in London. The Dumbarton Oaks Concerto, commissioned by Mr. and Mrs. Robert Woods Bliss, was written in 1937–38. During the 1939–40 season he was Charles Eliot Norton Professor at Harvard University, giving a series of six public lectures in French and holding conferences with music students. He has been living in Hollywood, California, since 1940. He was commissioned by the Elizabeth Sprague Coolidge Foundation (Library of Congress). The Chicago Symphony Orchestra commissioned a Fourth Symphony in 1940. In 1942 he wrote the "Circus Polka" commissioned by Ringling Bros. and Barnum & Bailey. In 1944 he wrote "Scènes de Ballet" for the Billy Rose production, "Seven Lively Arts." The "Ebony Concerto" was introduced by the swing bandleader Woody Herman at Carnegie Hall in 1946. His most recent work is the Symphony in Three Movements, dedicated to the New York Philharmonic-Symphony Society and played under the composer's direction in 1946.

The following major works have been recorded under the composer's direction or with his participation: "Duo Concertant," "Histoire du Soldat," "Les Noces," Octet, "L'Oiseau de Feu," "Petrouchka," excerpts from "Pulcinella," "Le Sacre du Printemps" and "Symphonie de Psaumes" by Columbia; the Concerto for Violin and Orchestra by French Polydor; "Jeu de Cartes" by Telefunken, and the Divertimento by Mexican Victor. Records of a number of his recent works are listed in both Columbia and Victor catalogues, and recently Concert Hall Society, Inc., has recorded the Sonata for Two Pianos and "5 Pièces Faciles" for four hands.

COMPOSITIONS WRITTEN IN AMERICA

ORCHESTRAL WORKS	DURATION	PUBLISHER	DATE
CIRCUS POLKA (composed for a young elephant)	4 minutes	Associated Music Publishers	1942
NORWEGIAN MOODS—four episodes	8 "	Associated Music Publishers	1942
ODE—in three parts	12 "	Associated Music Publishers	1943
SCHERZO À LA RUSSE	4½ "	Associated Music Publishers	1943
SCÈNES DE BALLET	15 "	Associated Music Publishers	1944
SYMPHONY IN THREE MOVEMENTS		Associated Music Publishers	1945
CHAMBER ORCHESTRA			
DANSES CONCERTANTES		Associated Music Publishers	1942
CHAMBER MUSIC			
TANGO FOR PIANO OR TWO PIANOS		Mercury Music Corp.	1940
SONATA FOR TWO PIANOS		Associated Music Publishers	1944
ÉLÉGIE FOR VIOLIN OR VIOLA SOLO		Associated Music Publishers	1944

IGOR STRAVINSKY (*Continued*)

STAGE WORKS	PUBLISHER	DATE
DANSES CONCERTANTES	Associated Music Publishers	1942
SCÈNES DE BALLET	Associated Music Publishers	1944

LAMAR STRINGFIELD

Born in Raleigh, North Carolina, in 1897. He received his academic education in the North Carolina public schools and at Mars Hill and Wake Forest colleges. Although he had planned to study medicine, his talent for music changed his career, and an interest in bands and orchestras gave him the chance to gain a playing knowledge of all the instruments. After serving for three years during the First World War, he began to study the flute in Asheville; a year later he entered the Institute of Musical Art in New York City to study with Barrère. In 1924 he graduated with the artist's diploma in flute playing. He received a prize in composition and continued his studies with Goetschius, Robinson and Wedge. He was a pupil of Clifton and Hadley in conducting. In 1928 he was awarded the Pulitzer Prize for his orchestra suite "From the Southern Mountains." He has employed American folklore in many of his compositions.

He has conducted and played in New York City chamber-music ensembles, has appeared as guest conductor with many of the symphony orchestras and is the Musical Director of the North Carolina Symphony Society, the first state symphony orchestra in the United States. From 1938 to 1939 he was Associate Conductor of the Radio City Music Hall Orchestra. He gave a course on American Music at the Juilliard School of Music for two summers, taught composition and advanced orchestration at the Graduate School of Claremont College (California), and during World War II, he spent fifteen months in an airplane factory.

A great many of his works, including "A Negro Parade," "The Legend of John Henry," "Moods of a Moonshiner" and "From the Southern Mountains," have been heard in New York, Boston, Philadelphia, Detroit and many other cities. There have been broadcasts over CBS and by NBC and BBC (London). "Cripple Creek" was recorded by Victor and was included in the International Radio Program sponsored by the NBC and the CBS.

COMPOSITIONS

ORCHESTRAL WORKS	DURATION	PUBLISHER	DATE
INDIAN LEGEND—symphonic poem	12 minutes	Manuscript for hire	1925
FROM THE SOUTHERN MOUNTAINS—suite	22 "	Carl Fischer, Inc.	1927
THE SEVENTH QUEUE—symphonic ballet	14 "	Manuscript for hire	1928
AT THE FACTORY—symphonic fantasy	10 "	Manuscript	1929

LAMAR STRINGFIELD (*Continued*)

ORCHESTRAL WORKS (*Continued*)	DURATION	PUBLISHER	DATE
A NEGRO PARADE—symphonic patrol	12 minutes	J. Fischer & Bro.	1931
THE LEGEND OF JOHN HENRY— symphonic ballad	14½ "	J. Fischer & Bro.	1932
MOODS OF A MOONSHINER—symphonic suite in 3 parts	17 "	M. Baron, Inc.	1934
FROM THE BLUE RIDGE—symphonic sketches (3 parts)	12 "	Manuscript	1936

CHAMBER ORCHESTRA

MOUNTAIN DEW—SERENADE FOR STRING ORCHESTRA	7 minutes	Sprague-Coleman	1937

CHAMBER MUSIC

MOUNTAIN SKETCHES *violin, cello, piano*	15 minutes	Carl Fischer, Inc.	1923
INDIAN SKETCHES *flute, string quartet*	12 "	Manuscript	1924
PRELUDE AND FUGUE *flute, string quartet*	9 "	Manuscript	1924
THE OLE SWIMMIN' HOLE *flute, viola, cello*	6 "	Manuscript	1924
CONCERT FUGUE *string quartet*	6 "	Manuscript	1924
INTRODUCTION AND SCHERZO *12 instruments*	10 "	Manuscript	1926
IMPROMPTU *flute, cello*	7 "	Manuscript	1927
AT EVENING *11 instruments*	6 "	Carl Fischer, Inc.	1927
FROM A NEGRO MELODY *12 instruments*	5 "	Manuscript	1928
FANTASY *5 instruments*	8 "	Manuscript	1932
A MOUNTAIN EPISODE (3 parts) *string quartet*	18 "	M. Baron, Inc.	1933
CHIPMUNKS *flute, clarinet, bassoon*	4½ "	Edition Musicus	1940
MOUNTAIN DAWN *flute solo with strings*	5½ "	Edition Musicus	1945

STAGE WORKS

TREAD THE GREEN GRASS—integral music to Paul Green's "Fantasy"	2¼ hours	Manuscript *for hire*	1930
THE MOUNTAIN SONG—opera in 3 scenes	1¾ "	Manuscript	1931
INTEGRAL MUSIC FOR "AEOLIK FRAGMENT"	2 "	Manuscript	1937
SHROUD MY BODY DOWN—integral music to Paul Green's play	2 "	Manuscript	1938
BORN CLIMBIN'—integral music to Cary F. Jacob's play	2½ "	Manuscript	1944

EDWIN JOHN STRINGHAM

Born in Kenosha, Wisconsin, in 1890. He graduated from Northwestern University, from which he received a Bachelor of Music degree. At the Cincinnati Conservatory he studied under Stillman-Kelley, and later studied

EDWIN JOHN STRINGHAM (*Continued*)

at the Denver College of Music. In Rome he was a pupil of Respighi and won a scholarship at the Royal Academy. He also received the Cromwell Traveling Fellowship in Germany.

He has been Director of the School of Music, Grand Forks. He was a member of the faculty of the University of Colorado, as well as Dean of the College of Music in Denver, and Chairman of the Music Board of the Colorado State Board of Education. He is the author of books on the history of music, a contributor to magazines, and has served as music critic of the *Denver Post* and *News*. He was on the editorial staff of the Carl Fischer music firm and music editor of the educational department of the Radio Music Corporation. From 1931 to 1938 he was Professor of Music at Teachers College, Columbia University, and also music editor of the American Book Company. During these same years he was Professor of Composition at Union Theological Seminary. From 1938 to 1944 he was founder and Chairman of the Music Department of Queens College of the City of New York and became Professor of Music there in 1944. In 1945 and 1946 he was Division Head of the Music Department of the Army University Study Center in Biarritz, France.

His orchestral works have been performed in New York, Rochester, Cincinnati, St. Louis, Chicago and other cities, and many of his works for chamber music have had frequent performances and have been broadcast. He is at present completing a symphonic narrative for full orchestra, called "Childe Roland," and a "Romanza" for violin and piano. His recent book, *Listening to Music Creatively,* is published by Prentice-Hall. He is co-author of *Advanced Harmony* (American Book Co.) and co-author of several books on acoustics and harmony to be published soon.

COMPOSITIONS

ORCHESTRAL WORKS	DURATION	PUBLISHER	DATE
THE PHANTOM—symphonic poem	20 minutes	Manuscript	1916
THREE PASTELS—short suite	6 "	Manuscript	1917
VISIONS—symphonic poem	23 "	Manuscript	1924
ANCIENT MARINER—symphonic poem	20 "	Manuscript	1926
SPRINGTIME—overture	8 "	Manuscript	1927
DANSES EXOTIQUES—symphonic suite	20 "	Manuscript	1928
SYMPHONY NO. 1, B FLAT MINOR	30 "	Manuscript	1929
NOCTURNE—symphonic poem	13 "	Carl Fischer, Inc. *for hire*	1932
SYMPHONIC SUITE		Manuscript	1937
NOCTURNE NO. 2	12 "	G. Schirmer, Inc. *for hire*	1938
FANTASY ON AMERICAN FOLK TUNE *violin, orchestra*	14 "	Manuscript	1942

CHAMBER ORCHESTRA			
NOTTURNO *12 woodwinds, 2 French horns, 1 harp*	9 minutes	Manuscript	1936

CHORAL WORKS			
PILGRIM FATHERS—cantata *mixed chorus, a cappella*	15 minutes	H. W. Gray Co., Inc.	1931

EDWIN JOHN STRINGHAM (*Continued*)

CHORAL WORKS (*Continued*)	DURATION	PUBLISHER	DATE
DREAM SONG	6 minutes	M. Witmark & Sons	1933
soprano, 2 altos, piano			
AVE MARIA	6 "	Manuscript	1937
mixed chorus, a cappella			
LONGING	4 "	M. Witmark & Sons	1944
women's voices			

CHAMBER MUSIC

STRING QUARTET IN F MINOR	25 minutes	Manuscript	1935

GUSTAV STRUBE

Born in Ballenstedt, Germany, in 1867. He came to America when he was a young man and for many years has lived in Baltimore, Maryland. He graduated from the Leipzig Conservatory, where he studied composition and violin, and then taught at the Mannheim Conservatory of Music.

He has held the position of Assistant Conductor of the Boston Symphony Orchestra, and he organized and conducted the Baltimore Symphony Orchestra for fifteen years. He has taught harmony, counterpoint, orchestration and composition at the Peabody Conservatory of Music. His book on *The Theory and Use of Chords* has been used extensively. He was awarded the National Federation of Music Clubs Prize.

His orchestral works have all been performed by orchestras in Washington, Baltimore, New York and Chicago, and the Sonatas for Viola, Cello and Violin have been played frequently.

COMPOSITIONS

ORCHESTRAL WORKS	DURATION	PUBLISHER	DATE
SYMPHONY IN G	35 minutes	Manuscript	1921
SINFONIETTA	20 "	Manuscript	1922
SYMPHONIC PROLOGUE	15 "	Manuscript	1924
VIOLIN CONCERTO IN B MINOR	25 "	G. Schirmer, Inc.	1924
VIOLIN CONCERTO IN D MINOR	32 "	G. Schirmer, Inc.	1930
SYLVAN SUITE	30 "	Manuscript	1930
AMERICANA	25 "	Manuscript	1930
HARZ MOUNTAIN SYMPHONIC POEM	15 "	Manuscript	1940
PEACE OVERTURE	8 "	Manuscript	1945

CHAMBER ORCHESTRA

DIVERTIMENTO FOR CHAMBER ORCHESTRA	20 minutes	Manuscript	1925
5 strings, 5 winds, piano			

CHORAL WORKS

LAZARUS	35 minutes	Manuscript	1926
solo quartet, chorus, orchestra			

CHAMBER MUSIC

	DURATION	PUBLISHER	DATE
STRING QUARTET	20 minutes	Manuscript	1923
SONATA FOR VIOLIN AND PIANO	25 "	G. Schirmer, Inc.	1923
SONATINA FOR VIOLIN AND PIANO	30 "	Manuscript	1923
SONATA FOR VIOLA AND PIANO	30 "	Manuscript	1924
SONATA FOR VIOLONCELLO AND PIANO	30 "	Manuscript	1925
TRIO FOR VIOLIN, VIOLONCELLO AND PIANO	20 "	Manuscript	1925
QUINTET FOR WOODWIND AND HORN	35 "	Manuscript	1930
STRING QUARTET	35 "	Manuscript	1936
TRIO FOR CLARINET, HORN AND PIANO	20 "	Manuscript	1936

LOUISE TALMA

She received her Bachelor of Music degree from New York University and her Master of Arts degree from Columbia University. She studied piano with Philipp and composition with Boulanger at the Fontainebleau School in France. She was also a student at the Institute of Musical Art.

She was a Professor of Solfege at the Fontainebleau School of Music and instructor at the Manhattan School of Music. At present, she is Assistant Professor of Music at Hunter College. She is a Fellow in the American Guild of Organists and a composer-member of the League of Composers. She received the Joseph Bearns Prize in 1932 and, in 1946, was awarded a Guggenheim Fellowship and the Juilliard Publication Award.

Her Toccata for Orchestra was premiered by the Baltimore Symphony under the direction of Stewart and was performed at the 1946 Columbia Festival of Contemporary Music by the NBC Symphony. It was also broadcast over a coast-to-coast NBC hook-up. The "Five Sonnets from the Portuguese" song cycle, the Piano Sonata and the "Alleluia for Piano" were presented by the League of Composers. The Piano Sonata was broadcast over WABF (FM) and was performed by the I.S.C.M. The "Terre de France" song cycle was broadcast over WABF and WNYC.

COMPOSITIONS

ORCHESTRAL WORKS	DURATION	PUBLISHER	DATE
TOCCATA	12 minutes	American Music Company	1944
INTRODUCTION AND RONDO GIOCOSO	10 "	Manuscript	1946

CHORAL WORKS

	DURATION	PUBLISHER	DATE
THREE MADRIGALS FOR WOMEN'S VOICES AND STRING QUARTET		J. Fischer & Bro.	1929
LA BELLE DAME SANS MERCI *baritone solo, women's chorus, organ*		Manuscript	1929
IN PRINCIPIO ERAT VERBUM *mixed chorus, organ*	10 minutes	Manuscript	1939

LOUISE TALMA (*Continued*)

CHAMBER MUSIC	DURATION	PUBLISHER	DATE
TERRE DE FRANCE—song cycle	16 minutes	Manuscript	1925
FIVE SONNETS FROM THE PORTUGUESE— song cycle		Manuscript	1934
PIANO SONATA	17 "	Manuscript	1943

ALEXANDRE TANSMAN

Born in Lodz, Poland, in 1897. He is a resident of Paris, but spent the years from 1942 to 1946 in Los Angeles.

In Europe he wrote several symphonies and string quartets, piano music and other works. He also wrote the music for several French films, among them "Poil de Carotte." He received the Coolidge Medal in 1941.

His Symphony No. 5 has been performed under the composer's direction in Washington, New York, San Francisco, Cincinnati, Minneapolis and elsewhere in the United States. Performances have been scheduled in Paris, London, Brussels, Amsterdam and other European cities. His Serenade No. 3 was given in St. Louis and Los Angeles and will also be heard in various European cities this year. "The Fall of Man" had its first performance in 1945 in Los Angeles. His earlier works have had many performances in Europe and the United States. "Two Polish Hymns" was first heard over Radio-Canada.

COMPOSITIONS WRITTEN IN AMERICA

ORCHESTRAL WORKS	DURATION	PUBLISHER	DATE
SYMPHONY No. 5 IN Γ	27 minutes	Associated Music Publishers	1942
SYMPHONIC ETUDES	16 "	Associated Music Publishers	1942
SYMPHONY No. 6 mixed choir, orchestra	22 "	Eschig	1943
SERENADE No. 3	12 "	Associated Music Publishers	1943
CONCERT PIECE FOR PIANO (left hand) AND ORCHESTRA			1943
SYMPHONY No. 7	28 "	Eschig	1944
SHORT SUITE FOR ORCHESTRA AND INSTRUMENTAL GROUPS		Delkas	1944
THE FALL OF MAN FROM "GENESIS" narrator, orchestra			1944
CONCERTINO FOR GUITAR AND ORCHESTRA			1945
ADAGIO ET ALLEGRO FOR ORCHESTRA			1945

CHAMBER ORCHESTRA			
VARIATIONS ON A THEME BY FRESCOBALDI string orchestra	14 minutes	Associated Music Publishers	1942–43
CARNIVAL MUSIC FROM "FLESH AND FANTASY" American band	12 "	Leeds Music Corp.	1942–43
FOUR IMPRESSIONS woodwind octet	10 "	Leeds Music Corp.	1945

ALEXANDRE TANSMAN (*Continued*)

CHORAL WORKS	DURATION	PUBLISHER	DATE
Two Polish Hymns	8 minutes	Manuscript	1945
mixed chorus, piano			
Two Prayers		Manuscript	1945
mixed chorus, solo, organ			

CHAMBER MUSIC			
Divertimento for Oboe, Clarinet, Trumpet, Cello, Piano	15 minutes	Associated Music Publishers	1943
String Quartet No. 6	22 "	Eschig	1944
Sonatine for Violin and Piano	15 "	Eschig	1944

STAGE WORKS			
He, She and I—ballet	25 minutes	Manuscript	1946
orchestra			

FILM MUSIC	STUDIO		
Flesh and Fantasy	Universal	Leeds Music Corp.	1942
concert version—suite		*for hire*	
Paris Underground	United Artists	Leeds Music Corp.	1945
concert version—suite	Constance Bennett Production		
Sister Kenny	R.K.O.	Leeds Music Corp.	1946
concert version—suite			

DEEMS TAYLOR

Born in New York City in 1885. He was educated at the Ethical Culture School and New York University. At an early age he began to write "musical shows." During his college years he wrote burlesques of grand operas, which were produced at student gatherings. He wrote the music for four comic operas, and one of them, "The Echo," was repeated in a Broadway production. Five years after graduating from college he began to study harmony and counterpoint seriously, and at the same time he worked as a journalist.

After holding various newspaper and magazine positions, he was made music critic on the *New York World* in 1921, where he remained for four years. He resigned in order to write his first opera, "The King's Henchman." After two years he again took up the field of journalism as Editor of *Musical America.* Then he became interested in the theater, and for a time he prepared the incidental music for a number of theatrical productions. He has been on the editorial staff of the *Encyclopedia Britannica* and the *Nelson Encyclopedia,* and also served as Associate Editor of *Collier's Weekly* and the *New York Tribune.* He was narrator for the Metropolitan Opera broadcasts in 1931–32, and for seven years, 1937–1944, was intermission commentator for the Philharmonic Symphony broadcasts. He is the Editor of the *Music Lovers Encyclopedia* and *A Treasury of Gilbert and Sullivan.* He is the author of *Of Men and Music, The Well-Tempered*

DEEMS TAYLOR (*Continued*)

Listener, and *A Pictorial History of the Movies.* He has been President of A.S.C.A.P. since 1942.

In 1913 he won first place in the National Federation of Music Clubs' competition. In 1914 he wrote "The Highwayman" for the MacDowell Festival in Peterboro, New Hampshire. In 1925 the Metropolitan Opera Company commissioned him and Edna St. Vincent Millay; the result of their collaboration was "The King's Henchman" in 1927. A second commission from the Metropolitan followed in close succession and in 1931 "Peter Ibbetson" had many performances in New York. The major orchestras in America and in Europe have presented his orchestral works and his choral and chamber music has been widely performed. Many of his compositions have been broadcast. Excerpts from his operas have been recorded by the Victor Company and Columbia has recorded "Through the Looking Glass."

COMPOSITIONS

ORCHESTRAL WORKS	DURATION	PUBLISHER	DATE
THROUGH THE LOOKING GLASS—suite	30 minutes	J. Fischer & Bro.	1922
CIRCUS DAY—suite	22 "	J. Fischer & Bro.	1934
BALLET FROM INCIDENTAL MUSIC TO "CASANOVA"	5½ "	J. Fischer & Bro.	1937
PROCESSIONAL	6 "	Manuscript	1941
FANTASY ON TWO THEMES	18 "		1925–43
MARCO TAKES A WALK—variations	14 "		1943
ELEGY FOR ORCHESTRA	14 "		1944

CHAMBER ORCHESTRA			
THE PORTRAIT OF A LADY *11 instruments*	15 minutes	J. Fischer & Bro.	1924

CHORAL WORKS			
THE CHAMBERED NAUTILUS—cantata *mixed chorus, orchestra*	15 minutes	Oliver Ditson Co.	
THE HIGHWAYMAN—cantata *mixed or women's chorus, orchestra*	30 "	Oliver Ditson Co.	
CHORIC SONG FROM "THE LOTUS EATERS" *two sopranos, alto*	3½ "		1940
YULETIDE—two Spanish Christmas songs *mixed chorus*	5 "		1942

CHAMBER MUSIC			
LUCRECE—suite *string quartet*	15 minutes	J. Fischer & Bro.	1936

STAGE WORKS			
A KISS IN XANADU—pantomime *2 scenes, 2 pianos*	20 minutes	J. Fischer & Bro.	1923
THE KING'S HENCHMAN—opera *3 scenes, full orchestra*	2½ hours	J. Fischer & Bro.	1926
PETER IBBETSON—opera *8 scenes, full orchestra*	2¾ "	J. Fischer & Bro.	1930
RAMUNTCHO—opera *5 scenes, full orchestra*	2½ "	J. Fischer & Bro.	1937

RANDALL THOMPSON

Born in New York City in 1899. He received his Bachelor of Arts degree from Harvard University in 1920 and his Master of Arts in 1922. Among his music professors were Spalding, Hill, Heilman, Davison and Bloch. He was a Fellow of the American Academy in Rome from 1922 to 1925 and received the Guggenheim Fellowship in 1929 and again in 1930. He received the Eastman Publication Award.

He was Assistant Professor of Music at Wellesley College from 1927 to 1929 and has also lectured at Harvard University. He was appointed Director for a Study of College Music by the Association of American Colleges. In 1931–32 he was Guest Conductor of the Dessoff Choirs and Conductor of the Juilliard School Madrigal Choir and Supervisors' Chorus. He returned to Wellesley College again in 1936 to lecture on music, and in 1937 he was appointed Professor of Music and Director of the University Chorus at the University of California at Berkeley. He was Director of the Curtis Institute of Music, 1931–1941, and Professor of Music and head of the Department of Music, University of Virginia, 1941–1945. He is now Professor of Theory and Composition at Princeton University. He is a member of the National Institute of Arts and Letters and the American Academy of Arts and Sciences.

"The Peaceable Kingdom," commissioned for the Harvard Glee Club by the League of Composers, has been presented in New York several times and in other cities. "Pierrot and Cothurnus," "The Piper at the Gates of Dawn," "Jazz Poem" and the Symphonies No. 1 and No. 2 have had performances in America, Italy, Germany, England and France. "The Testament of Freedom" was presented by the Boston Symphony and the Harvard Glee Club and by other choral groups in other parts of the United States. "Solomon and Balkis," commissioned by the League of Composers and CBS, received its radio première over CBS and later over BBC. It was given with stage first at the Juilliard School of Music and later at Cambridge, Rochester and in other cities. "Alleluia" and "Americana" have had frequent performances all over the United States, also in England, Mexico and South America, and have been broadcast. The String Quartet No. 1 was commissioned by Elizabeth Sprague Coolidge Foundation (Library of Congress) and broadcast from the Library of Congress in 1941. He received the Coolidge Medal for chamber music. The Suite for Oboe, Clarinet and Viola was commissioned by the League of Composers for a radio première which was broadcast over CBS. Many of his orchestral and choral works, as well as his chamber music, have had too many performances to list.

At present he is writing a third symphony which was commissioned by the Alice M. Ditson Fund (Columbia University) and a short orchestral work commissioned by the Cleveland Orchestra. Victor has recorded "The Testament of Freedom," "Song After Sundown," "Velvet Shoes" and "Tarantella." Decca (England) has recorded "Alleluia."

COMPOSITIONS

ORCHESTRAL WORKS	DURATION	PUBLISHER	DATE
PIERROT AND COTHURNUS	10 minutes	Manuscript	1922

RANDALL THOMPSON (*Continued*)

ORCHESTRAL WORKS (*Continued*)	DURATION	PUBLISHER	DATE
THE PIPER AT THE GATES OF DAWN	12 minutes	Manuscript	1924
JAZZ POEM *piano*	14 "	Manuscript	1928
SYMPHONY NO. 1	30 "	Carl Fischer, Inc.	1929
SYMPHONY NO. 2	28 "	Carl Fischer, Inc.	1931

CHORAL WORKS

ODES OF HORACE *mixed chorus, a cappella, except: Ode to Pyrrha, men's voices; Invocation to Venus, piano or orchestra*	23 minutes	E. C. Schirmer Music Co.	1925
PUERI HEBRAEORUM *8 part women's voices, a cappella*	3 "	E. C. Schirmer Music Co.	1927
FIVE SONGS FOR "NEW SONGS FOR NEW VOICES"		Harcourt, Brace and Co.	1927
ROSEMARY *women's voices, a cappella*	15 "	E. C. Schirmer Music Co.	1929
AMERICANA *mixed chorus, piano or orchestra*	20 "	E. C. Schirmer Music Co.	1932
THE PEACEABLE KINGDOM *mixed chorus, a cappella*	30 "	E. C. Schirmer Music Co.	1936
TARANTELLA *men's voices, piano or orchestra*	7 "	E. C. Schirmer Music Co.	1937
TWO SONGS *medium voice, piano*	6 "	E. C. Schirmer Music Co.	1937
THE LARK IN THE MORN *mixed chorus, a cappella*	4 "	E. C. Schirmer Music Co.	1938
ALLELUIA *mixed chorus, a cappella*	6 "	E. C. Schirmer Music Co.	1940
THE TESTAMENT OF FREEDOM *men's voices, piano, orchestra or band*	28 "	E. C. Schirmer Music Co.	1943

CHAMBER MUSIC

SONATA *piano*	15 minutes	Manuscript	1923
SUITE *piano*	8 "	Manuscript	1924
THE WIND IN THE WILLOWS *string quartet*	16 "	Manuscript	1924
SUITE FOR OBOE, CLARINET AND VIOLA	14 "	E. C. Schirmer Music Co.	1940
STRING QUARTET NO. 1, IN D MINOR	29 "	Carl Fischer, Inc.	1941

STAGE WORKS

THE STRAW HAT—incidental music			1926
GRAND STREET FOLLIES—music and score			1926
SOLOMON AND BALKIS—opera in one act *soloists, women's chorus, orchestra*	43 minutes	E. C. Schirmer Music Co.	1942

VIRGIL THOMSON

Born in Kansas City, Missouri, in 1896, of Scotch ancestry. He was educated in the public schools and graduated from Harvard University in 1922. He studied music with private instruction in piano, voice, organ, conduct-

VIRGIL THOMSON (*Continued*)

ing and composition; among his teachers were Gebhard, Davison, Goodrich, Scalero and Boulanger. He was awarded the Naumburg and Payne fellowships from Harvard University. Later fellowships from the École Normale de Paris and from the Juilliard School were granted to him.

In 1917–18 he became Second Lieutenant in the U. S. Military Aviation Corps. From 1920 to 1925 he was an assistant instructor in music at Harvard University and the conductor of the Harvard Glee Club. For several years he was also organist at King's Chapel in Boston and the conductor of the Chapel choir. He has been Music Critic for the *Boston Transcript, Vanity Fair* and *Modern Music* and became the Critic for the *New York Herald Tribune* in 1940. He has been a guest conductor in Paris, London, Chicago, Boston and New York, also Musical Director for the Friends and Enemies of Modern Music in Hartford from 1934 to 1937, as well as for several of the Federal Theaters in New York in 1936. From 1925 to 1932 he lived in Paris. There he came under the influence of Eric Satie and the Parisian "Six," and his associations in France had great influence upon his early works. Most of his songs are set to French verse.

His opera "Four Saints in Three Acts" is set to a text by the American writer Gertrude Stein. This had a large number of performances in 1934 in Hartford, New York and Chicago under the auspices of the Friends and Enemies of Modern Music; parts of it were broadcast in Hartford over NBC and included in the program "March of Time" in New York. His orchestral and chamber music has had many performances in Europe and America and has been broadcast in England, France and America. He was commissioned by the League of Composers in 1935 to write a choral work, which was performed at Town Hall by the Adesdi Chorus. "Stabat Mater" was presented at the Yaddo Festival of American Music. There have been repeated performances of the works he has written as incidental music for the stage. He has also written music for films.

COMPOSITIONS

ORCHESTRAL WORKS	DURATION	PUBLISHER	DATE
SYMPHONY ON A HYMN TUNE	19 minutes	Manuscript	1928
SYMPHONY NO. 2	21 "	Manuscript	1931
SUITE FROM "THE PLOUGH THAT BROKE THE PLAINS"	15 "	Music Press, Inc.	1936
SUITE FROM "THE RIVER"	18 "	Manuscript	1937
CANONS FOR DOROTHY THOMPSON	3 "	Manuscript	1942
MAYOR LA GUARDIA WALTZES	7 "	Manuscript	1942
SUITE FOR ORCHESTRA NO. 1	15 "	Manuscript	1944
SUITE FOR ORCHESTRA NO. 2	6¾ "	Manuscript	1944
ELECTION DAY—suite	15 "	Manuscript	1945

CHORAL WORKS			
THREE ANTIPHONAL PSALMS *women's voices, a cappella*	6 minutes	Manuscript	1924
MISSA BREVIS *women's voices, percussion*	14 "	Weaner-Levant	1934
MEDEA CHORUSES (Countee Cullen) *women's voices, percussion*	10 "	Weaner-Levant	1934
SCENES FROM THE HOLY INFANCY *mixed chorus, a cappella*	12 "	Weaner-Levant	1937

VIRGIL THOMSON (*Continued*)

CHAMBER MUSIC	DURATION	PUBLISHER	DATE
SYNTHETIC WALTZES *2 pianos*	6 minutes	Elkan-Vogel	1925
SONATA DA CHIESA *5 instruments*	25 "	New Music	1926
FIVE PHRASES FROM THE SONG OF SOLOMON *soprano, percussion*	8 "	Manuscript	1926
CAPITAL, CAPITALS (text by Gertrude Stein) *4 men's voices, piano*	18 "	Manuscript	1927
FIVE PORTRAITS *quartet of clarinets*	12 "	Manuscript	1929
PIANO SONATA NO. 1	20 "	Manuscript	1929
PIANO SONATA NO. 2	5 "	Manuscript	1929
VIOLIN SONATA NO. 1	14 "	Manuscript	1930
PIANO SONATA NO. 3	4 "	Mercury	1930
STRING QUARTET NO. 1	18 "	Arrow Music Press	1931
STABAT MATER (text by Max Jacob) *soprano, string quartet*	6 "	Cos Cob Press	1931
SERENADE IN FIVE MOVEMENTS *flute, violin*	5 "	Manuscript	1931
STRING QUARTET NO. 2	21 "	Arrow Music Press	1932
THE FORTY PORTRAITS *violin solo, violin and piano, piano solo*	40 "	Manuscript	1935
PIANO SONATA NO. 4	6 "	Elkan-Vogel	1940
SONATA FOR FLUTE ALONE	6 "	Elkan-Vogel	1943

STAGE WORKS

FOUR SAINTS IN THREE ACTS—opera (text by Gertrude Stein) *6 solo parts, double chorus, orchestra, ballet*	2 hours	Manuscript	1928
FILLING STATION—ballet	22 minutes	Arrow Press	
ANTONY AND CLEOPATRA		Manuscript	1937
THE TROJAN WOMEN—for radio (Euripides, in English)	25 "	Manuscript	1940
OEDIPUS TYRRANOS (Sophocles, in Greek) *men's voices, winds, percussion*		Manuscript	1941
THE MOTHER OF US ALL—opera (text by Gertrude Stein) *orchestra, soloists, chorus*	90 "	Manuscript	1947

FILM MUSIC

	STUDIO		
THE PLOUGH THAT BROKE THE PLAINS (concert version—suite)	U. S. Government		1936
THE RIVER (concert version—suite)	U. S. Government		1937
THE SPANISH EARTH (with Marc Blitzstein)	Contemporary His- torians, Inc.		1937
A TUESDAY IN NOVEMBER (concert version—"Election Day")	Paramount for U. S. Government		1945

DIMITRI TIOMKIN

Born in St. Petersburg, Russia, in 1899. His musical education was begun by his mother, who was an eminent pianist. In 1920 he graduated from the St. Petersburg Conservatory with high honors; his teachers were Blumenfeld and Glasounov. In 1921 he continued his studies in piano with Busoni and in composition with Leichtentritt. Following his first concert in 1921 with the Berlin Philharmonic, he toured extensively through Europe and introduced many compositions of contemporary composers. In 1927 he made his first appearance in New York and went on a coast-to-coast concert tour.

He gave the first European performance of George Gershwin's Concerto in F in the Paris Grand Opera House in 1928, and then continued concertizing until 1933, when he began composing for motion pictures in Hollywood. In addition to the numerous film scores he has written, he has composed the music for films used by the U. S. Army Signal Corp orientation program. His music for films and concert arrangements are listed here.

COMPOSITIONS

FILM MUSIC	STUDIO	PUBLISHER	DATE
ALICE IN WONDERLAND	Paramount		1934
(concert version—suite)			
THE ROAD BACK	Universal		1936
THE GREAT WALTZ	M.G.M.		1937
(concert version—Strauss suite)		Manuscript	
LOST HORIZON	Columbia		1937
(concert version)		Manuscript	
THE CORSICAN BROTHERS	United Artists		1937
THE WESTERNER	S. Goldwyn		1937
MR. SMITH GOES TO WASHINGTON	Columbia		1938
(concert version)		Manuscript	
THE MOON AND SIXPENCE	United Artists		1939
(concert version)		Manuscript	
SHADOW OF A DOUBT	Universal		1940
MEET JOHN DOE	Warner Bros.		1941
(concert version—suite)		Manuscript	
DUEL IN THE SUN	Selznick		1946
IT'S A WONDERFUL LIFE	Liberty		1946

ERNST TOCH

Born in Vienna, Austria, in 1887. He was educated in Vienna and at the University of Heidelberg, but as a composer he is self-taught.

He received the Mozart Prize in 1909, the Mendelssohn Prize in 1910 and also the Austrian State Prize for Composition. He has written music in practically every form, vocal as well as instrumental. He came to the United States in 1934 and was appointed Professor of Composition at the

ERNST TOCH (*Continued*)

New School for Social Research, New York. At present he is Professor of Composition at the University of Southern California, Los Angeles.

His works have been performed in all music centers of Europe and the United States. His opera, "The Princess on the Pea," which was written in Europe, was produced in New York in 1936, in Cleveland and in Houston, Texas. His works have been broadcast over the NBC, CBS and Mutual networks, and over stations in Boston, San Francisco and Los Angeles.

COMPOSITIONS WRITTEN IN AMERICA

ORCHESTRAL WORKS	DURATION	PUBLISHER	DATE
BIG BEN—variation-phantasy on the Westminster chimes	20 minutes	Associated Music Publishers	1934
PINOCCHIO—a merry overture	8 "	Associated Music Publishers	1936
THE IDLE STROLLER—suite	20 "	Manuscript	1938

CHORAL WORKS			
CANTATA OF THE BITTER HERBS soli, mixed choir, orchestra, narrator	45 minutes	Manuscript	1941
SONGS OF THE CYCLE soli, mixed choir, flute, piano, organ	20 "	Manuscript	1945

CHAMBER MUSIC			
TRIO violin, viola, cello	24 minutes	Manuscript	1936
QUINTET, OPUS 64 piano, strings	35 "	Delkas Music Publishing Co.	1938
POEMS TO MARTHA, OPUS 66—quintet for voice and strings	20 "	Delkas Music Publishing Co.	

FILM MUSIC	STUDIO	
PETER IBBETSON	Paramount	1935
CAT AND CANARY	Paramount	1938
THE GHOSTBREAKERS	Paramount	1939
LADIES IN RETIREMENT	Columbia	1941
FIRST COMES COURAGE	Columbia	1943
NONE SHALL ESCAPE	Columbia	1943
THE UNSEEN	Paramount	1944
ADDRESS UNKNOWN	Columbia	1944

GEORGE AMEDEE TREMBLAY

Born in Ottawa, Canada, in 1911. His father, Amedee Tremblay, gave him his early training in music. Later, he studied with David Patterson and Arnold Schoenberg.

He made his first public appearance in Canada at the age of nine as an improviser at the keyboard. He gave many performances later in Salt

GEORGE AMEDEE TREMBLAY (*Continued*)

Lake City, in Los Angeles, at the Modern Music Festival and at Modern Music Forums. He is at present teaching piano and composition. He has been a regular member of the musical-quiz program, "Are You Musical," broadcast over KMPC, Beverly Hills.

His compositions, which have been played in New York, Los Angeles, Paris and Buenos Aires, have also been broadcast over a CBS nation-wide hook-up. Wanda Landowska performed the Two Piano Sonatas over the Poste National Radio in Paris. The Co-Art Recording Company has recorded the Prelude and Dance and the "Modes of Transportation." At present, he is completing a symphonic piece for large orchestra.

COMPOSITIONS

ORCHESTRAL WORKS	DURATION	PUBLISHER	DATE
CHAPARRAL SYMPHONY	12 minutes	Manuscript	1939
CHAMBER MUSIC			
TWO PIANO SONATAS	10 minutes	New Music	1938
WIND QUINTET	6 "	Manuscript	1940
MODES OF TRANSPORTATION	12 "	Manuscript	1941
string quartet			

BURNET CORWIN TUTHILL

Born in New York City in 1888. Upon graduating from Columbia University in 1909 he entered upon a business career but continued his musical interests by conducting both the Columbia University Orchestra and the Peoples' Choral Union. He became librarian for the New York Oratorio Society and joined the Young Men's Symphony.

From 1922 to 1930 he was manager of the Cincinnati Conservatory of Music, and returned to his study of music at the College of Music in Cincinnati, where he received the degree of Master of Music in 1935. He was appointed Director of Music at Southwestern College in Memphis and in 1937 became Director of the Memphis College of Music. He founded the Society for the Publication of American Music in 1919 for the purpose of bringing good chamber music to the attention of musicians and music lovers; he also helped to organize the National Association of Schools in Music in 1924. In 1938 he organized the Memphis Symphony Orchestra and continues as its conductor. In 1945 he recruited the music faculty for the two U. S. Army universities set up in Europe and served as Chief of the Fine Arts Section of the one in Shrivenham, England.

His compositions have been performed in many cities of the United States, on tour in England, at the Berkshire Festival and on broadcasts over CBS, NBC and local networks. The Overture for Symphonic Band was played by the U. S. Marine Band in Washington, D. C., and on tour and was broadcast. He is now completing a Sonata for Oboe and Piano.

BURNET CORWIN TUTHILL (*Continued*)

COMPOSITIONS

ORCHESTRAL WORKS

	DURATION	PUBLISHER	DATE
BETHLEHEM, OPUS 8—pastorale	8 minutes	Published	1934
COME SEVEN, OPUS 11—rhapsody	6 "	Manuscript for hire	1935
LAURENTIA, OPUS 16—symphonic poem	14 "	Manuscript for hire	1936
SYMPHONY IN C, OPUS 21	22 "	Manuscript for hire	1940

CHAMBER ORCHESTRA

NOCTURNE *solo flute, strings*	4½ minutes	Private Printing	1933
INTRADA *13 instruments*	3 "	Manuscript	1935

CHORAL WORKS

BENEDICITE OMNIA OPERA, OPUS 2 *alto, tenor, a cappella*	4 minutes	H. W. Gray Co., Inc.	1932
BIG RIVER *soprano solo, women's chorus, orchestra*	15 "	Published	1942
SONG OF THE WHITE HORSE VALE *tenor solo, male chorus*	5 "	Published	1945

BAND MUSIC

DR. JOE, OPUS 5—march	4 minutes	Manuscript	1933
OVERTURE FOR SYMPHONIC BAND, OPUS 19	9 "	Manuscript	1937

CHAMBER MUSIC

INTERMEZZO FOR TWO CLARINETS *2 clarinets, bassethorn*	2 minutes	Carl Fischer, Inc.	1927
FANTASY SONATA, OPUS 3 *clarinet, piano*	9 "	Carl Fischer, Inc.	1932
NOCTURNE, OPUS 4 *flute, string quartet*	4½ "	Private Printing	1933
SONATINE, OPUS 7 (in canon form) *flute, clarinet*	8 "	Private Printing	1933
TRIO, OPUS 6 *piano, violin, cello*	15 "	Manuscript	1933
VARIATIONS ON "WHEN JOHNNIE COMES MARCHING HOME," OPUS 9 *woodwind quintet, piano*	4 "	Galaxy Music Corp.	1934
SAILORS HORNPIPE, OPUS 10, No. 1 *wind quintet*	3 "	Carl Fischer, Inc.	1935
DIVERTIMENTO, OPUS 10, No. 2 (in classic style) *wind quartet*	6 "	Carl Fischer, Inc.	1936
QUINTET, OPUS 15 *clarinet, strings*	22 "	Manuscript	1936
SONATA, OPUS 17 *violin, piano*	15 "	Manuscript	1937
SONATA, OPUS 20 *saxophone, piano*	18 "	Manuscript	1941

DONALD NICHOLS TWEEDY

Born in Danbury, Connecticut, in 1890. He graduated from Harvard University and received the degree of Bachelor of Arts magna cum laude in music; in 1917 he received a Master of Arts degree. He was a pupil of Heilman, Spalding and Hill. After studying in Europe he returned to the United States in 1912 to study counterpoint with Goetschius at the Institute of Musical Art.

He was instructor of music at Vassar College for two years. After the first World War he went to the Cleveland Museum of Art to take charge of the music under Surette. He taught music for two summer sessions at the University of California, and for seven years he was a member of the faculty of the Eastman School of Music. He was Professor of Music at Hamilton College and in 1945–46 was Associate Professor of Music at Texas Christian University. He is the author of *Manual of Harmonic Technic, Based on the Practice of J. S. Bach,* and has been editor of the program notes of the Cleveland Symphony Orchestra.

His compositions have been given by the Rochester Philharmonic, the Harvard Musical Society, the League of Composers, the Rochester Civic Orchestra and many other musical societies. "Three Dances for Orchestra" was broadcast over NBC and the Suite for Piano, over WQXR.

COMPOSITIONS

ORCHESTRAL WORKS	DURATION	PUBLISHER	DATE
L'ALLEGRO—symphonic study	15 minutes	Manuscript	1925
THREE DANCES FOR ORCHESTRA (from an unnamed ballet)	8 "	Manuscript	1934
MARCH IN B FLAT FOR STUDENT ORCHESTRA	4½ "	Manuscript	1940
SUITE FOR ORCHESTRA, WILLIAMSBURG	12 "	Manuscript	1941

CHORAL WORKS			
ANTHEM FOR LENT: OUT OF THE DEPTHS		H. W. Gray	1942
soprano, alto, tenor, bass, organ or piano			

CHAMBER MUSIC			
SONATA FOR VIOLA AND PIANO	25 minutes	Manuscript	1916
SONATA FOR VIOLIN AND PIANO	25 "	Manuscript	1920
SONATA FOR VIOLONCELLO AND PIANO	25 "	Manuscript	1930
SUITE FOR PIANO	15 "	Manuscript	1935

STAGE WORKS			
INCIDENTAL MUSIC FOR SIDNEY HOWARD'S "SWORDS"		Manuscript	1921
ALICE IN WONDERLAND—ballet	1 hour	Manuscript	1935
24–70 dancers, 40–50 players, complete mise-en-scène			

DAVID VAN VACTOR

Born in Plymouth, Indiana, in 1906. He entered the School of Music of Northwestern University in 1923, where he studied the flute, theory and composition. Upon graduation in 1928 he went to Vienna for advanced study in composition and flute and to Paris, where he studied under Dukas and Moyse.

In 1931 he became a flutist in the Chicago Symphony Orchestra. His symphonic prelude, "The Masque of the Red Death," won honorable mention in the Swift Competition in Chicago. In 1939 the Symphony in D won the New York Philharmonic Orchestra Prize and was presented in New York, Cleveland and Chicago. He was awarded the Frederick Stock Conducting Scholarship in 1939 and became Dr. Stock's understudy until the death of Stock in 1942. He received his Master's degree in music at Northwestern, where he became an instructor in composition. His "Overture to a Comedy No. 2" won the Juilliard Publication Prize in 1942. In 1941, with four other composers, he accepted the League of Composers sponsorship of a concert tour of Central and South America. His Quintet for Flute and Strings won the S.P.A.M. Award. He was commissioned to write a symphonic suite depicting the character of the United States Marine Corps in 1943 and composed "Music for the Marines." In the summer of 1945 he was invited by the Chilean Government to be a guest conductor of the Orquesta Sinfonica de Chile and Visiting Professor in the University of Chile. At present he is Associate Conductor of the Kansas City Philharmonic Orchestra and head of the Composition Department at the Conservatory of Music. He is preparing a suite of Chilean folk tunes for full orchestra.

His compositions have had performances by the principal symphonic societies, also by many of the string quartets. Many of his works have been broadcast over NBC, CBS and WOR. He has had several works recorded by Victor and the Office of War Information.

COMPOSITIONS

ORCHESTRAL WORKS

	DURATION	PUBLISHER	DATE
CHACONNE string orchestra	9 minutes	Manuscript	1928
FIVE SMALL PIECES FOR LARGE ORCHESTRA	17 "	Manuscript	1929
CRISTOBAL COLON—overture	21 "	Manuscript	1930
THE MASQUE OF THE RED DEATH—symphonic prelude	9 "	Manuscript	1932
PASSACAGLIA AND FUGUE IN D MINOR	11 "	Manuscript	1933
OVERTURE TO A COMEDY	13 "	Manuscript	1935
CONCERTO GROSSO 3 flutes, harp, orchestra	15 "	Manuscript	1935
SYMPHONY No. 1	32 "	Manuscript	1937
SYMPHONIC SUITE	19 "	Manuscript for hire	1938
CONCERTO FOR VIOLA	20 "	Manuscript for hire	1940
OVERTURE TO A COMEDY, No. 2	6 "	Juilliard Publications	1941
VARIAZIONE SOLENNE	9 "	Manuscript for hire	1941

DAVID VAN VACTOR (*Continued*)

ORCHESTRAL WORKS (*Continued*) DURATION		PUBLISHER	DATE
FANFARE, "SALUTE TO RUSSIA"	4 minutes	Manuscript for hire	1943
MUSIC FOR THE MARINES	25 "	Manuscript for hire	1943

CHAMBER ORCHESTRA

CONCERTO FOR FLUTE	20 minutes	Manuscript	1931
flute, 21 instruments			
FIVE BAGATELLES FOR STRINGS	20 "	Manuscript for hire	1938
24 strings or full orchestra			
DIVERTIMENTO	20 "	Manuscript	1939
small orchestra			

CHORAL WORKS

O HAUPT VOLL BLUT UND WUNDEN— chorale	7 minutes	Manuscript	1936
4 part mixed chorus, organ			
CREDO	20 "	Manuscript for hire	1941
mixed chorus, full orchestra			

CHAMBER MUSIC

QUINTET	21 "	G. Schirmer, Inc.	1932
flute, 2 violins, viola, cello			
SUITE FOR TWO FLUTES	15 "	Manuscript	1933
NACHTLIED (Nietzsche)	10 "	Manuscript	1935
soprano, string quartet			
STRING QUARTET IN C	10 "	Manuscript for hire	1940
GAVOTTE FOR WOODWIND QUINTET	4 "	Manuscript for hire	1940
TRIO FOR VIOLIN, VIOLA AND CELLO	10 "	Manuscript for hire	1942
SONATA FOR FLUTE	10 "	Manuscript for hire	1945
flute and piano			

STAGE WORKS

THE PLAY OF WORDS—ballet	22 minutes	Manuscript	1934
5 solo dancers, 1 stage set, 26 players			

CHARLES GILDERSLEEVE VARDELL

Born in Salisbury, North Carolina, in 1893. He graduated from Princeton University, where he received his Bachelor of Arts degree, and from the Eastman School of Music, where he received his Master of Arts and Doctorate degrees. He won the Shirley Cup for Composition in North Carolina in 1921, 1923 and 1926 and the Publication Award from the Eastman School of Music in 1937. He was Dean of the Music Department at the Flora Macdowal College in North Carolina from 1919 to 1923. Since 1928, he has been Dean of the School of Music at Salem College in North Carolina.

His works have been performed by many orchestras throughout the country. The 390th Army Service Forces Band and the First Combat Infantry Band presented "Exit the Axis." NBC and MBS have broadcast the "Carolinian Symphony," "Joe Clark Steps Out" and "Exit the Axis." "Joe Clark Steps Out" has been recorded by Victor.

CHARLES GILDERSLEEVE VARDELL (*Continued*)

COMPOSITIONS

ORCHESTRAL WORKS	DURATION	PUBLISHER	DATE
JOE CLARK STEPS OUT	4 minutes	Eastman School Publication *parts for hire*	1933
SYMPHONY IN G MINOR (Carolinian)	30½ "	Manuscript *for hire*	1938
NOCTURNE PICARESQUE	13½ "	Manuscript *for hire*	1939
THE SHELF BEHIND THE DOOR	16½ "	Manuscript *for hire*	1941
EXIT THE AXIS *orchestra or band*	3½ "	Manuscript *for hire*	1944
CHORAL WORKS			
THE INIMITABLE LOVERS *soprano, baritone solo, mixed chorus*	25 minutes	Carl Fischer, Inc. *vocal score pub. orch. score and parts for hire*	1928
CHRISTMAS PRAYER FOR A NATION AT WAR *soprano, contralto solos, women's chorus, piano*	25 "	Manuscript *for hire*	1944
STAGE WORKS			
THE HIGHLAND CALL (by Paul Green)—incidental overtures to Acts I and II *organ solo*	4 to 5 minutes each		

EDGAR VARESE

Born in Paris, France, in 1885, of French and Italian parentage. He was first interested in mathematics and science and was a student at the École Polytechnique. Later he developed a sufficient interest in music to make it his career. He joined the master class at the Paris Conservatory under Widor and studied also with Roussel and D'Indy at the Schola Cantorum. Competing for a prize given by the city of Paris, called the "Bourse Artistique," he won the first purse. Early in his career as composer he felt the inadequacy of the present symphony orchestra and claimed that new instruments were needed in order to express the spirit of a new age.

He has been very active in the development of a number of musical organizations. In Paris he founded and conducted the chorus of the Université Populaire and organized the concerts of the Chateau du Peuple. In Berlin he founded and conducted the Symphonische Chor for the performance of old motets. In 1919, shortly after he came to New York, he organized and directed the New Symphony Orchestra, the Pan American Society and later, with Carlos Salzedo's assistance, the International Composers' Guild.

EDGAR VARESE (*Continued*)

He toured as a conductor in Europe and was guest conductor with several of the American orchestras. Among his works, "Hyperprism," "Ameriques," "Arcana" and "Integrales" have been performed by orchestras in various cities of the United States, as well as in Berlin, Paris, Madrid and Havana. His chamber music and works for chamber orchestra have been played by the Austrian, Czech and Hungarian sections of the I.S.C.M. and in many cities in this country, as well as in Mexico. He is a member of the Acoustical Society of America.

COMPOSITIONS

ORCHESTRAL WORKS	DURATION	PUBLISHER	DATE
AMERIQUES	20 minutes	Editions Max Eschig	
ARCANA	18 "	*scores for sale*	
		parts for hire	
METAL—poem		Manuscript	1932
soprano, orchestra			
ESPACE		Manuscript	1937
SYMPHONY WITH CHORUS		Manuscript	1937

CHAMBER ORCHESTRA			
INTEGRALES	20 minutes		
OFFRANDES	10 "		
soprano voice			
HYPERPRISM	6 "		
IONISATION	6 "	Editions Max Eschig	1931
two groups of percussion—13 players		*for hire*	
DENSITY 21.5	3 "	Manuscript	1936
flute solo			
EQUATORIAL	10 "	Manuscript	1937
bass-baritone voice, organ, percussion,			
trumpets, trombones, theremin			
instrument			

JOHN WEEDON VERRALL

Born in Britt, Iowa, in 1908. He studied piano, cello and composition at the University of Minnesota with Ferguson and Roentgen and received his Bachelor of Arts degree in 1934. He attended the Royal College in London, where he studied with Morris, and the Liszt Conservatory in Budapest, where his teachers were Kodaly and Zsigmondy. He is also a pupil of Copland, Harris and Jacobi.

He taught composition and piano at Hamline University in Minnesota and at Mount Holyoke College in Massachusetts. From 1941 until 1945 he was a Sergeant in the U. S. Army.

His orchestral compositions have been performed by the Eastman Orchestra, the Minneapolis Symphony, the New York Philharmonic and the Honolulu Symphony. His chamber music has been played frequently in the United States and in Mexico. He has written the musical score for "Minnesota Document," a film produced by the Visual Education Center of the University of Minnesota.

COMPOSITIONS

ORCHESTRAL WORKS

	DURATION	PUBLISHER	DATE
Symphony No. 1	18 minutes	Manuscript	1940
Portrait of Man	20 "	Manuscript for hire	1941
Symphony No. 2	25 "	Manuscript for hire	1943
Six Variations	15 "	Manuscript for hire	1945
The Children—overture	5 "	Manuscript for hire	1945

CHAMBER ORCHESTRA

Concert Piece for Strings and Horns	15 minutes	Manuscript	1941

CHAMBER MUSIC

Sonata for Horn and Piano	15 minutes	Manuscript	1941
Sonata for Viola and Piano	18 "	Manuscript	1941
String Trio	12 "	Valley Press	1942
2 violins, viola			
Serenade for Clarinet, Horn and Bassoon	15 "	Manuscript	1942
String Quartet	18 "	Valley Press	1943

FILM MUSIC

	STUDIO
Minnesota Document	University of Minnesota

BERNARD WAGENAAR

Born in Arnhem, the Netherlands, in 1894. He studied at the Conservatory in Utrecht, where he had lessons in violin and piano and studied composition with Johan Wagenaar. From 1914 to 1920 he taught and conducted in the Netherlands. In 1921 he came to the United States and became a member of the New York Philharmonic Orchestra, playing first in the violin section and later playing the organ, celeste, harpsichord and piano. In 1923 he decided to devote himself to teaching theory and composition at the Institute of Musical Art. In 1927 he joined the faculty of the Juilliard Graduate School, where he now teaches fugue, orchestration and composition and also conducts private classes. He has conducted many programs of his own works throughout the country.

He is a member of the I.S.C.M., MacDowell Association, a Composer-Member of the League of Composers, the Netherland-America Foundation and various Dutch organizations. He was commissioned by CBS to write a

BERNARD WAGENAAR (*Continued*)

work for small orchestra for the "American School of the Air" program, which was broadcast in 1940. He was commissioned to write a work for the Netherland-America Foundation called "Song of Mourning," which was presented at the Metropolitan Opera House in 1944 and by the National Symphony Orchestra and had frequent performances and broadcasts, including an orchestral performance in Vancouver, B.C. He was commissioned by the League of Composers for their 20th Anniversary Program at the Museum of Modern Art, for which he wrote the Concertino for Eight Instruments. He received the Alice Ditson Award (Columbia University) for the chamber opera "Pieces of Eight," which was presented in 1944 at the Brander Matthews Theater. He was commissioned by Hans Kindler to write "Feuilleton for Orchestra," which had its first performance in 1942. He received the Eastman School Publication Award for Divertimento and also the Society for the Publication of American Music Award for a Sonata for Violin and Piano. The Sinfonietta was chosen to represent the I.S.C.M. at the Festival in Belgium.

His works have had frequent performances by the major orchestras in America, and many of his works have been played in Amsterdam, London, the Hague, Brussels, Liège, Paris, Zurich and in other cities. CBS and NBC have broadcast orchestral and chamber music. Columbia has recorded the Sonatina for Cello and Piano and the "Fanfare for Airmen." He is at present at work on his Fourth Symphony.

COMPOSITIONS

ORCHESTRAL WORKS

	DURATION	PUBLISHER	DATE
SYMPHONY NO. 1	30 minutes	Manuscript	1926
DIVERTIMENTO	20 "	C. C. Birchard & Co.	1927
SINFONIETTA	12 "	Cos Cob Press	1929
SYMPHONY NO. 2	25 "	Manuscript *for hire*	1930
TRIPLE CONCERTO *flute, harp, cello, orchestra*		Manuscript *for hire*	1935
SYMPHONY NO. 3	22 "	G. Schirmer, Inc.	1936
CONCERTO *violin, orchestra*		Manuscript *for hire*	1940
FANFARE FOR AIRMEN (Brass)		Boosey & Hawkes	1942
FEUILLETON		Manuscript *for hire*	1942

CHAMBER ORCHESTRA

FANTASIETTA ON BRITISH-AMERICAN BALLADS	3½ minutes	Manuscript *for hire*	1940
ARRANGEMENT OF TWO SPANISH FOLKSONGS	8 "	Manuscript *for hire*	1942
SONG OF MOURNING	7 "	Carl Fischer, Inc.	1944

CHAMBER MUSIC

THREE SONGS FROM THE CHINESE *voice, flute, harp, piano*	8 minutes	Juilliard Edition	1921
SONATA *violin and piano*	30 "	G. Schirmer, Inc.	1925

BERNARD WAGENAAR (*Continued*)

CHAMBER MUSIC (*Continued*)	DURATION	PUBLISHER	DATE
SONATA	10 minutes	Manuscript	1927
piano			
STRING QUARTET No. 2		Arrow Music Press	1931
SONATINA		Carl Fischer, Inc.	1934
cello, piano			
STRING QUARTET No. 3		G. Schirmer, Inc.	1936
CONCERTINO FOR EIGHT INSTRUMENTS		Carl Fischer, Inc.	1942
flute, clarinet, oboe, bassoon,			
French horn, violin, viola, cello			

STAGE WORKS

PIECES OF EIGHT—operatic comedy		Manuscript	1943
		for hire	

JOSEPH FREDERICK WAGNER

Born in Springfield, Massachusetts, in 1900. He graduated from the New England Conservatory of Music and the Boston University College of Music. Among his teachers were Converse and Casella in the United States and Boulanger, Monteux and Weingartner in Europe. He received the Endicott Prize in composition.

Upon his return home, he was organist and pianist in Providence, Boston and other cities. Later he became a member of the faculties of Boston University, Rutgers University and the University of Oklahoma, at which institutions he taught conducting, instrumentation and orchestration. In 1925 he founded the Boston Civic Symphony Orchestra, and for eighteen years he served as its musical director. He has appeared as a guest conductor throughout the United States, including performances with the Boston Symphony and the Buffalo Philharmonic Symphony. At present his home is in New York City. His compositions have been heard on many programs in Vienna, Paris and in the United States. Many of his works have been broadcast over coast-to-coast networks and local stations.

COMPOSITIONS

ORCHESTRAL WORKS	DURATION	PUBLISHER	DATE
DIVERTISSEMENT	18 minutes	Manuscript	1928
CONCERTO IN G MINOR	15 "	M. Witmark & Sons	1929
piano, small orchestra			
SYMPHONY No. 1	18 "	Manuscript	1934
SUITE No. 1 FROM BALLET "THE			
BIRTHDAY OF THE INFANTA"	18 "	Manuscript	1935
SUITE No. 2 FROM BALLET "THE			
BIRTHDAY OF THE INFANTA"	18 "	Manuscript	1935
VARIATIONS ON AN OLD FORM	9 "	C. C. Birchard & Co.	1939
HUDSON RIVER LEGEND—suite	8½ "	E. B. Marks Music Corp. *parts for hire*	1941
SYMPHONY No. 2	30 "	Manuscript *for hire*	1945
AMERICAN JUBILEE—overture	6 "	Manuscript *for hire*	1945

JOSEPH FREDERICK WAGNER (*Continued*)

CHAMBER ORCHESTRA	DURATION	PUBLISHER	DATE
RHAPSODY FOR CLARINET, PIANO AND STRINGS	10 minutes	R. D. Row & Co.	1928
SINFONIETTA AMERICANA	18 "	Manuscript for hire	1931
SINFONIETTA NO. 2		Manuscript	
A FUGAL TRIPTYCH *piano, percussion, strings*	17 "	Manuscript for hire	1936

CHORAL WORKS			
GLORIA IN EXCELSIS DEO *mixed chorus, small orchestra*	11 minutes	C. C. Birchard & Co.	1926
PSALM XIX *2 pianos or orchestra*	7 "	M. Witmark & Sons	1933
DAVID JAZZ *men's chorus, piano with small jazz band*	9 "	Richard D. Row Music Co.	1934
SONG OF ALL SEAS, ALL SHIPS *mixed chorus, organ*	10 "	Manuscript	1945

CHAMBER MUSIC			
TWO MOMENTS MUSICAL *string quartet or string orchestra*	8 minutes	Cranz	1927
QUINTET *piano, flute, clarinet, viola, cello*	15 "	Manuscript	1933
SERENADE *oboe, violin, cello*	12 "	Manuscript	1934
QUARTET IN C MINOR	22 "	Manuscript for hire	1940
SONATA FOR VIOLIN AND PIANO	17 "	Manuscript for hire	1941
SONATA FOR CELLO AND PIANO	16 "	Manuscript for hire	1943

STAGE WORKS			
THE BIRTHDAY OF THE INFANTA—ballet *one act, two scenes, moderate orchestra*	1 hour	Manuscript	1935
DANCE DIVERTISSEMENT—ballet	13 minutes	E. B. Marks Music Corp.	1937
HUDSON RIVER LEGEND—ballet	30 "	E. B. Marks Music Corp. parts for hire	1941

MAX WALD

Born in Litchfield, Illinois, in 1889. He taught himself to play the piano and also began his first study of theory without a teacher. He conducted an orchestra, producing operettas for a while; later he studied the piano with Oberndorfer and harmony with Keller in Chicago. At the American Conservatory in Chicago he studied composition and orchestration with Andersen. In 1922 he went to Paris to study with D'Indy. He received the **second prize in the National Broadcasting Company's Orchestral Awards in**

MAX WALD (*Continued*)

1932. While abroad he spent a number of years composing and teaching in Paris, Florence, London, and also in Austria. On his return he taught theory at the American Conservatory in Chicago. He has also taught piano and played in recitals; he is Chairman of the Theory Department at Chicago Musical College.

His orchestral works have been performed by the Chicago, the Cincinnati, the Illinois and other symphony orchestras and have been broadcast by NBC. Recently the "Cycle for Soprano and String Quartet" was heard over a CBS network. At present he is completing a Symphony in F.

COMPOSITIONS

ORCHESTRAL WORKS

	DURATION	PUBLISHER	DATE
SENTIMENTAL PROMENADES	20 minutes	Manuscript	1922
RETROSPECTIVES	10 "	Manuscript	1925
THE DANCER DEAD	12 "	Galaxy Music Corp. for hire	1931
COMEDY OVERTURE		Manuscript	1937
THE STREETS OF SPRING	12 "	Manuscript	1942
IN PRAISE OF PAGEANTRY	14 "	Manuscript	1945

CHAMBER ORCHESTRA

THREE SERENADES		Manuscript	1937

CHAMBER MUSIC

	DURATION	PUBLISHER	DATE
SONATA FOR VIOLIN AND PIANO	20 minutes	Manuscript	1922
SONATA FOR PIANO	15 "	Manuscript	1923
OCTOBER MOONLIGHT cycle for soprano, string quartet, flute, clarinet, piano		Manuscript	1937
SONATA NO. 2 piano			

STAGE WORKS

MIRANDOLINA—opera in 3 acts large orchestra		Manuscript	1936
GAY LITTLE WORLD—light opera in 2 acts soloists, chorus, orchestra		Manuscript	1942

EDWARD WARD

Born in St. Louis, Missouri, in 1897. He has been a musical director, composer and conductor for the New York stage. Since 1941, he has been writing comedy scores for the Hal Roach productions. His music for films and concert arrangements are listed here.

EDWARD WARD (*Continued*)

COMPOSITIONS

FILM MUSIC	STUDIO	PUBLISHER	DATE
BOYS TOWN	M.G.M.		1936
THE WOMEN	M.G.M.		1936
YOUNG TOM EDISON	M.G.M.		1937
NAVY BLUE AND GOLD	M.G.M.		1937
NIGHT MUST FALL	M.G.M.		1937
MY SON, MY SON	United Artists		1939
PHANTOM OF THE OPERA	Universal		1943
concert version—Piano Concerto		Published	
CLIMAX	Universal		1944
ALI BABA AND FORTY THIEVES	Universal		1944
concert version		Manuscript	
SALOME, WHERE SHE DANCED	Universal		1945

ROBERT E. WARD

Born in Cleveland, Ohio, in 1917. He studied at the Eastman School of Music with Hanson and Rogers, at the Juilliard Graduate School with Jacobi, Schenkman and Stoessel and at the Berkshire Music Center with Copland.

Before joining the U. S. Army, he was on the faculty of Queens College. In the Army, he was the bandleader of the Seventh Infantry Division and wrote the music for the all-soldier show, "Life of Riley." His First Symphony won the Juilliard Publication Award in 1942. He was awarded the Ditson Fellowship from Columbia University in 1945. In 1946, he received the American Academy of Arts and Letters and the National Institute of Arts and Letters grant.

His compositions, which have been performed in New York, Rochester, Denver, Washington, D. C., and Worcester, include the First Symphony, "Hush'd Be the Camps Today," Adagio and Allegro, and "Fatal Interview."

COMPOSITIONS

ORCHESTRAL WORKS	DURATION	PUBLISHER	DATE
FATAL INTERVIEW	8 minutes	Manuscript	1937
soprano, orchestra			
SYMPHONY NO. 1	15 "	Juilliard Publication	1941
ADAGIO AND ALLEGRO	12 "	Manuscript	1943
JUBILATION—overture	8 "	Broadcast Music Inc.	1946

CHORAL WORKS			
HUSH'D BE THE CAMPS TODAY	5 minutes	H. W. Gray Co., Inc.	1940
mixed chorus, orchestra			

STAGE WORKS			
LIFE OF RILEY—all soldier show		Manuscript	1942

FRANZ WAXMAN

Born in Konigshutte, Germany, in 1906. He studied music in Berlin and Dresden. Since he came to the United States in 1934, he has been a composer of film music and has written the music for a great many motion pictures. He has worked for Fox Studios and Metro-Goldwyn-Mayer and has been the head of the music department at Universal Studios. At present he is working at Warner Brothers.

"Athaneal, the Trumpeter," a comedy overture, was performed by Stokowski and by the Standard Symphony Orchestra and the University of Chicago Band. The "Elegy for Strings" and "Rebecca Suite" were also presented by the Standard Symphony Orchestra. The "Symphonic Fantasy from the Edge of Darkness" was played by the Los Angeles Philharmonic Orchestra. His music for films and concert arrangements are listed here.

COMPOSITIONS WRITTEN IN AMERICA

FILM MUSIC	STUDIO	PUBLISHER	DATE
CAPTAINS COURAGEOUS	M.G.M.		1937
REBECCA	Selznick Inter-		1939
concert version—Rebecca Suite	national	Manuscript	
SUSPICION	R.K.O.		1942
THE EDGE OF DARKNESS	Warner Bros.		1943
concert version—Symphonic Fantasy on "A Mighty Fortress"		Manuscript	
OLD ACQUAINTANCE	Warner Bros.		1943
concert version—Elegy for Strings		Manuscript	
THE HORN BLOWS AT MIDNIGHT	Warner Bros.		1944
concert version—"Athaneal the Trumpeter"—comedy overture		Manuscript	
AIR FORCE	Warner Bros.		1944
MR. SKEFFINGTON	Warner Bros.		1944
THE TWO MRS. CARROLLS	Warner Bros.		1945
OBJECTIVE BURMA	Warner Bros.		1945

POWELL WEAVER

Born in Clearfield, Pennsylvania, in 1890. He studied music at the Institute of Musical Art, New York City, and was an organ pupil of Dethier, Yon and Renzi. He was taught composition by Goetschius and Respighi.

As an accompanist he toured with many prominent singers. He is the organist of Temple B'nai Jehudah and also of the First Baptist Church in Kansas City, Missouri.

"The Vagabond" was given by the orchestras in Minneapolis, St. Louis and Kansas City. His works have also been given by the Boston Women's Symphony, the Kansas City Little Symphony and other organizations. The "Faun Suite" was broadcast over WOR. He is at present preparing a Fugue for String Orchestra and organ and choral works.

POWELL WEAVER (*Continued*)

COMPOSITIONS

ORCHESTRAL WORKS	DURATION	PUBLISHER	DATE
PLANTATION OVERTURE	12 minutes	Manuscript	1925
AN IMAGINARY BALLET	5 "	Manuscript	1925
THE FAUN—suite	12 "	Manuscript	1927
three movements			
THE VAGABOND—symphonic poem	14 "	Manuscript	1930
SYMPHONIC POEM		Manuscript	1937
DANCE OF THE SAND-DUNE CRANES—			
symphonic poem for piano and			
orchestra	12 "	Manuscript	1941
MOON-MARKETING	1¼ "	G. Schirmer, Inc.	
large and small orchestra			
THE SQUIRREL		Manuscript	
THE LITTLE FAUN	2½ "	Manuscript	

CHORAL WORKS			
HO! FOR WINDY WEATHER	2½ minutes	Oliver Ditson Co.	
mixed chorus, a cappella			
BOATING SONG		Oliver Ditson Co.	
mixed chorus, piano			
I WILL LIFT UP MINE EYES	2½ "	Lorenz Publishing Co.	
mixed chorus, organ			
SPIRIT OF GOD	2½ "	Galaxy Music Corp.	1938
NETTLETON CAROL	2¾ "	Galaxy Music Corp.	1939
COME THOU FOUNT OF EVERY BLESSING	2¾ "	Galaxy Music Corp.	1939
WHEN MORNING GILDS THE SKIES	3 "	Galaxy Music Corp.	
GOD IS WISDOM, GOD IS LOVE	2¼ "	Galaxy Music Corp.	
O GOD OUR HELP IN AGES PAST	3¼ "	J. Fischer & Bro.	
CHORAL RESPONSES—a volume			
of short responses		J. Fischer & Bro.	
SABBATH EVENING SERVICE	20 "	Bloch Publishing Co.	
(Hebrew)			
SABBATH EVENING SERVICE NO. 2	25 "	Manuscript	
(Hebrew)			
MOON-MARKETING	1¼ "	G. Schirmer, Inc.	
mixed or women's chorus			
THE HUMMING-BIRD	1¾ "	Galaxy Music Corp.	
trio women's voices			

CHAMBER MUSIC			
EXULTATION—PIECE SYMPHONIQUE	14 minutes	J. Fischer & Bro.	1933
organ, piano			
AN ODE—PIANO QUINTET	15 "	Manuscript	1936
piano, strings			
STRING QUARTET		Manuscript	1937
SONATA FOR VIOLIN AND PIANO	25 "	Manuscript	1945

ROY DENSLOW WEBB

Born in New York City in 1888. He attended the Collegiate School and Columbia University. His teacher was Julius Vogler.

He was a conductor for several musical comedies, including "Wildflower," "Garrick Gaieties," "Stepping Stones" and "Connecticut Yankee."

ROY DENSLOW WEBB (*Continued*)

In 1929 he went to R.K.O. to write for films and has continued to work there. The music for "Enchanted Cottage" was performed in the Hollywood Bowl. His music for films and concert arrangements are listed here.

COMPOSITIONS

FILM MUSIC	STUDIO	PUBLISHER	DATE
QUALITY STREET	R.K.O.		1936
LOVE AFFAIR	R.K.O.		1938
MY FAVORITE WIFE	R.K.O.		1939
ABE LINCOLN OF ILLINOIS	R.K.O.		1939
KITTY FOYLE	R.K.O.		1940
HITLER'S CHILDREN	R.K.O.		1942
THE FALLEN SPARROW	R.K.O.		1943
THE SEVENTH CROSS	M.G.M.		1944
THE ENCHANTED COTTAGE	R.K.O.		1945
concert version		Manuscript	
THE SPIRAL STAIRCASE	R.K.O.		1945

KARL WEIGL

Born in Vienna, Austria, in 1881. He studied composition under Zemlinsky and Fuchs at the Vienna Academy of Music and musicology under Guido Adler at the University of Vienna.

He was assistant coach at the Vienna State Opera under Gustav Mahler. In 1918 he became teacher of theory at the New Vienna Conservatory of Music, and, in 1930, he was appointed lecturer at the University of Vienna. During the Salzburg Festival months he gave summer courses for English and American students. He also taught composition, theory and conducting privately. He won the Grand Silver Medal and the Beethoven Prize of the Gesellschaft der Musikfreunde, Vienna, the Prize of the Philadelphia Mendelssohn Club for an a cappella composition in 1922, and the Prize of the City of Vienna for the Symphonic Cantata "World Festival" in 1924. He came to the United States in 1938 and lives in New York City. He has been a teacher of theory and composition for the Committee on Musical Training and Scholarships of the New York Philharmonic Society and at the Julius Hartt Music Foundation in Hartford. In 1943–45 he was on the faculty of Brooklyn College, and he gave a summer course at the Chicago Y.M.C.A. At present he is head of the Theory Department of the Boston Conservatory, at the same time teaching privately in New York.

His orchestral works have been performed by many of the European orchestras. His quartets have been played by the Busch Quartet, the Rosé Quartet and other groups. Some of his works have been broadcast over stations in Vienna, London, Birmingham and Danzig, as well as over WNYC and WQXR, New York, and WFIL, Philadelphia.

KARL WEIGL (*Continued*)

COMPOSITIONS WRITTEN IN AMERICA

ORCHESTRAL WORKS	DURATION	PUBLISHER	DATE
FESTIVAL PRELUDE	9 minutes	Fleisher Collection *for hire*	1938
VIENNA, THE CITY THAT WAS (dances from old Vienna)	15 "	American Music Center *for hire*	1939
RHAPSODY FOR PIANO AND ORCHESTRA, C MINOR	10 "	American Music Center *for hire*	1940
FOURTH SYMPHONY, F MINOR	35 "	Fleisher Collection *for hire*	1945
(FIFTH) APOCALYPTIC SYMPHONY, C MINOR	40 "	Manuscript *for hire*	1945

CHAMBER ORCHESTRA			
SPRING OVERTURE	5 minutes	American Music Center *for hire*	1939
SUMMER EVENING MUSIC *string orchestra*	6 "	Manuscript	1940

CHORAL WORKS			
TWO RELIGIOUS CHORUSES: "HYMN", "WHO KNOWS" *4-part mixed chorus, a cappella*	6 minutes	American Music Center *for hire*	1941
IN THE MACDOWELL WOODS *6-part mixed chorus, a cappella*	3 "	Boston Music Co.	1942
TWO SONGS OF THE TIME: "THY WILL BE DONE", "HYMN OF THE TIME" *4-part mixed chorus, a cappella*	6 "	American Music Center *for hire*	1942
THE WATCHMAN'S REPORT *baritone solo, 4-part mixed chorus, piano*	4 "	American Music Center *for hire*	1945

CHAMBER MUSIC			
TRIO IN D MINOR *violin, cello, piano*	25 minutes	Manuscript *for hire*	1939
SONATA FOR VIOLA AND PIANO, G MINOR	18 "	American Music Center *for hire*	1940
SERENADE FOR STRINGS *string quartet or string orchestra*	9 "	American Music Center *for hire*	1941

KURT WEILL

Born in Dessau, Germany, in 1900. He began to study music at the age of fourteen, and in 1918 he went to Berlin to study with Humperdinck for a year. From 1921 to 1924 he was a pupil of Busoni.

In 1919 he became conductor of opera, operetta, ballet and concerts in Lüdenscheid, Westphalia, and his tasks also included composition of incidental music for plays. The success of his opera "Der Protagonist," in 1926, prompted him to concentrate on music for the stage. He wrote eight

KURT WEILL (*Continued*)

operas, several operettas and musical comedies. He left Germany early in 1933 and lived for two years in Louveciennes, near Paris. He came to the United States in 1935 and lives in Rockland County, New York.

"Der Protagonist" was first performed by the Dresden State Opera in 1926 and "Der Zar lässt sich photographieren" was presented in Leipzig, in 1928. The first performance of "Die Dreigroschenoper," written in collaboration with Bert Brecht and based on the plot of the old "Beggar's Opera" by John Gay, was given in Berlin. This opera had many performances in other European cities and, in 1930, was made into a film. Another opera written to a libretto by Bert Brecht, "Aufstieg und Fall der Stadt Mahagonny," caused a hostile demonstration by the Nazis when first performed in Leipzig in 1930. The school opera, "Der Jasager," was first given in Berlin in 1931 and subsequently by school groups in Hamburg and other German cities. Excerpts from "Die Dreigroschenoper" have been recorded by Telefunken and French Polydor and vocal selections from "Marie Galante" by French Polydor.

COMPOSITIONS WRITTEN IN AMERICA

CHORAL WORKS	DURATION	DATE
THE BALLAD OF MAGNA CHARTA— cantata	20 minutes	1939

STAGE WORKS		
MY KINGDOM FOR A COW—comic opera		1935
JOHNNY JOHNSON—musical play		1936
THE ETERNAL ROAD—scenic oratorio		1937
KNICKERBOCKER HOLIDAY—operetta		1938
RAILROADS ON PARADE—World's Fair pageant		1939
LADY IN THE DARK—musical play		1941
ONE TOUCH OF VENUS—musical play		1943
THE FIREBRAND OF FLORENCE—operetta		1945
STREET SCENE—musical play (text by Elmer Rice)	1½ hours	1946

FILM MUSIC	STUDIO	
YOU AND ME	Paramount	1938
WHERE DO WE GO FROM HERE?	Twentieth Century Fox	1945

LAZAR WEINER

Born in Kiev, Russia, in 1897. He was educated in the State Conservatory and at the age of seventeen came to the United States. In New York City he studied composition with Jacoby, Bennett and Schillinger.

He has been coach and accompanist for prominent singers of the opera and the concert stage, and in 1922 he began to take an interest in workers'

LAZAR WEINER *(Continued)*

choruses. In the following year he organized and became the Conductor of the Freiheit Singing Society. In 1929 he organized the Jewish Culture Society and two years later he was made Conductor of the Workmen's Circle Chorus, a position which he still holds. At present he is also the Conductor of the Central Synagogue choir and of the Y.M.H.A. and Y.W.H.A. Chorus in New Jersey. He has directed the Mendelssohn Symphony Orchestra in Brooklyn and the I.L.G.W.U. Chorus. He is a member of the American Musicological Society.

His works have been performed in the United States and in Europe. Three of his piano compositions were chosen to be played at the Festival of American Composers in Rochester, and his choral works have been presented several times in New York. "Legend of Toil" was recorded by Musicraft.

COMPOSITIONS

ORCHESTRAL WORKS	DURATION	PUBLISHER	DATE
THEME AND VARIATIONS	15 minutes	Manuscript	1937
FUGUE AND POSTLUDE	12 "	Manuscript	1938

CHORAL WORKS			
LEGEND OF TOIL—cantata *soprano, tenor, baritone,* *mixed chorus, orchestra*	30 minutes	Transcontinental Music Co.	1933
SUITE FOR MIXED CHORUS AND PIANO *soprano, baritone*	15 "	Manuscript	1937
MAN IN THE WORLD—cantata *soprano, 2 tenors, baritone,* *bass, mixed chorus, orchestra*	40 "	Manuscript	1939
FIGHT FOR FREEDOM—choral-ballet *soprano, baritone, mixed* *chorus, two pianos*	40 "	Manuscript	1943
TO THEE, AMERICA—cantata *baritone, mixed chorus, orchestra*	14 "	Transcontinental Music Co.	1944

CHAMBER MUSIC			
TRIO *violin, cello, piano*	20 minutes	Manuscript	1929
STRING QUARTET	25 "	Manuscript	1937

STAGE WORKS			
TOG UN NACHT—incidental music *small orchestra*	20 minutes	Manuscript	1923
LAG BOIMER—first Jewish ballet *two pianos*	25 "	Manuscript	1929
ONCE UPON A TIME—musical comedy *small orchestra*	2½ hours	Manuscript	1932

ADOLPH WEISS

Born in Baltimore, Maryland, in 1891. He studied in Chicago with Weidig, then in New York with Lilienthal and Rybner, and later went to Vienna to study with Schoenberg. He has held the position of bassoonist with the

ADOLPH WEISS (*Continued*)

New York Philharmonic Orchestra, the New York Symphony Society, with the Chicago and Rochester Symphony orchestras and with radio orchestras. At present he is working with the Metro-Goldwyn-Mayer studios. He has taught harmony, counterpoint and composition and has coached many singers. In 1932 he was awarded a Guggenheim Fellowship. The Crescendo Club awarded the Concerto for Bassoon and String Quartet a prize in 1944.

The Concerto for Bassoon and String Quartet, the Passacaglia for Horn and Viola, and the Wind Quintet have been performed many times in various cities of the country. The Wind Quintet was performed on a South American tour in 1941, which was sponsored by the League of Composers. Others of his compositions have been presented in the United States and in Europe. The "Kammersymphonie" was broadcast in London over BBC and in New York over WNYC. Three of the songs for soprano and string quartet have been recorded by N.M.Q.R. and the Wind Quintet was recorded by Co-Art. He is now completing a Concerto for Trumpet.

COMPOSITIONS

ORCHESTRAL WORKS

	DURATION	PUBLISHER	DATE
I SEGRETI	12 minutes	Manuscript	1924
AMERICAN LIFE	6 "	New Music	1929
THEME AND VARIATIONS	13 "	Manuscript for hire	1931
SUITE FOR ORCHESTRA	20 "	Manuscript for hire	1941

CHAMBER ORCHESTRA

CHAMBER-SYMPHONY *10 instruments*	20 minutes	Manuscript	1928

CHORAL WORKS

LIBATION BEARERS (Aeschylus) *solo quartet, mixed chorus,* *orchestra, dance pantomime*	45 minutes	Manuscript for hire	1930

CHAMBER MUSIC

FIRST STRING QUARTET	20 minutes	Manuscript	1923
SECOND STRING QUARTET	20 "	Manuscript	1926
THIRD STRING QUARTET	20 "	Manuscript	1929
SONATA DA CAMERA *flute, viola*	8 "	New Music	1930
QUINTET *for winds*	10 "	Manuscript	1932
FOURTH STRING QUARTET	18 "	Manuscript	1932
VIOLIN SONATA	15 "	Manuscript	1936
TRIO *clarinet, flute, bassoon*		Boletin Latino- Americano	1937
SEVEN SONGS FOR SOPRANO AND STRING QUARTET	11 "	Manuscript for hire	1937
CONCERTO FOR BASSOON AND STRING QUARTET	15 "	Manuscript for hire	1943
PASSACAGLIA FOR HORN AND VIOLA	12 "	Manuscript for hire	1944
ODE TO THE WEST WIND *baritone, viola and piano*			1947

MARK WESSEL

Born in Coldwater, Michigan, in 1894. He studied with Schoenberg and received a music degree from Northwestern University. He was awarded a Guggenheim Fellowship and a Pulitzer Scholarship. He has taught theory and piano at Northwestern University and is now Professor of Piano and Composition at the University of Colorado. His interests are chamber and orchestral music, and he makes appearances as pianist.

His works, including Symphonie Concertante and Concertino, have been given in Chicago, New York City, Rochester, Budapest, Vienna and other cities and have been broadcast by the National Broadcasting Company and local stations.

COMPOSITIONS

ORCHESTRAL WORKS	DURATION		PUBLISHER	DATE
SYMPHONIE CONCERTANTE	26 minutes		Manuscript	1929
horn, piano, orchestra				
SYMPHONY	25	"	Manuscript	1932
HOLIDAY	6	"	Manuscript	1933
SONG AND DANCE	10	"	Manuscript	1933
PIANO CONCERTO NO. 1			Manuscript	
PIANO CONCERTO NO. 2			Manuscript	
TONE POEM			Manuscript	
CONCERTO	25	"	Manuscript	1942
piano, orchestra				

CHAMBER ORCHESTRA				
CONCERTINO	14 minutes		Manuscript	1928
flute, 16 or 20 instruments				
BALLADE	10	"	Manuscript	1932
violin, oboe, string orchestra				

CHORAL WORKS
SHORT COMMUNION SERVICE

CHAMBER MUSIC				
SEXTET	19 minutes		Manuscript	1928
flute, oboe, horn, bassoon,				
clarinet, piano				
SONATA	15	"	Manuscript	1930
violin, piano				
TRIO	18	"	Manuscript	1931
violin, cello, piano				
PRELUDE AND FUGUE	6	"	Manuscript	1931
string quartet				
STRING QUARTET	18	"	Manuscript	1931
SONATINE	8	"	Eastman School Publication	1935
piano				
BALLADE	12	"	Manuscript	1936
two pianos, also violin				
and piano				
PLAINS AND MOUNTAINS	12	"	Manuscript	1937
piano, string quartet				
SONATA FOR CELLO AND PIANO			Manuscript	
QUARTET FOR HORNS			Manuscript	
SONATINE	9	"	Manuscript	1942
trumpet, piano				
SONATA FOR CELLO AND PIANO	15	"	Manuscript	1943

STAGE WORKS				
THE KING OF BABYLON	1 hour		Manuscript	
chorus, large orchestra, mimers				

HERMANN HANS WETZLER

Born in Frankfort, Germany, in 1870 and died in 1944. He spent his childhood in the United States. In 1882 he returned to Germany to study at the Frankfort Conservatory under Schumann, Humperdinck, Heermann, and Scholz.

In 1892 he returned to New York City and was the organist of Trinity Church from 1897 to 1901. He organized the Wetzler Symphony Orchestra, which later gave the première of Strauss' "Symphonia Domestica." In 1905 Wetzler returned to Germany, where he devoted his efforts to conducting opera and concert programs. In 1905 he directed opera in Hamburg; later he held positions as a conductor in Elberfeld, Riga, Halle, Lubeck, and Cologne. He has been guest conductor of symphonic orchestras in many cities of Europe.

"As You Like It," an overture, "Symphonic Fantasy," "Visions," "Assisi," and "Symphonic Dance in Basque Style" have had performances in the United States, in Europe, in England, and South America. Broadcasts from Germany and Switzerland have been given of his works.

COMPOSITIONS

ORCHESTRAL WORKS

	DURATION	PUBLISHER	DATE
OVERTURE TO "AS YOU LIKE IT," OPUS 7	17 minutes	Simrock-Rahter, Leipzig	1917
SUITE FROM "AS YOU LIKE IT," OPUS 7	20 "	Simrock-Rahter, Leipzig	1917
SYMPHONIC FANTASY, OPUS 10	16 "	Simrock-Rahter, Leipzig	1922
VISIONS—SIX SYMPHONIC MOVEMENTS, OPUS 12	35 "	Max Brockhaus	1923
ASSISI, OPUS 13—legend for orchestra	18 "	C. F. Peters	1924
SYMPHONIC DANCE IN BASQUE STYLE, OPUS 14	17 "	Max Brockhaus	1927
SYMPHONIE CONCERTANTE, OPUS 15 violin, orchestra	22 "	Manuscript	1932

CHORAL WORKS

	DURATION	PUBLISHER	DATE
MAGNIFICAT, OPUS 16 solo soprano, boys' or women's voices, solo violin, organ	20 minutes	Manuscript for sale and for hire	1936

CHAMBER MUSIC

		PUBLISHER	DATE
STRING QUARTET IN C MINOR, OPUS 18		Manuscript	1937

STAGE WORKS

	DURATION	PUBLISHER	DATE
COMPLETE MUSIC TO "AS YOU LIKE IT," OPUS 7		Simrock-Rahter, Leipzig	1917
THE BASQUE VENUS—OPERA IN 5 PICTURES, OPUS 14	2½ hours	Max Brockhaus	1929

PAUL WHITE

Born in Bangor, Maine, in 1895. He began his early studies in his native city. In 1918 he graduated from the New England Conservatory in Boston, with highest honors in solo violin, quartet playing and theory, and was a pupil of Winternitz, Chadwick, Mason and Elson. For three years he studied violin with Ysaye and conducting and composing with Goossens.

He joined the Cincinnati Symphony Orchestra for three years as first violinist and has been concert master at the New England Conservatory of Music and conductor at the Eastman Theatre. He has also been a guest conductor with the Boston Symphony, Cincinnati Symphony, New York Philharmonic Stadium, and Rochester Philharmonic orchestras and an associate conductor of the Rochester Civic Concert and the Eastman School Symphony orchestras. He has a conducting class at the Eastman School of Music and is Musical Director at the Lake Placid Club.

There have been many performances of his works. "Five Miniatures" has been played by all of the major orchestras and in South America and Europe; it has also been recorded by RCA Victor. Other compositions have been presented by the Chicago, Cincinnati, Philadelphia, Indianapolis and Rochester symphonies, the Boston Pops Orchestra and the New York Philharmonic at the Stadium. CBS, NBC and Mutual have broadcast his works. "Sea Chanty" is recorded by Columbia.

COMPOSITIONS

ORCHESTRAL WORKS	DURATION	PUBLISHER	DATE
Lyric Overture	8 minutes	Manuscript	1919
Feuilles Symphoniques	12 "	Manuscript *for hire*	1920
Poem for Violin	8 "	Cranz	1922
Overture to Youth	7 "	Manuscript *for hire*	1924
Pagan Festival—overture	5 "	Manuscript *for hire*	1927
Voyage of the Mayflower	12 "	C. C. Birchard & Co.	1928
Symphony No. 1 in E minor	18 "	Manuscript *for hire*	1932
Five Miniatures	6 "	Elkan-Vogel Co.	1933
Lake Spray	8 "	Elkan-Vogel Co. *for hire*	1938
Boston Sketches	9 "	Carl Fischer, Inc. *for hire*	1938
College Caprice	5 "	For hire *published for Band*	1939
Lake Placid Scenes	16 "	For hire	1943
Idyl	5 "	Published	1944
Andante and Rondo for Cello and Orchestra	10 "	For hire	1945

CHAMBER ORCHESTRA			
Old Fashioned Suite *strings*	8 minutes	Manuscript	1921
Fantastic Dance *woodwinds*	5 "	Manuscript	1922
Little Romance and Tune and Variations *small orchestra*	10 "	Manuscript	1923

PAUL WHITE (*Continued*)

CHAMBER ORCHESTRA (*Continued*)	DURATION		PUBLISHER	DATE
SINFONIETTA FOR STRINGS	17 minutes		Elkan-Vogel Co.	1936
ANDANTE AND RONDO FOR CELLO AND ORCHESTRA	10	"	For hire	1945

CHORAL WORKS

	DURATION		PUBLISHER	DATE
VOYAGE OF THE MAYFLOWER *mixed chorus, orchestra*	12 minutes		C. C. Birchard & Co.	1928

CHAMBER MUSIC

	DURATION		PUBLISHER	DATE
STRING QUARTET	17 minutes		Elkan-Vogel Co.	1925
SONATA FOR VIOLIN AND PIANO	25	"	Elkan-Vogel Co.	1926
SEA CHANTY *harp, strings*	16	"	Published	1942

EMERSON WHITHORNE

Born in Cleveland, Ohio, in 1884. At the age of fifteen he started professional work as a pianist. He went to Vienna and studied with Leschetizky and Fuchs. He then spent some years in London, where he composed, taught piano and theory and wrote musical criticism for the *Pall Mall Gazette*.

In 1915, when he returned to America, he became Executive Editor of the Art Publications' Society of St. Louis and remained there until 1920. For the following two years (1921–23) he acted as Vice-President of the Composers' Music Corporation, which published a great many of the works of the younger composers.

His suite for piano, "New York Days and Nights," was chosen to represent America at the International Festival of Contemporary Music in Salzburg in 1923. "Saturday's Child" (text by Countèe Cullen) was commissioned and performed by the League of Composers. He has had performances of most of his orchestral scores by the major orchestras. The music for his ballet "Sooner and Later" was presented in New York and his chamber music has been played on the tours of many ensembles. He is a contributor to various magazines on musical subjects.

COMPOSITIONS

ORCHESTRAL WORKS	DURATION		PUBLISHER	DATE
LA NUIT	5 minutes		Manuscript *for hire* G. Schirmer, Inc.	1917
ADVENTURES OF A SAMURAI—suite	20	"	Manuscript	1919
THE AEROPLANE	4	"	Manuscript *for hire* Carl Fischer, Inc.	1920
NEW YORK DAYS AND NIGHTS—suite	20	"	Carl Fischer, Inc.	1923
POEM *piano, orchestra*	20	"	Carl Fischer, Inc.	1926
FATA MORGANA—symphonic poem	25	"	Cos Cob Press	1927

EMERSON WHITHORNE *(Continued)*

ORCHESTRAL WORKS *(Continued)*	DURATION	PUBLISHER	DATE
FIRST SYMPHONY	28 minutes	Associated Music Publishers *for hire*	1929
THE DREAM PEDLAR	16 "	Cos Cob Press *for hire*	1930
FANDANGO	8 "	Associated Music Publishers *for hire*	1931
VIOLIN CONCERTO	32 "	Associated Music Publishers *for hire*	1931
MOON TRAIL	16 "	Associated Music Publishers	1933
SECOND SYMPHONY	32 "	Associated Music Publishers	1935

CHAMBER ORCHESTRA

SATURDAY'S CHILD *soprano, tenor, 12 instruments, percussion*	20 minutes	C. C. Birchard & Co.	1926
THE GRIM TROUBADOUR *baritone, string quartet*	10 "	Carl Fischer, Inc.	1927
STROLLERS' SERENADE, OPUS 60 *string orchestra*	8 "	Associated Music Publishers	1943

CHAMBER MUSIC

GREEK IMPRESSIONS *string quartet*	16 minutes	Maurice Sénart	1917
PIANO QUINTET *piano, string quartet*	28 "	Carl Fischer, Inc.	1928
QUARTET, OPUS 51 *string quartet*	18 "	Cos Cob Press	1930
VIOLIN SONATA	17 "	Manuscript	1932
EL CAMINO REAL—piano suite		Carl Fischer, Inc.	1937

STAGE WORKS

SOONER AND LATER—ballet in 6 scenes *chorus, chamber orchestra*	2 hours	Maurice Sénart *2 piano score for hire*	1925

ROBERT S. WHITNEY

Born in Newcastle, England, in 1904, of American parentage. He first studied piano in Chicago with Oberndorfer and Reuter and theory with Anderson and Sowerby. He studied conducting under Delamarter and Stock of the Chicago Civic Orchestra. He was also a pupil of Koussevitzky.

From 1924 to 1931 he directed the Whitney Trio Chamber Music broadcasts over WMAQ. For two years the Whitney Chamber Music Ensemble over the NBC Red and Blue networks was under his direction. He was district supervisor in Chicago of the Federal Music Project.

His Concerto Grosso and the Symphony in E Minor have been heard with the orchestras in Chicago, San Francisco and other cities. The Concerto Grosso was broadcast by WGN and the Divertimento was heard in the NBC Music Guild series over the Red Network.

ROBERT S. WHITNEY (*Continued*)

COMPOSITIONS

ORCHESTRAL WORKS	DURATION	PUBLISHER	DATE
Concerto Grosso	14 minutes	Manuscript	1933
Symphony in E minor	27 "	Manuscript	1935
Sinfonietta	15 "	Manuscript	1939
Symphonic Essay	9 "	Manuscript	1943

CHORAL WORKS			
Four Pastoral Scenes *mixed chorus, orchestra*	17 minutes	Manuscript	1942

ALLAN ARTHUR WILLMAN

Born in Hinckley, Illinois, in 1909. At sixteen he was awarded a scholarship at the Knox College Conservatory of Music at Galesburg, Illinois. In 1928 he received a Bachelor of Music degree. He then entered Chicago Musical College and in 1930 was granted the degree of Master of Music. He has studied composition under Noelte and Otterstrom and was a pupil of Boulanger in Paris. His composition "Solitude" received the Paderewski Award in 1935.

He has been active as pianist, accompanist and arranger of music and has taught at the Chicago School of Music. At present he is Chairman of the Music Division of the University of Wyoming. From 1943 to 1945 he was in the U. S. Army, serving in various capacities; he also arranged music for army broadcasts, which were heard over CBS, Mutual and NBC networks.

His works, including "Solitude" and "A Ballade of the Night," have been heard in many cities of the United States and in Australia and Sweden. He is, at present, preparing a Quartet for Strings.

COMPOSITIONS

ORCHESTRAL WORKS	DURATION	PUBLISHER	DATE
Solitude—symphonic poem	10 minutes	Manuscript	1933
Symphonic Overture	12 "	Manuscript	1935

CHAMBER MUSIC			
Sonata *piano*	15 minutes	Manuscript	1930
A Ballade of the Night *medium voice, string quartet*	9 "	Manuscript	1936
Suite for Violin and Piano		Manuscript	1937

STEFAN WOLPE

Born in Berlin, Germany, in 1902. He studied harmony with Alfred Richter and counterpoint and composition with Otto Taubmann at the Klindworth-Scharwenka Conservatory and Paul Juon at the State Academy of Music in Berlin. He continued his studies under Ferrucio Busoni, Anton von Webern and Hermann Scherchen.

He has written several orchestral works, chamber music, a number of cantatas, as well as other choral works and many songs in Europe and Palestine. Between 1934 and 1938 he taught theory and composition at the Palestine Conservatory. He came to the United States late in 1938 and was the head of the Theory Department of the Settlement Music School in New York City from 1939 to 1944. At present he is teaching privately. He is working on a group of cantatas for different voices and chamber orchestra and on a symphonic work.

His cantata "About Sport" and the oratorio "The Passion of Man" were first performed in Berlin in 1931 and 1932, respectively. In 1934 the March and Variations for Two Pianos was given in Moscow. "Two Psalms for Soprano and Piano" had its first performance in New York in 1941, and the following year the sonata for Oboe and Piano and the Passacaglia were also performed in New York. The Dance Players, New York, gave his ballet "The Man from Midian." Some of his chamber-music works and songs have been broadcast over several New York stations.

COMPOSITIONS WRITTEN IN AMERICA

ORCHESTRAL WORKS	DURATION	PUBLISHER	DATE
THE MAN FROM MIDIAN	40 minutes	Manuscript	1942
CHAMBER ORCHESTRA			
CONCERTO FOR FLUTE, CLARINET, BASSOON, HORN, TRUMPET, TROMBONE, VIOLIN, CELLO, PIANO	35 minutes	Manuscript	1938
LAMENT FOR IGNACIO SANCHEZ MEJIAS (Garcia Lorca) *soprano, baritone, speaker, chamber orchestra*	37 "	Manuscript	1945
CHORAL WORKS			
FOUR SONGS FOR CHORUS—from the play "The Unknown Soldier" *mixed chorus, a cappella*	10 minutes	Manuscript	1938
ISRAEL AND HIS LAND—oratorio *baritone solo, speaker, chorus, orchestra*	1 hour	Manuscript	1939
UNNAMED LANDS—cantata *mixed chorus, orchestra*	20 minutes	Manuscript	1940
YIGDAL—cantata *baritone solo, mixed chorus, organ*	25 "	Manuscript	1945
CHAMBER MUSIC			
ZEMACH SUITE *piano*	18 minutes	Manuscript	1939
TRIO FOR CLARINET, VIOLIN AND CELLO	17 "	Manuscript	1945
SONATA FOR VIOLIN AND PIANO	36 "	Manuscript	1945
FILM MUSIC	STUDIO		
PALESTINE AT WAR—documentary	Palestine Labor Com.		1942

FREDERICK WOLTMANN

Born in Flushing, New York, in 1908. He began to study the piano at the age of eleven, and he sang in the boys' choir at the Metropolitan Opera House. His academic studies included chemistry and architecture. He was self-taught in composition and orchestration until his formal music studies began in 1933, when he was awarded a four-year scholarship at the Eastman School of Music. His teachers were Hanson and Rogers. He received a fellowship at the MacDowell Colony in 1936 and the Prix de Rome in 1937, when he studied at the American Academy in Rome with Pizzetti. He was awarded a prize by the National Academy of Arts and Letters in 1941.

His music has been performed by the Minneapolis Symphony, the New York Philharmonic Symphony, the Philadelphia Orchestra, the Rochester Philharmonic Symphony and by many orchestras abroad. His works have been heard over the CBS and NBC networks and by special short-wave broadcast from Italy. He is now preparing an opera based on Edith Wharton's "Ethan Frome."

COMPOSITIONS

ORCHESTRAL WORKS

	DURATION	PUBLISHER	DATE
SONG OF THE FOREST DWELLER *baritone solo*	3 minutes	Manuscript	1932
DANCE OF THE TORCH BEARERS	5 "	Manuscript	1932
POEM FOR FLUTE AND ORCHESTRA	6 "	Manuscript	1935
RHAPSODY FOR HORN AND ORCHESTRA	8 "	Manuscript	1935
LEGEND *cello, orchestra*	7 "	Manuscript	1936
SONGS FOR AUTUMN—symphony *soprano, baritone, orchestra*	25 "	Manuscript	1937
CONCERTO FOR PIANO AND ORCHESTRA		Manuscript	1937
THE POOL OF PEGASUS—tone poem		Manuscript	1937
VARIATIONS ON AN OLD ENGLISH FOLK SONG *piano, orchestra*	7 "	Manuscript	1938
FROM DOVER BEACH *voice, orchestra*	8 "	Manuscript	1938
THE COLISEUM AT NIGHT	6 "	Manuscript	1939
SOLITUDE	4 "	Carl Fischer, Inc.	1942
FROM LEAVES OF GRASS—symphony *voice, orchestra*	35 "	Manuscript	1946

CHAMBER ORCHESTRA

SONGS FROM A CHINESE LUTE *3 songs, medium voice, 33 instruments*	7 minutes	Manuscript	1936
POEM FOR HORN AND STRINGS	5 "	Manuscript	1936

CHORAL WORKS

AN INCANTATION *mixed chorus, orchestra*	6 minutes	Manuscript	1938

CHAMBER MUSIC

POEM FOR EIGHT INSTRUMENTS	4 minutes	Manuscript	1933
SCHERZO FOR EIGHT WIND INSTRUMENTS	5 "	Manuscript	1937
SUITE FOR JUDY	10 "	Manuscript	1944

JOSEPH WOOD

Born in Pittsburgh, Pennsylvania, in 1915. He attended Bucknell University and graduated from the Institute of Musical Art, where he studied with Roeder. He received a fellowship in composition at the Juilliard Graduate School and studied with Wagenaar. His opera, "The Mother," won the Juilliard Operatic Competition in 1942. He was awarded the Ditson Post-War Fellowship (Columbia University).

He was head of the Music Department at Union Junior College in New Jersey (1938–39). He was staff composer and musical consultant at the Chekhov Theatre Studio (1939–41). He composed and arranged radio and theatrical productions, including the incidental music for "Twelfth Night" and "Cricket on the Hearth." In 1943 he went into the Special Service of the U. S. Army.

His compositions have been heard in New York, New Jersey, Rochester and Washington. The Overture to "Twelfth Night" and the String Quartet No. 2 were broadcast over WJZ. The String Quartet was presented on the American Music Festival and played over WNYC. At present he is completing a Violin and Piano Sonata.

COMPOSITIONS

ORCHESTRAL WORKS	DURATION	PUBLISHER	DATE
SYMPHONY	25 minutes	Manuscript	1939
OVERTURE TO "TWELFTH NIGHT"	6 "	Manuscript	1941

CHAMBER ORCHESTRA			
ROMANZA *string orchestra*	8 minutes	Manuscript	1937

CHORAL WORKS			
THE NIGHT (Wordsworth) *mixed chorus, piano*	6 minutes	Manuscript	1937

CHAMBER MUSIC			
TRIO IN E MINOR *violin, cello, piano*	13 minutes	Manuscript	1938
STRING QUARTET No. 1	12 "	Manuscript	1938
SONATA FOR VIOLA AND PIANO	14 "	Manuscript	1939
STRING QUARTET No. 2	15 "	Manuscript	1941

STAGE WORKS			
TWELFTH NIGHT—incidental music *string quartet, organ, piano*	25 minutes	Manuscript	1940
CRICKET ON THE HEARTH—incidental music *string quartet, organ, piano*	15 "	Manuscript	1940
THE MOTHER (libretto Hurd Hatfield)—opera *2 sopranos, 2 altos, 2 baritones, small chorus, chamber orchestra*	35 "	Manuscript	1942
LAND OF FAME—incidental music *clarinet, trumpet, horn, Hammond organ*	20 "	Manuscript	1943

VICTOR YOUNG

Born in Chicago, Illinois, in 1900. At the age of eight he moved to Europe, where he graduated from the Conservatory of Warsaw. He returned to America to concertize as a violinist and later accepted the position as Concertmaster for the Chicago Theater. He became Director for the Brunswick Phonograph Company and for the Decca Recording Company. Today he is a composer and conductor for Paramount Studios and is also Musical Director for the Westinghouse Radio Program.

He has written orchestral and chamber music which has had performances, and Decca has recorded several of the concert versions of the music he has written for films. He has also written a great many popular songs which are not listed here.

COMPOSITIONS

ORCHESTRAL WORKS
ELEGY TO F.D.R.
WALT WHITMAN—tone poem

CHAMBER MUSIC
STRING QUARTET (based on
Stephen Foster)

FILM MUSIC	STUDIO	PUBLISHER	DATE
GULLIVER'S TRAVELS	Paramount		1939
THE LIGHT THAT FAILED	Paramount		1939
THE WAY OF ALL FLESH	Paramount		1939
GOLDEN BOY	Columbia Pictures		1939
REAP THE WILD WIND	Paramount		1941
FOR WHOM THE BELL TOLLS symphonic synthesis	Paramount	Manuscript *for hire*	1942
THE UNINVITED	Paramount		1943
TWO YEARS BEFORE THE MAST	Paramount		1944
THE STORY OF DR. WASSEL	Paramount		1944
FRENCHMAN'S CREEK	Paramount		1944
A MEDAL FOR BENNY	Paramount		1944
AND NOW TOMORROW	Paramount		1944
LOVE LETTERS	Paramount		1945
CALCUTTA	Paramount		1945
TO EACH HIS OWN	Paramount		1945
CALIFORNIA	Paramount		1946
SEARCHING WIND	Paramount		1946

EUGENE ZADOR

Born in Bataszek, Hungary, in 1895. He was a pupil of Heuberger, Reger, Albert and Volbach and received his Doctor of Music degree in 1921. He won the Grand Prix for Chamber Music in 1934, and later he became Professor of Music at the Academy in Budapest.

He was on the faculty of the Vienna Conservatory from 1922 to 1938, where he became a member of the Praesidium. He came to America in 1939 and has been teaching composition and writing for motion pictures and radio programs.

His compositions have been performed in Europe and the United States. The "Csardas Rhapsodie" was broadcast over major networks. Several of his operas and symphonies have been presented in this country. He is, at the present time, preparing a Symphony and an Introduction and Fugue for Strings.

COMPOSITIONS WRITTEN IN AMERICA

ORCHESTRAL WORKS	DURATION	PUBLISHER	DATE
CHRISTOPHER COLUMBUS—opera in concert form	1 hour	Associated Music Publishers	1939
CSARDAS RHAPSODIE	10 minutes	Manuscript	1939
TARANTELLA—scherzo	10 "	G. Schirmer, Inc.	1942
CHILDREN'S SYMPHONY	12 "	Mills Music, Inc.	1942
BIBLICAL TRIPTYCH	20 "	Manuscript	1944

EFREM ZIMBALIST

Born in Rostoff on the Don, Russia, in 1889. He began his musical training with his father and later went to the St. Petersburg Conservatory to study violin with Leopold Auer. He won a gold medal and received a scholarship. He made his début playing with the Berlin Philharmonic in Berlin in 1907. He toured the Continent and England, and, in 1911, he made his American début playing with the Boston Symphony. Since 1938 he has been on the faculty of the Curtis Institute of Music and is now the Director.

His works include "Slavic Dances" for violin and orchestra, a "Suite in Old Style" for violin and piano, an opera and many songs.

COMPOSITIONS

ORCHESTRAL WORKS	DURATION	PUBLISHER	DATE
AMERICAN RHAPSODY	11 minutes		1942
PORTRAIT OF AN ARTIST	18 "	Manuscript	1945

CHAMBER MUSIC

STRING QUARTET		G. Schirmer, Inc.
SONATA FOR VIOLIN AND PIANO		G. Schirmer, Inc.
SARASATEANA—suite of Spanish dances *violin, piano*		

A SUPPLEMENTARY LIST OF COMPOSERS

ADOMIAN, LAN
AJEMIAN, MARO
ALESSANDRO, VICTOR
ALEXANDER, JOSEPH
ALMAND, CLAUDE
AMES, WILLIAM T.
ANDERSON, FLORENCE
ANDREWS, JANE VAN ETTEN
ARHENDT, KARL
ARNOLD, MAURICE
AVSHALOMOFF, JACK

BACON, GLENN
BAILEY, PARKER
BALDWIN, RUSSELL
BALES, RICHARD
BALLANTINE, EDWARD
BALLAZS, FREDRIC
BALOGH, ERNO
BARAB, SEYMOUR
BARNES, EDWARD SHIPPEN
BARNETT, ALICE
BARNETT, DAVID
BARRYMORE, LIONEL
BARTHOLOMEW, MARSHALL
BARTLETT, PHILLIPS PAYSON
BAUM, RUSSELL
BEAL, NEWTON
BECKHELM, PAUL
BEESON, JACK
BERGH, ARTHUR
BERLIN, IRVING
BESTE, LAWRENCE
BESTOR, DOROTHEA NOLTE
BEYER, JOHANNA M.
BITTER, JOHN
BLOCK, FREDERICK
BLOOM, RUBE
BOATWRIGHT, HOWARD
BODENHORN, AARON
BOVE, HENRY
BOYD, HAROLD
BOYD, JEANNE
BOYLE, GEORGE FREDERICK
BRADLEY, JOHN

BRAINE, ROBERT
BRANT, CYR DE
BRAUN, EDITH EVANS
BRINDEL, BERNARD
BROCKWAY, HOWARD
BROOKS, ERNEST
BROWN, EDDY
BROWN, GERTRUDE M.
BROWN, HAROLD
BROWN, MERTON
BROWNING, MORTIMER
BUCHMAN, CARL
BUKETOFF, IGOR CONSTANTIN
BURLEIGH, H. T.
BURTON, ELDIN
BUSCH, ADOLF
BUSCH, CARL
BUUCK, PAUL

CANNING, THOMAS
CARNEVALE, LUIGI
CARPENTER, HOYLE
CARSTENS, JEANNE
CESANA, OTTO
CHALOFF, HERMAN
CHARLES, ERNEST
CHELIMSKY, SAMUEL E.
CLAPP, PHILLIP G.
CLARKE, HENRY LELAND
CLIFTON, CHALMERS
CLINE, J. DE FOREST
CLOKEY, JOSEPH W.
COBB, SCRIBNER
COLLINS, EDWARD
COLMAN, JOHN
COMFORT, ANNABELLE
CONE, HAROLD S.
COOKE, FREDERICK
COOLEY, CARLETON
COOPER, LOU
COUPER, MILDRED
COWLES, CECIL
CRANDALL, GEORGE
CRANE, ALICE
CREWS, LUCILE

395

DANIELS, NEIL MORET
DAVIDSON, HAROLD G.
DAVIS, LEONORE
DEIS, CARL
DELAMARTER, ERIC
DELANEY, EDWARD
DE LUCA, EDMOND
DICKINSON, CLARENCE
DILLER, ANGELA
DILLON, FANNIE CHARLES
DINSMORE, WILLIAM
DOELLNER, ROBERT
DONATO, ANTHONY
DUBENSKY, LEO
DU PAGE, RICHARD
DVORAK, ROBERT

EDMUNDS, JOHN
EFFINGER, CECIL
EITZEN, LEE
ELLINGTON, DUKE
ENGEL, CARL
EPHROS, GERSHON
EVETT, ROBERT

FELLMAN, HAZEL
FEIGIN, IRVING G.
FERGUSON, DONALD
FINE, IRVING GIFFORD
FISCHER, IRWIN
FISHER, WILLIAM ARMS
FLETCHER, GRANT
FORRELL, GENE
FOSTER, FAY
FOSTER, GEORGE
FREER, ELEANOR EVEREST
FREILICHER, JOHN
FRIEDHOFER, HUGO
FRIML, RUDOLPH
FUERSTNER, CARL

GAINES, SAMUEL RICHARDS
GANNETT, KENT
GAUL, HARVEY B.
GEBHARD, HEINRICH
GEHRM, LOUIS
GESENSWAY, LOUIS
GIDEON, HENRY
GILLETTE, JAMES R.
GODOWSKY, LEOPOLD
GOEB, RICHARD
GOLDMAN, MAURICE

GOLDSWORTHY, WILLIAM A.
GOODWIN, JACK
GORE, RICHARD TAYLOR
GOSSICK, BEN R.
GRASSE, EDWIN
GREENBERG, HERBERT
GRIMM, C. HUGO
GRISELLE, THOMAS
GRUEN, RUDOLPH
GRUNN, HOMER
GUNDER, JOHN
GUNTHER, FELIX
GUSIKOFF, MICHEL

HAGGERTY, RICHARD
HAINES, EDMUND
HANSEN, REGINA
HARLING, W. FRANKE
HARMAN, CARTER
HARRIS, VICTOR
HARRISON, LOU
HARTMANN, ARNOLD
HARWELL, SAMUEL
HAWLEY, OSCAR HATCH
HEADLEY, H. CLINE
HEILMAN, WILLIAM CLIFFORD
HELD, PAUL
HELLER, JAMES G.
HENDERSON, ARTHUR WILLIAM
HENDL, WALTER
HENIOT, HANS LEVY
HENRY, GEORGE
HENSLER, BERNICE
HERBERT, VICTOR
HEYMAN, KATHERINE RUTH
HIGGINSON, J. VINCENT
HITCHCOCK, ARTHUR B.
HOFMANN, JOSEF
HOLLANDER, FREDERICK
HOMER, SIDNEY
HORST, LOUIS
HOSMER, ELMER SAMUEL
HOUSMAN, ROSALIE
HOVHANESS, ALAN
HOWE, WALTER
HRUBY, FRANK
HUFFMAN, WALTER
HUHN, BRUNO
HULL, ALEXANDER
HUMPHREY, HOMER C.
HUNT, FREDERICK
HUTCHESON, ERNEST

IDE, CHESTER EDWARD
IMBRIE, ANDREW
ISAACS, LEWIS

JACKSON, HOWARD
JARECKI, TADEUSZ
JENCKS, GARDNER
JOHNS, LOUIS EDGAR
JOHNSON, J. ROSAMOND
JOHNSTONE, ARTHUR EDWARD
JONES, DORIS

KAPER, BRONISLAW
KAPLAN, SOL
KAUN, BERNARD
KELLER, WALTER
KENT, GARDNER
KERN, JEROME
KESSLER, JOHN J.
KILHAM, ROGER
KILPATRICK, JACK F.
KINGSFORD, CHARLES
KINNEY, GORDON
KIRBY, PAUL
KLEIN, JOHN
KLEMM, GUSTAVE
KOEHLER, EMIL
KOLAR, VICTOR
KORN, RICHARD
KOSAKOFF, REUVEN
KOUNTZ, RICHARD
KOVEN, REGINALD DE
KRAFT, LEO
KROEGER, ALFRED
KROLL, WILLIAM

LA FORGE, FRANK
LAIDLAW, ROBERT LEE
LANDAU, VICTOR
LANE, EASTWOOD
LANE, MARGARET RUTHVEN
LANGE, ARTHUR
LAVA, WILLIAM
LEGINSKA, ETHEL
LEICH, ROLAND
LEIDZEN, ERIK W. G.
LEIGHTER, HENRY CLOUGH
LENEL, LUDWIG
LEONARDI, LEONID
LEONE, FRANCESCO DE
LESTER, WILLIAM
LEVENSON, BORIS

LEVY, ELLIS
LEVY, HANS HENIOT
LEWIS, LEO RICH
LEWIS, URSULA
LIEBERSON, SAMUEL A.
LIEURANCE, THURLOW
LIPSKY, ALEXANDER
LLOYD, ARTHUR CLELAND
LLOYD, NORMAN
LOOMIS, CLARENCE
LORA, ANTONIO
LOWENS, IRVING

MACGIMSEY, ROBERT
MACKEE, CHESTER
MACKOWN, MARJORIE TRUELOVE
MADURO, CHARLES
MAESCH, LA VAHN
MAITLAND, MARGARET
MALOTTE, ALBERT H.
MANNEY, CHARLES FONTEYN
MARVEL, ROBERT
MATTFELD, JULIUS
MAYNARD, GEORGE
MCCLURE, J. CLARENDON
MCHOSE, ALLAN I.
MIDDLETON, JEAN B.
MIESSNER, OTTO
MILLER, ALEXANDER
MONTANDON, BLAZSE
MONTANI, NICOLA
MOORE, MARY CARR
MORITZ, EDWARD
MORSE, RICHARD W.
MOURANT, WALTER
MOWREY, DENT
MURPHY, HOWARD A.
MYERS, RICHARD

NANCARROW, CONLON
NAYLOR, WILLIAM
NELSON, ROBERT
NERO, PAUL
NEUBECK, W. HENRY
NEVIN, ARTHUR M.
NORDEN, N. LINDSAY
NORTON, SPENCER
NOVICK, NATHAN

O'GORMAN, EDWARD
OLDBERG, ARNE
OTTERSTROM, THORWALD

PARKER, MURIEL
PARRISH, CARL
PATTISON, LEE
PAYNE, HARRIET
PENDLETON, EDMUND
PIERCE, EDWIN HALL
PIKE, ALFRED
PINKHAM, DANIEL
PITTAWAY, RUDOLPH ALEXANDER
PLUMB, EDWARD H.
PORTER, COLE
POWERS, MAXWELL
PROCTOR, LELAND
PYLE, FRANCIS

QUASHEN, BEN

RALSTON, FRANCES MARION
RANDEGGER, G. ALDO
RAPHLING, SAM
RASBACH, OSCAR
RATNER, LEONARD
RAYMOND, LEWIS
REICHMANN, SAMUEL
REPPER, CHARLES
REVIL, RUDOLF
RICH, FRED
RISHER, ANNA PRISCILLA
ROBB, JOHN D.
ROBBINS, REGINALD C.
RODGERS, RICHARD
ROGERS, JAMES HOTCHKISS
ROGERS, JOHN WILLIAM
ROMBERG, SIGMUND
ROME, HAROLD
ROREM, NED
ROSE, DAVID
ROSENSTOCK, MILTON
ROYCE, EDWARD
RUDHYAR, DANE
RUDIN, HERMAN
RUNKEL, KENNETH E.
RUSSELL, ALEXANDER
RYBKA, FRANK

SALTER, H. J.
SANFORD, GRACE KRICK
SAPERTON, DAVID
SAWTELL, PAUL
SCHEER, LEO
SCHENCK, ELLIOTT
SCHIFFMAN, BYRON

SCHIMMERLING, H. A.
SCHROEDER, W. A.
SCHUYLER, PHILIPPA DUKE
SCOTT, THOMAS JEFFERSON
SEARCH, FREDERICK PRESTON
SEAY, VIRGINIA
SERLEY, TIBOR
SEVERN, EDMUND
SHARP, EARL C.
SHELLEY, HARRY ROWE
SHURE, R. DEANE
SIEGEL, JEANNETTE
SIEMONN, GEORGE
SILBERTA, RHEA
SILVER, MARK
SIMMONS, HOMER
SKILES, MARLIN
SKINNER, FRANK
SLAVIT, LOUIS
SMITH, JULIA
SMITH, ROGER M.
SNELL, DAVID
SNYDERMAN, TOBIE
SODERLUND, GUSTAVE
SODERO, CESARE
SOUVAINE, HENRY
SPALDING, ALBERT
SPEAKS, OLEY
SPIALEK, HANS
SPROSS, CHARLES GILBERT
STACKHOUSE, DAVID
STEINER, GEORGE
STEWART, GRAHAM
STOJOWSKI, SIGISMOND
STOLZ, ROBERT
STRASVOGEL, IGNACE
STRICKLAND, LILY
STRIMER, JOSEPH
SWIFT, KAY

TERRY, FRANCES
THATCHER, HOWARD
THOMPSON, VAN DENMAN
TOSAR, HECTOR
TROWBRIDGE, LUTHER
TUCKER, GREGORY
TURNER, GODFREY

USSACHEVSKY, VLADIMIR

VARDELL, MARGARET
VENTH, CARL

VINITSKY, RUTH
VRIONIDES, CHRISTOS
VYNER, LOUIS

WALDROP, GID
WALLACE, OLIVER G.
WANSBOROUGH, HAROLD
WARD, FRANK EDWIN
WARD, WILLIAM R.
WARFORD, CLAUDE
WARNER, PHILIP
WARNKE, F. M.
WARREN, ELINOR REMICK
WATTS, WINTTER
WEBER, BEN
WEHNER, GEORGE
WEIGEL, EUGENE
WEINBERG, JACOB
WEINZWEIG, JOHN
WEISGAL, HUGO
WEISGARBER, ELLIOTT
WERNER, JULIUS

WHITEFIELD, BERNARD
WHITMER, T. CARL
WIGGLESWORTH, FRANK
WILDER, ALEX
WILLIAMS, DAVID McK.
WILLIAMSON, ESTHER
WITTELL, CHESTER
WOLFE, JACQUES
WOODBRIDGE, C. LOUISE
WOODWARD, HENRY LYNDE, JR.
WORK, JULIAN
WRIGHT, KENNETH

YON, PIETRO
YORK, WYNN
YOST, GAYLORD
YOUMANS, VINCENT

ZADOKOFF, JAK
ZEISL, ERIC
ZUCCA, MANA